THE SAGE HANDBOOK of
ORGANIZATIONAL DISCOURSE

Editorial Board

THE SAGE HANDBOOK of
ORGANIZATIONAL DISCOURSE

Edited by

D. GRANT, C. HARDY, C. OSWICK
AND L. PUTNAM

SAGE Publications
London • Thousand Oaks • New Delhi

First published 2004

SAGE Publications Ltd
1 Oliver's Yard
55 City Road
London EC1Y 1SP

SAGE Publications Inc.
2455 Teller Road
Thousand Oaks, California 91320

SAGE Publications India Pvt Ltd
B-42, Panchsheel Enclave
Post Box 4109
New Delhi 110 017

British Library Cataloguing in Publication data

A catalogue record for this book is available from the British Library

ISBN 0 7619 7225 0

Library of Congress Control Number: 2004102661

Typeset by C&M Digitals (P) Ltd., Chennai, India
Printed in Great Britain by The Cromwell Press Ltd, Trowbridge, Wiltshire

Contents

List of Tables and Figures

LIST OF TABLES

LIST OF FIGURES

List of Contributors

EDITORS

David Grant is Professor in Work and Organizational Studies, the School of Business, at the University of Sydney. He is also a Co-director of the International Centre for Research on Organizational Discourse Strategy and Change and Visiting Senior Research Fellow at the Management Centre, King's College, London. His current research interests focus on the social constructivist effects of language in order to explain the implementation and impact of various organizational change initiatives. He has published in a range of refereed journals including *Academy of Management Review, Organization, Human Relations, The Journal of Management Studies, Organization Studies, The International Journal of Human Resource Management, International Studies in Management and Organization* and *The Journal of Applied Behavioral Science*. He has also co-edited *Discourse and Organization* (1998, with Tom Keenoy and Cliff Oswick), *Metaphor and Organizations* (1996, with Cliff Oswick) and *Organizational Development: Metaphorical Explorations* (1996, with Cliff Oswick).

Cynthia Hardy has been Professor of Management at the University of Melbourne, Australia since 1998. Before then, she was a professor in the Faculty of Management at McGill University in Canada. Her current research interests focus on organizational discourse theory and discourse analysis. In addition to co-editing this *Handbook*, she has recently published with Nelson Phillips a qualitative methods book on using discourse analysis to study organizations, and has co-edited a special issue of *Organization Studies* on organizational discourse with Dave Grant, Tom Keenoy, Cliff Oswick and Nelson Phillips. Her work on organizational discourse has been published in *Academy of Management Review, Organization Studies, Human Relations* and *Organization*. Cynthia Hardy has also conducted a number of critical studies of power and politics in organizations, especially with regard to inter-organizational collaboration and strategy making. In total, she has published 12 books and edited volumes, including the *Handbook of Organization Studies*, published by Sage, which won the 1997 George R. Terry Book Award at the Academy of Management. She has written over 60 journal articles and book chapters. Cynthia Hardy is also co-editor of *Organization Studies*.

Cliff Oswick (PhD, King's College, University of London) is Professor of Organization Theory and Discourse at The Management Centre, University of Leicester, UK. His current research interests are concerned with the application of aspects of discourse, dramaturgy, tropes, narrative and rhetoric to processes of management, organizing and consumption. He has co-edited several collections and has published widely on these topics in journals, including recent and forthcoming contributions to *Academy of Management Review, Journal of Management Studies, Journal of Applied Behavioral Science, Human Relations, Journal of Organizational Change Management* and *Organization*. He is also a Regional Editor of the *Journal of Organizational Change Management*.

Linda L. Putnam (PhD, University of Minnesota) is Professor of Organizational Communication in the Department of Communication at Texas A&M University. Her current research interests include negotiation and organizational conflict and language analysis in organizations. She is the co-editor of *The New Handbook of Organizational Communication* (Sage, 2001), *Communication and Negotiation* (1992), *Communication and Organization: An Interpretive Approach* (1983) and the *Handbook of Organizational Communication* (1987). She is a past President of the International Communication Association, a past President of the International Association of Conflict Management, and is a past Board Member-at-Large of the Academy of Management. She is a Fellow of the International Communication Association and a Distinguished Scholar of the National Communication Association.

AUTHORS

Susan Ainsworth is a Lecturer in Work and Organizational Studies at the University of Sydney, Australia. She recently completed a PhD at the University of Melbourne, studying the social construction of older worker identity using discourse analysis. Her other research interests include gender studies, public policy and critical organization studies. She holds a BA (Hons) in English Literature and Language and a Master of Commerce (Hons) from the University of Melbourne. She has published in *Organization Studies, Gender, Work and Organization* and *Tamara: Journal of Critical Postmodern Organization Science*.

Mats Alvesson is Professor of Business Administration at the University of Lund, Sweden. He has previously held positions in Montreal, Turku, Linköping, Stockholm and Göteborg and has been a visiting academic at the universities of Cambridge, Melbourne, Colorado and Oxford. He received his PhD from the University of Lund in 1984. Research interests include critical theory, gender, power, management of professional service (knowledge-intensive) organizations, organizational culture and symbolism, qualitative method and philosophy of science. Recent books include *Making Sense of Management: A Critical Introduction* (Sage, 1996, with Hugh Willmott), *Communication, Power and Organization* (de Gruyter, 1996), *Understanding Gender and Organizations* (Sage, 1997, with Yvonne Billing), *Reflexive Methodology* (Sage, 2000), *Doing Critical Management Research* (Sage, 2000, with Stan Deetz), *Postmodernism and Social Research* (Open University Press, 2002), *Understanding Organizational Culture* (Sage, 2002) and *Knowledge Work and Knowledge-intensive Firms* (Oxford University Press, 2004).

Donald Anderson, PhD, is a faculty member in applied communication at the University of Denver, Colorado. His research focuses on stability and change in organizational discourse, writing in organizations, and communication theory and the work of philosopher Mikhail Bakhtin. He has published in *Discourse Studies* and the *Journal of Business and Technical Communication.*

Karen Lee Ashcraft received her PhD in 1998 from the University of Colorado at Boulder. She is an Associate Professor in the Department of Communication at the University of Utah. Her research examines gender, power, professional identity and alternative organizational forms, and has appeared in such forums as *Communication Monographs*, *Administrative Science Quarterly* and the *Academy of Management Journal.* Her recent co-authored book with Dennis Mumby, *Reworking Gender*, explores the relationship between feminist and critical organization studies and proposes a communication approach to the study of gender and organizing.

Frank J. Barrett, PhD, is Associate Professor of Systems Management at the Naval Postgraduate School in Monterey, California where he is Director of the Center for Positive Change. He is also a Faculty Member in the School of Human and Organizational Development at the Fielding Graduate Institute. He received his BA in Government and International Relations from the University of Notre Dame, his MA in English from the University of Notre Dame, and his PhD in Organizational Behaviour from Case Western Reserve University. He has written and lectured widely on social constructionism, appreciative inquiry, organizational change, jazz improvisation and organizational learning. He has published articles in the *Journal of Applied Behavioral Science*, *Human Relations*, *Organization Science* and *Organizational Dynamics*, as well as numerous book chapters. He is co-editor of *Appreciative Inquiry and Organizational Transformation* (Greenwood Books, 2001).

Pablo J. Boczkowski (PhD, Science and Technology Studies, 2001, Cornell University) is Assistant Professor of Organization Studies at the Sloan School of Management, Massachusetts Institute of Technology, and holds the Cecil and Ida Green Career Development Chair at MIT. He studies how the construction and use of new media technologies affect work practices, communication processes, and interaction with consumers, focusing on organizations and occupations that have traditionally been associated with print media. He is the author of *Digitizing the News: Innovation in Online Newspapers*, MIT Press, 2004. His current project looks at issues of information intermediation and professional work through an examination of the transformations in librarianship that have taken place in relation to libraries' construction and use of new media technologies.

Kirsten Broadfoot (PhD, University of Colorado at Boulder) is currently a Lecturer in Management Communication at the University of Waikato, Hamilton, New Zealand. Her scholarly work is founded in dialogic approaches to organizational and cultural communication and the discursive construction of work, knowledge, technology and self for, and by, organizations and individuals. Using ethnographic methods and critical discourse analysis, Kirsten's current research interests explore new forms of working and workplaces, the discourse of genetics and its intersection with medicine. More specifically, her work examines the impact of such forces on diverse ways of knowing, being and speaking. Her research and teaching highlights the dialectical and tension-filled relationship between communicative micro-practices and organizing structures, and how these interact to foreclose opportunities for 'good work' in everyday life. She will join the Communication Faculty at Colorado State University in January 2005.

George Cheney is Professor of Communication at the University of Utah and Adjunct Professor in the Department of Management Communication, the University of Waikato, Hamilton, New Zealand. He has published four books and more than 70 journal articles and book chapters. George's research and teaching interests include identity and power in organizations, quality of worklife, corporate public discourse, employee participation and workplace democracy, and professional ethics. George is a past chair of the Organizational Communication Division of the National Communication Association, and he has lectured extensively in Western Europe and Latin America. He is committed to community engagement, service learning and positive social transformation.

Lars Thøger Christensen (PhD, Odense University) is Professor of Communications at the Department of Marketing, the University of Southern Denmark. Previously he was research professor at the Copenhagen Business School where he established the CBS Center for Corporate Communication. Lars's research and teaching interests include several themes within the broad fields of organizational and corporate communication, for example identity, issues management, integration, advertising and transparency. In addition to four books, his research is published in *Organization Studies*, *European Journal of Marketing*, *Consumption, Markets and Culture*, *The New Handbook of Organizational Communication*, *The Handbook of Public Relations*, *Communication Yearbook*, and elsewhere. Lars's contribution to this book was made possible by a grant from the Danish Social Science Research Council.

Charles Conrad is Professor of Organizational Communication and Organizational Rhetoric in the Department of Communication at Texas A&M University and editor of *Management Communication Quarterly*. His research focuses on the interface among organizational discourse, power and politics, and has appeared in the *Quarterly Journal of Speech*, *Journal of Applied Communication Research*, *Communication Monographs* and *Management Communication Quarterly*. He is currently involved in research on processes through which organization discourse influences public policy-making in the USA.

François Cooren is an Associate Professor in the Department of Communication of the University of Montreal, Canada. His research centres on the organizing properties of communication as displayed in high-reliability organizations, coalitions and board meetings. Recent publications include two articles – 'Translation and articulation in the organization of coalitions: The Great Whale River Case' (2001, *Communication Theory*) and 'Implicatures: A schematic approach' (2002, *Journal of Pragmatics*) – and a book, *The Organizing Property of Communication* (*John Benjamins*, 2000). He is currently editing two books titled *Interacting and Organizing: Analyses of a Board Meeting* and *Communication as Organizing: Practical Approaches to Research into the Dynamic of Text and Conversation* (with James R. Taylor and Elizabeth Van Every). He is also the recipient of the 2002 International Communication Association Young Scholar Award.

Barbara Czarniawska holds a Chair in Management Studies at Gothenburg Research Institute, School of Economics and Commercial Law, Gothenburg University, Sweden. Her research focuses on organizing in action nets, most recently in the field of big city management. In terms of methodology, she favours the narrative approach. She has published in the area of business and public administration in Polish, her native language, as well as in Swedish, Italian and English, the most recent positions being *A Narrative Approach to Organization Studies* (Sage, 1998), *Writing Management* (Oxford University Press, 1999), *A Tale of Three Cities* (Oxford University Press, 2003) and *Narratives in Social Science Research* (Sage, 2004). A member of both the Royal Swedish Academy of Sciences since 2000 and the Royal Swedish Academy of Engineering Sciences since 2001, Barbara was awarded the Wihuri International Prize in 2003.

Stanley Deetz, PhD, is Professor of Communication at the University of Colorado, Boulder, where he teaches courses in organizational theory, organizational communication and communication theory. He is co-author of *Leading Organizations through Transition* (Sage, 2000) and *Doing Critical Management Research* (Sage, 2000), and author of *Transforming Communication, Transforming Business* (Hampton, 1995) and *Democracy in an Age of Corporate Colonization* (SUNY, 1992), as well as editor or author of eight other books. He has published nearly 100 essays in scholarly journals and books. His academic interests include stakeholder representation, culture, and communication in corporate organizations. He has served as a consultant on culture, diversity and participatory decision-making for several major corporations in the USA and Europe. He is a Fellow of the International Communication Association and served as its President, 1996–97.

Norman Fairclough is Professor of Language in Social Life at Lancaster University in the UK. He has written extensively on critical discourse analysis, including *Language and Power* (2nd edition, Longman, 2000), *Discourse and Social Change* (Polity Press, 1992), *Discourse in Late Modernity* (Edinburgh University Press, 1999, with Lilie Chouliaraki), *New Labour, New Language?* (Routledge, 2000), *Analysing Discourse: Textual Analysis for Social Research* (Routledge, 2003).

Gail T. Fairhurst is a Professor of Communication at the University of Cincinnati, USA. Her research interests include leadership and language analysis in organizations. She has published over 40 articles and book chapters in management and communication journals. She also recently co-authored *The Art of Framing: Managing the Language of Leadership* (Jossey-Bass, 1996), which received the 1997 National Communication Association (USA) Organizational Communication Book of the Year Award. She is currently working on a book entitled, *Discursive Approaches to Leadership*.

Yiannis Gabriel is Professor in Organizational Theory, School of Management, Imperial College, having taught previously at Thames Polytechnic and Bath University. He has a degree in Mechanical Engineering from Imperial College London, where he also carried out postgraduate studies in industrial sociology. He has a PhD in Sociology from the University of California, Berkeley. His main research interests are in organizational and psychoanalytic theories, consumer studies, storytelling, folklore and culture. Gabriel is author of *Freud and Society*, *Working Lives in Catering* (both Routledge) and *Organizations in Depth* (Sage), co-author of *Organizing and Organizations*, *The Unmanageable Consumer: Contemporary Consumption and Its Fragmentation* and *Experiencing Organizations* (all Sage), and *Storytelling in Organizations* (Oxford University Press, 2000). Other publications include articles on computer folklore, organizational nostalgia, chaos and complexity in organizations, fantasies of organizational members about their leaders, organizational insults and research methodology using stories and narratives. He has been Editor of the journal *Management Learning* and is Associate Editor of *Human Relations*.

Kenneth J. Gergen is the Mustin Professor of Psychology at Swarthmore College. He is a leading figure in the development of social constructionist thought and practice, and the recipient of numerous awards, including honorary degrees in both Europe and the USA. Among his major works are *Toward Transformation in Social Knowledge*, *Realities and Relationships*, *The Saturated Self* and *An Invitation to Social Construction*. Professor Gergen is also the Director of the Taos Institute, a non-profit organization linking social constructionist theory to societal practices.

Mary Gergen is a Professor of Psychology and of Women's Studies at Pennsylvania State University, Delaware County. Her published work links social constructionism with feminist theory. Her most recent book is *Feminist Reconstructions in Psychology: Narrative, Gender and Performance* (Sage, 2001). She is also co-editor of *Readings in Social Construction* (Sage, 2003, with K.J. Gergen) and a co-author of *The Appreciative Organization*. As a founder of the Taos Institute, she has been involved in workshops and conferences that bring social constructionism and organizational practices into closer connection.

Christian Heath has held positions at the Universities of Manchester, Surrey, Nottingham and London, and visiting positions at the Universities of Constance, Paris and Lyon. He serves as a scientific consultant to various academic, service and industrial organizations in the UK and abroad, including the UK research councils and the European Commission. He also serves on various conference committees, and advisory and editorial boards. He teaches courses on research methods, social interaction, work and technology.

Loizos Heracleous earned his PhD at the Judge Institute of Management Studies, University of Cambridge. He is Associate Professor at the School of Business, National University of Singapore. From 2004 he will be Fellow in Strategy and Organization, Templeton College, Oxford University. His research interests include organizational discourse, organization change and development, and structurational approaches to organizational analysis. His work has been published in several journals, including the *Academy of Management Journal, Human Relations* and *Journal of Applied Behavioral Science*. He serves as a senior editor of *Organization Studies*, international consulting editor of the *Journal of Applied Behavioral Science* and is an editorial board member of the *Journal of Management Studies and of the Asia Pacific Journal of Management*.

Deborah Jones is a Senior Lecturer in the Victoria School of Management at Victoria University in Wellington, Aotearoa/New Zealand. She has degrees in English and Management Studies and teaches communication and organizational studies with a focus on difference and power. She is interested in national identity as well as gender, ethnicity and age at work, and has initiated an ongoing study of the New Zealand film industry from an organizational perspective.

Tom Keenoy is Reader in Management and Senior Research Fellow at the Management Centre, King's College, University of London. His most recent book is the co-edited *Discourse and Organization* (Sage, 1998) and he has published widely in international journals. His current research interests include organizational discourse analysis, organizational tropes, the construction of HRM, time and organization, the co-construction of management in cooperative organization, and the changing tempo of sense-making in academic work.

Mihaela Kelemen (DPhil, University of Oxford) is a Senior Lecturer in Quality Management and Organization Studies at Keele University in the UK. Her research concentrates on critical and postmodern approaches to quality management, Eastern European management and research methodologies and has been published in journals such as *Organization, Human Relations* and *Journal of Management Studies*. Her book on critical quality management was published by Sage in 2003.

Martin Kilduff (PhD, Cornell University) is a Professor of Organizational Behaviour at The Pennsylvania State University. He currently serves as an associate editor at both *Administrative Science Quarterly* and *Academy of Management Review*. His research focuses on how individuals help create the worlds that constrain and enable their behaviours. His recent work includes *Social Networks and Organizations* (Sage, 2003, with Wenpin Tsai) and the article 'Bringing ideas back in: Eclecticism and discovery in organizational studies', *Research in the Sociology of Organizations*, forthcoming (co-authored with Mihaela Kelemen).

Hubert Knoblauch (PhD, 1959) is Professor of Sociology at the Technical University of Berlin (since 2003). He studied Sociology, Philosophy and History at the University of Konstanz, FRG, and at the University of Sussex, UK, and has taught at the Universities of Konstanz, Sankt Gallen, Bern and Prague. He won the Christa-Hoffmann-Riem Award for Qualitative Sociology in 1997. He was Heisenberg Scholar, 1997–2000; Senior Research Fellow at King's College, London, 1998–99 and Professor for the Sociology of Religion at the University of Zurich, 2000–03.

Daniel J. Lair is a doctoral student in the Communication Department at the University of Utah. His research interests lie in organizational communication and rhetoric, with a particular focus on issues of work and identity, worklife and corporate discourse.

Paul Luff is a Senior Research Fellow at King's College, London. His research focuses on the relationships between studies of work and the development of new technologies. In particular, he is interested in how detailed analysis of work and interaction can assist in the design of computer systems to support collaborative work. He has published extensively in the fields of human–computer interaction, requirement engineering and computer-supported cooperative work.

Dennis K. Mumby (PhD, Southern Illinois University, 1985) is a Professor in the Department of Communication Studies at the University of North Carolina at Chapel Hill, USA. His research focuses on the relationships among discourse, power, gender and organization. He has published in journals such as *Academy of Management Review*, *Communication Monographs* and *Management Communication Quarterly*. He is the co-author (with Karen Ashcraft) of *Reworking Gender: A Feminist Communicology of Organization* (Sage, 2004).

Wanda J. Orlikowski is Professor of Information Technologies and Organization Studies at the Sloan School of Management and the Eaton-Peabody Chair of Communication Sciences at the Massachusetts Institute of Technology. Her primary research interest focuses on the dynamic relationship between organizations and information technologies, with particular emphases on organizing structures, cultural norms, communication genres and work practices. She is currently leading a five-year National Science Foundation project on the social and economic implications of Internet technologies.

Nelson Phillips (PhD, University of Alberta, 1995) is the Beckwith Professor of Management Studies at the Judge Institute of Management, University of Cambridge. His research interests include knowledge management, multinationals and international development, inter-organizational collaboration, and a general interest in management in cultural industries. He has published a number of academic articles in the *Academy of Management Journal*, *Academy of Management Review*, *Sloan Management Review*, *Journal of Management Studies*, *Journal of Management Inquiry*, *Business & Society*, *Journal of Business Ethics*, *Business Ethics Quarterly*, *Organization Science*, *Organization* and

Organization Studies. He has also written a methods book with Cynthia Hardy on discourse analysis and the study of organizations.

Craig Prichard is a former newspaper reporter who, through a strange mixture of accident and coincidence, turned to academic work when he took a job researching journalism education in UK regional newspapers. He graduated with a PhD from the University of Nottingham in 1998 after writing a thesis on the shift to managerialism in UK further and higher education, and is currently senior lecturer in the Department of Management at Massey University in New Zealand. While research topics range widely, recent work includes papers on death in the workplace, relations between Foucault and Marx in organization studies, social movement organizations, management identity and higher education management. A core theme of his work is how useful and important discourse analytic research is to understanding and changing people, organizations and societies.

Mike Reed is Professor of Organization Analysis and Deputy Director (Research) at Cardiff Business School, Cardiff University, Wales, UK. His research interests focus on the organization and control of 'expert work' in a range of institutional environments. In pursuing these research interests, Mike draws extensively on the philosophical, theoretical and methodological resources provided by critical realism in order to develop 'analytical histories' of organizational restructuring in contemporary capitalist societies and political economies. Recently, he has published on a wide range of theoretical and substantive issues, including the 'agency/structure' dilemma, 'new public management/new managerialism', the management of UK universities, and the putative emergence of 'network-based' organizational forms. He is working on a book, *Beyond The Iron Cage?: The Dynamics of Organizational Control in Contemporary Capitalism*. But, as his son Christopher never fails to remind him, this book should have been finished and published a long time ago! He is one of the founder editors of the journal *Organization*.

Ralph Stablein is the Academic Director of the DBA programme and a Professor in the Management Department of the Massey University College of Business, New Zealand. He received his BA in psychology and economics from Benedictine University, his MA in economics from Western Illinois University and his PhD in organization behaviour from the Kellogg Graduate School of Management at Northwestern University. Ralph has worked at the University of British Columbia, the University of Otago and Massey University. He has been a visiting scholar at Stanford University's Work, Technology and Organization Center, New York University, Benedictine University, South Florida University and the University of Western Sydney. Both his research and teaching focus on inquiry in organization studies. Ralph serves on the editorial board of the *Academy of Management Review, Asia Pacific Journal of Human Resources, Journal of Organizational Change Management* and *Organization Studies*. He is co-editor of the *Advances in Organization Studies* series published by John Benjamins and serves as the chair of the Critical Management Studies Interest Group of the Academy of Management.

Pete Thomas is a Senior Lecturer at Lancashire Business School with research interests in the development and dissemination of managerial and organizational discourses. At present his research is focused on the 'translation' process between management education and management practice, particularly in terms of the ways in which discourse is transformed into other moments of social practice. The political and power effects of management discourse is also a key interest area.

Karl E. Weick is the Rensis Likert Distinguished University Professor of Organizational Behavior and Psychology, and Professor of Psychology at the University of Michigan. His PhD is from Ohio State University in Social and Organizational Psychology. He is a former Editor of the journal *Administrative Science Quarterly* (1977–85) and former Associate editor of the journal *Organizational Behavior and Human Performance* (1971–77). His research interests include collective sense-making under pressure, medical errors, hand-offs and transitions in dynamic events, high-reliability performance, improvisation and continuous change.

Introduction: Organizational Discourse: Exploring the Field

David Grant, Cynthia Hardy, Cliff Oswick and Linda L. Putnam[1]

A growing disillusionment with many of the mainstream theories and methodologies that underpin organizational studies has encouraged scholars to seek alternative ways in which to describe, analyse and theorize the increasingly complex processes and practices that constitute 'organization'. One outcome of this search has been that 'organizational discourse' has emerged as an increasingly significant focus of interest. It is now difficult to open a management or organizational journal without finding that it contains some sort of discursive-based study, and there has been a recent flurry of books, edited collections and journal special issues dedicated to the topic (Boje et al., 2004; Grant et al., 1998a, 2001; Hardy et al., 2004; Iedema & Wodak, 1999; Keenoy et al., 1997, 2000a; Oswick et al., 1997, 2000a, 2000b; Phillips & Hardy, 2002; Putnam & Cooren, 2004). Interest also extends to the establishment of a biennial International Conference on Organizational Discourse, which has been running since 1994, and the creation of an International Centre for Research in Organizational Discourse, Strategy and Change[2] that links organizational researchers worldwide.

The growth in interest in organizational discourse has seen researchers apply a range of discourse analytic approaches to language and other symbolic media that are discernible in organizations. In so doing, they have been able to analyse, engage with and interpret a variety of organization-related issues in ways that would not have been otherwise achievable. At the same time, some have observed that this growth appears to have been achieved through the widespread use of broad, non-specific definitions and a bewildering array of methods, approaches and perspectives. In short, how people talk about and analyse organizational discourse varies considerably.

The variation in the way that researchers talk about and analyse organizational discourse can, in part, be attributed to its theoretical and disciplinary antecedents emanating from the broader domain of discourse analysis: discourse analysis is informed by a variety of sociological, socio-psychological, anthropological, linguistic, philosophical, communications and literary-based studies (Alvesson & Kärreman, 2000a, 2000b; Grant et al., 1998b, 2001; Keenoy et al., 2000a; Oswick et al., 2000a; Potter & Wetherall, 1987). Within the broader social sciences, it has been used in order to promulgate various positivist, social constructivist and postmodern perspectives about a range of social phenomena (Brown & Yule, 1983; Fairclough, 1995; Potter & Wetherell, 1987; Schiffrin, 1987; Silverman, 1993; Van Dijk, 1997a, 1997b). Despite some integration of work in, for example, pragmatics, socio-linguistics, sociology and ethnography, discourse analysis in the social sciences for the most part remains disparate and fragmented, and characterized by a number of debates and tensions. As Van Dijk (1997a, p. 3) puts it, 'given the different philosophies, approaches and methods in their various "mother disciplines", the various developments of discourse analysis [have] hardly produced a unified enterprise'.

The field of organizational discourse has borrowed extensively from the wider discourse analytic literature and exhibits similar characteristics. Unlike Van Dijk, however, we do not see this as problem. Rather, we see the diversity of approaches and perspectives as indicative of organizational discourse as a *plurivocal project* and argue that such an approach is the best way of ensuring that the field makes a meaningful contribution to the study of organizations. Accordingly, the purpose of this *Handbook* is to demonstrate the plurivocal nature of organizational discourse for the benefit of those who wish to familiarize themselves with the field or who are contemplating utilizing a discursive approach to the study of organizational phenomena for the first time, as well as those already carrying out organizational discourse research, and who wish to enhance their understanding of it.

The *Handbook* is divided into four sections. Part I, *Domains of Discourse*, focuses on specific discursive domains or 'forms' of organizational discourse. Part II, *Methods and Perspectives*, plots the contrasting methodological approaches and epistemological views that may be discerned among those studying organizational discourse. Part III, *Discourses and Organizing*, comprises chapters that draw on a variety of discursive perspectives and approaches in order to show how discursive activity produces and mediates different organizational phenomena. Part IV, the final section of the *Handbook*, is titled *Reflections*. It comprises three pieces in which eminent contributors consider the value of organizational discourse to the broader field of organizational studies, reflect on chapters presented in the *Handbook* and suggest future avenues of research.

The remainder of this chapter provides an introductory overview of the field of organizational discourse by using the structure and content of the *Handbook* to explore what organizational discourse comprises. We then discuss key areas of debate and discussion within the field, and identify some of the challenges it faces. We conclude by highlighting the significance of organizational discourse in terms of its contribution to our understanding of organization. However, we also note that while there has been a recent growth in the number of studies of organizational discourse, it remains a relatively under-utilized avenue of enquiry whose contributions have not been fully realized. We assert that there is considerable further scope for its application, and advocate more discourse-focused research on the basis of the potentially considerable insights that it offers.

EXPLORING ORGANIZATIONAL DISCOURSE

The term 'organizational discourse' refers to the structured collections of texts embodied in the practices of talking and writing (as well as a wide variety of visual representations and cultural artefacts) that bring organizationally related objects into being as these texts are produced, disseminated and consumed (Grant et al., 1998b; Parker, 1992; Phillips & Hardy, 2002). Consequently, texts can be considered to be a manifestation of discourse and the discursive 'unit' (Chalaby, 1996) on which the organizational discourse researcher focuses. They signify collections of interactions, media of communication (i.e., oral, print, electronic), or assemblages of oral and written forms (Putnam & Cooren, 2004). Such a definition demonstrates that those studying organizational discourse are often interested in the social constructionist (Berger & Luckmann, 1967; Searle, 1995) effects of language in organizational settings (Phillips & Hardy, 2002). As Mumby and Clair point out:

> Organizations exist only in so far as their members create them through discourse. This is not to claim that organizations are 'nothing but' discourse, but rather that discourse is the principle means by which organization members create a coherent social reality that frames their sense of who they are. (1997, p. 181)

In line with Mumby and Clair's observation, this *Handbook* shows how the everyday attitudes and behaviour of an organization's members, along with their perceptions of what they believe to be reality, are shaped and influenced by the discursive practices in which they engage and to which they are exposed or subjected. In short, the *Handbook* highlights the fact that discursive practices in organizations 'do not just describe things; they do things' (Potter & Wetherell, 1987, p. 6).

In studying how discourse shapes organizing processes, researchers engage with discourse in different ways. Table 1 distinguishes between studies that focus on domains of discourse, studies that highlight methodological and epistemological issues, and studies of discourses of organizing. Combined, this material provides helpful resources that can be used to explore the field of organizational discourse and build a more meaningful and useful definition than has hitherto been provided. In particular, it serves to demonstrate that organizational discourse is in fact a plurivocal project – one where a range of approaches and perspectives co-exist.

Domains of Organizational Discourse

Researchers have shown particular interest in specific domains or 'forms' of discourse that are to be found in organizational texts. Part I of this *Handbook* focuses on four domains that are particularly prevalent in studies of organizational discourse: conversation and dialogue, narratives and stories, rhetoric and tropes. In no way do we claim that these domains are exclusive – we have chosen them because they are widely studied in the field and make a significant contribution to our understanding of organizational discourse.

Table 1: *Organizational discourse by modes of engagement*

Domains of Discourse		Methodological & Epistemological Perspectives		Discourses & Organizing	
Texts are a manifestation of discourse and the discursive unit upon which the organizational discourse researcher focuses. A number of domains are regarded as constituting texts.		Methodological approaches and epistemological perspectives that inform the study of organizational discourse and the various texts therein.		Application of discourse analytic approaches to a variety of organizational phenomena.	
Examples	**Related Handbook chapter(s)**	**Examples**	**Related Handbook chapter(s)**	**Examples**	**Related Handbook chapter(s)**
Conversation & dialogue	Gergen et al., Ch. 1.	Language in use • Conversation analysis • Speech act schematics • Interaction analysis	Fairhurst & Cooren, Ch. 5.	Gender	Ashcraft, Ch. 12.
Narratives & stories	Gabriel, Ch. 2.	Context sensitive • Pragmatics • Socio-linguistics • Institutional dialogue • Social semiotics • Critical discourse analysis	Ainsworth & Hardy, Ch. 6. Heracleous, Ch. 7. Deetz et al., Ch. 8. Prichard et al., Ch. 9.	Power	Hardy & Phillips, Ch. 13.
Rhetoric	Cheney et al., Ch. 3.	Exposition of plurivocality	Mumby, Ch. 10. Kilduff & Keleman, Ch. 11.	Culture	Alvesson, Ch. 14.
Tropes	Oswick, Putnam & Keenoy, Ch. 4.			Technology	Heath et al., Ch. 15.
				New media	Orlikowski & Boczkowski, Ch. 16.
				Globalization	Fairclough & Thomas, Ch. 17.

CONVERSATION AND DIALOGUE Both conversation and dialogue have been defined as a set of interactions that are produced as part of the talk or message exchange between two or more people (Collins, 1981; Eisenberg & Goodall, 1993; Ford & Ford, 1995; Putnam & Fairhurst, 2001; Taylor & Van Every, 1993; Westley, 1990). Conversations happen over time and are connected through time. This means that texts only exist as part of the same conversation if they are in some way responsive to each other, either directly or indirectly (a rhetorical connection), and are produced through chronologically sequenced discursive acts (a temporal connection) (Collins, 1981; Ford & Ford, 1995; Westley, 1990). On this basis, consequential action in organizations is not so much the result of disconnected utterances or isolated texts but, rather, is produced through ongoing linguistic and textual exchanges among organizational actors that draw on broader discourses and produce discursive objects that act as resources for action and for further conversations (Fairclough, 1992; Taylor et al., 1996). Moreover, the texts that constitute conversations are 'intertextual' (see discussion of context-sensitive approaches to discourse and intertextuality below). For example, Ford and Ford (1995) show how the forms of conversation associated with initiating organizational change are those that identify a need for change. From a discourse perspective, any such 'need for change', be it in the shape of an environmental shift, an organizational problem or a political agenda, is a discursive object that, once produced, is available for use by other interested actors that can support it with reference to broader discourses, such as 'strategic change' or 'profitability' (see Hardy et al., 2003).

Studies of dialogue in organizations focus on it as a mode of communication that builds mutuality through awareness of others and as an instance of unfolding interaction (Eisenberg & Goodall, 1993; Putnam & Fairhurst, 2001). In this respect, and unlike conversation with its strong temporal and rhetorical orientation, dialogue can be seen more as a momentary accomplishment (Cissna & Anderson, 1998). Drawing on the work of, for example, Bakhtin (1981), Buber (1958), Bohm (1996), and Eisenberg and Goodall (1993), studies of dialogue in organizations have sought to show how it is used to generate new meaning and understanding, create space in which to question and critique, and play a mediating function that can lead to a convergence of views (Gergen, 1994, 1999; Gergen et al., 2001; Hawes, 1999; Thatchenkery & Upadhyaya, 1996).

In the opening chapter to the *Handbook* Kenneth Gergen, Mary Gergen and Frank Barrett demonstrate how texts acquire significance through dialogue and show the importance of this relational process to organizing. Their chapter shows how the generative, degenerative and transformational properties of dialogue may impact on the organization's well-being to the extent that they may restore its vitality or may lead to its demise. Given these properties and their potential effects, the authors express some concern with the way that the significance of dialogue has hitherto been downplayed in organizational studies and suggest that all too often organizations themselves neglect to institute practices that facilitate dialogue in the workplace. To these authors, an increasing interest in studies of organizational discourse is to be welcomed since it may encourage studies that expand our knowledge and understanding of dialogue and thus its practical application in organizational situations.

NARRATIVES AND STORIES   Another important domain of study within organizational discourse is that of narratives and stories. Narrative analysis takes into account the context in which the narrative is being used and constructed. In certain respects, it can be seen as a literary form of analysis, in that it approaches narratives and stories as symbolic and rhetorical devices. Organizational researchers have used narrative analysis to show how narratives and stories are produced through a variety of verbal and written discursive interactions. It is widely used in organizational studies, having become an especially popular approach to the study of discourse among critical and postmodern scholars. Narrative analysis focuses on the topics, ideas, characters and plots within a particular text or texts. Narratives are thematic in that they tell a story; sometimes true, sometimes fictional. Moreover, they are co-constructed; they are not only authored by those who introduce them, but also by their readers and various interlocutors, who engage with them and influence the direction that they may take. They may also function ideologically so as to represent the interests of a particular group (Boje, 1995, 2001; Czarniawska-Joerges, 1996, 1997, 1998; Gabriel, 1991, 1995, 1997, 1998; Mumby, 1987; Phillips, 1995). Several authors (Brown, 2000, 2004; Dunford & Jones, 2000; Wallemacq & Sims, 1998) have noted how narratives are integral to the process of sense-making (Weick, 1995) in organizations. In short, narratives are fundamental to the way in which we think about ourselves and how we interact with one another (Ochs, 1997).

By exploring the narrative content of various texts – for example, conversations, dialogue, official documentation, newspaper articles and Internet sites – narrative analysis can provide insight into how meaning is socially constructed and action is generated within organizations (Brown, 1990). Accordingly, narratives have been studied as elements of organizational culture (Hansen & Kahnweiler, 1993; Mahler, 1988; Salzer-Morling, 1998), as shared identity among organizational members (Brown, 1990; Meyer, 1993) and as expressions of political domination and opposition (Collinson, 1988, 1994; Gabriel, 1995; Rosen, 1984, 1985). They have also been used to examine organizational policy, strategy and change (Barry & Elmes, 1997; Beech, 2000; Boje, 1991; Brown, 2000; Brown & Humphreys, 2003; Currie & Brown, 2003; Dunford & Jones, 2000; Feldman, 1990; Washbourne & Dicke, 2001).

For Yiannis Gabriel, narratives and stories feature prominently as sense-making devices in organizations which, because of their constructed and contested nature, have important implications for the processes and practices of organizing. Gabriel uses his chapter to argue that, despite their current popularity with organizational researchers and consultants, stories and narratives are in fact quite special events in organizations and that our ability to identify the texts of such stories and narratives is all too often lost in a myriad of other discourses used to express information, opinions and theories that reflect preoccupations with efficiency, rationality and action. Gabriel also suggests that in recent years the concept of stories in particular has become 'too comfortable' to the extent that what once seemed a provocative and innovative approach to the study of organizational phenomena seems to have become an unquestioned truth and accepted norm. Thus, part of the purpose of this chapter is to 'reproblematize' the idea of stories by pointing out that they can be vehicles of oppression and can lead to dissimulation and oppression (Helmer, 1993; Mumby, 1987; Witten, 1993). Moreover, stories do not deny the importance or existence of facts; rather they allow them to be re-interpreted and embellished. They therefore become powerful and potentially dangerous tools in the hands of certain individuals within social, and more specifically, organizational contexts.

RHETORIC   Narrative and stories are but one domain of discourse, the study of which allows us to consider how discourse can be used in order to achieve particular ends. The study of rhetorical devices has also offered insights into this aspect of discourse. This approach looks at symbols within the organization to examine the way they shape messages and message responses (Putnam & Fairhurst, 2001; Watson, 1994, 1995). Approaches that focus on rhetoric draw on classic definitions and theories of argumentation in order to demonstrate how particular features and forms of discourse are used in relation to a variety of organizational practices. For example, several studies examine the way symbolic and rhetorical devices are used to communicate corporate image and strategy as well as to shift blame and distance the organization from a problem (Barton, 1993; Benoit & Brinson, 1994; Campbell et al., 1998; Coombs, 1995; Grant, 1999; Keenoy & Anthony, 1992). Other studies have looked at rhetorical devices, such as argumentation in relation to decision-making and bargaining and negotiation (Hamilton, 1997; Putnam, 2004; Putnam & Jones, 1982; Putnam et al., 1990; Roloff et al., 1989).

Rhetoric is the focus of George Cheney, Lars Christensen, Charles Conrad and Daniel Lair's chapter showing the way rhetoric is deployed in organizations and the reasons that lie behind its use. As such, it demonstrates that the study of the rhetoric in organizations, in contrast to most other domains of organizational discourse, is concerned primarily with discourse's strategic dimensions. Perhaps most significantly, it points out a natural link between rhetorical and organizational studies in that the persuasive effects of rhetoric are organizational and that rhetoric is embedded in what we take to mean 'organization'.

TROPES As Putnam and Fairhurst (2001) point out, rhetoric is infused with a variety of literary devices, the most significant of which are the four classic (or master) tropes of metaphor, synecdoche, metonymy and irony (Manning, 1979; Morgan, 1983; White, 1978). The trope of metaphor is the medium through which two separate conceptual domains are compared, with the more abstract one understood in terms of the more concrete one (Grant & Oswick, 1996a; Morgan, 1980). Synecdoche and metonymy are often confused. Both involve the mapping or connection between two things within the same domain (e.g., a part-whole or a whole-part substitution) or between closely connected domains (e.g., a cause and effect relationship) (for a detailed discussion of these features, see Gibbs, 1993). Finally, irony involves the use of the discourse in an unconventional way to describe something that is paradoxical or contradictory. It exists when an unexpected outcome or surprising twist comes from the way a situation evolves opposite of what was intended (Westenholz, 1993).

The study of the master trope of metaphor in particular has contributed to organizational analysis in a number of ways. Metaphor's generative qualities are perceived to enable new knowledge production and to provide innovative new perspectives of organizational theory and behaviour. Accordingly, metaphors have been variously used as theory-building and methodological tools (Alvesson, 1993; Brink, 1993; Grant & Oswick, 1996b; Morgan, 1980, 1983, 1986, 1996; Oswick & Grant, 1996a; Putnam et al., 1996; Tsoukas, 1991). There have also been numerous studies that have sought to examine metaphors that pervade organizational discourses related to particular organizational phenomena. For example, a raft of studies have sought to examine the role and application of metaphor in relation to organizational change (e.g., see Barrett & Cooperrider, 1990; Broussine & Vince, 1996; Clark & Salaman, 1996a, 1996b; Dunford & Palmer, 1996; Marshak 1993, 1996; Morgan, 1997; Oswick & Grant, 1996b; Oswick & Montgomery, 1999; Sackmann, 1989; Srivastva & Barrett, 1988; Warner-Burke, 1992).

To Oswick, Putnam and Keenoy tropes are a prevalent feature of any form of text and are thus an inevitable and unavoidable facet of organizational life. It is this feature that makes them a significant domain of study within organizational discourse. While research on the application of metaphor to the study of organizations is prevalent, these authors point out that other tropes have received much less attention. Their chapter explores the ways that metaphors are applied to organizations and concentrates on an alternative cluster of tropes, notably irony. This approach leads to an innovative framework that enables researchers to identify discrepancies and dissonance within organizations. In doing so, their chapter can be seen as extending the application of tropes to the study of organizations.

Methodological and Epistemological Perspectives

Some researchers are less interested in the specific domains of discourse and instead engage with organizational discourse through more explicit consideration of underlying methodological and epistemological issues, some of which are explored in Part II of the *Handbook*. A sweep of the pertinent literature (see, e.g., Alvesson & Kärreman, 2000a, 2000b; Grant et al., 1998a, 2001; Hardy et al., 2004; Iedema, 2003; Phillips & Hardy, 2002; Putnam & Fairhurst, 2001; Woodilla, 1998) suggests that one key methodological issue relates to whether studies place an emphasis on language in use as opposed to language in context, while an important epistemological issue relates to the exposition of plurivocality.

In considering methodological approaches we wish to draw attention to two important issues. First, we are not seeking to look at the specific methods of analysis that are applied as a result of the researcher adopting a particular methodological approach. In this respect we are drawing a distinction between methodology and methods along the lines advocated by Schwandt (1997, p. 93): '"Methodology" is ... the theory of how inquiry should proceed. It involves analysis of the principles and procedures in a particular field of inquiry that, in turn, govern the use of particular methods'. Secondly, we acknowledge that several classifications of the various methodological approaches used to examine organizational discourse have already been proposed. For example, Putnam and Fairhurst (2001) link methodology to many of the kinds of disciplinary distinctions to be found in descriptions of traditional linguistics and communications departments: socio-linguistics, semiotics, critical linguistics, pragmatics, and so on. In doing so, they provide a comprehensive overview of language research carried out in organizational settings. Focusing on related domains of enquiry, Woodilla offers a similar but somewhat simplified classification. She isolates three main areas of organizational research methods: conversational analysis, pragmatic linguistics and critical language theory (Woodilla, 1998, p. 32). In our view, however, it is important to move away from classifying methodologies purely by virtue of their disciplinary antecedents. While it remains useful to note these antecedents, the methodologies themselves no longer lend themselves to being delineated in terms of a particular field of academic provenance. As the following discussion demonstrates, any examination of the range of methodological approaches applied by those who practise organizational discourse research must therefore come to terms with the multiplicity of influences that currently pervades the field. It must also recognize that, as a result of the field's multifaceted nature, the methodological approaches employed are likely to be quite complex and overlapping. Consequently, studies of organizational discourse may draw on several methodologies at the same time.

LANGUAGE IN USE Approaches to the study of organizational discourse that focus on language in use seek to provide a detailed examination of talk and texts as instances of social practice. They concern talk-in-interaction (Silverman, 1999) and in many instances can be said to be ethnomethodological in orientation in that they explore the role of discourse in shaping social order in everyday organizational conduct (Boden, 1994; Pomerantz & Fehr, 1997; Sacks et al., 1974). For these studies what is important is to understand the organizing properties of discourse, that is how what happens during a particular discursive interaction impacts on the actions and behaviour of individuals. Accordingly, they place emphasis on capturing and analysing discourse as a discrete moment that occurs in the present.

Approaches that employ methodologies of language in use focus on 'the machinery', 'rules' and 'structures' that are located within a particular discursive interaction (Psathos, 1995). These approaches reveal the recurrent features of talk – known as 'interactive constants' (Schegloff, 1984, 1996). These include, participants' side sequences, repair strategies and turn-taking strategies. Language in use approaches also include examination of the ways in which people use particular words or phrases to invoke actions. While the term 'language in use' denotes an emphasis on verbal interactions, this interpretation is misleading. As Pomerantz and Fehr have pointed out when discussing conversation analysis (CA):

> Conversation analysts from the outset have been interested in both the verbal and the paralinguistic features of talk (that is, sound quality, pauses, gaps, restarts etc.) In fact the actions constituted in and through speaking can be difficult or impossible to identify without attention to both. Moreover, a number of researchers have expanded the scope of CA to include the visually available features of conduct such as appropriate orientation, hand-arm gestures, posture etc. (1997, p. 65)

Conversation analysis is one of three approaches to the study of language in use discussed by Gail Fairhurst and François Cooren. The other two are interaction analysis (Bakeman & Gottman, 1986; Holmes & Rogers, 1995) and speech act schematics (Cooren, 2001; Searle, 1969). Fairhurst and Cooren contrast these three approaches, noting that each has a different analytic focus and is based on different theoretical assumptions. They also distinguish among them by applying each approach to analyse the same piece of text – a police radio transcript. The result is a rich and fascinating insight into the organizing properties of language. While noting that each makes an important and distinctive contribution to our understanding of organizational life and what constitutes 'organization', they are careful to explain that the aim of their chapter is not to suggest that any one approach is better than the others, but rather to explain and preserve the analytical integrity of each.

CONTEXT-SENSITIVE APPROACHES Approaches that focus on language in use draw attention to the detailed aspects of discursive interaction. In certain instances this may have its merits, but it does leave these approaches open to accusations of having too narrow a focus and of not being sufficiently context sensitive (Segerdahl, 1998). For example, Iedema (2003, p. 38) has suggested that 'conversation analysis' concentration on the structural-technical and interactive details of short stretches of talk excludes this kind of analysis from having much to say about broader social and organizational processes and outcomes'. Writers such as Heritage (1984) have sought to counter these criticisms by suggesting that anything that is contextual will manifest itself in the micro-sociological details of the discursive interaction under scrutiny, although this line of argument has not satisfied many researchers. Instead, they employ methodological approaches that take account of the historical and social factors that reside beyond the text under scrutiny, factors which are adjudged to influence and shape the way a text is produced, disseminated and consumed. Examples of these context-sensitive approaches include studies that draw on pragmatics, socio-linguistics, institutional dialogue, systemics and critical discourse analysis.

Like approaches that focus on language in use, pragmatics focuses on the words and grammar of language as emergent in discursive interactions. However, pragmatics draws heavily on the philosophy of language, particularly Grice's (1957, 1971) theories of meaning and intentional communication and Austin (1962) and Searle's (1969, 1979) work on speech-act theory. The result is an approach to the study of language that goes beyond conventional conversation analysis in that:

> Words can mean more – or something other – than what they say. Their interpretation depends on a multiplicity of factors including familiarity with the context, intonational cues and cultural assumptions. The same phrase may have different meanings on different occasions and the same intention may be expressed by different linguistic means. (Blum-Kulka, 1997, p. 38)

The context-sensitive position, adopted by pragmatics offers interesting insights into, for example, cross-cultural communication (Tannen, 1986). However, context-sensitive studies of discourse in organizations have developed even further. Interactive socio-linguistics, for example, combines basic social variables such as age, class and gender with an understanding of the interpretive and assumptive frames of reference (Goffman, 1963) that people draw on when talking to one another and in their behaviour towards one another. Researchers such as Schiffrin (1994) have used this framework of analysis to demonstrate that people's cultural and social backgrounds are deeply implicated in the construction of social identity.

Social context in particular has also been brought to the fore in studies of dialogue and talk. For example, studies of institutional dialogue place an emphasis on how institutional context informs and shapes language and thus the way in which individuals perform and pursue their respective organizational tasks and goals (Drew & Sorjonen, 1997). As Drew and Heritage (1992) have observed, much of the institutional dialogue literature has tended to focus on the same, specific institutional settings that emanate from outside of organization theory (e.g., sociological studies of doctor–patient interactions [Fisher & Todd, 1983; Heath, 1986; Silverman, 1987]). More recently, however, organization theorists have started to focus on a variety of socially situated aspects of everyday talk, especially professional talk and dialogue, among organization members. This development has led to studies of the various forms of talk and dialogue (bargaining, argumentation, negotiation, generative dialogue, etc.) that appear in organizations and how they relate to the social construction of a reality that impacts on identity, roles and occupational constraints (e.g., Hamilton, 1997; Iedema et al., 2004; Putnam, 2004).

Systemic approaches to the study of organizational discourse, while still context-sensitive, are also concerned with the political nature of language. Systemic approaches such as socio-political linguistics (Halliday, 1978, 1994) and critical linguistics attempt to 'expose the inequitable distribution of opportunities for meaning making to different groups in society' (Iedema, 2003, p. 41). These days, socio-political and critical linguistics are apt to be regarded as integral to social semiotics – an approach that is not only concerned with the political intricacies of discourse, but also with the multi-modal features (language, gesture, dress, etc.) of meaning making (Hodge & Kress, 1988; Kress & van Leeuwen, 1990). This approach draws on the work of Foucault, who sought to uncover the representionalist discourse or principles that govern a particular aspect of society (Foucault, 1965, 1973, 1974, 1976, 1977, 1978, 1986). As such, social semiotic approaches reveal the political effects of discourse on a variety of organizational phenomena such as knowledge, power, identity construction and the operation and effect of rules and procedures (Fowler & Kress, 1979; Hodge et al., 1979; Iedema, 2003; Martin, 1993; Rose, 1990).

Perhaps one of the most influential context-sensitive approaches to the study of organizational discourse has been that of critical discourse analysis (CDA). CDA aims to reveal the role of language as it relates to ideology, power and socio-cultural change (Fairclough, 1992, 1995; Fairclough & Wodak, 1997; Van Leeuwen, 1993). It combines several of the aforementioned methodological approaches to epitomize their complex, blurred and interpenetrating nature. It is based on a 'three dimensional' framework whereby any discursive event is analysed on the basis of its being 'simultaneously a piece of text, an instance of discursive practice, and an instance of social practice' (Fairclough, 1992, p. 4). More specifically, what occurs is (i) examination of the actual content, structure and meaning of the text under scrutiny (*the text dimen*sion); (ii) examination of the form of discursive interaction used to communicate meaning and beliefs (*the discursive practice dimension*); and (iii) consideration of the social context in which the discursive event is taking place (*the social practice dimension*).

Like the systemic approaches of critical linguistics and social semiotics, CDA draws upon the theories and approaches of Bourdieu, Derrida, Lyotard and, in particular, Foucault, while at the same time utilizing systematic and detailed forms of textual analysis to be found in conversation analysis, studies of institutional dialogue and pragmatics. Crucially, it combines these forms of analysis with the concept of *intertextuality* (Bakhtin, 1986; Fairclough, 1992, 1995; Kress & Threadgold, 1988; Thibault, 1991). Intertextuality reminds us that while texts may be the discursive units on which the researcher focuses, discourse itself has an existence beyond any individual text from which it is constituted (Chalaby, 1996; Hardy, 2001; Heracleous & Barrett, 2001; Phillips et al., 2004). In short, any text is seen as 'a link in a chain of texts, reacting to, drawing in and transforming other texts' (Fairclough & Wodak, 1997, p. 262). The value of this approach is that it 'mediates the connection between language and social context, and facilitates more satisfactory bridging of the gap between texts and contexts (Fairclough, 1995, p. 189). Consequently, it takes us beyond simple examinations of verbal and written interaction and allows us to appreciate the importance of 'who uses language, how, why and when' (Van Dijk, 1997b, p. 2).

These features have made CDA and other intertextual approaches extremely attractive to organization theorists because they override representationist concerns that location cannot explain organization. Discourse analytic approaches that are intertextual thus suggest that to understand the constructive effects of discourse, researchers must contextualize discourses historically and socially. As Kress (cited in Hardy, 2001, p. 27) observes:

> Texts are the sites of the emergence of complexes of social meanings, produced in the particular history of the situation of production, that record in partial ways the histories of both the participants in the production of the text and of the institutions that are 'invoked' or brought into play, indeed a partial history of the language and the social system… (Kress, 1995, p. 122)

Four chapters in this *Handbook* demonstrate the significance of social and historical context, and the importance of intertextuality to studies of organizational discourse. In the first of these, Susan Ainsworth and Cynthia Hardy apply context-sensitive approaches (CDA, systemics and socio-linguistics) to the same piece of data (text from a novel) in order to study identity in organizational settings. Ainsworth and Hardy's approach to identity is essentially social constructionist in nature. Their point – derived from Hacking (2000) – is that constructionist studies of identity tend to focus on the 'product' of identity construction rather than the processes by which it comes about. They demonstrate how, combined, the various forms of discourse analysis can address this deficiency by allowing organizational researchers to examine the complex processes that constitute the construction of identity. As such, their chapter represents an attempt to 'revitalize' constructionist research in this area.

Earlier we noted that the language in use approaches to the study of organizational discourse downplay context. Ainsworth and Hardy's study challenges this criticism. Not only does it show the value of context-sensitive approaches to identity construction, it also shows that studies of language in use, notably conversation analysis, have an equally important role in investigating context. Language in use approaches can be used to demonstrate how rules and structures associated with particular discursive interactions constitute identities and how they lead to the institutionalization of these identities. Their chapter thus reminds us that while important, we should not necessarily seek to privilege context-sensitive approaches over those that focus on language in use. Both have something to offer the study of identity (as well as other socially and organizationally related phenomena). Moreover, their respective benefits are most apparent when they are used in a complimentary fashion.

The issue of discursive context is a central feature of Loizos Heracleous's chapter. For Heracleous, an important and often neglected feature of organizational discourse is the way in which historical and social context shapes or constructs its interpretation. To him, a failure to link the interpretation of discourse to context and to appreciate how and why this occurs has two interrelated and important repercussions. First, it contributes to and perpetuates a number of common misconceptions about the ontological and epistemological status of interpretivism, including that it is an abstract theoretical approach and a form of subjectivism. In so doing, it undermines the validity of interpretive discourse approaches (hermeneutics, rhetoric, metaphor, symbolic interactionism and critical discourse analysis). Secondly, it constrains our ability to understand how organizational members engage with, and make sense of, particular discourses and their associated texts and then act and behave as they do. For Heracleous, an understanding of this misconception and an appreciation of the significance of interpretivism are critical for the organizational discourse project to make progress. Accordingly, his chapter demonstrates the empirical and analytical rigour of interpretive-based approaches to the study of discourse, showing how, within a social constructionist framework, they can generate new and alternative understandings of a range of important organizational phenomena.

Like Heracleous, Stan Deetz, Kirsten Broadfoot and Donald Anderson remind us that it is not only the text under scrutiny that shapes interpretation, but also the other texts that interpreters invariably bring to the process. Their chapter demonstrates that texts can be linked to other texts and that this process is ongoing and recursive as texts are produced, reviewed and changed. In this respect Deetz and his co-authors address the intertextual properties of discourse. Their point is that no one theoretical or methodological approach can capture these properties. Instead, they suggest that researchers adopt a multi-level perspective of the organization and multiple discourse analytic methods. They draw on three approaches to examine the relationship between discourse and organization and go on to show how multi-level analyses would work. In using these three approaches they are able to enlarge their empirical and analytical focus and embrace the social and historical dynamics of organizational discourses. They do not, however, suggest that any one of the approaches is more valuable than the others. Instead they believe that a combination is most useful. In sum, Deetz and his colleagues advance the case for organizational discourse as a plurivocal project. Only by drawing on a combination of the many approaches available can this field of study progress.

Craig Prichard, Deborah Jones and Ralph Stablein also believe that adopting a context-sensitive approach to the study of organizational discourse is important. However, the context-sensitive approach they advocate differs in emphasis and purpose from those discussed so far. Their aim is for organizational discourse researchers to develop a reflexive understanding of their own context. Using Denzin and Lincoln's (2000) five research choice points, they demonstrate a number of questions that researchers need to ask about their own roles and the milieu in which they operate. Answers to these queries allow researchers to reflect on what might be the most appropriate discursive analytic approach to adopt in relation to the organizational phenomenon they wish to study. Prichard and his colleagues provide a chapter that enriches organizational discourse research practice. It is an invaluable aid to those who are novices to organizational discourse analysis.

EXPOSITION OF PLURIVOCALITY Methodological choices, such as those discussed above, are related to epistemological perspectives and, in this regard, we subscribe to a particular view of the way in which discourse 'does things'. Specifically, we believe that discourse does many things at the same time and over time, in many different arenas, and in ways that are not necessarily compatible or even visible. Thus, there can never be only one discourse that characterizes an organizational setting. Nor is there ever a definitive reading of organizational discourse. Researchers are only able to observe some of what is going on as a result of their methodological choices; and they promote particular readings of it depending on academic and professional considerations. Moreover, researchers are subjected to their own discursive orders that discipline what they see and think. Discourse is thus the site of a struggle that extends beyond organizational borders to encompass the academic project itself, and which is nested in multiple discourses. Accordingly, any particular research approach cannot but fail to capture the complexity of language use that occurs over time, in multiple sites, and in hidden ways: we make choices and trade-offs, some of which we are not even aware of. In advocating plurivocality, we subscribe to an epistemology that acknowledges the limitations of what we think we know, and provides space for different approaches and readings of organizational phenomena.

Not all researchers of organizational discourse take this approach, however. For example, a number of studies of organizational discourse, which might be described as positivist in their approach, see organizations as 'containers' of discourse and discourse as only one variable among many worthy of study. According to this perspective, discourse is a facet of organizational life; a communicative practice that can be empirically examined to determine its meaning and purpose. This 'containerization' of discourse has led to positivist approaches being described as viewing discourse in functional terms (Putnam et al., 1996): 'as a body of communicative actions that [serve as] tools at actors' disposal, emphasising the purposive and instrumental use of such communicative actions for the facilitation of managerially relevant processes and outcomes' (Heracleous & Barrett, 2001, p. 756). Drawing on, for example, conversation and rhetorical analysis, positivist studies of organizational discourse have undoubtedly provided valuable insights into organizational practices, such as decision-making, conflict management and leadership (Huisman, 2001; Westley & Mintzberg, 1989; Yeung, 1997). They use empirically derived data to identify patterns and regularities within the discursive interactions of various organizational actors (e.g., Brown, 1985; Crouch & Basch, 1997; Donnellon, 1994; Palmer & Dunford, 1996; Tannen, 1995).

The value of positivist studies, however, has been questioned on several important dimensions. Specifically, positivist approaches to the study of organizational discourse do not seek to uncover the ways that language constitutes and reconstitutes social arrangements (Putnam & Fairhurst, 2001). They do not, for example, dwell on how discourse is used by different groups to further their respective interests. Nor do they look at how discourse produces and maintains systems of power and control or how it is used to resist such systems. In some cases, such as Huisman's (2001) conversation analytic study of decision-making, this work demonstrates a limited recognition of the importance of context. These limitations lead to a flat, somewhat one-dimensional view of discourse and suggest that although positivist studies add considerably to our knowledge of practices and processes or 'functions of management' (Oswick et al., 1997), they reinforce rather than challenge the boundaries and constraints of organizing and organization.

Another limitation of the positivist approach to studying organizational discourse is an emphasis on a monological orientation (Eisenberg & Goodall, 1993; Grant et al., 1998b; Oswick, 2001) that presents a singular, coherent narrative or set of shared meanings among organizational members (Boje, 1995). Mumby and Clair term this a 'cultural/interpretative' approach which:

> tends to operate at a largely descriptive level, and focuses on the ways in which organization members' discursive practices contribute to the development of shared meaning. As such, the principal goal of this research is to demonstrate the connection between the shared norms and values of an organization on the one hand, and the means by which these norms and values are expressed on the other. (Mumby & Clair, 1997, pp. 182–3)

Perhaps the strongest condemnation of monological accounts of the organization comes from those who question the validity of such studies and the selective reading of data that leads to a reified, rhetorical analysis (Potter & Wetherell, 1987). They suggest that this can be avoided by utilizing the more dialogical (Eisenberg & Goodall, 1993) or polyphonic forms of analysis, to which we now turn.

In this regard, studies of organizational discourse that take a critical perspective expose the ways in which discourse constitutes and reconstitutes social arrangements in organizational settings. They emphasize how discourse is used to produce, maintain or resist power, control and inequality though ideology and hegemony (Mumby & Clair, 1997), and show discourse itself to be a power resource. More specifically, critical discourse studies see organizations as dialogical entities where discourses vie with each other for dominance (Oswick, 2001). They regard organizations as 'sites of struggle in which different groups compete to shape the social reality of organizations in ways that serve their own interests' (Mumby & Clair, 1997, p. 182) and in ways that enable them to exercise or resist social control. This, in turn, enables these studies to demonstrate how inequalities in power determine the ability to control the production, distribution and consumption of particular discourses (Clegg, 1975; Deetz, 1995; Giddens, 1979; Mumby & Stohl, 1991; Rosen, 1985). As Fairclough (1995, p. 2) explains, the 'power to control discourse is seen as the power to sustain particular discursive practices with particular ideological investments in dominance over other alternative (including oppositional) practices'.

The value of critical discourse studies, then, is that they explore how and why some organizational meanings become privileged, taken for granted and reified (Hardy, 2001). Similarly, they explain why power relations that appear fixed within organizations (Clegg, 1989) are really the result of ongoing discursive struggles in which any shared meaning is secured via a process of negotiation (Mumby & Stohl, 1991). Furthermore, they demonstrate that although some discourses may dominate, 'their dominance is secured as part of an ongoing struggle among competing discourses that are continually reproduced or transformed through day-to-day communicative practices' (Hardy, 2001, p. 28).

Critical organizational discourse studies draw on the work of a variety of social theorists such as Foucault (1978), Bourdieu (1991) and Giddens (1984) to reveal the political effects of discourse in relation to a variety of organizational phenomena. Moreover, they take an intertextual approach that is sensitive to historical and social context to explore how and why particular interests shape and are shaped by discourses that come to dominate (see above). Such studies utilize a variety of methodological approaches, including critical discourse analysis, socio-linguistics and critical linguistics. For example, focusing on the links between language and power, Fairclough has applied CDA to a variety of socio-cultural changes and trends as well as social and organizational discursive phenomena (Fairclough, 1992, 1995; Fairclough & Wodak, 1997). Others, such as Wodak and her colleagues, examine the effects of power structures and ideologies on individuals' organizational performances through a methodological approach consistent with socio-linguistics (Hein & Wodak, 1987; Muntigl et al., 1999; Wodak, 1996; Wodak & Matoushek, 1993).

Dennis Mumby's chapter contends that the critical perspective offers a highly effective means by which to understand how discourse constitutes and is constituted by social practices. In a detailed exposition of the links between discourse, power and ideology, he shows how discourse brings oppression and domination into existence and how these objects become material realities through the practices that they invoke. Mumby's argument is that discursive studies incorporating this perspective can unpack the complex power-related dimensions that permeate the construction of knowledge that fosters gendered and race-based identities within organizations. His chapter thus demonstrates how critical modes of engagement with organizational discourse influence 'the conditions that shape what may be said, who can speak within socially organized settings, the ways in which reality claims are made and the social practices that are invoked' (Hardy, 2001, p. 28). In this respect, critical discourse studies offer a rich insight into organizational processes and practices, one that is richer than findings drawn from positivist research.

Critical studies, however, have been criticized as being limited in their explanatory power. From a dialogical perspective, they assume that the organization is essentially a site of bi-vocal competition – a place where two competing discourses are in operation. These two discourses represent the forces of undue power and human emancipation (Chouliaraki & Fairclough, 1999, p. 34). Thus, while discursive studies of organizations tend to adopt a normative perspective of social relations in organizations, their ability to offer innovative insights into the complexities, paradoxes and contradictions that often characterize contemporary organizations is restricted. Postmodern modes of engagement overcome this problem by depicting the organization as a polyphonic (Oswick, 2001) entity that comprises paradoxical, fluid and contradictory processes. This perspective avoids reification of the concept 'organization', while offering a more complete explanation of the incoherence and inconsistency that underlies what organizations do to cope with the escalating demands of globalization and the increasing unpredictability of 'the market' (Tsoukas & Chia, 2002).

As with the critical perspective, postmodern approaches focus on the role of discourse in meaning construction and social relations within the organization, and hence adopt a social constructionist view. They are also highly intertextual in that they recognize the importance of the social and historical dynamics of discourse (Alvesson & Kärreman, 2000b; Boje, 1995, 2001; Burrell, 1996; Chia, 1998, 2000; Cooper, 1993; Keenoy et al., 1997; Parker, 2000). However, the postmodern perspective of organizational discourse challenges its critical and positivist counterparts in a number of significant respects. As Iedema (2003, p. 23) points out, postmodernism has acted as a rallying point for organization theorists who are becoming increasingly sceptical about the systematic and stable features of organization and who want to move beyond the patterns and regularities of conventional organizational theory. It does not commence with the premise that there is some pre-existing social object called 'organization', which is defined by its formal features and cohesive behaviours (Alvesson, 1995; Alvesson & Deetz, 1996; Chia, 1996; Czarniawska-Joerges, 1992; Gergen, 1992; Hassard, 1994; Kilduff & Mehra, 1997; Knights, 1997). Rather, it views the texts that constitute discourse as metaphors for organizing and as representing an array of multiple meanings. Consequently, they require careful deconstruction (Derrida, 1976) in order to reveal the concealed and marginalized elements within them and thereby open them up for alternative interpretations (Calás & Smircich, 1999; Putnam & Fairhurst, 2001). Studies adopting this approach examine the texts represented in a variety of discursive domains, including dialogue and conversation (Cissna & Anderson, 1998; Cooren, 1997, 1999, 2001; Cooren & Taylor, 1997, 1998; Eisenberg & Goodall, 1993; Groleau & Cooren, 1998; Isaacs, 1993, 1999; Kristiansen & Bloch-Poulsen, 2000; Taylor & Van Every, 2000) and narratives and stories (Boje, 1995, 2001; Czarniawska-Joerges, 1996; Gabriel, 1991, 1995, 1997, 1998).

The deconstruction of texts is the focus of Martin Kilduff and Mihaela Keleman's chapter. For them, the rise in organizational discourse studies is to be welcomed because it signals renewed appreciation of the importance of language and other symbolic media in understanding the social construction of organizations. However, although there has been a rise in the number of postmodern discourse studies, these often overlook the value of deconstruction in explicating the meanings of a given text. All too often, they argue, scholars apply discourse analytical approaches in ways that send them down predetermined paths towards self-evident meanings. The value of deconstruction, they argue, is that it enables the reader to examine the complexities of the text itself, does not prescribe any particular meaning to it and points out over-simplification on the part of previous non-deconstructive readings. To demonstrate these attributes, they deconstruct a classic organizational text, Chester Barnard's *The Functions of the Executive*, finding that this work should not be treated as a celebration of rationality, formal power structures and cooperation, but rather as a eulogy to the behaviour of the individual in the organization and his or her inherent need for camaraderie.

Postmodern studies acknowledge explicitly that the organization is a polyphonic entity comprising a multiplicity of discourses that reflect meanings of various participants (Grant et al., 1998b), and which result in fragmented, ambiguous and paradoxical meanings (Martin, 1992; Meyerson, 1991; Thatchenkery & Upadhaya, 1996). In so doing, they suggest that the organization is in fact an abstract notion that often fails to resonate with its members' lived reality. In this way, postmodernist studies of organizational discourse add a new dimension to what constitutes organization and organizing. Specifically, they suggest that what are often viewed as abstract principles underlie our shared understandings and experiences of organizations and that discourse inevitably plays an important role in both the social construction and deployment of these principles.

Taking a polyphonic approach to organizational discourse also leads postmodern studies to suggest that organizations are comprised of a multitude of 'organizational realities' which, although expressed in relatively autonomous discourses, may overlap and permeate each other. Accordingly, scholars can identify and analyse the many discourses and counter-discourses that actors use to make sense of their work, their colleagues and the organization. These assumptions permeate other epistemological positions and so, while the *Handbook* contains two separate chapters on the critical and postmodern perspectives, these boundaries blur as writers draw on and combine insights from both perspectives, as can be seen in, for example, the chapters on power, culture and globalization.

Discourses and Organizing

Parts I and II of the *Handbook*, in combination, represent studies that address the theoretical and conceptual features of organizational discourse and examine the methodological and epistemological perspectives that inform discourse analyses. The chapters in Part III focus on the discourses of organizing; that is, they use discourse analytic techniques as a 'vehicle' to scrutinize and analyse specific organizational phenomena (see Table 1). In so doing, they show how organizational discourses bring objects such as identity, knowledge and power relations (Alvesson, 1996; Du Gay & Salaman, 1992; Hardy et al., 1998, Phillips & Hardy, 1997) into existence and how they are manifested in organizational practices. Similarly, they show how studies have illuminated our understandings of organizational strategy (Knights & Morgan, 1991); negotiation processes (Putnam, 2004); decision-making (Huisman, 2001); interorganizational collaboration (Hardy et al., 1998); organizational change (Mueller et al., 2004); and workplace control (Knights & Wilmott, 1989). The chapters in Part III of this *Handbook* exemplify this approach, providing fresh insights into a variety of specific, organizationally related issues.

Karen Ashcraft's chapter examines the contribution of the discursive turn to the study of gender in organizations. Ashcraft notes how discourse constitutes – rather than simply reflects – gendered identity in organizational settings. She contends that this view highlights the ways in which discursive activity creates, solidifies, disrupts and alters gender identities. The discursive literature on gender, however, has given rise to a diversity of views that Ashcraft finds both useful and encumbering. Her chapter seeks to sensitize the researcher to this fact by identifying four dominant ways of framing the relationships among discourse, gender and organization. It does not, however, identify any one of these as the 'optimal' perspective, but instead clarifies points of agreement and tensions among them. Ashcraft concludes by calling for researchers to move from one frame of reference to another, suggesting that this process of interplay will evoke new ways of seeing.

Many studies of organizational discourse, particularly those that adopt a critical perspective, suggest that the social construction of discourse emerges from the power-laden contexts in which meanings are negotiated. Cynthia Hardy and Nelson Phillip's chapter reminds us that power and discourse are mutually constitutive. In short, discourse shapes power relations and power relations shape which actors are able to influence discourse. Hardy and Phillips propose a framework that offers a useful alternative to mainstream approaches to the study of power and politics in organizations. This framework melds the extant power literature and the work of Foucault and critical discourse analysts with the way that discourse shapes power. The resultant framework is essentially intertextual and highly sensitive to both temporal and spatial contexts. It enables the researcher to explain why some actors, as opposed to others, are better able to produce and modify texts that influence discourse in ways beneficial to these actors. It also demonstrates how power relations come about over a period of time and why they, and the discourses they invoke, change.

For Mats Alvesson, studies of organizational culture often downplay the importance of discourse and, instead, focus on shared, moderately stable forms of meaning that are only partially verbalized. Culture focuses on systems of meanings and symbolism that become taken for granted, and thus need to be deciphered. Myths, basic assumptions about human nature and perceptions of the organizational environment are often 'language-distant', that is, they are rarely espoused and form part of the sub-conscious. Conversely, discursive studies of culture look at language in use and view the meanings attached to culture as discursively constituted. This approach leads to identification of culture-related discourses and their effects on the organization. Alvesson uses his chapter to preserve the integrity of both the cultural and discursive approaches to the study of organizations, believing that both provide valuable insights into the phenomenon. Thus, he advocates an approach to culture that is sensitive to, but not solely focused on, the importance of language. He argues that preserving and applying this distinction will yield rich analytical insights.

Christian Heath, Paul Luff and Hubert Knoblauch's chapter synthesizes a body of research known as 'workplace studies'. These studies focus on a range of tools and technologies that are present in our day-to-day working lives. More specifically, they utilize discourse analytic methods to explore how these artefacts have become taken for granted in workplaces while simultaneously demonstrating that their use rests upon social and organizational interactions. For Heath and his colleagues, conventional studies of organizational discourse downplay the material aspects of an organization and the way these aspects affect language and talk at work. Thus, they demonstrate how language in use affects the tools and technology in the workplace. With workplace studies, the opposite holds true; using examples from a doctor–patient consultation and a television newsroom, they show how tools and technologies create socially enacted rules that impact on the form, content and meaning of discursive interactions. This relationship, argue Heath and his colleagues, provides an innovative, distinct and detailed analytical approach to the study of work and how it is accomplished.

Like Heath and his colleagues, Pablo Boczkowski and Wanda Orlikowski also focus on workplace technology and how it impacts on the accomplishment of work. Their chapter, however, examines research on new technology and the new media. New media refers to information, telecommunication and communication technologies, for example, electronic mail, videoconferencing, instant messaging and voice mail. For Boczkowski and Orlikowski, the communication literature continues to distinguish between face-to-face and mediated communication, despite the widespread integration of communication media. What is important, however, is whether the users of new media believe it to be synchronous – that is, whether they see it as a form of communication that allows for immediacy of interaction, direct connection to others and control over the pace and timing of the conversation. To examine the extent to which synchrony occurs, they develop an innovative framework – one in which the discourses of the new media users are analysed in conjunction with their actual practices. Boczkowski and Orlikowski argue that such an approach provides important insights into the dynamic, emergent nature of organizational discourse and how new media and its synchrony impacts these processes.

The final chapter in this section examines globalization as it impacts on the process of organizing. For Norman Fairclough and Pete Thomas an appreciation of how certain versions of the term 'globalization' have come to dominate our thinking about organizations is achieved by adopting a dialectical approach to the issue. This involves their drawing a distinction between what they call the 'discourse of globalization' and the 'globalization of discourse'. Discourses of globalization refer to texts about globalization. They crystallize globalization as a distinct social practice, and often present it as a reified object that emanates from an ongoing and inevitable flow. Fairclough and Thomas suggest that these discursive representations are resources developed by particular social agents to achieve particular social ends. Moreover, they reinforce the process of globalization in ways that these actors did not intend or anticipate. The globalization of discourse refers to the emergence of organizational discourses as global in reach and penetration. This process occurs, first, when the discourse of globalization is recontextualized into one that assimilates local pre-existing discourses and, second, when globalization is translated into moments of social action that change belief systems or social structures within and around organizations. The processes that Fairclough and Thomas identify as crucial to globalization are likely to apply to other social phenomena and how they impact on organizations. However, these processes are not only conceptually important, they are also politically significant in demonstrating how powerful, hegemonic discourses promote oppression and inequality. Fairclough and Thomas end on an optimistic note by pointing out that their chapter demonstrates the frailties, weaknesses and contradictions that occur within these processes. These contradictions can be exploited for resistance and the development of counter-emancipatory discourses.

In providing the above categorization for the chapters of the *Handbook* which, in turn, influences, and is influenced by, the chapters themselves as well as our own views of organizational discourse, we need to make two disclaimers. First, we have noted the plurivocal nature of the studies of organizational discourse in this *Handbook*. In this regard, we admit to privileging plurivocality as a feature of work on organizational discourse that we value highly. We offer no apologies for this, other than to say that a number of other researchers clearly agree that this is a useful way for the field to develop. We also acknowledge that, in setting up categories of disciplinary antecedents and epistemological positions, we inevitably reify 'false' distinctions. We do so for analytic purposes and concede that the various domains, methods and perspectives complement one another, and any apparent divisions among them should be regarded as blurred or interpenetrating. Accordingly, we do not see this categorization as a way in which particular authors or studies can be neatly pigeonholed or mapped on to a grid. Rather, it allows us to identify the key philosophical, theoretical, epistemological and methodological tenets of organizational discourse research and to provide greater understanding of the complex nature of the relationship between organizational discourse and the study of organizations.

ORGANIZATIONAL DISCOURSE: KEY ISSUES AND DEBATES

Several key issues and debates regarding organizational discourse surface in this *Handbook*. These pertain to the negotiation of meaning, intertextuality, cognitive approaches to organizational discourse, and reflexivity. These issues and debates are significant in assessing the contributions of organizational discourse to the study of organizations. They also set direction for future research in the field.

The Negotiation of Meaning

Collectively, the chapters in this *Handbook* contribute to the growing body of literature through examining how meaning is negotiated in organizations and how these struggles impact on organizing. Each chapter in its own way demonstrates how struggles around meaning are played out in organizations. Further, each one reminds us that organizations do not start out 'possessing' meaning; instead, meanings are created and contested through discursive interactions among organizational actors and organizational publics with divergent interests (Mumby & Clair, 1997). The emergence of dominant meanings arises as alternative discourses are subverted or marginalized. In highlighting this process, a number of *Handbook* chapters also demonstrate that the negotiation of meaning is influenced by discursive context and, more specifically, intertextuality. This brings us to our next point.

The Significance of Intertextuality

Our discussion of context-sensitive approaches to discourse, along with several of the chapters in the *Handbook* (e.g., Heracleous, Deetz et al., Fairclough & Thomas), demonstrates that the negotiation of meaning unfolds through the complex interplay of both socially and historically produced texts (Alvesson & Kärreman, 2000a; Keenoy & Oswick, 2004) that are part of a continuous, iterative and recursive process (Grant & Hardy, 2004; Taylor et al., 1996). This process means that the outcome of such negotiations are what produce 'organization', and that in so doing they also produce the context in which the discourse is embedded and from which new discourses emerge – what Iedema and Wodak (1999) have described as 'recontextualization'. Thus, when studying a particular discursive interaction, organizational researchers should consider other interactions that operate in different arenas and at different times, and which are linked to and inform interpretations of the discourse under scrutiny. As pointed out by Deetz and his co-authors in their chapter, this aspect of organizational discourse analysis remains under-theorized in two significant respects.

First, historical context imposes temporal constraints on intertextual studies in that a text that was produced in the past can only be linked to a text in the present (Keenoy & Oswick, 2004). It does not acknowledge that what is said in the past or present has a significant impact on what is said in the *future*. Keenoy and Oswick observe that only a handful of studies focus on the projective content of a discourse, that is, its implications, outcomes and aims. These studies include Pearce and Cronen's (1979) work on the way that social actors assess the potentially negative and positive consequences of their discursive actions for themselves and for others and act accordingly.

Secondly, Keenoy and Oswick (2004) also point out that intertextual approaches often focus only on context as a 'backdrop' to the discursive episode under scrutiny when what is actually needed is to see context as *embedded* within the episode itself, that is, 'the text actually forms part of the context and vice versa'. Similarly, Latour (2000) has argued that the micro and macro levels of discourse are in many ways indivisible, while Cooren (2001) has shown how micro-level utterances are mutually implicated with discourses on macro-level organizing. Drawing on the work of Adam (1998) and Schama (1995), Keenoy and Oswick conclude that organizational discourse researchers need to analyse what they call the 'textscape' of a discursive event in order to obtain a comprehensive understanding of its meaning. To achieve this, more studies need to assess simultaneously *both* the temporal and social dynamics of organizational discourse. In doing so they must recognize that the dynamics are blurred and interpenetrating and be appreciative of the fact that they are embedded in the text of the discursive event itself, rather than just surrounding or being linked to it.

Cognitive Approaches and the Study of Organizational Discourse

Cognitive approaches such as those advocated by cognitive linguists (Brown, 1970; Johnson, 1987; Lakoff, 1987) and cognitive psychologists (Graesser et al., 1997) have sought to map cognitive frameworks on to the study of discourse. Although they differ in emphasis, they nevertheless share a common interest in how the mind processes and constructs discourse (Forrester, 1996, pp. 5–7; Greene, 1986). This concern sets them apart from the methodological approaches discussed earlier in this chapter. Specifically, cognitive approaches show that a variety of verbal, written or symbolic forms of discourse evoke mental processes such as scripts, schemata and frames that are rooted in mental maps of cultural, social and organizational experiences (Lord & Kernan, 1987; Moch & Fields, 1985).

Within organizational studies, cognitive approaches fall into the broad category of sense-making (Putnam & Fairhurst, 2001). Studies adopting the cognitive approach show how the discursively constructed meanings that reside in our minds impact on collective sense-making and thus on the processes of organizing (Gioia, 1986; Weick, 1995). In so doing, these studies have looked at the impact of cognitive scripts and schema on such activities as performance appraisals (Gioia et al., 1989), negotiations and bargaining (Carroll & Payne, 1991; O'Connor & Adams, 1999) and superior–subordinate relationships (Gioia & Sims, 1983).

Despite this work, cognitive approaches to the study of organizational discourse are relatively underdeveloped. The organizational discourse literature exhibits a tendency to shy away from the cognitive aspects of words and their meanings in organizations. Indeed, the *Handbook* itself reflects this fact. No chapter is solely devoted to this issue and only a few integrate cognitive aspects of discourse into their analyses (see, e.g., Heracleous or Deetz et al.).

Marshak and colleagues (Marshak et al., 2000, pp. 250–1) suggest that this paucity of cognitive material stems from the infancy of organizational discourse studies and the dominance of researchers with organizational sociology rather than psychology backgrounds. They also suggest that many organizational discourse scholars feel more comfortable with conventional perspectives of language found in socio-linguistics and, more recently, the 'postmodern turn'. Consequently, the key metaphors and analogues they employ conceptualize organizational phenomena as 'narratives', 'texts', 'conversations' or 'discourses' and the methodological approaches adopted focus on discerning the social meaning(s) of discourse as opposed to individual motivations and the psychological origins of words. This dearth of cognitive research leads us to reiterate Marshak et al.'s (2000) call for more studies of organizational discourse that examine the psychosocial origins of organizational texts, narratives and meanings, which lie beneath the subtext of social interaction.

Reflexivity

As the chapters in this *Handbook* contribute to unpacking how organizational meanings are negotiated, it is important to acknowledge that we, as editors, are clearly negotiating meaning for organizational discourse. This interpretation of reflexivity is well embedded within the discourse of organizational discourse (e.g., Chia, 2000; Iedema, 2003; Keenoy et al., 2000b). As Alvesson and Kärreman (2000b, p. 145) have observed, organizational discourse provides researchers with the opportunity to reflect on the ambiguous and constructed nature of the data with which they must work, while at the same time allowing them space for bold ways of interacting with the material. We have directly addressed the issue of reflexivity in other writings (Grant & Hardy, 2004). Here, we adopt a different approach: we commissioned three eminent scholars to review the *Handbook*'s contents and to comment on the strength and limitations of this volume in contributing to our understanding of organization. Their reflections comprise the final section of the *Handbook* and represent an important contribution.

Barbara Czarniawska's contribution focuses on the benefits arising from an upsurge of interest in the discursive analysis of organizations and organizing. In doing so she highlights that the 'discursive turn' has been helpful in so far as it diverts attention away from the overly mechanical view of information transfer prevalent in traditional models of communication (i.e., those which emphasize issues around the sender, receiver, message, noise and feedback). Drawing upon the work of Paul Ricœur, Czarniawska provides an account of speaking and writing as separated discursive forms through the deployment of the concept of 'distanciation' (the processes by which text acquires a distance from speech). She goes on to assert that treating text *as* action and action *as* text is crucial within the field of organization studies.

Karl Weick's reflection on acting discursively in organizations also highlights the relationship between text and action. Referring to the image of smoke, Weick encourages researchers to focus on the dynamic, transient smoke-like character of evolving conversations. These images capture the interface among saying, doing, seeing and enacting that unites a lived world with a text world. Weick points out that the term 'discourse analysis' may convey a more static picture of discourse than researchers intended. He cautions theorists to avoid the trap of treating discourse as self-contained or de-contextualized and, instead, to see it as becoming, embedded in context, known in aftermath, and within flux.

The final reflection injects a cautionary note for those taken with organizational discourse as Mike Reed attempts to bring a sense of realism back into its study. He thus uses his reflections chapter as an opportunity to put forward a critical realist perspective of organizational discourse. To Reed there is a worrying propensity among those who research in the field to reduce social constructionism to being a purely discursively determined process. He asserts that this raises a number of crucial questions about the inherent explanatory aspirations and limits of discourse analysis within organization studies which cannot be ignored. Reed seeks to develop an alternative and more meaningful approach to organizational discourse analysis, one which by virtue of adopting a critical realist perspective recognizes that 'organization' comes about primarily as a result of non-discursive interactions between particular agents and the various structural conditions and contingencies that determine conditions of action. This is not, however, to deny a role to discourse where it is seen as a representational or performative practice that is located within and reproduced through generative mechanisms or structures. For Reed, the advantage of such an approach is that it more clearly demonstrates the ways in which, for example, organizational discourse reshapes ongoing struggles for power and reinforces institutionalized power structures. At the same time it is an approach based on the premise that discourse isn't everything!

CONCLUSION

In this introduction we have sought to explore the field of organizational discourse and, in doing so, to provide an overview that captures its value and purpose as well as its plurivocal nature. The chapter has shown that the field encompasses a number of domains of study and variety of methodological approaches and epistemological perspectives that enable researchers to investigate a range of organizational phenomena. These attributes often delimit the parameters of a particular research question and facilitate analysis of an enormous range of data types (Grant et al., 2001; Phillips & Hardy, 2002).

Organizational discourse has made several important contributions to our understanding of organization. Most notably, it has shown how discourse is central to the social construction of reality (Berger & Luckmann, 1967; Searle, 1995) and, more specifically, and as part of this process, the negotiation of meaning. As such, discourse 'acts as a powerful ordering force in organizations' (Alvesson & Kärreman, 2000b, p. 1127). Discourse analytic approaches therefore allow the researcher to identify and analyse the key organizational discourses by which ideas are formulated and articulated and to show how, via a variety of discursive interactions and practices, these go on to shape and influence the attitudes and behaviour of an organization's members. Many of the chapters in this volume exemplify this attribute. They have, for example, illuminated an understanding of globalization, technology, identity, power and culture.

Yet despite the contributions to our understanding of organizations that studies of organizational discourse have so far made, there remains the sense that its considerable potential remains relatively under-utilized – a point made all the more significant when we consider that most of the activity in organizations (i.e., organizing and managing) is primarily discursive. In this regard, the study of discourse in organizations is in many ways analogous to the notion of 'oceans on earth'. Both organizational discourse and the oceans form the largest part of the macro phenomena in which they are embedded but they remain the least explored, least understood and most under-utilized parts. More studies of organizational discourse are needed, studies that are undertaken from a variety of methodological and epistemological perspectives and which take into account its intertextual and cognitive features. We believe that for this to occur we need to integrate the insights of organizational discourse into organizational research even more broadly than has already been the case. There remains enormous scope to explore how discourse analysis relates to other theories that are familiar to organizational scholars, such as institutional theory, sense-making and actor-network theory, as well as drawing on work on discourse analytic approaches that has been undertaken in fields like psychology, sociology and political science. This is not to deny that some organizational researchers are already incorporating a wider frame of reference for their work; rather it is to encourage others to join those (e.g., Alvesson & Deetz, 2000; Alvesson & Kärreman, 2000a, 2000b; Burrell, 1997; Chia, 2000; Cooper, 1993; Deetz, 1992, 1995; Gergen, 1994, 1999; Keenoy et al., 1997; Kilduff, 1993; Knights, 1997; Parker, 2000; Reed, 2000; Tsoukas, 2000) who link discourse to broader social theory in order to provide new explanations and understanding of organizational structures and processes.

NOTES

1 This project was carried out under the auspices of The International Centre for Research in Organizational Discourse, Strategy and Change and with the financial support of the Universities of Melbourne and Sydney.
2 The International Centre for Research in Organizational Discourse, Strategy and Change comprises eight institutional partners: the University of Melbourne, Australia; the University of Sydney, Australia; the University of Leicester, UK; Texas A&M University, USA; The Judge Institute of Management, University of Cambridge, UK; Lund University, Sweden; McGill University, Canada; and King's College, London, UK. It provides a critical mass of expertise in organizational discourse and offers an innovative approach to the study of strategy and change in organizations.

REFERENCES

Adam, B. (1998) *Timescapes of modernity*. London: Routledge.
Alvesson, M. (1993) The play of metaphors. In J. Hassard & M. Parker (eds), *Postmodernism and organization* (pp. 114–31). London: Sage.
Alvesson, M. (1995) The meaning and meaninglessness of postmodernism: Some ironic remarks. *Organization Studies*, 16 (6): 1047–75.
Alvesson, M. (1996) *Communication, power and organization*. Berlin: Walter de Gruyter.

Alvesson, M. & Deetz, S. (1996) Critical theory and postmodernism approaches to organizational studies. In S. Clegg, C. Hardy & W. Nord (eds), *Handbook of organization studies* (pp. 78–99). London: Sage.

Alvesson, M. & Deetz, S. (2000) *Doing critical management research*. London: Sage.

Alvesson, M. & Kärreman, D. (2000a) Taking the linguistic turn in organizational research. *Journal of Applied Behavioral Science*, 36 (2): 136–58.

Alvesson, M. & Kärreman, D. (2000b) Varieties of discourse: On the study of organizations through discourse analysis. *Human Relations*, 53 (9): 1125–49.

Austin, J. (1962) *How to do things with words*. Oxford: Oxford University Press.

Bakeman, R. & Gottman, J.M. (1986) *Observing interaction: An introduction to sequential analysis*. Cambridge: Cambridge University Press.

Bakhtin, M.M. (1981) *The dialogic imagination: Four essays by M.M. Bakhtin*. Edited by C. Emerson & M. Holquist. Austin, TX: University of Texas Press.

Bakhtin, M.M. (1986) *Speech genres and other late essays*. Edited and trans. by C. Emerson & M. Holquist. Austin, TX: University of Texas Press.

Barrett, F.J. & Cooperrider, D.L. (1990) Generative metaphor intervention: A new behavioral approach for working with systems divided by conflict and caught in defensive perception. *Journal of Applied Behavioral Science*, 26 (2): 219–39.

Barry, D. & Elmes, M. (1997) Strategy retold: toward a narrative view of strategic discourse. *Academy of Management Review*, 22 (2): 429–52.

Barton, L. (1993) *Crisis in organizations: Managing and communicating in the heat of chaos*. Cincinnati, OH: College Divisions South-Western Publishing.

Beech, N. (2000) Narrative styles of managers and workers: A tale of star-crossed lovers. *Journal of Applied Behavioral Science*, 36 (2): 210–28.

Benoit, W.L. & Brinson, S.L. (1994) AT&T: 'Apologies are not enough'. *Communication Quarterly*, 42: 75–88.

Berger, P. & Luckmann, T. (1967) *The social construction of reality*. London: Penguin.

Blum-Kulka, S. (1997) Discourse pragmatics. In T.A. Van Dijk (ed.), *Discourse as social interaction: Discourse studies vol. 2 – A multidisciplinary introduction* (pp. 38–63). London: Sage.

Boden, D. (1994) *The business of talk: Organizations in action*. Cambridge: Polity Press.

Bohm, D. (1996) *On dialogue*. Edited by Lee Nichol. New York: Routledge.

Boje, D.M. (1991) The storytelling organization: A study of performance in an office supply firm. *Administrative Science Quarterly*, 36: 106–26.

Boje, D.M. (1995) Stories of the storytelling organization: A postmodern analysis of Disney as *Tamara*-Land. *Academy of Management Journal*, 38 (4): 997–1035.

Boje, D.M. (2001) *Narrative methods for organizational and communications research*. London: Sage.

Boje, D.M., Ford, J. & Oswick, C. (2004) Language and organization: The doing of discourse. *Academy of Management Review*, forthcoming.

Bourdieu, P. (1991) *Language and symbolic power*. Trans. G. Raymond & M. Adamson. Cambridge, MA: Harvard University Press.

Brink, T.L. (1993) Metaphor as data in the study of organizations. *Journal of Management Inquiry*, 2: 366–71.

Broussine, M. & Vince, R. (1996) Working with metaphor towards organizational change. In C. Oswick & D. Grant (eds), *Organization development: Metaphorical explorations* (pp. 557–72). London: Pitman.

Brown, A. (2000) Making sense of inquiry sensemaking. *Journal of Management Studies*, 37 (1): 45–75.

Brown, A. (2004) Authoritative sensemaking in a public inquiry report. *Organization Studies*, 25 (1): 95–112.

Brown, A.D. & Humphreys, M. (2003) Epic and tragic tales: Making sense of change. *Journal of Applied Behavioral Science*, 39 (2): 121–44.

Brown, G. & Yule, G. (1983) *Discourse analysis*. Cambridge: Cambridge University Press.

Brown, M.H. (1985) That reminds me of a story: Speech action in organizational socialization. *Western Journal of Speech Communication*, 49: 27–42.

Brown, M.H. (1990) Defining stories in organizations: Characteristics and function. In S. Deetz (ed.), *Communication yearbook* (Vol. 13, pp. 162–90). Newbury Park, CA: Sage.

Brown, R. (1970) *Psycholinguistics: Selected papers*. New York: Free Press.

Buber, M. (1958) *I and thou* (2nd edition). Trans. R.G. Smith. New York: Scribner. (Original work published 1923.)

Burrell, G. (1996) Normal science, paradigms, metaphors, discourses and genealogies of analysis. In S. Clegg, C. Hardy & W. Nord (eds), *Handbook of organization studies* (pp. 642–58). London: Sage.

Burrell, G. (1997) *Pandemonium: Towards a retro-organization theory*. London: Sage.

Calás, M. & Smircich, L. (1999) Past postmodernism? Reflections and tentative directions. *Academy of Management Review*, 24 (4): 649–71.

Campbell, K.S., Follender, S.I. & Shane, G. (1998) Preferred strategies for responding to hostile questions in environmental public meetings. *Management Communication Quarterly*, 11: 401–21.

Carroll, J.S. & Payne, J.W. (1991) An information processing approach to two-party negotiations. In J.S. Carroll & J.W. Payne (eds), *Research on negotiation in organizations* (pp. 3–34). Greenwich, CT: JAI Press.

Chalaby, J.K. (1996) Beyond the prison-house of language: Discourse as a sociological concept. *British Journal of Sociology*, 47 (4): 684–98.

Chia, R. (1996) *Organizational analysis as deconstructive practice*. Berlin and New York: Walter de Gruyter.

Chia, R. (ed.) (1998) *Organized worlds: Exploring the expanded realm of technology, organization and modernity*. London: Routledge.

Chia, R. (2000) Discourse analysis as organizational analysis. *Organization*, 7 (3): 513–18.

Chouliaraki, L. & Fairclough, N. (1999) *Discourse in late modernity: Rethinking critical discourse analysis*. Edinburgh: Edinburgh University Press.

Cissna, K.N. & Anderson, R. (1998) Theorizing about dialogic moments: The Buber–Rogers position and postmodern themes. *Communication Theory*, 8 (1): 63–104.

Clark, T. & Salaman, G. (1996a) The use of metaphor in the client–consultant relationship: A study of management consultants. In C. Oswick & D. Grant (eds), *Organizational development: Metaphorical explorations* (pp. 118–40). London: Pitman.

Clark, T. & Salaman, G. (1996b) Telling tales: Management consultancy as the art of storytelling. In D. Grant & C. Oswick (eds), *Metaphor and organizations* (pp. 166–84). London: Sage.

Clegg, S. (1975) *Power, rule and domination*. London: Routledge and Kegan Paul.

Clegg, S.R. (1989) *Frameworks of power*. London: Sage.

Collins, R. (1981) On the microfoundations of macrosociology. *American Journal of Sociology*, 86 (5): 984–1013.

Collinson, D.L. (1988) 'Engineering humour': Masculinity, joking and conflict in shop-floor relations. *Organization Studies*, 9 (2): 181–99.

Collinson, D.L. (1994) Strategies of resistance: Power, knowledge and subjectivity in the workplace. In J. Jermier, W. Nord & D. Knights (eds), *Resistance and power in organizations* (pp. 142–60). London: Routledge.

Coombs, W.T. (1995) Choosing the right words: The development of guidelines for the selection of the 'appropriate' crisis-response strategies. *Management Communication Quarterly*, 8: 447–76.

Cooper, R. (1993) Formal organization as representation: Remote control, displacement and abbreviation. In M. Reed & M. Hughes (eds), *Rethinking organization: New directions in organization theory and analysis* (pp. 254–72). London: Sage.

Cooren, F. (1997) Actes de langage et sémio-narrativité: une analyse semiotique des indirections. *Semiotica*, 116: 339–73.

Cooren, F. (1999) Applying socio-semiotics to organizational communication: A new approach. *Management Communication Quarterly*, 13 (2): 294–304.

Cooren, F. (2001) *The organizing property of communication*. Amsterdam/Philadelphia: John Benjamins.

Cooren, F. & Taylor, J.R. (1997) Organization as an effect of mediation: Redefining the link between organization and communication. *Communication Theory*, 7: 219–60.

Cooren, F. & Taylor, J.R. (1998) The procedural and rhetorical modes of the organizing dimension of communication: Discursive analysis of a parliamentary commission. *Communication Review*, 3 (1–2): 65–101.

Crouch, A. & Basch J. (1997) The structure of strategic thinking: A lexical content analysis. *Journal of Applied Management Studies*, 6 (1): 13–38.

Currie, G. & Brown, A.D. (2003) A narratological approach to understanding processes of organizing in a UK hospital. *Human Relations*, 56 (5): 563–86.

Czarniawska-Joerges, B. (1992) *Exploring complex organizations: A cultural perspective*. Newbury Park, CA: Sage.

Czarniawska-Joerges, B. (1996) Autobiographical acts and organizational identities. In S. Linstead, R. Grafton-Small & P. Jeffcutt (eds), *Understanding management* (pp. 127–49). London: Sage.

Czarniawska-Joerges, B. (1997) *Narrating the organization: Dramas of institutional identity*. Chicago: University of Chicago Press.

Czarniawska-Joerges, B. (1998) *A narrative approach to organization studies*. Newbury Park, CA: Sage.

Deetz, S. (1992) *Democracy in an age of corporate colonization*. Albany, NY: State University of New York Press.

Deetz, S. (1995) *Transforming communication, transforming business: Building responsive and responsible workplaces*. Cresskill, NJ: Hampton Press.

Denzin, N.K. & Lincoln Y.S. (eds) (2000) *Handbook of qualitative research* (2nd edition). Thousand Oaks, CA: Sage.

Derrida, J. (1976) *Of grammatology*. Baltimore, MD: Johns Hopkins University Press.

Donnellon, A. (1994) Team work: Linguistic models of negotiating differences. In R.J. Lewicki, B.H. Sheppard & R. Bies (eds), *Negotiations in organizations* (Vol. 4, pp. 71–123). Greenwich, CT: JAI Press.

Drew, P. & Heritage, J. (1992) Analysing talk at work: An introduction. In P. Drew & J. Heritage (eds), *Talk at work: Interaction in institutional settings* (pp. 3–65). Cambridge: Cambridge University Press.

Drew, P. & Sorjonen, M. (1997) Institutional dialogue. In T.A. Van Dijk (ed.), *Discourse as structure and process: Discourse studies Vol. 1 – A multidisciplinary introduction* (pp. 92–118). London: Sage.

Du Gay, P. & Salaman, G. (1992) The cult[ure] of the customer. *Journal of Management Studies*, 29 (5): 615–34.

Dunford, R. & Jones, D. (2000) Narrative and strategic change. *Human Relations*, 53 (9): 1207–26.

Dunford, R. & Palmer, I. (1996) Metaphors in popular management discourse: The case of corporate restructuring. In D. Grant & C. Oswick (eds), *Metaphor and organization* (pp. 95–109). London: Sage.

Eisenberg, E.M. & Goodall, H.L. (1993) *Organizational communication: Balancing creativity and constraint*. New York: St Martin's Press.

Fairclough, N. (1992) *Discourse and social change*. Cambridge: Polity Press.

Fairclough, N. (1995) *Critical discourse analysis: The critical study of language*. Language in Social Life Series. London: Longman.

Fairclough, N. & Wodak, R. (1997) Critical discourse analysis. In T.A. Van Dijk (ed.), *Discourse as social interaction: Discourse studies vol. 2 – A multidisciplinary introduction* (pp. 258–84). London: Sage.

Feldman, S.P. (1990) Stories as cultural creativity: On the relation between symbolism and politics in organizational change. *Human Relations*, 43 (9): 809–28.

Fisher, S. & Todd, D.D. (1983) *The social organization of doctor–patient communication*. Washington, DC: Center for Applied Linguistics.

Ford, J. & Ford, L. (1995) The role of conversations in producing intentional change in organizations. *Academy of Management Review*, 20 (3): 541–70.

Forrester, M.A. (1996) *Psychology of language: A critical introduction*. London: Sage.

Foucault, M. (1965) *Madness and civilization: A history of insanity in the age of reason*. New York: Vintage.

Foucault, M. (1973) *The birth of the clinic: An archeology of medical perception*. New York: Vintage.

Foucault, M. (1974) *The archeology of knowledge*. New York: Pantheon.

Foucault, M. (1976) Governmentality. *I&C*, 6: 5–21.

Foucault, M. (1977) *Discipline and punish: The birth of the prison*. Harmondsworth: Penguin.

Foucault, M. (1978) *The history of sexuality (Vol. I)*. Harmondsworth: Penguin.

Foucault, M. (1986) *The care of the self: The history of sexuality (Vol. III)*. Harmondsworth: Penguin.

Fowler, R. & Kress, G. (1979) Rules and regulations. In R. Fowler, B. Hodge, G. Kress & T. Trew, *Language and Control*. London: Routledge and Kegan Paul.

Gabriel, Y. (1991) Turning facts into stories and stories into facts. *Human Relations*, 44 (8): 857–75.

Gabriel, Y. (1995) The unmanaged organization: Stories, fantasies, subjectivity. *Organization Studies*, 16 (3): 477–501.

Gabriel, Y. (1997) The use of stories in organizational research. In D. Symon & N. Cassell (eds), *Qualitative methods in organizational research* (pp. 60–74). London: Sage.

Gabriel, Y. (1998) Same old story or changing stories? Folkloric, modern and post-modern mutations. In D. Grant, T. Keenoy & C. Oswick (eds), *Discourse and organization* (pp. 84–103). London: Sage.

Gergen, K.J. (1992) Organization theory in the postmodern era. In M. Reed & M. Hughes (eds), *Rethinking organization: New directions in organization theory and analysis* (pp. 62–81). London: Sage.

Gergen, K.J. (1994) *Realities and representations: Soundings in social construction*. Cambridge, MA: Harvard University Press.

Gergen, K.J. (1999) *An invitation to social construction*. London: Sage.

Gergen, K.J., McNamee, S. & Barrett, F. (2001) Toward transformative dialogue. *International Journal of Public Administration*, 24: 697–707.

Gibbs, R.W. Jr. (1993) Process and products in making sense of tropes. In A. Ortony (ed.), *Metaphor and thought* (2nd edition, pp. 252–76). Chicago: University of Chicago Press.

Giddens, A. (1979) *Central problems in social theory: Action, structure and contradiction in social analysis*. Berkeley, CA: University of California Press.

Giddens, A. (1984) *The constitution of society*. Cambridge: Polity Press.

Gioia, D.A. (1986) The state of the art in organizational social cognition. In H.P. Sims, Jr. & D.A. Gioia (eds), *The thinking organization* (pp. 336–56). San Francisco: Jossey-Bass.

Gioia, D.A. & Sims, H.P., Jr. (1983) Perceptions of managerial power as a consequence of managerial behavior and reputation. *Journal of Management*, 9: 7–26.

Gioia, D.A., Donnellon, A. & Sims, H.P., Jr. (1989) Communication and cognition in appraisal: A tale of two paradigms. *Organization Studies*, 10: 503–30.

Goffman, E. (1963) *Behaviour in public places*. New York: Free Press.

Graesser, A., Gernsbacher, M. & Goldman, S. (1997) Cognition. In T.A. Van Dijk (ed.), *Discourse as structure and process: Discourse studies vol. 1 – A multidisciplinary introduction* (pp. 292–319). London: Sage.

Grant, D. (1999) HRM, rhetoric and the psychological contract: A case of 'easier said than done'. *International Journal of Human Resource Management*, 10 (2): 327–50.

Grant, D. & Hardy, C. (2004) Struggles with organizational discourse. *Organization Studies*, 25 (1): 5–14.

Grant, D. & Oswick, C. (1996a) Getting the measure of metaphor. In D. Grant & C. Oswick (eds), *Metaphor and organizations* (pp. 1–20). London: Sage.

Grant, D. & Oswick, C. (eds) (1996b) *Metaphor and organizations*. London: Sage.

Grant, D., Keenoy, T. & Oswick, C. (eds) (1998a) *Discourse and organization*. London: Sage.

Grant, D., Keenoy, T. & Oswick, C. (1998b) Of diversity, dichotomy and multi-disciplinarity. In D. Grant, T. Keenoy & C. Oswick (eds), *Discourse and organization* (pp. 1–14). London: Sage.

Grant, D. Keenoy, T. & Oswick, C. (2001) Organizational discourse: Key contributions and challenges. *International Studies of Management and Organization*, 31 (3): 5–24.

Greene, J. (1986) *Language and understanding: A cognitive approach*. Milton Keynes: Open University Press.

Grice, H.P. (1957) Meaning. *Philosophical Review*, 67: 44–58.

Grice, H.P. (1971) Logic and conversation. In D. Steinberg & L. Jacobovits (eds), *Semantics: An interdisciplinary reader in philosophy, linguistics and psychology* (pp 32–56). Cambridge: Cambridge University Press.

Groleau, C. & Cooren, F. (1998) A socio-semiotic approach to computerization: Bridging the gap between ethnographers and system analysts. *Communication Review*, 3 (1–2): 125–64.

Hacking, I. (2000) *The social construction of what?* Cambridge, MA and London: Harvard University Press.

Halliday, M. (1978) *Language as social semiotic: The social interpretation of language and meaning*. Baltimore, MD: Edward Arnold.

Halliday, M.A.K. (1994) *An introduction to functional grammar* (2nd edition). London: Edward Arnold.

Hamilton, P.M. (1997) Rhetorical discourse of local pay. *Organization*, 4: 229–54.

Hansen, C.D. & Kahnweiler, W. (1993) Storytelling: An instrument for understanding the dynamics of corporate relationships. *Human Relations*, 46 (12): 1391–409.

Hardy, C. (2001) Researching organizational discourse. *International Studies of Management and Organization*, 31 (3): 25–47.

Hardy, C., Lawrence, T.B. & Phillips, N. (1998) Talk and action: Conversations and narrative in interorganizational collaboration. In D. Grant, T. Keenoy & C. Oswick (eds), *Discourse and Organization* (pp. 65–83). London: Sage.

Hardy, C. Lawrence, T. & Grant, D. (2003) *Discourse and collaboration: The role of conversations and collective identity*. University of Melbourne, working paper.

Hardy, C., Grant, D., Keenoy, T., Oswick, C. & Phillips, N. (2004) Organizational discourse. Special issue of *Organization Studies*, 25 (1).

Hassard, J. (1994) Postmodern organizational analysis: Toward a conceptual framework. *Journal of Management Studies*, 31 (3): 303–24.

Hawes, L.C. (1999) The dialogics of conversation: Power, control, and vulnerability. *Communication Theory*, 9: 229–64.

Heath, C. (1986) *Body movement and speech in medical interaction*. Cambridge: Cambridge University Press.

Hein, N. & Wodak, R. (1987) Medical interviews in internal medicine. *Text*, 7: 37–66.

Helmer, J. (1993) Storytelling in the creation and maintenance of organizational tension and stratification. *Southern Communication Journal*, 59: 33–44.

Heracleous, L. & Barrett M. (2001) Organizational change as discourse: Communicative actions and deep structures in the context of information technology implementation. *Academy of Management Journal*, 44: 755–78.

Heritage, J. (1984) *Garfinkel and ethnomethodology*. Cambridge: Polity Press.

Hodge, B. & Kress, G. (1988) *Social semiotics*. Cambridge: Polity Press.

Hodge, B., Kress, G. & Jones, G. (1979) The ideology of middle management. In R. Fowler, B. Hodge, G. Kress & T. Trew (eds), *Language and control* (pp. 81–93). London: Routledge and Kegan Paul.

Holmes, M.E. & Rogers, L.E. (1995) Let me rephrase that question: Five common criticisms of interaction analysis studies. Paper presented at the annual conference of the Western States Communication Association. Portland, Oregon.

Huisman, M. (2001) Decision making in meetings as talk-in-interaction. *International Studies of Management and Organization*, 31 (3): 69–90.

Iedema, R. (2003) *Discourses of post-bureaucratic organization*. Amsterdam: John Benjamins.

Iedema, R. & Wodak, R. (1999) Organizational discourses and practices. *Discourse and Society*, 10 (1): 5–20.

Iedema, R., Degeling, P., Braithwaite, J. & White, L. (2004) 'It's an interesting conversation I'm hearing': The doctor as manager. *Organization Studies*, 25 (1): 15–34.

Isaacs, W.N. (1993) Taking flight: Dialogue, collective thinking, and organizational learning. *Organizational Dynamics*, 22 (2): 24–39.

Isaacs, W. (1999) *Dialogue and the art of thinking together*. New York: Doubleday.

Johnson, M. (1987) *The body in the mind: The bodily basis of meaning, imagination, and reason*. Chicago: University of Chicago Press.

Keenoy, T. & Anthony, P.D. (1992) HRM: Metaphor, meaning and morality. In P. Blyton & P. Turnbull (eds), *Reassessing human resource management* (pp. 233–55). London: Sage.

Keenoy, T. & Oswick, C. (2004) Organizing textscapes. *Organization Studies*, 25 (1): 135–42.

Keenoy, T., Oswick, C. & Grant, D. (1997) Organizational discourses: Text and context. *Organization*, 4 (2): 147–57.

Keenoy, T., Marshak, R., Oswick, C. & Grant, D. (2000a) The discourses of organizing. *Journal of Applied Behavioral Science*, 36 (2): 511–12.

Keenoy, T., Oswick, C. & Grant, D. (2000b) Discourse, epistemology and organization: A discursive footnote. *Organization*, 7 (3): 542–5.

Kilduff, M. (1993) Deconstructing organizations. *Academy of Management Review*, 18: 13–31.

Kilduff, M. & Mehra, A. (1997) Postmodernism and organizational research. *Academy of Management Review*, 22 (3): 453–81.

Knights, D. (1997) Organization theory in the age of deconstruction: Dualism, gender and postmodernism revisited. *Organization Studies*, 18 (1): 1–19.

Knights, D. & Morgan, G. (1991) Strategic discourse and subjectivity: Towards a critical analysis of corporate strategy in organizations. *Organization Studies*, 12 (2): 251–73.

Knights, D. & Willmott, H. (1989) Power and subjectivity at work: From degradation to subjugation in social relations. *Sociology*, 23 (4): 535–58.

Kress, G. (1995) The social production of language: History and structures of domination. In P. Fries & M. Gregory (eds), *Discourse in society (systemic functional perspectives Vol. L): Meaning and choice in language (Series: Advances in Discourse Processes)* (pp. 115–40). Norwood, NJ: Ablex.

Kress, G. & Van Leeuwen, T. (1990) *Reading images*. Geelong, Victoria: Deakin University Press.

Kress, G. & Threadgold, T. (1988) Towards a social theory of genre. *Southern Review*, 21: 215–43.

Kristiansen, M. & Bloch-Poulsen, J. (2000) The challenge of the unspoken in organizations: Caring container as a dialogic answer? *Southern Communication Journal*, 65 (2–3): 176–90.

Lakoff, G. (1987) *Women, fire, and dangerous things: What categories reveal about the mind*. Chicago: University of Chicago Press.

Latour, B. (2000) *We have never been modern*. Hemel Hempstead: Harvester Wheatsheaf.

Lord, R.G. & Kernan, M.C. (1987) Scripts as determinants of purposive behavior in organizations. *Academy of Management Review*, 12: 265–77.

Mahler, J. (1988) The quest for organizational meaning: Identifying and interpreting the symbolism in organizational stories. *Administration and Society*, 20 (3): 344–68.

Manning, P.K. (1979) Metaphors of the field: Varieties of organizational discourse. *Administrative Science Quarterly*, 24: 660–71.

Marshak, R.J. (1993) Managing the metaphors of change. *Organizational Dynamics*, 22: 44–56.

Marshak, R.J. (1996) Metaphors, metaphoric fields and organizational change. In D. Grant & C. Oswick (eds), *Metaphor and organizations* (pp. 147–65). Thousand Oaks, CA: Sage.

Marshak, R., Keenoy, T. Oswick, C. & Grant, D. (2000) From outer words to inner worlds. *Journal of Applied Behavioral Science*, 36 (2): 245–58.

Martin, J. (1992) *Cultures in organizations: Three perspectives*. New York: Oxford University Press.

Martin, J.R. (1993) Technology, bureaucracy and schooling. *Cultural Dynamics*, 6 (1): 84–130.

Meyer, J.C. (1993) Tell me a story: Eliciting organizational values from narratives. *Communication Quarterly*, 43: 210–44.

Meyerson, D.E. (1991) Acknowledging and uncovering ambiguities in cultures. In P.J. Frost, L.F. Moore, M.R. Louis, C.C. Lundberg & J. Martin (eds), *Reframing organizational culture* (pp. 254–70). Newbury Park, CA: Sage.

Moch, M.K. & Fields, W.C. (1985) Developing a content analysis for interpreting language use in organizations. In S.B. Bacharach (ed.), *Research in the sociology of organizations* (4th edition, pp. 81–126). Greenwich, CT: JAI Press.

Morgan, G. (1980) Paradigms, metaphors and puzzle-solving in organization theory. *Administrative Science Quarterly*, 25: 605–22.

Morgan, G. (1983) More on metaphor: Why we cannot control tropes in administrative science. *Administrative Science Quarterly*, 28 (4): 601–7.

Morgan, G. (1986) *Images of organization* (1st edition). London: Sage.

Morgan, G. (1996) An afterword: Is there anything more to be said about metaphor? In D. Grant & C. Oswick (eds), *Metaphor and organizations* (pp. 227–40). London: Sage.

Morgan, G. (1997) *Images of organization* (2nd edition). London: Sage.

Mueller, F., Sillince, J., Harvey, C. & Howorth, C. (2004) 'A rounded picture is what we need': Rhetorical strategies, arguments and the negotiation of change in a UK hospital trust. *Organization Studies*, 25 (1): 75–94.

Mumby, D. (1987) The political function of narrative in organizations. *Communication Monographs*, 54 (2): 113–27.

Mumby, D. & Clair, R. (1997) Organizational discourse. In T.A. Van Dijk (ed.), *Discourse as structure and process: Discourse studies vol. 2 – A multidisciplinary introduction* (pp. 181–205). London: Sage.

Mumby, D.K. & Stohl, C. (1991) Power and discourse in organizational studies: Absence and the dialectic of control. *Discourse and Society*, 2: 313–32.

Muntigl, P., Weiss, G. & Wodak, R. (1999) *European Union discourses on un/employment*. Amsterdam and Philadelphia: John Benjamins.

Ochs, E. (1997) Narrative. In T.A. Van Dijk (ed.), *Discourse as structure and process: Discourse studies vol. 1 – A multidisciplinary introduction* (pp. 185–207). London: Sage.

O'Connor, K.M. & Adams, A.A. (1999) What novices think about negotiation: A content analysis of scripts. *Negotiation Journal*, 15 (2): 135–48.

Oswick, C. (2001) Organizational discourse(s): Modes of engagement. Paper presented at the American Academy of Management Conference (Professional Development Workshop), Washington DC (August).

Oswick, C. & Grant, D. (1996a) The organization of metaphors and the metaphors of organization: Where are we and where do we go from here? In D. Grant & C. Oswick (eds), *Organization and metaphor* (pp. 213–26). London: Sage.

Oswick, C. & Grant, D. (eds) (1996b) *Organization development: Metaphorical explorations*. London: Pitman.

Oswick, C. & Montgomery, J. (1999) Images of an organization: The use of metaphor in a multinational company. *Journal of Organizational Change Management*, 21 (5): 501–23.

Oswick, C., Keenoy, T. & Grant, D. (1997) Managerial discourses: Words speak louder than actions? *Journal of Applied Management Studies*, 6 (1): 5–12.

Oswick, C., Keenoy, T. & Grant, D. (2000a) Discourse, organizations and organizing: Concepts, objects and subjects. *Human Relations*, 52 (9): 1115–24.

Oswick, C., Keenoy, T., Grant, D. & Marshak, R. (2000b) Discourse, organization and epistemology. *Organization*, 7 (3): 511–12.

Palmer, I. & Dunford, R. (1996) Conflicting use of metaphors: Reconceptualizing their use in the field of organizational change. *The Academy of Management Review*, 21 (3): 691–717.

Parker, I. (1992) *Discourse dynamics*. London: Routledge.

Parker, M. (2000) 'The less important sideshow': The limits of epistemology in organizational analysis. *Organization*, 7 (3): 519–23.

Pearce, W. & Cronen, V. (1979) *Communication, action and meaning: The creation of social realities*. New York: Praeger.

Phillips, N. (1995) Telling organizational tales: On the role of narrative fiction in the study of organizations. *Organization Studies*, 16 (4): 625–49.

Phillips, N. & Hardy, C. (1997) Managing multiple identities: Discourse legitimacy and resources in the UK refugee system. *Organization*, 4 (2): 159–85.

Phillips, N. & Hardy, C. (2002) *Discourse analysis: Investigating processes of social construction*. Newbury Park, CA: Sage.

Phillips, N., Lawrence, T. & Hardy, C. (2004) Discourse and institutions. *Academy of Management Review* (forthcoming).

Pomerantz, A. & Fehr, B.J. (1997) Conversation analysis: An approach to the study of social action as sense making practices. In T.A. Van Dijk (ed.), *Discourse as social interaction: Discourse studies vol. 1 – A multidisciplinary introduction* (pp. 64–91). London: Sage.

Potter, J. & Wetherell, M. (1987) *Discourse and social psychology*. London: Sage.

Psathos, G. (1995) *Conversation analysis: The study of talk-in-interaction*. Beverley Hills, CA: Sage.

Putnam, L. (2004) Dialectical tensions and rhetorical tropes in negotiations. *Organization Studies*, 25 (1): 35–54.

Putnam, L.L. & Cooren, F. (2004) Textuality and agency: Constitutive elements of organizations. *Organization*, 11 (3).

Putnam, L. & Fairhurst, G. (2001) Discourse analysis in organizations: Issues and concerns. In F.M. Jablin & L. Putnam (eds), *The new handbook of organizational communication: Advances in theory, research and methods* (pp. 235–68). Newbury Park, CA: Sage.

Putnam, L.L. & Jones, T.S. (1982) Reciprocity in negotiations: An analysis of bargaining interaction. *Communication Monographs*, 49: 171–91.

Putnam, L.L., Phillips, N. & Chapman, P. (1996) Metaphors of communication and organization. In S.R. Clegg, C. Hardy & W. Nord (eds), *Handbook of organizational studies* (pp. 375–408). London: Sage.

Putnam, L.L., Wilson, S.R. & Turner, D.B. (1990) The evolution of policy arguments in teachers negotiations. *Argumentation*, 4: 129–52.

Reed, M. (2000) The limits of discourse analysis in organizational analysis. *Organization*, 7 (3): 524–30.

Roloff, M.E., Tutzauer, F.E. & Dailey, W.O. (1989) The role of argumentation in distributive and integrative bargaining contexts: Seeking relative advantage but at what cost? In M.A. Rahim (ed.), *Managing conflict: An interdisciplinary approach* (pp. 109–19). New York: Praeger.

Rose, N. (1990) *Governing the self: The shaping of the private self.* London: Routledge.

Rosen, M. (1984) Myth and reproduction: The conceptualization of management theory, method and practice. *Journal of Management*, 21 (3): 303–22.

Rosen, M. (1985) Breakfast at Spiro's: Dramaturgy and dominance. *Journal of Management Studies*, 11 (2): 31–48.

Sackmann, S. (1989) The role of metaphors in organization transformation. *Human Relations*, 42: 463–85.

Sacks, H., Schegloff, E.A. & Jefferson, G. (1974) A simplest systematics for the organization of turn-taking for conversation. *Language*, 50: 696–735.

Salzer-Morling, M. (1998) As God created Earth… A saga that makes sense? In D. Grant, T. Keenoy & C. Oswick (eds), *Discourse and organization* (pp. 104–18). London: Sage.

Schama, S. (1995) *Landscape and memory.* London: Harper Collins.

Schegloff, E. (1984) On some questions and ambiguities in conversation. In J.M. Atkinson & J. Heritage (eds), *Structures of social action: Studies in emotion and social interaction* (pp. 28–51). Cambridge: Cambridge University Press.

Schegloff, E. (1996) Turn organization: One intersection of grammar and interaction. In E. Ochs, E. Schegloff & S. Thompson (eds), *Interaction and grammar* (pp. 52–133). Cambridge: Cambridge University Press.

Schiffrin, D. (1987) *Discourse markers.* Cambridge: Cambridge University Press.

Schiffrin, D. (1994) *Approaches to discourse.* Oxford: Basil Blackwell.

Schwandt, T.A. (1997) *Qualitative inquiry: A dictionary of terms.* Thousand Oaks, CA: Sage.

Searle, J.R. (1969) *Speech acts: An essay in the philosophy of language.* London: Cambridge University Press.

Searle, J.R. (1979) *Expression and meaning: Studies in the theory of speech acts.* Cambridge and New York: Cambridge University Press.

Searle, J.R. (1995) *The construction of social reality.* London: Allen Lane.

Segerdahl, P. (1998) Scientific studies of aspects of everyday life: The example of conversation analysis. *Language and Communication*, 18: 275–323.

Silverman, D. (1987) *Communication and medical practice.* London: Sage.

Silverman, D. (1993) *Interpreting qualitative data. Methods for analysing talk, text and interaction.* London: Sage.

Silverman, D. (1999) Warriors or collaborators: Reworking methodological controversies in the study of institutional interaction. In S. Sarangi & C. Roberts (eds), *Talk, work and the institutional order: Discourse in medical, mediation and management settings* (pp. 401–25). Berlin: Mouton de Gruyter.

Srivastva, S. & Barrett, F. (1988) The transforming nature of metaphors in group development: A study in group theory. *Human Relations*, 41 (1): 31–64.

Tannen, D. (1986) *That's not what I meant.* New York: Ballantine Books.

Tannen, D. (1995) The power of talk: Who gets heard and why. *Harvard Business Review*, 74 (5): 138–48.

Taylor, J.R. & Van Every, E.J. (1993) *The vulnerable fortress: Bureaucratic organization in the information age.* Toronto, Canada: University of Toronto.

Taylor, J.R. & Van Every, E.J. (2000) *The emergent organization: Communication as its site and surface.* Mahwah, NJ: Lawrence Erlbaum Associates.

Taylor, J.R., Cooren, F., Giroux, N. & Robichaud, D. (1996) The communicational basis of organization: Between the conversation and the text. *Communication Theory*, 6 (1): 1–39.

Thatchenkery, T.J. & Upadhyaya, P. (1996) Organizations as a play of multiple and dynamic discourses: An example from a global social change organization. In D.J. Boje, R.P. Gephart & T.J. Thatchenkery (eds), *Postmodern management and organization theory* (pp. 308–30). Thousand Oaks, CA: Sage.

Thibault, P. (1991) *Social semiotics as praxis*. Minnesota: University of Minnesota Press.

Tsoukas, H. (1991) The missing link: A transformational view of metaphors in organizational science. *Academy of Management Review*, 16: 566–85.

Tsoukas, H. (2000) False dilemmas in organization theory: Realism or social constructivism? *Organization*, 7 (3): 531–5.

Tsoukas, H. & Chia, R. (2002) Organizational becoming: Rethinking organizational change. *Organization Science*, 13 (5): 567–82.

Van Dijk, T.A. (1997a) The study of discourse. In T.A. Van Dijk (ed.), *Discourse as structure and process: Discourse studies vol. 1 – A multidiciplinary introduction* (pp. 1–34). London: Sage.

Van Dijk, T.A. (1997b) Discourse as interaction society. In T.A. Van Dijk (ed.), *Discourse as social interaction: Discourse studies vol. 2 – A multidisciplinary introduction* (pp. 1–38). Newbury Park, CA: Sage.

Van Leeuwen, T. (1993) Language and representation. Unpublished doctoral thesis, University of Sydney.

Wallemacq, A. & Sims, D. (1998) The struggle with sense. In D. Grant, T. Keenoy & C. Oswick (eds), *Discourse and organization* (pp. 119–33). London: Sage.

Warner-Burke, W. (1992) Metaphors to consult by. *Group and Organization Management*, 17 (3): 255–9.

Washbourne, N. & Dicke, W. (2001) Dissolving organization theory? A narrative analysis of water management. *International Studies of Management and Organization*, 31 (3): 91–112.

Watson, T.J. (1994) *In search of management: Culture, chaos and control in managerial work*. London: Routledge.

Watson, T.J. (1995) Rhetoric, discourse and argument in organizational sense making: A reflexive tale. *Organization studies*, 16 (5): 805–21.

Weick, K.E. (1995) *Sensemaking in organizations*. Thousand Oaks, CA: Sage.

Westenholz, A. (1993) Paradoxical thinking and change in the frames of reference. *Organizational Studies*, 14: 37–58.

Westley, F. (1990) Middle managers and strategy: The microdynamics of inclusion. *Strategic Management Journal*, 11: 337–51.

Westley, F. & Mintzberg, H. (1989) Visionary leadership and strategic management. *Strategic Management Journal*, 10 (1): 17–32.

White, H. (1978) *Tropics of discourse*. Baltimore, MD: Johns Hopkins University Press.

Witten, M. (1993) Narrative and the culture of obedience at the workplace. In D.K. Mumby (ed.), *Narrative and social control: Critical perspectives* (pp. 97–118). Newbury Park, CA: Sage.

Wodak, R. (1996) *Disorders of discourse*. London: Longman.

Wodak, R. & Matouschek, B. (1993) We are dealing with people whose origins one can clearly tell just by looking: Critical discourse analysis and the study of neo-racism in contemporary Austria. *Discourse and Society*, 2 (4): 225–48.

Woodilla, J. (1998) Workplace conversations: The text of organizing. In D. Grant, T. Keenoy and C. Oswick (eds), *Discourse and organization* (pp. 31–50). London: Sage.

Yeung, L. (1997) Confrontation or resolution: Discourse strategies for dealing with conflicts in participative decision-making. *Journal of Applied Management Studies*, 6 (1): 63–75.

Part I

DOMAINS OF DISCOURSE

1

Dialogue: Life and Death of the Organization

Kenneth J. Gergen, Mary M. Gergen and Frank J. Barrett

There is a pervasive tendency in organizational studies to view acts of communication in terms of the individual agent. It is the individual who speaks, writes, gestures, and so on; it is the individual we credit for effective speaking, just as it is the individual's ineffective listening that invites discredit. This tendency to focus on individual acts of expression is indeed unfortunate because it suppresses perhaps the central feature of such actions, their function within relationships. Indeed, as we shall soon make clear, it is from the relational matrix that the very possibility of individual sense-making comes into being, and without the existence of ongoing relationship communicative acts lose their status as communication. As the editors of this *Handbook* have made clear, organizational worlds are created and sustained through discourse. This chapter makes it equally clear that it is through relational process that discourse acquires its significance. More broadly stated, it is by virtue of relational processes that organizations live or die.

THE CENTRALITY OF DIALOGUE: EARLY INTIMATIONS

In this chapter we focus on the dialogic dimension of relational process in organizations. Although dialogue as a topic of study has been little mentioned in traditional handbooks of organizational study, its importance to organizational functioning has been subtly apparent since the inception of the science. Even the earliest research in organizational development attests to the importance of dialogue in organizational change. For example, in Lewin's (1951) groundbreaking research, the attempt was to enlist housewives in serving unfashionable meat products (e.g., beef hearts, kidneys) as a contribution to the war effort. Comparisons were made between groups exposed to persuasive information and groups that received the information and then discussed its implications. The results revealed that the discussion groups were far more likely to purchase the meats. In effect, 'involved participation' in decision-making was critical to change. Yet, while this study is often credited with spawning the field of action research, we actually know very little about the essential process of dialogue itself.

Later studies continued in much the same vein. Classic research at Detroit Edison in 1948 aimed at improving work processes (Baumgartel, 1959). Again the researchers contrasted traditional training methods with group discussions. They conclude that 'Intensive, group discussion ... can be an effective tool for introducing positive change in a business organization (Baumgartel, 1959, p. 6). In their oft cited experiment, Coch and French (1948) tested organizational change in a clothing factory. Management informed one group of machine operators about changes in their job. In this group 'resistance developed almost immediately after the change', resulting in grievances, quitting and lowered productivity. In the experimental condition, groups discussed how working methods could be improved and how to eliminate unnecessary operations. In this case there were no signs of resistance. These early studies have stimulated a robust line of inquiry (see Porras & Robertson, 1992). And yet, because of the exclusive focus on outcome rather than process, we learn little about the actual process of dialogue.

ORGANIZATION OF THE CHAPTER

In the present chapter the process of dialogue takes centre stage. The discussion is composed of four parts. As a necessary précis we shall explore the myriad meanings of dialogue and develop what we view as a useful orienting platform: dialogue as *discursive coordination*. This orientation will enable us to consider the practical consequences of various forms of dialogic action. We then turn to the pivotal function of dialogue in the organizing process. We shall be especially concerned with developing a vocabulary of discursive action with practical consequences for effective organizing. After considering the uses of dialogue in creating organization, we turn to the problematic potentials of dialogue. A contrast between *generative* and *degenerative* dialogue enables us to explore how certain forms of coordination ultimately lead to organizational demise. Indeed, the very forms of dialogue required for organizational well-being may also establish the grounds for deterioration. In the final section we turn to dialogic practices that may restore vitality to the organization. Here we focus on transformational dialogue, that is, dialogic practices designed to break through naturally occurring barriers to communication.

DIALOGUE AS DISCURSIVE COORDINATION

In recent years scholars and practitioners have become increasingly excited about the potentials of dialogue for creating and transforming social worlds. However, such broad excitement is accompanied by a certain vagueness as to what is meant by dialogue. Choruses now sing hosannahs to dialogue, but seldom stop to consider that their praise may be directed towards entirely different practices. On a simple level, *The American Heritage Dictionary* offers the culturally common definition of dialogue as 'conversation between two or more people'. However, virtually no scholarly work on dialogue shares this definition; scholars of dialogue are not at all interested in mere conversation. Nor do such scholars typically share definitions with each other. In our view, the primary definitional criterion of most contemporary analyses of dialogue is derived from a vision of an ideal form of relationship; dialogue is defined in terms of the favoured ideal. For most contemporary analysts, merely having a conversation does not constitute true dialogue.

It is primarily the particular vision of the ideal that sets various dialogic scholars apart. David Bohm's popular book, *On Dialogue* (1996), defines dialogue as a form of communication from which something new emerges; participants must evidence a 'relaxed, non-judgmental curiosity, with the aim of seeing things as freshly and clearly as possible' (Bohm, 1996, p. ix). Yet, Robert Grudin's *On Dialogue* (1996) is not so much interested in relationships that create novelty as in a 'reciprocal exchange of meaning … across a physical or mental space' (Grudin, 1996, p. 11). In contrast, Putnam and Fairhurst (2001) are not centrally concerned with either generating novelty or exchanging meaning, but rather with the creation of convergence in views; they define dialogue as 'a mode of communication that builds mutuality through the awareness of others', and it does so through the 'use of genuine or authentic discourse, and reliance on the unfolding interaction' (Putnam & Fairhurst, 2001, p. 116). At the same time, for L.C. Hawes (1999), the central ingredient of dialogue is conflict reduction; for him dialogue is 'praxis for mediating competing and contradictory discourses' (p. 19). In further contrast, while many of the above scholars assume that dialogue is among equals, Eisenberg and Goodall (1993) are chiefly concerned with enhancing the voices of minorities. They see dialogue as 'providing parties with a chance to speak and be heard and to challenge the traditional positioning of authority' (1993, p. 9). Quite distinct from all these orientations, Isaacs (1993, p. 25) defines dialogue as 'a sustained collective inquiry into the processes, assumptions, and certainties that compose everyday experience'. Finally, for Tullio Maranhao (1990), it is not everyday life that dialogue should throw into question but all certainty of knowledge. For him dialogue is a logic of 'stating and questioning', with the aim of generating the kind of scepticism that invites continuous inquiry. For Maranhao, dialogue is a form of 'anti-epistemology'.

With such differing views of dialogue, each saturated as it is with values and visions, any general characterization of dialogue becomes perilous. In order to establish a more comprehensive analytic frame, while not sacrificing valuable distinctions embedded in these various accounts, it is useful to separate the normative from the descriptive. Rather than equating the term 'dialogue' with any particular vision of ideal interchange, we offer an elemental descriptive definition. Variations in the specific patterning of interchange may thus reflect the various ideal forms sought by differing scholars. In this way we return again to an elemental formulation, but leave room for broad expansion in specific forms and functions. We do not propose a return to the view of 'dialogue as conversation', as it does not serve our analytic ends here. The term 'conversation' is both ambiguous and conceptually thin. Rather, for present purposes we propose to define dialogue as discursive coordination in the service of social ends. To amplify this view and its implications, we propose the following:

1.   Dialogue originates in the public sphere. In understanding dialogue many theorists have drawn from the individualist tradition in which language is a reflection or expression of the individual mind. On this account, dialogue is a form of intersubjective connection or synchrony. The public actions are derivative of private meanings. In the present account we bracket the realm of subjectivity and focus on the public coordination of discourse. This enables us to avoid a number of intractable philosophical problems (e.g., the relation of mind to body, the problem of 'other minds', and the hermeneutic problem of accurate interpretation), and to focus on the relational function of various utterances within ongoing conversation. We are informed here, in part, by J.L. Austin's *How To Do Things with Words* (1962), in which the performatory character of speech is illuminated. Utterances are essentially actions performed with social consequences.

This orientation does not exclude psychological inquiry. However, it is to say that significant analyses of dialogue can ensue without recourse to psychological explanation. Effective analysis of dialogue need not refer to states of individual understanding, subjective biases or inattention, personality traits, and so on. This possibility was initially demonstrated in Garfinkel's (1967) groundbreaking work on ethnomethodology, and now more copiously in various forms of discourse and conversation analysis (Wetherell et al., 2001a, 2001b). If psychological inquiry is to proceed, our orientation here is most congenial with Vygotsky's (1986) view that higher order psychological processes are reflections of social process. This is to say that the process of thought is essentially public discourse carried out on a private site. This is essentially the view adopted by Bruner in *Acts of Meaning* (1990), and by Harré and Gillette in *The Discursive Mind* (1994). In our view, however, it is most useful to focus on the forms of public coordination that originate, sustain, transform and potentially terminate what participants take to be meaning.

2.   Dialogue is a form of coordinated action.   In foregrounding the concept of collaboration we mean to call attention to the relational foundation of dialogue. That is, meaning within dialogue is an outcome not of individual action and reaction, but of what Shotter (1984) calls joint-action, or the coordinated actions of the participants. In this sense, the meaning of an individual's expression within a dialogue depends importantly on the response of his or her interlocutor – what has elsewhere been called 'a supplement' (Gergen, 1994). No individual expression harbours meaning in itself. For example, what we might conventionally index as a 'hostile remark' can be turned into 'a joke' through a response of laughter; the 'vision statement' of a superior can be refigured as 'just more BS' through the shared smirk of the employees.

In this context, Wittgenstein's (1963) metaphor of the language game is also useful. The metaphor calls attention specifically to the coordinated or rule-governed activities of the participants in generating meaning. The words 'strike' and 'home run' acquire their meaning by virtue of the participation of the interlocutors in the rule-constrained talk of baseball. Words invented by a single individual (a 'private language' in Wittgenstein's terms) would not in themselves constitute meaningful entries into dialogue. In this sense, the traditional binary separating monologue and dialogue is misleading. The term 'monologue' cannot refer to the language of one person alone, for such a language would fail to communicate. The meaning of any utterance depends on its functioning within a relational matrix. Thus monologue is better understood as an extended (or dominating) entry of a single voice into a dialogue; in this sense monologue is an unevenly distributed dialogue.

3. **Dialogic efficacy is bodily and contextually embedded.** While our orientation to dialogue emphasizes discourse, we do embrace linguistic reductionism. Spoken (or written) language may be focal in our analyses but, other than for analytic purposes, we do not wish to separate out such language from the remainder of the life sphere entering into the production of meaning. Clearly the efficacy of spoken words within dialogue is fastened to the simultaneous movements of the speakers' bodies, tone of voice and physical proximity. Further, dialogic efficacy cannot ultimately be separated from the world of objects and spaces – the material context. The efficacy of one's words may importantly depend, for example, on whether one is clutching a gavel, a dagger or a bouquet of flowers. In the same way, the meaning of words within the dialogue may depend on whether they are expressed in an executive suite, in a bar room or over the Internet. Again to draw from Wittgenstein (1963), the language games in which we engage are embedded within broader forms of life. Thus, the meaning of 'strike' and 'home run' do not only depend on the rules of baseball talk, but on their function within a form of life that includes balls, bats, bases, fields, players, umpires, hotdogs, and so on.

4. **Dialogic efficacy is historically and culturally situated.** The contribution of any particular act of speech to dialogic coordination is contingent on its placement within a cultural context. In part this emphasis acknowledges Saussure's (1974) distinction between the synchronic and diachronic study of language. While we may effectively focus on contemporary forms of dialogue and their accomplishments (synchronic study), we must also be prepared for temporal transformations in what and how various ends are accomplished. For example, 'the boss's orders' were once very effective within Western organizations, but they are slowly losing their power to generate activity. As concerns with workplace democracy, diversity and organizational flattening become popular, an authoritative 'top-down' voice may become dysfunctional (Yankolovich, 1999).

Bakhtin (1981) also draws our attention to the heterogeneous cultural traditions that typically contribute to the shared language of a nation. This analysis prepares us for the possibility that partners in a dialogue may be polyvocal, capable of shifting from one mode or form of dialogue to another across the course of conversation (Hazen, 1993). At the same time, the focus on cultural heterogeneity prepares us for the difficulties that may be encountered when participants do not share discursive traditions. As the mounting literature on cross-cultural (mis)understanding makes clear (see, for example, Pearce, 1989; Rahim, 1994; Jandt, 2001; Ting-Toomey & Oetzel, 2001), such dialogues may be frustrating and ineffectual. The dialogic moves effective for achieving goals within one tradition may be counterproductive in conversations with those outside the tradition. Similarly, even within the same culture the dialogic forms effective in one condition may not carry over to another. (See, for example, Wells' (1999) discussion of optimal forms of classroom dialogue.) Whatever is said about dialogic efficacy within organizations must thus be tempered by consciousness of contingency.

5.   Dialogue may serve many different purposes, both positive and negative. Finally, by viewing dialogue as discursive coordination we attempt to avoid conflating normative and descriptive commitments. Coordination in itself is neither good nor evil. From our definitional framework, heated argument is as much a dialogue as an attempt to gain an appreciative understanding of another's 'point of view'. This is not to abandon concern with the kinds of ideal central to most contemporary analysts. Rather, it is to invite differentiation among forms of dialogue in terms of the ends they serve. Thus, while certain forms of dialogue may indeed succeed in reducing conflict, other moves in language may enable authority to be challenged, multiple opinions to be expressed, or taken-for-granted realities to be deliberated. Drawing again from Wittgenstein (1963, 6e): 'Think of the tools in a tool-box: there is a hammer, pliers, a saw, a screw-driver, a rule, a glue-pot, glue, nails, and screws. The function of words are as diverse as the functions of these objects'. From this perspective, inquiry is invited into the specific forms of dialogue required to achieve particular goals of value.

It is important to note here that the value placed on dialogic outcomes may vary significantly from one standpoint to another. For example, a vigorous argument, from an outsider's perspective, may seem aggressive and hostile. For the participants, however, such skirmishes can be enlivening fun, much like a game of chess. By the same token, the outcomes of any particular dialogue may be simultaneously both positive and negative (see also Thatchenkery & Upadhyaya, 1996). One may be pleased that a given dialogue succeeds in establishing intimate bonds with another, but simultaneously realize that certain critical capacities are simultaneously suspended. And also, what is accomplished in a dialogue may be judged differently in terms of what ensues at a later point in time. Many organizations have been disappointed by training exercises that generate immediate joy and communal good will, only to find that with Monday morning life returns to dull normal.

GENERATIVE DIALOGUE AND THE ORGANIZING PROCESS

If we understand dialogue as the process of relational coordination, it is immediately clear that certain forms of dialogue are essential to the process of building organizations. As people's words and actions become coordinated, so do forms of life come into being – friendships, marriages, families, and organizations large and small (see also Weick, 1995; Yankelovich, 1999; Taylor & Van Every, 2000). In this sense, there is no inherent difference in the process by which two children create a sand-castle, a family eats Sunday dinner together, a strike is planned, or the Ford motor company produces automobiles. Processes of dialogic coordination are at work in every instance. Yet, while we acknowledge the significant implications of understanding dialogue as relational coordination, we are still left without the kind of detailing essential for creating and sustaining an effective organization. Invited, in particular, is an account of those dialogic moves that facilitate the process of organizing. What moves contribute to what might be called generative dialogue, dialogue that brings into being a mutually satisfying and effective organization?

A full treatment of generative dialogue would require an examination not only of bodily movements, gestures and gaze, but also of the environment and the objects available to people in relationships. A focus on historical conditions contributing to various forms of generative dialogue would be helpful, as well as an account of cultural variations in effective dialogue. However, given limited space and the emphasis of the present volume on discourse, let us focus in particular on spoken and written language in the contemporary Western organization. This is no insignificant matter, as language is the chief means by which such organizations come into being and are sustained. However, it is important to be sensitive to the limitations of such an analysis.

Further, what we offer here may be viewed as a 'first cut'. That is, we work here without the benefit of a well-grounded literature specific to the topic. We must piece together significant ideas from a number of disparate areas to offer a preliminary scaffolding. At the same time, we hope that this unfinished structure will enable more detailed elaboration as future study moves in this direction.

It should be noted that we are guided in our present treatment by a social constructionist orientation (Gergen, 1994, 1999). In effect, we place a strong emphasis on the way in which discourse functions to structure both a sense of the real and the valuable within relationships. From the relational matrix, then, both ontology and ethics – agreement on what is, and what ought to be – can grow. And, as these agreements are cemented to action, local traditions (sub-cultures) emerge. In terms of generative dialogue, then, the central focus is on those kinds of dialogic moves that may bring realities and ethics into being and bind them to particular patterns of action. With the above provisos notwithstanding, we propose the following as central components in generative dialogue.

The pivotal act of affirmation

As proposed above, because meaning is born in relationship, an individual's lone utterance contains no meaning. Rather, it provides the potential for meaning, a potential that can only be realized through another's supplement. The supplement of affirmation may stand as the key building block to creating conjoint realities.

To affirm is to ratify the significance of an utterance as a meaningful act. It is to locate something within an expression that is valuable, to which one can agree or render support. Merely responding to the question 'How are you?' with 'Fine, thank you' is to render the question meaningful as a ritual of greeting. To respond with a blank stare would be to negate its significance as communication. In the act of affirmation elements of the initial utterance are also sanctioned as 'real' and are given rudimentary value. The response of 'Fine, thank you' simultaneously grants 'personal health' an existence in the world and places value upon it.

Affirmation is important for other reasons as well, partly deriving from the individualist tradition and the presumption that thoughts and feelings are individual possessions. As we say, 'It is my experience that…', or 'These are my beliefs'. To affirm such utterances is to grant worth to, or to honour, the validity of the other's subjectivity; failure to affirm places the identity of the other in question. Finally, in affirming an utterance one also sanctions the relationships from which it derives. If one dismisses a speaker's opinions, it is often to disparage the range of relations in which this opinion is embedded. To embrace a novel idea is to embrace new relationships, and possibly to threaten old ones.

Affirmation may take many forms depending on conversation and context. At the simplest level, careful or sympathetic attention provides a beginning. Curiosity or question-asking also serves as a simple form of affirmation, as it grants to the speaker's preceding utterance meaningful significance. To 'be moved' by another's expressions is a high form of affirmation. In her volume, *Conversation, Language, and Possibilities* (1997), Harlene Anderson speaks for many change agents when she proposes that therapy becomes effective when

> the therapist enters the therapy domain with a genuine posture and manner characterized by an openness to another person's ideological base – his or her reality, beliefs, and experiences. This listening posture and manner involve showing respect for, having humility toward, and believing that what a client has to say is worth hearing. (1997, p. 12)

More broadly, affirmation may be roughly equated with what many researchers call 'mutuality' in dialogue (Markova et al., 1995), and finds parallels in mother–child interaction as well as relations with non-human species. It should finally be noted that we are not proposing here that generative dialogue requires full agreement among interlocutors. Affirmation is not assent, a point to which we shall return momentarily.

Productive difference

While affirmation is of critical significance in building organization, it is important to draw a distinction between affirmation and duplication. At the most rudimentary level affirmation ratifies the reality and value of a preceding utterance. However, it functions in this way primarily against the backdrop of a contrasting possibility or domain that is negated. If another agrees with you, this agreement serves as an affirmation primarily when the other is apprised of what is not being affirmed or valued. When one shows signs of deliberating the issues, and then agrees, affirmation is achieved. If one is prepared to agree no matter what is proposed, we have duplication as opposed to affirmation.

The distinction is important in virtue of a more general theoretical point: the conjoint creation of meaning depends on the generation of difference. In the same sense that the meaning of a single word depends on its difference from other words (e.g., bit, bat, but), so does the meaning of any utterance in a dialogue acquire its meaning from its difference from other utterances. To echo each utterance spoken by the other is to destroy the meaning of these expressions. Thus, in a more general sense, generative dialogue depends on the continuous generation of differences. The meaning-making process is rendered robust by virtue of distinctive voices (see also Hazen, 1993).

With this said, however, a further distinction is essential between productive as opposed to destructive difference. Dialogic entries that sustain or extend the potentials of a preceding utterance may be viewed as productive; utterances that curtail or negate what has preceded are destructive. They essentially impede the process of constructing a mutually viable reality. For example, to offer an example of what has just been said, to add an associated idea or to ask about how an utterance might apply in a particular situation will typically function in a productive way. Adding new voices to the conversation may also make a robust contribution to productive difference (see also Barbules (1994) on 'building statements'). In contrast, to announce that another's utterance is 'just plain wrong' unintelligible or outrageous will typically bring dialogue to a halt. This is not at all to say that disagreement is essentially destructive. There are conversational conditions under which argument and mutual critique are both anticipated and welcomed (see Billig, 1987). A properly conducted debate, for example, may vitally extend the range of relevant considerations for effective decision-making.

The creation of coherence

The combination of affirmation and difference makes a potent contribution to the emerging world of the real and the good. However, in the same way that the meaning derived from a paragraph in a novel is highly dependent on its relationship to preceding paragraphs, so does meaning in dialogue depend on what precedes any particular turn-taking segment. To create a sustainable world thus requires dialogic acts that engender what is commonly termed conversational coherence (Craig & Tracy, 1983; Duck, 2002). Such acts enable preceding expressions to create a singular, ordered world about which to organize. Among the common dialogic inputs contributing to coherence are repeating conversational topics (*topoi*), offering comments relevant to a recognized issue, and providing answers to preceding questions (Barbules, 1994; Wells, 1999). On a more subtle level, we wish to call attention to *metonymic reflection* as a means of generating coherence. Metonymy refers to the use of a fragment to stand for a whole to which it is related. Thus, 'the golden arches' are used to signify the McDonald's restaurants, or the British flag (the so-called Union Jack) to indicate the United Kingdom. In the present case, metonymic reflection occurs when one's actions contain some fragment of the other's actions, a piece that represents the whole. If an interlocutor expresses doubts about a given policy, and her colleague responds by asking 'What's the weather report for tomorrow?', the expression of doubt fails to be represented in the reply. The reply fails to include some element of the initial utterance. If a response includes a metonymic fragment of what has just been said, then the interlocutor finds him or herself carried in the other. Collaborative coherence is achieved.

Narrative and temporal integration

As dialogue develops it leaves in its wake a repository of discourse and associated action. This repository may serve as both a resource for sustaining generativity and a potential threat to continuation. Its major contribution to the process of organizing stems from its integrative properties. That is, as interlocutors set about constructing a world of the real and the good, materials are required for solidification. This world must become compelling, reliable and significant. One major means of solidifying this world is through integrating materials from the past – accounts of events that can fortify the present, fill out its contours, add to its dimension, and/or ratify its value. Although all past events can be used in this way, the most important resources for such solidification come from events common to the interlocutors themselves. By inserting accounts of the past into ongoing dialogues, the interlocutors also create a reality with historical depth (Thatchenkery & Upadhyaya, 1996). They cease to speak in terms of 'what we are presently creating', but see the present as rooted in the past. The shaky quality of 'here and now' is replaced by the concept of 'tradition'. Evanescence gives way to a sense of temporal lodgement (for additional insights into the ways in which narratives serve as organizing devices, see Boje, 1991, 2001; Czarniawska, 1997).

EXPANDING THE ARENA OF GENERATIVE DIALOGUE

These four insertions into dialogue – emphasizing affirmation, productive difference, coherence and temporal integration – may be viewed as central to creating the forms of reality and value necessary for effective organization. At the same time, these are only entry markers in a scholarly effort of extended duration and scope. For the purposes of inviting collaborative expansion, we share here several additional contributions of significance.

Repetitive sequences

Generative dialogue may be compared to the fluid and synchronized movements of dancers. A key to the success of the dance is a history of practice. Yet, this is not the practice of isolated individuals, but of the collaborative unit. Their practice together readies each of them for the movements of the other. The slight pressure of the male's hand may send his partner into a swirl, at the end of which his open arms are prepared to receive her return. And so it is in the case of generative dialogue. If effective organization is to be achieved, so must there be repetitive scenarios of relationship, sequences of action that form a reliable core. This is not to propose that all relational sequences should move in the repetitive direction. The result would be a stagnation of meaning and the loss of flexibility. However, without major contributions to repetition, organizational efficacy will be lost. A significant degree of dialogic ritual is essential.

Reflexive punctuation

As dialogues unfold and repetition becomes more frequent, agreements will emerge as to what is real and good. However, because the meaning of what has been achieved is inherently ambiguous – subject to alteration as the conversation moves on – effective organization may require periodic reflection on what has been accomplished. Such punctuating insinuations into dialogue serve to collect and organize the sedimented realities and aspirations of the participants. Comments concerning 'what we have agreed to', 'our objectives' or 'our current plans' may all have this solidifying effect. Metaphors may play an especially important role in this case, as they have the capacity to tie together many disparate facets of conversation and action into a coherent whole. (See also Weick (1995) on significance of 'retrospective sense-making'.)

Constructing bonds and boundaries

Participants in an organization will often speak in the singular: 'my opinion...', 'what I think...', 'my hopes in this case...', and so on. In effect, such dialogic inputs construct the reality of isolated individuals. If fully sustained, such dialogue may invite division, alienation and destructive competition. Favoured for generative dialogue, then, is a shift from a discourse of individual entities to a collective 'we'. In speaking of 'our opinion', 'what we think' and 'our hopes', the 'imagined community' becomes a reality (Anderson, 1997). The result will be a bonding among the participants, the creation of an exterior to the organization, and an increased focus on the relations among participants.

In closing this discussion it is important to note that none of the discursive moves outlined here achieves its function until affirmed by one's interlocutors. While linguistic tradition forces us to single out specific 'moves', 'utterances' or 'speech acts', this tradition simultaneously obscures the conjoint creation of their meaning as moves, utterances or speech acts. Thus, for example, a narrative is not a narrative until another ratifies it as such. One may tell what conventionally counts as 'a story of a past success', but its reality as such depends on the affirmation of the listener. If the listener indexes the offering as a 'manipulative ploy' or 'a misleading distortion', the 'story of past success' is destroyed. In this sense, the analysis of dialogue is not congenial with strategic views of communication competence. The success of a given move does not depend on the rational calculus of the actor, but on its relationship to that which has preceded and follows.

DIALOGUE AND ORGANIZATIONAL DYSFUNCTION

While dialogic process is critical to the achievement of organization, it is also clear that not all forms of dialogue function in this way. The preceding discussion has attempted to pinpoint dialogic contributions that seem pivotal to organizing around a shared reality. Here we turn to the problem of organizational dysfunction. First, we inquire in a more general way into what forms of dialogue undermine or destroy organizations. Then we turn to the more subtle and ironic ways in which organizing processes themselves lay the groundwork for disorganization.

We shall not belabour the topic of dialogic dysfunction. In part this is because organizational failure is implied by the absence or inverse of the various dialogic moves just outlined. The failure to affirm, for example, can lead to relational disunity, failing to create coherence can undermine concerted action. Further, most of us well understand the destructive forms of dialogue by virtue of our participation in the rituals of everyday life. Common experience is perhaps our best teacher. However, two contributions to dysfunctional dialogue should be singled out for their ubiquitous deployment: negation and individual blame.

Negation

Echoing our discussion of destructive difference, the negative move within a dialogue is one that essentially destroys the meaning-making potential of a preceding utterance. This is not simply a failure to affirm, but the active obliteration of the utterance as a candidate for meaning. On a subtle level, active inattention serves as negation. Turning away from an interlocutor, reading a document, starting another conversation, or interrupting without acknowledging what has been said all serve as forms of negation. More blatantly, hostile critique or volatile arguments against the interlocutor's utterances can function as negation. Again, this is not to imply that critique and argument are always dysfunctional. As indicated above, much depends on the form (including tone of voice and bodily posture). However, it is to say that the latter forms of discourse must be employed with care and sensitivity. As suggested earlier, in the Western tradition one's words are virtually expressions of personal essence. To attack another's views is not, then, a mere linguistic exercise; it is to invalidate the originary essence of the self.

On a more subtle level, monologic discourse may function as negation. As previously proposed, we view monologue as an unevenly distributed form of dialogue. If extended indefinitely, it eliminates the space for the other's supplementation. In effect, the speaker pre-empts the affirmation process, placing the affirmation into the mouth of the otherwise mute listener. In this way, monologue subtly denies the listener participation in the creation of meaning. There is no recognition of a worthy essence within the other. Here we are sensitized as well to the relationship between dialogic forms and organizational structure. Monologic communication is traditionally a prerogative of rank. Indeed, the presumption remains in Western culture that the more senior the individual in the organization the more knowledge he or she should possess. In this sense, the failure to display monologic prowess may be viewed as a sign of weakness. However, monologic speech remains effective only so long as the senior commands the kind of respect necessary for the presumption of affirmation to find assent. In the wave of recent support for workplace democracy and diversity initiatives, such a presumption becomes questionable. Further, as organizations grow more complex and confront an increasingly chaotic world of meaning, monologic discourse seems increasingly counterproductive (Anderson et al., 2001).

Individual blame

From the Western ideology of 'the individual self' also sprouts the concept of individual responsibility. If individual minds are originary sources of action, then we may sensibly hold the individual responsible for his or her deeds – both good and bad. Such assumptions make their way into our institutions of law, into the application of rule systems within organizations, and into the rituals of daily life. In all cases, there is longstanding legitimation for blaming the individual for his or her untoward actions. Yet, in significant respects acts of individual blame function much like negations. They symbolically assault what is taken to be the centre core of self. Resistance is thus invited, a resistance that is further exacerbated by the typical sense of righteousness. From the present standpoint, individuals function within shared visions of the real and the good; there is no place in such worlds for 'choosing evil'. Such actions would be incomprehensible. From the personal standpoint, then, all actions are justified – 'right at the time'. Acts of blame, then, often seem unjustified, gratuitous and alien to those who are accused. In terms of dialogue, the challenge is to locate alternative conversational entries that may serve sanctioning purposes without resorting to acts of blame (see McNamee & Gergen, 1999).

ORGANIZATION AS DISORGANIZATION

Negation and individual blame may seriously impede the process of generative dialogue. However, there is a more subtle and ironic narrative of disorganization that requires special attention. To be succinct, we propose that successful organizing establishes the grounds for disorganization. To elaborate, consider Bakhtin's (1981) important distinction between dialogue that functions centripetally (bringing language into a centralized form of organization), as opposed to centrifugally (disrupting or disorganizing centralized forms of understanding). In this sense what we have characterized as generative dialogue essentially functions centripetally to create effective organization. However, dialogue that brings organizational participants together into a shared space of understanding also functions in such a way that the dialogic traditions in which they are otherwise engaged are disrupted, suppressed or, in a word, disordered. Essentially the participants may come to embrace a particular reality, set of values and practices that cut them away from other forms of life. The tendency is to become a 'company man', 'a bureaucrat', 'a true believer', or 'one dimensional'. The result is a subtle negation of that which lies outside the shining sphere of organization. The centripital process simultaneously functions centrifugally. (See also Baxter & Montgomery (1998) on dialectic change as inherent in dialogue.)

This problem is exacerbated by a small group pattern long familiar to the social sciences, namely that of 'in-group/out-group' formation. From the early work of Sherif (1966) to more recent accounts of group identity (Tajfel, 1981; Turner, 1991), researchers have noted a strong tendency for organized groups to become alienated from, or hostile to, those outside the group. In-group members come to celebrate their way of doing things, their ideals and their members; other groups form a devalued exterior. They are discredited and suspicious. In more contemporary terms, Foucault's (1980) views of power/knowledge are apposite. As groups develop a shared vision of the real and the good, they tend to incorporate or suppress alien discourses. The hegemonic thrust of discursive communities tends to marginalize or alienate those who fall outside. Or, in more practical terms, as organizations become larger, more complex and more geographically extended, so will multiple discursive communities emerge, each with a particular construction of the world, each with a potential distrust or animus towards the others. Pockets of local organization – effective for carrying out the daily duties as understood within – carry with them potential resistances to other enclaves of meaning within the organization. The Marketing division fails to appreciate the problems of Sales, Sales does not believe R&D is functioning effectively, the French subsidiary believes the home office in the USA is irrational, and so on. In sum, wherever dialogue is successful in organizing, there is a subtle undoing of organization, and unleashing of potentials for intergroup negation.

TOWARDS TRANSFORMATIVE DIALOGUE

In preceding sections we have focused on specific moves in dialogue that may contribute to both organization and disorganization. We turn finally to dialogic practices that may bridge the gap between alienated realities. Required here are moves in conversation that may sometimes differ substantially from those congenial to creating and sustaining a given reality, morality or way of life. The challenge is that of bringing into productive synchrony groups that share solidified visions of the real and the good. We may speak, then, of transformative dialogue, a relational accomplishment that creates new spaces of meaning and enables the organization to restore its generative potentials (Gergen et al., 2001). In what follows we will consider two forms of organized practice specifically focused on crossing boundaries. In each case we shall attempt to isolate those particular dialogic moves central to bringing about restorative change.

The Public Conversations Project

The Public Conversation Project, founded in 1989, seeks to create an alternative to polarized debate by creating constructive dialogues between parties (see Chasin & Herzig, 1994; Chasin et al., 1996). Typically, the project works with groups that have a history of marginalizing, demonizing and even eliminating the other. In some of their most important work, activists on both sides of the abortion debate were brought together in small groups for a two-day meeting. The meeting began with a dinner in which participants were free to talk to another about any issue except the issue of abortion. The dinner gave way to guided conversations in which, during the subsequent days, participants specifically addressed the following questions:

1. How did you get involved with this issue? What is your personal relationship or personal history with it?
2. We would like to hear a little more about your particular beliefs and perspectives about the issues surrounding abortion. What is at the heart of the matter for you?
3. Many people we've talked to have told us that within their approach to this issue they find some gray areas, some dilemmas about their own beliefs or even some conflicts. Do you experience any pockets of uncertainty or lesser certainty, any concerns, value conflicts, or mixed feelings that you may have and wish to share?

The first question enabled the participants to tell personal stories about events that shaped their views. Often they shared experiences from their own lives or the experience of a family member at a crisis moment. The second question gave participants an opportunity to express their personal, core beliefs about the abortion issue. Finally, participants were able to speak of their uncertainties or ambivalence. Participants in this and other projects have been almost univocal in their praises. Interestingly, in January 2001, six Boston women – public leaders from both sides of the abortion debate – revealed that they had been meeting in secret for six years after their participation in the project (Fowler et al., 2001). Among other things the participants felt they learned to abandon polemical language; continued meeting enabled them to see 'the dignity and goodness' of those they opposed. While not eschewing their original positions, they reported that they 'learned to avoid being over-reactive and disparaging the other side and to focus instead on affirming (our) respective causes'.

What are the discursive moves that enabled the boundaries of animosity to be traversed? At the outset we find that the practice included certain generative moves in dialogue and avoided two more destructive possibilities. In the generative case, both the conversation at dinner and the session in which participants spoke of the 'heart of the matter' for them, their 'opponents' were cast in the role of respectful listening. The act of listening without responding with contentious questions subtly served an affirming function. At the same time, by steering the conversation away from uncompromising theoretical issues, few destructive differences entered the conversation. Finally, the dialogue was arranged in such a way that acts of blame were not permitted. However, the public conversations format also points to the importance of narrative revelation and self-reflexivity.

NARRATIVE REVELATION Listening to the first-person narratives of those to whom one is otherwise opposed seems to have a powerful ameliorating effect. The reasons are several. First, such narratives are easily comprehensible; from our earliest years we are exposed to the narrative form common in personal storytelling, and we are more fully prepared to understand this form as opposed to abstract arguments. Further, stories can invite fuller audience engagement than does the explication of abstract ideas. In hearing stories we generate images, thrive on the drama, suffer and celebrate with the speaker. Finally, the personal story tends to generate acceptance as opposed to resistance. If it is 'your story, your experience', then the audience can scarcely say 'you are wrong'. Narratives do not invite opposition but indulgence.

SELF-REFLEXIVITY One unfortunate aspect of traditional conversation is that we are positioned as unified egos. That is, we are constructed as singular, coherent selves, not fragmented and multiple ones. To be incoherent is subject to ridicule; moral inconsistency is grounds for scorn. Thus, as we encounter people whose positions differ from ours, we tend to represent ourselves one-dimensionally, ensuring that all our statements form a unified, seamless whole. As a result, when we enter a relationship defined by our differences, commitment to unity will maintain our distance. And if the integrity or validity of one's coherent front is threatened by the other, we may move towards polarizing combat. In this respect the invitation to explore one's 'gray areas' or doubts releases the demand for coherence. In Baxter and Montgomery's (1998) terms, we demonstrate one of the most important dialogic skills, namely the 'ability to recognize multiple, simultaneously salient systems'. More broadly, self-reflexivity may be only one member of a family of moves that will inject polyvocality into the dialogue. For example, in their conflict work, Pearce and Littlejohn (1997) often employ 'third person listening', in which one member of an antagonistic group may be asked to step out of the conversation and to observe the interchange. By moving from the first-person position, in which one is representing a position, to a third-person stance, one can observe the conflict with other criteria at hand (e.g., 'Is this a productive form of interaction?', 'What improvements might be made?').

Appreciative inquiry

Appreciative inquiry (AI) is a second and highly effective transformative practice. Developed by David Cooperrider and his colleagues in the 1980s (Cooperrider & Srivastva, 1987; Cooperrider et al., 2000; Ludema et al., 2000; Fry et al., 2002), it is a method that aims to transform the capacity of human systems for positive change by deliberately focusing on positive experiences and hopeful futures. Traditional action research, they claim, has been constrained within a problem-solving ethos and girded with a deficit orientation in which participants are encouraged to notice and talk about breakdowns and plan action around solutions that address these problems. AI claims that organizations are not problems to be solved but are 'centers of infinite relational capacity, alive with infinite imagination, open, indeterminate, and ultimately – in terms of the future – a mystery' (Cooperrider & Barrett, 2002, p. 236).

AI practitioners begin with the belief that topic choice and question formation are the most important moves in shaping dialogue. Much effort is made towards creating questions around positive topics that guide attention towards peak experiences and strengths. The challenge is to ask questions that deliberately focus on those factors that contribute to the system operating at its very best. Questions are designed to encourage participants to search for stories that embody these affirmative topics. Participants are encouraged to develop an appreciative eye, to appreciate the possibility that every human system, no matter how dysfunctional or conflictual, has elements of beauty, goodness and value.

Although AI practices are frequently used to stimulate organizational change, they are particularly applicable to cases in which groups are locked in spirals of negation and vengeance. One case study in particular conveys the value of appreciative inquiry as a mode of creating transformative dialogue in a system under siege. (For a fuller description, see Barrett & Coopperrider, 1990.) In the early 1980s, The Medic Inn, a one-star hotel facility, was taken over by a larger enterprise and given the mandate to transform itself into a first class, four-star facility. The parent company invested in the property and upgraded the physical facilities. However, the quality of service was slow to change. Managers were locked in cycles of interpersonal conflict and interdepartmental turf wars. Interpersonal tension and competition were seemingly insurmountable obstacles to overcome. It was clear to the consultants that the managers needed to engage in a different kind of dialogue in order to overcome conflict and move towards a new standard of excellence.

The consultants in this case created a task force of managers to take a collective journey to Chicago's famous Tremont Hotel, one of the premier four-star properties in the county. Here they interviewed managers about the factors they felt contributed to excellence. A typical question was: What were the peak moments in the life of the hotel – the times when people felt most energized, most committed, and most fulfilled in their involvement? Later, the participants interviewed one another about their own peak experiences in their hotel, and then began to articulate aspirations for their possible future. In these discussions there were no traces of the cycles of blame and turf protection. The group returned to their hotel with a new cooperative spirit and a renewed capacity to generate consensus. They continued the dialogue that had begun with the appreciative inquiry at the Tremont and within a few months developed a collective strategic plan for excellence. Within a few years they had achieved a four-star rating from the Michelin rating service.

Appreciative inquiry seeds transformational dialogue in many ways. There is a premium placed on *mutual affirmation*; *productive differences* are encouraged, *individual blame* is avoided, and *personal narratives* create a strong sense of mutuality. At the same time, AI offers one highly significant addition to a vocabulary of transformative dialogue: the co-creation of new worlds.

THE CO-CREATION OF NEW WORLDS   As outlined earlier, transformative dialogue is essentially aimed at facilitating the collaborative construction of new realities. Needed in the dialogue are what might be called imaginary moments in which participants join in developing visions of common good. These imaginary moments not only sow the seeds for constructing a common reality and vision of the good, but also shift the position of the participants from combative to cooperative. As participants move towards common purpose, so do they redefine the other, and lay the groundwork for a conception of 'us'. This is precisely what is achieved as AI participants engage in designing new futures.

To be sure, the work of the Public Conversations Project and appreciative inquiry practitioners do not exhaust the possibilities for transformative dialogue. The interested reader is directed as well to the important work of the Public Dialogue Consortium on community change (see Pearce & Pearce, 2001; Spano, 2001). Further, a rich reserve of resources may be located through several websites, including: www.uia.org/dialogue; www.thataway.org/dialogue;www.study-circles.org; and www.un.org/Dialogue.

IN CONCLUSION

In the 1987 edition of *The Handbook of Organizational Communication* (Jablin & Putnam, 1987), there is no index entry for 'dialogue', nor does significant discussion of dialogue appear in any of the included chapters. We hope that the present chapter will signal a significant shift in attention, and serve as an animating springboard for new lines of inquiry. As we have attempted to demonstrate, dialogue is essential to the vitality of an organization, and neglect of dialogic practices can create internal schisms and ultimate collapse. In the present chapter we have developed a view of dialogue as discursive coordination, and within this framework moved on to consider dialogic practices that bring organization into being, that destroy organization, and that enable conflicting domains of meaning to be re-coordinated.

Yet, these are only beginnings. We have already noted the lack of attention in this analysis to non-verbal forms of discursive action, to material context, to cultural and historical variations. However, a full treatment of dialogue should also be attentive to issues of power. Deetz (1992) warns us that the relations of power in our ordinary institutions may preclude the kind of dialogue from which organizational change may ensue. In the same vein, we have not discussed the many possible relational configurations in which dialogue may take place. Various configurations of gender, age, kinship, friendship and the like might well reveal different forms of effective dialogue (Duck, 2002). Further, Myerson (1994) draws our attention to 'double arguability', essentially a distinction between the interactions of the interlocutors in a dialogue and the specific issue at stake. Ultimately we must consider the relationship between what is said, the way in which it is said and the form of relationship (Taylor, 1999). The present analysis has focused exclusively on the former domain, while neglecting potentially significant issues of dialogic content. Finally, our analysis has failed to make contact with issues of dialogic ethics. Should there be ethical imperatives for effective dialogue (see, for example, Krippendorff, 1989; Habermas, 1993; Baxter & Montgomery, 1998); are there ethical assumptions already implicit, or is it possible that ethical imperatives may interfere with the contextual necessities and generative potentials of dialogue? We favour, then, an infinite unfolding of the dialogue on dialogue.

REFERENCES

Anderson, H. (1997) *Conversation, language, and possibilities: A postmodern approach to therapy*. New York: Harper Collins.

Anderson, H., Cooperrider, D., Gergen, K.J., Gergen, M., McNamee, S. & Whitney, D. (2001) *The appreciative organization*. Swarthmore, PA: Taos Institute Publications.

Austin, J.L. (1962) *How to do things with words*. New York: Oxford University Press.

Darbules, N.C. (1994) *Dialogue in teaching*. New York: Teachers College Press.

Bakhtin, M.M. (1981) *The dialogic imagination: Four essays by M.M. Bakhtin*. Edited by C. Emerson & M. Holquist. Austin, TX: University of Texas Press.

Barrett, F.J. & Cooperrider, D. (1990) Generative metaphor intervention: A new approach to intergroup conflict. *Journal of Applied Behavioral Science*, 26 (2): 223–44.

Baumgartel, H. (1959) Using employee questionnaire results for improving organizations: The survey 'feedback' experiment. *Kansas Business Review*, December: 2–6.

Baxter, L. & Montgomery, B. (1998) *Relating: Dialogues and dialectics*. Hillsdale, NJ: Lawrence Erlbaum Associates.

Billig, M. (1987) *Arguing and thinking*. Cambridge, MA: Cambridge University Press.

Bohm, D. (1996) On dialogue. Edited by Lee Nichol. New York: Routledge.

Boje, D.M. (1991) Organizations as storytelling networks: The study of performance in an office supply firm. *Administrative Science Quarterly*, 36: 106–26.

Boje, D.M. (2001) *Narrative methods for organizational and communication research*. London: Sage.

Bruner, J. (1990) *Acts of meaning*. Cambridge, MA: Harvard University Press.

Chasin, R. & Herzig, M. (1994) Creating systemic interventions for the socio-political arena. In B. Berger-Gould & D. Demuth (eds), *The global family therapist: Integrating the personal, professional and political*. Boston, MA: Allyn & Bacon.

Chasin, R., Herzig, M., Roth, S., Chasin, L., Becker, C. & Stains, R. (1996) From diatribe to dialogue on divisive public issues: Approaches drawn from family therapy. *Median Quarterly*, Summer (13): 4.

Coch, J. & French, R.P. (1948) Overcoming resistance to change. *Human Relations*, 1 (4): 512–33.

Cooperrider, D.L. & Barrett, F.J. (2002) An exploration of the spiritual heart of human science inquiry: A methodological call of our time. *SOL Journal*, 3 (3): 56–62.

Cooperrider, D.L. & Srivastva, S. (1987) Appreciative inquiry in organizational life. In W.A. Pasmore & R.W. Woodman (eds), *Research in organization change and development* (Vol. 1, pp. 129–69). Greenwich, CT: JAI Press.

Cooperrider, D.L., Sorensen, P.F., Whitney, D. & Yaeger, T.F. (2000) *Appreciative inquiry: Rethinking human organization toward a positive theory of change*. Champagne, IL: Stipes.

Craig, R.T. & Tracy, K. (eds) (1983) *Conversational coherence*. Beverly Hills, CA: Sage.

Czarniawska, B. (1997) *Narrating the organization*. Chicago: University of Chicago Press.

Deetz, S. (1992) *Democracy in an age of corporate colonization*. Albany, NY: State University of New York Press.

Duck, S. (2002) Hypertext in the key of G: Three types of 'history' as influences on conversational structure and flow. *Communication Theory*, 12: 41–62.

Eisenberg, E.M. & Goodall, H.L., Jr. (1993) *Organizational communication: Balancing creativity and constraint*. New York: St Martin's Press.

Foucault, M. (1980) *Power/knowledge*. New York: Pantheon.

Fowler, A., Gamble, N., Hogan, F., Kogut, M., McComish, M. & Thorp, B. (2001) Talking with the enemy. *The Boston Globe*, 28 January.

Fry, R., Barrett, F., Seiling, J. & Whitney, D. (2002) *Appreciative inquiry and organizational transformation: Reports from the field*. Westport, CT: Quorum Books.

Garfinkel, H. (1967) *Studies in ethnomethodology*. Englewood Cliffs, NJ: Prentice-Hall.

Gergen, K.J. (1994) *Realities and relationships*. Cambridge, MA: Harvard University Press.

Gergen, K.J. (1999) *An invitation to social construction*. London: Sage.

Gergen, K.J., McNamee, S. & Barrett, F. (2001) Toward transformative dialogue. *International Journal of Public Administration*, 24: 697–707.

Grudin, R. (1996) *On dialogue: An essay in free thought*. New York and Boston, MA: Houghton Mifflin.

Habermas, J. (1993) *Justification and application: Remarks on discourse ethics*. Cambridge, MA: MIT Press.

Harré, R. & Gillette, G. (1994) *The discursive mind*. London: Sage.

Hawes, L.C. (1999) The dialogics of conversation: Power, control, and vulnerability. *Communication Theory*, 9: 229–64.

Hazen, M.A. (1993) Toward polyphonic organization. *Journal of Organizational Change Management*, 6: 15–26.

Isaacs, W.N. (1993) Taking flight: Dialogue, collective thinking, and organizational learning. *Organizational Dynamics*, 22: 24–39.

Jablin, F.M., Putnam, L., Roberts, K. & Porter, L. (eds) (1987) *The handbook of organizational communication*. Beverly Hills, CA: Sage.

Jandt, F.E. (2001) *Intercultural communication*. Thousand Oaks, CA: Sage.

Krippendorff, K. (1989) On the ethics of constructing communication. In B. Dervin, L. Grossberg, B. O'Keefe & E. Wartella (eds), *Rethinking communication. V.I Paradigm issues*. Newbury Park, CA: Sage.

Lewin, K. (1951) *Field theory in social science*. New York: Harper.

Ludema, J.D., Cooperrider, D.L. & Barrett, F.J. (2000) Appreciative inquiry: The power of the unconditional positive question. In P. Reason & H. Bradbury (eds), *Handbook of action research* (pp. 189–99). Thousand Oaks, CA: Sage.

Maranhao, T. (ed.) (1990) *The interpretation of dialogue*. Chicago: University of Chicago Press.

Markova, I., Graumann, C.F. & Foppa, K. (eds) (1995) *Mutualities in dialogue*. Cambridge: Cambridge University Press.

McNamee, S. & Gergen, K.J. (1999) *Relational responsibility*. Thousand Oaks, CA: Sage.

Myerson, G. (1994) *Rhetoric, reason and society*. London: Sage.

Pearce, W.B. (1989) *Communication and the human condition*. Carbondale, IL: Southern Illinois University Press.

Pearce, W.B. & Littlejohn, S. (1997) *Moral conflict: When social worlds collide*. Thousand Oaks, CA: Sage.

Pearce W.B. & Pearce, K. (2001) Extending the theory of the coordinated management of meaning (CMM) through a community dialogue process. *Communication Theory*.

Porras, J.I. & Robertson, P.J. (1992) Organizational development: Theory, practice, research. In M.D. Dunnette & L.M. Hough (eds), *Handbook of organizational psychology* (2nd edition, vol. 3, pp. 719–822). Palo Alto, CA: Consulting Psychology Press.

Putnam, L.L. & Fairhurst, G.T. (2001) Discourse analysis in organizations. In F.M. Jablin & L. Putnam (eds), *The new handbook of organizational communication: Advances in theory, research, and methods* (pp. 78–136). Thousand Oaks, CA: Sage.

Rahim, S.A. (1994) Participatory development communication as a dialogical process. In S. White, K. Sadanandan Nair & J. Ascroft (eds), *Participatory communication: Working for change and development*. New Delhi: Sage.

Saussure, F. de (1974) *Course in general linguistics*. London: Fontana.

Sherif, M. (1966) *In common predicament: Social psychology of intergroup conflict and cooperation*. Boston, MA: Houghton Mifflin.

Shotter, J. (1984) *Social accountability and selfhood*. Oxford: Blackwell.

Spano, S. (2001) *Public dialogue and participatory democracy*. Cresskill, NJ: Hampton Press.

Tajfel, H. (1981) *Human groups and social categories: Studies in social psychology*. London: Cambridge University Press.

Taylor, J.R. (1999) What is 'organizational communication'?: Communication as a dialogic of text and conversation. *Communication Review*, 3: 21–63.

Taylor, J.R. & Van Every, E.J. (2000) *The emergent organization: Communication as its site and surface*. Mahwah, NJ: Lawrence Erlbaum Associates.

Thatchenkery, T.J. & Upadhyaya, P. (1996) Organizations as a play of multiple and dynamic discourses: An example from a global social change organization. In D.J. Boje, R.P. Gephart & T.J. Thatchenkery (eds), *Postmodern management and organization theory* (pp. 308–30). Thousand Oaks, CA: Sage.

Ting-Toomey, S. & Oetzel, J.G. (2001) *Managing intercultural conflict effectively*. Thousand Oaks, CA: Sage.

Turner, J.C. (1991) *Social influence*. Milton Keynes, UK: Open University Press.

Vygotsky, L.S. (1986) *Thought and language*. Trans. Alex Kozulin. Cambridge, MA: MIT Press.

Weick, K.E. (1995) *Sensemaking in organizations*. Thousand Oaks, CA: Sage.

Wells, G. (1999) *Dialogic inquiry: Towards a sociocultural practice and theory of education*. Cambridge: Cambridge University Press.

Wetherell, M., Taylor, S. & Yates, S.J. (2001a) *Discourse as data: A guide for analysis*. London: Sage and The Open University Press.

Wetherell, M., Taylor, S. & Yates, S.J. (2001b) *Discourse theory and practice*. London: Sage and The Open University Press.

Wittgenstein, L. (1963) *Philosophical investigations*. Trans. G.E.M. Anscombe. London: Blackwell.

Yankelovich, D. (1999) *The magic of dialogue: Transforming conflict into cooperation*. New York: Simon & Schuster.

2

Narratives, Stories and Texts

Yiannis Gabriel

The facts:

> A routine visit to the doctor turns into something more serious. An urgent referral to the hospital, a batch of tests, an anxious wait, a diagnosis. Testicular cancer.

> A company take-over, a restructuring. An invitation to re-apply for a job. Notification of immediate termination of employment and a compensation package. A black eye.

> A chance meeting with an old school acquaintance at an airport lobby. Instant revival of relationship. Offer of a job.

Three sequences of events involving different people, or perhaps the same person, simultaneously or in succession. Notice immediately two temptations. First, to find other facts, missing from the descriptions above: Who are the 'subjects' of those events? What is their gender, age, class, race and so on? What are the prospects of alternative employment? Who got the black eye and how? What kind of job was being offered? Second, to find clues as to the significance of such facts: How advanced is the cancer? How did he take the diagnosis? How did she or he react to the letter? The two temptations – finding out more facts and finding out clues about their significance – are not unrelated, since it is through the juxtaposition and sequencing of facts, their 'engagement' with each other in a plot, that meaning begins to emerge. For instance, on the very day he was diagnosed with testicular cancer, he also received a notice of termination of employment. Or alternatively, the day after she was offered an alluring new job following a chance meeting with an old school acquaintance at an airport lobby, she received the letter of termination from her old job. Facts, even those seemingly trivial ones that feature in game shows, invite being placed in a story, through the magic of plot.

Notice too, a third temptation – the temptation to silence. Why bother about a case of testicular cancer, a termination, a black eye or a job offer? Why indeed care in the light of personal and world events that cry out for meaning and explanation? Of course, if the protagonists in the above incidents happen to be oneself, or one's spouse (whether loved or hated or both), one's son or daughter or one's close friend, then the search for meaning may be burning. But if the subject is one of the anonymous thousands who are diagnosed with testicular cancer, are fired from their jobs or receive unexpected job offers each month, then the search for meaning may all but vanish. The very requirement that meaning should reside in the facts disappears. They become mere statistics, data, information. The 'So what?' question is the abyss that faces every storyteller as soon as a story is announced (Labov, 1972, p. 360). A story has been announced and a challenge has been set – will it be delivered or will it wither away in the face of the dreaded 'So what?' question?

Facts rarely speak for themselves – and never in isolation. Narratives and stories enable us to make sense of them, to identify their significance, and even, when they are painful or unpleasant, to accept them and live with them. Narratives and stories feature prominently as sense-making devices, through which events are not merely infused with meaning, but constructed and contested. This chapter will review their nature and mutations in organizational settings, their usage and scope. It will demonstrate some of their unique qualities as sense-making devices, contrasting them to other devices employed by people in organizations. Of course, narratives and stories are not the only discursive devices enabling us to understand facts, to link them with meanings, to make decisions or to cope with suffering and pain. The argument that will be put forward in this chapter is that, in spite of their current popularity among researchers and consultants, narratives, but especially stories, are relatively special events in organizations, capable of great sense-making feats, but also easily drowned in the din of information, lists, numbers, opinions, rationalizations and theories that saturate many organizational spaces, or remaining still-born in environments dominated by relentless preoccupations with efficiency, rationality and action.

There is another point to this chapter. I have a strong feeling that, over the past ten years or so, the concept of story has become distinctly too comfortable. Ideas that once seemed crisp and provocative (e.g., 'The truth of a story lies in its meaning, not in its accuracy', 'We are all storytelling animals', 'Stories are repositories of knowledge' etc.) have assumed the standing of unquestioned truths, ossified in time; in short, they have become platitudes. I see it, therefore, as part of my purpose here to reproblematize the idea of story, to make it prickly, tricky and even dangerous once more. In particular, I would like to question some of the current enthusiasm with stories displayed by critical researchers, by pointing out that stories can be vehicles of contestation and opposition but also of oppression; that they can be vehicles to enlightenment and understanding but also to dissimulation and lying; and finally, that they do not obliterate or deny the existence of facts but allow facts to be reinterpreted and embellished – this makes stories particularly dangerous devices in the hands of image-makers, hoaxers and spin doctors.

TEXT, NARRATIVE, STORY AND DISCOURSE

Current interest in organizational storytelling and narrative is part of a broader tendency of narrativization of organizational theory, that is an emphasis on language, scripts, metaphors, talk, stories and narratives not as parts of some putative super-structure erected on top of the material realities of organizations, such as structure, power, technology and so forth, but rather as parts of the very essence of organization. This has challenged the 'standard platform' of organizational theory (Thoenig, 1998), built around the themes of bureaucracy, hierarchy and authority, and empha-sizes, if not the primacy, at least the relative autonomy of the symbolic dimension. This is itself part of the broader linguistic turn in the social and human sciences – a tendency to view many social and psychological phenomena as constituted through language, sustained through language and challenged through language. Facts them-selves can become 'denaturalized' (Fournier & Grey, 2000), the products rather than the instigators of discourse – note, for example, how 'the facts' in the first sequence described above change if 'testicular cancer' is replaced by 'malignant seminoma (survival rate 95 per cent)'.

As the linguistic turn has been played out in different fields of study, the mean-ings of four key terms, namely text, narrative, story and discourse, have multi-plied, merged and demerged, overlapped and fragmented. Attempts to order or police their usage through definitions have not been very successful. (For a good discussion of the definitional issues surrounding discourse, see Grant et al., 1998). Nor maybe should they be, since one of the qualities of the 'linguistic turn' has been a move away from adjudication by definition. Terms, concepts and so forth are approached not as immutable essences, but as elements of language in action. Stories are frequently used interchangeably with narratives, narratives with texts, and texts with discourse. In this chapter, I want to advocate a differ-ent view, one that regards not all discourse and not every text as narrative, and not every narrative as a story. My reason for doing so is not an obsession with semantic policing, but a belief that viewing every type of text as story obliterates those qualities that make stories vivid and powerful but also fragile sense-making devices, obscures the skill and inventiveness entailed by storytelling and reduces the usefulness of studying stories in organizations. In particular, it sup-presses those unique and interrelated properties of stories which make them effective as vehicles of both sense-making and contestations in and out of organizations – their ambiguous relation to truth or reality, their unmanaged and unmanageable qualities, and their vindication of experience as a source of knowl-edge against the claims of science and information.

Narratives are particular types of text. Unlike definitions, labels, lists, recipes, logos, proverbs, hypotheses, theories, or neurotic symptoms, buildings, clothes, musical instruments, cooking utensils or numerous other texts, all of which can be 'read', narratives involve temporal *chains* of interrelated events or actions, undertaken by characters. Narratives are no simple signs, icons or images, still less are narratives material objects and physical movements (all of which may, to please Barthes (1966/1977), be regarded as texts but not narratives). Rather, narratives require verbs denoting what characters did or what happened to them. They are not mere snapshot photographic images, but require *sequencing*, something noted by most systematic commentators on narratives (Bruner, 1990; Culler, 1981/2001; Czarniawska, 1997, 1999; Labov, 1972; MacIntyre, 1981; Polkinghorne, 1988; Ricœur, 1984; Van Dijk, 1975; Weick, 1995). As we move from narrative to story we are forced to recognize the increasing importance of *plot*, which 'knits events together', allowing us to understand the deeper significance of an event in the light of others (Czarniawska, 1999, p. 64f; Polkinghorne, 1988, pp. 18–19).

If plot (involving characters, sequencing, action, predicaments, etc.) is a crucial feature of stories, their second key feature is a seminal ambiguity – the characters and events in the plot may be *real or imagined*, the product of *experience or fantasy* (Czarniawska, 1999, p. 15; Gabriel, 2000, p. 239; Ricœur, 1984, p. 150). This creative ambiguity gives stories a unique combination of two qualities, those of having a plot at the same time as representing reality. Stories purport to relate to facts that happened, but also discover in these facts a plot or a meaning, by claiming that facts do not merely happen but that they happen in accordance with the requirements of a plot. In short, stories are not 'just fictions' (although they may be fictions), nor are they mere chronologies of events as they happened. Instead, they represent poetic elaborations of narrative material, aiming to communicate *facts as experience*, not facts as information (Benjamin, 1968). This accords the storyteller a unique narrative privilege, *poetic licence*, that enables him/her to maintain an allegiance to the effectiveness of the story, even as he/she claims to be representing the truth.

Poetic licence is a feature of a *psychological contract* between the storyteller and his/her audience, that allows a storyteller to poetically mould the material for effect, to exaggerate, to omit, to draw connections where none are apparent, to silence events that interfere with the storyline, to embellish, to elaborate, to display emotion, to comment, to interpret, while he/she claims to be representing reality. All of these poetic interventions are justified in the name of giving a voice to experience. Thus poetic licence enables the storyteller to buy the audience's suspension of disbelief in exchange for pulling off a story which is *verisimilar*. The story, then, is a poetic elaboration on events, one that accords with the psychological needs of the teller and the audience, and one that requires considerable ingenuity on the part of the narrator. If the 'So what?' indicates that the plot is failing to carry meaning, 'Who are you kidding?' indicates that it fails to carry verisimilitude. Treading this tightrope between two questions which threaten the psychological contract is what sets the storyteller apart from narrators of other narratives, such as chronicles, reports, myths and films.

STORIES, FICTIONS AND SENSE-MAKING

This then is where the skill and imagination of the storyteller resides – in spinning a yarn which at once makes events meaningful and maintains their standing as facts. This type of poetic work can be thought of as 'story-work', a work of creative imagination which does not lose contact with events but always seeks to uncover a deeper meaning in them. If I resist the temptation of calling this 'narrative labour' after the precedents of emotional labour (Hochschild, 1983) and aesthetic labour, it is because story-work is both emotional, in as much as it seeks to generate emotions appropriate to the situation, and aesthetic, in as much as it seeks to deliver a fulfilling artefact.

How does story-work operate? It seems to me that in making sense of events, storytellers make use of a number of interpretive devices to which I refer as 'poetic tropes' (Gabriel, 2000, p. 36). Each one of these tropes represents a way of either making sense of specific parts in the narrative or making connections between different parts. Eight such poetic tropes can be noted:

1 *Attribution of motive* – this is maybe the most important trope, one that turns individuals into agents, seeking to influence events and achieve their purposes consciously or unconsciously; motives cannot be established by observation, but can be established by inference.

2 *Attribution of causal connections* – here chronological sequence is turned into causal chain, earlier events causing subsequent ones; causal connections in stories tend to be simple and mechanical rather than complex, statistical and probabilistic.

3 *Attribution of responsibility, namely blame and credit* – here an evaluation is implicit between praiseworthy events, for which credit is attributed, and reversals, which call for the attribution of blame; credit and blame are attributed to single agents, minimizing the influence of chance and accident.

4 *Attribution of unity* – where an entire class of people or objects are treated as indistinguishable and, therefore, may substitute each other in the plot; any one person or object can stand for the entire class under such circumstances.

5 *Attribution of fixed qualities, especially in opposition* – here individuals, objects or classes of people and objects are seen as possessing natural or supernatural qualities (strength, intelligence, perfidiousness, cunning, sorcery) which are immutable, unless the plot accounts for their transformation.

6 *Attribution of emotion* – whereby individuals act in emotional ways and derive specific emotions from the events in the plot; emotion is frequently attributed in conjunction with motive.

7 *Attribution of agency* – whereby inanimate objects (such as volcanoes, machines, weather, etc.) are seen as capable of acting in a motivated way.

8 *Attribution of providential significance* – whereby an event is seen as meeting the plot's requirement for justice or injustice, as though it were engineered by a superior benevolent or malevolent intelligence or fate.

How does the deployment of poetic tropes affect the representation (mimesis) of events by the storyteller? Within stories specific incidents may be accorded great emphasis. Because they establish the significance of other events, other incidents may be silenced altogether or modified. Juxtaposition of different accounts of the same sequence of events suggests that, in drawing out meaning, storytellers use 'facts' in a plastic way, moulding them to the requirements of the plot which is itself a reflection of the needs of the audience (Boje, 1994; Czarniawska, 1997). A plot that delivers verisimilitude to one audience fails to do so to another. This moulding of events to accord with the requirements of the plot takes place in different ways. These may include the following:

1 *Framing* – here various events or characters are placed at the heart of the narrative, while others are placed near the edges or left out altogether.
2 *Focusing* – extends the idea of framing by according special emphasis on a single cluster of events or characters, diminishing the importance of others.
3 *Filtering* – whereby specific events or characters are taken out of the narrative, in spite of their closeness to some of the central characters or events.
4 *Fading* – whereby specific events or characters are brought in or out of focus for specific aspects of the plot and then silenced as though their usefulness and significance were extinguished.
5 *Fusing* – whereby two or more characters or events are merged into a single one, collapsing temporal and other distinctions.
6 *Fitting* – whereby specific events or characters are re-interpreted or represented in accordance with the plot.

HOW TRUTHFUL THEN ARE STORIES?

Such moulding of events allows the storyteller to construct plots and deploy the poetic tropes in identifying meaning. Does this amount to falsification? Undoubtedly, if the criterion of truth is accuracy of reporting. If, however, the criterion of truth is something different, then it may be that distortions, omissions and exaggerations serve a deeper truth. What may such a deeper truth be? The answer often given to this question is that the truth of the story lies not in its accurate depiction of facts but in its *meaning* (see, for example, Reason & Hawkins, 1988). Poetic licence and all the falsifications that it justifies aim at generating a deeper truth, one which gives us greater insight into a situation than the literal truth. 'Let's create a fiction that is truer than truth', says one of the characters in Pirandello's *Six characters in search of an author*. But is it possible for fiction to be truer than reality? This is a question that has preoccupied philosophers through the ages. In *The Republic*, Plato challenged precisely this view, in his critique of poetic and mythical narratives as longstanding repositories of deeper truths and wisdom. Instead, he proffered philosophy as a superior source of knowledge, subject to rational examination and analysis. He criticized poets and storytellers (even revered ones, like Homer) as persuasive peddlers of untruths and stirrers or irrational emotions, famously allowing them no place his Republic. At the heart of Plato's critique was his theory of *mimesis* – stories imitate the world of appearances which is itself only a pale imitation of the world of forms, and are therefore twice removed from the real world of ideas or deep truths.

Aristotle, in his *Poetics*, sought to salvage poetry and storytelling from Plato's critique, by counterposing his uniquely illuminating theory, namely that poetry and art imitate not the real but the general, the ideal, the deeply true. Mimesis in art is no mere imitation and carries no pejorative connotation – instead of imitation, it becomes representation. Reality as represented by the work of art is more true and more profound than that represented by the historian or the chronicler – instead of imitating mere superficial appearance, it represents the essence, the general. A literal untruth, according to this view, may be closer to the true nature of things than a literal truth which remains superficial and mundane. Where literal representation accurately imitates the veil, the façade, the surface, poetry has transcendental qualities, reaching out towards the systematically hidden from sight, the enduring. It thus reveals a deeper truth, a poetic truth. Consider, for instance, caricatures, cartoons or painted portraits – all of these forms of representation aim at something deeper and more general, seeking to go beyond the accuracy of photographic reproduction. Could it then be said that storytelling too seeks to represent events in this deeper manner, reaching beyond the world of mere appearances?

I have long found the view that the truth of a story lies in its meaning rather than in its accuracy very compelling. I have now developed serious doubts and have come to regard it as a comforting but inadequate rhetorical gesture where proper argument is called for. It is reminiscent of the psychoanalytic view, which has always made psychoanalysis a target to criticism, that what matters is the experience of trauma, not whether the events causing the trauma actually happened or not. Likewise, if the experience described by a story is authentic, it matters little whether the events described therein actually took place or not. This view asserts the *primacy of experience* over other ways of establishing truth (Eagleton, 1996) above all else (including Plato's philosophy and science) as a source of knowledge. When the knowledge of experts is routinely devalued (and often for excellent reasons), knowledge from introspection, divination or faith is virtually dismissed, and facts become infinitely accommodating of diverse interpretations and spin, we are left with knowledge and truth from authentic personal experience, and the different voices that it takes (art, story, memoir, reminiscence), which assumes pride of place. Far from storytelling then being overwhelmed by other modernist narratives and texts as some theorists of modernity imagined (Benedict, 1931; Benjamin, 1968), storytelling enables people to discover a *voice* through which they can build truth on their experience, communicate it, debate it and share it with other people.

Yet, I think that this approach has weaknesses of its own and we have reasons to be sceptical towards it. Instead of representing the reflexive 'finding' of a voice rooted in experience, storytelling can represent a *discursive strategy of dissimulation*. Consider two recent imbroglios involving two memoirs which represent the literary genre that voices experience. Both achieved great success by combining the qualities of authenticity and verisimilitude that marked them as authentic expressions of people who had experienced extraordinary events. In *I, Rigoberta Menchú* (Menchú & Burgos-Debray, 1984), a Guatemalan Indian woman (later honoured with the Nobel Peace Prize) painted a torrid account of the brutality inflicted on her family and village by wealthy landowners and the government who were trying to drive them off their land. Subsequently, David Stoll (1999), an American anthropologist sympathetic to the plight of Guatemalan Indians, challenged substantial parts of Menchú's narrative. With the help of interviews with numerous villagers, Stoll offered convincing evidence (both narrative and factual) that some of the reported atrocities had not actually happened to Menchú's own family and that many of her claims were inaccurate (not least her claim to have been illiterate or that her father was a landless peasant). Stoll, more significantly, also challenged Menchú's contention that the Mayan Indians had been enthusiastic recruits by the *focista* guerrillas. Instead he makes a very convincing argument that they were caught between two armies, both of which bullied and brutalized them. Even more devastating was the discovery that *Fragments: Memories of a wartime childhood*, an award-winning Holocaust memoir written by Binjamin Wilkomirski (Wilkomirski, 1996) was a fake, its author being neither a Jew nor a Holocaust survivor (Maechler, 2001; Peskin, 2000; Suleiman, 2000). Both of these memoirs represent unspeakable suffering told by the presumed victims and generate powerful emotions in the reader – compassion for the victims as well as admiration for their courage, and outrage against the oppressor. However, when we learn that the events could not have taken place as told, we feel that the authors have abused our trust, exceeding the limits of poetic licence to present fictions as facts.

Some have defended Menchú and Wilkomirski on similar grounds. Israel Gutman, for example, the director of the revered Yad Vashem and a Holocaust survivor, defended Wilkomirski on the grounds that 'Wilkomirski has written a story which he has experienced deeply; that's for sure. … He is not a fake. He is someone who lives this story very deeply in his soul. The pain is authentic' (Finkelstein, 2000, p. 61). Others have argued that Menchú and Wilkomirski speak not just for themselves but with a collective voice, on behalf of a whole class of disempowered and silenced victims. Some indeed have seen this as a perfectly legitimate defence, refusing to acknowledge any difference between factual truth and a presumed symbolic truth (Binford, 2001; Gledhill, 2001). The mere contestation of testimonies like Menchú's and Wilkomirski's, according to such defendants, amounts to a denial of every survivor's experience, a virtual blasphemy. 'I was there, not you', exclaimed Wilkomirski to his detractors, implying that no historical research, not even by distinguished Holocaust scholars like Raoul Hilberg and Yehuda Bauer, could cast any doubt on his testimony.

In spite of attempts to defend the authenticity of the voice of experience (with all its inexactitudes, artifices and partialities), it seems to me incontestable that incidents like the above (and numerous less well-publicized others) alert us to the possibility of grave breaches of the psychological contract between author and reader. In each case, knowingly or unknowingly, the authors have exceeded the prerogatives of poetic licence and ventured into the field of misrepresentation. Once this breach of contract has occurred, in spite of their possible literary and other merits, the fundamental credibility of such narratives has been broken.

Verisimilitude has given way to dissimulation. The narrator is no longer a creditable one. Through an application of the trope of attribution of fixed qualities, having proven untrustworthy once, he/she remains so forever – his/her narrative damaged beyond repair. This in itself generates a new type of literary narrative, the literary exposé, which has emerged as the antithesis of the memoir, establishing its own psychological contracts between authors and their audiences.

What is true of literary memoirs is also true of stories – breaches of the psychological contract between storyteller and audience and subsequent discrediting of a story undermine our confidence that the 'truth of stories lies in their meaning, not in their accuracy', since the meaning of stories is altered and distorted once some aspects of a story's accuracy have been called into question. Instead, what we appreciate is that one means of contestation of stories lies in the ability to corrupt the credibility of the storyteller, by showing that he/she has broken his/her contract. To the two questions feared by every storyteller – 'So what?' and 'Who are you kidding?' – we must now add a third one, 'Who are you to speak?' In addition to delivering meaning and verisimilitude, a story must be sustained by numerous hidden assumptions about legitimate and non-legitimate forms of representation. For a storyteller to say 'I witnessed it with my own eyes' may be legitimate distortion for effect in some instances or entirely fraudulent in others. Poetic truth, therefore, becomes a product of this contract, which we may legitimately call '*narrative contract*', which continuously defines legitimate and non-legitimate deviations from the facts, legitimate and non-legitimate forms of representation (Veyne, 1988).

Stories are subject to programmes of truth which are continuously negotiated through the narrative contract between the storyteller and the audience in the course of the storytelling process itself. Storytelling, then, is liable to collapse for a number of reasons – if the audience is not interested or does not have the time to listen, if the narrative does not deliver verisimilitude by failing to 'resonate', i.e. to touch those important wishes and desires that give it vibrancy and meaning, if the trust in the storyteller's ability, integrity or authority are undermined. For all these reasons, stories must be seen as fragile and delicate types of narrative, requiring much skill and sensitivity in order to be successful.

STORIES AND NARRATIVES IN ORGANIZATIONS

What can be said of stories and narratives in organizations that does not apply to stories and narratives in general? In the first place, I would contend that they have to compete with other sense-making devices which find, in organizations, a very hospitable environment. A person or a group seeking to understand an action or an event may very well resort to purely rationalistic explanations which do not require a supportive cast of characters, chronology or plot. 'Why did Tourism International lay off a hundred people? Because, in the light of the current crisis facing the tourist industry, the organization was facing bankruptcy and it had to reduce costs.' This may not be an explanation that possibly makes sense to those hundred people or their families, but it makes perfectly good sense to numerous others. In addition, many actions and events in organizations can be understood in terms of bureaucratic rules and procedures from which they emanate. 'Why was X fired by organization Y? Because he was found guilty of gross professional misconduct and, according to the organization's disciplinary code, he was summarily dismissed.' This type of rationalistic and legalistic explanation may not exhaust the sense-making requirements of outsiders and often of insiders, but it would be wrong to dismiss them as either infrequent or inadequate – they perform their functions very well much of the time in organizations.

If stories and narratives as sense-making devices are far from hegemonic in organizations, they are even more severely contested as means of communication. Here organizations mobilize formidable resources which prima facie stand in the way of narratives and include rule-books and manuals, recipe books and reports, instructions and orders conveyed by word of mouth, paper and electronic means, circulars, and so forth. Undoubtedly, these frequently invite narrative support or qualification (for a good discussion see Tsoukas, 1998). 'What is the story?' is usually an invitation to offer a narrative elaboration on what appears factual and definitive. Yet, on innumerable occasions, instructions are followed, procedures are adhered to and information is assimilated without a call for such narrative elaborations. Even where symbolic elaborations are called for to reinforce or to contest rationalistic or legalistic explanations or to support other information, they are not limited to stories and narratives. Various non-narrative linguistic devices can do so, for instance metaphors, labels and platitudes (Czarniawska-Joerges & Joerges, 1990).

There are additional qualities to organizations which inhibit narratives. Organizational controls on time, movement, space and on what people are allowed to say often inhibit the delicate and time-consuming narrative process. Many people work in organizations where they have little time for storytelling (as tellers or listeners) or where the emphasis on factual accuracy is such that storytelling is severely impaired. Even when stories do emerge, they frequently have to compete with official narratives and reports, often being silenced in a din of information and data. Numerous people simply do not have the time, the inclination or, indeed, the skill to tell stories. Many narratives are fragmented, cursory or incomplete – they are hardly narratives at all, only embryonic narrative fragments that may be regarded as 'proto-stories', but contain hardly any plot or characters. To all these difficulties, we must add a generalized *narrative deskilling*, a feature of modernity which was commented upon by Walter Benjamin (Benjamin, 1968), while late modernity has rediscovered narratives in a wide variety of contexts and media, including journalism, advertising, political and other commentary, memoirs, etc. It can scarcely be said to represent a storytelling culture in the way that traditional cultures were (Gabriel, 2000).

All in all then, organizations are not 'natural' storytelling communities, communities where stories represent the only or even the main currency for sense-making and communication. In proposing the interesting term 'antenarrative' to describe organizations, David Boje offers a similar conceptualization of organizations (even though he defines 'story' differently from other authors, such as Czarniawska, Watson and myself), as spaces full of 'unconstructed and fragmented' stories which have not yet been told (narrated) (Boje, 2001, p. 3). He argues, that in telling a story, storytellers 'take a bet' that what they are about to say, in interaction with their audience, will amount to a story, although this is frequently not the case (since, as Boje acknowledges, most such tellings end up not having coherent plots). Of course, stories and narratives do exist in organizations in different measures. The importance of stories and narratives in organizations lies precisely in their ability to create symbolic spaces where the hegemony of facts, information and technical rationality can be challenged or side-stepped. This is the domain that I refer to as the *unmanaged organization*, that dimension of organizational life where fantasies and emotions can find expressions in often irrational symbolic constructions. Emotional truths, half-truths and wishful fantasies inhabit this domain, which evades or side-steps organizational controls, and allows individuals and groups to seek pleasure and meaning in stories, gossip, jokes, graffiti, cartoons and so on (Gabriel, 1995).

The unmanaged terrains in organizations are not the same as the informal or unofficial organization. For the greatest part, these are part of the managed organization, patrolled and policed in more or less subtle ways as we are now well aware, thanks mostly to the work of theorists from the critical management perspective. Nor should all narratives, individual or shared, be thought of as part of the unmanaged organization – such a view would fly in the face of the massive resources devoted to the creation and propagation of *corporate fantasies* for both internal and external consumption and the current fad in turning storytelling into another management tool of control and performance by those whom Sievers entirely appropriately called 'merchandisers of meaning' (Sievers, 1986). Those with power can attempt to dictate their own sense-making on others. They may use propaganda, officially-sponsored texts which usually come not as stories but as slogans, logos, lists of values, images, etc., to this effect.

Some such manufactured and merchandized narratives may aspire to becoming stories, celebrated and reproduced by organizational members, but in my experience, few become so. The majority of stories I collected from my study of storytelling in organizations were either indifferent to official narratives or sought to subvert them (Gabriel, 2000). My findings are consistent with those of Watson, who carried out a one-year ethnographic study of management at a British telecommunications company. He too discovered that

> the bulk of Ryland tales were negative ones. Almost totally dominating the stories told to me, when I asked the managers I interviewed to pass on stories they thought were typical of the ones told on the site, were anecdotes, myths and jokes with Ted Meadows [CEO] as the villain or butt. (Watson, 1994, p. 193)

Due to their plastic relation to reality, stories make perfect inhabitants for the unmanaged organization. They slip furtively in and out of sight, they evade censors, they are easily camouflaged and they can rapidly join forces with each other to provide mutual reinforcement and support. They are notoriously difficult to suppress since in doing so the result is to add to their currency and appeal. In this way, stories often cross the boundary between unmanaged and managed organization in different guises. The narrative about the man inventing adhesive tape in his spare time, or the loyal employee who discharges his/her mission against all odds may be adopted as parts of official organizational discourse. These may crystallize into organizational scripts, which may then generate pride, cynical derision or indifference among different groups of people. These, in turn, may reappear in the unmanaged organization with a new twist, such as that the erstwhile hero was subsequently fired or fell foul of management. Other narratives may cross the boundary in a different manner, not as potential supports for organizational practices but as open, visible challenges to such practices. Stories of victimized employees who dispute management decisions, of morally outraged individuals who become whistleblowers and criticize their organization in public, or of individuals who have the fortitude to directly confront their superiors, intervene in the control–resistance domain of their organization and risk bringing its organized power upon themselves. Their narratives are no longer treated as stories, but they become claims, allegations, 'lies' and 'facts'.

Stories continuously test and re-draw the boundaries between the managed and the unmanaged. Within the context of narrative contracts, individuals continuously make assumptions about what can properly be discussed, the meanings attached to different texts, emotional reactions, and so forth. Thus stories rarely emerge fully shaped. Their telling requires minuscule judgements depending on how the narrative is being received and engagements with questions, suggestions and hints from listeners which may indicate loss of interest, loss of understanding or, worst of all, loss of credibility. Stories are sometimes aborted altogether, when one of the listeners or even the teller him/herself quickly steers the narrative back to verifiable facts or to official stories, the precincts of the managed organization. At times, the mere presence of a certain person or a particular look may be enough to put an end to a venture in the unmanaged terrain. Alternatively, a story started by one individual may be finished by another (Boje, 1991) or different variants may be discussed and compared. Stories in the unmanaged organization are far more plastic than their counterparts embedded in official 'mythologies', and frequently tend to mutate into other stories and merge with them. The unmanaged organization can then be seen as a kind of organizational dreamworld, where fantasy obtains a precarious advantage over reality and pleasure over work.

STORIES AND NARRATIVES IN ORGANIZATIONAL RESEARCH

Twenty years ago, it was not uncommon for researchers to complain that narratives and stories were not taken seriously in organizational research. One still hears such complaints though they are far less justified. The climate of opinion has changed. While some research on organizations has remained indifferent to them, scholars have increasingly turned to narratives and stories for a wide range of organizational studies, including strategy, power and politics, emotion and rationality, ethics and morality, management learning and practice, aesthetics and identity, as well as the more predictable ones such as sense-making, communication and culture. As was suggested earlier, much of this work has challenged the standard platform of organizational theory and has sought to reconceptualize organizations as narrative spaces, where discourse is, if not hegemonic and constituting, at least constitutive of what organizations stand for.

Numerous benefits have accrued. We have now become far more alert to the role of language in shaping perceptions and understanding, in discursive forms of control which operate in a subtle and often invisible manner, as well as discursive forms of opposition and contestation. We have been able to observe and study emotions and fantasies operating in organizations and note that, far from being extra add-ons, they are vital in many aspects of organizational life. We have realized that much knowledge and information in organizations is disseminated and transformed through narrative processes. Our understanding of leadership and management has turned increasingly on the discursive resources deployed, which are every bit as important as material and human resources. Numerous aspects of organizational functioning which were either invisible or opaque have gradually come into view. All this is to the good.

Is there a downside to these developments? Until the events of 11 September 2001, I would have argued that the biggest danger of the linguistic turn in the social sciences (and organizational theory) was the tendency to deny the existence or the recalcitrance of facts along with the conviction that virtually any interpretation and symbolic construction can be made to stick. This seems to me less of a danger now. I am not at all sure that following the events of 11 September 2001 in New York and Washington, social scientists can continue to pretend that facts do not exist or do not matter, or that they are dissolved into 'intersubjective and emerging realities'. Facts exist, aeroplanes exist, buildings exist, fanatics exist, hijackings exist, planes crashing into buildings exist and thousands of people dead (whether in New York or in Kabul) exist – as facts. Likewise, bombing raids exist and people die, irrespective of whether they are discursively constructed as 'heroes', 'martyrs' or 'collateral damage'. We may dispute and quarrel about such things (their causes and meanings) till the end of time, but to deny their 'facticity' seems to me preposterous. We may weave ('emplot') facts into stories of heroism, martyrdom, betrayal, hubris, retribution and a thousand different meanings, but these are built on the facts. And facts are recalcitrant – they cannot be modified at will unless people are 'in denial'. It is a fact that Wilkomirski was not a concentration camp inmate, just as it is a fact that Rigoberta did not witness the execution-by-burning of one of her brothers, even if both of these individuals insist that they 'experienced' these events with total conviction. None of this, of course, implies that people are not liable to disregard or deny facts that are unwelcome or invent 'facts' that are useful.

This brings me to the second and, in my view, more important danger – the increasing hegemony in the field of knowledge of personal experience, as expressed in 'voice'. While science has often been guilty of discounting personal experience and adopting a hegemonic voice of uncontested authority, we now run the risk of accepting the voice of personal experience as the uncontested and authentic source of understanding and sense-making. While 'silencing' this voice of experience can no longer be justified, neither can its elevation to unquestioned and unquestionable authority. As Moore and Muller have argued

> The reduction of knowledge to the single plane of experience through the rejection of 'depth analysis' and its epistemology (that allows for and requires a separate and autonomous non-mundane language of theory) produces differences of identity alone, but differences that are, in essence, all the same. The postmodern proclamation that there is only 'surface' echoes the earlier phenomenological claim that science is simply another species of commonsense – an everyday accomplishment of members of the science community or form of life. ... The world is viewed [as] a patchwork of incommensurable and exclusive voices or standpoints. Through the process of sub-division, increasingly more particularized identity categories come into being, each claiming the unique specificity of its distinctive experience and the knowledge authorized by it. (Moore & Muller, 1999, p. 199)

As Maton has argued, this leads to a reduction of knowledge discourse to 'knower discourses', which

> base their legitimation upon the privileged insight of a knower, and work at maintaining strong boundaries around the definition of the knower – they celebrate difference where 'truth' is defined by the 'knower' or 'voice'. As each voice is brought into the choir, the category of the privileged 'knower' becomes smaller, each strongly bounded from one another, for each 'voice' has its own privileged and specialized knowledge ... In summary, with the emergence of each new category of knower, the categories of knowers become smaller, leading to proliferation and fragmentation within the knowledge formation. (Maton, 1998, p. 17) (Also cited in Moore & Muller, 1999, p. 199)

Instead of accepting all voices of experience as equally valid and worthy of attention, I would argue that it is the job of researchers to interrogate experiences, seeking to examine not only their origins, but also those blind spots, illusions and self-deceptions that crucially and legitimately make them up. Far from being an unqualified source of knowledge, experience must be treated with scepticism and suspicion. Joining the postmodern choirs of ever smaller voices does little credit to academic research. Disentangling these voices, understanding them, comparing them, privileging those which deserve to be privileged and silencing those that deserve to be silenced, questioning them, testing them and qualifying them – these seem to me to be essential judging qualities that mark research into storytelling and narratives as something different from the acts of storytelling and narration themselves. Deception, blind-spots, wishful thinking, the desire to please or manipulate an audience, lapses of memory, confusion, and other factors may help mould a story or a narrative. It is the researcher's task not merely to celebrate the story or the narrative but to seek to use it as a vehicle for accessing deeper truths than the truths of undigested personal experience.

20 THESES ON ORGANIZATIONAL STORYTELLING

Rather than providing a conventional conclusions section to this chapter, I wish to propose 20 theses on organizational storytelling that emanate from the preceding discussion:

1 Narratives and stories are important though precarious sense-making and communication devices.

2 They are by no means the only sense-making or communication devices, competing as they do in organizations and societies with numerous other ones, including theories, reports, statistics and numbers, opinions, platitudes, images, clichés, acronyms, logos, and so forth.

3 Nor should sense-making be privileged in the study of organizations and societies at the expense of other political, economic and psychological processes.

4 Storytelling is especially tested in organizations, due to their emphasis on rationality, economy, time-keeping and formal control, all of which inhibit storytelling processes.

5 All the same, stories and narratives serve important functions in and out of organizations, including the creation of unmanaged spaces, the offering of consolations and the giving of warnings.

6 Stories may equally serve interests of emancipation, development and enlightenment and those of oppression, exploitation and obscurantism.

7 Stories do not eliminate facts, but are poetic elaborations on facts which reveal much about unconscious wishes and desires.

8 These elaborations are accepted by storytellers and audiences as prerogatives of poetic licence, though they can turn stories into misrepresentations, untruths and lies; the legitimacy of such prerogatives is constantly negotiated through a psychological contract linking storyteller and audience, described as narrative contract.

9 Not all stories are good stories and not all storytellers are good storytellers; storytelling in late industrial societies has become more fragmented and less imaginative as a result of narrative deskilling, itself the product of technological, political and cultural processes of late modernity.

10 Good storytelling requires considerable time and narrative skill, sensitivity and patience.

11 Not all stories deserve to be heard and often poor stories are cut short for very good reasons.

12 Stories involve plots and characters, generate emotion and may be the product of fantasy or experience.

13 Stories and narratives have careers – they develop, they split, they unite, they mutate and they crystallize.

14 What remains relatively constant through such careers are the characters and the plots; to a much lesser extent, the emotions and symbolism.

15 The researcher's own accounts may assume many forms, including theories, statistics, narratives and reports, as well as stories.

16 Such stories, like other stories, are based on interpretations of narrative material, but the researcher's interpretations are of a different order (neither better nor worse) than those of the storyteller; the former are analytic interpretations aimed at uncovering the deeper meanings of a narrative, the latter are poetic interpretations seeking to infuse facts with meaning.

17   While experience is one of the two major sources of stories (the other being imagination), it is not an undisputed and unproblematic source of knowledge; much experience is the product of wish-fulfilling and other illusions which is what makes stories and narratives powerful avenues towards knowledge but not parcels of knowledge.

18   Unlike storytellers and narrators, researchers cannot disregard the facts or pretend that facts do not exist or matter – the same story has entirely different meanings, depending on whether its narrative foundation is factual or imaginary (cf. hoaxes and imbroglios like Wilkomirski).

19   All the same, researchers may become fellow-travellers on stories and narratives, suspending disbelief or forensic tendencies and concentrating on symbolism and meaning.

20   It is inevitable and natural that each person privileges his/her own stories and those of their friends, allies and companions over those of others; it takes great feats of courage and fortitude to be able to engage with stories fundamentally at odds with one's own.

REFERENCES

Aristotle (1963) *The poetics*. London: Dent.

Barthes, R. (1966/1977) Introduction to the structural analysis of narratives. In S. Heath (ed.), *Image – Music – Text* (pp. 79–124). Glasgow: Collins.

Benedict, R. (1931) Folklore. In *The Encyclopaedia of the Social Sciences* (Vol. VI). New York: Longman.

Benjamin, W. (1968) The storyteller: Reflections on the works of Nikolai Leskov. In H. Arendt (ed.), *Walter Benjamin: Illuminations* (pp. 82–110). London: Jonathan Cape.

Binford, L. (2001) Empowered speech: Social fields, testimonio, and the Stoll–Menchú debate. *Identities – Global Studies in Culture and Power*, 8 (1): 105–33.

Boje, D.M. (1991) The storytelling organization: A study of story performance in an office-supply firm. *Administrative Science Quarterly*, 36: 106–26.

Boje, D.M. (1994) Organizational storytelling: The struggles of pre-modern, modern and postmodern organizational learning discourses. *Management Learning*, 25 (3): 433–61.

Boje, D.M. (2001) *Narrative methods for organizational and communication research*. London: Sage.

Bruner, J. (1990) *Acts of meaning*. Cambridge, MA: Harvard University Press.

Culler, J. (1981/2001) *The pursuit of signs: Semiotics, literature, deconstruction* (Routledge Classics edition). London: Routledge.

Czarniawska, B. (1997) *Narrating the organization: Dramas of institutional identity*. Chicago: University of Chicago Press.

Czarniawska, B. (1999) *Writing management: Organization theory as a literary genre*. Oxford: Oxford University Press.

Czarniawska-Joerges, B. & Joerges, B. (1990) Linguistic artifacts at service of organizational control. In P. Gagliardi (ed.), *Symbols and artifacts: Views of the corporate landscape* (pp. 339–75). Berlin: Walter de Gruyter.

Eagleton, T. (1996) *The illusions of postmodernism*. Oxford: Blackwell.

Finkelstein, N.G. (2000) *The Holocaust industry: Reflections on the exploitation of Jewish suffering*. London: Verso.

Fournier, V. & Grey, C. (2000) At the critical moment: Conditions and prospects for critical management studies. *Human Relations*, 53 (1): 7–32.

Gabriel, Y. (1995) The unmanaged organization: Stories, fantasies and subjectivity. *Organization Studies*, 16 (3): 477–501.

Gabriel, Y. (2000) *Storytelling in organizations: Facts, fictions, fantasies*. Oxford: Oxford University Press.

Gledhill, J. (2001) Deromanticizing subalterns or recolonializing anthropology? Denial of indigenous agency and reproduction of northern hegemony in the work of David Stoll. *Identities – Global Studies in Culture and Power*, 8 (1): 135–61.

Grant, D., Keenoy, T. & Oswick, C. (1998) Introduction: Organizational discourse: Of diversity, dichotomy, and multidisciplinarity. In D. Grant, T. Keenoy & C. Oswick (eds), *Discourse and Organization* (pp. 1–13). London: Sage.

Hochschild, A.R. (1983) *The managed heart: Commercialization of human feeling*. Berkeley, CA: University of California Press.

Labov, W. (1972) *Language in the inner city*. Philadelphia: University of Pennsylvania Press.

MacIntyre, A. (1981) *After virtue*. London: Duckworth.

Maechler, S. (2001) *The Wilkomirski Affair*. Basingstoke: Picador.

Maton, K. (1998) Recovering pedagogic discourse: Basil Bernstein and the rise of taught academic subjects in higher education. Paper presented at the Knowledge, Identity and Pedagogy Conference, University of Southampton, Southampton, July.

Menchú, R. & Burgos-Debray, E. (1984) *I, Rigoberta Menchú: An Indian woman in Guatemala*. Trans. E. Burgos-Debray. London: Verso.

Moore, R. & Muller, J. (1999) The discourse of 'voice' and the problem of knowledge and identity in the sociology of education. *British Journal of Sociology of Education*, 20 (2): 189–206.

Peskin, H. (2000) Memory and media: 'Cases' of Rigoberta Menchú and Binjamin Wilkomirski. *Society*, 38 (1): 39–46.

Plato (1993) *Republic*. Trans. R. Waterfield. Oxford: Oxford University Press.

Polkinghorne, D.E. (1988) *Narrative knowing and the human sciences*. Albany, NY: State University of New York Press.

Reason, P. & Hawkins, P. (1988) Storytelling as inquiry. In P. Reason (ed.), *Human inquiry in action: Developments in new paradigm research* (pp. 71–101). London: Sage.

Ricœur, P. (1984) *Time and narrative* (Volume 1). Chicago: University of Chicago Press.

Sievers, B. (1986) Beyond the surrogate of motivation. *Organization Studies*, 7 (4): 335–51.

Stoll, D. (1999) *Rigoberta Menchú and the story of all poor Guatemalans*. Boulder, CO and Oxford: Westview Press.

Suleiman, S.R. (2000) Problems of memory and factuality in recent Holocaust memoirs: Wilkomirski/Wiesel. *Poetics Today*, 21 (3): 543–59.

Thoenig, J.-C. (1998) How far is a sociology of organizations still needed? *Organization Studies*, 19 (2): 307–20.

Tsoukas, H. (1998) Forms of knowledge and forms of life in organized contexts. In R.C.H. Chia (ed.), *In the realm of organization: Essays for Robert Cooper*. London: Routledge.

Van Dijk, T.A. (1975) Action, action description, and narrative. *New Literary History*, 6: 275–94.

Veyne, P. (1988) *Did the Greeks believe in their myths?* Trans. P. Wissing. Chicago, IL: University of Chicago Press.

Watson, T.J. (1994) *In search of management: Culture, chaos and control in managerial work*. London: Routledge.

Weick, K.E. (1995) *Sensemaking in organizations*. London: Sage.

Wilkomirski, B. (1996) *Fragments: Memories of a wartime childhood*. New York: Random House.

3

Corporate Rhetoric as Organizational Discourse

George Cheney, Lars Thøger Christensen,
Charles Conrad and Daniel J. Lair

THE NATURE OF RHETORIC IN
AN ORGANIZATIONAL WORLD

Definition of rhetoric and its relevance to organizations

Rhetoric is the humanistic tradition for the study of persuasion. Identified most closely with the ancient Greeks and Romans, rhetoric's classical emphasis is best captured by Aristotle's famous definition 'the faculty of observing in any given case the available means of persuasion' (1954. p. 3). This means analysing the art of using symbols to *persuade* others to change their attitudes, beliefs, values or actions. In contrast to persuasion are processes through which auditors are *coerced* to act in particular ways through the use of inartistic strategies such as threats, torture or contracts. The 'rhetorical situation' envisioned by Aristotle and Cicero (1942) was comparatively simple by today's standards because it involved an educated, propertied, male speaker addressing a homogeneous audience about an issue of the day for which the speaker and the audience had a shared interest. Aristotle understood keenly how inductive and deductive structures of argument work in the persuasive process: thus, he spoke of the power of 'the example' (or narrative) and the *enthymeme* (an interactive syllogism) in the enterprise of convincing others. Moreover, Aristotle understood the interplay of three dynamics in the use of discourse to influence others: the speaker or source dynamic, *ethos*; the message or logical dynamic, *logos*; and the audience's emotional and value-oriented dynamic, *pathos*. Therefore, *from its inception, rhetoric was concerned about the way discourse is intertwined with human relations.*

Rhetoric held a vaulted place among the disciplines in the ancient and early medieval worlds since it was part of the *trivium*, along with grammar and logic. During the Renaissance and Enlightenment periods, however, rhetoric lost its status as its domain of concern was narrowly circumscribed. Rhetoric was therefore distanced from truth-seeking and relegated to the world of speculation, to conditions of uncertainty, and to the ornamentation of language. This devaluation of rhetoric and its reduction to technical matters of elocution have contributed to the pejorative use of this term. In the mid-twentieth century, rhetoric's scope was expanded and its broad societal functions rediscovered, as evident, explicitly or implicitly, in the works of scholars such as Austin (1970), Burke (1969), Searle (1970) and Wittgenstein (1953). Today there are 'rhetorics' of fields as diverse as sociology (Brown, 1977), economics (McCloskey, 1994) and physics (Pera, 1994). In each case, the central symbols of those disciplines (including models, metaphors and images) come under examination for their persuasive capacities (Simons, 1990). Moreover, rhetorical scholars have widened their focus beyond the impact of individual orators to encompass a wide range of symbolic action, including social movements, architecture and broader discourses of society. In this way, rhetorical theorists have re-conceptualized persuasion to focus on the dialectical processes that link social actors, texts and communicative situations (Burke, 1969; Perelman & Olbrechts-Tyteca, 1969). For example, Burke's 'Dramatism' includes non-deliberate influences (e.g., when a subordinate anticipates what a 'boss' might want to have done; see Sennett, 1980), self-persuasion (e.g., when public presentations by an organization's representative serve as internal communication; see Bullis & Tompkins, 1989), and numerous linkages between discourse and other types of symbol (e.g., when a manager conflates the power of a formal position with his/her own power; see Kanter, 1977).

In addition, influences from social theory, including the Frankfurt school, post-structuralism, deconstruction, feminisms, postmodernism, and post-colonialism, have interacted with rhetorical theory and criticism (see Foss et al., 1991). The overall effect is to orient rhetoric towards societal roles (Foucault, 1984) and to bring it into direct concern with social and institutional power (e.g., Habermas, 1979). In both respects, the study of rhetoric now addresses the roles that organizations and institutions play in the modern world.

Relationship of rhetoric to other perspectives on discourse

In a multidisciplinary volume such as this *Handbook*, it is important to position rhetoric in relation to other discourse-based approaches in the study of organizations. The comprehensive scheme developed by Putnam and Fairhurst (2001) describes eight different forms of 'organizational discourse' that relate in various ways to rhetoric, including logic and formal argument, pragmatics, interaction and conversational analysis, semiotics, narrative theory, and critical discourse analysis. Limited chapter lengths for this volume prohibit an extensive treatment of each relationship; hence, we offer only a few general comments.

First, we view disciplines, theories and scholarly perspectives as networks of researchers. Thus, when we speak of 'the rhetorical tradition', we refer to certain families of scholarship and ways of understanding society. We are also talking about a specific intellectual history, a lineage of ideas and a core set of concepts in a 'membership' group characterized by paradigmatic ways of seeing language, symbols and society (Brown, 1987). In the area of logic and formal argument, rhetoric shares with pragmatics a concern for the actual or potential effects of messages, especially those that are not abstracted from their social contexts. In contrast to conversation or interaction analyses, rhetoric attends to the social situations beyond the micro-interpersonal or group episode. And, rhetoric's mode of explanation is usually less concerned with rules or norms of interpersonal interaction than are other approaches to the study of 'talk'. Rhetoric shares with semiotics a sensitivity to the ways that symbols are interrelated, but rhetoric is less structural in its approach to analysis than is semiotics. Narrative theory has influenced rhetoric by elevating storytelling and inductive reasoning to positions alongside deductive forms of communication. In contrast to ethnography of speaking, organizational rhetoric is oriented to formal, *public* messages and discourses (e.g., CEO speeches, mission statements, public relations campaigns and discourses regarding organizational efficiency and change). Finally, while rhetoric centres on persuasion and identification, critical discourse analysis (CDA) orients its work to the concept of power (Fairclough, 1989). In this way, the two methodological and philosophical traditions of rhetorical criticism and CDA offer complementary and overlapping schemes for analysing language in organizations (see Cheney et al., 1999).

Characteristic concerns of organizational rhetoric

The defining concerns of rhetoric include:

- Situations of uncertainty and possibility (for instance, when a corporation seeks subsidies or tax breaks from a governmental unit but cannot guarantee economic advantages to the community commensurate with the magnitude of the request).
- Situations in which the 'intent' of a message is ambiguous for the speaker and/or audience (as when managers of a hospital argue that fundamental organizational changes are being imposed on them by market forces, without admitting or recognizing that the anticipated changes will transform the underlying values of the institution from an ethic of care to an efficiency model).
- Situations in which the credibility or the *ethos* of the source is problematic (as when energy companies argue that self-regulation is sufficient for environmental protection).
- Situations in which the nature of the audience(s) for a message is unclear or complex (for instance, when the World Health Organization must simultaneously speak to and coordinate with governments and health-care institutions at all levels).
- Situations in which the likelihood of persuasion as the message effect is context-dependent (e.g., the persuasiveness of a corporate ad *campaign* on 'diversity' as opposed to the success of an individual advertisement).

These defining concerns differ from a classical approach which positions rhetoric in tension with logic, particularly formal models, such as the syllogism. The syllogism can be 'true' or made true through its adherence to certain abstract principles. The most famous of all syllogisms is: 'All men are mortal; Socrates is a man; therefore, Socrates is mortal.' This categorical syllogism is true by virtue of its form and the scientific accuracy of its premises. Both the form and the definition of truth are a priori and independent of tests in interaction. In contrast, a rhetorical syllogism employs probability statements whose 'truth' depends on conformity to the audience's beliefs and the functions of the syllogism in everyday talk.

Thus, *organizational rhetoric is embedded in or implied in interaction* that deals with contingencies, uncertainties and ambiguities. While classical rhetoric emphasized the intentionality of the speaker, contemporary rhetoric examines a range of communication situations, including organizational socialization (Allen, in press; Clair, 1996), in which intentions are not tied to one person or decision-maker.

Credibility or ethos can be linked with authority and rationality. In an important essay, Tompkins (1987) compares Weber's (1978) ideal types of rationality and authority (charismatic, traditional and legal-rational) with Aristotle's (1954) 'artistic proofs' of persuasion – *ethos, pathos* and *logos*. That is, Weber's three main types of rationality (or four, if you add a values-based type, see Rothschild-Whitt, 1979; Satow, 1975) represent logics of human relations, ones that have their counterparts in discourses about work, decision-making and organizational life. This parallel suggests that rhetoric serves a constitutive function in organizations. The rhetoric of bureaucracy, for instance, surfaces as a broad discourse that privileges value neutrality, universality, standardization, roles and fairness (Cheney et al., 2004).

The audience becomes considerably more complex in moving from the classical 'rhetorical situation', with a clearly defined orator and audience, to contemporary organizational rhetoric in which messages are removed from their sources and audience boundaries are unclear and shifting. For example, in today's organizational society, the line between 'internal' and 'external' corporate communications is not distinct (Cheney & Christensen, 2001). Advertising to outside audiences may simultaneously affect employees, just as messages to employees may affect consumers.

Functions of rhetoric in organizations

The application of rhetoric in organizational contexts can be categorized along three dimensions: the specific form of rhetoric, its general direction and the role of strategy. These three dimensions array in the following dialectical pairs:

- 'Texts/Artifacts' versus 'Discourse/Fragments'
- 'Internal' versus 'External' Forms
- Strategic versus Non-strategic Understandings

For the first dimension, the contemporary field of rhetoric differs as to what constitutes the specific form or an appropriate object for rhetorical analysis. Leff (1987) advocates a traditional focus on bounded, discrete 'texts'. Traditionally, these texts consist of speeches presented orally, but the analysis of discrete texts also includes other messages such as CEO letters (Hyland, 1998), mission statements (Swales & Rogers, 1995), marketing campaigns (Christensen, 2001b), or corporate architecture (Berg & Kreiner, 1990). By contrast, McGee (1990) argues that bounded 'texts' are illusions and that rhetoric consists of discursive 'fragments' or scraps of messages that loosely cohere and never come together into a finished product, but they are packaged for the critic. However, even if they are not complete, some texts *appear* as 'apparently finished texts' (McGee, 1990).

The tension, then, lies between focusing on the persuasive effect of distinct messages or the critique of a broader set of discursive patterns in society. This situation is analogous to the tension in mass communication between tracing the persuasive impact of a particular violent television show to tracking the 'cultivation' effects of violence on television in general. While the former approach examines instances of aggression spawned by television viewing, the latter one focuses on the broader cultural implications of viewers' perceptions of a violent world (Gerbner, 1994). Organizational rhetoric operates at both levels. On the one hand, organizations employ 'finished' messages in their efforts to persuade, as for example, issue advertisements (e.g., Crable & Vibbert, 1983; Heath, 1980) or corporate *apologia* in response to a specific crisis (Benoit, 1995). On the other hand, the same organizations create broad programmes of messages to socialize their members (Cheney, 1983a, 1983b; Clair, 1996) or to frame discussions of public policy issues (Conrad & McIntush, 2003).

The second dimension focuses on the intended direction of persuasive efforts. Even though the boundaries between the inside and outside of the organizational 'box' are not clear, an *internal* audience of organizational members and an *external* audience of stakeholder groups clearly exist. There are important practical ways in which employees are 'inside' an organization; for example, they receive a salary from the organization and can get fired. As a consequence, their motivations are likely to differ from those of consumers, investors, the general public and other groups. Organizations may direct their rhetorical efforts internally by attempting to persuade members to identify with organizational goals and to adopt organizationally desired decision premises (Bullis, 1993; Tompkins & Cheney, 1985), or they may focus on external audiences, in an effort to restore tattered organizational images (Cheney, 1992) or to influence the grounds on which an upcoming policy initiative will be decided (Vibbert & Bostdorff, 1993). Nevertheless, internally- and externally-focused messages are not mutually exclusive; that is, organizations are engaged in multiple rhetorical efforts simultaneously. The same persuasive efforts can be aimed at both internal *and* external audiences, not only because organizational employees simultaneously are members of various external stakeholder groups but also because they typically ascribe more significance to messages posted in high-status media like advertising. For example, when an organization sells itself in an advertisement as composed of 'dedicated employees who never sleep', it aims to advance a positive image while reinforcing the value of hard work to its members (Christensen, 1995, 1997).

The third dimension relates to the strategic function of organizational messages. When organizations act rhetorically, they make strategic decisions regarding the types and audiences of their messages. 'Strategy' is a cornerstone of traditional rhetorical practice in that persuasion relies on targeted assessments of purpose, audience and message. *Rhetoric, thus, seeks to have an impact beyond a self-contained effect*, such as aesthetic appreciation (in poetics). It is the conscious, deliberate and efficient use of persuasion to bring about attitudinal or behavioural change. In this way rhetoric can be seen as a capacity, an instrument and a dimension of human communication and social relations, highlighting and exploiting opportunities for influence. Perhaps one of the best encapsulations of the strategic function of rhetoric comes from the notion of adjusting 'ideas to people and people to ideas' (Bryant, 1953), an aim that extends to external discourses of public relations and issues management with the goal of 'adjusting organizations to environments and environments to organizations' (Crable & Vibbert, 1986).

The links between rhetorical and organizational studies seem natural because considerable persuasion in contemporary society *is organized and is organizational* (Cheney & McMillan, 1990; Conrad, 1993; Crable, 1990; Tompkins, 1987). This is not to say that the individual *rhetor* is completely eclipsed by the institutional one, but that much of public persuasion today is embedded in institutional arrangements and processes. Contemporary everyday rhetoric is also diffused, just as, for example, the impact of violence on television may be seen in terms of the larger 'text' in addition to the effects of specific programmes or scenes. This idea applies to the realms of sales, marketing and advertising, as well as to the formal and informal ways identities and issues are managed by and in organizations. In this respect, examining the effects of 'corporate advocacy' and 'corporate issues management' broadly (e.g., Heath, 1980; Crable & Vibbert, 1983) makes sense. This perspective recognizes not only the *announced* persuasive strategies of organizations, such as Exxon's PR campaign in the wake of the Exxon-Valdez oil spill of 1989 (Leeper, 1996), but also the complex messages that come to define an organization's image, identity and culture. 'Strategy' then covers both explicit persuasive campaigns and the wider arena in which influence is exercised – including *un*intended consequences (Cheney & Vibbert, 1987; Perrow, 2002). The question of strategy in broad institutional arrangements is thus linked to reformulations of intention and agency in the move from the individual to the collective unit of analysis.

In contrast to other forms of discourse analysis, a *rhetorical* approach is concerned primarily with the *strategic dimensions* of discourse. This focus does not imply that *strategizing* is a strictly rational endeavour, or that the impact of a particular strategy is within the control of an organization. Research in psychology and philosophy, especially in the areas of discourse processing and practical reasoning, has challenged the rational perspective on strategy (see, for example, Cascio, 1993;

Dooley & Fryxell, 1999; Levinthal & March, 1993; Simon, 1947; Weick, 1979). Indeed, organizational theorist Petro Georgiou (1981) asserts that no organization has any other primary goal than its own continuance and aggrandizement. Consistent with *auto-poesis* or theories of self-creation, organizations as living systems interact with their surroundings to create and recreate themselves (Krippendorff, 1984; Luhmann, 1990; Maturana & Varela, 1980). Through the related notion of 'auto-communication' (Lotman, 1990), scholars have demonstrated that corporate speeches, mission statements, advertising campaigns, marketing strategies and market analyses are *meta*-messages that help organizations *confirm themselves* to internal as well as external audiences (Broms & Gahmberg, 1983; Christensen, 1997). The self-generative, self-identifying and self-protective modes of organizational performance may ultimately overwhelm other functions and provide an interesting twist on the neo-Weberian model of bureaucratic organizations as rational(ized) systems.

Finally, not only are organizations often unsuccessful in their attempts to persuade, they may also be unaware of the ultimate effects of their rhetoric. For example, Heath (1990) demonstrates how the asbestos industry, in its efforts to convince the public of the safety of its product, ultimately convinced *itself* that asbestos was safe, leaving it incapable of adequately responding to the chaotic environment faced by the industry once the harmful effects of asbestos were widely recognized. Marketers often employ strategy precisely when the benefits of their activities are least clear or are most difficult to measure. When asked about *the effects* of an image campaign, organizations may respond that it is part of a long-term strategy and thus beyond simple measurement. Thus, strategy and rationality emerge discursively, *qua* argument, especially when the exhortation 'Be rational!' is used both to win and to terminate a dispute. A rhetorical view of organizational discourse, then, focuses on the *strategic possibilities of discourse in action*. Thus, strategy as a rhetorical concept is considerably more complicated than the persuasive intent of organizations alone.

CENTRAL ISSUES IN THE STUDY OF ORGANIZATIONAL RHETORIC

Key terms from classical and contemporary rhetorical theory

Basic concepts from classical or contemporary rhetorical theory appear in Table 3.1 (reprinted from Cheney, in press). These concepts include such issues as intention and effect, categories of classical rhetoric, the dynamics of the rhetorical situation, the dialectic between inductive and deductive forms, and the shift from persuasion (Aristotle, 1954) to identification (Burke, 1969). The remainder of this essay references and highlights terms from Table 3.1.

Major strategies of organizational rhetoric

Concepts of rhetoric apply specifically and broadly to diverse situations and forms of organizational communication. Discourse is used to perform the essential

Table 3.1   *Some core concepts from the rhetorical tradition as applied to organizations*

1. **Locus** of Study: Messages and their *actual or potential effects* (Wichelns, 1925); compares with pragmatics

2. **Function** in Society: 'Adjusting ideas to people and people to ideas' (Bryant, 1953); similar to modern PR (see Crable & Vibbert, 1986)

3. '**Faculty** of observing in a given case the available means of persuasion' (Aristotle, 1954, p. 3); parallels social-psychological persuasion research

4. Principal **dynamics** of rhetoric (compare Aristotle, 1954; Booth, 1988; Weber, 1978; Tompkins, 1987):
   (a) Speaker or source (Ethos or character)/'Entertainer's stance'/Charismatic authority
   (b) Message (Logos or logic)/'Pedant's stance'/Rational-legal authority
   (c) Audience or listeners (Pathos or emotional appeal)/'Advertiser's stance'/Traditional authority

5. The **Canons** or key principles of rhetoric (Greco-Roman traditions)
   (a) **Invention**, or the sources of ideas
   (b) **Arrangement**, or the organization/structure of ideas
   (c) **Style**, or the use of language and other symbols
   (d) **Delivery**, or the nature of the presentation of the message itself
   (e) **Memory**, 'the forgotten canon' (central to the oral tradition, with its analogues in written and electronic forms of literacy)

6. **Types** or Classes of Rhetoric (Aristotle, 1954; Perelman & Olbrechts-Tyteca, 1969)
   (a) **Deliberative** – arriving at a decision – chiefly future-oriented
   (b) **Forensic** – passing judgement – chiefly past-oriented
   (c) **Epideictic** – issuing praise or blame, celebrating values, self-promotion – chiefly present-oriented (compare Cheney & Vibbert, 1987; Crable & Vibbert, 1983; Cheney & McMillan, 1990)

7. **Topoi**, topics, 'commonplaces', or areas used as resources for ideas and claims; also, points of reference or 'pools' of meaning (Aristotle, 1954; Karpik, 1978)

8. **Stasis**, or the status of an issue: When is an issue active, latent or dead? Through what processes does the status of an issue change? (Aristotle, 1954; Crable & Vibbert, 1986)

9. **Central Terms:**
   (a) Of ancient rhetoric: *persuasion* (Aristotle) *or inspiration – movere* (Cicero, 1942)
   (b) Of contemporary (post-Aristotelian, post-Marxist, post-Freudian) rhetoric: *identification* (Burke, 1969)

10. **Kernel Elements** (Aristotle, 1954)
    (a) The *Example*: the building block of inductive rhetorical form (compare Fisher's (1987) narrative _____ form)
    (b) The *Enthymeme*: the building block of the deductive rhetorical form – drawing upon premises of fact or value already held by the audience to lead them towards a particular conclusion (compare Sproule's (1988) non-enthymemic 'managerial' rhetoric and Tompkins & Cheney's (1985) 'enthymeme 2' in corporate discourse)

11. **The Rhetorical Situation:**
    (a) For Aristotle: identifiable single speaker addressing a homogeneous audience in a largely one-way manner with a discrete message
    (b) For Bitzer (1968): Exigencies (Needs), Audience, and Constraints (Parameters)
    (c) For Burke (1973): 'congregation' and 'segregation' (in the universal human condition)
    (d) In the organizational context: 'corporate' or organized bodies addressing multiple audiences, including one another, through multiple means, and in an elusive search for stable identities, in an exploding/imploding universe of communication (Cheney & Christensen, 2001)

persuasive functions of the modern organization as well as to achieve specific organizational goals. Organizational rhetors typically employ several broad strategies (or categories of strategies), often by a variety of professions, media and messages. (The appendix to this chapter presents additional specific discursive/ rhetorical strategies.) These typical categories of strategy are:

- Responding to existing rhetorical situations
- Anticipating future rhetorical situations
- Shaping or framing projected rhetorical situations
- Shaping organizational images and identities

Responding to existing rhetorical situations

Bitzer's (1968, 1980) famous re-conceptualization of the rhetorical situation has played a highly influential role in thinking about rhetorical strategies. He purports that a speaker responds to a particular *exigence*, which can be remedied through discourse to influence an *audience* within given *constraints*. *This view of rhetoric's role as reactive and targeted certainly describes what organizations seek to accomplish when they attempt to persuade.* Thus, when faced with crises such as an oil spill, as was Exxon in 1989 (Leeper, 1996), accused of operating sweatshops, as was Nike in 1998 (Stabile, 2000), or simply confronted with a record of poor performance, as was Chrysler in the mid-1980s (Seeger, 1986), organizations aim to persuade the public that the crisis is either not their fault or that the organization can resolve the urgent situation. Public relations was actually born out of responses to such crises when oil companies, railroads and other monopolies came under public attack in the last two decades of the nineteenth century (Cheney & Vibbert, 1987). Often, such *responsive* persuasive efforts take the form of an *apologia*, or attempts to restore lost credibility (see Benoit, 1995). However, focusing solely on reactive rhetoric would limit the range of persuasive efforts that an organization can adopt. Organizations also anticipate and plan for the development of rhetorical situations and employ discourse strategically to influence the situations they face, as did US airlines when they anticipated the economic effects of the 2003 invasion of Iraq and sought additional governmental aid.

Anticipating future rhetorical situations

Another way in which organizations anticipate future rhetorical situations is to act rhetorically to prevent a crisis from occurring in the first place. In fact, one of the primary purposes of issues management is to anticipate and adapt to changes before they occur (Kuhn, 1997). As a corporate communications strategy, issues management surfaced in the mid-1970s when US petroleum companies began an aggressive campaign to speak about values, issues and identities and to shift attention away from their products, services and policies. *At a first-order level of*

strategy, issues management contributes to strategic planning by allowing organizations
to anticipate and adapt to changes before they occur – through what is called
'environmental scanning' (Forbes, 1992). Anticipating changes in environmental
pressures offers several advantages. The information-gathering process necessary
for any issues management campaign yields information that then can be used to
set the stage for future policies and message campaigns (Heath, 1990). For example, Heath argues that proactive issues management enables an organization to
identify shifting societal ethical standards and to align company policy and corporate image management accordingly. Extending this view, Mobil Oil executive
Schmertz (1986) contends that issues management allows businesses to represent
their side of the story before their opposition presents it for them. Finally, Littlejohn
reaffirms that PR's importance lies in 'being harnessed to assist directly in the
pursuit of strategic goals' (1986, p. 109). While traditional managerial practice
separates the act of strategizing from communicating about it, more recent commentaries treat planning and communication functions as being inextricably
intertwined. And, to the extent that PR is less defensive and more proactive, these
links to strategic planning and management seem natural.

Shaping rhetorical situations

Organizations also act rhetorically at a *second-order level of strategy* by attempting to shape, rather than simply anticipate, the rhetorical situations they might
face. They do so by influencing popular attitudes and public policies. Rather than
simply designing or prescribing measures that adapt to changes in 'what's out
there', PR, marketing and related disciplines recognize that organizations need to
set changes in motion that they hope will become true tomorrow (e.g., Berg,
1989; Brown & Eisenhardt, 1998; Hamel & Prahalad, 1994). This idea is built
into the logic of contemporary marketing, though it exists somewhat in tension
with the democratic ethos of marketing: 'give 'em what they want' (Christensen,
1997). For example, organizations that market lifestyle products increasingly
employ 'cool hunters', postmodernist market researchers who do not simply
chase what's cool, but who also participate actively in the construction of 'cool-
ness' (Gladwell, 1997).

   The same proactive and comprehensive orientation towards corporate communications is also applied to documents and web-based material such as vision,
mission and ethics statements. Although little empirical evidence exists to confirm
that employees and consumers care about these documents or that they contribute
to organizational success (Bart, 1998), corporations and consultants make powerful claims for their persuasiveness and for the value of having an overall strategic
communication plan (Begley & Boyd, 2000; Stone, 1996). And Duncan (1995)
insists that marketing 'a cause' – such as the core values of a company – allows
an organization to invest in a single symbol (or set of symbols) as the repository
of the organization's values, identities and culture, with long-range implications
beyond the immediate campaign. This wide-ranging, proactive perspective is
analogous to Crable and Vibbert's (1986) *catalytic* issues management strategy

and is *the essence of 'strategizing' on the second-order level – the calculated attempt to shape the very conditions of strategy making*. Thus, organizations not only react to issues in their surroundings but also initiate and stimulate the advent of certain trends and developments. Such persuasive efforts lay the groundwork for future rhetorical endeavours, but the power of an organization's own mechanisms may be masked in the process.

One function of organizational rhetoric is to try to influence *topoi* or beliefs and general assumptions held by the public. For many contemporary organizational rhetors, at least in the private sector, the most valuable *topos* is the myth of the free market or what Soros (1998) calls 'free market fundamentalism': that is, the presumption that free market capitalism is superior to any other economic system and that government 'interference' in that system is inevitably futile and perverse (Aune, 1994, 2001). The myth of the free market became increasingly dominant during the last two decades of Western neo-liberal ascendancy, through the concerted, strategic efforts of organizational rhetors (Krugman, 1994; Kuttner, 1997). Because it is inherently unstable, the ideological edifice of 'free market capitalism' requires strong persuasive buttresses. What seems 'natural' and 'inevitable' in fact relies on constant messaging (Aune, 2001; Lindblom, 1977; Madrick, 2002). But, if the major premise of 'free market' superiority is sufficiently reinforced, the myth is available to rhetors in almost any organization and industry to legitimize almost any organizational policy or practice.

Consider several examples. First, in a number of Western capitalist democracies, 'privatization' has become a god-term as well as a broad practical trend. The term articulates an unquestioned premise that carries notions of individual incentive, economic efficiency, smooth management and organizational effectiveness. During the 1980s and 1990s, even comparatively egalitarian nations such as New Zealand rushed to see how quickly and how completely they could dismantle the welfare state and convert formerly public domains to private organizations (Gray, 1998). Due to the persuasive power of the free market ideology, this revolution took place without a systematic comparative analysis of the performance of different organizations in the private and public sectors (Kuttner, 1997). Even in nations that have questioned privatization more vigorously, as in Scandinavia, a growing suspicion associated with public sector jobs and activities is found (see, for example, Czarniawska-Joerges, 1994). As a result, most public service organizations in Sweden, Norway and Denmark must demonstrate their worth by embracing management principles developed and celebrated in private business (for a critical analysis, see Stokes & Clegg, 2002).

Even industries whose practices seem indefensible exploit the broad premises of market fundamentalism. In the 1990s, rhetors in the tobacco industry found that standard *topoi* failed to mollify hostility to the industry – both in the US Senate and with the US public. However, corporate rhetors reframed the debate from the issue of industry behaviour to a question of government interference in the free market. The corporations did this by attacking a proposed tax on tobacco, which would have compromised the positions of working- and middle-class consumers. Thus, the tobacco companies portrayed themselves as champions of working people and as defenders of a free market, thereby sidestepping the issues of how they promote tobacco addiction in the USA and the rest of the world.

In sum, organizations have a broad forum for the promulgation of their issues and corporate images. They have the resources, access and expertise to engage widely in the management of public issues, and the gradual expansion of 'corporate free speech' in recent decades extends this influence. Corporate rhetoric serves two primary functions: it draws on existing cultural assumptions to support/condemn and/or legitimize/ de-legitimize particular policies, and, more importantly, it reproduces and reinforces the cultural assumptions on which it is based.

However, in addition to moulding popular attitudes and images, organizational rhetors can manage the regulatory and political environments they face through strategically manipulating political structures and practices (Austin, 2002; Ryan et al., 1987). The most important strategy is also the simplest one, doing public business in private (Baumgartner & Leech, 1998). The post-September 11 bailout of the US airline industry, for example, was developed during private meetings among corporate lobbyists, a handful of members of the US Congress and the George W. Bush administration. Even ranking members of US congressional committees and executive departments were excluded from these deliberations (Wayne, 2002). *In these cases, public discourse became relevant only after the policies had been made in private, and thus the discourse was focused on justifying the decisions or the process itself.* Invariably those justifications assert that the policy would benefit all citizens, not just a privileged few (Stone, 1988).

Even when policy debates 'go public', organizational rhetors have a number of structural advantages. Pro-business rhetors and those who represent economic elites are more tightly organized than groups that represent other interests. At least, they typically have greater resources and prestige, are better able to utilize the decision processes of legislative bodies, are better equipped to obtain and use private information provided by politicians, and are able to inflate their political power in the minds of policy-makers (Schattschneider, 1935; Stone, 1988; Wilson, 1973). Through multiplex and private networks, organizational rhetors can (1) influence the way in which 'problems' are defined and policy questions are framed, (2) mould public opinion on issues, and (3) define the terms of an upcoming public policy debate (Baumgartner & Jones, 1993).

In the rare cases in which definitional strategies fail and an undesirable proposal reaches the policy agenda, organizational rhetors often employ blocking strategies to 'contain' an issue or to limit its popular appeal. In this way, rhetorical strategies come full circle to become reactive and responsive. Some strategies involve little or no risk to the organization and its image. These practices include refusing to acknowledge that a problem exists, denying knowledge of the problem, not recognizing the legitimacy of groups that are pushing for policy change, and 'anti-patterning' or arguing that a problem is an isolated incident not worthy of systematic attention (Ibarra & Kitsuse, 1993). More risky but potentially more effective strategies include launching *ad hominem* attacks on advocates of change or resorting to 'symbolic placation', including efforts to define a problem as a 'private sector' or 'law enforcement' concern rather than a matter for public policy. Hall and Jones (1997) show that this strategy is especially effective in blunting calls for increased regulation following periods of business malpractice; Conrad (2003) offers a parallel analysis of its role in blunting reform after the Enron scandal.

Shaping their own identities

Organizations act rhetorically also by *attempting to shape their very image as rhetors*. Image and identity management, which became popular in consulting venues during the 1980s (Olins, 1989), is revisited in the efforts of 'integrated marketing communications' to unify communication practices (i.e., from employee communications to identity management to branding) and to develop a grand strategy under a highly appealing name. Even though marketing has always regarded itself as an integrative practice of coordinating the promotion mix (advertising, sales promotions, packaging, etc.), scholars of integrated marketing communications envision 'integration' as far more comprehensive. Recognizing that contemporary organizations communicate with their stakeholders on dimensions typically ignored by marketers (e.g., employee behaviours, investment policies, retirement benefits and waste disposal), they aim for the organization to speak with 'one voice' through coordinating all relevant 'contact points' between the organization and its surroundings (e.g., Caywood, 1997; Schultz et al., 1994; Yeshin, 1998).

Rhetorically speaking, then, integrated marketing communications takes seemingly disparate messages, melds them into one, gives them a voice and provides them with a strategically designed persona. The resulting label radiates technical competence as well as confidence. Ironically, this 'new' strategy harks back to early twentieth-century efforts by major corporations to 'give a folksy persona' to an organization, so that it would not be seen as a massive, cold and distant institution (see Marchand, 1998). At the same time, these comprehensive rhetorical strategies often fail to appreciate the ambiguities inherent in corporate logos and symbols, the sub-cultures that exist within the organizations, and the fact that many audiences are relatively disinterested in the identities in which organizations invest so much time, energy and resources to construct (Christensen & Cheney, 2000).

PREDICAMENTS AND CHALLENGES
FOR ORGANIZATIONAL RHETORS

As organizations exercise specific and broader influences, they face several important challenges. To some extent, these difficulties are associated with a postmodern communication environment. Three challenges are especially important:

- The communication implosion as well as explosion
- The management of 'univocality' versus 'multivocality'
- Maintaining credibility and legitimacy across circumstances and over time

The communication explosion as an implosion

James March remarked that 'the most conventional story of contemporary futuro-logy is a story that observes and predicts dramatic changes in the environments of organizations' – changes spurred by increased competition, globalization and new information technologies (1995, p. 428). Increasingly, this story is phrased in terms of corporate communications and organizational rhetoric. Thus, organizations continuously reaffirm that the communication environment in which they operate is turbulent and volatile and shaped by a virtual explosion in the number of messages and images that shout to be heard and taken seriously (Blythe, 2000; Ries & Trout, 1981; Schultz et al., 1994). Contributing to the generally negative portrayals of the communication environment are depictions of audiences as apathetic, critical and sometimes cynical (see also Baudrillard, 1988; Ewen, 1988). Taken together, these assumptions reduce conventional communication campaigns to dubious undertakings (Bond & Kirshenbaum, 1998; Morgan, 1999). With the additional realization that mass media are 'fragmented', contemporary organizations feel hard-pressed to adopt new ways of reaching their audiences (Belch & Belch, 1998; Fill, 1999). *Indeed, even though communication often produces the very problems it claims to solve, the pressure to seek distinctiveness through rhetorical means is more pronounced than ever.*

Ironically, one primary rhetorical method that organizations use to distinguish themselves is recycling *pre-existing* messages. In an influential series of articles for *Advertising Age*, later published as the book *Positioning: The Battle for Your Mind*, Al Ries and Jack Trout (1981) argue that the problem of *over*-communication can be attributed, in part, to the limited mental capacities of audiences. Put simply, the human mind can only recall a limited number of brands and brand names, forcing marketers to work from what the consumer already knows or believes about the market, that is, to adopt enthymematic arguments. Thus, some companies 'position' themselves by trading off images of major competitors, for example, Avis's 'We Try Harder' campaign of the 1970s and 1980s played on its second-place market position behind Hertz, 7-Up famously marketed itself as the 'Un-Cola', and Apple urged consumers to 'Think Different' in response to IBM's widely recognized slogan 'Think'. Such strategies increasingly go beyond product categories to employ sophisticated forms of 'intertextuality' (e.g., Allen, 2000) as, for example, when Sisley Underwear – in a witty reference to the famous motto of Nike – suggests: 'Just *Un*do It'. And Sprite intentionally plays on advertising strategies such as Gatorade's 'Be Like Mike' slogan, using celebrity athletes to endorse and confirm what consumers already know, that is, drinking their product will not make the consumer any more like that athlete. Some organizations, such as Absolut Vodka and Silk Cut cigarettes, engage in *self-referential advertising*, acting with 'autonomized' images without reference to anything but themselves or what Perniola (1980) and Baudrillard (1994) call *simulacra*. These various responses, in turn, become messages that *other* organizations inevitably play on to position *themselves* in the crowded communication climate. Thus, the communication environment creates its own dynamics and turbulence, one in which even established positions are exposed and vulnerable (Christensen, 2001a, 2001b). The crowded communication climate, in effect, functions as a pool of messages on which organizations inevitably draw, reflecting their traditional rhetorical concerns for *topoi*, the argumentative resources on which a rhetor may draw.

Managing 'Univocality/Multivocality'

At the same time that organizations draw from a common pool of *topoi*, they must simultaneously manage the tension between casting themselves as either univocal or multivocal rhetors. As discussed earlier, organizational messages are received and interpreted by multiple audiences. Organizational mission statements, for example, not only foster member identification with corporate value systems but also *announce* those value systems to external audiences such as consumers (Swales & Rogers, 1995). Simultaneously, the *organizations themselves* are audiences of their own mission statements and can become so infatuated with the view of the corporation portrayed in them that they believe it *is* the organization (Langelar, 1992). In this way, organizations are susceptible to their own persuasive efforts, an outcome that underscores the challenges organizational rhetors face as they try to manage multiple audiences. These challenges are heightened as organizations attempt to navigate an increasingly global environment and are held accountable to a broadened array of stakeholders, many of whom are likely to be antagonistic to them (e.g., Argenti, 1998; Fombrun & Rindova, 2000; Van Riel, 2000).

As organizations manage the way they communicate with a wide range of audiences, they must inevitably negotiate the tension between presenting a message in an integrated, univocal manner or tailoring it in a multivocal fashion to the needs of various audiences (see Balmer, 2001). Within the broad field of marketing and advertising, an ongoing debate exists on the possibility and desirability of standardizing corporate messages *across* different audiences and different markets. On the one hand, marketing and rhetoric share an ethos of tailoring messages to the audiences they are intended for and anecdotes in books such as *Big Business Blunders* (Ricks, 1983) remind organizations of the failures that loom by ignoring cultural differences. On the other hand, Theodore Levitt (1983) has argued, with much influence, that to survive in a competitive market, corporations must operate as if the world is one large market, ignoring 'superficial regional and national differences', a need which the Internet's pressures towards global convergence and homogenization continues to magnify (Hennessey, 1999).

In response, some marketing scholars claim that Levitt's analysis is impervious to cultural differences and therefore contend that corporations will receive greater returns by adapting their products and marketing strategies to the specifics of individual markets (e.g., Kotler, 1985). Other scholars claim that the convergence thesis is unsubstantiated and blind to the fact that numerous companies adapt their product lines to idiosyncratic country preferences (Douglas & Wind, 1987). In the midst of this controversy, the larger question of corporate globalization is left unchallenged.

To address this question, many organizations devote their persuasive efforts to advancing a particular image of the *organization itself*. Here, organizational rhetoric is aimed at a level 'above' products and services, namely, what an organization *does*, *what* its identity or image is, and what the organization itself *is*. Promoting a vision of a 'one-voice company' in which all communication is coordinated into a consistent, coherent and seamless expression, integrated marketing communications and corporate branding aim to help organizations create a synergy of persuasive voices (Thorson & Moore, 1996). Rather than branding individual products and consequently sending off different kinds of message in different directions, the logic of integration and corporate branding is to create a platform of symbols, a master brand that can inform and shape all forms of market-related communications. Thus, for example, the LEGO Corporation has for many years taken the position that *LEGO is a global product* and that, accordingly, it should focus on similarities across global markets, making its products available in a similar form (Cheney & Christensen, 2001).

Whether the ideal of adapting messages to the interests and concerns of local audiences was ever implemented, that ideology shaped almost everything organizations said or did in the past. But now, the literature on corporate communication speaks *against* such an adaptive approach and promotes the ideal of 'one corporate voice' (Balmer, 2001). The irony of corporations insisting on univocality while simultaneously claiming to listen and adapt to their customers cannot go unnoticed; yet very few organizations acknowledge this contradiction in their practices. The co-existence of these trends means that the corporate sector is successful at talking about dialogue and adaptation while doing all it can to control the communication agenda. After all, to bend significantly in the direction of audience adaptation really is to surrender to uncertainty (e.g., Chase & Tansik, 1983).

Maintaining credibility

The pressure to maintain univocality in the face of divergent stakeholders also reflects the rhetorical concern for *ethos*, as corporations strive to create and maintain credibility and legitimacy. The disciplines of marketing and corporate communication argue that consistency and univocality in corporate communication not only facilitate the creation of a distinct identity but also help an organization build credibility among its various audiences (e.g., Backer, 2001; Christensen, 2002; Ind, 1997; Kunde, 2000). Once established, this credibility becomes a resource for additional communication campaigns. Within the context of integrated communications, global consistency and univocality refer to securing maximum impact in a crowded marketplace, a goal that is broader than just the alignment of messages. It also implies an ongoing effort to ensure concordance between organizational words and action. Thus organizations tell themselves to 'walk their talk'. While this ideal formerly meant that managers should practise what they preach, it now extends to organizational behaviour *in toto*. Having publicized vision statements, values and corporate stories that highlight ideal futures and business practices, organizations expect to be held to their word. Or, put another way, company and consumer jointly expect that today's corporate 'messages' will sound something like yesterday's rhetoric. By subscribing to this ideal, corporations open themselves to a new type of critique that crosses formal organizational boundaries and confirms the observation that internal and external communications are no longer distinct practices (Cheney & Christensen, 2001).

What does this change suggest to organizations about their discourses and strategies? Although some stakeholders (e.g., journalists, interest organizations and investors) occasionally question the values and visions of organizational practices, *it is probably too early to tell how the call for consistency and integration will affect responses to corporate strategic communication.* Weick (1995) has speculated that the practice of walking the talk, while reducing hypocrisy, also stifles innovation and risk-taking; that is, 'People act in order to think … When told to walk their talk, the vehicle for discovery, that walking, is redirected. It has been pressed into service as a testimonial that a handful of earlier words are the right words' (Weick, 1995, p. 183). Still, few organizations can ignore the call to let their actions follow their words. To the extent that organizations educate their audiences to demand new practices, stakeholders and consumers are likely to hold organizations responsible for their communication. Whether such attempts will give rise to a more sophisticated critique of corporate rhetoric, only time will tell. Certainly this trend will give rise to new discursive strategies, and new will likely make reference to old.

EPILOGUE

In this essay we have argued that viewing organizational discourse as a rhetorical process has great theoretical and practical potential. In this process, we have ignored a number of important issues. For example, we have elided our treatment of organizational agency, legitimacy and ethics. Of course, we recognize that the question of *agency* is central to an understanding of organizational rhetoric, just as it is pivotal to problems in social theory, political theory and law. It is also difficult to decipher the roles of organizational actors in society, especially at a time when many of them take the form of networks and when their messages are distanced from policy-makers, individuals and groups. We also realize that *legitimacy* strikes at the heart of society's rationalizations of itself and of organizations' claim on societal resources. Also, a full understanding of legitimation entails a broadranging consideration of power relations between sectors – public, private and 'independent' – and the reception of it by citizen-consumers. *Ethics* are bound up in the practice and study of organizational rhetoric, both in the inherently *suasory* nature of language and in organizational campaigns based on values. For corporate rhetoric and organizational discourse, these three issues demand urgent attention.

APPENDIX: RHETORICAL AND DISCURSIVE STRATEGIES COMMON IN ORGANIZATIONAL/ INSTITUTIONAL MESSAGES

(adapted slightly from Cheney et al., 2004)

- Identification: for example, linking one issue with another
  Think how often 'sex and violence on television' is expressed as an indivisible unit.

- Differentiation: that is, declaring an issue to be unrelated to another or separating the organization from responsibility
  e.g., 'Guns don't kill people; people kill people.'

- Juxtapositioning: simply putting one thing next to another, regardless of connection
  This is especially common in the verbal and visual elements of advertising, for example, placing a beautiful body on top of a sleek new car.

- Strategic ambiguity
  e.g., 'We cannot say for certain that smoking causes cancer.'

- Denial: that is, asserting that the issue is not relevant or is not even an issue
  e.g., 'The loss of that part of the work force will have no effect on quality.'

- Containment: that is, minimizing an issue
  e.g., 'Don't mind his flirting and talking about sex at work. He's harmless.'

- Reification: treating something as solid and unchangeable
  e.g., 'You can't even suggest changing the policy. That's the way it is.'

- Enhancement: that is, stressing the importance of an issue
  e.g., 'We are in a crisis; that much is certain.'

- Substitution or diversion: that is, trying to move the discussion to another issue
  e.g., 'The problem with energy resources is not over-consumption but under-exploration.'

- Bolstering or self-promotion: for example, through the build-up of the status or credibility of the organization
  e.g., 'In the union's generous proposal to management yesterday, we offered ...'

- Dismissal: denigrating an opposing viewpoint or opposing source
  e.g., 'Only narrow-minded resistors of change would reject this proposal.'

- Partial reporting: for example, taking a statistic or a result out of a larger context
  'The unemployment rate is at an all-time low.'

- Totalizing: declaring a concern to be overriding, of superordinate importance, or overshadowing all other issues
  e.g., 'Global warming is unquestionably the most important issue of our time.'

- Apology: using excuses or justifications for past actions admitted to be harmful
  e.g., 'We admit we made a few mistakes, but have taken action to correct them.'

- Misrepresentation: that is, offering highly questionable assertions or conclusions from data
  e.g., 'The proposed tax cut will benefit all *citizens.'*

- Concealment of identity: that is, hiding or renaming the source of a message
  Think of ads that barely mention the source, give it a misleading name, or don't even list it.

- Self-expansion: suggesting that an organization or a consensus is really larger than it is
  e.g., 'Our employees overwhelmingly support the new performance appraisal system.'

- Reframing and reversal: using an ironic or surprising shift to create a new idea
  Consider recent attempts to make the term 'corporate welfare' stick.

- Non-response: that is, ignoring an issue that has been raised by a person or group
  Consider cases in meetings where a passionate speech on the part of an individual is ignored by the group.

- Propaganda: that is, suggesting that only one view is reasonable or possible
  In advertising, this is often manifested through the illusion of two alternatives; for example, 'You must choose Coke over Pepsi' or 'If you don't buy this facial cream, you'll ...'
  At work: 'In this organization, there are achievers and there are slackers.'
  And in politics: 'If you do not support this bill, you are part of the problem.'

REFERENCES

Allen, B.J. (in press) *Difference matters in organizational communication.* Prospect Heights, IL: Waveland Press.

Allen, G. (2000) *Intertextuality.* London: Routledge.

Argenti, P.A. (1998) *Corporate communication* (2nd edition). Boston, MA: Irwin McGraw-Hill.

Aristotle (1954) *The Rhetoric*. Trans. W. Rhys Roberts. New York: The Modern Library.

Aune, J. (1994) *The rhetoric of Marxism*. Boulder, CO: Westview Press.

Aune, J. (2001) *Selling the free market*. New York: Guilford Press.

Austin, J. (1970) *How to do things with words*. New York: Oxford.

Austin, A. (2002) Advancing accumulation and managing its discontents: The US anti-environmental movement. *Sociological Spectrum*, 22 (1): 71–104.

Backer, L. (2001) The mediated transparent society. *Corporate Reputation Review*, 4 (3): 235–51.

Balmer, J.M.T. (2001) Corporate identity, corporate branding and corporate marketing: Seeing through the fog. *European Journal of Marketing*, 35 (3/4): 248–91.

Bart, C. (1998) Mission matters. *The CPA Journal*, 68 (8): 56–67.

Baudrillard, J. (1988) *The ecstasy of communication*. New York: Semiotext(e).

Baudrillard, J. (1994) *Simulacra and simulation*. Ann Arbor, MI: The University of Michigan Press.

Baumgartner, F. & Jones, B. (1993) *Agendas and instability in American politics*. Chicago: University of Chicago Press.

Baumgartner, F. & Leech, B. (1998) *Basic interests*. Princeton, NJ: Princeton University Press.

Begley, T. & Boyd, D. (2000) Articulating corporate values through human resource policies. *Business Horizons*, 43 (4): 8–12.

Belch, G.E. & Belch, M.A. (1998) *Advertising and promotion: An integrated marketing communications perspective* (4th edition). Boston, MA: Irwin McGraw-Hill.

Benoit, W.L. (1995) *Accounts, excuses, and apologies: A theory of image restoration strategies*. Albany, NY: State University of New York Press.

Berg, P.O. (1989) Postmodern management? From facts to fiction in theory and practice. *Scandinavian Journal of Management*, 5 (3): 201–17.

Berg, P.-O. and Kreiner, K. (1990) Corporate architecture: Turning physical settings into symbolic resources. In P. Gagliardi (ed.), *Symbols and artifacts: Views of the corporate landscape* (pp. 41–67). Berlin: Walter de Gruyter.

Bitzer, L.F. (1968) The rhetorical situation. *Philosophy and Rhetoric*, 1 (1): 1–14.

Bitzer, L.F. (1980) Functional communication. In E. White (ed.), *Rhetoric in Transition* (pp. 21–38). University Park, PA: Pennsylvania State University Press.

Blythe, J. (2000) *Marketing communications*. Harlow, UK: Financial Times–Prentice Hall.

Bond, J. & Kirshenbaum, R. (1998) *Under the radar: Talking to today's cynical consumer*. New York: Adweek Books.

Booth, W.C. (1988) *The vocation of a teacher*. Chicago: University of Chicago Press.

Broms, H. & Gahmberg, H. (1983) Communication to self in organizations and cultures. *Administrative Science Quarterly*, 28: 482–95.

Brown, R.H. (1977) *A poetic for sociology*. New York: Cambridge University Press.

Brown, R.H. (1987) *Society as text*. Chicago: University of Chicago Press.

Brown, S.L. & Eisenhardt, K.M. (1998) *Competing on the edge: Strategy as structured chaos*. Boston, MA: Harvard Business School Press.

Bullis, C. (1993) Organizational socialization research. *Communication Monographs*, 60: 10–17.

Bullis, C.A. & Tompkins, P.K. (1989) The forest ranger revisited: A study of control practices and identification. *Communication Monographs*, 56: 287–306.

Burke, K. (1969) *A rhetoric of motives*. Berkeley, CA: University of California Press.

Burke, K. (1973) The rhetorical situation. In L. Thayer (ed.), *Communication: Ethical and moral issues* (pp. 263–75). London: Gordon & Breach.

Bryant, C.D. (1953) Rhetoric: Its functions and its scope. *Quarterly Journal of Speech*, 39: 401–24.

Cascio, W.F. (1993) Downsizing: What do we know? *Academy of Management Executive*, 7 (1): 95–104.

Caywood, C. (ed.) (1997) *The handbook of strategic public relations and integrated communications.* New York: McGraw-Hill.

Chase, R.B. & Tansik, D.A. (1983) The customer contact model for organization design. *Management Science*, 29 (9): 1037–50.

Cheney, G. (1983a) On the various and changing meanings of organizational membership. *Communication Monographs*, 50: 342–62.

Cheney, G. (1983b) The rhetoric of identification and the study of organizational communication. *The Quarterly Journal of Speech*, 69: 143–58.

Cheney, G. (1992) The corporate person (re)presents itself. In E.L. Toth & R.L. Heath (eds), *Rhetorical and critical approaches to public relations* (pp. 165–83). Hillsdale, NJ: Lawrence Erlbaum Associates.

Cheney, G. (in press) Theorizing about organizational rhetoric: Classical, interpretive and critical aspects. In S.K. May & D.K. Mumby (eds), *Organizational communication theory*. London: Sage.

Cheney, G. & Christensen, L.T. (2001) Organizational identity: Linkages between internal and external organizational communication. In L.L. Putnam & F.M. Jablin (eds), *The new handbook of organizational communication* (pp. 231–69). Thousand Oaks, CA: Sage.

Cheney, G., Christensen, L.T., Zorn, T.E. & Ganesh, S. (2004) *Organizational communication in the age of globalization: Issues, reflections, and practices.* Prospect Heights, IL: Waveland Press.

Cheney, G., Garvin-Doxas, K. & Torrens, K. (1999) Kenneth Burke's implicit theory of power. In B. Bock (ed.), *Kenneth Burke for the 21st century* (pp. 133–50). Albany, NY: State University of New York Press.

Cheney, G. & McMillan, J.J. (1990) Organizational rhetoric and the practice of criticism. *Journal of Applied Communication Research*, 18 (2): 92–114.

Cheney, G. & Vibbert, S.L. (1987) Corporate discourse: Public relations and issue management. In F.M. Jablin, L.L. Putnam, K.H. Roberts & L.W. Porter (eds), *Handbook of organizational communication* (pp. 165–94). Newbury Park, CA: Sage.

Christensen, L.T. (1995) Buffering organizational identity in the marketing culture. *Organization Studies*, 16 (4): 651–72.

Christensen, L.T. (1997) Marketing as auto-communication. *Consumption, Markets & Culture*, 1 (3): 197–227.

Christensen, L.T. (2001a) *Reklame i selvsving.* København: Samfundslitteratur.

Christensen, L.T. (2001b) Intertextuality and self-reference in contemporary advertising. In F. Hansen & L.Y. Hansen (eds), *Advertising research in the Nordic countries* (pp. 351–6). København: Samfundslitteratur.

Christensen, L.T. (2002) Corporate communication: The challenge of transparency. *Corporate Communications: An International Journal*, 7 (3): 162–8.

Christensen, L.T. & Cheney, G. (2000) Self-absorption and self-seduction in the corporate identity game. In M. Schultz, M.J. Hatch & M.H. Larsen (eds), *The expressive organization* (pp. 246–70). Oxford: Oxford University Press.

Cicero (1942) *De Oratore: Books I, II & II.* Trans. E.W. Sutton and H. Rackham. Cambridge, MA: Harvard University Press.

Clair, R.P. (1996) The political nature of the colloquialism, 'a real job': Implications for organizational socialization. *Communication Monographs*, 66: 374–81.

Conrad, C. (1993) The ethical nexus: Conceptual grounding. In *The ethical nexus* (pp. 7–22). Norwood, NJ: Ablex.

Conrad, C. (2003) Stemming the tide: Corporate discourse and agenda denial in the 2002 'corporate meltdown'. *Organization*, 10: 549–60.

Conrad, C. & McIntush, H. (2003) Organizational rhetoric and healthcare policymaking. In T. Thompson, A. Dorsey, K. Miller & R. Parrott (eds), *Handbook of health communication* (pp. 403–22). Mahwah, NJ: Lawrence Erlbaum Associates.

Crable, R.E. (1990) 'Organizational rhetoric' as the fourth great system: Theoretical, critical, and pragmatic implications. *Journal of Applied Communication Research*, 18 (2): 115–28.

Crable, R.E. & Vibbert, S.L. (1983) Mobil's epideictic advocacy: 'Observations' of prometheus-bound. *Communication Monographs*, 50: 380–94.

Crable, R.E. & Vibbert, S.L. (1986) Managing issues and influencing public policy. *Public Relations Review*, 11 (2): 3–16.

Czarniawska-Joerges, B. (1994) Narratives of individual and organizational identities. In S.A. Deetz (ed.), *Communication yearbook 17* (pp. 193–221). Thousand Oaks, CA: Sage.

Dooley, R. & Fryxell, G. (1999) Attaining decision quality and commitment from dissent. *Academy of Management Journal*, 42: 389–402.

Douglas, S.P. & Wind, Y. (1987) The myth of globalization. *Columbia Journal of World Business*, 22 (Winter): 19–29.

Duncan, T. (1995) Why mission marketing is more strategic and long-term than cause marketing. *American Marketing Association*, Winter: 469–75.

Ewen, S. (1988) *All consuming images: The politics of style in contemporary culture.* New York: Basic Books.

Fairclough, N. (1989) *Language and power*. London: Longman.

Fill, C. (1999) *Marketing communications: Contexts, contents and strategies.* London: Prentice Hall.

Fisher, W.R. (1987) *Human communication as narration.* Columbia, SC: University of South Carolina Press.

Fombrun, C.J. & Rindova, V.P. (2000) The road to transparency: Reputation management at Royal Dutch/Shell. In M. Schultz, M.J. Hatch & M.H. Larsen (eds), *The expressive organization* (pp. 77–96). Oxford: Oxford University Press.

Forbes, P. (1992) Applying strategic management to public relations. *Public Relations Journal*, 48: 32.

Foss, S.K., Foss, K.A. & Trapp, R. (1991) *Contemporary perspectives on rhetoric* (2nd edition). Prospect Heights, IL: Waveland Press.

Foucault, M. (1984) *The Foucault reader.* Edited by P. Rabinow. New York: Pantheon.

Gerbner, G. (1994) Reclaiming our cultural mythology: Television's global marketing strategy creates a damaging and alienated window on the world. *In context*, Spring: 40.

Georgiou, P. (1981) The goal paradigm and notes toward a counter-paradigm. In M. Zey-Ferrell & M. Aiken (eds), *Complex organizations: Critical perspectives*. Glenview, IL: Scott, Foresman & Co.

Gladwell, M. (1997) The coolhunt. *The New Yorker*, 17 March: 78–88.

Gray, J. (1998) *False dawn.* New York: New Press, distributed by W.W. Norton.

Habermas, J. (1979) *Communication and the evolution of society.* Boston, MA: Beacon Press.

Hall, B. & Jones, B. (1997) Agenda denial and issue containment in the regulation of financial securities. In R.W. Cobb & M.H. Ross (eds), *Cultural strategies of agenda denial* (pp. 40–69). Lawrence, KS: Kansas University Press.

Hamel, G. & Prahalad, C.K. (1994) *Competing for the future: Breakthrough strategies for seizing control of your industry and creating the markets of tomorrow.* Boston, MA: Harvard Business School Press.

Heath, R.L. (1980) Corporate advocacy: An application of speech communication skills and more. *Communication Education*, 29: 370–7.

Heath, R.L. (1990) Effects of internal rhetoric on management response to external issues: How corporate culture failed the asbestos industry. *Journal of Applied Communication Research*, 18 (2): 153–67.

Hennessey, H.D. (1999) View from here. *The Ashridge Journal*, July: 23–4.

Hyland, K. (1998) Exploring corporate rhetoric: Metadiscourse in the CEO's letter. *The Journal of Business Communication*, 35 (2): 224–45.

Ibarra, P. & Kituse, J. (1993) Vernacular constituents of moral discourse: An interactionist proposal for the study of social problems. In G. Miller & J. Holstein (eds), *Constructionist controversies: Issues in social problems theory* (pp. 97–128). New York: Aldine Press.

Ind, N. (1997) *The corporate brand.* London: Macmillan Press.

Kanter, R.M. (1977) *Men and women of the corporation.* New York: Basic Books.

Karpik, L. (1978) Organizations, institutions, history. In L. Karpik (ed.), *Organizations and environment: Theory, issues and reality.* Thousand Oaks, CA: Sage.

Kotler, P. (1985) Global standardization – courting danger. Panel discussion at the 23rd American Marketing Association Conference, Washington, DC.

Krippendorff, K. (1984) An epistemological foundation for communication. *Journal of Communication*, 34: 21–36.

Krugman, P. (1994) *Peddling prosperity.* New York: W.W. Norton.

Kuhn, T. (1997) The discourse of issues management: A genre of organizational communication. *Communication Quarterly*, 45 (3): 188–210.

Kunde, J. (2000) *Corporate religion: Building a strong company through personality and corporate soul.* London: Financial Times–Prentice Hall.

Kuttner, R. (1997) *Everything for sale.* New York: Alfred A. Knopf.

Langelar, G. (1992) The vision trap. *Harvard Business Review*, March–April: 46–55.

Leeper, R.V. (1996) Moral objectivity: Jürgen Habermas's discourse ethics, and public relations. *Public Relations Review*, 22 (2): 133.

Leff, M. (1987) The habitation of rhetoric. In J. Wenzel (ed.), *Argument and critical practice: Proceedings of the Fifth SCA/AFA Conference on Argumentation.* Annandale, VA: Speech Communication Association.

Levinthal, D. & March, J. (1993) The myopia of learning. *Strategic Management Journal*, 14: 95–112.

Levitt, T. (1983) The globalization of markets. *Harvard Business Review*, 61 (3): 92–101.

Lindblom, C. (1977) *Politics and markets.* New York: Basic Books.

Littlejohn, S.E. (1986) Competition and cooperation: New trends in corporate public issue identification and resolution. *California Management Review*, 29 (1): 109–23.

Lotman, Y.M. (1990) *Universe of the mind: A semiotic theory of culture.* London: I.B. Tauris.

Luhmann, N. (1990) *Essays of self-reference.* New York: Columbia University Press.

Madrick, J. (2002) Devotion to free market makes for ineffectual policy. *The New York Times on the Web*, 5 September.

March, J. (1995) Disposable organizations and the rigidities of imagination. *Organization*, 2 (3/4): 427–40.

Marchand, R. (1998) *Creating the corporate soul: The rise of public relations and corporate imagery in American big business.* Berkeley, CA: The University of California Press.

Maturana, H.R. & Varela, F.J. (1980) *Autopoiesis and cognition: The realization of the living.* Dordrecht, Holland: Reidel.

McCloskey, D. (1994) *Knowledge and persuasion in economics.* Cambridge: Cambridge University Press.

McGee, M.C. (1990) Text, context, and the fragmentation of contemporary culture. *Western Journal of Speech Communication*, 54: 274–89.

Morgan, A. (1999) *Eating the big fish: How challenger brands can compete against brand leaders.* New York: John Wiley & Sons.

Olins, W. (1989) *Corporate identity: Making business strategy visible through design.* New York: Thames & Hudson.

Pera, M. (1994) *The discourses of science.* Chicago: University of Chicago Press.

Perelman, C. & Olbrechts-Tyteca, L. (1969) *The new rhetoric: A treatise on argumentation.* Notre Dame, IN: University of Notre Dame Press.

Perniola, M. (1980) *La societê dei simulacri*. Bologna, Italy: Capelli.

Perrow, C. (2002) *Organizing America*. Princeton, NJ: Princeton University Press.

Putnam, L.L. & Fairhurst, G.T. (2001) Discourse analysis in organizations: Issues and concerns. In L.L. Putnam & F.M. Jablin (eds), *The new handbook of organizational communication* (pp. 78–136). Thousand Oaks, CA: Sage.

Ricks, D.A. (1983) *Big business blunders: Mistakes in multinational marketing*. Homewood, IL: Dow Jones-Irwin.

Ries, A. & J. Trout (1981) *Positioning: The battle for your mind*. New York: Warner Books.

Rothschild-Whitt, J. (1979) The collectivist organization: An alternative to rational-bureaucratic models. *American Sociological Review*, 44: 509–27.

Ryan, M.H., Swanson, C.L. & Buchholz, R.A. (1987) *Corporate strategy, public policy, and the Fortune 500*. Oxford: Basil Blackwell.

Satow, R.L. (1975) Value-rational authority and professional organizations: Weber's missing type. *Administrative Science Quarterly*, 20: 526–31.

Schattschneider, E.E. (1935) *The semisovereign people*. Hinsdale, IL: The Dryden Press.

Schmertz, H. (1986) *Goodbye to the low profile: The art of creative confrontation*. Boston, MA: Little, Brown & Co.

Schultz, D.E., Tannebaum, S.I. & Lauterborn, R.F. (1994) *The new marketing paradigm: Integrated marketing communications*. Chicago: NTC Business Books.

Searle, J. (1970) *Speech acts*. Cambridge: Cambridge University Press.

Seeger, M.W. (1986) CEO performances: Lee Iacocca and the case of Chrysler. *The Southern Speech Communication Journal*, 52: 52–68.

Sennett, R. (1980) *Authority*. New York: Knopf.

Simon, H.A. (1947) *Administrative behavior*. New York: Free Press.

Simons, H. (1990) *The rhetorical turn*. Chicago: UC Press.

Soros, G. (1998) *The crisis of global capitalism*. New York: Public Affairs Press.

Sproule, J.M. (1988) The new managerial rhetoric and the old criticism. *Quarterly Journal of Speech*, 74: 468–86.

Stabile, C.A. (2000) Nike, social responsibility, and the hidden abode of production. *Critical Studies in Media Communication*, 17 (2): 186–204.

Stokes, J. & Clegg, S. (2002) Once upon a time in the bureaucracy. *Organization*, 9: 225–47.

Stone, D.A. (1988) *Policy paradox and political reason*. Glenview, IL: Scott, Foresman & Co.

Stone, R.A. (1996) Mission statements revisited. *SAM Advanced Management Journal*, 61 (1): 31–7.

Swales, J.M. & Rogers, P.S. (1995) Discourse and the projection of corporate culture: The Mission Statement. *Discourse & Society*, 6 (2): 223–42.

Thorson, E. & Moore, J. (eds) (1996) *Integrated communication: Synergy of persuasive voices*. Mahwah, NJ: Lawrence Erlbaum Associates.

Tompkins, P.K. (1987) Translating organizational theory: Symbolism over substance. In F.M. Jablin, L.L. Putnam, K.H. Roberts & L.H. Porter (eds), *Handbook of Organizational communication: An interdisciplinary perspective* (pp. 70–96). Newbury Park, CA: Sage.

Tompkins, P.K. & Cheney, G. (1985) Communication and unobtrusive control in contemporary organizations. In R.D. McPhee & P.K. Tompkins (eds), *Organizational communication: Traditional themes and new directions* (pp. 179–210). Beverly Hills, CA: Sage.

Van Riel, C.B.M. (2000) Corporate communications orchestrated by a sustainable corporate story. In M. Schultz, M.J. Hatch & M. Holten Larsen (eds), *The expressive organization* (pp. 157–81). Oxford: Oxford University Press.

Vibbert, S. & Bostdorff, D. (1993) Issue management and the 'lawsuit crisis'. In C. Conrad (ed.), *The ethical nexus* (pp. 103–20). Norwood, NJ: Ablex.

Wayne, L. (2002). Tighter rules for options fall victim to lobbying. *New York Times on the Web*, 20 July.

Weber, M. (1978) *Economy and society* (2 vols). (Trans. G. Roth and C. Wittich). Berkeley, CA: University of California Press.

Weick, K.E. (1979) *The social psychology of organizing* (2nd edition). Reading, MA: Addison-Wesley.

Wieck, K.E. (1995) *Sensemaking in organizations.* Thousand Oaks, CA: Sage.

Wichelns, H.A. (1925) The literary criticis of oratory. In A.M. Drummond (ed.), *Studies in rhetoric and public speaking in honor of James A. Winans* (pp. 181–216). New York: Century.

Wilson, J.Q. (1973) *Political organizations.* New York: Basic Books.

Wittgenstein, L. (1953) *Philosophical investigations.* Trans. G.E.M. Anscombe. London: Macmillan.

Yeshin, T. (1998) *Integrated marketing communications: The holistic approach.* Oxford: Butterworth Heinemann.

4

Tropes, Discourse and Organizing

Cliff Oswick, Linda L. Putnam and Tom Keenoy

> Good analysis rests not on just spotting ... 'which metaphor fits best', but in using metaphor to unravel multiple patterns of significance and their interrelations. (Morgan, 1986, p. 342)

Tropes[1] are an inevitable and unavoidable aspect of organizational life. They pervade the everyday interaction of organizational stakeholders and they inform and underpin the study of organizations (Manning, 1979). More generally, they are sense-making imagery used to describe, prescribe and circumscribe social reality (Burke, 1969b; White, 1978), and in the process, they also project, constitute and theorize particular constructions of those realities. Tropes are figures of speech in which words are used in non-literal ways, that is, words and phrases function symbolically to evoke meanings and ideas.

Although prominent in literary and rhetorical analyses, the study of tropes has recently developed explanatory power in a large number of disciplines, including history, geography, linguistics, philosophy and psychoanalysis (D'Angelo, 1987; Smith, 1996; White, 1978). The majority of this work centres on the four primary or master tropes – metaphor, metonymy, synecdoche and irony (Burke, 1969b; D'Angelo, 1992) from which other figures of speech are derived. The four tropes are known as the classic topoi or sets of categories that symbolize relationships among concepts, for example, resemblance, substitution, part–whole and contradiction, respectively (D'Angelo, 1987).

While there has been considerable interest in applying metaphor to the study of social phenomena, other tropes have received far less attention, even within linguistic work, where research on the other three tropes is 'not nearly so extensive as that on metaphor' (Gibbs, 1993, p. 253), and in management where 'if we disregard metaphor, research which examines the nature and application of tropes within the field of organization theory is scarce' (Oswick & Grant, 1996a, p. 222).

Organizational scholars have used metaphor to contrast theoretical perspectives and paradigms in organization science and organizational communication (Clegg & Gray, 1996; Keys, 1991; Morgan, 1980, 1986; Putnam et al., 1996; Tinker, 1986) and to unpack the debates between constructionist and non-constructionist views, literal and figurative meanings, and analogical reasoning and knowledge generation in organizational theory (Morcol, 1997; Oswick, Keenoy & Grant, 2003; Pinder & Bourgeois, 1982; Reed, 1990; Tsoukas, 1991, 1993a).

Other scholars employ metaphors to distinguish different schools of thought and to recast organizational constructs such as career ladders, globalization, industrial relations, human resources, negotiation, organizational change and organizational socialization (Buzzanell & Goldzwig, 1991; Dunn, 1990; Grant, 1996; Keenoy & Anthony, 1992; Marshak, 1996; Oswick, 2001a; Smith & Turner, 1995; Stutman & Putnam, 1994). Analyses of organizational metaphors are also central to the study of organizational culture (Deetz, 1986; Hirsh & Andrews, 1983; Koch & Deetz, 1981; Krefting & Frost, 1985; Smith & Eisenburg, 1987; Yanow, 1992) and to work on consulting, intervention techniques and organizational changes (Akin & Schultheiss, 1990; Barrett & Cooperrider, 1990; Clark & Salaman, 1996; Keizer & Post, 1996; Pondy, 1983). The latter approach draws on the use of metaphor to engender creative thinking and unique approaches to problem-solving. Throughout most of these studies, metaphor functions as a tool, one that presumes rather than explicates the complex relationship among language, thought and meaning (Inns, 2002).

In like manner, studies of metonymy, synecdoche and irony employ tropes as analytical tools. Unlike metaphor, however, this work is typically empirical, even though scholars have used irony and paradox to promote theory building (Poole & Van de Ven, 1989). Moreover, these studies address the links between language and meaning as they situate tropes in organizational practices, such as the evolution of issue definition in labour–management negotiations (Putnam, 2004), making argumentative appeals for courses of action (Hamilton, 1997, 2003) and making sense of ironic remarks (Hatch, 1997). By reviewing the work on tropes in general, we explore the unstated presumptions that reside in extant research and learn more about the role of discourse in organizational tropes.

This chapter summarizes issues on the use of tropes in organizational analysis and attempts to redress the under-representation of the 'lesser' tropes within organizational theory. Our purpose is to elaborate the role, status and utility of tropes within the field. The first section provides a discussion of the dominant tropes in use, particularly the four master tropes and the debate about their relationship to each other. Then the chapter sets forth ways that the master tropes can be distinguished from each other through projecting resonance or developing dissonance images. Within this framework, we review organizational research on the master tropes and the contributions and limitations each offers for organizational analysis. Finally, we present a research agenda for how scholars could enrich organizational analyses through the study of tropes in the workplace.

DEFINITIONS AND RELATIONSHIPS
AMONG THE MASTER TROPES

As an area for study, tropes are closely linked to literary theory. Often called *figures of speech*, some scholars presume that tropes are language patterns used for expression or ornamentation. Tropes, however, are not just 'extraneous adornments fitted onto plain language'; rather they function as a form of invention or a way of knowing through analytical reasoning and through creative processes that help us understand the world (D'Angelo, 1987, p. 39). Tropes, then, are *figures of thought* in which language is used strategically and rhetorically to set up types of relationship (Smith, 1996).

Distinguishing between and delineating relationships among the four master tropes are matters of some debate. Metaphor, clearly the most popular and best understood of the master tropes, uses language to tie the unfamiliar and abstract to the familiar and concrete (Inns, 2002; Lakoff & Johnson, 1980). Metaphor, then, involves the projection of certain attributes of one object or concept (i.e., a concrete one) on to another (i.e., an abstract one) to generate new or novel insights (Lakoff & Johnson, 1980, 1999; Ortony, 1975; Schön, 1993). Thus, it carries over or crosses 'one element of experience into another' (Morgan, 1996, p. 227).

Considerable confusion surrounds metonymy and synecdoche. These two closely related tropes involve the substitution of an attribute of a phenomenon to represent the phenomenon itself (Oswick et al., 2002). Unlike metaphor, they are not contingent on mapping across different domains. Metonymy works within the same domain by using language to substitute for particular relationships, such as the instrument for the agent, the cause for the effect or the sign for the thing. Using the term 'The Crown' to refer to 'a political monarchy' or using the phrase 'the sisters' to signify 'the feminist movement' illustrates language patterns that function as metonymy (Morgan, 1996, p. 230).

In contrast, synecdoche relies on a classification process – the substitution of the whole for the part or vice versa, for example, substituting the genus for the species or a microcosm for a macrocosm. What differentiates synecdoche from metonymy is that the word used to represent the phenomenon is classified into the same language category with it. For example, managerial use of 'the market' to legitimate or disguise an unwelcome company decision draws upon the way a subset (i.e., competition, economic conditions and sales figures) relates to the whole market. Also, words that become shorthand expressions for a category function as synecdoche, for example, the term *Biro* – the name of the Hungarian inventor of the ballpoint pen – to refer to any ballpoint pen or the term *Google* used as an expression for an Internet search. Both examples illustrate a specific label or brand name that refers to general categories of ballpoint pens or Internet searches, respectively.

Irony, the final master trope, uses language to depict something in a contradictory way, that is, it calls on the reader or recipient to interpret the message in a way that is opposite of what is said. Like metaphor, irony entails mapping across two domains, but one based on the 'juxtaposing of opposites' (Brown, 1977, p. 174).

By keeping multiple contradictory processes in play, irony evokes the unexpected, typically through invoking a meaning that is opposite of a word's standard definition. Thus, the reader or recipient of a message must confront the contingency of language and its inability to capture the complexity of discourse (Trethewey, 1999). Morgan's (1983) use of anarchy as a form of 'effective' organizing provides a succinct illustration of irony at work, as evidenced in Sabrosky, Thompson and McPherson's (1982) study of the military bureaucracy as organized anarchy.

The four tropes are interrelated, but each functions with a different relationship of language to thought. Metaphor is holistic and works through comparison and contrast while metonymy is dispersive and works through reduction. Synecdoche, in turn, is both inductive and deductive and works by integrating words within their constituent categories. Irony, in turn, is reflective and functions through incongruity and ambiguity (D'Angelo, 1987).

Although the respective roles of the four master tropes are relatively well established, their utility and status within the field of organization theory is contested (Keenoy et al., 2003; Oswick & Grant, 1996a; Oswick, Keenoy & Grant, 2003; Oswick, Keenoy & Jones, 2003). For some scholars, metaphor is the primary trope and the other figures of speech are subservient (D'Angelo, 1987; Levin, 1993; Morgan, 1996; Searle, 1993), while for other theorists the four tropes are equally valuable figurative devices (Manning, 1979). According to Morgan (1983, p. 602), metaphor 'makes meaning in a primal way' and metonymy, synecdoche and irony are 'secondary forms within the domain or context forged through metaphor'.

Somewhat paradoxically, other commentators have inverted the hierarchy of tropes. White (1978) contends that metaphor is the least sophisticated of the master tropes. For him, the ascending order of utility and value goes from metaphor to metonymy to synecdoche and finishes with irony. Sharing this view, Winner and Gardner (1993) and Kellner (1989) claim that irony requires a higher order of cognitive development than does the deployment of metaphor. Metaphor rests on a firm grasp of similarity between domains while irony requires a deep understanding of the nuances of opposition, as well as similarity, to generate alternative representations of reality. Kennedy (1998), in turn, adds another twist to this debate by casting metonymy and synecdoche as the 'natural rhetorical tropes' that function through signals and non-verbal cues (such as a dog's leash or a totem pole that stands for a whole tribe) as well as linguistic symbols.

In our view, the relative ranking of tropes is ultimately not a productive endeavour. Since figurative devices are a critical element in sense-making (Weick, 1995), our more immediate concern is on the processes through which different tropes employ similarity and dissimilarity in sense-making. Understanding the way tropes project resonance and dissonance is critical to showing how the four tropes could work together to enhance organizational analyses. Table 4.1 summarizes the analytic schema for examining the role of tropes in organizational research.

Table 4.1 *Contrasting applications and forms of trope in organizational analysis*

	Resonance tropes	Dissonance tropes
Dominant form	Metaphor	Irony
Alternative/subsidiary forms	Metonymy, synecdoche, allegory, simile and analogy	Paradox, sarcasm, parody, satire and anomaly
Basis of analysis	Functions through resemblances developed from comparison/contrast, substitution, representation, and reduction	Functions through incongruity developed from ambiguities and contradictions
Surface/figurative applications in organizational discourse	Makes meanings visible by generating Gestalt-like, insights and/or providing discursive embellishment	Makes meanings visible by generating contradiction, humour, understatement or caustic commentary
Deeper/cognitive applications in organizational analysis	Crystallizing a particular view and/or disseminating pre-existing knowledge	Undermining prevailing view and/or challenging conventional knowledge
Potential meta-level implications for organizational theorizing	Mechanisms for paradigm reinforcement	Mechanisms for paradigm disruption

RESONANCE TROPES, DISCOURSE AND ORGANIZING

Resonance refers to the way that tropes are used to establish figure–ground relationships through resemblances. That is, meaning occurs for metaphor, metonymy and synecdoche through the familiarity of the links between two domains – a source and a target (Stern, 2000). Resonance is epitomized in the way that metaphor 'proceeds through implicit or explicit assertions that A *is* (or is like) B' (Morgan, 1986, p. 13). The use of the term *like* privileges the similarities or *figure* between domains and diverts attention away from the dissimilarities, tension or ground (Ortony, 1975). A comparable process exists with synecdoche in which the part/whole correspondence is contingent on the degree of contiguity or representativeness of the 'part' as a proxy for 'whole' (and vice versa). The part/whole has to resonate sufficiently with the whole/part to ensure that the trope is a viable and effective figure of speech.

In like manner, 'the conceptual basis of metonymy is best demonstrated by the similarity between various metonymic expressions' (Gibbs, 1996, p. 234). For example, the phrase, 'the entire ship rejoiced' sets up the term *ship* to substitute for *passengers* by accenting the link between the people aboard, their emotions and reactions, and their physical location. Resonance occurs through making salient the link between the people and their physical containment and ignoring the many features that differentiate a ship from a body of people.

Drawing upon the work of Gentner (1983), Tsoukas (1993a) identifies four domains in which tropes function through resonance: *abstractions*, based on relational similarities between the target and source domains (e.g., 'the organization as a control system'); *analogies*, based on identifiable structures or sets of characteristics that link target and source domains (e.g., 'Orchard Road is to

Singapore what Oxford Street is to London'); *literal similarities*, which transfer both relationships and attributes from the source to the target domains (e.g., 'milk is like water'); and *mere appearances*, based on transferring specific attributes, but not relationships, between the source and target domains (e.g., 'the surface of the lake was calm and clean like a mirror') (Tsoukas, 1993a, pp. 337–8).

This classification underscores the analytic significance of resemblance between domains. Resonance tropes, then, are contingent on an adequate degree of domain comparison. Greater resemblance, however, does not result in greater resonance. Just as it is possible to have too little overlap between domains, it is also possible to have too much overlap. Effective resonance then requires a middle range of domain overlap in so far as 'too much or too little similarity means that the point may not be understood and no successful metaphor will have been created' (Alvesson, 1993, p. 116).

Surface and Deep Analysis of Resonance

Analytic distinctions have also been drawn between metaphors that are 'deep' and 'surface' (Schön, 1993), 'strong' and 'weak' (Black, 1979) and 'superficial' and 'meaningful' (Oswick & Grant, 1996a). Despite differences in terminology, these dualisms reflect an underlying concern with 'effective' resonance through presumptions about the links between language and meaning in context. A synthesis of these positions suggests that metaphors can be seen as superficial devices when they act as mere embellishments (Bourgeois & Pinder, 1983; Pinder & Bourgeois, 1982); they have limited image-generating potential (Grant & Oswick, 1996); and/or they have become so conventional that they are literal descriptors and, as such, function as 'dormant' or 'dead' metaphors (Lakoff & Johnson, 1980; Tsoukas, 1991). For example, the word *inflation* is a conventional metaphor that treats the economy as 'blown up like a balloon'; however, inflation is now a dead metaphor in that the word has become a literal descriptor; thus an analysis of the concept of 'inflation as a balloon' would fit a surface use of metaphor. In a similar way, the metaphor of an organization as a decision-making system is so deeply ingrained and taken for granted that it operates only at a surface level (Boland & Greenberg, 1988).

By contrast, deep, strong and meaningful metaphors are perceived as producing powerful, evocative and vivid imagery (Ortony, 1975; Oswick & Grant, 1996b; Oswick & Montgomery, 1999), providing novel ways of thinking (Morgan, 1980, 1986), having a generative capacity (Schön, 1993), and potentially liberating and illuminating (Barrett & Cooperrider, 1990; Ortony, 1993).

A deep-level analysis relies on the way that tropes constitute a given world-view or ideology in a particular context. One way to examine a set of tropes in context is through employing 'second-order' resemblances (Alvesson, 1993). For example, a second-order metaphor refers to the way it is framed or informed by other metaphors and tropes, even contradictory ones. Second-order metaphors shift the analysis to a recursive level that enables the examination of subsets of 'metaphorical entailments' or related metaphors linked to the deeper cognitive framework of language (Lakoff & Johnson, 1980). Oswick and Grant (1996a) illustrate this second-order analysis:

> In addition to permitting an initial surface comparison to be made, the 'organization as family' metaphor also accommodates a deeper form of analysis by considering second-order comparisons, such as the existence of metaphoric counterparts to: the father role, the mother, the children, family feuds, family values and so on. (Oswick & Grant, 1996a, pp. 217).

This form of deep analysis parallels the abstraction category that focuses on a multiplicity of relationships between the source and target domains. According to Tsoukas (1993a, p. 338), abstractions are the most effective means of generating organizational knowledge because they 'operate at a high level of generality, reveal the generic properties of a variety of phenomena and can thus be used to explain phenomena across widely different domains'. In effect, the set of relationships present in the abstraction, 'the organization *as* family', is constituted through a complex bundle of sub-metaphors (e.g., a senior manager *as* father figure, norms *as* family values and customers as extended family members) that intertextually produce resonance.

Imposing and Exposing Resonance

Organizational scholars also differ in the ways that they impose or expose patterns of resonance among tropes. Just as scholars embrace different presumptions about surface- and deep-level analyses, researchers use tropes often in normative ways to impose or project metaphors on ideas, theories and organizational practices (Gibbs, 1996). Two types of study that impose resonance appear in the literature – those that use metaphors as theoretical models to cluster perspectives and images of organizing and those that prescribe particular metaphors as a means to some organizational end.

IMPOSING RESONANCE FOR THEORY BUILDING   One approach to imposing metaphors is to use them as images to depict diverse organizational perspectives. This approach employs metaphor to generate new theory, decentre old ones and unpack nuances of various schools of organizational thought (Cazal & Inns, 1998). The most popular and ubiquitous approach is Morgan's (1980, 1981, 1983, 1986, 1989, 1993, 1996) extensive and seminal contribution of the work on images of organizations. Researchers and scholars in a variety of related fields have adopted this framework to illustrate how organizations function as: machines, organisms, brains, psychic prisons, cultures and holograms (Keys, 1991; May, 1993). In a similar vein, Putnam, Phillips and Chapman (1996) employ alternative metaphors to unpack the way that researchers depict organizational communication in terms of a conduit, a lens, linkage systems, performances, symbols, multiple voices or discursive forms.

Other scholars cast organizations as analogous to: theatres (Mangham & Overington, 1987), human entities (Kumra, 1996), soap bubbles (Tsoukas, 1993b), garbage cans (Cohen et al., 1972), icebergs (Selfridge & Sokolik, 1975), predatory animals and zoos (Brink, 1993; Oswick, 2001b), triune-brains (Broekstra, 1996), journeys (Brink, 1993), competitive sports teams (Deetz, 1986; Koch & Deetz, 1981; Morgan, 1997), organizational gardening (Keating, 1993; Mitroff, 1987) and cars and car parts (Oswick & Montgomery, 1999). These images typically arise from discursive patterns linked to particular metaphors. For example, Weick (1979, pp. 49–50) and Deetz (1986) show how military language pervades the business world through the use of such phrases as 'waging campaigns', 'gathering intelligence', 'conferring with the brass', 'chain of command', 'insubordination' and 'bypassing'. The combat and war metaphors are particularly problematic as they lead to policies and practices consistent with this imagery (Stohl, 1995).

For some scholars, this work emanates from a desire to decipher the metaphors of a field or the way knowledge production has evolved in the sciences, social sciences and organizational sciences (Gross, 1990; McCloskey, 1985, 1988; Prelli, 1989, Tietge, 1998). For other scholars, it has become a shorthand way to impose or project particular images on organizations. When researchers use this metaphorical imagery to colour *all* organizational behaviours or to superimpose it on particular institutions, it becomes prescriptive and premeditated. In short, the demands of resonance can result in metaphors being imposed on organizational life rather than being revealed within it (Mangham, 1996).

IMPOSING RESONANCE FOR ORGANIZATIONAL PROBLEM-SOLVING   A second way that scholars impose tropes is casting them as a means to some organizational end, such as problem-solving or organizational change (Inns, 2002). Consultants, teachers and trainers often employ Morgan's seminal work as tools for making changes in organizations. In this approach managers are encouraged to eliminate, replace or control organizational metaphors (Keely, 1980; Krefting & Frost, 1985; Pinder & Bourgeois, 1982); to use metaphoric thinking to solve problems (Smith & Simmons, 1983); to serve as a catalyst for stimulating organizational change (Keizer & Post, 1996); to influence the way organizational members interpret planned changes (Sackmann, 1989); and to persuade and influence clients in the consultant industry (Clark & Salaman, 1996). In a similar way, Hopfl and Maddrell (1996) demonstrate how a direct marketing organization draws upon evangelical metaphors such as 'live the dream', 'the élite chosen ones' and 'amazing grace' to arouse emotions, inspire visions and transform employees into accepting changes.

A variation of this approach draws from the generative power of metaphor to aid problem formulation, to develop imagination and to engage in creative thinking. Specifically, students who use organic metaphors formulate problems more broadly and favour decentralized solutions more often than do those who use mechanistic images of organizations (Boland & Greenberg, 1988). In organizational development, practitioners use metaphors to foster unity and reframe disparities in work experiences (Akin & Schultheiss, 1990), to develop strategies and plans for implementing changes through using corrective metaphors (Cleary & Packard, 1992) and to liberate groups from cyclical patterns of conflict and defensive behaviours (Barrett & Cooperrider, 1990).

As this review suggests, planting, eliminating and replacing metaphors are ways of imposing tropes to attain particular ends. Yanow (1992, p. 103) contends that metaphors can 'no more be replaced by different metaphors than they can by literal language without changing [the] perception and understanding of [the organizational] context'. To suggest that organizational members can implant, change or control the multiple meanings that tropes engender ignores the fact that language is embedded in an organization's culture in a particular time and place.

Overall, several problems emanate from imposing tropes on organizational experiences. First, imposing tropes often reduces them to singular and fixed meanings that blind organizational members to other courses of action, as is evident in the concept of 're-engineering', a metaphor equated with downsizing. By denying the ambiguity of tropes, researchers equate language with reality and presume that meaning resides in words. Secondly, imposing tropes, even as diagnostic tools for critical evaluations, ignores the power of language to shape how we see and make sense of the world, particularly through chains of associations that often function in complex ways.

EXPOSING RESONANCE   An alternative approach to resonance is to expose the tropes that are used in everyday practice in organizations. Studies of language in use in organizations encompass a variety of tropes, even though the vast majority of them focus on metaphors. Unlike the normative stance evident in imposing resonance, studies that expose tropes involve scrutiny and interpretation of texts and conversations, typically through in-depth descriptions, critical analyses and deconstructions (Inns, 2002). Informed by Lakoff and Johnson's (1980) seminal work on metaphor, these studies centre on the way that tropes evoke multiple meanings, reveal root metaphors and legitimate actions.

Metaphors in use refer to the different words that form images, such as viewing *arguments* as *war*, which is manifested in such everyday expressions as 'claims being indefensible', 'criticism is on target', and 'attacking, demolishing and shooting down positions' (Lakoff & Johnson, 1980, 1999; Lakoff & Turner, 1989). Metaphors are also interwoven within and across social groups. While some individuals view arguments as war, others see them as *journeys*, represented by phrases as 'not getting anywhere', 'taking the wrong path' and 'following the lead' (Lakoff & Johnson, 1980). Examining the way that members negotiate differences in metaphorical use is a key to understanding the dynamic and evolutionary nature of organizational realities (Deetz, 1986).

EXPOSING RESONANCE THROUGH MULTIPLE MEANINGS   The metaphor of *teams* is one that evokes multiple meanings in everyday language. As an intermediate metaphor that organizational actors consciously use (Oswick & Grant, 1996a), the *team* image is a broad heuristic which reveals cognitive frameworks for collective action (Morgan, 1997). Contrasting students' with managers' images of teams, Gribas and Downs (2002) demonstrated that novices held distinctively different metaphorical entailments than did practising managers, ones rooted in sports, cooperation and unity. Managers, in turn, invoked a 'meeting' metaphor and saw *teams* as problem-centred, time wasting and condescending.

Multiple meanings of the team metaphor are particularly salient with new organizational forms. Using the metaphor of Protean Places from the Greek sea god, Shockley-Zalabak (2002) examined the transcripts of a dynamic ten-member virtual team. Her data revealed that the team shifted form by maintaining its core values while continually changing; by using language such as 'crossing time and space'; by embracing both trust and distrust, stability and change and formal and informal processes; and by viewing the team as a 'sense of place' rather than a unified collective. Thus, the metaphor of Protean Places effectively characterized the features of this virtual team. Both studies reaffirmed Morgan's (1997) contention that the *team* metaphor is too ambiguous and elusive to function as a common symbolic construction; rather, it parallels an archetype with multiple meanings.

EXPOSING RESONANCE THROUGH ROOT METAPHORS   Archetypal metaphors are closely linked to the concept of *root metaphor*, that is, images that provide rich summaries of the world and function as dominate ways of seeing (Smith & Eisenberg, 1987). Research on root metaphors illustrates how they differ across contexts. Koch & Deetz (1981) examined intra-organizational memos and transcripts of member conversations to isolate metaphorical expressions at a university news service. Through a thematic analysis, they identified three root metaphors – organization is coach ('sport talent scouts' and 'all star teams'), conduit ('channelling the news') and a machine ('going like clockwork' and 'putting things in the wrong gear'). Their analysis demonstrated the prevalence of root metaphors in everyday discourse and the importance of examining multiple metaphors and their internal coherence.

Differences in root metaphors also distinguished growth from non-growth firms. Using transcriptions of autobiographical tapes of owner-managers for 16 firms, Perren and Atkin (1997) discovered that growth firms embraced a *journey* or *life cycle* root metaphor, in which owners viewed their firms as passing through stages of development, as seen in the expressions, 'working my way up' or 'building a house'. Owners of these firms had a combative approach to the external environment, evident in statements like 'fight to get it', 'hold people to ransom' and 'treading on toes'. In contrast, the root metaphor for non-growth firms was *a victim*, with the relationship to the environment cast as dependent, burdensome and heavy. In this case, root metaphors revealed orientations to organizational environment that were not immediately visible or readily understood by organizational members.

Contrasting root metaphors can also lead to conflicts among organizational members. Yanow (1992) describes how the founders of a community centre in Israel employed 'a functional supermarket' as a root metaphor to shape the programme offerings, employee roles and evaluation criteria. The centre was to be 'multifaceted', 'offer pre-packaged goods', 'value high turnover of services' and be evaluated based on 'volume of sales'. But this metaphor clashed with the norms of professional community practices in Israel which required the director to 'leave the store', 'interact with clients in natural settings' and 'avoid pre-packaged programmes'. The juxtaposition of the supermarket metaphor with professional norms continued to generate conflict, leading to the closing of the centre and signifying the importance of exposing tacit understandings of metaphors in use.

In a similar way, Smith and Eisenberg (1987) illustrated how management's root metaphor of Disneyland as a *drama* clashed with the employees' metaphor of it as a *family*, leading to Disney's biggest labour strike. Disney managers referred to personnel as 'casting', employee jobs as 'scripts' or 'roles', the park as a 'show' and customers as 'guests', while employees viewed Disney as a family, complete with images of Walt as the patriarch, the corporation as caretaker and lifetime family membership. Management's violation of the 'family rules' through layoffs and salary cuts ran counter to the employees' root metaphor and led to major changes in organizational culture.

Another study that focused on multiple root metaphors was Dunford and Palmer's (1996) textual analysis of the popular management literature on downsizing. Their extensive review revealed three root metaphors that underlay the reasons given for downsizing: *military/violence* justified through 'combating rising costs', 'engaging in wars with competitors' and 'riding the stormy seas'; *horticultural/nature* justified as natural and inevitable 'pruning' and 'getting rid of the dead wood'; and *medical/health* justified as necessary for long-term survival through 'becoming lean', 'slimming down' and 'getting fit' (Dunford & Palmer, 1996, pp. 100–3). In general, root metaphors, as universes of meaning, are rarely explicit and are mostly taken for granted. Moreover, they are emotionally charged and seen as inevitable. Thus, when conflicts arise over clashes between symbolic constructions, root metaphors remain hidden, continuing to be aligned with resonance.

EXPOSING RESONANCE THROUGH LEGITIMATING ACTIONS   Research that demonstrates how tropes legitimate actions investigates organizational uses of metonymy and synecdoche as well as metaphors. In a study of a variety of tropes, Hamilton (1997) focused on the use of metonymy in shop stewards' talk to demonstrate how employees of the National Health Service invoked a pendulum swing that resulted in an arbitrated agreement of a no-strike policy (Hamilton, 1997). For example, the phrase 'get their butts down to that area fast' signified negotiation representatives who were not pulling their weight and substituted for the negotiation process. Similarly, Watson (1995) used metonymy as a rhetorical device to study managerial deliberations about a new development programme. A phrase such as 'going down the road' substituted for the general set of organizational principles and the terms 'pay package' and 'brown envelope' signified rewards and dismissal in deciphering whether the programme was a 'con'.

Another project focused specifically on synecdoche to illustrate how this trope legitimated actions around local control of pay in the National Health Service Trust, using such language such 'controlling our paybill' to stand for the whole of 'controlling the organization' (Hamilton, 2003, p. 1577). References to 'professionalism' and 'professional groups', such as 'speech and language therapists', were used to convince management that employees *en masse* were changing to local pay. In both studies, organizational members use metonymy and synecdoche in everyday talk to support courses of action and legitimate decisions.

Some studies take a critical read on tropes by exposing how they legitimate inequities. For example, Putnam (2004) adopted a dialectical perspective to demonstrate how words used as metonymy and synecdoche shifted across time in a labour–management negotiation. She examined terms like 'language' and 'money', as different synecdoches for the bargaining contract, to show how they folded into each other to become a commodity (also a metonymy) that reinforced tacit norms, repeated bargaining formulae and enacted a duality of control. Even though tropes legitimated actions, they also revealed inequities as both sides lost opportunities for creative settlements.

Shifting to metaphor and particularly the *marketplace* metaphor, Anderson (1998) described the way an academic organization institutionalized unfairness. In a time of severe budget cuts, 'allocation of resources' became transformed into 'allocation of scarcity' such that salaries were set through comparison to same-sex norms, particularly the scarcity principle of 'don't ask too often and too early'. For women, who were told not to overturn the salary structure of senior women, it meant no discretionary increase. For men, the marketplace metaphor fostered 'equity adjustments' to level the playing field with other males. The market-place metaphor, then, redefined 'equity' not in terms of individual discrepancies, but in comparison with broad socio-economic groups.

With a similar critical slant, Kent (2001) examined the language patterns of 'Web 21's One Hundred Hottest Web Sites' to uncover the packed ideology of the medium. Through analysing both content and form, he deduced that the dom-inant metaphor for the web was *consumerism*, not education, information or democ-racy. Language patterns that revealed self-contained slogans, eclipsed messages, disembodied content and anonymity made the web sites *commercial attractions* rather than *information superhighways*.

These studies draw attention to the potential ideological role of tropes in con-structing a preferred relationship for the 'target domain' (Tinker, 1986). It also sug-gests that a focus on tropes in use – because the observer has less direct personal ownership of the symbols in question – may lead to critical analyses as well as insights as to how resonance occurs. Morgan's insightful approach has privileged resonance and promoted analytic coherence, but, as research illustrates, the produc-tion and consumption of tropes can also result in dissonance and ambiguity.

DISSONANCE TROPES, DISCOURSE AND ORGANIZING

Unlike tropes that project resonance, other figures of speech reflect the incon-gruities in organizational life, thus revealing dissonance. If metaphor operates as the generic term for resonance tropes, then irony, which embodies paradox, sarcasm, satire, parody and understatement, is the dominant trope of dissonance (Booth, 1974; Knox, 1961; Muecke, 1969). It also serves a range of quite different functions, including the humorous (Hatch, 1997), the dramatic (Burke, 1969a,

1969b; Sedgewick, 1935), the romantic (Muecke, 1970), and the critical (Hutcheon, 1994; Kierkegaard, 1966; Sim, 2002). Given this heterogeneity, irony is far more complex than are resonance tropes and therefore more difficult to pin down.

Dissonance in this sense means more than binary oppositions. Often associated with sarcasm or sardonic observation, irony is 'saying one thing but meaning the opposite' (Booth, 1974, p. 34) or using words to express something other than what they suggest. It involves an element of surprise, the unexpected or unconventional interpretations that move outside existing frames of reference (Westenholz, 1993). This contrast between the apparent and intended meaning requires knowledge of the context or the situation in which the ironic reference occurs. Thus, irony is rooted in contradictions between text and subtexts of what a situation purports and what it actually is (Putnam, 1986).

Irony is also closely tied to ambiguity and to humour. Ambiguity is central to irony since this trope keeps multiple and contradictory meanings at play concomitantly and operates at implicit levels of understanding. Ironic humour with its simultaneous aim to evoke surprise, be funny and undercut the 'sacred', capitalizes on this ambiguity (Johansson & Woodilla, 2000).

Irony also has a distinctively moral or political edge that resonance tropes do not (Purdy, 1998). It turns an orthodox way of thinking on its head by using levels of meaning to make a commentary, by 'decentring the subject' (Lemert, 1979) and by 'making the familiar strange' (Foucault, 1977). These functions stand in contrast to uses of metaphor that, to some extent, make the 'familiar more familiar'.

Overall, irony works from a presumed association between a source and a target domain, but in an unexpected and often contradictory fashion. The 'ironical' feature of irony, whether spoken or enacted, is that it alludes to resemblances in oppositional ways. In this sense a high degree of dissonance between two disparate domains is crucial, but with counter-intuitive points of similarity, ones that make alternative meanings visible.

Inversion and Subversion of Dissonance

Although the terms 'deep' and 'surface' are not explicitly applied to dissonance-generating tropes, irony functions at discernibly different levels. In Hutcheon's (1994) view, the figurative or surface role of irony involves linguistic *inversion*, such as the greeting 'Nice day, isn't it?', stated when it is raining outside. Moreover, irony is often used in certain discursive communities to signify communicative competence or as 'purely decorative, subsidiary and non-essential' language (Hutcheon, 1994, p. 48). This kind of 'in-group' irony has a reinforcing quality that makes parody, sarcasm and humour benign (Booth, 1974; Muecke, 1970). Another form of inversion is 'ludic irony' that results from affectionate teasing, innocuous humour and general playfulness (Hutcheon, 1994). Such forms of verbal irony are widely reported in the literature on humour in organizations (Duncan et al., 1990; Lynch, 2002; Meyer, 1997, Vinton, 1989).

Hutcheon (1994) contrasts these surface forms with *subversion* in which irony articulates antithetical positions embedded in organizational practices. Such usage offers a challenge to the 'very' sites of discourse, those based on hierarchical social relations of dominance (Hutcheon, 1994, p. 30). In this sense, irony exposes and destabilizes existing power structures. For example, Rodrigues and Collinson (1995) examined the way employees at a Brazilian-owned telecommunication company used irony, humour and satire to resist management. Highlighting inconsistencies between what managers said and their actual autocratic practices, union members published satirical cartoons that symbolized the irony of everyday experiences.

Other scholars have suggested that irony facilitates 'transformative' and 'transgressive' outcomes (Stallybrass & White, 1986) and undermines hegemony to foster new ways of acting and being (Rorty, 1989). For instance, Trethewey (1999) used irony to analyse the taken-for-granted paradoxes of confessional discourse in a women's social service agency. These discourses, often perceived as 'instruments of power', were ironically liberating through providing clients with fortification to resist bureaucratic practices, break the rules, mock confessional technologies and revise personal relationships. Dependent relationships with social workers, while reinforcing the roles of deficient females, ironically empowered the clients and enabled them to get their needs met.

Intentional and Situational Dissonance

DISSONANCE THROUGH INTENTIONAL IRONY   Although some studies focus on the liberating and transformative outcomes of irony, the majority of research on organizational irony casts it as a conscious process of engagement, one that typically reinforces the prevailing power structures. Perhaps because of its roots, irony is frequently *intentional* or the product of planned agency (Booth, 1974). These roots go back to Socrates, who feigned ignorance and then asked informed questions of his adversaries to confuse them (Kierkegaard, 1966). Intentional irony can arise through real-time exchanges at the surface level (e.g., contrived sarcasm) or, more typically, based on a sustained synthesis of opposing perspectives (e.g., deliberate subversion).

Specifically, Joseph Heller's famous novel, *Catch-22* (1964), exemplifies an 'ideal type' of subversive intentional irony through the way that fragility and power in Weber's legal-rational authority are displayed in eponymous rule. Heller's success was not merely that he wrote an anti-war novel through the medium of irony, but also that his account resonated with experiences in contemporary organizations.

Subversion as a form of intentional irony demasks hypocrisy and reveals prejudice, but rather than liberating or transforming power relations, it helps to distance the oppressed from the oppressor, often by creating and preserving isolated sub-cultures. The use of irony to create a reaction that distances organizational members is evident in Kunda's (1992) ethnography of a high-tech engineering corporation. In an organization characterized by strong normative control, employees relied on ironic slogans and humour to depersonalize their actions and distance themselves from corporate immersion that engulfed personal and emotional lives. In another example of distancing, Collinson's (1988) research on shop-floor workers demonstrated how sarcasm and ironic humour enacted a divide between labour and management, one in which the workers' masculine prowess reified a sub-culture that positioned them ironically as powerless victims.

This paradox of control is also evident in Hatch and Ehrlich's (1993) analysis of irony used in routine meetings of senior managers in a multinational computer company. In discussions of security issues, managers constructed multiple meanings that cast themselves as both prisoners and guards. Subsequent analysis revealed that this ironic disposition allowed them to interpret emotional experiences in contradictory ways and to distance themselves from impending organizational changes (Hatch, 1997).

In effect, organizational members use irony and ironic humour intentionally to distance themselves from management, to preserve a sense of self, and to embrace paradoxes of control. The multiple meanings created through irony provide organizational members with a symbolic distance to cope with normative systems while inadvertently reinforcing the power structures that put them in place.

DISSONANCE THROUGH SITUATIONAL IRONY   Not all forms of irony are conscious, intentional or planned. For example, irony also occurs serendipitously through unintended and unexpected circumstances or through the evolution of situations. *Situational irony* focuses on the surprising and inevitable fragility of the human condition, in which the consequences of actions are often the opposite of what was expected (Lucariello, 1994). Also known as the 'irony of fate' (Muecke, 1970) and the 'irony of events' (Booth, 1974), this form of irony creates dissonance through comparing events to the logic (or illogic) of the situation. As an example, Johansson and Woodilla (2000, p. 7) report on an organization in which employees worked less and less in teams while ironically receiving more and more team training. They also illustrate situational irony in an example of the way that Sweden casts women workers as equal with men in pay, competence and achievements, yet this country has far fewer women in top management than do many other nations.

Another type of situational irony is 'perspectives by incongruity', in which seemingly opposite occurrences are really similar (Burke, 1969b). For example, Manning (1979) compared the police world of morality to the drug world of immorality and found that undercover cops parallel drug dealers in ironic ways, including keeping strange hours, dressing like criminals, frequenting similar hangouts, and being paid on a different basis. In this way situational irony draws on both dissonance and resonance to reveal ironic circumstances.

IMPLICATIONS FOR ORGANIZATION ANALYSIS

Our discussion of the role of resonance and dissonance tropes highlights four main approaches in organizational studies (see Figure 4.1). Resonance entails two

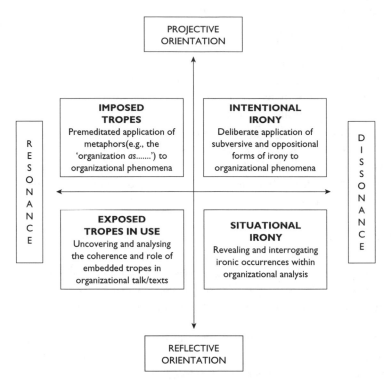

Figure 4.1   *Tropological approaches to the analysis of organization discourse*

practices – imposing tropes to enhance organizational theory-building and problem-solving and examining the way that tropes in use engender multiple meanings, expose root metaphors and legitimate actions. Our examination of dissonance tropes centres on two approaches to the study of irony – the way organizational members incorporate it intentionally and the way it surfaces through circumstances and unplanned situations.

Our critique and suggestions for future studies, however, derive from the vertical axes of Figure 4.1, that which distinguishes projective from reflective orientations. Clearly, the majority of work on tropes in organizational analysis falls into the upper quadrants of 'imposed tropes' and 'intentional irony'. No doubt, imposing tropes on organizational phenomena has revealed many aspects of target domains that were heretofore hidden. This discovery process occurs through mapping across domains to crystallize assumptions, makes the implicit known and articulates the inexpressible. In this way, tropes assist sense-making through identifying resemblances that invoke emotional, cognitive and experiential connections (i.e., resonance). However, the process of selecting resonance tropes and applying them to organizational analyses is not unproblematic or neutral.

To generate resonance, organizational scholars select metaphors or other related tropes that have the potential for 'high resemblance' or that intuitively have a 'good fit'. As a consequence, the connection or links in metaphorical projection often seem self-fulfilling or self-evident. In short, the act of imposing metaphors may lead to explicitly confirming what we already knew implicitly.

In contrast, if scholars avoid selecting metaphors that do not resonate, they may choose a different set of tropes inadvertently – for example, anomaly (domains that do not fit) or irony (domains that are antithetical) – leading to a shift to dissonance. Meaning, then, is not inherent in words or relationships among them, but in the larger context in which organizational actors use words, interpret them, co-construct meanings and institutionalize them. Blindly imposing tropes overlooks the contextual roots that originally inspired their use.

The reflective orientation depicted in Figure 4.1 focuses on tropes in use and situational irony – two areas that are clearly under-represented in organizational research. As this chapter reveals, studies of metaphors in use are growing. This work, however, needs redirecting in two ways: developing chains of association among metaphors and privileging the context in which different forces impinge on metaphor use.

First, researchers of metaphors in use often enact a point of closure by locking these tropes into fixed categories. Metaphors, however, highlight some features while suppressing others; hence, no one metaphor can capture the nuances of organizational phenomena. To address this concern, researchers often develop a laundry list of metaphors, ones that are detached from their constitutive context and their dynamic relationships.

Analysis of metaphors in use, then, needs to focus on chains of associations or the ways that meanings shift and enable the ground to become the figure for another metaphor. These chains could capture the fluid nature of meanings and the reflexivity that typifies organizational discourse. Understanding metaphors in use would then become less an issue of representation and more a concern for repertoires of meaning (Lacan, 1986). Smith and Turner's (1995) study that critiques and reconfigures metaphors of organizational socialization provides a model for this type of analysis.

Secondly, unpacking metaphors' meaning entails privileging language in context rather than isolating symbols. Stern (2002) contends that studies of metaphor need to filter the meanings that have high contextual salience through schemas that combine valence, prior familiarity and facets of resemblance. Analysts also need to decipher the schemas of relevant organizational groups, particularly their polysemic interpretations of symbols.

Our analysis of the reflective orientation also reveals an imbalance within resonance tropes and between resonance and dissonance tropes. In particular, there is a paucity of organizational research on metonymy, synecdoche and irony. In a 'postmodern world characterized by rapid changes and fragmentation' (Putnam et al., 1999, p. 138), dissonance tropes offer an escape from the positivist dogma that pervades organizational life. Consequently, the use of intentional as well as situational irony seems central to a critical management agenda of 'subversion' (Hutcheon, 1994) and 'transgression' (Stallybrass & White, 1986).

To summarize, organizational scholars need to move beyond the relative comfort and security of 'imposed resonance' engendered through 'safe abstractions'.

If we are to make sense of the complex, turbulent and plurivocal world in which we live, we need to engage actively with dissonance tropes (i.e., 'intentional irony' and 'situational irony') and challenge taken-for-granted metaphors by exposing 'tropes in use'.

NOTE

1 We are primarily concerned in this chapter with the way tropes function as discursive devices to constitute organizational phenomena. While recognizing the fundamental importance of tropes to social construction, we do not directly address the philosophical issues raised by Lakoff and Johnson (1999) in their analysis of metaphor.

REFERENCES

Akin, G. & Schultheiss, E. (1990) Jazz bands and missionaries – OD through stories and metaphors. *Journal of Managerial Psychology*, 5 (4): 12–18.

Alvesson, M. (1993) The play of metaphors. In John Hassard & Martin Parker (eds), *Postmodernism and organizations* (pp. 114–31). London: Sage.

Anderson, J.W. (1998) The role of the marketplace metaphor in creating gender inequities. *The New Jersey Journal of Communication*, 6 (1): 41–58.

Barrett, F. & Cooperrider, D. (1990) Generative metaphor intervention: A new behavioral approach for working with systems divided by conflict and caught in defensive perception. *Journal of Applied Behavioral Science*, 23 (4): 219–44.

Black, M. (1979) More about metaphor. In Andrew Ortony (ed.), *Metaphor and thought* (pp. 19–41). Cambridge: Cambridge University Press.

Boland, R.J. & Greenberg, R.H. (1988) Metaphorical structuring of organizational ambiguity. In Louis R. Pondy, Richard J. Boland Jr. & Howard Thomas (eds), *Managing ambiguity and change* (pp. 17–36). New York: John Wiley & Sons.

Booth, W.C. (1974) *A rhetoric of irony*. Chicago: University of Chicago Press.

Bourgeois, V.W. & Pinder, C.C. (1983) Contrasting philosophical perspectives in administrative science: A reply to Morgan. *Administrative Science Quarterly*, 28 (4): 608–13.

Brink, T.L. (1993) Metaphor as data in the study of organizations. *Journal of Management Inquiry*, 2 (4): 366–71.

Broekstra, G. (1996) The triune-brain metaphor: The evolution of the living organization. In David Grant & Cliff Oswick (eds), *Metaphor and organization* (pp. 53–73). London: Sage.

Brown, R.H. (1977) *A poetic for sociology*. New York: Cambridge University Press.

Burke, K. (1969a) *A grammar of motives*. Berkeley, CA: University of California Press.

Burke, K. (1969b) *A rhetoric of motives*. Berkeley, CA: University of California Press.

Buzzanell, P.J. & Goldzwig, S.R. (1991) Linear and nonlinear career models. *Management Communication Quarterly*, 4: 466–505.

Cazal, D. & Inns, D. (1998) Metaphor, language, and meaning. In David Grant, Thomas Keenoy & Cliff Oswick (eds), *Discourse and organization* (pp. 177–92). London: Sage.

Clark, T. & Salaman, G. (1996) The use of metaphor in the client–consultant relationship: A study of management consultants. In Cliff Oswick & David Grant (eds), *Organization development: Metaphorical explorations* (pp. 154–74). London: Pitman.

Cleary, C. & Packard, T. (1992) The use of metaphors in organizational assessment and change. *Group and Organizational Management*, 17 (3): 229–41.

Clegg, S. & Gray, J. (1996) Metaphors in organizational research: Of embedded embryos, paradigms and powerful people. In David Grant & Cliff Oswick (eds), *Metaphor and organization* (pp. 74–93). London: Sage.

Cohen, M.D., March, J.G. & Olsen, J.P. (1972) A garbage can model of organizational choice. *Administrative Science Quarterly*, 17: 1–25.

Collinson, D. (1988) Engineering humor: Masculinity, joking and conflict in shop-floor relations. *Organization Studies*, 9: 181–99.

D'Angelo, F.J. (1987) Prolegomena to a rhetoric of tropes. *Rhetoric Review*, 6 (1): 32–40.

D'Angelo, F.J. (1992) The four master tropes: Analogues of development. *Rhetoric Review*, 11 (1): 91–107.

Deetz, S.A. (1986) Metaphors and the discursive production and reproduction of organizations. In Lee Thayer (ed.), *Organization–communication: Emerging perspectives* (pp. 168–82). Norwood, NJ: Ablex.

de Man, P. (1978) The epistemology of metaphor. In S. Sacks (ed.), *On metaphor*. Chicago: Chicago University Press.

Duncan, W.J., Smeltzser, L.R. & Leap, T.L. (1990) Humor and work: Applications of joking behavior to management. *Journal of Management*, 16 (2): 255–78.

Dunford, R. & Palmer, I. (1996) Metaphors in popular management discourse: The case of corporate restructuring. In David Grant & Cliff Oswick (eds), *Metaphor and organization* (pp. 95–109). London: Sage.

Dunn, S. (1990) Root metaphor in the old and new industrial relations. *British Journal of Industrial Relations*, 28: 1–31.

Foucault, M. (1977) *The archaeology of knowledge*. London: Tavistock.

Gentner, D. (1983) Structure mapping: A theoretical framework for analogy. *Cognitive Science*, 7: 155–70.

Gibbs, R.W. (1993) Process and products in making sense of tropes. In Andrew Ortony (ed.), *Metaphor and thought* (2nd edition, pp. 252–76). Cambridge: Cambridge University Press.

Gibbs, R.W. (1996) Metaphor as a constraint on text understanding. In B.K. Britton & A.C. Grasesser (eds), *Models of understanding texts* (pp. 215–40). Hillsdale, NJ: Lawrence Erlbaum Associates.

Grant, D. (1996) Metaphors, human resource management and control. In Cliff Oswick & David Grant (eds), *Organizational development: Metaphorical explorations* (pp. 193–208). London: Pitman.

Grant, D. & Oswick, C. (1996) Getting the measure of metaphor. In David Grant & Cliff Oswick (eds), *Metaphor and organization* (pp. 1–20). London: Sage.

Gribas, J. & Downs, C. (2002) Metaphoric manifestations of talking *Team* with team novices. *Communication Studies*, 53: 112–28.

Gross, A.G. (1990) *The rhetoric of science*. Cambridge, MA: Harvard University Press.

Hamilton, P.M. (1997) Rhetorical discourse of local pay. *Organization*, 4 (2): 229–54.

Hamilton, P.M. (2003) The saliency of synecdoche: The part and the whole of employment relations. *Journal of Management Studies*, 40 (7): 1569–85.

Hatch, M.J. (1994) Reading irony in the humor of a management team: Organizational contradictions in context. *Copenhagen Business School – Papers in Organization Series*, No. 17.

Hatch, M.J. (1997) Irony and the social construction of contradiction in the humor of a management team. *Organization Science*, 8 (3): 275–88.

Hatch, M.J. & Ehrich, S. (1993) Spontaneous humor as an indicator of paradox and ambiguity in organizations. *Organization Studies*, 14: 505–26.

Heller, J. (1964) *Catch-22*. London: Transworld Publishers.

Hirsch, P.M. & Andrews, J.A.Y. (1983) Ambushes, shootouts, and knights of the round-table: The language of corporate takeovers. In Louis R. Pondy, Peter J. Frost, Gareth Morgan & Thomas C. Danridge (eds), *Organizational symbolism* (pp. 145–55). Greenwich, CT: JAI Press.

Hopfl, H. & Maddrell, J. (1996) Can you resist a dream? Evangelical metaphors and the appropriation of emotion. In David Grant & Cliff Oswick (eds), *Metaphor and organization* (pp. 200–12). London: Sage.

Hutcheon, L. (1994) *Irony's edge: The theory and politics of irony*. London: Routledge.

Inns, D. (2002). 'Metaphor in the literature of organizational analysis: A preliminary taxonomy and a glimpse at a humanities-based perspective. *Organization*, 9 (2): 305–30.

Johansson, U. & Woodilla, J. (2000) The double dimension of irony: A way both to keep and to change existing reality constructions. Paper presented at the International Conference on Organizational Discourse, London.

Keating, K.E. (1993) Organizational gardening: A metaphor for the new business paradigm. In P. Barrentine (ed.), *When the canary sings: Women's perspectives on transforming business* (pp. 54–70). San Francisco: Berrett-Koehler.

Keeley, M. (1980) Organizational analogy. *Administrative Science Quarterly*, 25 (2): 337–62.

Keenoy, T. & Anthony, P. (1992) HRM: Metaphor, meaning and morality. In P. Blyton & P. Turnbull (eds), *Reassessing HRM* (pp. 233–55). London: Sage.

Keenoy, T., Oswick, C. & Grant, D. (2003) The edge of metaphor. *Academy of Management Review*, 28 (2): 191–2.

Keizer, J.A. & Post, G.J.J. (1996) The metaphoric gap as a catalyst of change. In Cliff Oswick & David Grant (eds), *Organizational development: Metaphorical explorations* (pp. 90–105). London: Pitman.

Kellner, H. (1989) *Language and historical representation: Getting the story crooked*. Madison, WI: University of Wisconsin Press.

Kennedy, G. (1998) *Comparative rhetoric*. Oxford: Oxford University Press.

Kent, M.L. (2001) Managerial rhetoric as the metaphor for the World Wide Web. *Critical Studies in Media Communication*, 18 (3): 359–75.

Keys, P. (1991) Operational research in organizations: A metaphorical analysis. *The Journal of Operational Research Society*, 42 (6): 435–46.

Kierkegaard, S. (1966) *The concept of irony, with constant reference to Socrates*. London: Collins.

Knox, N. (1961) *The word irony and its context, 1500–1755*. Durham, NC: Duke University Press.

Koch, S. & Deetz, S. (1981) Metaphor analysis of social reality in organizations. *Journal of Applied Communication Research*, 9: 1–15.

Krefting, L.A. & Frost, P.J. (1985) Untangling webs, surfacing waves, and wildcatting: A multiple metaphor perspective on managing organizational culture. In Peter J. Frost, Larry F. Moore, Meryl Reis Louis, Craig C. Lundberg & Joanne Martin (eds), *Organizational culture* (pp. 155–68). Beverly Hills, CA: Sage.

Kumra, S. (1996) The organization as a human entity. In Cliff Oswick & David Grant (eds), *Organization development: Metaphorical explorations* (pp. 35–53). London: Pitman.

Kunda, G. (1992) *Engineering culture: Control and commitment in a high-tech corporation*. Philadelphia, PA: Temple University Press.

Lacan, J. (1986) *The four fundamental concepts of psycho-analysis*. Harmondsworth: Peregrine.

Lakoff, G. & Johnson, M. (1980) *Metaphors we live by*. Chicago: University of Chicago Press.

Lakoff, G. & Johnson, M. (1999) *Philosophy in the flesh: The embodied mind and its challenge to western thought*. New York: Basic Books.

Lakoff, G. & Turner, M. (1989) *More than cool reason: A field guide to poetic metaphor*. Chicago: University of Chicago Press.

Lemert, G.C. (1979) *Sociology and the twilight of man*. Carbondale, IL: Southern Illinois University Press.

Levin, S.R. (1993) Language, concepts, and worlds: Three domains of metaphor. In Andrew Ortony (ed.), *Metaphor and thought* (2nd edition, pp. 222–51). Cambridge: Cambridge University Press.

Lucariello, J. (1994) Situational irony: A concept of events gone awry. *Journal of Experimental Psychology/General*, 123 (2): 126–46.

Lynch, O. (2002) Humor as communication: Finding a place for humor in communication research. *Communication Theory*, 12 (4): 423–45.

Mangham, I. (1996) Some consequences of taking Gareth Morgan seriously. In David Grant & Cliff Oswick (eds), *Metaphor and organization* (pp. 21–36). London: Sage.

Mangham, I. & Overington, M. (1987) *Organizations as theatres: A social psychology of dramatic appearances*. Chichester: Wiley.

Manning, P. (1979) Metaphors of the field: Varieties of organizational discourse. *Administrative Science Quarterly*, 24: 660–71.

Marshak, R. (1996) Metaphors, metaphoric fields and organizational change. In David Grant & Cliff Oswick (eds), *Metaphor and organization* (pp. 147–65). London: Sage.

May, S.K. (1993) A communication course in organizational paradigms and metaphors. *Communication Education*, 42: 234–54.

McCloskey, D.N. (1985) *The rhetoric of economics*. Madison, WI: University of Wisconsin Press.

McCloskey, D.N. (1988) The theater of scholarship and the rhetoric of economics. *Southern Humanities Review*, 22: 241–9.

Meyer, J.C. (1997) Humor in member narratives: Uniting and dividing at work. *Western Journal of Communication*, 61 (2): 188–208.

Mitroff, I. (1987) *Business NOT as usual*. San Francisco: Jossey-Bass.

Morcol, G. (1997) The epistemic necessity of using metaphors in organizational theory: A constructivist argument. *Administrative Theory and Praxis*, 19 (1): 43–57.

Morgan, G. (1980) Paradigms, metaphors and puzzle solving in organization theory. *Administrative Science Quarterly*, 25: 605–22.

Morgan, G. (1981) The schismatic metaphor and its implications for organizational analysis. *Organization Studies*, 2 (1): 23–44.

Morgan, G. (1983) More on metaphor: Why we cannot control tropes in administrative science. *Administrative Science Quarterly*, 27: 601–7.

Morgan, G. (1986) *Images of organization*. Beverley Hills, CA: Sage.

Morgan, G. (1989) *Creative organization theory*. Newbury, CA: Sage.

Morgan, G. (1993) *Imaginization: The art of creative management*. London: Sage.

Morgan, G. (1996) Is there anything more to be said about metaphor? In David Grant & Cliff Oswick (eds), *Metaphor and organization* (pp. 227–40). London: Sage.

Morgan, G. (1997) *Images of organizations* (2nd edition). Beverley Hills, CA: Sage.

Muecke, D.C. (1969) *The compass of irony*. London: Methuen.

Muecke, D.C. (1970) *Irony: The critical idiom*. London: Methuen.

Ortony, A. (1975) Why metaphors are necessary and not just nice. *Educational Theory*, 2: 45–53.

Ortony, A. (1993) Metaphor, language and thought. In Andrew Ortony (ed.), *Metaphor and thought* (2nd edition, pp. 1–17). Cambridge: Cambridge University Press.

Oswick, C. (2001a) The globalization of globalization: An analysis of a managerialist trope in action. In J. Biberman & A. Alkhafaji (eds), *The business research yearbook* (Vol. VIII. pp. 522–7). IABD Press.

Oswick, C. (2001b) The etymology of corporate predatorship: A critical commentary. *Journal of Critical Postmodern Organizational Science*, 1 (2): 20–4.

Oswick, C. & Grant, D. (1996a) The organization of metaphors and the metaphors of organization: Where are we and where do we go from here? In David Grant & Cliff Oswick (eds), *Organization and metaphor* (pp. 213–26). London: Sage.

Oswick, C. & Grant, D. (eds) (1996b) *Organization development: Metaphorical explorations*. London: Pitman.

Oswick, C. & Montgomery, J. (1999) Images of an organization: The use of metaphor in a multinational company. *Journal of Organizational Change Management*, 12 (6): 501–23.

Oswick, C., Keenoy, T. & Grant, D. (2002) Metaphors and analogical reasoning in organization theory: Beyond orthodoxy. *Academy of Management Review*, 27 (2): 294–303.

Oswick, C., Keenoy, T. & Grant, D. (2003) More on metaphor: Revisiting analogical reasoning in organization theory. *Academy of Management Review*, 28 (1): 10–12.

Oswick, C., Keenoy, T. & Jones, P. (2003) Rethinking organizational metaphors: Beyond (*M*)*organ*-ization theory. In A.P. Muller & A. Kieser (eds), *Communication in organizations: Structures and practices* (pp. 135–48). Berlin: Peter Lang.

Perren, L. & Atkin, R. (1997) Owner–manager's discourse: The metaphors-in-use. *Journal of Applied Management Studies*, 6 (1): 47–61.

Pinder, C. & Bourgeois, V. (1982) Controlling tropes in administrative science. *Administrative Science Quarterly*, 27: 641–52.

Pondy, L.R. (1983) The role of metaphors and myths in organization and in the facilitation of change. In Louis R. Pondy, Peter J. Frost, Gareth Morgan & Thomas C. Danridge (eds), *Organizational symbolism* (pp. 157–66). Greenwich, CT: JAI Press.

Poole, M.S. & Van de Ven, A. (1989) Using paradox to build management and organization theories. *Academy of Management Review*, 14: 562–78.

Prelli, L.J. (1989) *A rhetoric of science: Inventing scientific discourse*. Columbia, SC: University of South Carolina Press.

Purdy, J. (1998) Age of irony. *American Prospect*, 39: 84–90.

Putnam, L.L. (1986) Contradictions and paradox in organizations. In Lee Thayer (ed.), *Organization-communication: Emerging perspectives* (pp. 151–67). Norwood, NJ: Ablex.

Putnam, L.L. (2004) Dialectical tensions and rhetorical tropes in negotiations. *Organization Studies*, 25 (1): 35–53.

Putnam, L.L., Phillips, N. & Chapman, P. (1996) Metaphors of communication and organization. In Stewart Clegg, Cynthia Hardy & Walter Nord (eds), *Handbook of organizational studies* (pp. 375–408). London: Sage.

Putnam, L.L., Phillips, N. & Chapman, P. (1999) Metaphors of communication and organization. In S. Clegg, C. Hardy & W. Nord (eds), *Managing organizations: Current issues* (pp. 125–58). London: Sage.

Reed, M. (1990) From paradigms to images: The paradigm warrior turns post-modern guru. *Personnel Review*, 19: 35–40.

Rodrigues, S.B. & Collinson, D.L. (1995) Having fun?: Humour as resistance in Brazil. *Organization Studies*, 16 (5): 739–68.

Rorty, R. (1989) *Contingency, irony and solidarity*. Cambridge: Cambridge University Press.

Sabrosky, A.N., Thompson, J.C. & McPherson, K.A. (1982) Organized anarchies: Military bureaucracy in the 1980s. *Journal of Applied Behavioral Science*, 18 (2): 137–53.

Sackmann, S. (1989) The role of metaphors in organization transformation. *Human Relations*, 42 (6): 463–85.

Schön, D. (1993) Generative metaphor: A perspective on problem setting in social policy. In Andrew Ortony (ed.), *Metaphor and thought* (2nd edition, pp. 135–61). Cambridge: Cambridge University Press.

Searle, J.R. (1993) Metaphor. In Andrew Ortony (ed.), *Metaphor and thought* (2nd edition, pp. 83–111). Cambridge: Cambridge University Press.

Sedgewick, G.G. (1935) *Of irony, especially in drama*. Toronto: University of Toronto Press.

Selfridge, R.J. & Sokolik, S.L. (1975) A comprehensive view of organization development. *Business Topics*, Winter: 10–14.

Shockley-Zalabak, P. (2002) Protean places: Teams across time and space. *Journal of Applied Communication Research*, 30 (3): 231–50.

Sim, S. (2002) *Irony and crisis: A critical history of postmodern culture*. Cambridge: Icon Books.

Smith, J.M. (1996) Geographical rhetoric: Modes and tropes of appeal. *Annals of the Association of American Geographers*, 86 (1): 1–20.

Smith, K. & Simmons, V. (1983) A Rumpelstiltskin organization: Metaphors on metaphors in field research. *Administrative Science Quarterly*, 28 (3): 377–92.

Smith, R.C. & Eisenberg, E.M. (1987) Conflict at Disneyland: A root-metaphor analysis. *Communication Monographs*, 54: 367–80.

Smith, R.C. & Turner, P. (1995) A social constructionist reconfiguration of metaphor analysis: An application of *SCMA* to organizational socialization theorizing. *Communication Monographs*, 62: 152–81.

Stallybrass, P. & White, A. (1986) *The politics and poetics of transgression*. London: Methuen.

Stern, J. (2000) *Metaphor in context*. Oxford and New York: Oxford University Press.

Stohl, C. (1995) *Organizational communication: Connectedness in action*. Thousand Oaks, CA: Sage.

Stutman, R.K. & Putnam, L.L. (1994) The consequences of language: A metaphorical look at the legalization of organizations. In Sim B. Sitkin & Robert J. Bies (eds), *The legalistic organization* (pp. 281–302). Thousand Oaks, CA: Sage.

Tietge, D.J. (1998) The role of Burke's four master tropes in scientific expression. *Journal of Technical Writing and Communication*, 28 (3): 317–24.

Tinker, T. (1986) Metaphor or reification: Are radical humanists really libertarian anarchists? *Journal of Management Studies*, 25: 363–84.

Trethewey, A. (1999) Isn't it ironic: Using irony to explore the contradictions of organizational life. *Western Journal of Communication*, 63 (2): 140–67.

Tsoukas, H. (1991) The missing link: A transformational view of metaphors in organizational science. *Academy of Management Review*, 16 (3): 566–85.

Tsoukas, H. (1993a) Analogical reasoning and knowledge generation in organization theory. *Organization Studies*, 14: 323–46.

Tsoukas, H. (1993b) Organizations as soap bubbles: An evolutionary perspective. *Systems Practice*, 6 (5): 501–15.

Vinton, K.L. (1989) Humor in the workplace is more than telling jokes. *Small Group Behavior*, 20: 151–66.

Watson, T.J. (1995) Rhetoric, discourse. and argument in organizational sensemaking: A reflexive tale. *Organization Studies*, 16 (5): 805–21.

Weick, K.E. (1979) *The social psychology of organizing* (2nd edition). Reading, MA: Addison-Wesley.

Weick, K.E. (1995) *Sensemaking in organizations*. Thousand Oaks, CA: Sage.

Westenholz, A. (1993) Paradoxical thinking and change in the frames of reference. *Organization Studies*, 14: 37–58.

White, H. (1978) *Tropics of discourse*. Baltimore, MD: Johns Hopkins University Press.

Winner, E. & Gardner, H. (1993) Metaphor and irony: Two levels of understanding. In Andrew Ortony (ed.), *Metaphor and thought* (2nd edition, pp. 425–55). Cambridge: Cambridge University Press.

Yanow, D. (1992) Supermarkets and culture clash: The epistemological role of metaphors in administrative practice. *The American Review of Public Administration*, 22 (2): 89–109.

Part II

METHODS AND PERSPECTIVES

5

Organizational Language in Use: Interaction Analysis, Conversation Analysis and Speech Act Schematics

Gail T. Fairhurst and François Cooren

The popularity of discourse to the study of organizations has grown in recent years (Alvesson & Kärreman, 2000a, 2000b; Grant et al., 1998; Putnam & Fairhurst, 2001). Part of the fascination derives from the fact that organizational discourse analysts are not just concerned with what is *discursive about organizations*; they are also concerned with what is *organizing about discourse*. A concern with the former reinforces the conception of discourse as a modifying feature of an already formed organization (Cooren & Taylor, 1997; Fairhurst & Putnam, 2004). This view is not necessarily incorrect, but it eludes questions about the dynamic processes of the organization. Because people exchange messages and only messages, how can we explain the origin and maintenance of an organization in the absence of discourse? As Hawes (1974) suggested, how do organizations organize in the first place, continue to stay organized, and sometimes un-organize?

As discourse analysts ponder these questions, the fundamentally organizing nature of discourse begins to reveal itself. Analysts pay particular attention to the ways that organizational members orient to one another through discourse: in speech acts such as requests versus commands that signal relational differences (Cooren, 2001a); in membership categorizations like 'boss' or 'employee' that confer high or low status (Boden, 1994); in powerful versus powerless speech forms (e.g., interruptions, hesitations, non-fluencies, forms of address) and turn-taking patterns that signal dominance or submission (Fairhurst, 1993); through narrative structures that hierarchically organize action into embedded sub-routines (Cooren, 2001a; Taylor & Van Every, 2000); and in constellations of talk, ideas and assumptions that form power/ knowledge systems related to the construction of key organizational roles (du Gay et al., 1996; Knights & Wilmott,

1992). In studies such as these, discourse becomes a building block – the very foundation upon which organizational life is built.

Many scholars who study the organizing properties of discourse frame organizations as discursive constructions (e.g., Alvesson & Kärreman, 2000a; Boden, 1994; Cooren & Taylor, 1997), although such framing is subject to a variety of interpretations. According to Fairhurst and Putnam (2004), the organization can be conceptualized: (1) as an already formed object with discursive features or outcomes; (2) in a state of becoming *vis-à-vis* the organizing properties of discourse; or (3) as grounded in action, anchored in social practices amd discursive forms. Conceptions of organizational discourse also vary from language in use and interaction process to general and enduring systems of ideas in historically situated time (Alvesson & Kärreman, 2000b). The former focuses on the study of talk and text in social practices, whereas the latter emphasizes the powerful forces that reside beyond the text (e.g., through power/ knowledge relations that become established in culturally standardized discourse [Foucault, 1976, 1980]).

This chapter focuses on the study of talk and text in social practices, specifically the organizing potential of language in use. Despite the merits of broader conceptions of discourse, the organizing properties of language hold the key to understanding how social structure is locally and practically achieved (Garfinkel, 1967). As Boden wrote: 'When people talk, they are simultaneously and reflexively talking their relationships, organizations, and whole institutions into action or into "being"' (1994, p. 14). Issues of power, status, affect and affiliation are continuously worked out in an interaction process through such patterns as turn-taking and floor dominance, but also in language choices that frame and focus attention, categorize and signal similarity or difference, link and transfer properties, and/or perform actions. It is through the ordering properties of discourse that organizations come to life as processes of organizing.

Our goal in this chapter is to examine three discursive approaches – interaction analysis, conversation analysis and speech act schematics – to determine what is 'organizational' in their discursive forms. A host of other approaches focus on language in use (e.g., linguistics, sociolinguistics, content analysis, literary analyses, textual analyses), yet remain less influential perhaps because they tend to downplay the organizational context (Keenoy et al., 1997; Putnam & Fairhurst, 2001). Interaction analysis, conversation analysis and speech act schematics all combine an interest in linguistic form; yet, they focus on context and discourse as action in different ways. They have different analytic foci and different assumptions about the link between discourse and organization. Far more than methodological choices, they also embrace diverse theoretical positions, each offering a unique lens with which to view organizational life. Our goal is to preserve the analytic integrity of each perspective and highlight its distinctive contribution to understanding the organizing properties of discourse.

We begin with interaction analysis, which pays particular attention to the nature of sequence and temporal form in interaction systems. Next we examine conversation analysis, which examines the social organization of talk-in-interaction and how it enables individuals to make sense of their worlds. Finally, we discuss speech act schematics, which focuses on the performative character of language and its episodic ordering. We conclude with an analysis of a police radio transcript that facilitates comparison across these three perspectives.

INTERACTION ANALYSIS

Interaction analysis (IA) involves the categorization of discourse units according to a predefined set of codes (Bakeman & Gottman, 1986). It is a quantitative approach to discourse analysis that draws from message functions and language structures to assess the frequency and types of verbal interaction. Particular emphasis is given to the sequences and stages of interaction, their redundancy and predictability, and the links between interactional structures and the organizational context (Putnam & Fairhurst, 2001). As such, analysis of interaction is temporal through forms or patterns of ongoing message exchange (Gottman, 1982). Interaction analysts are particularly interested in mapping long chains of behaviour, examining more inclusive levels of temporal form and depicting the general nature or shape of an interaction (Holmes & Rogers, 1995).

The organizational IA literature clusters into five groups of studies that often differ in their observational mode (real-time observation, time-sampling or coding from tapes and transcripts); unit of analysis (speaking turn, thought unit, speech act; act, interact, double interact; act-to-act or phase); study design (simulation or naturally occurring conversation); length of interactions studied (20 minutes or more); nature of the coding scheme (a priori or derived from the data); type of coding required (univocal or multifunctional); type of analysis (distributional or sequential); and theoretical base (e.g., systems or structuration theories) (Fairhurst, 2004). In the following discussion, a sample of the research from each area is reviewed.

Among the earliest interaction analyses are those based on Bales' (1950) *Interaction Process Analysis*. This was a coding scheme for analysing the task/instrumental and socio-emotional/expressive functions of group communication and served as a forerunner to organizational studies on autocratic and democratic leader behaviours (Keyton & Wall, 1989; Sargent & Miller, 1971). *Behaviorist studies* are a second type of IA, ones that draw from reinforcement theory and the principles of operant conditioning to assess the impact of leader monitoring on work unit performance and managerial effectiveness (Gioia & Sims, 1986; Gioia et al., 1989; Komaki, 1986, 1998; Sims & Manz, 1984).

Negotiation research forms a third approach, utilizing IA to study the stages or phases of negotiations, message patterns or sequences of bargaining tactics, and the enactment of rules and norms in this context (Bednar & Curington, 1983; Donohue, 1981a, 1981b; Donohue et al., 1984; Olekalns et al., 1996; Putnam, 1990; Putnam & Jones, 1982; Weingart, Prietula et al., 1999; Weingart, Thompson et al., 1990). This research is heavily weighted towards understanding the effects of bargaining tactics, strategies and sequences on distributive versus integrative outcomes.

Adaptive Structuration Theory (AST) utilizes an interpretive form of interaction analysis to study the mutual influence of technology (e.g., Group Decision Support Systems) and social processes on organizational change. Drawing from Giddens (1979, 1984), DeSanctis and Poole (1994) and Poole and DeSanctis (1992) document the ways that structures arise from and occur within the discourse, demonstrating how groups' appropriation of the same technology can yield differential results (see also DeSanctis et al., 1992; Poole et al., 1991; Zigurs et al., 1988).

Finally, *systems-interactional* research, a fifth type of IA, draws from systems theory (Bateson, 1972; Watzlawick et al., 1967) to focus on control in routine work interaction. To discern control patterns, researchers adopt relational coding where each turn at talk is coded as to whether it asserts, accepts or neutralizes the control move of the previous utterance (e.g., Ellis, 1979; Rogers & Farace, 1975). Several studies demonstrate the deleterious effects of excessive dominance by one person, usually the manager or authority, and the positive outcomes associated with shared control (Courtright et al., 1989; Fairhurst et al., 1995; Glauser & Tullar, 1985; Tullar, 1989; Walther, 1995; Watson, 1982; Watson-Dugan, 1989).

In summary, interaction analysis typically examines organizational constructs such as leadership, strategies and tactics of negotiation, and faithful or unfaithful appropriations of technology as they evolve from communication systems. Especially for AST and systems-interactional research, what constitutes a 'system' can be a relationship, an organization or an institution. All are predicated on the view that systems emerge over repeated interactions that evolve into multi-level orders of pattern (Bateson, 1972). However, most interaction analyses focus on relational processes in which an organization is cast as an already formed entity whose features constrain relationships (Fairhurst, 2004).

As one approach to language in use, IA has been criticized for proliferating category systems, relying on a priori categories, and specifying and categorizing the meanings of utterances that are more ephemeral, malleable and negotiable than coding schemes allow (Firth, 1995; Gronn, 1982). Conversation analysis, in turn, moves away from coding schemes and assigned meanings to actors' meanings as interactional accomplishments.

CONVERSATION ANALYSIS

Like interaction analysis, conversation analysis (CA) has an abiding interest in sequential and temporal form. Unlike interaction analysis, CA eschews any a priori analytic concepts like relational control, arguing instead that actors' talk-in-interaction must first establish its relevance (Pomerantz & Fehr, 1997). CA focuses on the detailed organization of talk-in-interaction, but its main purpose is to discern how people use various interactional methods and procedures to produce their activities and make sense of their worlds (Sacks, 1984). The interpretive practices and competencies of actors in 'the-world-as-it-happens' (Boden, 1990) mark both CA and ethnomethodology, from which CA draws much of its theoretical framework (Atkinson & Heritage, 1984; Drew & Heritage, 1992; Psathas, 1979; Sudnow, 1970).

Several CA studies analyse profit-based corporations, although work is expanding to include education, courts, social welfare agencies, service encounters, media, negotiations and medical settings (e.g., Atkinson, 1984; Clayman, 1992; Firth, 1994; Hutchby, 1996; Peräkylä, 1995). This work clusters into five areas – conversational openings and closings, turn-taking, adjacency pairs, topic shifts, and disclaimers and alignments.

Conversational openings and closings attend to the initial and final statements of an interaction. Research in hospital settings reveals that spatial positioning, word choice and ambiguity play a critical role in shaping identities and managing impressions (Pomerantz et al., 1997). In a study of conversational closings in job interviews, summaries, positive statements, and interactional continuity helped recruiters manage impressions of their companies (Ragan, 1983).

Studies of *turn-taking* and floor dominance reveal that bargainers manipulate speech rate, hesitations, volume and interruptions to gain control of the floor, signal agreements (Neu, 1988), and set agendas, give reports and make decisions in organizational meetings (Boden, 1994; Gronn, 1983). Turn-taking is also a manifestation of power, particularly by male supervisors who talk longer and interrupt their colleagues more often than do female supervisors (James & Clarke, 1993; Kennedy & Camden, 1983; Woods, 1988).

Adjacency pairs refer to message/response sequences that occur in a predictable manner such as question/answer, request/acceptance or demand/response. Studies of emergency response calls examine question/answer pairs as dispatchers attempt to elicit information, manage emotions and routinize the crisis (Whalen & Zimmerman, 1987; Whalen et al., 1988; Zimmerman, 1984, 1992a, 1992b).

Typically seen as a way to control interaction, *topic shifts* refer to changes in the themes or subject matter from one utterance to the next. Research reveals that male physicians use topic shifts to exert control in decision-making (Ainsworth-Vaughn, 1992), while organizational mediators use them to reduce emotional outbursts and move disputants towards settlements (Frances, 1986; Greatbatch & Dingwall, 1994).

Finally, *disclaimers* qualify the force of an utterance through the use of meta-talk, hedges, tag questions and qualifiers. They function as feedback strategies aimed at avoiding conversational breakdowns, reducing expert power and credibility, softening criticism, maintaining social distance and facilitating group discussion (Adkins & Brasher, 1995; Dubois & Crouch, 1975; Holmes, 1984; Preisler, 1986). Similar to disclaimers, *alignments* refer to the way that speakers use formulations, meta-talk, accounts and side sequences to buffer or anticipate disruptions, clarify misunderstandings, convey intentions and repair conversations (Fisher & Groce, 1990; Morris, 1988; Ragan, 1983; Ragan & Hopper, 1981; Stokes & Hewitt, 1976).

For conversation analysts, the organization is literally 'talked into being' (Boden, 1994; Heritage, 1997; Tulin, 1997).[1] Its social structure is an ongoing production; hierarchy is an interactional accomplishment created by the asymmetries of talk and conversational procedures (Molotch & Boden, 1985). Such procedures may include: *turn-taking*, the procedures of which transform individual actions into collective achievements; *membership categorization* that flexibly groups people, objects or activities, thereby delimiting organizational boundaries; *agenda-setting* that translates the organizationally abstract into going concerns; and *decision-making* that surfaces in finely laminated strips of interaction that only retrospectively look like decisions (Boden, 1994). Unlike interaction analysts who see the organization *qua* system emerging in the patterns of joint action, conversation analysts treat organizations as enactments that arise through a laminated accounting process. In this process, actors draw from past circumstances, rules and other structural forms to account for their behaviour. Each selective orientation to the past made relevant in the here and now laminates or layers upon the other as conversations unfold. Organizations surface from this laminated accounting process in which the global, enduring and structural collapse into the immediacy of action in a self-organizing system of relevancies (Boden, 1994).

Like all conversation analysts, Boden (1994) maintains indifference towards the macro–micro distinction, preferring to focus on social practices and the primacy of text (Cooren & Fairhurst, 2002a). Yet, it is this unconditional attention to text that many see as a restricted view of the context, one that calls into question the assumptive basis of talk-in-action. Haslett (1987) and van Dijk (cited in Titscher et al., 2000) question what belongs to the text itself and what resides beyond the text, given that so much within a text is implied or presupposed. This assumption leads to a number of inferential leaps in conversational analysis, not the least of which is a greater role for analyst assigned meanings than is typically acknowledged, a similarity shared with speech act schematics.

SPEECH ACT SCHEMATICS

Initiated by Austin (1962, 1975) and formalized by Searle (1969, 1979, 1989), speech act theory contends that discourse should be analysed for its capacity to create new states of affairs. In this approach, language is *performative* in that words such as 'promising', 'baptizing', 'ordering' or 'apologizing' perform particular actions. Speech act theorists set forth six categories or types of action: assertives, directives, commissives, declaratives, expressives and accreditives (Cooren, 2001a; Searle, 1979; Vanderveken, 1990–91). However, the majority of organizational studies focus on directives or efforts to bring a state of affairs into existence (Donohue & Diez, 1985; Jones, 1992; Linde, 1988; Murray, 1987).

Early speech act research treated a speaker's motives and intentions as evolving from what was said, thereby neglecting the interpretive role of the listener. However, when speech acts are examined within the context of their use, intentions become an effect of the speech act, not a precursor (Cooren & Taylor, 1997; Taylor, 1993, 1995). From this premise, a second speech act tradition, speech act schematics (SAS), examines the larger episodic or schematic forms that arise from stringing speech acts together. Using Greimas's (1987) narratology, Cooren (2001a) and Taylor and Van Every (2000) summarize the different phases of an episode constituted by speech acts. Specific categories of speech acts constitute the opening of schemas (directives, assertives), their enactment (commissives, accreditives, assertives) and their closure (expressives). The closure of episodes makes it possible to *embed* them in larger schematic forms, which analysts then seek to explain. For this reason, researchers who employ SAS never analyse episodes from an a priori structure because organizing processes are subject to bifurcation, diversion or disruption.

Scholars have used SAS to study coalition-building strategies during ecological controversies (Cooren 2001b; Cooren & Taylor, 2000), the management of public town council meetings (Robichaud, 1998, 2001), a company vision and diverse employee interests (Cooren & Fairhurst, 2002b), corporate board meetings (Taylor & Lerner, 1996), computerization processes (Groleau & Cooren, 1998; Taylor et al., 2001), and parliamentary commissions (Cooren & Taylor, 1998).

In SAS, the organizing capacity of discourse reveals itself in the ways that speech acts are sequenced and episodes are embedded in talk. Taylor (1995) and Cooren (2001a) show how organizations are built and rebuilt through speech agency, whether through speech acts performed by organizational members or organizational texts (memos, rules, policies, contracts, etc.). Thus, the organization is tantamount to its organizing processes. The main criticism of this approach stems from its reliance on a model of language (speech act theory) that lacks empirical grounding (Levinson, 1983; Schegloff, 1988). Other critics claim that organizations as material entities cannot be reduced to the discursive, as some interpretations of SAS imply (Fairclough, 1992, 1995; Reed, 2000). However, this criticism is countered by less radical forms of SAS in which scholars acknowledge materiality through the recognition of non-human agency (Cooren, 2001a; Cooren & Taylor, 2000). Using these overviews, we now develop an exemplar by using these approaches to analyse an organizational episode.

ANALYSES OF A POLICE RADIO TRANSCRIPT

To illustrate the three language in use approaches, we analysed a police radio transcript. The transcript depicts the 1998 shooting of a 23-year-old Cincinnati, Ohio (USA) police officer, Katie Conway, by a 41-year-old male assailant who hijacked her cruiser. Although the officer was shot four times with a .357 Magnum handgun, she returned fire, killing the suspect with her gun. The transcript describes the officer's initial panicked call for help when the assailant was still in control of her cruiser, the police dispatcher's efforts to identify her location, and conversations with other officers who sought to assist her. The four minute and fifteen second transcript is a self-contained example of communication within a high reliability organization (HRO), one whose goal is to resist performance failures in police emergency response calls (Weick & Sutcliffe, 2001; Weick et al., 1999). A complete copy of the transcript appears in the appendix.

Due to space limitations, we can only highlight the organizing potential of language in use for each approach rather than dwell on specific methods or analysis.

Interaction analysis

Systems-interaction, the first approach, is a form of interaction analysis utilizing relational control coding. The Rogers and Farace (1975) coding scheme examines the control aspects of relationships by examining how people establish rights that define and direct the relationship. The focus of this scheme is in the form of an utterance. Although content is expected to vary widely, the form of a person's utterance, its 'command' (Bateson, 1951) or 'relationship' aspects (Watzlawick et al., 1967), are thought to produce relatively fixed and reproducible patterns. The coding scheme assigns a 'one-up' move to messages that exert control, a 'one-down' move to messages that accept or request control, and a 'one-across' move to non-demanding or levelling messages. The assignment of a specific code is heavily dependent upon the communicative context created by the previous utterance as the coding scheme captures both the grammatical form of an utterance (e.g., assertion, question, talkover) and the response to the previous message (e.g., support, non-support, extension, answer, instruction, order). The coding process begins with a series of translated texts from event to recording, recording to written transcript, and written to coded transcript. Coding moves from a single utterance to a two-unit utterance–response to larger sequential patterns in the interaction.

The analysis of the police radio transcript assumes that this particular call is just one of many that would be analysed in order to calculate coding scheme reliability and employ stochastic methods like lag sequential or Markov chain analysis. Systems-interactionists would analyse the control patterns that constitute the relationship between police officers and their dispatcher, patterns that are critical to assessing the dynamics of HROs under crisis conditions. In manufacturing firms, relational analyses reveal an extremely high number of one-across control moves (Courtright et al., 1989; Fairhurst et al., 1995), but such patterns could prove fatal in a crisis in which leaders need to coordinate a timely rescue through controlling the situation (Ansari, 1990). In addition, the dispatcher, a non-police officer, plays the facilitator role with multiple officers with whom she interacts. Since an authority structure exists, well-defined control patterns should emerge in this crisis situation.

We focus specifically on the role of the dispatcher (because on-scene police interactions are face to face and not radioed), and we demonstrate how she enacts her subordinate role. Basically, she defers to police supervisors (Police ↑ Dispatcher ↓, .44) more frequently than they do to her (D ↑ P ↓, .11), she never challenges an officer (P ↑ D ↑ or D ↑ P ↑, .00), and she engages in little discussion (D → P → .00, P → D → .12). She also plays a key role in eliciting information and confirming its receipt. When these moves are sequenced with the questions and acknowledgements of the police officers, a submissive symmetry pattern of successive one-down moves (↓↓↓ or more) emerges. The need to acknowledge ('Copy 1627 Central'), assist ('Car 15 responding'), question ('Is homicide responding?'), and confirm ('I'm notifying now') occurs in this submissive pattern as the following examples reveal:

91	**Disp**:	Copy 1627 Central	↓	
92		(1.0)		
93	**1215**:	Car 15 responding	↓	↓↓
94		(1.0)		
95	**Disp**:	Car 15 copy.	↓	↓↓↓
101	**1230**:	Get the aircare to stand by. And we have the	↑	
102		night chief responding		
103		(0.5)		
104	**Disp:**	The night chief is responding	↓	↑↓
105	**1230**:	Is homicide responding?	↓	↑↓↓
106		(2.5)		
107	**Disp**:	I'm notifying now.	↓	↑↓↓↓
108	**???**:	Ok, so do you know who might have done this?	↓	↑↓↓↓↓

Submissive symmetry plays an instrumental role in eliciting information and building sufficient redundancy to avoid error in the coordination of messages from multiple officers. This finding parallels the way redundancy operates in various forms (e.g., duplication, back-ups, cross-checking) in HROs to guard against simplification, complacency and missed information (Weick et al., 1999). As the submissive symmetry and other patterns demonstrate, the appeal of IA is based on the centrality of control to organizing and the ability to examine its enactment via temporal processes and the patternedness of messages.

Conversation analysis

Like interaction analysis, conversational analysis (CA) deals with transcripts of talk-in-interaction. Unlike interaction analysis, CA's transcripts are extremely detailed with markings for pronunciations, pauses, intonations and talkovers. CA is also characterized by 'unmotivated looking', which means that researchers let the data speak for itself versus analysing it through an a priori set of categories (Psathas, 1995). Such an analysis reveals Conway's role shift from victim to police officer. To understand this role shift, we drew from the rich tradition of CA work analysing 911 emergency assistance calls to the police (Whalen & Zimmerman, 1987, 1998; Whalen et al., 1988; Zimmerman, 1984, 1992a, 1992b). Of particular interest in both 911 calls and this police radio call is the need to disregard the stressful circumstances and routinize the emergency, in this instance, by collecting needed information as efficiently as possible in order to activate police support and emergency services. This is exactly what the dispatcher does by immediately launching into the interrogative series (lines 3, 8,10) in response to Conway's hysteria[2] and break from protocol in communicating with the dispatcher.[3] However, unlike 911 calls, *all* parties to the police radio traffic are trained to routinize emergencies as members of the same HRO. Indeed, Conway routinizes her own emergency at lines 25–26 and 33, as compared to her displays of hysteria at lines 1, 4 and 7.

1	**Cy**:	Help! I need assistance! I'm shot in the (car)!
2		(2.0)
3	**Disp**:	<u>Where</u> do you need it?
4	**Cy**:	Help! I need help!
5		(1.5)
6	**1030**:	1238 Elm. I believe, 1030, I believe I heard shots fired there.
7	**Cy**:	[((Unintelligible screaming)) please!
8	**Disp**:	[-Location?
9		(1.0)
10	**Disp**:	1212, what's your location?
11		(6.5)
24	**Disp**:	1212, what's your location?
25	**Cy**:	Distress. I've been involved in a shooting (0.3) on Central
26		Parkway (0.5) north (.) of Liberty. I need some help hhh
31	**Disp**:	1212, are you hurt?
32		(0.3)
33	**Cy**:	That's affirmative.

Conway's displays of hysteria (lines 1, 4, 7) come in the midst of struggling with her assailant, but by line 24 when the dispatcher again asks for her location, Conway has shot and killed the assailant. Conway answers, but not before prefacing it with a membership category (Sacks, 1992), consistent with her training.[4] Conway uses the word 'distress', as in 'distress call', a category used by the police to typify emergencies requiring immediate assistance. In much calmer tones and slower speech rate, Conway then answers the dispatcher's question about her location and repeats her request for help. The attempt by Conway to routinize her own emergency is all the more striking because she has been shot four times. Conway thus switches from the role of victim (lines 1, 4 and 7) to police officer (lines 25–26), which continues when she answers, 'That's affirmative' to a yes/no question from the dispatcher regarding her condition (lines 31–33).

Why is Conway's use of conventional police vernacular so critical in this HRO? Perhaps because HROs must have a commitment to resilience, which includes both the ability to bounce back from errors and cope with surprises (Weick et al., 1999). One mark of successful HRO police training is to gauge the point of Conway's role shift, which signals *her* routinization of this emergency to fellow officers. Finally, for CA, this example powerfully reflects how the institutional setting introduces itself as a practical matter – in the way it is oriented to, and made relevant in, the interaction by actors who will hold each other accountable for displaying contextually sensitive actions (Heritage, 1997; Zimmerman, 1992a).

Speech act schematics

In contrast to the previous approaches, SAS examines the organizing effects of different speech acts performed during an episode. To illustrate, consider lines 10–25 from the police radio transcript. What is 'organizing' or 'structuring' in this interaction? First, the dispatcher's question (line 10: '1212, what's your location?' a directive according to Searle's classification) creates a *tension* that is only resolved when Conway answers the question (lines 25–26: 'Distress. I've been involved in a shooting (0.3) on Central Parkway (0.5) north (.) of Liberty', which is an assertive). Similarly, Conway's response that she is in distress and needs help opens a schema within which other talk sequences can be *inserted* or *embedded*. Moreover, each opening determines more or less clearly what will count as a closure or the end of the sequence. For example, the fact that Conway answers the question (lines 25–26) counts as closure for the sequence that the dispatcher previously opened (line 10). On the issue of location, the matter becomes closed because the dispatcher now knows where Conway is, which was the object of her questions (lines 3, 10 and 24). Similarly, Conway's response opens up another sequence that, in turn, will close when she receives some help. Sequences are not always as short as these, but it is in their extension that organizing occurs through insertions.

To illustrate, consider the beginning of this excerpt. From the initial moment of Conway's distress call (line 1: 'Help, I need assistance! I'm shot in the (car)!'), participants are oriented towards resolving the tension that Conway introduces. In effect, Conway's initial distress call sets up the conditions for the active coordination of each participant's behaviour. For example, the dispatcher's question on line 3 ('Where do you need it?') makes sense because it is inserted within the logic of the sequence that Conway initiates. Committed to the resolution of Conway's distressful situation, the dispatcher must know Conway's location in order to send help. This question then opens up a sequence that does not end until lines 25–26 when Conway is finally able to respond.

Meanwhile, two other attempts help the dispatcher close the sequence that she opened on line 3. The first one is Officer 1030's speculation on line 6 as to Conway's whereabouts ('1238 Elm. I believe…'). By proposing a location, Officer 1030 tries to close the sequence that Conway opened. However, before the dispatcher can acknowledge this contribution, Conway screams again, thus leading the dispatcher to repeat her location question (lines 8–10). Regardless of whether or not the dispatcher could respond to Officer 1030, the insertion of 1030's contribution into the sequence remains problematic since it does not come from Conway. Line 14 reinforces this point when the dispatcher responds, 'Negative', to Officer 1080's inquiry about Conway's location.

Note, however, that the dispatcher uses 1030's speculation when she makes her first county-wide announcement at lines 16–18. The location is declared unknown, but she provides Officer 1030's information about Conway's possible location. Three seconds later, this speculation is rejected when Officer 1080 reports that Conway is not located on 12th and Elm (line 20). The sequence is still open when a second attempt to close it occurs when Officer 1240 asks the dispatcher to play the tape back (see line 22). The implication is that the dispatcher and officers may have missed something that could lead to Conway's whereabouts. However, the dispatcher does not acknowledge this directive. Instead, she reiterates her question to Conway (line 24: '1212, what's your location'), who finally responds (lines 25–26: 'Distress. I've been involved in a shooting…').

As this brief analysis illustrates, speech acts open and close sequences that can be inserted into each other, thus shaping the organizing of action. Each speech act category enacts part of an episode, such as the dispatcher's directive initiated in the above example. Interestingly, this analysis also illustrates HROs' commitment to resilience (Weick & Sutcliffe, 2001). Through ordered improvisation, the police officers and dispatcher maintain the objectives of the intervention (they all consistently orient to Conway's location and final rescue), while innovating ways to achieve such results.

CONCLUSION

As the foregoing discussion reveals, interaction analysis, conversation analysis and speech act schematics share some common themes: a bottom-up or constructed view of the organization, a view of language in use as inherently organizing, and an emphasis on sequence and temporal form. However, these three approaches offer a rich diversity of perspectives on each of these themes.

For example, even though all three approaches see organizations as discursive constructions, the status of the 'the organization' varies widely. Interaction analysts assert that the organization emerges in the patterned regularity of interaction. However, the interactional system of primary interest tends to be relationships that occur within an already formed organization whose features constrain them in some way. The organization remains a privileged phenomenon whose ontological status is unquestioned; thus, interaction analysts preserve the traditional split between the macro and micro levels of analysis. In CA, organizations exist in local and concrete moments of joint action.[5] As seen in Conway's role shift, the institutional setting introduces itself in the ways it is oriented to and made relevant in the interaction. The organization emerges in a laminated accounting process, hence Boden's (1994) focus on the temporal and sequential details of organization rather than on organizations as preformed objects. Analysts who employ SAS also view the macro and micro as inseparable and inherent in the everyday interactive order, but they endorse a realist stance in which organizations, once constructed, become objects with material constraints around which actors must orient (Searle, 1995). Thus, casting organizations as discursive constructions is a unifying metaphor for these three approaches, but unpacking the metaphor reveals a diversity of positions on the status of 'the organization'.

Likewise, all three perspectives focus on the organizing properties of language in use, but the operational differences among the three are striking. Systems interaction analysts examine the control aspects of messages and the way people define and direct their relationships. Every turn-at-talk has meaning, but message content is ignored in lieu of the way a message is communicated. By contrast, conversation analysts would neither ignore content, nor reduce talk-in-interaction to a single, a priori category. They examine details of interaction to decipher the meaning and intelligibility of the patterns *vis-à-vis* the nature of organizing. Finally, SAS proponents analyse the actions organizational members perform in using language (e.g., baptize, authorize, certify), but always in the context of the unfolding, episodic character of action. Organizing is synonymous with the positioning and inserting of speech acts nested within episodes and initiated and closed by other speech acts. Thus, in all three perspectives, language in use organizes as it situates actors in relation to other actors, contexts, goals and objects.[6]

All three approaches also focus on the sequence and temporal form of the interaction process. They share a view of structure in action, where action coheres as a sequence and regular patterns of discourse occur in identifiable sequences (Boden, 1994). However, IA is the only approach that actually tests for patterned regularities. CA centres on the intelligibility of patterns and *how* conversations work sequentially and interactionally, while SAS focuses on the structural possibilities of sequential patterns.

Regardless of how claims about structure are supported, the critical question is what does this type of research mean for the study of organizations? Given the HRO exemplar analysed in this chapter, we contend that IA can uncover specific control patterns as signs of reliable or unreliable performances. The submissive symmetry pattern that introduced redundancy into police radio communication is a case in point. CA reveals *how* and *which* breaks from protocol are oriented to and by *whom*. Conway's shift from victim to police officer is noteworthy in this regard. The resiliency she displays in the resumption of protocol through the use of standardized jargon and reliance on emotion minimization mark the effectiveness of her HRO training – a move that may have saved her life. Finally, SAS demonstrates the role of improvisation in highly reliable performances. To wit, improvisation functions through the opening and closing of schemas that serve as constraints in this interaction. Closing a schema often implies the opening and closing of other schemas, a phenomenon that illustrates how participants coordinate and subordinate their respective activities. If HROs rely on both routines and capacities for improvisation (Murphy, 2001), they enact basic schematic forms that constitute the organizational building blocks of coordinated action.

Finally, Weick and Sutcliffe (2001) claim that the principles that dictate the success of HROs, so-called 'smart systems', could be applied to more conventional types of organization. If these authors are correct, then the attention to detail afforded by discursive approaches that focus on language in use could prove very useful in explaining organizational functioning and why HRO processes succeed or fail.

NOTES

The authors would like to thank Paul Denvir, Alan Hansen, Anita Pomerantz, Sean Rintel and Robert Sanders for their insightful comments on the transcript. Special thanks to Linda Putnam, Bob McPhee, Anita Pomerantz, Edna Rogers and Karl Weick for comments on this chapter.
1 Heritage (1997, p. 163) observes that while an organization is 'talked into being', the reality invoked is not confined to talk but exists in documents, buildings, legal arrangements.

2   Whalen and Zimmerman (1998) define hysteria as sobbing, screaming, using profanity and 'shock tokens' such as 'Oh God!' and/or pleading for immediate assistance.

3   The police protocol for communicating with the dispatcher is to identify oneself by car number, wait for the dispatcher's acknowledgement, then proceed with the message by utilizing standardized police jargon (e.g., lines 96–102). Conway and her supervisors break from this protocol in the heat of the crisis.

4   Drawing from Sacks (1992), a membership category is a way of typifying and grouping people, objects, or activities.

5   Following Hilbert (1990), the emphasis on the concrete and local should not be mistaken for a preoccupation with microstructure. The macro and micro is a distinction neither ethnomethodologists nor conversation analysts make.

6   Clearly what is 'organizing' in all three perspectives shifts with the linguistic focus, and all three approaches miss the organizing aspects of non-linguistic behaviour. However, recent developments in SAS focus on the macro dimensions (Latour, 1996a, 1999) achieved through the way actors mobilize technologies in their interaction (Cooren, 2001a; Cooren & Fairhurst, 2002a, 2002b). Far from being entities that dictate the structure of interaction, macro concerns surface as the product of interaction by focusing on the effects of *globalization* (Latour, 1996b). 'Globalizing' suggests that every local situation is 'dis-located' somewhat through the mobilization of technologies (documents, machines, tools, etc.). For example, the interaction in the police dispatch transcript moves to a global level in lines 16, 37, and 70 when the dispatcher issues three county-wide calls to all officers in the general vicinity, regardless of the district or law enforcement affiliation. Thanks to a transmission device that channels the interactions, what the dispatcher says at the local level is translated in each patrol car, an effect of globalization/dislocation that explain how the micro *scales up* to the macro (Taylor & Van Every, 2000). Moreover, consistent with Weick's (1990) notion of technology as equivoque, this example demonstrates that organizations are *both* technological and discursive constructions because technologies, like language forms, are enabled, deployed and managed within a sequence of events. Thus, future studies of language in use should consider the technologies and other material conditions that enable or constrain interactions.

APPENDIX: TRANSCRIPT OF THE EMERGENCY CALL

 1   **Cy**:   Help! I need assistance! I'm shot in the (car)!
 2   (2.0)
 3   **Disp**:   <u>Where</u> do you need it?
 4   **Cy**:   Help! I need help!
 5   (1.5)
 6   **1030**:   1238 Elm. I believe, 1030, I believe I heard shots fired there.
 7   **Cy**:   [((Unintelligible screaming)) please!
 8   **Disp**:   [-Location?
 9   (1.0)
10   **Disp**:   1212, what's your location?
11   (6.5)
12   **1080**:   1080, we got a location?
13   (1.0)
14   **Disp**:   Negative
15   ((line sounds))
16   **Disp**:   Officer needs assistance, District One, unknown location.

17		12th 12th and Elm. Officer needs assistance, 12th and
18		Elm. Possibly shots fired.
19		(3.0)
20	**1080**:	1080 35, 12th and Elm, do not <u>see</u> them.
21		(2.5)
22	**1240**:	1240. Play the tape back
23		(2.5)
24	**Disp**:	1212, what's your location?
25	**Cy**:	Distress. I've been involved in a shooting (0.3) on Central
26		Parkway (0.5) north (.) of Liberty. I need some help hhh
27		(0.5)
28	**1080**:	1080, I [copy that. Check on her safety.
29	**Disp**:	[are you hurt?
30		(0.5)
31	**Disp**:	1212, are you hurt?
32		(0.3)
33	**Cy**:	That's affirmative.
34		(0.5)
35	**1080**:	1080, I'll be there in five seconds. Blockin' it off with four cars.
36		((line sounds))
37	**Disp**:	Attention all cars, all departments. An officer
38		has been <u>in</u>jured. Possible shooting offense hh
39		at 12th and Central Parkway.=Repeating,
40		Cincinnati officer needs assistance hhh at
41		12th and Central Parkway, a possible <u>shoot</u>ing
42		offense. =The officer reporting she is injured,
43		approach with caution.
44		(0.3)
45	**1080**:	She's at. Correct-correction, she's at <u>Liberty</u> (.) and, uh, Elm.
46	**1240**:	1240
47	**Disp**:	[12...
48	**1240**:	[1240, no more cars.
49		((unintelligible sounds))
50	**Disp**:	1240, are you on the scene?
51	**1080**:	Come on you guys=
52	**1240**:	=Assist assist! All emergency traffic. Let me talk.
53	**Disp**:	Go ahead
54	**1240**:	OK. We're about, uh, we're about just about north of uh
55		(.) uh Central Parkway. We're going to need a couple
56		rescue units. We've got an officer in the car shot.
57		((sirens in the background))
58	**Disp**:	OK, I you need to go slower.
59	**1080**:	Where are you?
60	**Disp**:	Where are you?
61	**1240**:	1240. We are at the corner of Central Parkway, just north
62		of ((sounds)) No more cars.

63 **Disp**: OK. Parkway, north of <u>what.</u>
64 **1240**: North of Liberty. West <u>L</u>iberty street
65 **Disp**: OK. You got any other cars with [you?
66 **1240**:   [I -] need (.) a rescue unit.
67   I need a rescue unit!
68   (2.5)
69   ((line sounds))
70 **Disp**: Attention, all cars all departments. <u>No</u> additional officers
71   are to respond hh reference the officer shot (0.5) on
72   Central Parkway, just North of Liberty. Repeating
73 **1240**: 1240=
74 **Disp**: =No other units are to respond on the assistance.
75   (1.5)
76 **Disp**: 1240
77 **1240**: Hey!
78 **Disp**: 1240, go ahead.
79 **1240**: Hey. I will take care of it on the scene here. We have the
80   perimeter secure. We need a fire company to <u>ex</u>pedite.
81 **Disp**: Fire company is responding. (.) Other units
82 **1240**: No other units to transmit at this point. I'm also gonna need
83   the uh recall list
84 **Disp**: OK. I need, if you can give us a call to know the condition
85   right now also.
86 **1240**: I'll give you one in two minutes
87   (1.0)
88   ((unintelligible sounds))
89 **1240**: We've got the address right. 1627 Central Parkway.
90 **Disp**: Copy 1627 Central
91 **Disp**: Copy 1627 Central
92   (1.0)
93 **1215**: Car 15 responding
94   (1.0)
95 **Disp**: Car 15 copy
96 **1230**: 1230
97   (0.5)
98 **Disp**: 1230 copy
99 **1230**: 12 (.) 1230
100 **Disp**: Car 1230.
101 **1230**: Get the aircare to stand by. And we have the
102   night chief responding
103   (0.5)
104 **Disp**: The night chief is responding.
105 **1230**: Is homicide responding?
106   (2.5)
107 **Disp**: I'm notifying now.
108 **???**: Okay, so do you know who might have done this?

REFERENCES

Adkins, M. & Brashers, D.E. (1995) The power of language in computer-mediated groups. *Management Communication Quarterly*, 8: 289–322.

Ainsworth-Vaughn, N. (1992) Topic transitions in physician–patient interviews: Power, gender, and discourse change. *Language in Society*, 21: 409–26.

Alvesson, M. & Kärreman, D. (2000a) Taking the linguistic turn in organizational research. *The Journal of Applied Behavioral Science*, 36: 136–58.

Alvesson, M. & Kärreman, D. (2000b) Varieties of discourse: On the study of organizations through discourse analysis. *Human Relations*, 53: 1125–49.

Ansari, M.A. (1990) *Managing people at work: Leadership styles and influence strategies.* New Delhi: Sage.

Atkinson, J.M. (1984) *Our masters' voices: The language and body language of politics.* London: Methuen.

Atkinson, J.M. & Heritage, J. (eds) (1984) *Structures of social action: Studies in conversation analysis.* Cambridge: Cambridge University Press.

Austin, J.L. (1962) *How to do things with words.* Cambridge, MA: Harvard University Press.

Austin, J.L. (1975) *How to do things with words* (2nd edition). Cambridge, MA: Harvard University Press.

Bakeman, R. & Gottman, J.M. (1986) *Observing interaction: An introduction to sequential analysis.* Cambridge: Cambridge University Press.

Bales, R.F. (1950) *Interaction process analysis.* Reading, MA: Addison-Wesley.

Bateson, G. (1951) Information and codification: A philosophical approach. In J. Ruesch & G. Bateson (eds), *Communication: The social matrix of psychiatry.* (pp. 168–211). New York: W.W. Norton.

Bateson, G. (1972) *Steps to an ecology of the mind.* New York: Ballantine.

Bednar, D.A. & Curington, W.P. (1983) Interaction analysis: A tool for understanding negotiations. *Industrial and Labor Relations Review*, 36: 389–401.

Boden, D. (1990) The world as it happens: Ethnomethodology and conversation analysis. In G. Ritzer (ed.), *Frontiers of social theory: The new synthesis* (pp. 185–213). New York: Columbia University Press.

Boden, D. (1994) *The business of talk: Organizations in action.* Cambridge: Polity Press.

Clayman, S. (1992) Footing in the achievement of neutrality: The case of news interview discourse. In P. Drew & J. Heritage (eds), *Talk at work: Interaction in institutional settings* (pp. 163–98). Cambridge: Cambridge University Press.

Cooren, F. (2001a) *The organizing property of communication.* Amsterdam/Philadelphia, PA: John Benjamins.

Cooren, F. (2001b) Translation and articulation in the organization of coalitions: The Great Whale River case. *Communication Theory*, 11: 178–200.

Cooren, F. & Fairhurst, G.T. (2002a) Dislocation and stabilization: How to scale up from interactions to organization. Paper presented at the annual conference of the National Communication Association, New Orleans.

Cooren, F. & Fairhurst, G.T. (2002b) The leader as a practical narrator: Leadership as the art of translating. In D. Holman & R. Thorpe (eds), *The manager as a practical author* (pp. 85–103). London: Sage.

Cooren, F. & Taylor, J.R. (1997) Organization as an effect of mediation: Redefining the link between organization and communication. *Communication Theory*, 7: 219–60.

Cooren, F. & Taylor, J.R. (1998) The procedural and rhetorical modes of the organizing dimension of communication. Discursive analysis of a parliamentary commission. *Communication Review*, 3: 65–101.

Cooren, F. & Taylor, J.R. (2000) Association and dissociation in an ecological controversy: The Great Whale River case. In N.W. Coppola & B. Karis (eds), *Technical communication, deliberative rhetoric, and environmental discourse: Connections and directions* (pp. 171–90). Stamford, CT: Ablex.

Courtright, J.A., Fairhurst, G.T. & Rogers, L.E. (1989) Interaction patterns in organic and mechanistic systems. *Academy of Management Journal*, 32: 773–802.

DeSanctis, G. & Poole, M.S. (1994) Capturing the complexity in advanced technology use: Adaptive structuration theory. *Organization Science*, 5: 121–47.

DeSanctis, G., Poole, M.S., Lewis, H. & Desharnais, G. (1992) Using computing in quality team meetings: Initial observations from the IRS-Minnesota Project. *Journal of Management Information Systems*, 8: 7–26.

Donohue, W.A. (1981a) Analysing negotiation tactics: Development of a negotiation interact system. *Human Communication Research*, 7: 272–87.

Donohue, W.A. (1981b) Development of a model of rule use in negotiation interaction. *Communication Monographs*, 48: 106–20.

Donohue, W.A. & Diez, M.E. (1985) Directive use in negotiation interaction. *Communication Monographs*, 52: 305–18.

Donohue, W.A., Diez, M.E. & Hamilton, M. (1984) Coding naturalistic negotiation interaction. *Human Communication Research*, 10: 403–25.

Drew, P. & Heritage, J. (1992) *Talk at work: Interaction in institutional settings.* Cambridge: Cambridge University Press.

Dubois, B.L. & Crouch, I. (1975) The question of tag questions in women's speech. *Language in Society*, 4: 289–94.

duGay, P., Salaman, G. & Rees, B. (1996) The conduct of management and the management of conduct: Contemporary managerial discourse and the constitution of the 'competent manager'. *Journal of Management Studies*, 33: 263–82.

Ellis, D.G. (1979) Relational control in two group systems. *Communication Monographs*, 46: 156–66.

Fairclough, N. (1992) *Discourse and social change.* Cambridge: Polity Press.

Fairclough, N. (1995) *Critical discourse analysis: The critical study of language.* London: Longman.

Fairhurst, G.T. (1993) The leader–member exchange patterns of women leaders in industry: A discourse analysis. *Communication Monographs*, 60: 321–51.

Fairhurst, G.T. (2004) Textuality and agency in interaction analysis. *Organization*, 11: 335–53.

Fairhurst, G.T., Green, S.G. & Courtright, J.A. (1995) Inertial forces and the implementation of a socio-technical systems approach: A communication study. *Organization Science*, 6: 168–85.

Fairhurst, G.T. & Putnam, L.L. (2004) Organizations as discursive constructions: *Communication Theory*, 14: 1–22.

Firth, A. (1994) 'Accounts' in negotiation discourse: A single case analysis. *Journal of Pragmatics*, 23: 199–226.

Firth, A. (ed.) (1995) *The discourse of negotiation: Studies of language in the workplace.* Oxford: Pergamon.

Fisher, S. & Groce, S.B. (1990) Accounting practices in medical interviews. *Language in Society*, 19: 225–50.

Foucault, M. (1976) *The history of sexuality:* Volume 1. New York: Pantheon.

Foucault, M. (1980) *Power/knowledge. Selected interviews and other writings 1972–1977.* New York: Pantheon.

Frances, D.W. (1986) Some structures of negotiation talk. *Language in society*, 15: 53–79.

Garfinkel, H. (1967) *Studies in ethnomethodology.* Englewood Cliffs, NJ: Prentice-Hall.

Giddens, A. (1979) *Central problems in social theory.* Berkeley, CA: University of California Press.

Giddens, A. (1984) *The constitution of society.* Berkeley, CA: University of California Press.

Gioia, D.A., Donnellon, A. & Sims, H.P., Jr. (1989) Communication and cognition in appraisal: A tale of two paradigms. *Organization Studies*, 10: 503–30.

Gioia, D.A. & Sims, H.P., Jr. (1986) Cognition-behavior connections: Attribution and verbal behavior in leader-subordinate interactions. *Organizational Behavior and Human Decision Processes*, 37: 197–229.

Glauser, M.J. & Tullar, W.L. (1985) Citizen satisfaction with police officer–citizen inter-action: Implications for changing the role of police organizations. *Journal of Applied Psychology*, 70: 514–27.

Gottman, J.M. (1982) Temporal form: Toward a new language for describing relation-ships. *Journal of Marriage and Family*, 44: 943–62.

Grant, D., Keenoy, T. & Oswick, C. (1998) Organizational discourse: Of diversity, dichotomy and multi-disciplinarity. In D. Grant, T. Keenoy & C. Oswick (eds), *Discourse and organization* (pp. 1–13). London: Sage.

Greatbatch, D. & Dingwall, R. (1994) The interactive construction of interventions by divorce mediators. In J.P. Folger & T.S. Jones (eds), *New directions in mediation* (pp. 84–109). Thousand Oaks, CA: Sage.

Greimas, A.J. (1987) *On meaning. Selected writings in semiotic theory*. Trans. Paul J. Perron & Frank H. Collins. London: Frances Pinter.

Groleau, C. & Cooren, F. (1998) A socio-semiotic approach to computerization: Bridging the gap between ethnographers and system analysts. *Communication Review*, 3: 125–64.

Gronn, P.C. (1982) Neo-Taylorism in educational administration? *Education Administration Quarterly*, 18: 17–35.

Gronn, P.C. (1983) Talk as the work: The accomplishment of school administration. *Administrative Science Quarterly*, 28: 1–21.

Haslett, B.J. (1987) *Communication: Strategic action in context*. Hillsdale, NJ: Lawrence Erlbaum Associates.

Hawes, L.C. (1974) Social collectivities as communication: Perspectives on organizational behavior. *Quarterly Journal of Speech*, 60: 497–502.

Heritage, J. (1997) Conversation analysis and institutional talk. In D. Silverman (ed.), *Qualitative research: Theory method and practice* (pp. 161–82). London: Sage.

Hilbert, R.A. (1990) Ethnomethodology and the micro-macro order. *American Sociological Review*, 55: 794–808.

Holmes, J. (1984) Hedging your bets and sitting on the fence. *Te Reo*, 27: 47–62.

Holmes, M.E. & Rogers, L.E. (1995) 'Let me rephrase that question': Five common criti-cisms of interaction analysis studies. Paper presented at the annual conference of the Western States Communication Association, Portland, Oregon.

Hutchby, I. (1996) *Confrontation talk: Argument, asymmetries and power on talk radio*. Hillsdale, NJ: Lawrence Erlbaum Associates.

James, D. & Clarke, S. (1993) Women, men and interruptions: A critical review. In D. Tannen (ed.), *Gender and conversational interaction* (pp. 231 80). Oxford: Oxford University Press.

Jones, K. (1992) A question of context: Directive use at a Morris team meeting. *Language in Society*, 21: 427–45.

Keenoy, T., Oswick, C. & Grant, D. (1997) Organizational discourses: Texts and contexts. *Organization*, 4: 147–57.

Kennedy, C.W. & Camden, C.T. (1983) A new look at interruptions. *Western Journal of Speech Communication*, 47: 45–58.

Keyton, J. & Wall, V.D. (1989) SYMLOG: Theory and method for measuring group and organizational communication. *Management Communication Quarterly*, 2: 544–67.

Knights, D. & Wilmott, H. (1992) Conceptualizing leadership processes: A study of senior managers in a financial services company. *Journal of Management Studies*, 29: 761–82.

Komaki, J.L. (1986) Toward effective supervision: An operant analysis and comparison of managers at work. *Journal of Applied Psychology*, 71: 270–9.

Komaki, J.L. (1998) *Leadership from an operant perspective*. New York: Routledge.

Latour, B. (1996a) On interobjectivity: *Mind, Culture, and Activity*, 3: 228–45.

Latour, B. (1996b) *Aramis or the love of technology*: Cambridge, MA: Harvard University Press.

Latour, B. (1999) *Pandora's hope: Essays on the reality of science studies*. Cambridge, MA: Harvard University Press.

Levinson, S.C. (1983) *Pragmatics*. Cambridge: Cambridge University Press.

Linde, C. (1988) The quantitative study of communicative success: Politeness and accidents in aviation discourse. *Language in Society*, 17: 375–99.

Molotch, H.L. & Boden, D. (1985) Talking social structure: Discourse, domination and the Watergate Hearings. *American Sociological Review*, 50: 273–88.

Morris, G.H. (1988) Accounts in selection interviews. *Journal of Applied Communication Research*, 15: 82–98.

Murphy, A.G. (2001) The flight attendant dilemma: An analysis of communication and sensemaking during in-flight emergencies. *Journal of Applied Communication Research*, 29: 30–53.

Murray, D.E. (1987) Requests at work: Negotiating the conditions for conversation. *Management Communication Quarterly*, 1: 58–83.

Neu, J. (1988) Conversation structure: An explanation of bargaining behaviors in negotiations. *Management Communication Quarterly*, 2: 23–45.

Olekalns, M., Smith, P.L. & Walsh, T. (1996) The process of negotiating: Strategies, timing, and outcomes. *Organizational Behavior and Human Decision Processes*, 68: 68–77.

Peräkylä, A. (1995) *AIDS counselling: Institutional interaction and clinical practice*. Cambridge: Cambridge University Press.

Pomerantz, A. & Fehr, B.J. (1997) Conversation analysis: An approach to the study of social action as sense making practices. In T.A. Van Dijk (ed.), *Discourse as social interaction* (Vol, 2, pp. 64–91). London: Sage.

Pomerantz, A., Fehr, B.J. & Ende, J. (1997) When supervising physicians see patients. *Human Communication Research*, 23: 589–615.

Poole, M.S. & DeSanctis, G. (1992) Microlevel structuration in computer-supported group decision-making. *Human Communication Research*, 91: 5–49.

Poole, M.S., Holmes, M. & DeSanctis, G. (1991) Conflict management in a computer-supported meeting environment. *Management Science*, 37: 926–53.

Preisler, B. (1986) *Linguistic sex roles in conversation*. Berlin: Mouton de Gruyter.

Psathas, G. (ed.) (1979) *Everyday language: Studies in ethnomethodology*. New York: Irvington Press.

Psathas, G. (1995) *Conversation analysis: The study of talk-in-interaction*. London: Sage.

Putnam, L.L. (1990) Reframing integrative and distributive bargaining: A process perspective. In B.H. Sheppard, M.H. Bazerman & R.J. Lewicki (eds), *Research on negotiation in organizations* (pp. 3–30). Greenwich, CT: JAI Press.

Putnam, L.L. & Fairhurst, G.T. (2001) Discourse analysis in organizations. In F.M. Jablin & L.L. Putnam (eds), *The new handbook of organizational communication* (pp. 78–136). Thousand Oaks, CA: Sage.

Putnam, L.L. & Jones, T.S. (1982) Reciprocity in negotiations: An analysis of bargaining interaction. *Communication Monographs*, 49: 171–91.

Ragan, S.L. (1983) A conversational analysis of alignment talk in job interviews. In R. Bostrum (ed.), *Communication yearbook 7* (pp. 502–16). Beverly Hills, CA: Sage.

Ragan, S.L. & Hopper, R. (1981) Alignment talk in the job interview. *Journal of Applied Communication Research*, 9: 85–103.

Reed, M. (2000) The limits of discourse analysis in organization analysis. *Organization*, 7: 524–30.

Robichaud, D. (1998) Textualization and organizing: Illustrations from a public discussion process. *Communication Review*, 3: 103–24.

Robichaud, D. (2001) Interaction as a text: A semiotic look at an organizing process. *American Journal of Semiotics*, 17: 141–61.

Rogers, L.E. & Farace, R.V. (1975) Relational communication analysis: New measurement procedures. *Human Communication Research*, 1: 222–39.

Sacks, H. (1984) Notes on methodology. In J.M. Atkinson & J. Heritage (eds), *Structures of social action: Studies in conversation analysis* (pp. 413–29). Cambridge: Cambridge University Press.

Sacks, H. (1992) Lectures on conversation. In G. Jefferson (ed.), (vol. 1 & 2). Oxford: Blackwell.

Sargent, J.F. & Miller, G.R. (1971) Some differences in certain communication behaviors of autocratic and democratic group leaders. *Journal of Communication*, 21: 233–52.

Schegloff, E.A. (1988) Presequence and indirection. Applying speech act theory to ordinary conversation. *Journal of Pragmatics*, 12: 55–62.

Searle, J.R. (1969) *Speech acts: An essay in the philosophy of language*. London: Cambridge University Press.

Searle, J.R. (1979) *Meaning and expression: Studies in the theory of speech acts*. Cambridge: Cambridge University Press.

Searle, J.R. (1989) How performatives work. *Linguistics and Philosophy*, 12: 535–58.

Searle, J.R. (1995) *The construction of social reality*. New York: Free Press.

Sims, H.P., Jr. & Manz, C.C. (1984) Observing leader verbal behavior: Toward reciprocal determinism in leadership theory: *Journal of Applied Psychology*, 69: 222–32.

Stokes, R. & Hewitt, J.P. (1976) Disclaimers. *American Sociological Review*, 40: 1–11.

Sudnow, D. (ed.) (1970) *Studies in social interaction*. New York: Free Press.

Taylor, J.R. (1993) *Rethinking the theory of organizational communication: How to read an organization*. Norwood, NJ: Ablex.

Taylor, J.R. (1995) Shifting from a heteronomous to an autonomous worldview of organizational communication: Communication theory on the cusp. *Communication Theory*, 5: 1–35.

Taylor, J.R., Groleau, C., Heaton, L. & Van Every, E. (2001) *The computerization of work: A communication perspective*. Thousand Oaks, CA: Sage.

Taylor, J.R. & Lerner, L. (1996) Making sense of sensemaking: How managers construct their organization through their talk. *Studies in Cultures, Organizations and Societies*, 2: 257–86.

Taylor, J.R. & Van Every, E. (2000) *The emergent organization: Communication as its site and surface*. Mahwah, NJ: Lawrence Erlbaum Associates.

Titscher, S., Meyer, M., Wodak, R. & Vetter, E. (2000) *Methods of text and discourse analysis*. London: Sage.

Tulin, M.F. (1997) Talking organization: Possibilities for conversation analysis in organizational behavior research. *Journal of Management Inquiry*, 6: 101–19.

Tullar, W.L. (1989) Relational control in the employment interview. *Journal of Applied Psychology*, 74: 971–77.

Vanderveken, D. (1990–91) *Meaning and speech acts*. Cambridge: Cambridge University Press.

Walther, J.B. (1995) Relational aspects of computer-mediated communication: Experimental observations over time. *Organization Science*, 6: 186–203.

Watson, K.M. (1982) An analysis of communication patterns: A method for discriminating leader and subordinate roles. *Academy of Management Journal*, 25: 107–20.

Watson-Dugan, K.M. (1989) Ability and effort attributions: Do they affect how managers communicate performance feedback information. *Academy of Management Journal*, 32: 87–114.

Watzlawick, P., Beavin, J.H. & Jackson, D.D. (1967) *Pragmatics of human communication*. New York: W.W. Norton.

Weick, K.E. (1990) Technology as equivoque: Sensemaking in new technologies. In P.S. Goodman & L. Sproull (eds), *Technology and organizations* (pp. 1–44). San Francisco: Jossey-Bass.

Weick, K.E. & Sutcliffe, K.M. (2001) *Managing the unexpected: Assuring high performance in an age of complexity*. San Francisco: Jossey-Bass.

Weick, K.E., Sutcliffe, K.M. & Obstfeld, D. (1999) Organizing for high reliability: Processes of collective mindfulness. *Research in organizational behavior*. (Vol. 21, pp. 81–123). Stamford, CT: JAI Press.

Weingart, L.R., Prietula, M.J., Hyder, E.B. & Genovese, C.R. (1999) Knowledge and the sequential processes of negotiation: A Markov chain analysis of response-in-kind. *Journal of Experimental Psychology*, 36: 366–93.

Weingart, L.R., Thompson, L.L., Bazerman, M.H. & Carroll, J.S. (1990) Tactical behavior and negotiation outcomes. *The International Journal of Conflict Management*, 1: 7–31.

Whalen, J. & Zimmerman, D.H. (1987) Sequential and institutional calls for help. *Social Psychology Quarterly*, 50: 172–85.

Whalen, J. & Zimmerman, D.H. (1998) Observations on the display and management of emotion in naturally occurring activities: The case of 'hysteria' in calls to 9-1-1. *Social Psychology Quarterly*, 61: 141–59.

Whalen, J., Zimmerman, D.H. & Whalen, M.R. (1988) When words fail: A single case analysis. *Social Problems*, 35: 335–62.

Woods, N. (1988) Talking shop: Sex and status as determinants of floor apportionment in a work setting. In J. Coates & D. Cameron (eds), *Women in their speech communities* (pp. 141–57). London: Longman.

Zigurs, I., Poole, M.S. & DeSanctis, G.L. (1988) A study of influence in computer-mediated group decision making. *MIS Quarterly*, December: 625–44.

Zimmerman, D.H. (1984) Talk and its occasion: The case of calling the police. In D. Schiffrin (ed.), *Meaning, form, and use in context: Linguistic applications* (pp. 210–28). Washington, DC: Georgetown University Press.

Zimmerman, D.H. (1992a) Achieving context: Openings in emergency calls. In G. Watson & R.M. Seiler (eds), *Text in context* (pp. 35–51). Newbury Park, CA: Sage.

Zimmerman, D.H. (1992b) The interactional organization of calls for emergency assistance. In P. Drew & J. Heritage (eds), *Talk at work: Interaction in institutional settings* (pp. 418–69). Cambridge: Cambridge University Press.

6

Discourse and Identities

Susan Ainsworth and Cynthia Hardy

It seemed to Vernon that he was infinitely diluted; he was simply the sum of all the people who had listened to him, and when he was alone, he was nothing at all. When he reached in solitude for a thought, there was no one there to think it. His chair was empty; he was finely dissolved throughout the building from the City Desk on the sixth floor where he was about to intervene to prevent the sacking of a long-serving sub[editor] ... to the basement where parking allocation had brought the senior staff to open war and an assistant editor to the brink of resignation. Vernon's chair was empty because he was in Jerusalem, the House of Commons, Cape Town and Manila, globally disseminated like dust; he was on TV and radio, at dinner with bishops, giving a speech to the oil industry, or a seminar to European Union specialists. In the brief moments during the day when he was alone, a light went out. Even the ensuing darkness encompassed or inconvenienced no one in particular. He could not say for sure that the absence was his. (Ian McEwan, *Amsterdam* (London: Vintage), 1998, pp. 29–30)[1]

This description of Vernon is emblematic of our view of identities in the poststructuralist, socially constructed tradition, which has helped to spark the growing interest in organizational discourse. Vernon's identities are fragmented, distributed, and marked by absence as much as an organizationally constituted presence. In this chapter, we draw on some of the identities constructed in *Amsterdam* to explore how discourse analysis can help us to understand the construction of identities in organizational settings – fictional identities to illustrate the made-up identities that make up our organizations. In this regard, the novel provides a resource for organizational analysts. And, why not? Novelists are experienced in the art of identity construction, and the insights of the 'linguistic turn' infiltrated their work a lot earlier and, some would argue, to far greater effect than in organization and management theory. Language is at the heart of their proficiency and their texts shape our discourse. Besides, they write better than academics.

DISCOURSE, ORGANIZATIONS AND IDENTITIES

This chapter builds on the work of the last chapter, by applying different forms of discourse analysis to data – in this case, 'data' in the form of text from a novel. In this way, we aim to show how discourse analysis can contribute to the study of identities in organizational settings as well as some of the different approaches to discourse analysis.

We use the term 'discourse' to refer to interrelated sets of texts that 'systematically form the objects of which they speak' (Foucault, 1972, p. 49). Discourses thus constitute the social world by bringing certain phenomena into being (Parker, 1992), including objects of knowledge, categories of social subjects, forms of 'self', social relationships and conceptual frameworks (Deetz, 1992; Fairclough, 1992; Fairclough & Wodak, 1997). Discourse analysis thus focuses on bodies of texts and the way in which texts are related to each other (Phillips & Hardy, 2002), as well as how any individual text 'responds to, reaccentuates, and reworks past texts, and in so doing helps to make history and contributes to wider processes of change' (Fairclough, 1992, p. 102).[2]

Within this broad interest in the constructive or performative effects of discourse, there is considerable variation in how research is carried out. Accordingly, we explore different approaches by contrasting some of the different sites where discourse analysis is conducted, namely language, talk, narrative, and interdiscursivity and social practice. This categorization, albeit artificial and overlapping, allows us to reflect on the ways in which different theoretical perspectives have constructed their object of study. For example, language is how sociolinguistics and some critical discourse analysts have formulated their site for investigation through their interest in the more systemic and linguistic aspects of a text. Talk has been studied by conversation analysts and discursive psychologists. Narrative is also the interest of discursive psychology, as well as sociolinguistics, social theory and cultural studies. Foucault and critical discourse analysts such as Fairclough (1995) have broadened the site to include the interdiscursive and extradiscursive, which includes a focus on practices of textual production, distribution and consumption (Phillips & Hardy, 2002), the way in which texts are constituted from diverse discourses (Fairclough, 1995), as well as social practices that include architecture, bodies, equipment, etc. (Foucault, 1976).[3]

It is not our intention to review different schools of thought *per se*. Instead, we explore the role that four sites of discourse research – language, talk, narrative and interdiscursivity – can reveal about the construction of identities. In this way, we hope to show how identities are constructed, whether it be 'Vernon' in the quotation above, *The Judge* – the newspaper of which he is Editor – or the very concept of a 'man', an 'editor', a 'newspaper'. In addition, we can show the value discourse analysis has for exploring identities, following the 'death' of the subject, by which we refer to the substitution of a view of the stable, unitary, essential subject with a more fluid, fragile construction (e.g., Baack & Prasch, 1997). Constructionist studies of identity have become commonplace and 'tired' according to Hacking (2000) because of the widespread focus on the products, rather than the processes, of social construction. Discourse analysis provides a range of ways that can address this neglect, allowing organizational researchers to examine the complexity of processes of construction of identity, thereby revitalizing constructionist research.

Identities are linked to organizations in that, not only are organizations settings in which identities are constructed, identities are 'materials out of which larger, more recognizably '"social" or "institutional" identities are built' (Antaki & Widdicombe, 1998b, 10). A discursive approach is also relevant to the concept of collective or organizational identity. In organizational research, collective identity has been predominantly understood as members' convergent beliefs about central, enduring and distinctive attributes of their organization (Albert & Whetten, 1985), which affects the way that members interpret and act on issues facing the organization (e.g., Gioia & Thomas, 1996). While recent work has highlighted the importance of tensions (e.g., Fiol, 2002), the longstanding emphasis on convergence in cognitively held beliefs leaves this body of theory lacking empirical means to explore them. A discursive perspective, by situating collective identity in the language in use among members, shifts attention from the intentions and attitudes of individuals to their observable linguistic practices and the effects of those practices on social relationships and action (Potter & Wetherell, 1987). Accordingly, a discursive approach allows us to view an organization as something that is always in the act of 'becoming' rather than as a discrete entity (Tsoukas & Chia, 2002).

In each of the following four sections, we examine some of the relevant research, review how it contributes to our understanding of how identities are constructed, and present some brief examples of particular studies.[4] We then use quotations from *Amsterdam* to illustrate the ways in which different discursive elements influence processes of identity construction and how identities and organizations emerge from the interplay among them.

Language and identities

The study of language is integral to discourse analysis – not as a transparent, reflective form of communication, but as a situated, interpretable phenomenon that serves to construct social reality, including identities. This site of research builds on the work of de Saussure (1983), who conceptualized language as a system of relational difference: words derived their meaning not from the relationship to their referent, but from their relationship to other words. Discourse researchers have developed this idea, exploring how processes of linguistic categorization construct identities that are defined by their relationship to, and difference from, other identities (Gergen, 2001; Wodak, 1996). However, Saussurean linguistics focused on language as an abstract system, rather than 'language in use' and its social context (Kress, 2001). These two issues – how language is used and the social context of its use – are particularly important to organizational discourse research on identity. Such research has explored the construction of organizationally-based identities (such as 'consumer' or 'worker') as well as how identity construction is affected by organizational contexts, in which other social identities, such as gender and ethnicity, overlap and which reflect and embed power differences between social groups.

For example, one area where the use of language in constructing identities has received considerable attention is in the field of advertising. As Dyer (1982, p. 185) notes: advertising 'validates consumer commodities and a consumer lifestyle ... We come to think that consuming commodities will give us our identities.' Language is critical in this regard, and advertisers are expert in their use of it. Piller (2001) analysed more than 1,000 advertisements to show how English was used to construct the identities of the German viewer or reader as a cosmopolitan, successful, future-oriented or goal-directed, affluent, educated, professional and predominantly male consumer. In the form of English voice-overs, slogans and headlines (often with distinguishing graphic devices compared to the details and factual information given in German), it was the 'authoritative voice' that reinforced and closed off the meaning of the advertisement. This strategic use of language constructs the reader/consumer in a very particular way.

> If you read English, fine; if not, you are an outsider. Tough luck. The advertisement is about an elite target group, 'the global class of decision makers and opinion leaders ... [who] move easily across continents and cultures'. The readers are not addressed as a member of that elite; instead, its opinions and practices are set up as an example for readers to emulate. For the reader who wants to belong to this global elite – rather than being an outsider – the product, the *IHT* [*International Herald Tribune*], is there to make aspirations to success come true. (Piller, 2001, p. 168)

Similar processes can be found at work in the construction of organizational identities through the language (and other symbols) used in advertising, marketing, issue management and public relations (e.g., Cheney & Christensen, 2001).

Another stream of research has focused on the way in which power is embedded in language use and, in particular, the way in which certain identities are disadvantaged. For example, it has been argued that 'women's language' has certain characteristics that make it less influential (Lakoff, 1975), although other writers argue that the characteristics may be related more to social position than gender *per se* (Lee, 1992). However, the relationship between discourse, gender and organizational research is complex (see Ashcraft, in this volume). Cameron (1995, 1996) suggests the need to problematize the construction of gender identity through processes of linguistic categorization and argues that much of the linguistics research that presupposes difference in language use of men and women actually operates to reify polarized gender identities. Rather than valuing gender difference, Cameron asserts that such research has contributed to women's disadvantage by being appropriated by the 'self-help' genre (e.g., Gray 1992), which offers advice based on a 'deficit' model of gender identity: in organizational settings as well as in personal relationships, women are urged to adjust their ways of speaking to emulate or accommodate men. Instead, Cameron suggests reversing the traditional assumptions: rather than assuming gender identity precedes and gives rise to linguistic practice, she argues that it is through linguistic practices that gender identities are produced (see also Butler, 1990). Thus language use is not viewed as an outcome of gender identity but as being produced through language use.

While acknowledging the power relationship involved in the binary oppositions (Derrida, 1979, 1981), embedded in linguistic categorizations of social identities where identity construction is a 'process of differentiation, a description of one's own group and simultaneously a separation from the "others"' (Wodak, 1996, p. 126), the 'other' is usually not only 'different', but also less desirable, less acceptable, less powerful (Hall, 1997a, 1997b). This orientation in linguistics and identity research recognizes that these meanings – of the 'other' and of the various categorizations that constitute identity – are not fixed. They change over time, in different contexts, and as a result of ongoing language use. In this way, we are reminded of Bakhtin's 'heteroglossia' of a 'dynamic multiplicity of voices, genres and social languages' (Maybin, 2001, p. 67), as meaning, including the evaluative or moral accent of language, derives from the struggle and ambiguity of daily life. In other words, actors are active in using language and, in using it, construct meaning for it, but this meaning is negotiated in dialogue among speakers in particular times and places.

To summarize this section, studies of language and identities draw our attention to the role of language in constructing identities. They include the active use of language to construct one's own and other's identities, the way in which broader social inequities are reflected and reproduced in language use, especially in the use of categorizations to differentiate and demarcate identities, and the struggles that occur around language and meaning. Box 6.1 returns to Vernon, to illustrate how these different processes play out.

**BOX 6.1: LANGUAGE
AND IDENTITIES**

Vernon Halliday is Editor of *The Judge* newspaper and a longstanding friend of Clive Linley, a composer. Both are former lovers of Molly Lane, a restaurant critic and photographer, as was Julian Garmony, a government minister. The novel begins with Molly's funeral, following which Vernon acquires some photographs, taken by Molly, in which Julian is posing dressed in women's clothes. Vernon decides to publish the photographs, disrupting Julian's identity as a Conservative politician through the revelation that he is also a transvestite. In so doing, he seeks to reaffirm his own identity, as a publisher who will change the country's future – and his paper's circulation – for the better. He tells his plan to Clive, who thinks it is a terrible idea. Clive asks Vernon:

'Tell me this. Do you think it's wrong in principle for men to dress up in women's clothes?' Vernon groaned...
...'You were once an apologist for the sexual revolution. You stood up for gays. ... Isn't this the kind of sexual expression you're so keen to defend? What exactly is Garmony's crime that needs to be exposed?'
...'His hypocrisy, Clive. This is the hanger and flogger, the family values man, the scourge of immigrants, asylum seekers, travellers, marginal people'.
'Irrelevant', Clive said.
'Of course it's relevant. Don't talk crap'.
'If it's OK to be a transvestite, then it's OK for a racist to be one. What's not OK is to be a racist.' ... Clive had found his trope. 'If it's OK to be transvestite, then it's OK for a family man to be one too. In private, of course. If it's OK to—'
'Clive! Listen to me. You're in your studio all day dreaming of symphonies. You've no idea what's at stake. If Garmony's not stopped now, if he gets to be prime minister in November, they've got a good chance of winning the election next year. Another five years! There'll be even more people living below the poverty line, more people in prison, more homeless, more crime, more riots, like last year. The environment will suffer. ... He wants to take us out of Europe. Economic catastrophe! It's all very fine for you' – here Vernon gestured around at the enormous kitchen – 'but for most people ...' (Ian McEwan, *Amsterdam*, 1998, pp. 73–4)

This quotation draws our attention to how language is used as a resource by Clive and Vernon (as well as the author) in constructing their identities and those of others, in particular Julian Garmony's. In addition to the use of evocative language (e.g., *the hanger and flogger*), both engage in a series of categorizations where identities are juxtaposed against each other in order to create meaning out of difference. They do so by using identity categorizations in different ways, negotiating their social legitimacy and acceptability. For example, Vernon juxtaposes Garmony as Conservative MP, potential Prime Minister and family values man, against Garmony as transvestite in order to highlight contradiction and hypocrisy. Either one is understandable and possibly even bearable (although not necessarily desirable), but the combination is intolerable. In contrast, Clive juxtaposes Garmony as transvestite and racist to highlight that transvestism is acceptable, while racism is not. In other words, Vernon compares identities to place Garmony in a more marginalized subject position, while Clive attempts to legitimate his transvestism by comparing it to racism. This process of categorization is then extended to each other: Clive contrasts Vernon as defender of freedom of sexual expression with Vernon as judge and jury; Vernon responds by contrasting Clive as privileged in comparison with most ordinary people. In doing so, they engage with each other in a struggle to define Garmony's identity, as well as their own. The quote also shows how the words used to construct categories relate to and derive meaning from the context. Language choice is not *ad hoc*: Vernon selects categories with reference to the current political context (*Europe, homeless, the poverty line*), while Clive refers back to an earlier context of sexual liberation and freedom. Both contexts imbue particular words with different meanings, as well as the moral or evaluative accents that underpin the power differentials embedded in the categorization process.

Talk and identities

Research informed by conversation analysis (Schegloff et al., 1996) and ethnomethodology (Garfinkel, 1974) views identity as a local achievement accomplished through social interaction (Antaki & Widdicombe, 1998a). It is concerned with understanding how participants in conversation make sense of, and co-produce, their social interaction, and focuses on naturally occurring talk to discover how 'participants understand and respond to one another in their turns at talk, with a central focus on how sequences of interaction are generated' (Hutchby & Woolfitt, 1998, p. 14). Traditional conversation analysis examines how certain identities or relationships are implicated in the ways social interaction proceeds by identifying structures of talk, for example, turn-taking, opening and closings of conversations, adjacency pairs (Sacks et al., 1974), or whether speakers refer to people in ways that suggest particular identities or activities (Pomerantz & Fehr, 1997). Some researchers adopt a broader orientation and work on talk-in-interaction[5] (Hutchby & Woolfitt, 1998; Psathas, 1995), which examines how social order is achieved through the way in which talk is organized (Jaworski & Coupland, 1999).

Silverman's (1997) study of HIV counselling provides an example that shows how identities are locally produced through shared understandings of social membership categories, which he refers to as membership categorization devices, and the activities associated with identity categories. Membership categorization devices allocate people to one category of a collection of categories that go together, for example, 'mother' from the collection of 'family', or 'patient' – 'doctor'. By invoking one identity, we imply other identities. Further, by describing activities we also indicate corresponding social identities. If, for example, we say that someone is seeking treatment, we provide him or her with a social identity – as a 'patient' – which also implies a certain range of appropriate behaviours. Thus Silverman's work builds on the oppositional 'othering' noted under the section on language and, in addition to examining the meaning of these classifications, he shows how shared understandings of such categorizations are used in social interaction in ways that have implications for behaviour and practice.

Studies of 'institutional dialogue' (Drew & Sorjonen, 1997; Heritage, 2001) also consider interactional effects of identity construction. They are concerned with how social institutions are accomplished in such talk as education, medical and legal interactions (Drew & Heritage, 1992; Heritage, 2001). Researchers examine how individuals refer to themselves and other people (e.g., adopting an institutional or representative, rather than a personal, identity); their use of technical vocabularies; how expression is constructed in certain grammatical forms; how participants locally manage their interaction through turn-taking; and participants' understandings of the meaning of their activities within that institutional context (Pomerantz & Fehr, 1997). In this way, institutional and organizational settings are created through multiple interactions that construct the relevant identities, mark out the relations and power differentials among them, and map out the behaviour associated with each (e.g., Boden, 1994; Kärreman & Alvesson, 2001; Schegloff, 1991, 1997).

The study of talk involves examining how identity is constructed from both the activity as well as what is said. Some writers emphasize activity over content. For example, Collins (1981) argues that it is the repeated actions of communicating – not what is said – that creates beliefs in common realities.

[S]ocial order must necessarily be physical and local ... peoples' activities always occur at a particular physical location and at a particular time. The inexpressible context upon which everybody depends, and upon which all tacit understandings rest, is the physical world, including everyone's own body, as seen from a particular place within it. (Collins, 1981, p. 995)

He argues that conversational interactions imply membership in different groups which, in turn, produce shared understandings of a group identity that shape the way in which individuals see and act on the world. In this way, identities and emotions are discursively constructed in conversation, providing a resource for action (Hardy et al., 1998).

Other writers iteratively juxtapose action and content – conversation and text. Texts are produced as acts of conversation and are turned into textual representations: an actor makes sense of the utterances of another and embeds the interpretation in a second conversational act and, in so doing, objectifies and shares background assumptions (Taylor & Van Every, 2000; Taylor et al., 1996). By encompassing both conversation and text, Taylor and colleagues build on the performative effects of language (discussed in the last section) to combine it with an understanding of processes of textualization (see also Iedema, 1998).[6] As talk is turned into text and increasingly distanced from the point of production, assumptions about the organizational setting embedded in the talk become increasingly objectified, generalized and anonymous. In this way, texts provide important links between 'the immediate circumstances of organizational conversations' and 'the organizing properties of the [larger] network in which they figure' (Cooren & Taylor, 1997, p. 223).

To summarize this section, research on talk and identities has shown how the rules and structures associated with interactions in a particular setting help to constitute identity; how these rules and structures can be used strategically; how locally situated talk enacts broader social structures in the form of organizational and institutional identities (see Box 6.2).

BOX 6.2: TALK AND IDENTITIES

One of his [Vernon's] few successful innovations, perhaps his only one so far, was to have reduced the daily conference [meeting] from forty to fifteen minutes by means of a few modestly imposed rules: no more than five minutes on the post-mortem – what's done is done; no joke telling and, above all, no anecdotes; he didn't tell them, so no one else could. He turned to the international pages and frowned. 'An exhibition of pottery shards in Ankara? A news item? Eight hundred words? I simply don't get it, Frank.'

Frank Dibben, the deputy foreign editor, explained, perhaps with a trace of mockery. 'Well, you see Vernon, it represents a fundamental paradigm shift in our understanding of the influence of the early Persian Empire on ...'

'Paradigm shifts in broken pots aren't news, Frank.'

Grant McDonald, the deputy editor, who was sitting at Vernon's elbow, cut in gently. 'Thing is, Julie failed to file from Rome. They had to fill the ...'

'Not again. What is it now?'

'Hepatitis C.'

'So what about AP?'

Dibben spoke up. 'This was more interesting.'

'You're wrong. It's a complete turn-off. Even the TLS wouldn't run it.'

They then moved on to the day's schedule. In turn, the editors summarized the stories on their lists.

(Ian McEwan, Amsterdam, 1998, p. 35)

We selected this quotation as a fictional and stylized illustration of 'institutional dialogue' – a meeting central to the operation of the newspaper, where the identity of Vernon, the managing editor, is enacted within the context of shared understandings of the structure of the interaction and the 'identity' of the organization. Here, Vernon sets the ground rules of how the meeting will proceed; he initiates the discussion and asks questions of the other editors. In this way, his identity as managing editor is enacted in the interaction as participants understand and cooperate in the organization of the meeting, taking turns to present summaries of their stories. In doing so, their organizational identities – responsibilities, role in the hierarchy, reporting relationships, etc. – are also (re)constructed and performed. The meeting works because the participants possess and draw upon shared knowledge and acceptance of the conventions of the newspaper business, and the organizational hierarchy and roles of the The Judge newspaper in particular. While the individual deputy editors may disagree over the content of the newspaper, Vernon's role in controlling the interaction is not challenged and the deputy editors cooperate by filling in missing information and providing summaries of potential stories. By sharing a technical vocabulary and knowledge of the operations of the newspaper industry, they construct the identities of other newspapers (e.g., TLS – the Times Literary Supplement). In debating which stories constitute 'news', the participants are also constructing versions of the identities of their readers and of The Judge newspaper, which they differentiate from other newspapers. The meeting also represents fictional 'institutional talk', which enacts or performs the business and institutional identity of the newspaper: reporting news items, filing stories, deciding what is newsworthy. Stylistically, the interruptions in dialogue and the highly abbreviated sentences in the meeting suggest the dynamism and urgency of the newspaper business. The repeated participation of these individuals in such meetings builds shared meanings that co-produce organizational and individual identities and provide the basis for collective action.

Narrative and identities

Other writers also attend to the content of talk in their studies, but less in terms of the power of language *per se*, and more in terms of the role of narrative in constructing identities (e.g., Boje, 1995; see Chapter 2 by Gabriel and Chapter 9 by Mumby). Narratives are a discursive resource (Gergen, 1994) used to make sense of experience (Riessman, 1993), including the meaning of the self and relationships with others. Identities are thus constructed in the stories people tell about themselves (Lieblich et al., 1998). Personal stories are not merely 'a way of telling someone about one's life; they are the means by which identities may be fashioned' (Rosenwald & Ochberg, 1992, p. 1). Self-identity is constituted as actors attempt to construct a coherent, continuous biography where their 'life-story' is the sensible result of a series of related events or cohesive themes (Gergen, 1994). According to Bourdieu (2000), such a narrative is a 'rhetorical illusion' designed to conform to cultural expectations of the self as rational, consistent and unified. In constructing a particular version of their own identities, an actor also constructs identities of others (Davis & Harré, 1990). Moreover, as narratives are fashioned more generally to explain events, excuse failures, promote particular outcomes, etc., both individual and organizational identities are constructed (e.g., Boje, 1995; Cobb, 1993). Thus a 'figured world' (Kitchell et al., 2000) emerges of different identities and relationships among them (Gergen, 1994).

In telling a story, the narrative is addressed to an audience, actual or imagined (Bakhtin, 1981). Narratives therefore have to be negotiated within the particular social context if they are to be accepted as legitimate (Riessman, 1993). For example, in a study of Alcoholics Anonymous, Kitchell, Hannan and Kempton (2000) found that older members narratively 'corrected' new members' stories when they deviated from the shared group identity of a 'non-drinking alcoholic'. Similarly, in her study of the Swedish public sector, Czarniawska (1997) uses narrative analysis to show how organizational identities are the product of a recursive process between actors within the context of a particular narrative. In this case, the quest for a new identity for the Swedish public sector occurred through changes in the dominant rhetoric used in organizational narratives and through social interactions where actors oscillated between old and new identities. Organizational identities and institutional structures emerged from collective action as the narratives were enacted, but only when accepted by other actors. The meaning of a narrative is thus negotiated between the teller and the listener (Czarniawska, 1997; Umphrey, 1999), and constructions of identities and social relationships have to be accepted by others to be judged intelligible (Gergen, 1994).

Accordingly, attempts to construct new identities may not always be successful. Humphreys and Brown (2002) provide an illustration of resistance to organizational identity change from both internal and external stakeholders. They argue that one reason for the failure of this organizational identity change – in a further education institution pursuing university status – was that senior managers constructed a monolithic narrative and attempted to suppress the plurality of other narratives. In effect, they tried to replace or erase, rather than incorporate or build on, existing narratives. Employees and other stakeholders responded in a variety of ways to reconcile narratives of their individual identity with that of the organization. Their alternative narratives challenged the attempts of senior managers to construct a new narrative and, as a result, the quest to attain a 'university' identity was unsuccessful. The construction of individual and organizational identity is thus an interrelated process: people author narratives 'not just to account for their organizations and other communities, but to "enact" versions of themselves and their relationships to other social categories' (Humphreys & Brown, 2002, p. 439).

Since narratives constitute a purposeful form of social action (Gergen, 1994), actors may attempt to increase the power of their narrative. Cobb (1993) argues that narrative potency is derived from two factors: closure and cultural resonance.

Closure can be achieved through narrative structures, such as the use of a linear plot and contextualizing explanation, that reduce the range of possible interpretations at points where the narrative could be contested; and adhering to established conventions of an intelligible self-narrative, such as establishing a desirable goal, providing an explanation for the outcome, and representing characters as possessing a coherent identity over time, except where the transformation of identities is itself the point of the story (Gergen, 1994). Cultural resonance can be achieved through the use of familiar metaphors that allow actors to access the power of dominant cultural stories whose meaning has already been stabilized.

Narratives, however, are always negotiated *in situ* (Gubrium & Holstein, 1999). Rather than treating narratives as discrete objects or artefacts with clear beginnings and endings (e.g., Boje et al., 2001; Reissman, 1993), they should be recognized as situated, ongoing processes of social action (Cobb, 1993; Gergen, 1994). Thus while studies of narratives often highlight human agency and creativity, choices in the construction of narratives (e.g., the relevance of events, the representation of characters, the organization of the plot and the narrative form or genre) are constrained by cultural conventions. 'One is not free to have simply any form of personal history. Narrative conventions do not ... command identity, but they do invite certain actions and discourage others' (Gergen, 1994, p. 255). Actors can only choose from the broader cultural repertoire of discursive resources. In addition, access to such cultural repertoires is not equally distributed among social groups. For example, women are less likely to tell linear narratives: Mary Gergen (1992) found that women's autobiographies exhibited less narrative stability and closure – they were organized around multiple endpoints and included information and events that were unrelated to endpoints. In institutional settings that privilege linear narratives, women are clearly at a disadvantage (Cobb, 1993). Some actors are never able to tell a story at all. Boje (1995) examined how the animators who participated in the 1941 strike were literally written out of the official story about the Disney organization.

Narratives are, then, particularly important to the study of identities because of the way in which they operate as a form of social action that helps to produce the identities of themselves and others. They represent a potential resource in identity construction, but one that has to be negotiated among and accepted by other actors. In addition, not all actors have the opportunity to tell stories or, if they do, not all narratives are equally powerful in influencing ongoing social relationships in a particular context (see Box 6.3).

BOX 6.3: NARRATIVE AND IDENTITIES

Vernon's plan to publish the photographs in the newspaper is pre-empted by Julian's wife, who makes a press statement prior to the intended publication date.

Mrs Garmony ... cleared her throat and prepared to make her statement. She began with a little history of her marriage ... Her voice was relaxed, even intimate, and derived its authority not so much from class, or status as a Cabinet Minister's wife, as from her own professional eminence ... Right at the beginning, she said, Julian told her something about himself, something rather startling, even a little shocking. But it was nothing that love could not absorb, and over the years it had endeared itself to her and she had come to regard it with respect, as an inseparable part of her husband's individuality ... She said calmly that she knew a newspaper with a political agenda of its own intended to publish this photograph and others tomorrow in the expectation of driving her husband from office. She had only this to say: the newspaper would not succeed because love was a greater force than spite. ... [When] asked whether she had any particular message for the editor of The Judge. *Yes, she said ... 'Mr Halliday, you have the mentality of a blackmailer and the moral stature of a flea.'* (Ian McEwan, *Amsterdam*, 1998, pp. 124–5)

A broad consensus emerged over the weekend that The Judge *had gone too far and was a disgusting newspaper, that Julian Garmony was a decent fellow and Vernon Halliday ('The Flea') was despicable and his head was urgently needed on a plate. In the Sundays, the life style sections portrayed the new supportive wife who had her own career and fought her husband's corner. The editorials concentrated on the few remaining neglected aspects of Mrs. Garmony's speech including 'love is greater than spite'.* (Ian McEwan, *Amsterdam*, 1998, p. 127)

In this press statement, Mrs Garmony is constructing a narrative of her marriage as well as her and her husband's identities. She is able to tell a convincing story that bridges the contradiction between her husband as Conservative politician and as transvestite through a narrative of 'individuality'. She uses the device to provide thematic coherence and re-establish a consistent and stable identity for her husband. She also draws on a culturally familiar narrative archetype – that of the romance. Within this framework, her love and relationship with her husband are depicted as triumphing over the 'spite' of the newspaper editor. In telling her story, she constructs not only her husband's identity but also her own and Vernon's identities. Julian's identity is no longer contradictory and hypocritical, but individual and loving. Her identity as a wife and a professional is important in constructing her as the authentic – and believable – author of the story and, in telling the story and co-authoring her husband's identity, her identity is reinforced and enhanced. She becomes a symbol of the spirit of the times and representative of the contemporary supportive wife, who is also an independent professional. In stark contrast, Vernon is cast as the villain. The fact that she tells her story before Vernon is able to tell his makes her story more powerful. The acceptance of her narrative is evident in its reproduction in the media, which repeats the narrative identities she has constructed and the culturally familiar romantic form – 'love is greater than spite'.

Interdiscusivity, social practice and identities

We refer to the final site of discourse analysis as 'interdiscursivity and social practice' to differentiate research that adopts a Foucauldian perspective and focuses on the ways in which broader discourses are used to construct subject positions that both enable and limit a range of social practices. Foucault's work has had a significant impact on the theorization of the relationship between discourse and identities (e.g., Du Gay, 1996; Garsten & Grey, 1997; Grey, 1994). According to this view, discourses, such as the enterprise culture (Du Gay, 1996), human resources management (Townley,

1993), racism (Wetherell & Potter, 1992), patriarchy and class (Homer-Nadesan, 1996) produce the power/ knowledge relations within which subjects are positioned, subjectivities are constructed, and bodies are disciplined. Discourse thus regulates not just what can be sensibly said about a particular object but also who can speak and from what position (Barker, 2000). Discourse in this sense refers to what Alvesson & Kärreman (2000, p. 1133) call 'Grand Discourse' – 'an assembly of discourses, ordered and presented as an integrated frame' – that represents a field of power in which actors are required to take up particular subject positions in order to speak (Parker, 1992; Potter & Wetherell, 1987), and from which particular practices follow (e.g., Phillips & Hardy, 1997).

For example, in tracing the development of the Tavistock Institute from the early twentieth century, Miller and Rose (1988) show how employee subjectivity became a focus for the Institute's expertise. Problems of productivity, absenteeism and organizational performance became defined as issues of the psychological welfare of employees and their relationships at work, particularly group relations. Groups were constructed as a mechanism for the social integration of individual employees into the organization. In this way, knowledge concerning organizational problems also constituted certain forms of identities that had effects on the ways in which individuals could act in organizations.

In Fairclough's terms (1995, p. 134), research must focus on interdiscursivity – the 'seemingly limitless possibilities of creativity in discursive practice' (i.e., the production, distribution and consumption of a text) as well as the way in which a discursive event is related to the order of discourse (or Grand Discourse). Foucault's work broadens the site of research even further from a concern with text to incorporate the extra-linguistic. For example, Tretheway's (1999) study explores Foucault's notion of the body as the site of power and how the intersection of gendered and organizational discourses resulted in a complex discursive field where women had to carefully negotiate their embodied identities. She examines how women professionalize their own bodies, that is, how they manage and control their bodies in routine ways in order to attain a professional identity. This included controlling bodily weight to appear fit, body language that signified interest in but did not threaten men, and dress that concealed or downplayed the 'femaleness' of their bodies. Revealing the 'femaleness' of a body at work was to risk being assigned a sexual, rather than a professional, identity, although women still had to dress in an appropriately feminine way. The professionalism of women's embodied identities was thus a product of the monitoring and judgements of others and self-management.

One criticism of Foucault's work has been its insensitivity to the way in which actors contribute to the deployment of discursive practices (Hollway, 1984). Subjects are 'done to' rather than 'doing' (Newton, 1998, p. 428).

[W]ithin a Foucauldian framework it is hard to gain a sense of how active agential selves 'make a difference' through 'playing' with discursive practices. To emphasize such agency is not to posit some essential subject, but rather to argue that understanding how the subject is constituted in discourse requires attention to the social processes through which people actively manoeuvre in relation to discursive practice. (Newton, 1998, pp. 425–6)

Accordingly, research has been undertaken that focuses more directly on agency (see Chapter 13 by Hardy & Phillips). Hardy, Palmer and Phillips (2000) show how a manager was able to change the identity of an organization from an 'international' non-governmental organization (NGO) to a 'local' one (and back again) through discursive means. He did so by making a series of discursive 'statements'. He introduced a new discourse of localization, and made increasing use of local symbols and narratives about localization, engaging in actions that were appropriately grounded in the prevailing discursive context. So, for example, the concept of a local NGO was well embedded in this particular context; the symbols and narratives he used were commonly recognized among the various actors; and he occupied a subject position from which he could speak. His activities helped to associate the existing organization with a new concept – a local NGO – and thereby create a new object, but only because his actions had meaning in the broader discursive context.

Equally, an interest in the disciplinary effects of discourse need not rule out resistance. Knights and Vurdubakis (1994) have argued that the existence of multiple, overlapping and contradictory discourses provide people with flexibility, reflexivity, dialogue and some choice in the identities with which they identify and this, in turn, provides scope for resistance. For example, in their study of a 'Big Six' accounting firm, Covaleski, Dirsmith, Heian and Samuel (1998) explore two management techniques – mentoring and management by objectives (MBO) – and how they relate to the construction of two competing professional identities – the 'autonomous professional' who deals with clients and technical matters and the 'business person' who is concerned with the financial performance of the firm. Mentoring was a relatively successful disciplinary practice whereby new or junior employees learned how to be and act within the organization, transforming their identities through a close relationship with a more senior person who personified the successful corporate identity. MBO produced hierarchies of differentiation as individuals were assessed and classified against established objectives that became the basis for corrective action, normalizing those whose performance was measured as below the norm and requiring individuals to encode standards of behaviour that benefitted the organization. However, the disciplinary practice of MBO was resisted by accountants identifying themselves as 'autonomous professionals', who were concerned with client relationships rather than the alternative identity of 'businessperson'. In other words, the existence of incomplete and contradictory discourses provides employees with opportunities to 'counter-identify or dis-identify with managerial formulations of their identity' (Holmer-Nadesan, 1996, p. 50), regardless of how much 'identity regulation' in which managers engage (Alvesson & Willmott, 2002).

To summarize this section, studies of discourse show how disciplinary techniques and normalization produce embodied identities and create limited subject positions from which only certain identities can speak. At the same time, while the discursive activities of individuals may be constrained, there is some scope for agency and resistance, and discursive activity is, as a result, likely to engender struggles around identities, regardless of how fixed they may appear to be (Box 6.4).

BOX 6.4: INTERDISCURSIVITY, SOCIAL PRACTICE AND IDENTITIES

Around five o'clock that afternoon, it occurred to the many newspaper editors who had bid for Molly's photographs that the trouble with Vernon's paper was that it was out of step with changing times. As a leader on one broadsheet put to its readers on Friday morning: 'it seems to have escaped the attention of the editor of The Judge that the decade we live in now is not like the one before. Then, self-advancement was the watchword, while greed and hypocrisy were the rank realities. Now we live in a more reasonable, compassionate and tolerant age in which the private and harmless preferences of individuals, however public they may be, remain their own business ...

Front-page headlines divided more or less equally between 'blackmailer' and 'flea' ... two thousand members of the Transvestite Pink Alliance marched on Judge House in their high heels, holding aloft copies of the disgraced front page ... the parliamentary party seized the moment and passed an overwhelming vote of confidence [in Garmony]. ... The Prime Minister suddenly felt emboldened to speak up for his old friend ... The matter was rather more complex for The Judge's board of directors. ... How could they sack an editor to whom they had given a unanimous vote of support last Wednesday?

Finally ... George Lane [one of the directors] had a good idea.

'Look, there was nothing wrong in purchasing those photographs ... [but] he was quite wrong to have gone ahead [and published them]. On Friday the paper was made to look ridiculous. He should have seen which way the wind was blowing and got out. If you're asking me, it was a serious failure of editorial judgement.' (Ian McEwan, *Amsterdam*, 1998, p. 126–8)

In this quotation, we can see how people are positioned within broader discourses that change over time. Vernon, the editor of *The Judge*, appears to have misjudged his audience by drawing on outmoded discourses of politics and sexual identity. Instead of marginalizing Garmony's subject position, Garmony's transvestism becomes a symbol of a new social decency that rests on tolerance of difference and respect for individual privacy. This opens up space for action by a series of subject positions, including not just organized, collective action by an alliance of transvestites, but also statements and actions by other newspapers, the parliamentary party, and the Prime Minister, all of whom are now able to speak and act in a way that supports Garmony's identities. This is not to suggest that these subject positions have free agency – occupants must continue to conform to prevailing discourses. Therefore, transvestites must appear in pink and in heels, while *The Judge's* Board of Directors must make a sensible and legitimate business decision, if both are to retain their identities within these ongoing processes of the negotiation of meaning.

CONCLUSIONS

The research reviewed above shows the complex ways in which identities are constructed: the overlapping and interwoven influences of language, interactions, stories and discourses; the tensions between discursive constraints and agential action; the struggles that underpin the negotiations among actors; the basis of broader institutional forms in locally situated talk; the way in which identity is a resource in and an outcome of these processes. It is from this confluence of complex relationships that identities emerge. It is also clear that the construction of identities has important implications for organization. First, organizations are one setting in which identities are constructed and the organizational identities of individuals are one of the myriad of categories of identities by which they are categorized. Second, collective identities that relate to particular organizations are formed in language and other discursive acts in the same way as individual identities. Third, identity and organization implicate each other: as identities are formed so too are organizations, as local meanings are scaled up and objectified.

The relationships and processes that we have described are clearly complex. One reaction to such complexity is to propose, in keeping with the normal conventions of academia, that future research should attend to the interplay of all these different aspects. Of course, we also know that such research is difficult – multiple, contested theorizations exist and in any individual empirical project, certain sets of relationships will inevitably figure over others. So, we are also inclined to say let us do the best we can, the novelists can do the rest.

Finally, we have used discourse analysis to explore the discursive construction of identity and our own academic identities are implicated in this process: we must acknowledge that our writing does not stand apart from these processes – our words have the same status as those we have analysed. So, rather than finish with a conclusion to stabilize and reinforce our interpretations of discursive approaches to identity, we have labelled the following box a 'coda' (literally a 'tail' at the end of a musical movement). This is a reference to the musical motif in the quotation below (Box 6.5) and a means of revisiting issues in our discussion but also developing them in new directions.

BOX 6.5: CODA

Throughout the novel, Clive's identity as a composer is suffering from his inability to complete his latest composition. Finally:

And it was almost done. Wednesday night into Thursday morning Clive revised and perfected the diminuendo. All that was required now was to go back several pages in the score to the clamorous restatement and vary the harmonies perhaps, or even the melody itself, or devise some form of rhythmic undertow, a syncopation that cut into the leading edge of the notes. To Clive this variation had become a crucial feature of the work's conclusion; it needed to suggest the future's unknowability. When that by now familiar melody returned for the very last time, altered in a small and significant way, it should prompt insecurity in the listener; it was a caution against clinging too tightly to what we know. (Ian McEwan, Amsterdam, 1998, p. 136)

In writing this coda, we are obviously responding to the ubiquitous demand for 'reflexivity' but does this coda really represent reflexivity? Are we genuine or cynical? Has reflexivity itself become a 'set piece' – a ritualistic hurdle that one must jump over – or at least ease under – in order to occupy a valid subject position within the broader realm of discourse analysis and social constructionism in organizational studies?

NOTES

We would like to thank Margie Wetherell and Karen Ashcraft for their helpful and supportive comments on the draft of this chapter.

1 Extract from *Amsterdam* by Ian McEwan published by Jonathan Cape, copyright © 1999 and 1998 Ian McEwan. All the quotations from this work are used with permission of the author c/o Coleridge & White Ltd, 20 Powis Mews, London W11 1JN, with permission of the Random House Group, and with permission of Doubleday, a division of Random House, Inc.

2 Also see Chapter 13 by Hardy & Phillips.

3 We are grateful to Margie Wetherell for helping us reframe our categorization in this way.

4 Some of this discussion appears in Ainsworth (2003).

5 Talk-in-interaction is considered by a number of writers to be a preferable term to conversation analysis, although some (e.g., Zimmerman, 1998) use the term 'discourse' to refer to talk-in-interaction, a quite different usage of 'discourse' from the one we employ in this chapter.

6 We are grateful to Karen Ashcraft for pointing this out.

REFERENCES

Ainsworth, S. (2003) The discursive construction of older worker identity. Unpublished PhD thesis.

Albert, S. & Whetten, D. (1985) Organizational identity. In L.L. Cummings & B.M. Staw (eds), *Research in organizational behavior* (Vol. 7, pp. 263–95). Greenwich, CT: JAI Press.

Alvesson, M. & Kärreman, D. (2000) Varieties of discourse: On the study of organizations through discourse analysis. *Human Relations*, 53 (9): 1125–49.

Alvesson, M. & Willmott, H. (2002) Identity regulation as organizational control: Producing the appropriate individual. *Journal of Management Studies*, 39 (5): 619–44.

Antaki, C. & Widdicombe, S. (eds) (1998a) *Identities in talk*. London and Thousand Oaks, CA: Sage.

Antaki, C. & Widdicombe, S. (1998b) Identity as an achievement and as a tool. In C. Antaki & S. Widdicombe (eds), *Identities in talk* (pp. 1–14). London and Thousand Oaks, CA: Sage.

Baack, D. & Prasch, T. (1997) The death of the subject and the life of the organization: Implications of new approaches to subjectivity for organizational analysis. *Journal of Management Inquiry*, 6 (2): 131–41.

Bakhtin, M.M. (1981) *The dialogic imagination: Four essays by M.M. Bakhtin*. Edited by M. Holquist, trans. by C. Emerson & M. Holquist. Austin, TX: University of Texas Press.

Barker, C. (2000) *Cultural studies: Theory and practice*. London and Thousand Oaks, CA: Sage.

Boden, D. (1994) *The business of talk: Organizations in action*. Cambridge: Polity Press.

Boje, D.M. (1995) 'Stories of the storytelling organization: a postmodern analysis of Disney as '*Tamara*-land'. *Academy of Management Journal*, 38 (4): 997–1035.

Boje. D.M., Alvarez, R.C. & Schooling, B. (2001) Reclaiming story in organization: Narratologies and action sciences. In R. Westwood & S. Linstead (eds), *Language and organization* (pp. 132–75). London: Sage.

Bourdieu, P. (2000) The biographical illusion. In P. du Gay, J. Evans & P. Redman (eds), *Identity: A reader* (pp. 297–310). London: Sage.

Butler, J. (1990) *Gender trouble: Feminism and the subversion of identity*. London: Routledge.

Cameron, D. (1995) *Verbal hygiene*. London and New York: Routledge.

Cameron, D. (1996) The language–gender interface: Challenging co-optation. In V.I. Bergvall, J.M. Bing & A.F. Freed (eds), *Rethinking language and gender research: Theory and practice* (pp. 31–53). London and New York: Longman.

Cheney, G. & Christensen, L.T. (2001) Organizational identity: Linkages between internal and external communication. In F.M. Jablin & L.L. Putnam (eds), *The new handbook of organizational communication: Advances in theory, research and methods*, (pp. 231–69). Thousand Oaks, CA: Sage.

Cobb, S. (1993) Empowerment and mediation: A narrative perspective. *Negotiation Journal*, July: 245–59.

Collins, R. (1981) On the microfoundations of macrosociology. *American Journal of Sociology*, 86 (5): 984–1013.

Cooren, F. & Taylor, J.R. (1997) Organization as an effect of mediation: Redefining the link between organization and communication. *Communication Theory*, 7 (3): 219–59.

Covaleski, M.A., Dirsmith, M.W., Heian, J.B. & Samuel, S. (1998) The calculated and the avowed: Techniques of discipline and struggles over identity in big six public accounting firms. *Administrative Science Quarterly*, 42: 293–327.

Czarniawska, B. (1997) *Narrating the organization: Dramas of institutional identity*. Chicago: University of Chicago Press.

Davis, B. & Harré, R. (1990) Positioning: The discursive production of selves. *Journal for the Theory of Social Behaviour*, 20 (1): 43–65. Reading 19 taken from M. Wetherell, S. Taylor & S.J. Yates (eds) (2001) *Discourse theory and practice: A reader* (pp. 261–71). London: Sage in association with the Open University.

Deetz, S. (1992) *Democracy in an age of corporate colonization: Developments in communication and the politics of everyday life*. Albany, NY: State University of New York.

De Saussure, F. (1983) *Course in general linguistics*. Trans. and annotated by Roy Harris. London: Gerald Duckworth & Co.

Derrida, J. (1979) *Spurs: Nietzsche's styles*. Trans. B. Harlow. Chicago: University of Chicago Press.

Derrida, J. (1981) *Positions*. Trans. A. Bass. Chicago: University of Chicago Press.

Drew, P. & Heritage, J. (1992) Analysing talk at work: An introduction. In P. Drew & J. Heritage (eds), *Talk at work: Interaction in institutional settings* (pp. 3–65). Cambridge: Cambridge University Press.

Drew, P. & Sorjonen, M.-L. (1997) Institutional dialogue. In T.A. Van Dijk (ed.), *Discourse studies: A multidisciplinary introduction*. Vol. 2: *Discourse as Social Interaction* (pp. 92–119). London: Sage.

Du Gay, P. (1996) *Consumption and identity at work*. London: Sage.

Dyer, G. (1982) *Advertising as communication*. London & New York: Methuen.

Fairclough, N. (1992) *Discourse and social change*. Cambridge: Polity Press.

Fairclough, N. (1995) *Critical discourse analysis*. London: Longman.

Fairclough, N. & Wodak, R. (1997) Critical discourse analysis. In T.A. Van Dijk (ed.), *Discourse studies: A multidisciplinary introduction*. Vol. 2: *Discourse as social interaction* (pp. 258–84). London: Sage.

Fiol, M. (2002) Capitalizing on paradox: The role of language in transforming organizational identities. *Organization Science*, 13 (6): 653–66.

Foucault, M. (1972) *The archaeology of knowledge*. London: Tavistock.

Foucault, M. (1976) *The birth of the clinic*. London: Tavistock.

Garfinkel, H. (1974) On the origins of the term 'ethnomethodology'. In R. Turner (ed.), *Ethnomethodology* (pp. 15–18). Harmondsworth: Penguin.

Garsten, C. & Grey, C. (1997) How to become oneself: Discourses of subjectivity in post-bureaucratic organizations. *Discourse and Organization*, 4 (2): 211–28.

Gergen, K.J. (1994) *Realities and relationships: Soundings in social construction*. Cambridge, MA: Harvard University Press.

Gergen, K.J. (2001) *Social construction in context*. London: Sage.

Gergen, M.M. (1992) Life stories: Pieces of a dream. In G.C. Rosenwald & R.L. Ochberg (eds), *Storied lives: The cultural politics of self-understanding* (pp. 127–44). New Haven, CT: Yale University Press.

Gioia, D.A. & Thomas, J.B. (1996) Identity, image and issue interpretation: Sensemaking during strategic change in academia. *Administrative Science Quarterly*, 41: 370–403.

Gray, J. (1992) *Men are from Mars, women are from Venus*. New York: Harper Collins.

Grey, C. (1994) Career as a project of the self and labour process discipline. *Sociology*, 28 (2): 479–98.

Gubrium, J.F. & Holstein, J.A. (1999) At the border of narrative and ethnography. *Journal of Contemporary Ethnography*, 28 (5): 561–73.

Hacking, I. (2000) *The social construction of what?* Cambridge, MA and London: Harvard University Press.

Hall, S. (1997a) The work of representation. In S. Hall (ed.), *Representation: Cultural representations and signifying practices* (pp. 15–64). London: Sage in association with the Open University.

Hall, S. (1997b) The spectacle of the other. In S. Hall (ed.), *Representation: Cultural representations and signifying practices*, (pp. 233–79). London: Sage in association with the Open University.

Hardy, C., Lawrence, T. & Phillips, N. (1998) Talking action: Conversations, narrative and action in interorganizational collaboration. In D. Grant, T. Keenoy & C. Oswick (eds), *Discourse and Organization* (pp. 65–83). London: Sage.

Hardy, C., Palmer, I. & Phillips, N. (2000) Discourse as a strategic resource. *Human Relations*, 53 (9): 1227–47.

Heritage, J. (2001) Goffman, Garfinkel and conversation analysis. In M. Wetherell, S. Taylor & S.J. Yates (eds), *Discourse theory and practice: A reader* (pp. 47–56). London: Sage in association with the Open University.

Hollway, W. (1984) Gender difference and the production of subjectivity. In J. Henriques, W. Hollway, C. Urwin, C. Venn & V. Walkerdine (eds), *Changing the Subject*, (pp. 227–63). London: Methuen. Reading 20 in M. Wetherell, S. Taylor & S.J. Yates (eds) (2001) *Discourse theory and practice: A reader* (pp. 272–83). London: Sage in association with the Open University.

Holmer-Nadesan, M. (1996) Organizational identity and space of action. *Organization Studies*, 17 (1): 49–81.

Humphreys, M. & Brown, A.D. (2002) Narratives of organizational identity and identification. *Organization Studies*, 23 (3): 421–48.

Hutchby I. & Woolfitt, R. (1998) *Conversation analysis: Principles, practices and applications*. Cambridge: Polity Press.

Iedema, R.A.M. (1998) Institutional responsibility and hidden meanings. *Discourse & Society*, 9 (4): 481–500.

Jaworski, A. & Coupland, N. (1999) Introduction: Perspectives on discourse analysis. In A. Jaworski & N. Coupland (eds), *The discourse reader* (pp. 1–44). London and New York: Routledge.

Kärreman, D. & Alvesson, M. (2001) Making newsmakers: Conversational identity at work. *Organization Studies*, 22 (1): 59–89.

Kitchell, A. Hannan, E. & Kempton, W. (2000) Identity through stories: Story structure and function in two environmental groups. *Human Organization*, 59 (1): 96–105.

Knights, D. & Vurdubakis, T. (1994) Foucault, power, resistance and all that. In J.M. Jermier, D. Knights & W.R. Nord (eds), *Resistance and power in organizations* (pp. 167–98). London: Routledge.

Kress, G. (2001) 'From Saussure to critical sociolinguistics: The turn towards a social view of language. In M. Wetherell, S. Taylor & S.J. Yates (eds), *Discourse theory and practice: A reader* (pp. 29–38). London: Sage in association with the Open University.

Lakoff, R. (1975) *Language and woman's place*. New York: Harper & Row.

Lee, D. (1992) *Competing discourses*. London: Longman.

Lieblich, A., Tuval-Mashiach, R. & Zilber, T. (1998) *Narrative research: Reading, analysis and interpretation*. Thousand Oaks, CA: Sage.

Maybin, J. (2001) Language, struggle and voice: The Bakhtin/Volosinov writings. In M. Wetherell, S. Taylor & S.J. Yates (eds), *Discourse theory and practice: A reader* (pp. 64–71). London: Sage in association with the Open University.

Miller, P. & Rose, N. (1988) The Tavistock programme: The government of subjectivity and social life. *Sociology*, 22 (2): 171–92.

Newton, T. (1998) Theorizing subjectivity in organizations: The failure of Foucauldian studies? *Organization Studies*, 19 (3): 415–47.

Parker, I. (1992) *Discourse dynamics*, London: Routledge.

Phillips, N. & Hardy, C. (1997) Managing multiple identities: Discourse, legitimacy and resources in the UK refugee system. *Organization*, 4 (2): 159–85.

Phillips, N. & Hardy, C. (2002) *Discourse analysis: Investigating processes of social construction*. Thousand Oaks, CA: Sage.

Piller, I. (2001) Identity constructions in multilingual advertising. *Language in Society*, 30: 153–86.

Pomerantz, A. & Fehr, B.J. (1997) Conversation analysis: An approach to the study of social action as sense-making practices. In T.A. Van Dijk (ed.), *Discourse studies: A multidisciplinary introduction*. Vol. 2: *Discourse as Social Interaction* (pp. 64–91). London: Sage.

Potter, J. & Wetherell, M. (1987) *Discourse and social psychology: Beyond attitudes and behaviour*. London: Sage.

Psathas, G. (1995) *Conversation analysis: The study of talk-in-interaction*. Thousand Oaks, CA: Sage.

Reissman, C.K. (1993) *Narrative analysis*. Newbury Park, CA: Sage.

Rosenwald, G.C. & Ochberg, R.L. (1992) *Storied lives: The cultural politics of self understanding*. New Haven, CT: Yale University Press.

Sacks, H., Schegloff, R. & Jefferson, G. (1974) A simplest systematics for the organization of turn-taking for conversation. *Language*, 50: 696–735.

Schegloff, E.A. (1991) Reflections on talk and social structure. In D. Boden & D. Zimmerman (eds), *Talk and Social Structure* (pp. 44–70). Cambridge: Polity Press. Taken from A. Jaworski & N. Coupland (eds) (1999) *The discourse reader*, (pp. 107–20). London and New York: Routledge.

Schegloff, E.A. (1997) Whose text? Whose context? *Discourse and Society*, 8 (2): 165–87.

Schegloff, E.A, Ochs, E. & Thompson, S.A. (1996) Introduction. In E. Ochs, E.A. Schegloff & S.A. Thompson (eds), *Interaction and grammar* (pp. 1–51). Cambridge: Cambridge University Press.

Silverman, D. (1997) The construction of 'delicate' objects in counselling. In *Discourses of counselling: HIV counselling as social interaction* (Chapter 4). London: Sage. Reading 10 in M. Wetherell, S. Taylor, & S.J. Yates (eds) (2001) *Discourse theory and practice: A reader* (pp. 119–37). London: Sage in association with the Open University.

Taylor, J.R. & Van Every, E.J. (1993) *The vulnerable fortress: Bureaucratic organizations and management in the information age*. Toronto: University of Toronto Press.

Taylor, J.R., Cooren, F., Giroux, N. & Robichaud, D. (1996) The communicational basis of organization: Between the conversation and the text. *Communication Theory*, 6 (1): 1–39.

Townley, B. (1993) Foucault, power/knowledge and its relevance for human resource management. *Academy Management Review*, 18 (3): 518–45.

Trethewey, A. (1999) Disciplined bodies: Women's embodied identities at work. *Organization Studies*, 20 (3): 423–50.

Tsoukas, H. & Chia, R. (2002) On organizational becoming: Rethinking organizational change. *Organization Science*, 13 (5): 567–82.

Umphrey, M.M. (1999) The dialogics of legal meanings: Spectacular trials, the unwritten law, and narratives of criminal responsibility. *Law & Society Review*, 33 (2): 293–324.

Wetherell, M. & Potter, J. (1992) *Mapping the language of racism: Discourse and the legitimation of exploitation*. London: Harvester Wheatsheaf.

Wodak, R. (1996) The genesis of racist discourse in Austria since 1989. In C.R. Caldas-Coulthard & M. Coulthard (eds), *Texts and practices: Readings in critical discourse analysis* (pp. 107–28). London: Routledge.

Zimmerman, D.H. (1998) Identity, context and interaction. In C. Antaki & S. Widdicombe (eds), *Identities in talk* (pp. 87–106). London and Thousand Oaks, CA: Sage.

7

Interpretivist Approaches to Organizational Discourse

Loizos Th. Heracleous

INTERPRETIVISM AND THE LINGUISTIC TURN

There is a broad range of theoretical approaches within the interpretive tradition, with varying ontological and epistemological positions (Burrell & Morgan, 1979). However, a key unifying factor is their focus on achieving a *meaningful understanding* of the actors' frame of reference, what Weber (1922) referred to as *verstehen*. In Weber's view, this ability and desire to achieve an in-depth, first-order understanding was what distinguished the social from the natural sciences. Meaningful understanding is often contrasted with *explanation* (Ricœur, 1991), the search for causal, law-like deterministic regularities that is to be found in the positivist tradition – a tradition based on the methodology of the natural sciences. This simple contrast, however, does not do justice to the potential for meaningful understanding and explanation to operate in a complementary manner.

Interpretivism should not be equated with subjectivism. This perspective is based upon the misconception that interpretivism lacks 'objectivity' and instead affords primacy to the idiosyncratic meanings of single actors with no necessary relation to a more shared, intersubjective and verifiable reality. If interpretivism were to assume more subjective properties, this would suggest a potential for unlimited interpretations of observations and textual data, with no means of verification or validation. Such a characterization is at the heart of Denzin's (1983) criticism that interpretivists reject generalization since each instance of observed social interaction is unique and social settings are complex and indeterminate.

Interpretive understanding does not, however, mean a degeneration to subjectivism, unlimited interpretations and the inability to make any sort of generalization, and several scholars emphasize this point. For Weber (1922), for example, the search for generalizations derived inductively from first-order data was compatible with, and indeed dependent on, the need for meaningful understanding of social action. His ideal types were aimed inductively to derive second-order frameworks based on regularities and patterns of observed phenomena. Eco's (1990) 'limits of interpretation', in addition, is an eloquent statement of the position that having unlimited interpretations does not imply that all interpretations are equally likely or valid. Textual interpretations can be informed, limited or constrained by such features as the semantic meaning of the words used, the internal coherence of the text and its cultural context, as well as the interpreter's own frame of reference (Eco, 1990). Ricœur (1991) and Giddens (1979, 1987) have also proposed criteria for validity of textual interpretations as a counter to subjectivism and relativism, that will be discussed below in the section on hermeneutics. Finally, Williams (2000), argues that interpretivists do in fact generalize, and that generalization in interpretive research is 'inevitable, desirable and possible'. He distinguishes between total generalizations (deterministic laws or axioms), statistical generalizations (where the probability of a situation or feature occurring can be calculated from its instances within a sample representative of a wider population), and *moderatum* generalizations (where aspects of a situation are examples of broader sets of features). He suggests that interpretive research does not aim to make total or statistical generalizations but can make moderatum generalizations, within the limits of the inductive problem (that one cannot generalize from a small number of cases to unknown cases) and the ontological problem of categorical equivalence (that generalizations within one category of experience of domain may not apply to other categories).

Interpretive discourse analysis is thus not content with merely identifying the subjective meanings attached to single texts; it considers multiple texts where they constitute bodies of discourse[1]. In doing so, it aims to identify discursive structures and patterns across these texts such as enthymemes, central themes or root metaphors, and to explore how these structures influence and shape agents' interpretations, actions and social practices (e.g., Hardy & Phillips, 1999; Heracleous & Barrett, 2001).

The linguistic turn in the social sciences has drawn attention to the way language shapes or constructs actors' first-order interpretations and actions and thus its role in shaping social practices and social reality. This orientation goes against earlier 'correspondence' or 'representational' views of language, as accurately representing (but not constructing) the world, and merely functioning as a conduit for the transfer of pre-determined communicative messages. Wittgenstein's *Philosophical Investigations* (1968) was instrumental in advancing this constructive view of language, interestingly repudiating his earlier representational theory of language advanced in his *Tractatus Logico-Philosophicus* (1955).

The next section addresses the question of the discursive construction of reality. Interpretive approaches assume that reality is socially constructed and that discourses (as collections of texts using the raw material of language) have a central role in this process. We thus set the context for discussing interpretive approaches by discussing the process of discursive reality construction. Within this process, a useful way to view discourse is as situated symbolic action (Heracleous & Hendry, 2000). The generation and interpretation of discourses is context-dependent or situated in broader contexts; discourse is action in the sense that its originators aim to achieve certain outcomes through communication; and discourse is symbolic not only in a textual, semantic sense, but in a more substantive sense indicating actors' assumptions, values and beliefs through actors' discursive choices (conscious or subconscious) that construct and evoke frames of reference for interpreting issues. The last part of this section on 'discourse and cognition' adopts a cognitive perspective to suggest that discourse constructs social reality through its constructive effects on actors' cognitions.

The third section discusses interpretive approaches to organizational discourse, and in particular the fields of hermeneutics, rhetoric, metaphor, symbolic interactionism and critical discourse analysis. These theoretical fields all share a constructive ontology of social phenomena, ascribe a central role to discourse in this process, and offer complementary ways of understanding it. In other words, these are not simply abstract theoretical approaches, but also offer more concrete analytical directions for conducting discourse analyses (Table 7.1 summarizes the main conceptual orientations and potential analytical directions of these fields). Finally, the conclusion includes a brief outline of the main ideas in this chapter, and highlights the value of the interpretive discourse approaches discussed here.

DISCOURSE AS CONSTRUCTIVE OF SOCIAL REALITY

Social constructionism and the fluidity of social reality

How does discourse construct social reality? Underlying this question is the realization that social phenomena do not have the same solidity, stability and amenability to experimental observation as natural phenomena. They are defined by actors themselves and can thus be better understood if we take into account first-order meanings of the actors involved; a phenomenological view that became a cornerstone of the interpretive paradigm (Burrell & Morgan, 1979). Social phenomena are characterized by high degrees of latitude in how they are portrayed as well as interpreted by social actors. Consequently, actors can both take control or manipulate how they present issues, as well as employ selective perception in order to protect and maintain their routinized or comfortable ways of perceiving issues. As Hardy and Phillips (2002, p. 2) put it, 'the things that make up the social world – including our very identities – appear out of discourse … without discourse, there is no social reality, and without understanding discourse, we cannot understand social reality, our experiences, or ourselves'.

Early social constructivisits provide some interesting insights into this process. Berger and Luckmann (1966) suggested that social reality is known to individuals in terms of symbolic universes constructed through social interaction. They viewed language as the 'most important sign system of human society' (1966, p. 51), the primary means through which 'objectivation', the manifestation of subjective meanings through actions, proceeds. Language makes subjective meanings 'real', and at the same time typifies these meanings through creating 'semantic fields or zones of meaning' (1966, p. 55) within which daily routines proceed. Language also creates mental frames that are 'metacommunicative' (Bateson, 1972, p. 188), simultaneously highlighting certain meanings and excluding others, evoking particular typifications and associations through framing and connotation (Phillips & Brown, 1993, p. 1564). Language, in this perspective, creates conditioned (rather than universal) rationalities as widespread ways of thinking within particular social systems, which become elements of those systems' social realities (Gergen & Thatchenkery, 1996; Heracleous & Barrett, 2001).

Social reality, seen as shared mental schemes or, as Moscovici (1981) has termed them, social representations, is thus mainly based on *discursive* interaction. Social representations are 'largely acquired, used and changed, through text and talk' (Van Dijk, 1990, p. 165). More generally, 'all concepts, categories, complex representations, as well as the processes of their manipulation, are acquired and used mostly in social contexts of perception, interpretation and interaction' (Van Dijk, 1988, p. 134).

Discourse as situated symbolic action

One useful way of understanding the nature of discourse and its effects on social reality is to view it as situated symbolic action. Speech act theory (Austin, 1962; Searle, 1975) offers a compelling statement of *discourse as action*. Austin (1962, p. 12) challenged the traditional assumption of the philosophy of language, that 'to say something … is always and simply to *state* something', that is either true or false, and developed the influential thesis that 'to *say* something is to *do* something' (emphases in original). Austin went on to distinguish analytically between locutionary speech acts (the act of saying something) (1962, p. 94), illocutionary speech acts (what individuals intend to achieve in saying something) (1962, p. 98), and lastly perlocutionary speech acts (the actual effects of utterances on their audience) (1962, p. 101). In practice, however, an utterance can perform all three simultaneously. The insights of speech act theory formed the theoretical foundation for discourse pragmatics, the study of language in use (Blum-Kulka, 1997).

Speech act theory, however, essentially remains at the micro level of single utterances without extending to the broader level of discourse as patterned collections of texts, so that it cannot analyse what Van Dijk (1977) has termed 'macro' speech acts, or Alvesson and Kärreman's (2000) 'grand' or 'mega' discourses. To achieve this, a more contextually sensitive and holistic approach would be needed, such as hermeneutic or rhetorical analysis. At the same time discourse is also *symbolic* in that it conveys actors' values and beliefs, and constructs or evokes frames for interpreting the issues at hand, as social constructionism highlights (Berger & Luckmann, 1966). Discourse is also *situated* in that discursive interaction takes place within embedded contexts that condition intended and perceived meanings, and pose rules of discursive and behavioural appropriateness, as vividly shown by ethnographies of communication (Gumperz & Levinson, 1991; Hymes, 1964).

Discourse and cognition: constructing first-order realities

Cognition has been posed as the 'missing link' (Van Dijk, 1993, p. 251) between discourse and action. The interaction of discourse and cognition can be elucidated through the key concept of schema (Condor & Antaki, 1997). Originally developed by Head and Bartlett, the concept of schema has since become a central construct of cognitive psychology (Rumelhart, 1984). A schema is 'a cognitive structure that consists in part of the representation of some stimulus domain. The schema contains general knowledge about that domain, including a specification of the relationships among its attributes, as well as specific examples or instances of the stimulus domain' (Taylor & Crocker, 1981, p. 91). Interpretive schemes and discourse are mutually constituted in a process of continuous interaction, where 'understanding is accomplished and communicated mainly by means of symbols (most notably in the form of metaphorical language) that are then retained in a structured or schematic form via scripts. The scripts subsequently serve as a basis for action that further facilitates the meaning construction and sensemaking processes' (Gioia, 1986, p. 50). In this perspective discourse is not merely informative, but 'transformative' (Phillips & Brown, 1993, p. 1548). Cognitive structures can be affirmed, elaborated or challenged when discourse is both interpreted and produced through them (Eoyang, 1983, p. 113).

Discourse influences not only the functioning of existing schemata, but also the long-term delineation of their parameters. Linguistic labels learned through social interaction influence cognitive development, and during communication or even during actors' reflections, linguistic labels evoke and utilize cognitive schemata. When schemata are developed, they are then heuristically employed as interpretative tools in the long term (Bloom, 1981).

Interpretive schemes and agents' (discursive) actions are interrelated in a continuously dialectic fashion; action arises out of interpretive schemes, and new experiences or reflections influence interpretive schemes and thus subsequent action (Gioia, 1986). Discursive social interaction is therefore central to the construction of social reality and to agents' actions based on this reality (Berger & Luckmann, 1966; Moscovici, 1981). This interactive view between cognition and discursive action emphasizes the relatively malleable nature of interpretive schemes, which can progressively be re-defined through the addition or attrition of concepts, the transformation of perceived causal associations, or the altered salience of concepts (Eoyang, 1983).

INTERPRETIVE APPROACHES TO ORGANIZATIONAL DISCOURSE

In this section five prominent interpretive approaches to the study of discourse are discussed: hermeneutics, rhetoric, metaphor, symbolic interactionism and critical discourse analysis. All of these fields deserve a place in a discussion of interpretive approaches to organizational discourse for the following four reasons. First, they all assume a constructive ontology of social phenomena. Second, they ascribe a central role to discourse (or texts that constitute discourses, or language as the raw material of texts) in the constructive process. Third, they view, in their own particular ways, discourse as context-dependent or situated; as a form of action where textual communications are intended to achieve things in their social context; and as symbolic, not only in a semantic sense but in a more substantive sense of indicating agents' assumptions, values and beliefs and invoking frames of reference for interpreting issues. Fourth, these fields do not remain at an abstract level but provide more specific directions for conducting discourse analyses, which can shed light on different angles of the discursive construction of social reality and its effects on agents' actions, social practices, organizations and societies. Table 7.1 portrays the main conceptual orientations and potential analytical directions suggested by the five fields discussed.

Hermeneutics

The roots of the word 'hermeneutics' lie in the Greek term *hermeneuein*, or 'to interpret'. The earliest usage of the term referred to principles of biblical interpretation, but this was subsequently broadened to refer to general rules of philological exegesis. Hermeneutics involves both the task of textual interpretation as well as the reflexive concern with the nature of understanding and interpretation itself (Palmer, 1969). Hermeneutics has had a rich conceptual history. Key figures in the development of hermeneutic thought include Schleiermacher, who sought to develop a 'general hermeneutics' whose principles could serve as the foundation for all kinds of textual interpretation; Dilthey, who saw hermeneutics as the core discipline which could serve as the foundation for all humanistic studies; Heidegger, who developed a view of hermeneutics as the phenomenological explication of human existence; and Gadamer, who followed the lead of Heidegger's work to develop 'philosophical hermeneutics', the encounter with Being through language (see Ricœur, 1991, pp. 53–74 for an overview of these scholars' work).

Ricœur's work returned the focus of hermeneutics to its initial concerns with textual interpretation. He has defined hermeneutics as the 'art of interpreting texts' (Ricœur, 1997, p. 66), posing as a fundamental concern the fact that once discourse is inscribed as 'text' it is severed from its author, and its meaning as interpreted by new audiences may not necessarily coincide with the author's original intentions (Ricœur, 1991, pp. 105–24). Thus, the hermeneutical task, according to Ricœur, becomes the interpretation of texts in contexts different from

Table 7.1 *Conceptual orientations and analytical directions*

Theoretical approach	Main conceptual orientations	Potential analytical directions
Hermeneutics Giddens, 1979, 1987; Palmer, 1969; Ricœur, 1991	• Focus on interpretation of texts and on nature of interpretation itself • Removal from subjectivist stance; some textual interpretations more valid than others, based on textual context • Commitment to in-depth textual interpretation through researchers' longitudinal immersion in texts' social and organizational context	• Textual interpretations in context and over time, being sensitive to alternative interpretations • Search for central themes, thematic constructions and thematic interconnections • Triangulation of patterns in ethnographic and textual data
Rhetoric Aristotle, 1991; Gill & Whedbee, 1997	• Rhetoric as both functional and constructive, employed in both grand oratory and everyday life • Focus on study of rhetoric in use, and on its situational, temporal and social contexts	• Aim to identify agents' rhetorical strategies and their central themes • Identity how themes are constructed in positive/normative orders • Identification of enthymemes and their functions in context
Metaphor Black, 1979; Lakoff, 1990; Lakoff & Johnson, 1980	• Emphasis on constructive role of metaphors in agents' conceptual systems and their influence on social action • Nature of epistemic and ontological correspondences between source and target domains	• Identification of root metaphors and aspects highlighted by actors over time and in context • Mapping target and source domains and their implication complexes • Mapping inter-metaphor systematicity and its implications
Symbolic interactionism Mead, 1912, 1913, 1922, 1925; Blumer, 1969	• Meanings arise and are modified through social interaction • Action arises out of subjective meanings that agents attach to situations • Actors' identity itself arises through social interaction	• Focus on social interaction and on the meanings involved in interaction • Study of discourse in use and its relation to subjective meanings • How does discourse in use embody and construct subject identities?
Critical discourse analysis Fairclough & Wodak, 1997; Van Dijk, 1993	• Discursive reality construction is hegemonic, biased in favour of dominant interests • Social practices viewed as 'natural' are a surreptitious consequence of dominant discourses aligned with the powerful • Subjects' subjectivity and identity is constructed by dominant discourses	• Focus on links between discourse and power • Aims to uncover the ways though which discursive reality construction is skewed in favour of dominant interests • Analysis is contextual and often historical, relating discourses to social practices and to powerful interests

that of the author and the original audience, with the ideal intent of discovering new avenues to understanding.

Ricœur notes that there may be several interpretations of texts depending on readers' pre-understandings (interpretive schemes) and their particular interpretations of a text in relation to their own perceived situation (1991, pp. 1–20). Acknowledging the possibility of various textual interpretations, however, does not necessitate a lapse to relativism, the resignation to the idea that there is no way to arrive at certain textual interpretations that are more valid than other potential interpretations. In contrast to poststructuralist approaches, for example, where the text is seen as having a plurality of indeterminate and irreducible meanings and which 'practises the infinite deferment of the signified' (Barthes, 1977, p. 158), hermeneutic approaches assume that some meanings are more valid than others, given a text's particular social-historical context (Phillips & Brown, 1993). For Ricœur (1991, pp. 144–67), for example, a text displays a limited field of potential interpretations as opposed to being a repository of potentially unlimited meanings.

Giddens suggests that the interpretive validity of texts can be improved through ethnographic inquiry in the settings of production of the text, the intellectual resources the author has drawn on and the characteristics of the audience it is addressed to (Giddens, 1987, p. 106). He emphasizes the necessity of studying texts as 'the concrete medium and outcome of a process of production, reflexively monitored by its author or reader'. Inquiry into this productive process involves exploring the author's or speaker's intentions as well as the practical knowledge involved in writing or speaking with a certain style for a particular audience (1979, p. 43).

Researchers employing hermeneutical discourse analysis search for central themes in texts, for thematic unity (how central themes are interrelated in broader argumentations both within texts and intertextually), and often relate these to patterns in ethnographic data over time. The analysis is treated as a process of discovery, going round the hermeneutic circle, from part to the whole and vice versa, each time further enriching the interpretations (Kets de Vries & Miller, 1987; Thatchenkery, 1992).

Rhetoric

Rhetorical discourse analysis is highly versatile (van Graber, 1973) and has been extensively utilized in organizational analysis (e.g. Finstad, 1998; Hopkins & Reicher, 1997; Huff, 1983; Watson, 1995). Rhetoric can explore the situation, the audience, the rhetor and textual features such as structure and temporality, enthymemes, metaphor and iconicity, not for their own sake, but in order to discover how rhetorical discourse can influence actors' understandings, values and beliefs by eloquently and persuasively espousing particular views of the world (Gill & Whedbee, 1997). Rhetorical principles have thus been fruitfully applied to wider, macro-level discourses to explore the discourses' constructive effects on peoples' understanding of pressing social issues (e.g., Charland, 1987; Gronbeck, 1973). Analyses can also focus on how apparently plain speaking can actually be rhetorical (Gowler & Legge, 1983) through the use of certain ideas but not others, through the particular implications and connotations of the ideas used, through the construction of certain kinds of subject, and through what the 'frame' evoked by the ideas used highlights or excludes (Bateson, 1972; Harré, 1981).

Rhetorical principles and processes have often been perceived as morally questionable, a view initiated since Plato's condemnation of rhetoric as inducing 'belief without knowledge' and as 'ignoble and bad' (Kinneavy, 1971, pp. 221–2). One can see the Platonic view of rhetoric as a tool for making manipulative representations in work, such as Keenoy (1990) or Alvesson (1993). Although views of rhetoric diverge in their evaluative standpoint, they do presuppose an understanding of rhetoric as a potent tool for constructing social reality. Rhetoric, for example, can be used to manage social representations (Moscovici, 1981), to initiate change (Bitzer, 1968), to sustain existing socio-political arrangements in ways that advantage certain social groupings at the expense of others (Gowler & Legge, 1983), or to achieve 'appropriate' self-presentation of actors to a community of peers (Harré, 1981).

Rhetorical strategies most often take the form of enthymemes, which are not necessarily consciously evoked, being located in actors' practical consciousness rather than discursive consciousness (Giddens, 1984, pp. 44–5). Rhetoric, in this perspective, is not some sort of grand oratory, but a mundane, everyday aspect of human competence (Watson, 1995). Enthymemes are rhetorical structures of argumentation. In contrast to syllogisms in logic, enthymemes are usually not fully expressed, one or more of their premises being taken for granted or assumed by the audience (Eemeren et al., 1997). The premises in enthymemes are only generally or probably true in a particular social context; their truth or rationality is not universal, but is conditioned by and arises from the socio-cultural features in that context (Gergen & Thatchenkery, 1996).

In terms of organizational discourse analysis, therefore, persistent patterns in argumentations, which pervade and operate in diverse situational, organizational and temporal contexts, can be seen as actors' rhetorical strategies (Heracleous, 2002). Identification and analysis of enthymemes, and particularly their unstated and assumed premises, can enable researchers to uncover the taken-for-granted values and beliefs of actors in a particular social context (Gill & Whedbee, 1997; Heracleous & Barrett, 2001).

Metaphor

It has been recognized since Aristotle that metaphor is more than just a figure of speech. Seeing A in terms of B, metaphor is not only the archetype of related tropes such as metonymy, synecdoche, simile and analogy, but more importantly, it is constructive of both social reality (Lakoff, 1990; Lakoff & Johnson, 1980) and scientific inquiry (Heracleous, 2003; Morgan, 1980, 1983, 1986), through inducing, in actors' minds, ontological and epistemic correspondences between otherwise distinct domains (Lakoff, 1990).

Literal views of metaphor see it as merely a statement of similarity or analogy that is potentially expendable, since what was stated metaphorically could also be stated literally (Black, 1979). This perspective is identified by Tsoukas (1993) as consistent with objectivist approaches in social science that view the use of metaphor as not only unnecessary but also distorting of the 'facts' that should be expressed in literal language (e.g., Pinder & Bourgeois, 1982; see Morgan, 1983 for a reply).

Constructionist views of metaphor, on the other hand, such as the 'interaction' view (Black, 1979), hold that metaphor is involved in fundamental thought processes through the projection of 'associated implications' of a secondary subject on a primary subject, where individuals select, emphasize, suppress and organize features of the primary subject by applying to it statements isomorphic with the secondary subject's implicative complex. Lakoff and Johnson's (1980) seminal study on the metaphorical structuring of experience emphasizes the status of metaphor as a constructive influence on social actors' conceptual systems in terms of which thought and action occurs. Lakoff provided a compelling statement of the constructionist view of metaphors through his 'invariance hypothesis', where he suggested that metaphors involve both ontological correspondences (where entities in the target domain correspond systematically to entities in the source domain), as well as epistemic correspondences (where knowledge about the source domain is mapped on to knowledge about the target domain) (Lakoff, 1990, p. 48).

The creative potential of metaphors has formed the basis for metaphorical typologies. Schön, for example, distinguished generative metaphors from non-generative ones by the former's ability to generate new perceptions, explanations and inventions (Schön, 1979, p. 259) and Black (1979) distinguished strong from weak metaphors by the former's possessing a high degree of 'implicative elaboration' (1979, p. 27). But are metaphorical statements creative by revealing aspects of the target domain which were already there, or by constituting such aspects by virtue of the two domains that they bring into interaction? Black argues that the latter is possible in the form of his 'strong creativity thesis' (Black, 1979, pp. 37–9). The creative potential of metaphorical statements depends upon there being sufficient differences between the two domains for a creative tension to exist (Morgan, 1983). As Aristotle has put it, 'metaphors should be transferred from things that are related but not obviously so' (1999, 3: 11: 5).

The link between metaphor and action rests markedly on metaphors' evaluative loading. This evaluative loading points implicitly towards what 'ought' to be done under situations framed metaphorically, the 'normative leap' resulting from metaphors' naming and framing processes (Schön, 1979, pp. 264–5). As Hirsch and Andrews have noted in the context of their analysis of the language of corporate takeovers, 'once the roles and relations are assigned, proper procedures and/or proper outcomes can be readily deduced. Sleeping Beauty must be liberated and wed; the shark must be annihilated; the black-hat brought to justice; the honorable soldier must fight doggedly, and so on' (1983, p. 149).

The potency of metaphor to re-frame situations and move individuals to action in a particular direction has been illustrated by the significant amount of research in organization theory on the role of metaphors in facilitating organizational change (e.g., Marshak, 1993; Pondy, 1983; Sackmann, 1989). Metaphors can offer new ways of looking at existing situations (Crider & Cirillo, 1991; Lakoff, 1990; Morgan, 1980, 1983), while simultaneously acting as a bridge from a familiar to a new state (Pondy, 1983). The high latitude of interpretation afforded by metaphorical statements can help to accommodate the interpretations of organizational groups perceiving their interests to be mutually incompatible (Crider & Cirillo, 1991), and unstructured situations can be made more concrete and comprehensible through the use of metaphor (Sackmann, 1989).

Metaphorical discourse analysis can focus on the root metaphors underlying a certain discourse, on the nature of the target and source domains and their implication complexes, on the presence of inter-metaphor systematicity (interrelations between metaphors underlying a discourse), or on the longitudinal shifts in root metaphors and the aspects of their implication complexes highlighted by actors in a social system.

Potential disagreements and ambiguities in metaphor use remain, however, for example whether a single or several metaphors should be used to understand a given situation, to what extent politics are involved in metaphor use, to what extent literal language is needed (or is feasible) in analysing organizations, or to what extent different metaphors are incommensurable or complementary (Palmer & Dunford, 1996). These ambiguities raise the importance and desirability of researcher reflexivity, a central issue in organizational discourse; the need to clarify one's assumptions and ideological biases and to consider how these shape various aspects of the research process (Heracleous, 2001).

Symbolic interactionism

Symbolic interactionism as a term was first used by Herbert Blumer (1969), drawing primarily on the work of Mead, to propose a new paradigm for the study of social issues. While symbolic interactionism originated as a reaction to the dominant positivist paradigm in sociology, many of its core premises have progressively been accepted in mainstream research (Fine, 1993). For symbolic interactionism, meanings do not reside in objects themselves, as distinct from social interaction. Symbolic interactionism assumes that individuals' action arises out of the meanings that situations have for them, that meanings arise from social interaction with others, and that individuals modify meanings in the process of thinking through issues and interacting further with other individuals (Blumer, 1969, p. 2; Thomas & Thomas, 1970). The main distinguishing factor of human from animal behaviour, from a symbolic interactionist perspective, is the use of language and other forms of symbolic communication.

Methodologically, symbolic interactionism has a dual focus on social interaction and on the meanings involved in interaction (Prasad, 1993). Its preferred methods involve participant observation and intensive in-depth interviewing. Even though it favours qualitative methods, however, symbolic interactionism also encourages generalizations derived inductively from qualitative data, consistent with other fields discussed in this chapter.

George H. Mead, the intellectual precursor of symbolic interactionism, was particularly concerned with the nature of the self, which he conceptualized as a social object arising out of a process of social interaction (Mead, 1912, 1913), and primarily through 'vocal gesture' or talk, suggesting that 'the "me" is a man's reply to his own talk' (1912, p. 405). The self becomes a social object when it 'assumes ... the attitudes of generalized others' (1925, p. 275). For Mead, not only self but mind was also discursively constituted. When individuals talk to themselves as they talk to others, 'in keeping up this conversation in the inner forum constitutes the field ... of mind' (Mead, 1922, p. 160).

Through discursive symbolic interaction, therefore, meanings become institutionalized or 'objectified' (Berger & Luckmann, 1966), acquiring a longer-term solidity and reification. Institutionalized meanings have their discursive correlates in the form of discursive deep structures that are intertextual, persist in the long term, are constructive as opposed to merely communicative, transcend individual situations, and are implicit, residing in actors' practical consciousness (Heracleous & Hendry, 2000).

Critical discourse analysis

Critical discourse analysis shares with the above approaches the interpretive concern with exploring the social construction of reality, and with the role of discourse in this process. It emphasizes, however, that this process is not neutral or unbiased. Symbolic universes function not only as communicational and sense-making mechanisms but also as legitimating ones (Giddens, 1984), representing different and potentially conflicting views of reality. Confrontations of symbolic universes are thus in effect power confrontations, where 'he who has the bigger stick has the better chance of imposing his definitions of reality' (Berger & Luckmann, 1966, p. 127). Critical discourse analysis aims to demystify situations and perceptions that may be viewed as 'natural', but that have in effect been discursively constructed over time by groups in power aiming to skew social reality and institutional arrangements to their own advantage (Barthes, 1972; Gramsci, 1971).

Critical discourse analysis consists of a variety of approaches drawing from strands of critical theory within Western Marxism (Fairclough & Wodak, 1997), as well as from other critical theorists such as Foucault, particularly his later genealogical work (1980) focusing on the intimate links between discourse and power. Critical discourse analysis is ethically committed to unmasking the processes through which discourses promote social constructions that support and perpetuate the interests of dominant groups or classes (Fairclough & Wodak, 1997; Wodak, 1990). In this connection, discourses are not seen as neutral or unbiased, but as 'sites of power' (Mumby & Stohl, 1991, p. 316) and as entrenched 'social practices' (Fairclough & Wodak, 1997, p. 258) that produce particular sorts of subjectivity and identity (du Gay & Salaman, 1992) and influence organizational practices in particular ways (Jacobs & Heracleous, 2001).

Discourses are thus seen as imbued with ideological hegemony, the process by which dominant classes attempt to construct and perpetuate belief systems that support their own interests, and make the *status quo* appear commonsensical and natural (Barthes, 1972; Gramsci, 1971). Critical discourse analysis assumes that social representations (shared cognitions) are principally constituted through discourse or, more succinctly, that 'managing the mind of others is essentially a function of text and talk' (Van Dijk, 1993, p. 254).

Critical discourse analyses thus follow interpretive, context-sensitive, often historical methodologies to analyse discourses empirically, to discover how ideologies permeate and manifest in these discourses, and highlight discourses' organizational and societal effects. In using this approach, analysts aim to bring about demystification and challenge of the *status quo* and thus, ideally, social change. The foci of analysis are often pressing social problems, such as racism, gender relations or ethnic tensions, not merely as a scholarly endeavour but as a committed form of social intervention (Van Dijk, 1993; Fairclough & Wodak, 1997; Wodak, 1990).

CONCLUSION

In the introduction to this chapter, the meaning of interpretivism was outlined as the commitment to in-depth understanding of actors' first-order interpretations. Interpretivism was distinguished from subjectivism in terms of interpretivism's acceptance of more general frameworks derived inductively from data that extends beyond individual subjective viewpoints. Organizational discourse analysis, in this vein, focuses on bodies of texts that constitute discourses, and on the discursive structures and patterns that pervade these texts rather than on individual texts, seeking to relate such structures to the social practices associated with specific discourses.

The second section of the chapter expanded on discourse as constructive of social reality, noting the constructive ontology of social phenomena and the potential of actors to manage social representations through discourse. Discourse was discussed as action that is situated in particular social contexts, and as symbolic in terms of portraying actors' values and beliefs and invoking frames for interpreting the issues it refers to. Finally, the section addressed the constructive effects of discourse on interpretive schemes, adopting a cognitive perspective.

In the third section, five prominent interpretive approaches to organizational discourse were discussed: hermeneutics, rhetoric, metaphor, symbolic interactionism and critical discourse analysis. Both their conceptual orientations as well as potential analytical directions for conducting discourse analyses were outlined, and summarized in Table 7.1.

Discussion of the nature of discourse as composed of numerous texts that share certain structural features, that engender conditioned rationalities and influence agents' interpretations, actions and social practices has shown that interpretive discourse research, as promoted by the interpretive approaches discussed in this chapter, is far from subjectivist (in the sense of delivering only idiosyncratic findings that cannot support the discovery of broader understandings of social systems or suggest any types of generalization).

At the same time, inductive research grounded in field data and, where possible, supported by field observations of agents' actions and social practices, would certainly not support uncontrolled generalizations that go beyond what can reasonably be supported by the data. As Eco, Ricœur, Giddens and others have suggested, there are criteria for textual validity that severely undermine the notion of unlimited interpretation as an avenue to useful understanding of social processes. Even though, in a narrow sense, a text can mean what its reader wants it to mean, at the same time the nature of the text itself (and of bodies of texts that constitute discourses) cannot be completely ignored, manipulated or violated. For example, words have a semantic meaning on which communication is based and this presupposed meaning, as it were, provides the foundation for interpretations and re-interpretations of texts. If those researching organizational discourse keep in mind the criteria for interpretive validity that Eco, Ricœur, Giddens and others have proposed, and view the issue of multiple interpretations in a reasoned and substantive way, then some interpretations will be found to be more valid, useful and insightful than others. The approaches discussed in this chapter offer a number of ways by which to explore and develop them profitably.

NOTES

I am grateful to Professors David Barry, David Grant, Cliff Oswick and Hari Tsoukas for their valuable feedback and suggestions on earlier versions of the manuscript. Research funding from National University of Singapore research grant R–313–000–038–112 is also gratefully acknowledged.
1   Both discourse and related terms, such as language, text or narrative, have been conceptualized and categorized in diverse ways in organization theory (e.g., Grant, Keenoy & Oswick, 1998; Mumby & Clair, 1997), as evidenced in this *Handbook*. Interpretive-based approaches to discourse analysis view discourses as collections of texts situated in social contexts, sharing certain structural features and having both functional and constructive effects in their contexts. Texts are thus manifestations of discourses and language is the raw material of discourses.

REFERENCES

Alvesson, M. (1993) Organizations as rhetoric: Knowledge-intensive firms and the struggle with ambiguity. *Journal of Management Studies*, 30: 997–1015.

Alvesson, M. & Kärreman, D. (2000) Varieties of discourse: On the study of organizations through discourse analysis. *Human Relations*, 53: 1125–49.

Aristotle (1991) *On rhetoric*. Trans. G.A. Kennedy. New York: Oxford University Press.

Austin, J.L. (1962) *How to do things with words*. Cambridge, MA: Harvard University Press.

Barthes, R. (1972) *Mythologies*. Trans. A. Lavers. London: Vintage.

Barthes, R. (1977) *Image, music, text*. London: Fontana.

Bateson, G. (1972) *Steps to an ecology of mind*. London: Intertext.

Berger, P. & Luckmann, T. (1966) *The social construction of reality*. London: Penguin.

Bitzer, L.F. (1968) The rhetorical situation. *Philosophy & Rhetoric*, 1 (1): 1–14.

Black, M. (1979) More about metaphor. In A. Ortony (ed.), *Metaphor and thought* (pp. 19–43). Cambridge: Cambridge University Press.

Bloom, A.H. (1981) *The linguistic shaping of thought*. Hillsdale, NJ: Lawrence Erlbaum Associates.

Blum-Kulka, S. (1997) Discourse pragmatics. In T.A. Van Dijk (ed.), *Discourse studies: A multidisciplinary introduction* (Vol. 2, pp. 38–63). Beverly Hills, CA: Sage.

Blumer, H. (1969) *Symbolic interactionism: Perspective and method*. Berkeley, CA: University of California Press.

Burrell, G. & Morgan, G. (1979) *Sociological paradigms and organizational analysis*. Aldershot: Gower.

Charland, M. (1987) Constitutive rhetoric: The case of the peuple Quebecois. *Quarterly Journal of Speech*, 73: 133–50.

Condor, S. & Antaki, C. (1997) Social cognition and discourse. In T.A. Van Dijk (ed.), *Discourse studies: A multidisciplinary introduction* (Vol. 1, pp. 320–47). Beverly Hills, CA: Sage.

Crider, C. & Cirillo, L. (1991) Systems of interpretation and the function of metaphor. *Journal for the Theory of Social Behavior*, 21: 171–95.

Denzin, N. (1983) Interpretive interactionism. In G. Morgan (ed.), *Beyond method: Strategies for social research* (pp. 126–46). Beverly Hills, CA: Sage.

Eco, U. (1990) *The limits of interpretation*. Bloomington, IN: Indiana University Press.

Eemeren, F.H., Grootendorst, R., Jackson, S. & Jacobs, S. (1997) Argumentation. In T.A. Van Dijk (ed.), *Discourse Studies: A multidisciplinary introduction* (Vol. 1, pp. 208–29). Thousand Oaks, CA: Sage.

Eoyang, C. (1983) Symbolic transformation of belief systems. In L.R. Pondy, P.J. Frost, G. Morgan & T.C. Dandridge (eds), *Organizational symbolism*, (pp. 109–21). Greenwich, CT: JAI Press.

Fairclough, N. & Wodak, R. (1997) Critical discourse analysis. In T.A. Van Dijk (ed.), *Discourse studies: A multidisciplinary introduction* (Vol. 2, pp. 258–84). Beverly Hills, CA: Sage.

Fine, G.A. (1993) The sad demise, mysterious disappearance, and glorious triumph of symbolic interactionism. *Annual Review of Sociology*, 19: 61–87.

Finstad, N. (1998) The rhetoric of organizational change. *Human Relations*, 51: 717–40.

Foucault, M. (1980) *Power/Knowledge: Selected interviews and other writings, 1972–77*. New York: Pantheon.

du Gay, P. & Salaman, G. (1992) The cult(ure) of the customer. *Journal of Management Studies*, 29: 615–33.

Gergen, K.J. & Thatchenkery, T. (1996) Organization science as social construction: Postmodern potentials. *Journal of Applied Behavioral Science*, 32: 356–77.

Giddens, A. (1979) *Central problems in social theory*. London: Macmillan.

Giddens, A. (1984) *The constitution of society*. Cambridge: Polity Press.

Giddens, A. (1987) *Social theory and modern sociology*. Cambridge: Polity Press.

Gill, A.M. & Whedbee, K. (1997) Rhetoric. In T.A. Van Dijk (ed.), *Discourse studies: A multidisciplinary introduction* (Vol. 1, pp. 157–83). Thousand Oaks, CA: Sage.

Gioia, D.A. (1986) Symbols, scripts and sensemaking: Creating meaning in the organizational experience. In H.P. Sims, Jr. & D.A. Gioia (eds), *The thinking organization*: (pp. 49–74). San Francisco: Jossey-Bass.

Gowler, D. & Legge, K. (1983) The meaning of management and the management of meaning. In M. Earl (ed.), *Perspectives in management* (pp. 197–233). Oxford: Oxford University Press.

van Graber, M. (1973) Functional criticism: A rhetoric of Black power. In G.P. Mohrmann, C.J. Stewart & D.J. Ochs (eds), *Explorations in rhetorical criticism* (pp. 207–22). University Park, PA: Pennsylvania State University Press.

Gramsci, A. (1971) *Selections from the prison notebooks of Antonio Gramsci*. Edited by Q. Hoare & G. Nowell-Smith. London: Lawrence & Wishart.

Grant, D., Keenoy, T. & Oswick, C. (1998) Organizational discourse: Of diversity, dichotomy and multi-disciplinarity. In D. Grant, T. Keenoy & C. Oswick (eds), *Discourse and organization* (pp. 1–13). London: Sage.

Gronbeck, B.E. (1973) The rhetoric of social-institutional change: Black action at Michigan. In G.P. Morhmann, C.J. Stewart & D.J. Ochs (eds), *Explorations in rhetorical criticism* (pp. 96–123). University Park, PA: Pennsylvania State University Press.

Gumperz, J.J. & Levinson, S.C. (1991) Rethinking linguistic relativity. *Current Anthropology*, 32: 613–23.

Hardy, C. & Phillips, N. (1999) No joking matter: Discursive struggle in the Canadian refugee system. *Organization Studies*, 20: 1–24.

Hardy, C. & Phillips, N. (2002) Discourse analysis: *Investigating processes of social construction*. Qualitative Research Methods Series, 50. Thousand Oaks, CA: Sage.

Harré, R. (1981) Rituals, rhetoric and social cognitions. In J.P. Forgas (ed.), *Social cognition: Perspectives in everyday understanding* (pp. 211–24). London: Academic Press.

Heracleous, L. (2001) An ethnographic study of culture in the context of organizational change. *Journal of Applied Behavioral Science*, 37: 426–46.

Heracleous, L. (2002) *A tale of three discourses: The dominant, the strategic and the marginalized*. Working Paper, School of Business, National University of Singapore.

Heracleous, L. (2003) A comment on the role of metaphor in knowledge generation. *Academy of Management Review*, 28: 190–1.

Heracleous, L. & Barrett, M. (2001) Organizational change as discourse: Communicative actions and deep structures in the context of information technology implementation. *Academy of Management Journal*, 44: 755–78.

Heracleous, L. & Hendry, J. (2000) Discourse and the study of organization: Toward a structurational perspective. *Human Relations*, 53: 1251–86.

Hirsch, P.M. & Andrews, J.A. (1983) Ambushes, shootouts, and knights of the round table: The language of corporate takeovers. In L.R. Pondy, P.J. Frost, G. Morgan & T.C. Dandridge (eds), *Organizational symbolism* (pp. 145–55). Greenwich, CT: JAI Press.

Hopkins, N. & Reicher, S. (1997) Social movement rhetoric and the social psychology of collective action: A case study of anti-abortion mobilization. *Human Relations*, 50: 261–86.

Huff, A.S. (1983) A rhetorical examination of strategic change. In L.R. Pondy, P.J. Frost, G. Morgan & T.C. Dandridge (eds), *Organizational symbolism* (pp. 167–83). Greenwich, CT: JAI Press.

Hymes, D. (1964) Toward ethnographies of communication. *American Anthropologist*, 66 (6), part 2: 12–25.

Jacobs, C. & Heracleous, L. (2001) Seeing without being seen: Towards an archaeology of controlling science. *International Studies of Management and Organization*, 31 (3): 113–35.

Keenoy, T. (1990) Human resource management: Rhetoric, reality and contradiction. *International Journal of Human Resource Management*, 1: 363–84.

Kets de Vries, M.F.R. & Miller, D. (1987) Interpreting organizational texts. *Journal of Management Studies*, 24: 233–47.

Kinneavy, J.L. (1971) *A theory of discourse*. Englewood Cliffs, NJ: Prentice-Hall.

Lakoff, G. (1990) The invariance hypothesis: Is abstract reason based on image schemas? *Cognitive Linguistics*, 1: 39–74.

Lakoff, G. & Johnson, M. (1980) *Metaphors we live by*. Chicago: Chicago University Press.

Marshak, R.J. (1993) Managing the metaphors of change. *Organizational Dynamics*, 22: 44–56.

Mead, G.H. (1912) The mechanism of social consciousness. *Journal of Philosophy, Psychology and Scientific Methods*, 9 (15): 401–6.

Mead, G.H. (1913) The social self. *Journal of Philosophy, Psychology and Scientific Methods*, 10 (14): 374–80.

Mead, G.H. (1922) A behavioristic account of the significant symbol. *Journal of Philosophy*, 19 (6): 157–63.

Mead, G.H. (1925) The genesis of the self and social control. *International Journal of Ethics*, 35 (3): 251–77.

Morgan, G. (1980) Paradigms, metaphor and puzzle solving in organization theory. *Administrative Science Quarterly*, 25: 660–71.

Morgan, G. (1983) More on metaphor: Why we cannot control tropes in administrative science. *Administrative Science Quarterly*, 28: 601–7.

Morgan, G. (1986) *Images of organization*. Beverly Hills, CA: Sage.

Moscovici, S. (1981) On social representations. In J.P. Forgas (ed.), *Social cognition: Perspectives on everyday understanding* (pp. 181–209). London: Academic Press.

Mumby, D.K. & Clair, R.P. (1997) Organizational Discourse. In T.A. Van Dijk (ed.), *Discourse as social interaction* (pp. 181–205). Beverly Hills, CA: Sage.

Mumby, D.K. & Stohl, C. (1991) Power and discourse in organization studies: Absence and the dialectic of control. *Discourse and Society*, 2: 313–32.

Palmer, I. & Dunford, R. (1996) Conflicting uses of metaphors: Reconceptualizing their use in the field of organizational change. *Academy of Management Review*, 21: 691–717.

Palmer, R.E. (1969) *Hermeneutics*. Evanston, IL: Northwestern University Press.

Phillips, N. & Brown, J.L. (1993) Analyzing communication in and around organizations: A critical hermeneutic approach. *Academy of Management Journal*, 36: 1547–76.

Pinder, C.C. & Bourgeois, V.W. (1982) Controlling tropes in administrative science. *Administrative Science Quarterly*, 27: 641–52.

Pondy, L.R. (1983) The role of metaphors and myths in organization and the facilitation of change. In L.R. Pondy, P.J. Frost, G. Morgan & T.C. Dandridge (eds), *Organizational symbolism* (pp. 157–66). Greenwich, CT: JAI Press.

Prasad, P. (1993) Symbolic processes in the implementation of technological change: A symbolic interactionist study of work computerization. *Academy of Management Journal*, 36: 1400–29.

Ricoeur, P. (1991) *From text to action*. Evanston, IL: Northwestern University Press.

Ricoeur, P. (1997) Rhetoric-poetics-hermeneutics. In W. Jost & M.J. Hyde (eds), *Rhetoric and hermeneutics in our time: A reader* (pp. 60–72). New Haven, CT: Yale University Press.

Rumelhart, D.E. (1984) Schemata and the cognitive system. In R.S. Wyer, Jr. & T.K. Srull (eds), *Handbook of social cognition*: (pp. 161–88). Hillsdale, NJ: Lawrence Erlbaum Associates.

Sackmann, S. (1989) The role of metaphors in organization transformation. *Human Relations*, 42: 463–85.

Schön, D.A. (1979) Generative metaphor: A perspective on problem-setting in social policy. In A. Ortony (ed.), *Metaphor and thought* (pp. 254–83). Cambridge: Cambridge University Press.

Searle, J. (1975) Indirect speech acts. In P. Cole & J. Morgan (eds), *Syntax and semantics 3: Speech acts* (pp. 59–82). New York: Academic Press.

Taylor, S.E. & Crocker, J. (1981) Schematic bases of social information processing. In E.T. Higgins, C.P. Herman & M.P. Zanna (eds), *Social cognition* (pp. 89–134). Hillsdale, NJ: Lawrence Erlbaum Associates.

Thatchenkery, T. (1992) Organizations as 'texts': Hermeneutics as a model for understanding organizational change. *Research in Organization Change and Development*, 6: 197–233.

Thomas, W.I. & Thomas, D.S. (1970) Situations defined as real are real in their consequences. In G.P. Stone & H.A. Faberman (eds), *Social psychology through symbolic interaction* (pp. 154–6). Toronto: Xerox College Publishing.

Tsoukas, H. (1993) Analogical reasoning and knowledge generation in organization theory. *Organization Studies*, 14: 323–46.

Van Dijk, T.A. (1977) *Text and context: Explorations in the semantics and pragmatics of discourse*. London: Longman.

Van Dijk, T.A. (1988) Social cognition, social power and social discourse. *Text*, 8: 129–57.

Van Dijk, T.A. (1990) Social cognition and discourse. In H. Giles & W.P. Robinson (eds), *Handbook of language and social psychology* (pp. 163–83). Chichester: Wiley.

Van Dijk, T.A. (1993) Principles of critical discourse analysis. *Discourse and Society*, 4: 249–83.

Watson, T.J. (1995) Rhetoric, discourse and argument in organizational sense making: A reflexive tale. *Organization Studies*, 16: 805–21.

Weber, M. (1922) *Economy and society: An outline of interpretive sociology*. Trans. G. Roth & G. Wittich. New York: Bedminster.

Williams, M. (2000) Interpretivism and generalization. *Sociology*, 34: 209–24.

Wittgenstein, L. (1955) *Tractatus logico-philosophicus*. London: Routledge & Kegan Paul.

Wittgenstein, L. (1968) *Philosophical investigations*. Oxford: Blackwell.

Wodak, R. (1990) Discourse analysis: problems, findings, perspectives. *Text*, 10: 125–32.

8

Multi-levelled, Multi-method Approaches in Organizational Discourse

Kirsten Broadfoot, Stanley Deetz and Donald Anderson

Competing and contradictory organizing discourses embody and carry with them diverse understandings of the nature and sources of expertise, the relationship between the institution and the public, the relationship between professions and larger groups, and the nature and control of one's own body. When we unthinkingly adopt the discourse of a new management programme, we potentially absorb without reflection, a range of meanings on work and employment. Moreover, organizing discourses pervade our non-work experiences as well when we blend home and work languages in both locales. What does the language of a new popular management programme (for example, total quality management, or business process re-engineering) tell us about what it means to work in the corporate world? What do conversations and meanings about maternity leave and work groups as 'families' imply about the relationship and boundaries between work and family life?

'Organization', like discourse, is constantly in action. Hence, when scholars engage in the analysis of either process, we analyse their fleeting and temporary products or snapshots of such flows. As a result, no single theoretical or methodological account can provide a full understanding of organizing life. This chapter outlines our vision of a dialogic research orientation to the relationship between the processes and products of discourse and organization. Such a research and analytical orientation involves a commitment to the symmetrical, or equal treatment of nested moments or sites and practices of discourse and organization, as well as the application of diverse empirical and analytical methods. Organizational scholars need to consider diverse discourses symmetrically, or treat as equally important, the complementary functions and sites of language or discourses as presented in the previous chapters, in order to explore the organizing phenomena produced and captured at the confused overlaps of these multiple and often contradictory discourses. Conceptualizing the relationship between discourse and organization as mutually constitutive allows scholars to explore the productive duality inherent in both discourse and organization. As a result, 'discourse' and 'organization' are considered as both producer and product.

To weave a complex and vivid picture of discourse and organizing life, we propose that while diverse discourses and their instantiations can be separated out and the levels separated for specific analytic purposes, much is gained by maintaining the same complexity and tensions in the process of study and report as presumed in naturally occurring organizing discourse. Macro-level discourses-as-structures can be seen as existing only to the extent that they are endlessly reproduced in the language and knowledge resources deployed by individuals engaged in organizing processes. Thus, focusing on the concrete procedures, strategies, techniques and vocabularies individuals and institutions use to construct stable, coherent and meaningful images of reality, provides insight into the ways discursive formations become articulated, negotiated and deployed to organize and pursue practical interests as well as reproduce relatively stable, sedimented social resources in interaction. As a result, analysis moves beyond the text itself to offer insights into the nature of text production and consumption and to reflect upon the societal discourses created and implicated therein. Scholars can continue to ask different questions at different moments, but holding them in dialogue and productive tension with each other accentuates the overlaps in discursive practices and forces through which the ambiguous, indeterminate, fleeting and highly adaptive phenomenon of organization becomes stable, coherent, fixed, unitary and consistent, yet subject to change as discursive and material changes emerge (Weick, 1979).

Our argument is not one of methodological promiscuity or theoretical infidelity. We do not suggest that researchers should have fleeting or fickle scholarly commitments. Rather, that often these theoretical notions and commitments are left implicit and key conceptions under-theorized (we use 'theoretical' here to indicate a lens or way of thinking and talking about discourse rather than a set of assumptions or postulates) in the study of organization and discourse. For our own part, we look at discourse using a poststructural lens focusing on the ways language constitutes social reality. In this sense, we examine the ways in which language use makes particular forms of social organization possible and actual. Such a theoretical attachment leads us to consider 'organizations' and organizing processes as defined and contested in the discourses through which we represent our selves and our relationship to our material existence (Althusser, 1972). Any discursive analysis of organizing life undertaking this approach describes the constitutive and reproductive nature of discursive practices associated with larger discursive formations and the stabilizing actions of discursive closure required to achieve specific conceptualizations of 'organization'. It also reveals sites of possible fracture and fissure at the sutured seams of discourses, where diverse interpretations and alternative forms of speaking, knowing and being lie latent, awaiting reassertion. Finally, a poststructuralist approach highlights how definitions and meanings attached to organizing phenomena such as 'knowledge', 'technology', 'self' and 'work' are not the sovereign territory of larger, power-full institutions, but co-constructed and highly dependent on the choices and contributions of all interactional others for their evolution.

Combined with a theoretical commitment to poststructuralism, a dialogic research orientation approaches organizing phenomena as sites of struggle between diverse forms of discourse and focuses on the multiple and diverse ways in which people discursively construct, contest and understand organizing phenomena and processes. The critical engagement and evaluation of organizing phenomena from this perspective provides insight into the messy, moment-to-moment manner in which people fashion what appear to be coherent, complete, organizing worlds out of essentially hidden, partial and fragmented pieces of discourse (Alvesson & Deetz, 2000; Deetz, 1996). Focusing on discursive and organizing phenomena as situated, dynamic, interrelated, heterogeneous and contingent provides a picture of organizing life as a richly textured tapestry. In the following section, we describe three different contemporary analytical approaches which engage the discourse–organization relationship from different angles, and then provide recent research exemplars from scholars in organizational communication as guides in how to implement such a dialogic orientation.

THE ORDER(ING) OF ORGANIZATIONAL DISCOURSE: A POSTSTRUCTURALIST PERSPECTIVE

The term 'poststructuralism' or 'poststructuralist thought' is generally applied to work inspired by Althusser, Foucault, Lacan, Derrida and Kristeva. Poststructuralist thought is based on the founding insight that language is constitutive of social reality. Language is where actual and possible forms of social organization and their consequences are defined and contested, and the discourse through which we represent to ourselves our lived relations to our material conditions of existence (Althusser, 1972). Thus, as Weedon claims:

> how we live our lives as conscious subjects and how we give meaning to the material and social relations in which we live depends on the range and social power of existing discourses, our access to them and the political strength of the interests they represent. (1997, p. 34)

Multiple discourses make up the public consciousness of any given historical period and society but must connect with others and insert themselves into material practices to become powerful. Once articulated together as a group of statements and conceptual figurations (discursive formations), a set of anonymous rules and structural principles (discursive practices), complex interrelations across sites (discursive fields) and when joined by the non-discursive (discursive apparatus), discourses produce objects, subjects and relationships demonstrating how power is deployed and meanings are shaped in historically-specific discourse (Weedon, 1997). Articulation, the establishment of non-necessary relationships between individual elements, can systemically transform the meaning of each individual element (Laclau & Mouffe, 2001). As a result, any coherence that appears in a discursive formation has to be accomplished through the regular dispersion of these individual discourses in multiple institutions, material practices and subjects (i.e., discourses must become grounded in everyday interaction to exert influence).

However, due to the evolving socio-historical conditions in which discourses emerge and exist, there are always discursive elements that exist outside a discursive formation yet to be sutured, highlighting the always incomplete nature of any discursive formation (Laclau & Mouffe, 2001). Moreover, because discourses are systems of signification, the meanings of any objects and subjects constructed discursively are necessarily vulnerable, fleeting and temporary as they depend on the sustenance and longevity of the specific discourses through and by which they are constituted (Weedon, 1997). The plurality and diversity of discourses present in any given historical period or society provide diverse sets of resources for justifying and transforming opposing orientations to practical problems and the kinds of meaning attached to experience (Miller, 1994; Weedon, 1997). Thus, discursive formations as articulated series or collages of discourses always carry the seeds of their own transformation and restructuring in the form of alternative others that lie latent, awaiting the necessary social and historical context in which to become dominant.

'Organization' as a product or result of a temporary freezing or arrest of organizing processes is a discursively contingent effect generated through larger discursive articulations and relationships which lead to consistent, hierarchical, orderly centres of material arrangements (Law, 1994). However, the creation, stabilization and perpetuation of dominant discourses and forms of organizing rationality require organizational subjects to police extensive, random, reverse or hypercritical discourses (Foucault, 1981; Therborn, 1980). First, discourses are restricted, authorized and shielded from 'unauthorized' others. Discursive sites are also delimited so the appropriation and reception of discourse is restrictively situated (Therborn, 1980). Individuals can also deploy a variety of practices to effect discursive closure to regulate the production and control of conflict and knowledge both internally and externally and maintain order (Deetz, 1992). The stability of a discursive formation and organizing rationality is maintained by disqualifying subjects and denying expression, access or legitimate expertise, privileging certain discourses, presenting a unified and coherent value-free interest, avoiding certain topics, rendering all difference as a matter of opinion, and appealing to moral or rational values to legitimate decisions and discount the importance or solvability of a problem (Deetz, 1992). As a result of all these discursive actions, the fleeting and temporary nature of organizing phenomena begins to stabilize and cohere, resulting in forms of 'organization' and 'organizations'. Discourse is hence productive of the very institutional forms that constrain and direct it. The produced and producing remain in a potential tension, a tension that is often difficult to see given the presumed finished artifact as a cover.

Through such processes, important organizing conflicts are suppressed and contestation becomes shallow. By reducing, suppressing and eliminating alternative interpretations, definitions, meanings and voices, at both institutional and individual levels, official versions, accounts and definitions of organizing life emerge (i.e., organization becomes determinate and coherent). These selective and selected definitions close off forms of knowledge and vocabularies of action to enforce a particular rationality and representation–a specific form of government and order (Foucault, 1981; Treichler, 1991). Finally, the 'organization' becomes less able to satisfy the needs of its many stakeholders, its creativity in addressing core issues is reduced, the customization of processes and products to members and customers declines, and commitments of all constituent groups become more tenuous.

But any such 'stable' or coherent picture of organizing life is fleeting. Once we conceptualize the discourse–organization as mutually constitutive and productive, we move away from conceptualizing either discourse or organization as producer or product. Rather, we begin to see the duality of discourse and organization as producers and products or simultaneously and mutually productive. As such, any change in one party can spiral into the other, transforming their relationship to each other in a continuous spiral upwards and onwards, through time and space. These changes, wrought by individuals or institutions, draw on their awareness of, accessibility to, and appropriation of alternative repertoires of conduct, knowledge, instruments, artifacts and vocabularies to form alternative ways of speaking, being and knowing organizing life (Rose, 1994). As a result, any analysis of a discursive formation or discourses as structure involves the analysis of discourse in use to expose discursive presences and absences, voices and silences, macro and micro practices in the search for alternative and transformative repertoires.

In summary, examining the practices and processes through which discourses become articulated together and their grounding in the interdependent nature and role of institutions and individuals provides a useful way to think about organizing phenomena from within a theory of discourse. By conceptualizing 'organization' as observable, recurring patterns and conventions of interactive and interpretive activities, the examination of social settings foregrounds the shifting formations of diverse conventions, organizing issues and realities that are effected through the deployment of categories and vocabularies reflecting assumptions about human nature and reality (Miller, 1994). In line with a dialogic research orientation to the discourse–organization relationship, our empirical focus now alights on the discursive and material resources and procedures, vocabularies, strategies and techniques used by participants in these settings to construct and maintain a coherent, stable representation of reality.

LOOKING AT ORGANIZING DISCOURSE DIALOGICALLY

A dialogic approach to discourse and organizing life requires the researcher to be sensitive to the messy moment-to-moment manner in which people and institutions fashion coherent, complete worlds out of essentially partial, incomplete, hidden, fragmented points of discursive struggle (Alvesson & Deetz, 2000;

Deetz, 1996). Focusing on the multiple and diverse ways people discursively construct, contest and understand social phenomena and communicative accomplishments in process, a dialogic orientation to research approaches social phenomena as the sites of struggle between diverse forms of knowing, being and speaking. What kinds of research design and commitment are appropriate for such objects of attention? How can researchers hold in tension and treat symmetrically, or equally, different discursive moments (levels of discourse) to illuminate the necessary articulations in play to produce a coherent representation of 'organization'? What methodological tools do we have available to us to complete such a treatment of discourse–organization?

Analysing organizing life from a dialogic orientation requires researchers to consider the structure of specific discourse, understand them within larger social contexts, and investigate the sedimented institutional forms left as residues, always available as resources in organizing interaction. Any investigation quickly dissolves into a swamp of theoretical and methodological contradictions if the attempt is to look at all at once or to integrate them into a coherent analysis. Alternatively, we propose to examine different levels and sites of discursive practices as 'moments', where the analysis of each moment is contextualized by and recontextualizes earlier ones without being subsumed, maintaining a productive tension as moments turn to and articulate with other moments (see Deetz, 1996).

Maintaining this productive tension between moments and holding them in dialogue with each other allows scholars to identify the transformative resources drawn from the diverse, partial and contradictory range of discourses present (Fairclough, 1992). As described earlier, discursive formations or discourses as structures are series of articulated discourses which are always incomplete and vulnerable to the manipulation of their inherent polysemy and instability. By examining diverse texts and discourses in use, as well as sites of discursive action, scholars are able to track the passage of certain discourses and the closure of others, providing generative alternatives to the ways 'organization' has been studied. Latent issues and moments of conflict and resistance, as well as the shifting balance of collaboration and competition, are thus situated and analysed specifically and temporally. This process allows organizing phenomena to be conceptualized as socially produced and validated, autonomous and often idiosyncratic, co-constructed *in situ* and organized in their encounters and engagements with other forms of discourses and rationalities (Atkinson, 1995; Lupton, 1997).

With such analytical goals in mind, an extended case study provides the methodological design necessary to explore the emergence and reproduction of discursive formations as manifested across multiple levels and contexts. Extended case studies demonstrate how the micro practices of a social situation under examination are shaped by, shape and condition the external forces operating around and through the interaction and context (Burawoy, 1991). In a holographic fashion, it assumes that micro discursive practices are made of similar components to the macro discursive structure. Thus, scholars can use similar tools to engage multiple levels and examine the reopening, closing and suppressing of moments of discourse (Latour, 1991). While cognizant of the material nature of any social setting, extended case study designs also allow for the conceptualization of any 'organization' as observable, recurring patterns and conventions of interactive and interpretive activities. We highlight the shifting formations of diverse conventions, organizing issues and realities through the deployment of categories and vocabularies that constitute social settings (Miller, 1994).

Moving through material sites and discursive moments, the extended case study design focuses on the discursive and material specificities of a setting but also how these specificities vary across time and space. As a result, this research design engages the nested and interconnected nature of discursive moments, resources and procedures, vocabularies, strategies and techniques that are used by institutions and individuals to construct and sustain a coherent, stable representation of 'organization'. In order to engage nested moments of discursive action, scholars apply a combination of ethnographic and discursive methods and practices, such as interviewing, participant observation, textual analyses and audio-taped recordings of interaction. This combination of methods captures the ways in which diverse structures of discourse possessing systems of values, knowledge and belief can situate themselves in organizing practices *in situ* and the forms of language used, patterns of interaction and the routines in which 'organization' becomes structured (Chouliaraki & Fairclough, 1999; Fairclough, 1992; Mokros & Deetz, 1996). All empirical material (ethnographic field notes, interview and interaction transcripts and other documents) is then treated symmetrically to identify and put into dialogue emergent discursive themes, practices and resources, illuminating instances of ambiguity, absence or silence, diversity and stabilization, patterns of fragmentation and integration, destabilization, fixation and orchestration (Alvesson & Deetz, 2000).

In summary, a dialogic research orientation and extended case study design seek to treat all moments of discursive action and accomplishment symmetrically or equally, requiring scholars of the discourse–organization relationship to track the passages and closures of diverse discourses as they swarm, storm and transform each other through, around and in organizing processes. In order to uncover the ways in which these discursive practices accomplish (or not) organizing phenomena, researchers must remain sensitive to the latent alternative or potentially transformative discursive resources available, even if they are not accessed currently. This requires the researcher to utilize multiple methodological tools for the symmetrical collection and analysis of empirical material.

EXAMPLE RESEARCH APPROACHES

Several research programmes operate in similar ways to the general approach outlined above. Three of the more successful ones have been labelled critical discourse analysis (CDA), intertextual analysis (ITA) and coordinated management of meaning (CMM). The first two are fairly well known within organization studies and the last one is more often applied to the analysis of interpersonal interaction.

Critical discourse analysis

Critical discourse analysis, or CDA, is a research tradition developed primarily over the last fifteen years by scholars in Europe. It seeks to understand 'the role of discourse in the (re)production and challenge of dominance' (Van Dijk, 1993, p. 249). Explicit statements about the goals and aims of critical discourse analytic work can be found in Fairclough (1992), Van Dijk, (1993) and Wodak (1997). A major journal founded in 1989, *Discourse & Society*, functions as an outlet for critical discourse analyses.

While there are as many kinds of CDA as there are analysts, most critical discourse analytic research aims to make explicit and visible the masked ways that discourse functions ideologically. To make these claims, most critical discourse analyses presume that individual instances of discourse tend to function as the by-product of social relations, while those relations themselves are constituted by, in part, the collective instances of discourses that serve them. In critical discourse analytic work, dominant discursive forms relate to broader social and cultural processes and practices, and it is the naturalized ideologies inherent in these forms that legitimate their serving as agents of power relations. Because we are often not aware of how discourse functions in these ways, the CDA agenda is to make them conscious for us. Thus, the connection between any given situated text and broader societal problems is of crucial concern to critical discourse analysts.

To accomplish this agenda, Fairclough (1992) lays out an ambitious statement of the various functions and levels of discourse. He theorizes a three-part relationship between discourse as text, as an instance of a discursive practice, and as a social practice. The first dimension he describes, 'discourse as text', refers to the linguistic and structural practices of any instance of text, broadly defined. Analysis of this dimension includes attention to the vocabulary, grammar, cohesion and text structure of the text. The second dimension, the level of 'discursive practices', consists of the analysis of the production, distribution, circulation and consumption of texts. This dimension consists of a wide-ranging degree of analyses of how texts are created, moved from situation to situation, analysed and interpreted, acted on or ignored. Finally, the third dimension is of the 'discourse as an instance of social practices'. This dimension consists of the analysis of the ideological or hegemonic relationships that a text demonstrates and in which it participates.

Such an approach to language and discourse in context aims to reveal the explicit and implicit rules and power structures of social domains embodied in institutions by social power relationships and specific divisions of labour (Wodak, 1997). Everyday life in organizing sites is characterized by conflicts and disorders discursively, which, like contradictions, are often obscured and suppressed by myths and other organizing symbols. Taking a critical discourse analytical perspective uncovers how structures are constantly being produced and reproduced in each specific interaction (Wodak, 1997).

The metaphor of a 'staircase' or 'ladder' of discourse captures the way researchers using this approach conceptualize the relationship between discourse and 'organization'. Researchers gather instances of narrative talk, rituals, formal texts and everyday talk to uncover how routine discursive practices and patterns of interaction occur in organizing settings. Underlying this analytical approach lies the assumption that institutional and individual texts and talk reflect and draw upon larger, more dominant cultural discourses that operate ideologically to restrict opportunities for voice and action in the organizing setting. Thus, empirical investigations focus on the links between language and ideology, the rule and role of dominant groups, discourses, interests and ideas. Focusing more carefully on levels of discourse as opposed to levels of 'organization', critical discourse analysis asks which discourses dominate and does not examine how these discourses became dominant, or the choices individuals and institutions may have had between discursive resources.

Primarily textually-based, critical discourse analysis examines and highlights the discursive 'warps' of the organizing fabric as they flow from the top, elite groups of society down to individual instances of talk and rarely back up the staircase or ladder. Discourse and organization are conceptualized as unitary, singular and consistent as hegemonic processes near completion and alternative discourses are closed off. In a like manner, our understandings of organizing life are closed off, as the critical discourse analyst accepts this data as representative of organizing reality, and does not interrogate the mechanisms through which it was produced. This process and its resulting understandings beg the historical, social, economic and political insights gathered through participation in the site and exposure to external texts to highlight how consensus has been produced and alternative discussions foreclosed (Alvesson & Deetz, 2000).

Intertextual analysis

While CDA foregrounds the links between discourse in use in terms of particular aspects of a text and its distribution and function at a societal level, it may not fully explore the ways in which individuals and institutions as sites of discourse appropriate discursive resources from one situation to another. This passage of discourses across situations, sites and interpretations highlights the fragmentation, development, evolution and change of meaning as it happens through interaction. This passage of discourses is the concern of intertextual analysis.

Intertextuality is a term coined by Julia Kristeva in the late 1960s (see Kristeva, 1984, for the English translation). Following Bakhtin, Kristeva proposes that a text does not exist only on its own, but exists in an interconnected dialogue with other texts. The text itself is a manifestation of this interconnection, as it borrows words, quotations and meanings from other situations, genres and speakers. For example, a speaker may report to a co-worker on a conversation she had with the department manager, replaying the conversation through reported quotes from herself and from the manager. It is the interplay of the current conversation with the past conversation that becomes of interest to the intertextual analyst.

The metaphor of a 'web' or a 'chain' of discourses is an apt one to use in understanding intertextuality. Linell writes that intertextual conversations are those in which 'we deal with several discourses, conversations, texts, etc. which form links in chains of communication situations, in which "the same issue" is recurrently reconstructed, reformulated, and recontextualized' (1998, p. 149). It is the movement and repetition as well as the borrowing and blending of voices and texts that becomes the focus of this kind of analytic method. Fitch (1998, p. 94) gives a metaphor for her ethnographic view of context as a particular children's book she references, a metaphor appropriately extended to understanding intertextual analysis as well. The first page of the book shows an abstract form and, on the next page, this abstraction is seen to be a rooster's comb. The third page shows children staring at the rooster, looking outside their window. Further on the reader realizes that the entire setting is but a picture on a postage stamp, and so on. The lesson to be gained is this: with the enlargement of empirical focus across texts, we gain access to more discursive moments and can create different interpretations and meanings of texts in use. These texts in use remain part of the current picture of organizing life but are then augmented and transformed by this new discursive moment.

Adopting the intertextuality/interdiscursivity approach begins to question the very notion that discourses exist 'inside' an 'organization'. Instead, discourses produce and transform, borrow and contribute to the ongoing and never completed process of organization. Discourses and organization are mutually constitutive. Two research examples demonstrate what a difference this re-conceptualization of the relationship between discourse and organization makes: Boje's (1995) use of the metaphor of 'Tamara' to see 'organizations' as a set of interconnected multiple discourses and Taylor's (1999) study of a Mormon bookstore.

'Tamara' is the name of a long-running Los Angeles play in which the audience follows the play not as a passive observer of action, but by literally and physically following the actors from one room to another. When a 'scene' is completed, the audience has the choice of whom to follow to the next room. Two different members of the audience, because they came to a certain interaction by way of a certain 'path' through the story, can leave an interaction with a completely different meaning of what has occurred in the scene. The 'Tamara' metaphor is so powerful because it resonates with our practical, everyday understanding and experience of how interaction in 'organizations' occurs: we run into one person, share a story, idea or interpretation, leave an interaction and share that idea with another. Only later, based on multiple interactions and new perspectives, do we realize that we have a new lens through which we can interpret the first conversation. Seen in this light, interaction is no longer the site of a single shared meaning, but a fractured site of diverse meanings. There can be no fruitful way to discover an 'organization's' 'central' meaning – there is none – the process of constructing and interpreting meaning is ongoing, concurrent and decentred among different organizing subjects and sites.

Taylor's (1999) study of a Mormon bookstore also provides a good example of intertextual analysis in practice. Taylor (1999) describes how employment in a Mormon bookstore requires employees to demonstrate competence as both organizing members and Mormons. Organizing performances (conversations) rely on employees reading and interpreting texts by carefully walking a balance between the cultural practices of the local organization and the 'host' culture of the Mormon church. Employees identifying a text as a 'good book', for example, created confusion about which organizing identity was being called upon: 'good book' could mean one which is 'well-crafted', or 'good book' could mean 'morally clean' and appropriate for bookstore clientele (Taylor, 1999, p. 85). These conversations simultaneously call upon a member's knowledge of what positive evaluation means to both cultures (through the term 'good'). It is the dual performance of Mormonism and organizing culture that characterizes the textual blending of conversations in this setting.

In both these examples, we see a focus on the movement of discursive practices across sites and subjects of interactional understanding. Taylor's participants draw on cultural discourses to achieve organizing action in everyday life, reproducing Mormon cultural membership in a faith-based organizing site. Taylor's analysis of these discursive accomplishments is inflected with understandings and resources gleaned through ethnographic practices and interviewing in the site to capture accounts of cultural context, resources and membership and how these become embedded and used in interaction. Boje's account of the '*Tamara*' experience allows us to see how participants in organizing processes travel diverse paths and texts which delimit as well as enable diverse experiences, productions and interpretations of organizing life. Both exemplars highlight the socially validated and constructed, yet autonomous and idiosyncratic, nature of organizing phenomena.

In demonstrating how plural and diverse discursive resources and sites become chained together horizontally and how people appropriate each other's talk to effect organizing action, we begin to visualize 'organizations' as hypertext or layered, interrelated and linked texts, where engagement with one text can lead to a network of diverse texts in diverse sites. 'Organizations' are now constituted and productive through, in and around discourse. This horizontal movement of discourses demonstrated in intertextual analyses, in contrast to the vertical travel of dominant discourse proposed in CDA, can be conceptualized as the 'weft', or series of horizontal discursive threads which weave together with the vertical 'warp' threads to construct the fabric of 'organization'. Such a combination of analytical approaches provides an appreciation of the rich and deeply textured nature of organizing life. However, we are still left without an understanding of the forces and necessary points of tension at work between and across discursive moments which simultaneously constrain and enable the stability and coherence of this discursive tapestry. As any weaver knows, the quality, durability and resilience of a fabric is dependent on these tensions between the warp and weft. From a dialogic perspective, the points at which discursive threads and moments come together are sites of potential transformation. As a result, to unduly privilege the warp or weft of a fabric is to create a sense of imbalance, where figures and objects created out of the weaving activity lose their shape, blur into each other, mutate or even disappear from view. The final research approach we discuss, CMM, attempts to meet this challenge of balancing discursive moments.

Coordinated management of meaning

The 'coordinated management of meaning' (CMM) was developed as a theoretical and methodological perspective by Barnett Pearce and Vernon Cronen primarily to describe and explain complex family systems (Pearce, 1989; Pearce & Cronen, 1980). While not applied to the study of organization and discourse in any contin- ued and systematic way, clearly useful ways of understanding the discursive forces and tensions that hold organizing fabrics together can be developed from it.

Within CMM lie the assumptions that people strive to create systems of mean- ing even when and where none is provided and that we organize meaning hierar- chically and temporally. As a result, institutional and individual behaviour is uninterpretable without taking into account the large discursive forces and resources at work which enable and constrain courses of action available in inter- action. Built initially for operation at the dyadic level, the application of CMM to organizing life has yet to be extensively explored. In one such attempt, Rose (1985) explained organizational adaptation using systems theory and CMM. Treating the 'organization' as a container in which action takes place, Rose (1985) argues that the nature of an organization's 'rules' for action constrain its ability to adapt to its environment in a hypothetical planning situation. Rose's rather simplistic application of the rules described in CMM overlooks much of what makes Pearce and Cronen's approach insightful and useful for the exami- nation of discourse and 'organization'.

Basically, Pearce and Cronen demonstrate that systems operate through a num- ber of intersecting logics. Specific logics are socially distributed across systems and individuals. Such distribution means that the available logic repertoire may be deficient in some circumstances; that logics that advantage some individuals and groups may be more actively reproduced and available than others; and that individuals and groups may have difficulty coordinating their activities and talk as they draw on different logics. Focusing on 'how things get done' rather than 'what is done', these authors argue that intersecting logics impel people to under- stand/interpret/act in certain ways and as resources drawn upon for practical accomplishments. Thus, logics are endlessly evoked, used and reproduced in dis- course. Therefore, a specific act of expression in an interaction can be understood as an outcome of a number of 'forces' (see Figure 8.1).

In Pearce and Cronen's work, an act is conditioned by four forces: contextual, prefigurative, practical and implicative forces. 'Prefigurative force' is an expres- sion of the sense of obligation one experiences based on a logical relation between previous acts and one's response. For example, if one follows or evokes a logic that aggression must be countered by aggression, a perceived act of aggression obligates an act of aggression. This is not a one-way street, suggest- ing a direct causal link between two actions, but rather the presence of this logic makes the perception or interpretation of aggression both possible and more likely (i.e., it gives it 'force').

Talk both responds to and puts into play the logical sequence and obligation. Hence, the complement of 'prefigurative' force is the 'practical force' of an act.

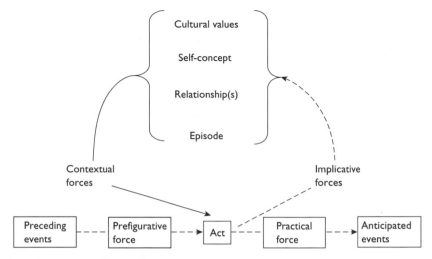

Figure 8.1   *Four aspects of logical force*

'Practical force' is an expression of the obligation felt from the desire to achieve. If the salient logic suggests that hard work will lead to success, if I wish to succeed, then I must work hard. Practical forces consider the anticipated 'end' of an act– that is, what the actor wishes to accomplish.

Both prefigurative and practical forces of an act are influenced by 'contextual' and 'implicative' forces. These forces are the conditions or resources an actor applies to select and mediate between potential responses to an act, or moves an actor makes, to achieve something in the future. Pearce and Cronen identified four resources: cultural values, definitions of self and other, the nature of the relationship and the definition of the situation (episode). While these resources are nested hierarchically, in every interaction, this ordering may be different according to the individual, highlighting the highly contingent nature of coordinating meaning in any interaction. People layer their perceptions of themselves, their relationships and episodes in which they participate. Resources for action are always determined by the ordering of the resources individuals and institutions bring to the situation or interaction at hand (Pearce, 1989).

None of these 'resources' is 'unitary' or psychologically or cognitively based. Values and definitions of the self, for example, are discursive accomplishments. They have no power of their own until used and reproduced in interaction. 'Cultural values' are the full set of complex and contradictory conceptions of what is perceived as worthwhile and prized. Specific values are connected to action choices by specific logics. Values, like other discursive resources, are evoked to justify and legitimate activities through the way they entail obligations. 'Definitions of self and other' are produced identities and identifications. One may be both an engineer and a manager of a tech company. Such identities require both their counterpart– others who are engineers or people to play subordinate to the manager–and larger systems in which these relations are embedded and interpreted–the engineering profession and company. Each definition of self produces different obligations and logics of action. 'Relationships' draw attention to the rights and obligations between interactants. Friendship obligates in ways different from supervisor/subordinate relations. We are often 'friends' with our 'bosses' or 'employees' which makes episodes such as a layoff difficult to accomplish due to the complicating nature of the different rights and obligations of these relationships. 'Episode' specifies the social form, the 'what' we are doing. For example, Schwartzman (1989) describes in detail the organizing accomplishment of meeting and the interpretations and obligations it entails.

Flowing out of these resources and their hierarchy are 'contextual forces' and 'implicative forces'. 'Contextual forces' express the sense of obligation one feels based on the presence of cultural values, definitions of the self and other, the nature of the relationship, the definition of the situation, etc. 'Implicative force' expresses the obligation one feels based on the perceived consequences the action will have on these resources. These forces are often reflected in our conversations in statements like 'What will people think of me?', 'I am not a bad person', 'That is not the IBM way', 'Men don't cry', 'This is a community', etc.

Approaching the relationship between discourse and organization from within the CMM perspective requires moving across levels (horizontally) as CMM analysis tries to unravel the logics of each speech act in the form of forces that obligate it and give it meaning (vertically). For example, let's take a simple discussion. Let us assume that person A is hurt by person B. Person A can find it to be appropriate, wise, and even obligatory to talk to B about it. This can come from a prefigurative force of hurt obligates complaint and a practical force that complaint leads to apology and repair. Cultural values of fairness, a concept of self as up-front and a friendship relationship seeking apology all form contextual and implicative forces on A's desire to discuss the problem with B. But let us assume that B sees complaint as obligating a shifting of blame and negating the extent of harm. Person B may base his/her interpretation and response on different prefigurative and practical logics, for example, a conception of self as a good person who wouldn't hurt anyone. With this set up, A's anticipated coordinated interaction–complaint leads to apology which leads to both feeling better and a strengthened relationship–may not be achieved. Instead he or she may get: complaint leads to shifting blame and minimization leading to stronger statements of harm leading to more shifting of blame and minimization and finally a destroyed relationship.

Such an analysis can have a practical payoff in looking at problematic organizing discourse. The driving force of CMM is to show the reciprocal relationship between individual actions and forms of social order. The nested nature of CMM allows us to consider resources gleaned from diverse sites and experiences as well as how organizing life is in constant creation and definition. At the minimum, Pearce and Cronen would hope that coordination might be improved by understanding a wider range of logics and developing the ability to talk about logics rather than simple acting out of them. This requires a particular sensitivity to the unintended consequences of practices. Moreover, CMM and its emphasis on 'cosmopolitan communication' does not deny the existence and inherent humanity of other resources and action (Pearce, 1989). By treating all resources as equal, or symmetrical, meaning and action can be coordinated without the reconciliation between incommensurate social realities, just as diverse discourses can be articulated together to form a coherent sense of reality. However, our dependence on some discursive resources over others, and our accessibility and awareness of these resources all impact on what we accomplish in interaction. CMM begins to illuminate the ways in which certain discursive practices and resources close others off, effectively reducing alternative courses of action or interpretation. When these closures are effected, by institutions or individuals, wider purposes are served and the social distribution and ability to use certain logics clearly advantages some people at the expense of others.

ORGANIZING CASES

Dialogic research poses questions at the boundaries, de-coding and re-coding grounds of collective order and diversity, listening to sounds and voices for who speaks, when, why and for whom (Clifford & Marcus, 1986; Deetz, 2001; Van Maanen, 1995). In the sections above, we have argued for the use of multiple methods for data collection and analysis to capture how organizing discourse is embedded in both larger social formations, which give it a specific life, sense and meaning, and the micro practices of discourse use, which evoke and reproduce these formations. Rather than discourse and organization being conceptualized as integrated and unitary, a dialogic orientation contends that the discourse – organization relationship, like its components, is ambiguous, tension filled and unsettled (Deetz, 1996). This enables strategic ambiguity, hidden domination and possibilities as well as creativity and resistance. The following empirical cases highlight the nature of this relationship more than others and show most clearly why multi-levelled analysis is important.

Bill Kinsella's (1996, 1997, 1999) studies of the Princeton Plasma Physics labs is one such case. The product of this lab was knowledge about fusion energy through the running of experiments that produced relatively small amounts of electricity from atomic fusion. Large amounts of energy were required to produce fusion, thus a complicated set of instruments and readings were needed to determine if additional energy was actually produced. This meant that the 'science' itself required much discourse and the active processes of knowledge construction were somewhat more explicit. Additionally, the lab was totally dependent on large amounts of federal grant money, which was dependent in large part on public perception of scientific merit and success.

Organizing discourse thus always involved three very different sets of discursive resources and audiences. First, 'science talk' was essential for the practice of science and the construction of scientific knowledge inside the labs. Second, 'organization process' talk involved the running of a rather large 'organization' with real deadlines, pay distributions, authority relations, etc. that often conflicted with the expectations and obligations of science talk as well as with each other. Finally, 'big science talk' required involvement of the mass media and public perceptions of science and scientific process in order to garner more resources for the 'organization'. In order to capture these different forms of discourse, their moments and links, Kinsella gathered documentary, observation and interview data to examine science as organized work, science as epistemology and science–society relations. Big science talk often conflicted with the other two, leading Kinsella to conclude that scientists acted as bricoleurs, selecting and arranging elements from the discourses of diverse cultures (the project team, the lab, the community of physics, big science) to assemble and legitimate their projects. However, even these cultures are internally diverse, which means that scientists of all kinds and at all levels must engage in discursive work to construct and reconstruct their own legitimation (Kinsella, 1996). As a result, discourse in the 'organization' could only be understood when put in relation to all three larger discourses. The decisions of which experiments to run and when didn't just appeal to different constituent needs–science needs, management needs, cultural industry needs–but required multilingual talk since each discourse had a very different logic. Such talk evoked and appealed to conflicting self-definitions and forms of expertise. In each turn it qualified and disqualified different people in different ways, it both used and made power.

Kirsten Broadfoot's (2003) work shows much the same in a very different organizing setting. Her work uses ethnographic methods of participant observation and interviewing, coupled with audio-taped interaction of both medical professionals and patients involved with genetic counselling interviews, to examine how the discourse of the gene is transforming medicine as organized work. All three forms of empirical material – field notes, interview and interaction transcripts – are treated symmetrically and then analysed according to critical discourse analysis. Discursive themes and structures emerging from this analysis are then subjected to the dialogic technique of defamiliarization to construct counter texts and work with negation to uncover the 'underbelly' of the discursive formations present and the dialectical tensions present in the empirical materials (Alvesson & Deetz, 2000; Martin, 1990; Thomas, 1993).

Again, three very different discourses and sets of discursive practices come together to organize knowledge, work and self in this context. In this case, 'medical talk' appeals to and borrows from the discourse of the medical profession with its specific values, expectations and knowledge of genetic science and technologies. 'Patient talk' is connected to the larger public and culture industry's understanding and discourse of the gene, genetic science and testing, with its own expectations and understandings. Finally, 'clinic talk' is the ever constant reminder that the clinic is an 'organization' of workers, payrolls and profit margins, as well as part of a larger health-care system. The end result of these discursive overlaps is a tapestry of tangled discursive threads such as clinical *vs* commercial interests, the relationship between biology and biography, the need for knowledge and the preservation of mystery and, finally, the simultaneous fragmentation and integration of medicine as organized work. It is not as if each of these discursive threads and interests simply impacts differentially on the talk in the interview. All are endlessly negotiated out there as power relations shift, metaphors are mixed across discourses, interactants borrow and deploy the talk of each other, and mis- and different understandings are let pass. These actions flow back out to their larger originating discursive sources – medical, patient or clinic – and transform our understandings of self, knowledge, technology and work, as well as the larger institution of 'medicine' in a society increasingly constructed within, through and around the science of genetics. As a result, clinic and professional participants emerge as negotiators, coordinators and mediators as the network of complexity that is medicine as organized work, as well as the truly unpredictable nature of all clinical futures, is revealed.

CONCLUSION

Cases like these are much the norm of contemporary organizing life. These are complex polysemic environments and times. Neither models of directional macro effects on micro practices, nor mere micro production/reproduction of larger dis- courses, capture the tension-filled, complex and evolving nature of organizing fabrics. Neither 'discourse' nor 'organization' can be separated from the forces that make them what they are. As a result, if our scholarly intent is to examine the ways in which organizing phenomena are discursively accomplished, then we need to enlarge our empirical and analytical focus to consider the interactive nature of this relationship and what it means for organizing social life.

Scholars of 'organization' and discourse can uncover conversations-in-wait- ing and demonstrate how language constructs multiple identities, objects and reality locally by using multiple methods of collecting empirical material, treat- ing all these forms of data symmetrically and applying complementary analyti- cal perspectives. As Richardson (1994) contends, the presentation of multiple and complex rationalities as a guiding objective requires that symmetry and sub- stance should be present in multiple dimensions, levels and perspectives to pre- serve the contradictions within and between discourses, and to privilege the partial, multiple and situated nature of our understandings of social worlds.

'Organization', like discourse, is constantly in action. Hence, when scholars engage in the analysis of either process, we analyse their fleeting and temporary products, or snapshots, of such flows. In contrast, this chapter outlines our vision of a dialogic research orientation to the relationship between the processes and products of discourse and organization.

REFERENCES

Althusser, L. (1972) *Lenin and philosophy*. New York: Monthly Review Press.
Alvesson, M. & Deetz, S. (2000) *Doing critical management research*. London: Sage.
Atkinson, P. (1995) *Medical talk and medical work: The liturgy of the clinic*. London: Sage.

Boje, D.M. (1995) Stories of the storytelling organization: A postmodern analysis of Disney as '*Tamara*-land'. *Academy of Management*, 38 (4): 997–1035.

Broadfoot, K. (2003) Disarming genes and the discursive reorganizing of knowledge, technology and self in medicine. Unpublished doctoral dissertation, University of Colorado.

Burawoy, M. (1991) *Ethnography unbound: Power and resistance in the modern metropolis*. Berkeley, CA: University of California Press.

Chouliaraki, L. & Fairclough, N. (1999) *Discourse in late modernity*. Edinburgh: Edinburgh University Press.

Clifford, J. & Marcus, G. (eds) (1986) *Writing culture: The poetics and politics of ethnography*. Berkeley, CA: University of California Press.

Deetz, S. (1992) *Democracy in an age of corporate colonization: Developments in communication and the politics of everyday life*. Albany, NY: State University of New York Press.

Deetz, S. (1996) Describing differences in approaches to organizational science: Rethinking Burrell and Morgan and their legacy. *Organization Science*, 7: 191–207.

Deetz, S. (2001) Conceptual foundations for organizational communication studies. In F.M. Jablin & L.L. Putnam (eds), *The new handbook of organizational communication: Advances in theory, research, and methods* (pp. 3–46). Thousand Oaks, CA: Sage.

Fairclough, N. (1992) *Discourse and social change*. Cambridge: Polity Press.

Fitch, K. (1998) Text and context: A problematic distinction for ethnography. *Research on language and social interaction*, 31 (1): 91–107.

Foucault, M. (1981) *History of Sexuality: Volume 1*. Harmondsworth: Penguin.

Kinsella, W. (1996) A 'fusion' of interests: Big science, government, and rhetorical practice in nuclear fusion research. *Rhetoric Society Quarterly*, 26: 65–81.

Kinsella, W. (1997) Communication and the construction of knowledge in a scientific community: An ethnographic study. Unpublished doctoral dissertation. Rutgers University, New Brunswick, NJ.

Kinsella, W. (1999) Discourse, power, and knowledge in the management of 'big science': The production of consensus in a nuclear fusion research laboratory. *Management Communication Quarterly*, 13: 171–208.

Kristeva, J. (1984) *Revolution in poetic language*. New York: Columbia University Press.

Laclau, E. & Mouffe, C. (2001) *Hegemony and socialist strategy: Towards a radical democratic politics* (2nd edition). London: Verso.

Latour, B. (1991) Technology is society made durable. In J. Law (ed.), *A sociology of monsters: Essays on power, technology and domination* (pp. 103–31). London: Routledge.

Law, J. (1994) *Organizing modernity*. Oxford: Blackwell.

Linell, P. (1998) *Approaching dialogue: Talk, interaction and contexts in dialogical perspectives*. Amsterdam: John Benjamins.

Lupton, D. (1997) Foucault and the medicalisation critique. In A. Petersen and R. Bunton (eds), *Foucault, health and medicine* (pp. 94–110). Routledge. London.

Martin, J. (1990) Deconstructing organizational taboos: The suppression of gender conflict in organizations. *Organization Science*, 1 (4): 339–59.

Miller, G. (1994) Towards ethnographies of institutional discourse: prospects and suggestions. *Journal of Contemporary Ethnography*, 23 (3): 280–306.

Mokros, H.B. & Deetz, S. (1996) What counts as real? A constitutive view of communication and the disenfranchised in the context of health. In E.B. Ray (ed.), *Communication and disenfranchisement: Social health issues and implications* (pp. 29–44). Mahwah, NJ: Lawrence Erlbaum Associates.

Pearce, W.B. (1989) *Communication and the human condition*. Carbondale, IL: Southern Illinois University Press.

Pearce, W.B. & Cronen, V.E. (1980) *Communication, action and meaning: The creation of social realities*. New York: Praeger.

Richardson, L. (1994) Writing: A method of inquiry. In N.K. Denzin & Y.S. Lincoln (eds), *Handbook of qualitative research* (pp. 516–29). Thousand Oaks, CA: Sage.

Rose, N. (1994) Medicine, history and the present. In C. Jones & R. Porter (eds), *Reassessing Foucault: Power, medicine and the body* (pp. 48–71). London: Routledge.

Rose, R.A. (1985) Organizational adaptation from a rules theory perspective. *Western Journal of Speech Communication*, 49 (4, Fall): 322–40.

Schwartzman, H.B. (1989) *The Meeting*. New York: Plenum.

Taylor, B.C. (1999) Browsing the culture: Membership and intertextuality at a Mormon bookstore. *Studies in Cultures, Organizations, and Societies*, 5: 61–95.

Therborn, G. (1980) *The ideology of power and the power of ideology*. London: Verso.

Thomas, J. (1993) *Doing critical ethnography*. Newbury Park, CA: Sage.

Treichler, P.A. (1991) How to have theory in an epidemic: the evolution of AIDS treatment activism. In C. Penley & A. Ross (eds), *Technoculture* (pp. 57–106). Minneapolis, MN: University of Minnesota Press.

Van Dijk, T. (1993) Principles of critical discourse analysis. *Discourse & Society*, 4: 249–83.

Van Maanen, J. (1995) *Representation and ethnography*. Newbury Park, CA: Sage.

Weedon, C. (1997) *Feminist practice and poststructuralist theory* (2nd edition). Oxford: Blackwell.

Weick, K. (1979) *The social psychology of organizing* (2nd edition). Reading, MA: Addison-Wesley.

Wodak, R. (1997) Critical discourse analysis and the study of doctor–patient interaction. In B. Gunnarsson, P. Linell & B. Nordberg (eds), *The construction of professional discourse* (pp. 173–200). London: Longman.

9

Doing Research in Organizational Discourse: The Importance of Researcher Context

Craig Prichard, Deborah Jones and Ralph Stablein

What's involved in doing research in organizational discourse? In this chapter we attempt to answer this question by using five phases of the research process, as identified by Denzin and Lincoln (2000), to guide an examination of the sub-fields of organizational discourse analysis (ODA) (see Table 9.1). Our first aim is to help those new to discourse analysis in organization studies to get started in this field. We also want to encourage researchers who are already using ODA to clarify their own positions and consider a wider repertoire of approaches. The chapter is organized into five sections that address each of Denzin and Lincoln's five choice points in the research process. At each point we interrogate how one of the sub-fields of organizational discourse undertakes this part of the research process. So, for example, the second choice point involves adopting a theoretical frame or position. Here we discuss frames or positions available in narrative research. In relation to the third choice point – adopting a strategy of inquiry – we discuss strategies used in Foucauldian discourse analysis. As this is a handbook, and not a textbook, we are attempting to strike a balance between helping researchers and engaging critically with the published work itself. In pursuing these aims we have been forced to be highly selective. While we make no apology for this, we would ask the reader to bear this in mind. 'Organizational discourse' is not a homogeneous field. It is a series of sub-fields linked together by a substantive concern with language and practice in organizations and organizing. In this chapter we provide particular kinds of 'snapshots' of research practice in four of these sub-fields: narrative, linguistic Foucauldian and deconstructive discourse analysis (see Table 9.1).

A key feature of research practice in Denzin and Lincoln's approach, and one that we strongly support, is developing a reflexive understanding of the context in which researchers find themselves. This practice not only enriches the research practice, it also provides much of the 'between the lines' knowledge that can lead to successful research outcomes. The opening section of the chapter – the first choice point – addresses this issue directly. We also open each section with a narrative that profiles the work of *different* fictional researchers, each named Andy Andrews, as they tackle a different phase of the work.[1]

Table 9.1 *Character map of organizational discourse analysis*

	Narrative	Foucauldian	Linguistic	Deconstruction
Choice Point 1: Who am I?! Locating the researcher	The context in which the researchers find themselves plays a crucial part in the shaping of the research work. Differences that attach to region, institution and academic disciplines are intermixed here with gender, race and class processes. These dimensions shape the nature, purpose and direction of the research undertaken.			
Choice point 2: Which theoretical frame?	Critical and interpretive	Critical	Positivist, interpretive and critical depending on field	Philosophical/critical
Choice point 3: Which research strategy?	Case-specific textual analysis	Historical, archival practice analysis	Samples from large corpus	Textual analysis
Choice point 4: Which form of data gathering and analysis?	Spoken and written texts	Documentary research in historical and contemporary archives, also ethnographic analysis of practice	Spoken and written texts analysed against theoretical/conceptual frameworks	Key texts, organizational texts, theoretical texts, experimental texts
Choice point 5: Which form of presentation and for what purpose?	**Presentation:** Research report and paper **Purpose:** To improve understanding of others	**Presentation:** Public debate and writing, academic papers, books **Purpose:** Political engagement, public critique	**Presentation:** Academic paper **Purpose:** Accumulation of knowledge	**Presentation:** Public academic texts **Purpose:** Academic critique of established knowledge
Key examples used in chapter	Boje, 1991, 1995; Brown, 2000; Gabriel, 2000	Brewis, 2001; Jacques, 1996; Pei-Chia, 2001	Erera-Weatherley, 1996; Fairclough, 1992, 2001; Titscher et al., 2000	Game, 1994; Martin, 1990; Mumby and Stol, 1991

> ## CHOICE POINT 1: SITUATING ONESELF
>
> *Andy Andrews cuts an impressive figure. Born in the South Pacific on the Island of Upolo, Western Samoa, she studied business at Auckland University in New Zealand before taking a job as a customer service representative in an insurance firm. She made team leader and finally section manager before quitting to take a fulltime Masters degree in Business Studies at the University of Auckland. While she might later reflect on the circumstances that led to her departure from the firm and her return to education, she did well in her early research endeavours and began to consider the possibility of pursuing an academic career. She began to explore the qualitative research and non-traditional forms of organization theory that had become part of her studies. Some of her lecturers spoke of management as rhetorical, dialogic and discursive, and of organizations as narratives, discourses and subject to deconstruction Whereas initially she regarded them as a bunch of self-indulgent wankers she began to find their approach illuminating and engaging.*

The first question to ask, in approaching research in organizational discourse analysis (ODA), is about you. One needs to develop a reflexive awareness of the conditions and circumstances in which one finds oneself. What positions are available for you to do the research? In this section we explore the influences on possible researcher positions for doing ODA.

The researcher position is not simply an intellectual stance drawn from a community of researchers, a school of thought or a particular research conversation through which we must position or frame research *vis-à-vis* the relevant research audience (Booth et al., 1995; Huff, 1999). The researcher position resides in a physical body that requires physical space, sustenance, an income to support ongoing effort and to pay for computer, paper and access to electronic databases. Researcher positions are constituted through a web of intellectual, institutional, economic and political relations. Important aspects would include the opportunities to develop and train in the skills required to write theses that will be accepted, the opportunities to publish, and regional and disciplinary differences in intellectual tradition and organizational practices.

ODA usually places the researcher in the business school, rather than the linguistics, sociology, psychology or social work department. The researcher position within the business school also strongly influences likely publication outlets, conference attendance and publishers considered. Most business schools find themselves embedded in universities that require significant revenue from the business school and question the academic respectability of business research. Thus the researcher position is enmeshed in heavy demands for teaching many students, demands for high quantity and quality publications, and often contract research and executive education duties as well (Near, 1996; Willmott, 1995). Balancing this, income and support are generally better than in, say, a cultural studies department. Research students are likely to benefit from the better financial position of the business school. For non-tenured faculty (North America and Canada) or staff (UK/Australasia), pressures are likely to be at the most intense. However, with tenure, more space to explore alternative perspectives and time to develop new skills may be available.

The location of the business school will make a difference as well. North American business schools are dominated by positivist approaches to science. Here, ODA will be an interesting but marginal, even odd, approach to the study of organization. Training, senior faculty support and co-authors may be hard to come by. In the absence of exposure to qualitative research training, one may feel too insecure to proceed, or one can suffer the hubris of assuming that anyone who can talk and read can do discourse analysis. In the UK and Europe, ODA fits well with the more mainstream interpretive and critical traditions. In Australasia, 'refugees' from North American and UK systems mix with Kiwis (New Zealanders) and Aussies in more intellectually diverse departments.

All of the non-US researcher positions must relate to the American domination of the intellectual field, hierarchical ranking of journals, etc. (Clegg & Linstead, 2000). And then there are the non-anglophone schools with their own situations. French and German institutions have been the source of much of the theoretical and empirical work in linguistics (see Wodak & Meyer, 2001) and poststructuralism that English-speaking ODA draws on. Personal biography, that is a nationality, mother tongue, family background, education, work experience, intellectual interests and moral commitments, project us into one of these researcher positions (Ellis & Bochner, 2000). Once we are occupied by or fill the researcher position, a range of choices are already made for us, while other choices open up to us.

Some of this positioning may well be experienced as constraint. However, though constitutive of the researcher position, much of it is simply not consciously experienced at all. Our upwardly mobile, intellectually curious, Auckland-based Andy Andrews above is unlikely to conceive even the possibility of pursuing a course in cultural studies. The business school is the place to be. She knows that her studies need to guarantee economic security. But what if we 'morph' Andy into the following?

Andy Andrews is an impressive figure. Son of two New York accountants, he studied sociology and psychology at Oberlin (an elite liberal arts college in the Midwest). For the next few years, Andy worked for a major multinational corporation on a series of corporate office projects as the personal assistant to a family friend. An MBA from the Kellogg GSM at Northwestern University followed. On graduation, he went to work in the Big Apple as a junior account executive with a multinational marketing and promotions firm. He made senior account executive in mid-2001 but late that year, following the bombing of the World Trade Centre, he quit his all-consuming job to take care of his two young children. He and his partner now job share an arts promotion post in his hometown. He recently signed on for a Master's degree in organizational analysis with ...

This 'WASPy' Andy has a choice. He will consider a range of possibilities, especially as he continues to reflect on the true meaning of life. Consider the question of which university to attend. WASPy Andy will clearly attend a top-10 graduate school in the USA. Nothing else is conceivable to him. There is no experience of constraint. Our NZ-based Andy will likely receive advice from her mentors suggesting overseas study. Traditionally, the universities of the UK would be the destination. But now the intellectual and financial inducement of the US or Australian universities beckon. Or, she could continue on to doctoral work at Auckland (she may qualify for a Pacific Island scholarship). In any case, she will have to choose.

Andy's differing experiences will unfold in different researcher positions. Both Andys may receive a good training but they will be exposed to different disciplines and intellectual traditions and they'll have various resource spaces available to them. Our WASPy Andy will attend the annual Academy of Management and will experience organizational discourse as an intriguing, exotic and slightly odd alternative approach. For New Zealand-based Andy, on the other hand, the understanding of organization as a set of discursive practices may be central to her developing work.

The importance of these reflections is the effect that knowing 'my' place and choosing 'my' position has on the character of the subsequent research practice. For example, writing from the margins (New Zealand and Australia, for instance) for a US management journal will require more emphasis on the explicit rigour of analysis. European reviewers will be less concerned about this aspect of the manuscript. Re-location may be possible, but it is time- and energy-consuming. If you are struggling for tenure against the standard of top-rated US journals, starting a family and settling in a new community, it may not be realistic.

CHOICE POINT 2: THEORETICAL FRAMES

'But what is this research for?' Andy had been explaining the tensions between the interpretive and critical traditions in organizational discourse analysis during a guest lecture for honours students. 'That's a great question!' said Andy, and the student went on: 'With all due respect, I'm just wondering how this relates to the real world?' Andy skipped her usually derisive comments about the 'real' and went straight to an example. 'OK, so you're sitting around a table at work. The accountant is talking rate of return, the HR bloke is doing a line on developing a learning culture and the strategy person is pressing home the importance of 'competitive advantage'. Your project, the one you so passionately want to be supported, is caught at what seems like a discursive crossroads. Discourse analysis can help. How can it help? Well ... Andy hesitated briefly then decided to go with her strongest pitch. 'It depends if your aim is to control, understand or emancipate your colleagues from their various discursive blinders.'

The second question to ask is how will we *frame* the study? Which theoretical framework will we use? Framing is about connecting to an intellectual community. One way to explore this question is to consider the purpose of the study (Stablein, 1996). At a broad level, and at the risk of some simplification, we follow Habermas (1971) and suggest that the organizational sciences are built on three core purposes: a technical interest in control, a practical interest in action-oriented meaning-making, and an emancipatory interest in human autonomy and responsibility. Pursuit of these diverse purposes produces the three traditions or frames from which to undertake research: the positivist, interpretive and critical traditions, respectively. The critical tradition always depends on research in the positivist and interpretive traditions, but adds the important corrective of attention to power relations. The positivist and interpretive traditions tend to accept existing power relations.

Critical scholars have found that exploring the power relations involved in the construction of meanings, and in the connection of meanings to organizational practices, provides valuable insight. While in the sections below we will present some examples of content analysis that draw on the positivist tradition, organization discourse as a field draws almost exclusively on the interpretive and critical traditions (Alvesson & Kärreman, 2000; Heracleous & Hendry, 2000; Phillips & Hardy, 2002).

Framing is an important choice point. The dimensions discussed above powerfully shape such a choice. As the stories of our Andy character make clear, one's choice of frame will be shaped by institutional, disciplinary and geographic contexts and biographical concerns. The particular research community will play a part here.

Research communities tend to be reproduced by key authors. Such authors may be on the advisory boards of key journals and regular speakers and guests at conferences. Their work carries with it some authority to speak and some resources through which to speak. These provide researchers facing the somewhat bewildering variety of potential framings with established intellectual positions to appropriate. By way of illustration we discuss below the frames provided by three prominent authors working with narrative resources in the field of organizational discourse.

Research positions in narrative discourse analysis

Narrative analysis forms a sub-field of organizational discourse (OD) studies. The substantive focus of research varies widely across a range of organizational topics and issues, for example, strategic management (Barry & Elmes, 1997), organizational change and innovation (Deuten & Rip, 2000; Feldman, 1990), and managerial practice (Ng & de Cock, 2002). Positionings are, as Davies and Harré identify (1990), sets of discursive practices. In this case, such practices include the researcher 'voice', the background theoretical resources, the substantive research topic, one's orientation to research subjects, and relations with one's audience. Narrative analysis in organization discourse studies includes at least three strong positionings in these terms. We briefly discuss these positions via well-cited examples produced by three prominent authors in this field, namely, David Boje, Yiannis Gabriel and Andrew Brown.

STORY LIBERATOR – BOJE David Boje's path-breaking case study of the Disney Corporation provides a strong positioning for the critical narrative analyst in organization discourse. Published in the *Academy of Management Journal*, the article institutes a researcher's position that regards work organizations as being oppressive and exploitative structures. Their central features are practices, including storytelling practices, that deny and marginalize the skills and efforts of the many for the benefit of the few. Drawing on archive and secondary literature sources, Boje's article moves between official company discourse, non-official commentaries and theoretical texts to detail the various controlling practices (including particular kinds of storytelling) used to institute, shape and reproduce the Disney Empire. For example, Boje discusses Walt Disney's paternalist narrative of the firm as a 'family' while at the same time he was paying workers below market rates (Boje, 1995, p. 1014). Theoretical support for this critical positioning is drawn from a wide range of sources, and Boje provides a brief biographical sketch of his own 'conversion' from functional organization researcher to sceptical critical analyst:

> As the analysis proceeded … I began to see how the stories I grew up accepting about Walt Disney and his Magic Kingdom were being resisted by marginalized accounts. I therefore began to shift from a 'functional' analysis (how stories sell) to a more sceptical one (how one side of a story masks another). (1995, p. 1008)

Through his work Boje provides an entry point for researchers to do narrative-based discourse analysis where power, inequality, oppression and exploitation are the substantive subjects of studies in organizational discourse.

STORY THERAPIST – GABRIEL While not necessarily at odds with Boje's work, Yiannis Gabriel's psychoanalytic-leaning critical narrative research (1995, also 1991) provides an alternative positioning. Rather than explore the interdependence of power and organizational storytelling, Gabriel's work highlights the subversive, resistive and downright unmanageable character of storytelling in organizations. Storytelling here is a *particular* practice that rebuffs, momentarily at least, rationalization, organizational control, oppression and exploitation. The researcher's positioning is with 'the people', who, by dint of their ability to gossip, dream and appropriate story resources, are never far from turning management practice into objects of amusement and cynicism. While we might identify Boje's positioning as one of critical organizational conscience and story liberator, Gabriel's position is more therapist, confidante or voyeur. The position's emancipatory interests are in supporting workers and managers by celebrating the pleasure of subversive storytelling.

> The researcher may become a fellow-traveller in a fantasy, sharing its emotional tone, seeking to expand it, enrich it, and ultimately sustaining its disengaged, wish-fulfilling qualities. This is the approach of one eager to appreciate a good story and willing to free-associate around it. It is the approach which I adopted. (1995, p. 401).

In terms of theoretical resources, the strength of Gabriel's researcher position – and where it also differs from that provided by Boje – is its use of folkloric, literary and psychoanalytic traditions. For Gabriel, stories are not everywhere, but rather they constitute very specific forms of organizational discourse. Their value is largely therapeutic. While Gabriel's researcher position is one of story celebrant, he also retains a residual role as organizational therapist. Here stories and dreams (1995) become material for the therapist's craft of attempting to change people's attachment to, and identification with, destructive organization practices and relations.

STORY ANALYST – BROWN There are some important points of contrast between Boje and Gabriel's positionings and that provided by our third author, Andrew Brown. As a point of difference, Brown's work with narrative draws on the social psychology of Karl Weick (1995). The upshot is that Brown's reading of narrative is less directly political than Boje's and draws from a different psychological tradition from that of Gabriel. Narratives for Brown are the form that people's cognitive sense-making takes as they individually and collectively struggle to understand and successfully enact the complex situations in which they find themselves. Narratives *do* carry forward particular interests and extend or defend the hegemonic positions of particular groups (Brown, 1998). But this is a latent rather than a deliberate strategy or tactic and more likely an effect of routinized and habituated modes of making sense.

In a series of papers that explore sense-making and narratives in particular organizations (Humphreys & Brown, 2002), public inquiries (Brown, 2000; Brown & Jones 2000) and change processes (Brown, 1998), Brown and his collaborators assert an interpretive analyst's position. The purpose here is to contribute to our *understanding* (note the difference from Gabriel and Boje) of how narratives are produced and used. Such a positioning has some similarities with those found in positivist science. For instance, the narrative analyst tends to be removed from the 'action' and speaks from 'above'. Yet such a position is not entirely secure. Recent challenges to positivist science, and the importance of researcher reflexivity, prompt Brown to make the following notes in a section of one paper in which he analyses the Report of the UK Allitt Inquiry (2000).[2] These comments provide useful insights into the problematics of researcher positioning in narrative analysis. Brown identifies the Allitt Inquiry Report as an artful text designed to persuade readers of a particular narrative. He argues that such a narrative seeks to absolve Allitt's medical colleagues of blame and maintain the legitimacy of the medical profession. In the methodological section of the paper, Brown makes the same claim for his own text: 'It is explicitly acknowledged that this paper is an artful product designed not just to inform but to persuade, and that the illusion of objectivity is not more than an authorial strategy, i.e. illusory' (2000, p. 50).

Brown follows this with comments that highlight some tensions over what is required to perform the interpretive analyst's position:

> That an acknowledgement of this effect has now become a condition (at least in certain European journals) for a scholarly audience to received interpretive work as authentic and credible (Jeffcutt, 1994), is an interesting symptom of how conventions governing the representation of qualitative research have altered in recent years. (2000, pp. 50–1)

Brown's comment identifies some loss of security or legitimacy over the interpretive analyst's position. The issue is one of equivalence. If the researcher claims that the targets of analysis are artfully-produced political documents that seek to defend particular interests, then equivalence would demand that we ask what interests artfully-researched documents defend or serve. In his article Brown offers little to guide us at this point. But his broader response might be that the authorities that support research at least attempt to guarantee 'a minimum of counter-intuitive and counter-conventional theory' (Brown, 2000, p. 67).

In sum, we have identified the taking up of a researcher position as a core practice in the doing of research. Such positions are created afresh when we begin research work. Taking a researcher's position involves taking up one or a mix of what we have termed theoretical perspectives, interpretive frames or paradigms. These are made available to us in the work of prominent scholars in a particular field of inquiry. We have argued that even within a sub-field, such as narrative analysis in OD, multiple and variably contradictory positions are available for the doing of discourse analytic research in organization studies.

CHOICE POINT 3: STRATEGIES OF INQUIRY

'I don't know how you can read that stuff ', said Michelle, grimacing as she pointed to Andy's copy of Discipline and Punish (Foucault, 1991), 'public disembowelling and all that. What has all that historical stuff got to do with politics now? How can you relate it to what you're doing on anti-racism in Aotearoa?' 'OK', agreed Andy, 'Yes it is revolting. But how come at that time everyone thought disembowelling was OK, and now we mostly would think it was grotesque and completely unjustifiable? How come people used to think slavery was OK, or think that seizing Maori land is OK or that racism is OK? Foucault is trying to figure out how we can analyse what is happening in these situations, how we come to see certain truths as self-evident. What is it we are taking for granted now about "race" and racism? How does it affect our strategies to change organizations?' 'Right, but that's history isn't it?', asked Michelle. 'Are you doing history? I thought you were looking at racism now.' 'Yes, well I am, I'm interviewing people. But I'm still trying to analyse how come we take certain ideas for granted, and how that affects our strategies.'

At this third choice point a researcher must generate a research strategy. According to Denzin and Lincoln, this involves a 'flexible set of guidelines that connect theoretical paradigms first to strategies of inquiry and second to methods of collecting empirical material' (2000, pp. 21–2). This phase of the research process is also described as methodological as it 'anchors', in Denzin and Lincoln's words (2000, p. 22), the researcher's question, standpoint, epistemology and theoretical framework in specific empirical sites. Decisions are made here about what we could call 'operationalizing' research questions, deciding on a field of inquiry and on methods of collecting and analysing data.

In conducting discourse analysis, it is critical at this juncture to be clear about how 'discourse' will be defined and treated. A wide range of types of research use 'discourse' as data – that is, they use verbal and visual material, such as interview transcripts or organizational documents. In such research 'primary' data (e.g., interview transcripts) are typically distinguished from 'secondary' data (e.g., organizational documents). In many types of discourse analysis, this distinction is problematized. 'Secondary' data (e.g., organizational documents) may be treated as of primary interest, or they may be treated as on the same plane with 'primary' data (e.g., interview transcripts), where both are regarded as examples of organizational discourse. A research strategy for 'discourse analytic' research (Burman &

Parker, 1993) will foreground the discursive element to the study, looking at discourse as a phenomenon in itself, as a form of meaning-making or as communication. Another possibility is to theorize 'discourse' in ways that completely re-frame the way it is used to carry out research – as in Foucauldian research, discussed in this section.

Michel Foucault's work has been hugely influential in triggering the new interest in discourse in organizational studies, and has informed a wide range of work that draws on a Foucauldian idea of discourse to theorize phenomena. Foucault's work has pushed the boundaries of what we take to be 'discourses': they go beyond the idea of 'language' to include forms of knowledge, together with the social practices, forms of subjectivity and power relations inherent in this knowledge. These social practices include language but they go beyond the verbal or linguistic.

It is not easy to operationalize 'discourse' in the Foucauldian sense (Sawyer, 2002). In his earlier work, discourses are relatively narrowly conceived, based around official writings and records (Foucault, 1972, 1991). In later work, as in the *History of Sexuality* (Foucault, 1978) and in subsequent seminars and interviews (Foucault, 1988, 1996), discursive practices are framed in a much more open way as 'technologies of the self', so that discourses are the condition for all social experience.

Foucault saw discourse analysis as the 'exercise of a perspective' in 'analysing sociopolitical relations'. This is rather different from simply applying discourse analysis 'methods' or seeing discourse as a kind of data.

> It is not at all obvious to those who wish to get on with the work of analysing sociopolitical relations how to move logically or practically from the analysis of language to the analysis of human relations. Yet a move from the analysis of linguistic or discursive practices to the analysis of human conduct requires little more than *the exercise of a perspective*, one that rejects a radical distinction between discursive practices and nondiscursive (real, actual, what can we call them?) practices. (Foucault, cited in Shapiro, 1981, p. 127, Shapiro italics)

By comparison with other interpretive, semiotic or broadly social constructionist approaches to organizational analysis, Foucault specifically refuses 'analysis couched in terms of the symbolic field or the domain of signifying structures' in favour of an analytic model of war or battle: 'relations of power, not relations of meaning' (Foucault, 1980, p. 114). Foucault is interested in questions of what discourse *does* rather than what it *means*. The implication for organization scholars is that an analysis of organizational discourse is inseparable from an analysis of power relations.

Roy Jacques' study, *Manufacturing the Employee* (1996), is akin to Foucault's classic historical studies (Foucault, 1970, 1978, 1994) in that he takes a particular discursive formation – 'American management discourse' (Jacques, 1996, p. xii) – and tracks it over time. To carry out an 'archaeology' of this 'archive' (Foucault, 1972) means collecting samples that will make up the data set. Jacques relates his research design to his experiences as a management practitioner, student and academic in the USA. For him, the samples are historical management texts, more specifically texts emerging from 'industrial-era US values' (Jacques, 1996, p. xiii).

His genealogical work, like Foucault's, creates a 'history of the present' (Foucault, 1991) which shows 'contemporary management knowledge' to be – rather than a set of universal best practices arrived at through progress in organizational science – 'a culturally and historically specific way of thinking about work and society' (Jacques, 1996, p. vii). The critical issue is not to produce new historical material, but to organize the archive 'in a way that may contribute to thinking differently about problems' (ibid., p. x). This strategy has several implications: Jacques argues that seeing this discourse in historical context shows how limited it is, for managers as well as academics, for confronting issues of the present. He also argues that 'contextualizing the history of management as culturally bound up with the Euro-American tradition' (p. xiv) allows us – from inside and outside this tradition – to produce 'many localized stories' of management in the place of 'one cultural system' (p. xv).

A Foucauldian archive strategy tends to focus on broad discourse formations in which 'official' knowledges and truth regimes are implicated along with associated organizational practices (Hollway, 1991; Townley, 1994). Joanna Brewis has also used management texts as her archive in studying 'knowledge on sexual harassment' (Brewis, 2001, p. 37). Like Jacques, her strategy is to position her archive – contemporary harassment knowledge – as 'no more and no less than a historical artefact, rather than some kind of enduring truth about modern organizational life' (ibid. 2001, p. 38). The difference is that she 'historicizes' her archive by an analysis of her texts within the wider contemporary discourse of sex, considering how identities and power relations are discursively constituted by 'the particular way sexual harassment is spoken, written and thought about within harassment knowledge' (p. 37). Brewis strongly emphasizes the distinction between a Foucauldian approach to analysing the archive, which sets out to problematize the truth regimes within which we ourselves are implicated, and a more traditional critical stance, where intellectuals consider themselves to be in a privileged position to comment on the archive and to uncover its 'truth'. In arguing that harassment knowledge may reproduce the very positions of harasser and recipient that practitioners may be setting out to abolish, Brewis resonates with feminist Foucauldian scholars who set out to upset identities – especially gendered identities – through discourse analytic work, often turning the focus on feminist discourse itself by way of auto-critique (Butler, 1990; Weedon, 1987).

A key aspect of Foucault's radical idea of discourse is to extend analysis from language to bodies, practices, identities and subjectivities. In Foucault's own work, the discursive construction of the body can be studied from the historical archive but, more recently, ethnographic case studies have been used to include contemporary data such as in-depth interviews and observation in the research design. Pei-Chia Lan's study of the body in cosmetics retailing compares two ethnographic case studies of service workers (Pei-Chia, 2001). Her work exemplifies the importance of the theoretical context for Foucauldian work. Arguing that a Foucauldian theory of 'the microphysics of labor control in regards to constructing workers' bodies' (ibid. 2001, p. 83) is required for an adequate theoretical and empirical analysis of the labour process, she explicitly splices labour process theory (LPT) with Foucauldian theory in her research design. Setting out to challenge the 'blindness to the body' in LPT, Pei-Chia selected case studies based on service workers because typically they 'interact with customers via their bodily performances' (ibid., p. 83). By choosing cosmetic retailers, she intensifies still further the focus on the body, as this work explicitly revolves around the physical appearance of both customers and workers. She draws on Foucault's theory of self-discipline, integrating it with studies of emotional labour (Hochschild, 1983) to depict workers who *voluntarily exploit their own bodies'* (Pei-Chia, 2001, p. 91, original italics).

Foucauldian methodologies have also been developed to include life history research (Middleton, 1993), extended ethnographic case studies (Kondo, 1990) and studies based on interviews and/or observations of specified populations (Austrin, 1994; Tretheway, 1999). Careful attention to power relations and broader discursive contexts, and the use of radical conceptions of discourse to de-naturalize contemporary knowledges, distinguish these as Foucauldian strategies of discourse analysis.

**CHOICE POINT 4: METHODS
OF COLLECTION AND ANALYSIS**

Andy Andrews felt apprehensive as she looked around at the unfamiliar audience. She wondered if she wasn't a bit of an impostor at the discourse analysis seminar. Everyone else there was from the arts faculty, and they had quite a different take on 'discourse'. As she listened to the first presenters, she started to get interested. These linguists had some great techniques for collecting data. They were analysing actual conversations for instance, interactions in their organizational contexts. They were recording meetings and putting microphones on factory workers to track their conversations over a day. This was much more specific stuff than you usually found in management research. And their analysis was detailed too – right down to who interrupted who, and the kinds of words they used. It was amazing how much they could explain about work relationships out of analysing one short exchange. Hmmm – her mind started to spin with speculations. This seemed to be quite positivist, realist stuff – could the techniques be used for analysing discourse from a more interpretive perspective? Was she going to have to study linguistics or could she just appropriate some methods? Would that be cheating?

At this choice point the researcher decides on methods of collecting and analysing empirical materials. Although in Denzin and Lincoln's research process model this is presented as one point (Denzin & Lincoln, 2000, pp. 20–1), in practice both data collection and analysis may be iterative and emergent. New sites or types of data may open up, and early forms of analysis may suggest incorporating new analytic methods later on to make sense of emerging data patterns. Denzin and Lincoln take the position that 'data', rather than pre-existing for the researcher to discover and 'collect', are created by the researcher through interaction with sites and through interactive practices (Denzin & Lincoln, 2000, p. 633). The choices of data types and analytic techniques in ODA require careful thought. Key questions include how data are defined or framed as 'discourse', what 'discourse analysis' may involve in terms of commitments to theories of discourse, and what its relationship is to other social phenomena such as organization, identity and power.

Some genres of discourse analysis are traditionally associated with various specific types of data and data analysis – content analysis, for instance, is strongly associated with published texts, and the collection of organizational stories frequently provides data for narrative analysis. However, innovations in ODA are often being produced by new combinations of data and analytic methods. For example, Anne Opie has collected transcripts of teamwork discussions, which would traditionally be analysed using some form of linguistic and conversational analysis, and has instead used a Foucauldian approach in tracing the interaction of professional discourses and their professional and political consequences (Opie, 1997, 2000).

'Organizational discourse analysis' has two main 'perspectives' on data collection and analysis:

- theorizing all social practices as discursively constituted and thus as potential data for discourse analysis (as in Foucauldian perspectives); and
- taking a new interest in discourse in its more traditional sense – as language use in organizational contexts.

While the two perspectives may be combined, our focus in this section is on the second – on discourse as text. This text may be writing, perhaps transcription of spoken language, less frequently visual imagery. Language has been a traditional focus of research in fields such as linguistics and communication studies, which provide a depth of expertise in both theorizing and analysing language. In these fields, specific analytic techniques pay close attention to texts as *language in use,* as opposed to the more broadly interpretive use of texts as data in qualitative research. Here we discuss data collection and analysis from two of the most influential perspectives on language in organizational research – content analysis and critical discourse analysis.

Content analysis

In organizational studies the term 'content analysis' is sometimes used in a very wide sense. Traditional content analysis looks at the communicative aspects of texts, setting out to systematically and objectively identify their characteristics (Titscher et al., 2000). In other words, content analysis seeks to reveal what is 'there' in a text – to describe its 'manifest content' (Berelson, 1952, also cited Titscher et al., 2000, p. 57). This kind of content analysis is a realist project by which the contents of published materials – usually media texts or organizational documents – are assessed through a combination of quantitative and qualitative methods. On the most basic level, it determines the presence of certain words and contents in texts.

The 'classical' form of content analysis is the quantitative version (Ryan & Bernard, 2000, pp. 785–6). But there has been a more recent proliferation of 'qualitative content analyses' that are difficult to separate from other forms of text analysis. Content analysis could be stretched to include any methods 'which somehow approach texts by means of categories' (Titscher et al., 2000, p. 55). It refers to the coding of ethnographic material, for instance, in a study of the culture of oil rigs (Collinson, 1999), and to the analysis of interviews in a study of how welfare supervisors cope with stress (Erera-Weatherley, 1996). In the latter case, content analysis is described as a variant of 'open coding', a term originally associated with the first stage of grounded theory analysis (Strauss & Corbin, 1990) and now used as a more general term for coding of qualitative data.

A distinction can be made between content analysis in the *sociological tradition*, which 'treats text as a window into human experience', and the *linguistic tradition*, which 'treats text as an object of analysis in itself' (Ryan & Bernard, 2000, p. 769). In the context of ODA, it is the linguistic tradition we draw on. For example, the content analysis research carried out by Carmelo Mazza and Jose Luis Alvarez (2000) on the business press lies within this linguistic tradition. It sets out to analyse the communicative effects of the texts. It uses both quantitative and qualitative content analysis to look at a specific management issue: 'how the business press creates, diffuses and legitimates management theories and practices' (2000, p. 574). The preliminary data set consists of all articles on human resource management (HRM) from two key Italian business newspapers in the period 1988–96.

Quantitative analysis, presented in graphed formats, provides evidence for conclusions on questions such as the sources of HRM knowledge in the media. Peaks in frequency of articles on HRM are related to 'the wider debate on corruption' in Italian organizations, both by reference to 'well-known' recent public events that coincided with fluctuations in the publication of HRM-related articles, and via a reading of the articles themselves (2000, p. 577). Qualitative analysis of the data 'focuses on the relations between the words in a text' (p. 576) and 'reconstructs' (p. 578) the legitimization of HRM methods by showing how they are linked in the media texts with business success.

'Content analysis' of organizational data is attractive to many organizational researchers and audiences because it can be carried out within a familiar positivist research framework, and need not require re-theorizing of either discourse data or of discourse analysis. And because many media and organizational texts are now easily accessible in electronic formats, computer-based forms of analysis of very large data sets are now much more feasible and correspondingly seductive.

Critical discourse analysis

Within the field of linguistics itself, new uses of discourse analysis are being hotly debated. While traditional analytic methods are criticized for their failure to couple close linguistic analyses with social theory, on the other side of the spectrum there is criticism of 'studies which pronounce on the nature of discourses, without getting down to the business of studying what is actually uttered or written' (Billig, 1999, p. 544) – a challenge which can be made to current trends in ODA. Linguistic approaches offer a wide range of methods for 'getting down to the business' of analysing the data of workplace interaction (Stubbe et al., 2000), and linguists are increasingly taking an interest in workplace data (Holmes & Stubbe, 2003).

Critical discourse analysis (CDA) offers a range of methods that can be used to collect and analyse data in organizational research. Norman Fairclough, the most prominent exponent of CDA, argues that 'discourse analysis should best be regarded as a method for conducting research into questions which are defined outside it' (Fairclough, 1992, p. 226), and that CDA is 'critical' in the sense of a 'commitment to progressive social change' (Fairclough, 2001, p. 230). Fairclough's own micro-analyses of a wide range of discourse – interviews, pamphlets, advertisements, mass media, packaging, and policy documents (Fairclough, 1992, 2001) – are placed within the context of changes in the broader discursive formations of contemporary Britain: the commodification of educational discourse (Fairclough, 1992); the discourse of New Labour (Fairclough, 2001); and the language of the new capitalism (Chiapello & Fairclough, 2002; Fairclough, 2000).

In his discussion of data collection, Fairclough uses the linguistic concept of a 'corpus', a series of discourse samples which can give adequate information about the 'archive' (Fairclough, 1992, p. 227). Using his example of research into quality circles, the corpus might consist of video recordings of meetings, audiotaped interviews and organizational documents. Because the corpus is usually extensive and linguistic analysis is often very detailed, careful selection of examples from the corpus is critical. Fairclough advocates a focus on 'moments of crisis' which problematize or de-naturalize discursive practice, spotlighting points of change or power struggle (1992, p. 230).

Fairclough draws on a range of analytic methods related to linguistics, distinguished by close and detailed analysis at a number of levels of discourse, from defining social problems to paying close attention to lexical items (see his exemplary analysis of a government Green Paper on work, Fairclough, 2001). While analysis at all these levels is not required in any one discourse analysis project, Fairclough's work offers not only a menu of possible methods but an insistence that the researcher must be aware of the complex relationships between language and social processes in collecting and analysing discourse as data.

CHOICE POINT 5: PRODUCING RESEARCH TEXTS

Andy's knees were knocking. He nodded to the chairperson thanking her for the invitation to speak. He stood up, cleared his throat a little and started, quietly at first, then slowly building the volume until his voice filled the small room. His song, a waiata learned from friends and colleagues, opened his conference paper. It seemed to make statues of his fellow conference goers. He sang two lines and as he began the third his colleagues at the rear of the room stood and joined him. Curving their voices into one, their song spoke of home, family and the pursuit of knowledge.

Doing of research involves a complex set of often highly embodied practices (as our Andy narrative above suggests), including the creation of what Denzin calls the 'public text' (2000, p. 23), that is reports, papers, theses, presentations and performances. Such texts may seek to make their contribution to the welfare of clients and sponsors and may be for their eyes and ears only. Academic research texts are grounded in the ethic of public contribution to a field of knowledge where publication is in the public domain.

Producing and deconstructing the public text

The making of a public (research) text is both a creative and political process, particularly in a relatively new field such as organizational discourse (Phillips & Hardy, 2002). The substantive foci of the research in the field remain relatively broad, and methodological debates are 'in-process' (Oswick et al., 2000). Some disorder and conflict is inevitable as contributors draw on a range of analytical resources, some of which feature competing or conflicting assumptions and practices. The published research text can be regarded as a site where the 'appropriate' conventions are supported, and what 'counts' as research is established. The major cleavage in ODA is between the critical and interpretive research traditions (Heracleous & Hendry, 2000). A key tension between these fields is the extent to which critical reflexivity over the production of knowledge becomes a textual feature of the public text. Some of the features of this tension are highlighted below with respect to work that draws on deconstruction.

Deconstruction, as Marta Calás and Linda Smircich (1999) note, is centrally concerned with reflexive and critical investigation of the practice of knowledge production. While not a method of research as such, deconstruction can be regarded as a form of textual, philosophical and political analysis that attempts to identify how texts function in ways that stabilize meanings and practices in the face of the 'messiness' of organizational life and the more general instability of the process of meaning-making. Writings that take up this mode of analysis explicitly use the public research text as the site of engagement, and are involved in attempting to challenge and intervene in established knowledge.

While the 'taxonomy urge' (Chia, 1995) is a frequent target of deconstruction, we can nevertheless identify two forms of writing that draw on deconstruction. Each takes a different approach to the question of whether the public text should include an engagement with *its own* textuality.

Far and away the largest group of works that 'apply' deconstruction in organization studies take the field's canonical studies texts or particular organizational texts such as policies, speeches and stories as their target (Farmer, 1997; Learmouth, 1999; Martin, 1990; Mumby & Stohl, 1991; Peterson & Albrecht, 1999; Rhodes, 2000). A compelling example here is Dennis Mumby and Cynthia Stohl's deconstruction of an organizational story about the different treatment received by male and female secretaries in a US bank:

> With female secretaries he [the manager] dealt in a crisp professional manner, softened with banter and jokes, with me [the male secretary] he pretended that I wasn't really a secretary at all. It wasn't as if he ignored me; every half hour or so he would emerge from his office to talk sports with me and exchange dirty jokes. (Mumby & Stohl, 1991, p. 325)

Mumby and Stohl argue that deconstruction can show how people's effort to 'make sense' in organizations, which has some very real material effects (e.g., the different treatment of men and women), is ordered by a system of absence and presence. In this case:

> The 'male secretary' presents organizational members with a simultaneous presence (male [executive]) and absence (female secretary) which cannot both have meaning ('make sense') and preserve the ongoing system of privilege and marginality characteristic of contemporary organizations. (Mumby & Stohl, 1991, p. 326)

The boss's over-attention to the man's masculinity – the half-hourly sports and dirty jokes sessions – is then a way of alleviating anxiety over this simultaneous presence and absence.

Despite this, the work does not extend analysis to its own textuality and thus, from a critical position, the text can be said to harbour an inconsistency. Deconstruction, read from within an interpretive frame, involves 'helping the reader to understand the extent to which the [target] text's objectivity and persuasiveness depend on a set of strategic exclusions' (Kilduff, 1993, p. 15). But read from within a critical frame, deconstruction would also challenge the reader to explore the strategic exclusions that produce the analytical text itself. While some might regard this as simply an issue of genre, the critical impulse is to explore the *significance* of genre differences.

What does this difference tell us? Some might say that the interpretive tradition, with its liberal humanist accompaniments, has extracted deconstruction's critical purpose – domesticated deconstruction. If we were looking to deconstruction for a radical renegotiation of the familiar positivist-influenced textual formats of organization studies, then the 'encounters' to date are disappointing. Such works use conventional normalizing practices. These tell us what we *must* learn to do in presenting research and the voice – the familiar authorial/legislative voice (Bauman, 1987) – in which this should be done (see Chia, 1994; Kilduff, 1993; and Noorderhaven, 1995, for examples of work on canonical texts). This all too familiar authorial position remains untroubled by the content of the research. There is no acknowledgment that such a voice is itself an effect of a system of strategic exclusions.

There are deconstructive works where non-conventional textual features appear. These probe the limits of traditional textual production and point towards the fragility in the authorial position (see Burrell, 1992, 1993, 1996; Calás & Smircich, 1991; Game, 1994; Jacques, 1992; Letiche, 1996; O'Doherty, 2002; Rhodes, 2000). In some cases such features have been 'smuggled in' once the familiar textual practices have been rehearsed. What we learn from this textual 'geography' is that producers of public texts must affirm (sedate?) the eye/ear of a journal's accepted audience position, and *then* tempt, provoke or seduce that eye/ear with other 'pleasures': a poem (Chia, 1994), a fictional piece of dialogue (Calás and Smircich, 1991; Jacques, 1992), or a biographical aside.

In Joanne Martin's (1990) celebrated and well-cited deconstruction of the CEO's comments on an employee's calendared Caesarean section, this is done in an intriguing fashion. Martin tells readers of the journal article of her indecision over including some features in the text. She advises readers to skip the section if they are uncomfortable with psychosexual topics:

The analysis below discusses sexuality in an overt manner quite alien to the usual forms of organization discourse. Readers uncomfortable with this approach may find this section of this paper particularly inappropriate or ill-founded. I was tempted, therefore, to delete this material rather than risk dismissal of the entire paper. However, resistance may well be a natural reaction to the discussion of a taboo topic. I decided to include this section because any resistance experience may be conceptually germane and potentially a useful source of insight into the ways sexual taboos operate in the context of organizational discourse. (Martin, 1990, pp. 349–50)

This is cleverly written. It ruefully affirms the appropriate sensibilities of the journal's ear/eye, but then tempts the reader out of this position with recourse to the heroic scientific subject position. Here knowledge is pursued beyond disgust or discomfort.

Ann Game's short autobiographical deconstruction of her position as head of her university department (Game, 1994) locates her as the object and subject of her text. She describes her new positioning by her colleagues as 'mother'. The piece neatly contrasts with Mumby and Stohl's (1991) paper, discussed above. In contrast, Game's text might seem rambling and confused. This is just the point! It is a disruptive text. Taking the licence offered by the invitation to write in this way, the article moves back and forward between organizational problem, philosophical position and personal experience. It seeks to show both how the structure of meaning is folded into each of these spaces and practices, and how the deconstructive approach challenges this process through the use of non-conventional textual practice. For example, Game concludes her piece with this kind of gesture. In the last paragraph of the paper she writes: 'Organizations are stories. I told a story [in the paper] about the organization of my work, a story which is itself an organization of this particular piece of academic work' (Game, 1994, p. 50). This might have been the last sentence of the article, but then she returns and adds a postscript (a practice normally reserved for more informal discourse). This offers a disruptive reading of her own paper. She suggests that even with non-conventional formats established systems of thought reappear as the desire for a 'clever end' or for 'a safe theoretical conclusion', and that even if she would wish to undo such practices she has not 'left behind the position of pure academic' (Game, 1994, p. 50).

In sum, we have argued that the production of the public research text is a critical 'choice point' in the doing of research. Producing such texts involves learning the appropriate disciplinary practices. As a way of illustrating this learning we have discussed the limits of experimentation and change in the format of the public text. Even within the sub-field of ODA identified by the term 'deconstruction', only on very rare occasions have scholars effectively 'dropped their tools' (Calás & Smircich, 1999, p. 664, quoting Weick, 1996).

BRINGING IT ALL BACK TOGETHER

We opened this chapter by posing the seductively simple question 'What's involved in doing research in organizational discourse?' Our response has been to follow Denzin and Lincoln's phases of research practice, and engage each by discussing research work from a sub-field of ODA. Through this process we hoped to 'show' as well as 'tell' what's involved in research in the field. A key feature of Denzin and Lincoln's approach, and a key reason for drawing on it, is the emphasis it places on contextualizing the researcher. For us, reflection on the institutional, geographical and academic context in which research takes place is a crucial feature of research practice, and developing this 'between the lines' knowledge is crucial to the task of doing successful research. The disciplinary practices and conventions of academic writing tend to guard against the inclusion of such understandings in finished texts. But developing an engaged and constructive understanding of how this context *already* shapes research practice enriches such practice and provides a sound basis for critically interrogating the boundaries, limitations and assumptions of work produced by others.

At the same time we recognize that the approach taken above has a number of limitations. Readers may regard Denzin and Lincoln's format as overly stylized and unrealistic (2000, p. 12). We would agree. Any typology of research practice is but a set of headings for organizing material and does not necessarily identify research practice as it is played out. Other readers may question the overly tidy way we have 'packaged' our discussion of the purpose of research. Again, we agree. Such purity is analytically useful but may limit the development of research practice. Some readers may wonder if the sub-fields we discuss are indeed those *most* representative of 'organizational discourse analysis'. We would regard this as an empirical question that we did not set out to answer. Instead, our choice of sub-fields was driven by our concern to show some of the diversity of research approaches available in organizational discourse. In turn, readers may challenge our selection of work drawn from the sub-fields we have chosen. Our aim was not to provide a balanced review of work in a particular sub-field, but to choose works that offer readers a snapshot of the field as it relates to a particular 'phase' of research practice.

For those new to research in organizational discourse, the field's rich diversity can seem confusing and anxiety-invoking. We hope that this chapter has been of some assistance in addressing this. Another response, which Victoria Grace neatly encapsulates below, is to treat this 'unsettled-ness' as space for creativity and exploration:

> The need to develop a method for each specific project ... is an extremely creative part of the research process, involving a hermeneutic engagement simultaneously with the research questions, the theoretical agendas, the politics of the research context, and understandings of 'discourse' and what one is doing in text. (Grace, 1998)[3]

In other words, what counts as methodology in ODA is not 'settled'. The excitement of epistemological instability is one of the features that has drawn some researchers to discourse analysis in organization studies. Another attraction is the conceptual promise of the field itself, as it has provided an invigorating means of engaging some of the endemic theoretical puzzles of organization studies: the qualities of change, identity, communication, control, power and hierarchy. The burgeoning of higher education and the explosive growth in business education have also played a part in the development of 'organizational discourse analysis'.

Scholars from 'outside' conventional business education have brought discourse analysis theories 'in' to business schools.

Some of the promise of 'organizational discourse' is to be found in its provision of space to raise these issues about the context of research work (Hardy et al., 2001). As we have noted, the first question to ask as a researcher is 'who am I?' Such questions locate us as historical, political and socially-situated subjects, and begin to raise our awareness of the way our 'choice' of interpretative frame, research strategy, the method of data collection and analysis and the form of research presentation are already shaped (and can be contested).

Our engagement with the various moments that make up the doing of research in organizational discourse has highlighted the somewhat unnerving but nevertheless creative state of the practice of research in this field. Such a state of affairs invites and, we suggest, requires reflexivity in the practices of doing research.

NOTES

1 One of the distinctive features of the organizational discourse is that to varying degrees (depending on the 'sub-field') it raises the issue of how particular genres of academic writing are intimately connected to the production of certain effects, e.g. claims as to the validity of statements. In part we include our 'Andy Andrews' narratives here to illustrate this point. 'Organizational discourse' also provides some space for the incorporation of unconventional genres into academic studies of work and organization, and following the path-breaking efforts of colleagues in previous handbooks (Calás & Smircich, 1996; Ellis & Bochner, 2000) we include these short narratives here to support this tradition.

2 The public inquiry investigating the deaths and injury of 13 children while at Grantham and Kesteven General Hospital in 1991. A junior nurse, Beverley Allitt, was convicted of charges of murder in relation to these deaths.

3 This sentence is quoted from a 1997 pre-publication version of Grace's paper, but has been edited from the final version.

REFERENCES

Alvesson, M. & Kärreman, D. (2000) Taking the linguistic turn in organizational research: Challenges, responses, consequences. *Journal of Applied Behavioural Sciences*, 36 (2): 136–58.

Austrin, T. (1994) Positioning resistance and resisting position: Human resource management and the politics of appraisal and grievance hearing. In J. Jermier, D. Knights & W. Nord (eds), *Resistance and power in organizations* (pp. 199–218). New York: Routledge.

Barry, D. & Elmes, M. (1997) Strategy retold: Toward a narrative view of strategic discourse. *Academy of Management Review*, 22 (2): 429–52.

Bauman, Z. (1987) *Legislators and interpreters: On modernity, post-modernity, and intellectuals*. Cambridge: Polity Press.

Berelson, B. (1952) *Content analysis in communication research*. New York: Free Press.

Billig, M. (1999) Whose terms? Whose ordinariness? Rhetoric and ideology in conversation analysis. *Discourse & Society*, 10 (4): 543–82.

Boje, D.M. (1991) The storytelling organization: A study of story performance in an office-supply firm. *Administrative Science Quarterly*, 36 (3): 106–26.

Boje, D.M. (1995) Stories of the storytelling organization: A postmodern analysis of Disney as 'Tamara-land'. *Academy of Management Journal*, 38 (4) 997–1035.

Booth, W.C., Colomb, G.G. & Williams, J.M. (1995) *The craft of research*. Chicago: University of Chicago Press.

Brewis, J. (2001) Foucault, politics and organizations: (Re)-constructing sexual harassment. *Gender, Work and Organization*, 8 (1): 37–60.

Brown, A.D. (1998) Narrative, politics and legitimacy in an IT implementation. *Journal of Management Studies*, 35 (1): 35–58.

Brown, A.D. (2000) Making sense of inquiry sensemaking. *Journal of Management Studies*, 37 (1): 45–75.

Brown, A.D. & Jones, M. (1998) Doomed to failure: Narratives of inevitability and conspiracy in a failed IS project. *Organization Studies*, 19 (1): 73–88.

Brown, A.D. and Jones, M. (2000) Honourable members and dishonourable deeds: Sensemaking, impression management and legitimation in the 'Arms to Iraq' affair. *Human Relations*, 53 (5): 655–89.

Burman, E. & Parker, I. (eds) (1993) *Discourse analytic research: Repertoires and readings of texts in action*. London: Routledge.

Burrell, G. (1992) The organization of pleasure. In M. Alvesson & H. Willmott (eds), *Critical management studies* (pp. 66–89). London: Sage.

Burrell, G. (1993) Eco and the Bunnymen. In J. Hassard & M. Parker (eds), *Postmodernism and organizations* (pp. 71–82). London: Sage.

Burrell, G. (1996) Normal science, paradigms, metaphors, discourses and genealogies of analysis. In S. Clegg, C. Hardy & W.R. Nord (eds), *Handbook of Organization Studies* (pp. 642–58). London: Sage.

Butler, J. (1990) *Gender trouble: Feminism and the subversion of identity*. London: Routledge.

Calás, M. & Smirchich, L. (1991) Voicing seduction to silence leadership. *Organization Studies*, 12 (4): 567–602.

Calás, M. & Smirchich, L. (1996) From 'the woman's' point of view: Feminist approaches to organization studies. In S. Clegg, C. Hardy & W.R. Nord (eds), *Handbook of Organization Studies* (pp. 218–57). London: Sage.

Calás, M. & Smircich, L. (1999) Past postmodernism? Reflections and tentative directions. *Academy of Management Review*, 24 (4): 649–71.

Chia, R. (1995) From modern to postmodern organizational analysis. *Organization Studies*, 16 (4): 579–604.

Chiapello, E. & Fairclough, N. (2002) Understanding the new management ideology: A transdisciplinary contribution from critical discourse analysis and new sociology of capitalism. *Discourse & Society*, 13 (2): 185–208.

Clegg, S. & Linstead, S. (2000) Only penguins: A polemic on *organization* theory from the edge of the world. *Organization Studies,* 21: 103–18.

Collinson, D. (1999) Surviving the rigs: Safety and surveillance on North Sea oil installations. *Organization Studies*, 20 (4): 579–600.

Davies, B. and Harré, R. (1990) Positioning: The discursive production of selves. *Journal of the Theory of Social Behaviour*, 20 (1): 43–63.

Denzin N.K. (2000) The practices and politics of interpretation. In N.K. Denzin & Y.S. Lincoln (eds), *The handbook of qualitative research* (pp. 897–922). London: Sage.

Denzin, N.K. & Lincoln, Y.S. (eds) (2000) *The handbook of qualitative research* (2nd edition). Thousand Oaks, CA: Sage.

Deuten, J.J. & Rip, A. (2000) Narrative infrastructure in product creation processes. *Organization*, 7 (1): 69–93.

Ellis, C. & Bochner, A.P. (2000) Autoethnography, personal narrative, reflexivity researcher as subject. In N. Denzin & Y. Lincoln (eds), *Handbook of qualitative research* (pp. 733–68). London: Sage.

Erera-Weatherley, P. (1996) Coping with stress: Public welfare supervisors doing their best. *Human Relations*, 49 (2): 157–70.

Fairclough, N. (1992) *Discourse and social change*. Cambridge: Polity Press.

Fairclough, N. (2000) *Language in the new capitalism. A new, revised, and enlarged version of the programmatic document for the LNC network*. [Online]. Posted 02/02/00. http://www.cddc.vt.edu/host/lnc/CA-15egd.doc

Fairclough, N. (2001) The discourse of New Labour: Critical discourse analysis. In M. Wetherell, S. Taylor & S. Yates (eds), *Discourse as data: a guide for analysis* (pp. 229–66). London: Sage/Open University Press.

Farmer, D.J. (1997) Derrida, deconstruction and public administration. *American Behavioral Scientist*, 41 (1): 12–27.

Feldman, S.P. (1990) Stories as cultural creativity: On the relation between symbolism and politics in organizational change. *Human Relations*, 43 (9): 809–28.

Foucault, M. (1970) *The order of things: An archaeology of the human sciences*. London: Routledge.

Foucault, M. (1972) *The archaeology of knowledge*. London: Routledge.

Foucault, M. (1978) *The history of sexuality: An introduction* (Vol. 1). London: Penguin.

Foucault, M. (1980) Truth and power (interview). In C. Gordon (ed.), *Power/knowledge: Selected interviews and other writings 1972–1977* (pp. 109–33). New York: Pantheon.

Foucault, M. (1988) Technologies of the self. In L. Martin, H. Gutman & P. Hutton (eds), *Technologies of the self: A seminar with Michael Foucault* (pp. 16–49). Amhurst, MA: University of Massachusetts Press.

Foucault, M. (1991) *Discipline and punish: The birth of the prison*. London: Penguin.

Foucault, M. (1994) *The birth of the clinic: An archaeology of medical perception*. New York: Vintage Books.

Foucault, M. (1996) Ethics of the concern for self as a practice of freedom. In S. Lotringer (ed.), *Foucault live: Interviews, 1961–1984* (pp. 432–49). New York: Semiotext(e).

Gabriel, Y. (1991) On organizational stories and myths – why it is easier to slay a dragon than to kill a myth. *International Sociology*, 6 (4): 427–42.

Gabriel, Y. (1995) The unmanaged organization: Stories, fantasies and subjectivity. *Organization Studies*, 16 (3): 477–501.

Gabriel, Y. (2000) *Storytelling in organizations: Facts, fictions and fantasies*. London & Oxford: Oxford University Press.

Game, A. (1994) 'Matter out of place': the management of academic work. *Organization*, 1 (1): 47–50.

Grace, V. (1998) Researching women's encounters with doctors: Discourse analysis and method. In R. Du Plessis & L. Alice (eds), *Feminist thought in Aotearoa/New Zealand: Differences and connections* (pp. 111–19). Auckland: Oxford University Press.

Habermas, J. (1971) *Toward a rational society: Student protest, science and politics*. Trans. Jeremy J. Shapiro. London: Heinemann.

Hardy, C., Phillips, N. & Clegg, S. (2001) Reflexivity in organization and management theory: A study of the production of the research 'subject'. *Human Relations*, 54 (5): 31–60.

Heracleous, L. & Hendry, J. (2000) Discourse and the study of organization: Toward a structurational perspective. *Human Relations*, 53 (10): 1251–86.

Hochschild, A. (1983) *The managed heart: Commercialization of human feeling*. Berkeley, CA: University of California Press.

Hollway, W. (1991) *Work psychology and organizational behaviour: Managing the individual at work*. London: Sage.

Holmes, J. & Stubbe, M. (2003) *Power and politeness in the workplace*. Harlow: Pearson Education.

Humphreys, M. & Brown, A.D. (2002) Narratives of organizational identity and identification: A case study of hegemony and resistance. *Organization Studies*, 23 (3): 421–47.

Huff, A.S. (1999) *Writing for scholarly publication*. Thousand Oaks, CA: Sage.

Jacques, R. (1992) Critique and theory building – producing knowledge from the kitchen. *Academy of Management Review*, 17 (3): 582–606.

Jacques, R. (1996) *Manufacturing the employee: Management knowledge from the 19th to the 21st centuries*. London: Sage.

Jeffcutt, P. (1994) From interpretation to representation. In J. Hassard & M. Parker (eds), *Postmodernism and organization* (pp. 25–48). London: Sage.

Kilduff, M. (1993) Deconstructing organizations. *Academy of Management Review*, 18 (1): 13–31.

Kondo, Dorinne K. (1990) *Crafting selves: Power, gender, and discourses of identity in a Japanese workplace*. Chicago: University of Chicago Press.

Learmouth, M. (1999) The National Health Service manager, engineer and father? A deconstruction. *Journal of Management Studies*, 36 (7): 999–1012.

Letiche, H. (1996) Postmodernism goes practical. In S. Linstead, R.G. Small & P. Jeffcutt (eds), *Understanding Management* (pp. 193–211). London: Sage.

Martin, J. (1990) Deconstructing organizational taboos: The suppression of gender conflict in organizations. *Organization Science*, 1: 1–21.

Mazza, C. & Alvarez, J.H. (2000) *Haute couture* and *pret-à-porter*: The popular press and the diffusion of management practices. *Organisation Studies*, 21 (3): 567–88.

Middleton, S. (1993) *Educating feminists: Life histories and pedagogy*. New York: Teachers College Press.

Mumby, D. & Stohl, C. (1991) Power in organization studies: Absence and the dialectic of control. *Discourse and Society*, 2 (3): 313–32.

Near, P. (1996) Stakeholders and you. In P.J. Frost & S. Taylor (eds), *Rhythms of academic life: Personal accounts of career experiences in academia*. Thousand Oaks, CA: Sage.

Ng, W. & De Cock, C. (2002) Battle in the boardroom: A discursive perspective. *Journal of Management Studies*, 39 (1): 23–49.

Noorderhaven, N. (1995) The argumentational texture of transaction cost economics. *Organization Studies*, 16 (4): 605–23.

O'Doherty, D. (2002) Writing professional identities: (In)between structure and agency. In M. Dent & S. Whitehead (eds), *Managing professional identities: knowledge, performativity and the 'new' professional* (pp. 217–34). London: Sage.

Opie, A. (1997) Teams as author: Narrative and knowledge creation in case discussions in multi-disciplinary health teams. *Sociological Research Online*, 2 (3).

Opic, A. (2000) *Thinking teams/thinking clients: Knowledge-based teamwork*. New York: Columbia University Press.

Oswick, C., Keenoy, T., Grant, D. & Marshak, B. (2000) Discourse, organization and epistemology. *Organization*, 7 (3): 511–12.

Pei-Chia, L. (2001) The body as contested terrain for labor control: Cosmetics retailers in department stores and direct selling. In R. Baldoz, C. Koeber & P. Kraft (eds), *The critical study of work: Labor, technology and global production* (pp. 83–105). Philadelphia, PA: Temple University Press.

Peterson, L. & Albrecht, T. (1999) Where gender/ power/politics collide: Deconstructing organizational maternity leave policy. *Journal of Management Inquiry*, 8 (2): 168–81.

Phillips, N. & Hardy, C. (2002) *Discourse analysis: Investigating processes of social construction*. London: Sage.

Rhodes, C. (2000) Reading and writing organizational lives. *Organization*, 7 (1): 7–29.

Ryan, G. & Bernard, H. (2000) Data analysis and management methods. In N.K. Denzin & Y.S Lincoln (eds), *Handbook of qualitative research* (2nd edition, pp. 769–802). Thousand Oaks, CA: Sage.

Sawyer, R.K. (2002) A discourse on discourse: An archeological history of an intellectural concept. *Cultural Studies*, 16 (3): 433–56.

Shapiro, M. (1981) *Language and political understanding: The politics of discursive practices*. New Haven, CT: Yale University Press.

Stablein, R. (1996) Data in organization studies. In S. Clegg, C. Hardy & W.R. Nord (eds), *Handbook of Organization Studies* (pp. 509–25). London: Sage.

Strauss, A. & Corbin, J. (1990) *Basics of qualitative research: Grounded theory techniques and procedures.* London: Sage.

Stubbe, M., Lane, C., Hilder, J., Vine, E., Vine, B., Holmes, J., Marra, M. & Weatherall, A. (2000) Multiple discourse analyses of a workplace interaction. *Wellington Working Papers in Linguistics*, 11: 39–85.

Titscher, S., Meyer, M., Wodak, R. & Vetter, E. (2000) *Methods of text and discourse analysis.* London: Sage.

Townley, B. (1994) *Reframing human resource management: Power ethics and the subject at work.* Thousand Oaks, CA: Sage.

Tretheway, A. (1999) Disciplined bodies: Women's embodied identities at work. *Organization Studies*, 20 (3): 423–50.

Weedon, C. (1987) *Feminist practice and poststructuralist theory.* London: Basil Blackwell.

Weick, K. (1995) *Sensemaking in organizations.* London: Sage.

Weick, K. (1996) Drop your tools: An allegory for organization studies. *Administrative science quarterly*, 41: 310–13.

Willmott, H. (1995) Managing the academics: Commodification and control in the development of university education in the UK. *Human Relations*, 48 (9): 993–1027.

Wodak, R. & Meyer, M. (2001) *Methods of critical discourse analysis.* London: Sage.

10

Discourse, Power and Ideology: Unpacking the Critical Approach

Dennis K. Mumby

A quick perusal of the management and organization studies literature reveals that the study of 'organizational discourse' has become a veritable cottage industry, with a number of books and special issues of journals reflecting the exponential growth of published essays on this topic (Alvesson & Kärreman, 2000a, 2000b; Grant et al., 1998; Keenoy et al., 2000; Oswick et al., 2000; Putnam & Fairhurst, 2001). The critical approach represents a particular intervention in this growth. Drawing on nineteenth- and twentieth-century developments in hermeneutics (Gadamer, 1989; Palmer, 1969), phenomenology (Heidegger, 1977; Merleau-Ponty, 1960), and humanist Marxism (Gramsci, 1971; Habermas, 1984; Horkheimer & Adorno, 1988; Korsch, 1971; Lukács, 1971), critical organization scholars articulate a 'discourse of suspicion' (Mumby, 1997a; Ricœur, 1970), exploring underlying structures of domination, resistance, and interest-driven discursive strategies that lurk beneath ostensibly consensual meaning systems (Hardy et al., 2000; Mumby, 1987; Young, 1989).[1] In this sense, organizations are conceived as political sites where various organizational actors and groups struggle to 'fix' meaning in ways that will serve their particular interests (Deetz, 1982, 1992; Mumby & Clair, 1997).

The critical perspective invokes one version of the modernist, Enlightenment project, with its efforts to emancipate human beings from conditions of domination and oppression. Within this version of modernism, writers such as Marx (1967), Gramsci (1971), Lukács (1971), and various members of the Frankfurt School (Adorno, 1973; Habermas, 1984, 1987; Horkheimer, 1986; Horkheimer & Adorno, 1988) provide systematic critiques of capitalist forms of exploitation and the various economic, political and cultural processes through which the ideas of the ruling class are produced and reproduced. Critical studies, then, are *both* modernist *and* social constructionist – a position that goes against the general tendency to equate modernism with positivism and postmodernism with 'linguistic turn' social constructionism (e.g., Hekman, 1990; Stewart, 1991).

In this chapter I will be examining research on organizational discourse that takes seriously the following critical modernist tenets: (1) communication and discourse constitute, and are constituted by, meaningful social practices; (2) the critical analysis of power relations is central to an understanding of these social practices; and (3) such critical analysis suggests the possibility of social and organizational transformation by social actors. This chapter unfolds in the following manner. In the next section I first provide a brief discussion of critical discourse analysis and its role in understanding the connections among discourse, power and organizing; this is followed by a description of the various research traditions that inform critical organization studies. In the next, main section of the chapter, I address the body of critical research by suggesting that it can be divided into two broad research domains: (1) critical analysis as ideology critique, and (2) critical analysis as an exploration of the dialectics of power and resistance. The final, concluding section suggests directions for future research.

FRAMING CRITICAL ORGANIZATIONAL DISCOURSE STUDIES

Critical discourse analysis

According to Fairclough and Wodak (1997), critical discourse analysis (CDA) involves the close examination of the relationship between discourse and power. Consistent with the discourse of suspicion addressed earlier, CDA attempts to:

> systematically explore often opaque relationships of causality and determination between (a) discursive practices, events and texts, and (b) wider social and cultural structures, relations and processes; to investigate how such practices, events and texts arise out of and are ideologically shaped by relations of power and struggles over power; and to explore how the opacity of these relationships between discourse and society is itself a factor securing power and hegemony. (Fairclough, 1993, p. 135)

Key to this statement is the notion that discourse, as a social practice, does ideological work that shapes social actors' relationships to the world in ways that are not always apparent to the social actors themselves. Discourse functions ideologically not by simply fixing or determining people's relationships to each other and to the wider society, but rather by mediating that relationship through social practice. In other words, ideology is not merely ideational, but is enacted and embodied in everyday practices. For example, gender and race are not just internal mental constructs through which people make sense of the world; rather, they are enacted and realized in the moment-to-moment, and in institutional contexts that do not necessarily give equal access to discursive, cultural and political resources (West & Fenstermaker, 1995; West & Zimmerman, 1987). Meaningful difference, then, is not a fixed state but an ongoing discursive, practical accomplishment. Discourse as ideology thus predisposes people towards certain sense-making practices, but by no means exhausts the interpretive possibilities in which people can engage. In this sense, discursive attempts to fix meanings ideologically are always contested processes. As Hall states, ideology 'sets limits to the degree to which a society-in-dominance can easily, smoothly and functionally reproduce itself' (1985, p. 113). Thus, critical discourse analysis is concerned with the process of ideological struggle, examining the ways in which social realities are produced, reproduced, resisted and transformed.

Gramsci's (1971) concept of hegemony is central to our understanding of this process of ideological struggle. While this concept has been widely interpreted to refer to ideological domination of one class or group by another, it is more appropriately read as a construct that frames power as a dialectical struggle between competing groups in the realm of civil society (Grossberg, 1986; Mumby, 1997b). In this context, hegemony is not simply consent to, and active support of, a dominant system of meaning, but rather involves complex articulations of discourses that represent and embody efforts to fix meanings in particular ways over and against other possible discursive articulations. In examining critical approaches to organizational discourse, then, we will be interested in the ways in which organizational members and interest groups engage in hegemonic struggle through discourse as a social practice.

Four research traditions in critical studies of organizational discourse

Historically speaking, there appear to be three relatively distinct but connected research traditions whose boundaries are at times porous, at times fairly impermeable. Together, however, they constitute a generally coherent and thematic body of critical work. First, there is a tradition of critical management research whose foundations can be traced in part to the series of Vancouver, BC, summer conferences held in the late 1970s and early 1980s (Frost, 1980). While much of this work was interpretive/cultural rather than critical in orientation (e.g., Frost et al., 1985; Smircich, 1983), it nevertheless helped to frame discourse studies as more than just a marginal presence in the field of management.

Second, the field of organizational communication was engaged in a similar enterprise. Publications resulting from a 1981 conference in Alta, Utah, laid much of the conceptual groundwork for the emergence of an interpretive, discourse-centred approach to organizational communication – a perspective that is now very much part of the mainstream in that field (Pacanowsky & O'Donnell-Trujillo, 1982; Putnam, 1983; Putnam & Pacanowsky, 1983). Interestingly, a distinct critical perspective emerged together with the nascent interpretive tradition, with essays by Deetz and colleagues (Deetz, 1982; Deetz & Kersten, 1983; Deetz & Mumby, 1985) and Conrad (Conrad, 1983; Conrad & Ryan, 1985) establishing the significance of examining power and politics as intrinsic features of organizational sense-making processes. Apart from the occasional cross-disciplinary publication, however (e.g., Deetz, 1985; Riley, 1983), early critical research in these two fields shows little evidence of cross-fertilization (although Frost's (1987) review essay in the *Handbook of Organizational Communication* (Jablin et al., 1987) is an early effort to draw connections between these two traditions).

Third, a distinctly European critical-cultural tradition emerged with the start of the journal *Organization Studies* in 1979 under the aegis of the European Group on Organization Studies (EGOS). While this tradition and critical management studies are far from mutually exclusive, the work of EGOS has been particularly important in generating both theory and research regarding the intersection of discourse, power, identity, organizing, and so forth (e.g., Alvesson, 1985; Clegg, 1981, 1989; Collinson, 1988; Linstead & Grafton-Small, 1992; Parker, 1995). Indeed, a series of theoretical publications on major continental thinkers has done much to introduce difficult philosophical work to a wider management and organization studies audience (Burrell, 1988, 1994; Cooper, 1989; Cooper & Burrell, 1988). More recently, the founding of the journal *Organization* signals the emergence of an international perspective on organizational discourse studies, suggesting the breaking down of some of the epistemological boundaries created by large bodies of water.

Finally, the establishment of a bi-annual conference on organizational discourse at King's College, London in the last ten years (founded and organized by several of the editors of this volume) has produced a body of research – published in edited volumes and special journal issues – that has further raised the profile of discourse studies among business and management scholars (Grant et al., 1998; Keenoy et al., 1997, 2000; Oswick et al., 2000).

Taken together, these four research traditions represent a 'critical mass' of literature examining the relationships among discourse, power and organizing. In the remainder of this chapter, I want to examine that research more closely, suggesting themes that have emerged as theory and research have developed dialectically.

CRITICAL STUDIES OF ORGANIZATIONAL DISCOURSE: IDEOLOGY CRITIQUE AND THE DIALECTICS OF POWER AND RESISTANCE

While there are a number of ways to review and classify the body of research in critical organizational discourse studies, I suggest for the purposes of this chapter that such research can be characterized by two broad themes. These are: (1) Critical organizational discourse analysis as ideology critique, and (2) Critical organizational discourse analysis as an exploration of the dialectics of power and resistance. Early critical work, I would suggest, tended to coalesce strongly around a theme of ideological domination. The principal goal of much of this work was to expose the ways in which dominant forms of ideological meaning functioned to reproduce extant power relations and foreclose possibilities for resistance and emancipation. This body of work can be characterized as rooted principally in 'ideology critique'. Alternatively, a second – and more recent – critical research agenda has moved beyond the rather functionalist, reproduction-oriented approach of ideology critique, and has focused instead on power as a dialectical phenomenon characterized by interdependent processes of struggle, resistance and control. While it would be inaccurate to view these two approaches as completely separate (there is certainly a good deal of overlap), invoking this analytic distinction is useful as a means to explore the evolution of critical organizational discourse studies over the last twenty years. Below, I explore this distinction in more detail, and then go on to discuss the ways in which these two perspectives have been taken up in the empirical study of three discursive domains of organizational life: storytelling, rites and rituals, and talk.

As I have already suggested, 'ideology' has played a central, defining role in critical organization studies, operating as the principal analytic construct to explain the relationship between discourse and structures of power. However, 'ideology' is a theoretically slippery and rather intractable term that has produced much definitional debate in neo-Marxist circles (see, for example, Geuss, 1981; Larrain, 1979; Therborn, 1980; Thompson, 1984). Within critical organization studies a prevailing conception closely links ideology to processes of control and domination. From a discourse perspective, Giddens' (1979) conception of ideology as linking systems of signification to relations of domination typifies this orientation. When linked with the concept of hegemony, the focus on control and domination has been further reinforced. For example, the 1998 special issue of *Administrative Science Quarterly* (Jermier, 1998) on organizational control, while certainly not overlooking issues of resistance, generally examines 'how societies control their members by clothing the iron fist of power in a velvet glove' (Jermier, 1998, p. 236).

The early focus of critical organization studies on ideology critique reflects, I think, an effort to theorize organizational power in a more complex and textured fashion than extant models. By focusing on processes of meaning construction and ideology formation, critical studies enable power to be conceived as something rooted in more than observable behaviour and decision-making (Bachrach & Baratz, 1962; Dahl, 1957) or in the control of material resources (Pfeffer, 1981), and instead as fundamental to the ways in which basic forms of perception and social reality get constructed (Lukes, 1974). From this latter perspective, power is seen as a deep-structure phenomenon that is manifest (though in a distorted, ideological manner) in the daily, mundane enactment of discourse processes that constitute webs of meaning. The goal of ideology critique, then, is to unpack the ways in which deep- structure, inequitable relations of power become normalized and naturalized through a process of ideological obfuscation. Within this frame, organizational discourse is both medium and product of the ideological production and reproduction of deep-structure power relations.

While critical studies conducted from an ideology critique perspective are extremely useful in terms of their insights into the relations among discourse, ideology and organizational power, much of this research evinces a distinct bias towards a domination model of organizational power. From such a perspective, organizational power is often conceived as pervasive, all-encompassing and relatively immune to resistance and transformation. Indeed, any strong sense of the agency of everyday social actors is largely missing from such work. Where agency *is* highlighted, it is generally read as functioning to reproduce the existing dominant relations of power and forms of social control (Burawoy, 1979; Willis, 1977). The critical model of ideology critique, then, does little to conceive of the relations among discourse, ideology and power as a contested terrain characterized by contradiction, resistance and struggle over (relatively) contingent meaning structures.

On the other hand, a dialectical approach to organization studies examines the inherent tensions and contradictions between agency and structure, between the multiple interpretive possibilities that exist in every discourse situation and institutional efforts to impose or fix meaning in particular ways (Benson, 1977; Giddens, 1979; Papa et al., 1995). In Giddens' (1979) sense, the dialectic of control recognizes the agentic possibilities, the ability to 'act otherwise' that inheres in all social actors, however limiting the context. Consistent with Hall's (1983) notion of a 'Marxism without guarantees', this dialectical approach to discourse and power recognizes that just as there are no completely monolithic and all-encompassing power structures, neither are there any pristine, authentic spaces of resistance that challenge dominant power relations.

The dialectical approach, then, recognizes that resistance and domination are not simple binary oppositions, but exist rather in a mutually implicative relationship. As such, organizational discourse can be constitutive simultaneously of moments of domination and resistance. In this sense, discourse – stories, talk, rituals, etc. – cannot be 'read off' as embodying organizational resistance or domination, but must rather be examined in terms of the ways in which it is taken up by competing organizational interests. Dialectical analyses of power and resistance thus suggest possibilities for multiple and contradictory meanings and realities existing in the same discursive space.

In the last few years, critical organization studies has begun to explore this dialectical struggle in more rich and textured ways. Rather than viewing organizations as systems of domination *tout court*, researchers have started to examine the complex struggles over meaning that simultaneously embody domination and resistance (e.g., Clair, 1994; Mumby, 1997b). In this context, there is a much greater sensitivity to social actors as knowledgeable agents who have insight into the discursive and political conditions that shape the ways in which they engage with the world.

In the remainder of this section I will explore three different discursive forms – stories, rites and rituals, and talk – and examine them in terms of the two critical approaches to organizational discourse discussed above.

Organizational storytelling

Organizational storytelling has been the focus of a large body of research over the last twenty years. While only some of this work is critically oriented, all of it recognizes narrative as a constitutive feature of organization members' sense-making processes (e.g., Boje, 1991; Boyce, 1996; Ehrenhaus, 1993; Gabriel, 2000; Mumby, 1987; Smith & Keyton, 2001; Trujillo & Dionisopoulos, 1987). As an endemic feature of human sociality (Gabriel, 2000), many researchers view storytelling as a defining feature of the human condition (Bruner, 1991). Indeed, in elaborating a 'narrative paradigm' rooted in a logic of 'good reasons', Walter Fisher has labelled human beings 'homo narrans' (Fisher, 1984, 1985).

From a perspective of ideology critique, this conception is extended to suggest that – precisely because of its discursive power and embeddedness in organizational life – narrative functions ideologically to privilege certain interests and social realities over others. Consistent with a discourse of suspicion, ideology critique suggests that organizational storytelling is a particularly powerful vehicle for simultaneously reifying and obscuring deep-structure power relations beneath the taken-for-grantedness of everyday discourse.

For example, Witten (1993) argues that the very structure of storytelling and the way in which it functions in everyday talk predisposes organization members towards a 'culture of obedience' and the acceptance of the organizational *status quo*. She suggests that the structure of the narrative context as one involving a teller and an audience does not – in a Habermasian sense – lend itself well to the testing of validity claims. Audience members are much less likely to challenge the veracity of truth claims made in a storytelling context than they are in a regular conversational context. As Witten argues, 'Narrative discourse suspends ordinary conversation, departing from a state of turn-by-turn talk among co-participants. Thus it is inappropriate for the listener to raise a challenge to a truth claim implicit in a narrative even if the faulty claim is recognized' (1993, p. 106).

Witten's narrative analysis raises two concerns. First, one might argue that she is making a rather arbitrary distinction between storytelling and regular conversation; storytelling might instead be viewed as a constitutive and regulative feature of everyday conversation that helps to grease the wheels of social interaction. Second, Boje (1991) has suggested that, far from being the province of a single teller, storytelling is actually an interactional accomplishment involving the coordination of several interactants' talk. However, while such a claim challenges Witten's conception of the storytelling process, it does not necessarily undermine her case for the power of narrative in constructing a culture of obedience. In fact, we might argue that a more interactive, dialectical model of the storytelling process suggests a greater level of investment by the participants in the reality created by the storytelling. Such a reading is consistent with the model of 'concertive control' developed by a group of organizational communication scholars to explain the paradox of team-based organizations that appear to exercise greater control over employees than more traditional centralized bureaucracies (Barker, 1993, 1999; Barker & Cheney, 1994; Tompkins & Cheney, 1985).

Other narrative studies worth mentioning under the rubric of 'ideology critique' are my own critical 'depth hermeneutic' of a single organizational story (Mumby, 1987, 1988), and Helmer's (1993) field study of storytelling at a harness racing track. My study submits to close analysis the widely quoted and circulated IBM story involving a confrontation between CEO Tom Watson, Jr. and a security guard named Lucille Burger. Invoking Giddens' (1979) three functions of ideology – denying contradictions, representing sectional interests as universal, and reification – I suggest that, far from telling the tale of a lowly employee's triumph over the CEO, the story functions politically to reinscribe and reproduce gendered relations of domination. In many respects I am invoking an Althusserian, rather functional reading of narrative as ideology, framing it principally as an interpretive mechanism that reproduces capitalist relations of production. There is little or no sense that the story might be read as an act of resistance by a low-level employee who is using the only resources available to her to upset the smooth functioning of IBM's patriarchal organizational bureaucracy.

Helmer's (1993) field study of a harness racing track provides a much richer analysis of the relationship between narrative and stratified relations of organizational power. Arguing that organizational narratives produce and reproduce certain binary oppositions that function as interpretive frames for members, he shows how different interest groups appropriate these narrative oppositions to position themselves and others in the organization. For example, the binary tension of 'men versus women' gets played out through storytelling in a number of ways, but is frequently used both to highlight sexism in the horse-racing business and to produce and reproduce tensions among women in the profession; that is, between those who are seen as succeeding on their own merits and those who are perceived as succeeding by virtue of who they sleep with. As such, while these stories function to identify the patriarchal nature of the industry, they also serve to undermine the potential for solidarity among women in the profession.

From a critical perspective, narrative studies such as Helmer's raise several important issues. First, it suggests the need to see narrative not as a static, artifactual product of organizational life, but rather as something that is accomplished, as process. In this sense, Helmer focuses on the dynamic practice of storytelling, addressing Marshak's (1998) concerns about the false dichotomy between talk and action. Second, Helmer's study suggests that the ideological functioning of stories cannot be derived from a purely textual analysis, but requires a close examination of the relationships among narratives, social structure and the competing interpretive processes of different interest groups. Critical narrative analysis, then, should be sensitive to the ongoing power dynamics of daily organizational life.

Organizational storytelling is a discursive site *par excellence* for the critical analysis of the dialectic of control and resistance. Given the ubiquity, complexity and reproducibility of the narrative form, critical scholars are particularly drawn to analyses of the ways in which stories embody and discursively mediate the contradictions and tensions of organizational life (Boje et al., 1999; Brown, 1998; Czarniawska, 1998; Dunford & Palmer, 1998; Ewick & Silbey, 1995; Scheibel, 1996, 1999). From this perspective, narratives are *both* discursive mechanisms of control *and* interpretive frames for strategies of resistance and emancipation. In other words, narratives are inherently political.

In this vein, Langellier (1989) suggests that narratives be conceived as political praxis; that is, as raising questions about relations among power, knowledge, ideology and identity. When viewed as political praxis, narratives are seen not as fixed texts but as performances that are 'embodied, material, and concrete' (1989, p. 267), occurring with and reproducing/resisting particular relations of power. Ewick and Silbey (1995) reflect a similar orientation, arguing that 'Narratives are not just stories told *within* social contexts; rather, *narratives are social practices*, part of the constitution of their own context ... [and as such] are as likely to bear the imprint of dominant cultural meanings and relations of power as any other social practice' (1995, p. 211, emphasis in original).

Ewick and Silbey make a useful, interesting distinction between hegemonic and subversive narratives, suggesting that the former function by appealing to general understandings of the world that remain implicit (and thus unexamined), and that the latter work precisely because they make explicit the connection between the particular and the general. In a subversive story, therefore, the everydayness of the sense-making process is shown to be political, and hence framed within larger social and economic processes. Hence, 'subversive stories are narratives that employ the connection between the particular and the general by *locating the individual within social organization*' (1995, p. 220, emphasis in original).

Ewick and Silbey's 'sociology of narrative' provides an insightful account of the relationship between domination and resistance. However, its bifurcation of hegemonic and subversive narratives is problematic. While certainly some can be read as predominantly hegemonic and others as subversive, it makes more sense to see narratives as sites of ideological and discursive struggle where different, conflicting interests get played out. If we see narratives not as fixed texts but rather as living, embodied performances that are contextualized politically and culturally, then they become open to appropriation and articulation within various discourses. Just as Hall's (1985) analysis of the racial term 'black' shows how its meaning is shaped by its articulation within particular chains of signification, so the meaning(s) of particular narratives is/are a product of their articulation and performance within certain ideological frames, by certain tellers, to particular audiences.

Imagine, for example, the IBM story not as a disembodied text, but as a living story told by Lucille Burger to her co-workers, or by Tom Watson to a group of vice presidents, or by a middle-level manager to his or her secretary. In each case, the story as a site of ideological struggle takes on a very different resonance and, indeed, has multiple interpretive possibilities in each context. Would Lucille Burger frame the story to her co-workers as reflecting her commitment to duty, or as demonstrating her political savvy and ability to put one over on the jerk who pays her minimum wage? Furthermore, this particular narrative will probably evolve through the course of multiple tellings, with each performance embodying the interests of the particular speaker and audience. Finally, the narrative does not function in isolation, but is articulated with other narratives, texts, social practices, and so forth, to create a complex and often contradictory discursive terrain that is the medium and outcome of relations of organizational power, domination and resistance.

The goal of a critical-dialectical approach to organizational narrative (and discourse generally), then, is not to frame stories as either hegemonic or subversive, but rather to critically analyse such narratives as performances within complex discursive articulations that both enable and constrain possibilities for human communicative praxis (O'Connor, 2000). That is, in what ways are social actors, as knowledgeable agents, both subjects and objects of narrative processes? How are organization members differentially positioned in terms of the narrative/ discursive resources upon which they are able to draw (Hardy et al., 2000; Hardy & Phillips, 1999)? In what ways do narrative performances embody contradictions that suggest possibilities for insight and organizational change? These are complex questions that have no straightforward answers, and which generally require complex and long-term ethnographic studies. Needless to say the number of narrative studies that address these issues in any detail is relatively limited, although Brown's (1998) ethnography of the implementation of information technology at a hospital and Scheibel's (1996) critical reading of medical students' stories about gynaecological exam training both effectively illuminate narrative as the site of complex ideological struggle. Clearly this is an area that requires further empirical investigation.

Rites and rituals

While rites and rituals might be seen as falling outside of the scope of organizational discourse, I include them here in so far as they form a domain of organizing that bridges the gap between talk and action (Marshak, 1998). That is, they are simultaneously the material instantiation of discourse, and are made sense of discursively. Here I will discuss briefly a couple of studies that address organizational rites and rituals from the perspective of ideology critique. Rosen's (1985, 1988) critical ethnography of an advertising firm examines the ways in which organizational rituals function to reproduce organizational relations of domination. His study is premised on the notion that meaning is a negotiated social process conducted within particular social structures, and that organizational dramas play a key role in shaping that process and predisposing organization members towards certain interpretive frames over others.

Rosen's analyses fall comfortably within the discourse of suspicion in that much of his focus is on showing the ways in which rituals function as forms of social control by obscuring underlying organizational contradictions. For example, his critical analysis of a corporate breakfast (Rosen, 1985) draws attention to the ways in which the event creates a sense of 'communitas' and shared purpose among members, while simultaneously obscuring the contradictions between this shared reality and the ways that surplus value is appropriated by elite organization members. Similarly, Rosen's (1988) analysis of a Christmas party at the same organization exposes how an ostensibly 'carnivalesque' (Bakhtin, 1984) atmosphere, complete with skits that lampoon elite organization members, reinforces rather than undermines extant relations of power. Indeed, Rosen's general orientation towards the ideological role of organizational ritual is well summed up by the following statement:

> Beyond the messages of fraternity and solidarity, Shoenman and Associates is a formal organization in which the labour process is controlled to gain production and profit from

the labour of its employees. This results in antagonisms, uncertainties, discomforts, and conflicts, many of which are presented during the various skits. While these conditions are recognized as difficult, they are at the same time glossed over insofar as they are comically portrayed and communally laughed at, and further, they are not seriously challenged. (Rosen, 1988, p. 479)

In short, from a critique of ideology perspective, organizational rituals operate as carefully choreographed discursive moments that reify the relationship between meaning and social control. Indeed, as an ideological mechanism that is explicitly performative, rituals can be seen as an embodiment of Althusser's claim that ideological processes operate in social *practice* rather than ideationally: 'kneel down, move your lips in prayer, and you will believe' (Althusser, 1971, p. 168).

The dialectical study of rites and rituals points to the ways in which such organizational events provide possibilities for both the re-instantiation of dominant corporate values and the playing out of alternative, resistant ways of constituting organizational reality. While rituals provide opportunities for an almost carnivalesque parodying of received organizational dogma, from a dialectical perspective parody and dogma, resistance and domination, are intertwined in complex and contradictory ways in the same events.

Collinson's (1988, 1992) critical ethnography of male shopfloor workers in a truck factory illustrates the complex relations among resistance, control and gendered identity as they get played out in various worker rituals and discourses. Such rituals neither reproduce the dominant corporate culture in a simplistic manner, nor do they represent pristine, authentic spaces resistant to that culture. Instead, Collinson illustrates how rituals function both to resist management efforts to control the labour process, and to reproduce working-class, hegemonic masculinity on the shopfloor. For example, hazing rituals both reproduce hegemonic masculinity and create a culture that instils an ethos that resists management efforts to improve productivity.

Perhaps the most important dimension of Collinson's study, however, is the way in which he problematizes worker identity(s), viewing it as constituted through the contradictory discursive and social practices of the workplace. In this sense, identity is not unproblematically linked to class or gender, or described in global terms as a manifestation of the culture; rather, it is explored as a complex, shifting and tension-filled product of particular discursive articulations and sense-making practices. Consistent with a critical-dialectical approach, Collinson thus examines discourse as communicative praxis (Schrag, 1986), that is, as the material, embodied, performative process through which social actors construct their identities in a dynamic, contradictory and precarious fashion. From such a perspective, identities are produced, reproduced and transformed through an ongoing process of struggle within relations of power within systems of enablement and constraint (Eisenberg & Goodall, 2001).

Young's (1989) ethnography of women workers in a rainwear factory also explores identity and meaning construction as it gets played out in the relationship between ritual behaviour and structures of power. Starting from the official corporate line that the women on the shopfloor constitute a single, familial culture, with various rites and rituals reproducing that culture, he shows how this culture actually embodies a significant rift between two sub-cultures – one of younger, female, occasional employees, and the other of older, full-time, female employees. This rift, he demonstrates, arises out of a complex articulation of gendered identities, age and the constitutive role of certain workplace rituals – employee outings, the wearing of St George's Day roses, and the maintenance of a 'Royalty Board' consisting of a pictorial and textual homage to the royal family – that shapes the everyday politics of the shopfloor. In brief, the age, apparent laziness and temporary employment status of the younger women leads to their marginalization by the older women and the instantiation of that marginality through their peripheral role in the shopfloor rituals. To wit, they do not get invited to contribute to the Roses fund, are excluded from factory outings, and are never given the coveted role of maintaining the Royalty board. The young women, in turn, re-frame these rituals as reflecting a traditional, conservative culture of 'old biddies', embodying an identity that they explicitly reject. Most significantly, Young's critical-dialectical analysis suggests a degree of cultural and political complexity that is invisible from a 'God's eye', managerial perspective.

In sum, a critical-dialectical approach suggests that organizational rites and rituals are a rich site of interpretive struggle. At one level such rituals function to crystallize extant relations of power, cementing hierarchy and reproducing social order. Alternatively, however, they always harbour transgressive possibilities, providing opportunities for ironic and parodic interpretations of dominant meanings. As Murphy (1998) illustrates in her critical study of flight attendance resistance to a highly gendered work culture, flight attendants quickly become adept at 'illegal' behaviour that occurs beyond the purview of company surveillance, or which appropriates and transforms aspects of the official culture. Rites and rituals, then, simultaneously harbour certainty and ambiguity in a complex and ever-shifting manner.

Organizational talk

A few critical scholars have examined everyday conversation as a way to understand power as a mundane, constitutive feature of organizing. Again, this research is far from voluminous, perhaps because of the difficulty of collecting verbatim, real-time conversational data. In addition, organization researchers generally have eschewed the kind of micro-analyses of talk that conversation analysts in the tradition of Sacks, Schegloff and others have developed in the last thirty years or so (see Boden, 1994, for an exception). However, such work is significant in so far as it recognizes that organizing is a practical accomplishment that is achieved through talk and interaction (Cooren, 2000; Taylor et al., 1996). Boden (1994), for example, brings together conversation analysis and structuration theory to illustrate the chimerical status of the action–structure distinction. Against this dichotomy, she argues that talk is not a feature of organization, but is rather both medium and outcome of organizing itself.

Forester's (1989, 1992, 1993) work is an effort to apply a Habermasian framework to examining organizational talk. Habermas (1979) argues that all speech has embedded in it claims to validity that are potentially open to discursive testing by interlocutors. Thus, every speech act makes claims to truth (regarding 'factual' conditions in the world), legitimacy (invoking social norms), sincerity (expressions of inner states of self), and intelligibility (invoking particular forms of language use). Forester (1992) suggests that the examination of organizational talk using these validity conditions helps us empirically to explore just how complex, how contingent and how rich, social and political actions actually are. From this perspective, the analyses show that organizational talk is far from purely instrumental in orientation, but constitutes efforts to shape belief and to manage consent to organizational values and political structures. For example, Forester's (1992) analysis of a brief extract from a city planning meeting examines the various turns in talk for the ways in which they construct patterns of belief about the world, develop and reproduce norms of action, and articulate social status and order among themselves. In this sense, Forester's work 'enables us to explore the continuing performance and practical accomplishment of relations of power' (1992, p. 62) as they unfold organizationally.

Huspek and Kendall's (1991) critical ethnography of a lumber yard is similarly interested in the ways that power relations are produced and reproduced through talk. In this case, the focus is on how lumber workers position themselves as a 'non-political' speech community in the face of what they see as the politicized nature of the workplace. Through the development of an alternative vocabulary, they carve out a resistant, 'insulated discursive space' (1991, p. 14) that legitimates political inaction and non-participation in the dominant culture. Thus, although the workers engage in a form of discursive penetration of that culture, their own vocabulary condemns them to powerlessness and lack of voice. Such conclusions are remarkably similar to Willis's (1977) analysis of 'the lads' resistant sub-culture discussed above.

On the other hand, the emergence of post-Fordist, team-based organizational structures has thrown a particularly bright spotlight on the ways in which organization members coordinate their collective sense-making processes through everyday talk. While more centralized, bureaucratic structures of power and decision-making leave comparatively little room for interpretive ambiguity, the new decentralized team structures require constant sense-making efforts on the part of their members as they figure out what it means to be 'self-managing'. In the latter case, control and coordination is an ongoing, dynamic process that is negotiated through everyday talk. In terms of the political economy of the workplace, the shift to team structures suggests a reversal of the Fordist separation of conception and execution of work (Braverman, 1974; Ezzamel & Willmott, 1998), and a greater involvement on the part of workers in the design of the labour process.

From a critical-dialectical perspective interest lies in how team structures function around the dialectic of empowerment and control. In recent years, critical organization scholars have closely examined the ways that team members negotiate this dialectic. On the one hand, the decentralized decision-making structures appear to suggest greater possibilities for participative work environments, while on the other hand, some critical scholars have argued that such structures simply 'tighten the iron cage' of bureaucracy through processes of worker self-surveillance or 'concertive control' (Barker, 1993, 1999; Tompkins & Cheney, 1985). Other critical scholars have provided evidence that the implementation of team structures is by no means as unproblematic as it seems, and that management is often confronted with workers who are highly resistant to change (Ezzamel & Willmott, 1998). In either case, critical research focuses on how team members employ everyday talk as the medium and outcome of organizational sense-making as it unfolds in the context of the dynamics of control and resistance.

In this context, the notion of 'accounting' plays a central role. That is, the team-based system of control appears to place much greater emphasis on how individuals must account for their behaviour and performance to other team members. Through everyday talk and interaction, members negotiate among themselves the meaning of 'appropriate' behaviour in a relatively uncertain organizational environment. Both Mumby and Stohl (1992) and Barker (1993), for example, have illustrated how the meaning of workplace absenteeism becomes more contested in a team environment. Mumby and Stohl analyse a fragment of conversation from a team meeting in a tyre plant to show how social control functions through the invocation of particular definitions of 'absence'. In this instance, the team talk is not seen as merely reflecting an already fixed power structure, but rather as dynamically constituting team member identities in a way that discursively positions them as having to provide accounts for any 'deviant' behaviour. Interpretive struggles over concepts like 'absence', then, play a key role in the creation of worker identities as they negotiate the politics of enablement and constraint. Similarly, Barker illustrates how workers in a newly organized team environment quickly develop a complex – and eventually institutionalized – system of sense-making to account for and monitor member absence – a system that, in many ways, is much more disciplinary than the previous bureaucratic system.

As Ezzamel and Willmott (1998) argue, however, the dynamic of teamwork is frequently more complex than these studies suggest. A focus on member talk cannot occur in the absence of an understanding of the larger political economy of the workplace. In their study of a large manufacturing company, they show how the decision to shift to teamwork had less to do with management's desire to empower workers, and more to do with a system of accounting that recognized the need for greater productivity in a more competitive global economy, thus providing a 'rhetoric of value added' (1998, p. 391). The ultimate failure of the team system, however, was due largely to management's lack of recognition that workers' identities were strongly tied up with the old line system and their identification with each other as 'mates' and fellow machinists. The new self-managing, group reward system violated a sense of identity in which individual performance was rewarded and each worker was responsible to no one but him/herself. The devolution of control to lower levels thus threatened the prevailing 'narrative of self' (1998, p. 392) and was actively resisted.

These studies, then, suggest a complicated picture of the relationship among discourse, sense-making and the dialectic of control and resistance. While the emergence of teamwork presents an important development in critical scholars' efforts to understand the dynamics of organizational control, such understanding must necessarily be framed within the context of larger concerns with the political economy of work. For example, it is hard to compare Barker's (1993, 1999) study of the introduction of teams in a small electronics company with Graham's (1993) critical ethnography of teams within the Japanese *Kaizen* model – a highly developed, minutely calibrated system that provides very little actual autonomy for team members. In each instance, the larger political economy of the workplace provides the backdrop against which workers' sense-making processes and discourse practices must be understood.

CONCLUSION AND DIRECTIONS FOR FUTURE RESEARCH

In this chapter I have provided an overview of critical organizational discourse studies that arise out of what I have termed a 'discourse of suspicion' – a perspective that focuses on the relationships among discourse, ideology and deep-structure relations of power. Furthermore, I argued that such studies tend to fall into one of two domains: first, those that privilege domination and control over resistance and that adopt an ideology critique, 'reproduction' view of organizing processes; and second, those that adopt a more dialectical perspective and examine the ways in which knowledgeable agents negotiate the contradictions and tensions of organizational relations of power. To conclude, I briefly address some issues that I believe critical scholars should be concerned with as they continue to explore the relations among discourse, meaning, identity and power.

First, one of the things that most surprised me in reviewing research for this chapter was the relative dearth of data-rich studies. Critical researchers spend a lot of time theorizing about organizational discourse, and many engage in ethnographic work, but relatively little time is spent in close analysis of the dynamics of discursive processes. There are certainly a number of exceptions to this rule (e.g., Clegg, 1975; Collinson, 1992; Helmer, 1993; Kunda, 1992; Rosen, 1985), but for the most part there are few studies that explore the richness of organizational discourse at close quarters. This is problematic for a couple of reasons. To begin with, the issue of 'voice' is central to critical organizational research (Mumby & Stohl, 1996), that is, how can organization members be viewed as knowledgeable social agents whose 'discursive penetration' (Giddens, 1979) of organizational life contributes substantially to our understanding of organizational power dynamics? The lack of focus on actual discourse results in the elimination of that voice as researchers mostly speak for organization members. Furthermore, much journal space has been devoted to discussions of discourse as constitutive of organizational reality, and yet relatively little time is spent actually examining the micro practices of such discourse and its relation to larger macro processes of organizational power. Indeed, it seems that researchers frequently make rather large conceptual leaps based on relatively little actual data. Critical research, then, needs to make a significant shift towards more richly textured analyses of actual discourse processes.

Second, and related, the linguistic/interpretive turn in organization studies has resulted in important insights into organizations as socially constructed phenomena. However, one of the unfortunate side effects of this important shift has been the tendency to view it as a move from examining the objective features of organizational life to examining its subjective features. In some ways, this shift has preserved the Cartesian subject–object dichotomy (Deetz, 1996). Rather than viewing discourse as simply mediating between these inner and outer worlds (Oswick et al., 2000), I would argue rather for a model of communicative praxis in which the self–world relation is constituted in an ongoing, performative fashion through everyday discursive processes. In this sense, discourse does not mediate but constitutes the very possibility of a self–world relation. Self and world are created in relation to each other, and have no meaning as independent spheres of existence.

Given this perspective, I suggest that one of the most fruitful avenues of research for critical discourse studies is the examination of (gendered, raced) identities as they are communicatively accomplished in a quotidian fashion in the context of complex and contradictory relations of organizational power. Such a position moves beyond discourse-as-text (though it does not eschew it), to an examination of discourse as dynamic, material and political (Conquergood, 1991). In this way, the relationship between discourse and identity becomes precisely that which must be made problematic and examined. For example, Dorinne Kondo's (1990) feminist ethnography of a Japanese pastry factory is an excellent exemplar of such work, as it explores gendered identities as ongoing, situational, and often contradictory accomplishments, enacted within the context of particular power relations and structures of meaning. Certainly some postmodern scholars have theorized the discourse–subject relation in interesting ways, informed particularly by the work of Foucault (e.g., Knights & Morgan, 1991; Knights & Vurdubakis, 1994; Newton, 1998), but few if any have explored subjectivity as a complex, communicative accomplishment that is 'born of contradiction' (Ashcraft, 1998, p. 587).

Finally, I suggest that critical organizational discourse studies help to remind us that organizations are real structures that have real consequences for real people. Yes, that reality is socially constructed, but I think we must be careful not to forget the material consequences of that social construction process. The Derridian claim that there is 'nothing outside the text' should not reduce critical organizational analyses to a textual solipsism that overlooks the incorrigibility of organizational life and its consequences for ordinary people. In this sense, the roots of critical studies lie in connecting the everyday to larger political and economic questions.

NOTE

1 Again, I am making a somewhat arbitrary distinction here. There are certainly so-called 'interpretive' scholars who argue that they are most definitely interested in issues of power (e.g., Trujillo, 1992).

REFERENCES

Adorno, T. (1973) *Negative dialectics*. Trans. E.B. Ashton. New York: Continuum.

Althusser, L. (1971) *Lenin and philosophy*. New York: Monthly Review Press.

Alvesson, M. (1985) A critical framework for organizational analysis. *Organization Studies*, 6: 117–38.

Alvesson, M. & Kärreman, D. (2000a) Taking the linguistic turn in organizational research: Challenges, responses, consequences. *The Journal of Applied Behavioral Science*, 36: 136–58.

Alvesson, M. & Kärreman, D. (2000b) Varieties of discourse: On the study of organizations through discourse analysis. *Human Relations*, 53: 1125–49.

Ashcraft, K.L. (1998) 'I wouldn't say I'm a feminist, but…': Organizational micropractice and gender identity. *Management Communication Quarterly*, 11: 587–97.

Bachrach, P. & Baratz, M. (1962) Two faces of power. *American Political Science Review*, 56: 947–52.

Bakhtin, M. (1984) *Rabelais and his world*. Trans. H. Iswolsky. Bloomington, IN: Indiana University Press.

Barker, J.R. (1993) Tightening the iron cage: Concertive control in self-managing teams. *Administrative Science Quarterly*, 38: 408–37.

Barker, J.R. (1999) *The discipline of teamwork: Participation and concertive control*. Thousand Oaks, CA: Sage.

Barker, J.R. & Cheney, G. (1994) The concept and practices of discipline in contemporary organizational life. *Communication Monographs*, 61: 19–43.

Benson, J.K. (1977) Organizations: A dialectical view. *Administrative Science Quarterly*, 22: 1–21.

Boden, D. (1994) *The business of talk*. Cambridge: Polity Press.

Boje, D.M. (1991) The storytelling organization: A study of story performance in an office-supply firm. *Administrative Science Quarterly*, 36: 106–26.

Boje, D.M., Luhman, J.T. & Baack, D.E. (1999) Hegemonic stories and encounters between storytelling organizations. *Journal of Management Inquiry*, 8: 340–60.

Boyce, M.E. (1996) Organizational story and storytelling: A critical review. *Journal of Organizational Change Management*, 9 (5): 5–26.

Braverman, H. (1974) *Labor and monopoly capital: The degradation of work in the twentieth century*. New York: Monthly Review Press.

Brown, A.D. (1998) Narrative, politics and legitimacy in an IT implementation. *Journal of Management Studies*, 35: 35–58.

Bruner, J. (1991) The narrative construction of reality. *Critical Inquiry*, 18: 1–21.

Burawoy, M. (1979) *Manufacturing consent: Changes in the labor process under monopoly capitalism*. Chicago: University of Chicago Press.

Burrell, G. (1988) Modernism, postmodernism and organizational analysis 2: The contribution of Michel Foucault. *Organization Studies*, 9: 221–35.

Burrell, G. (1994) Modernism, postmodernism and organizational analysis 4: The contribution of Jürgen Habermas. *Organization Studies*, 15: 1–19.

Clair, R.P. (1994) Resistance and oppression as a self-contained opposite: An organizational communication analysis of one man's story of sexual harassment. *Western Journal of Communication*, 58: 235–62.

Clegg, S. (1975) *Power, rule, and domination*. New York: Routledge & Kegan Paul.

Clegg, S. (1981) Organization and control. *Administrative Science Quarterly*, 26: 545–62.

Clegg, S. (1989) Radical revisions: Power, discipline and organizations. *Organization Studies*, 10: 97–115.

Collinson, D. (1988) 'Engineering humor': Masculinity, joking and conflict in shop-floor relations. *Organization Studies*, 9: 181–99.

Collinson, D. (1992) *Managing the shop floor: Subjectivity, masculinity, and workplace culture*. New York: De Gruyter.

Conquergood, D. (1991) Rethinking ethnography: Toward a critical cultural politics. *Communication Monographs*, 58: 179–94.

Conrad, C. (1983) Organizational power: Faces and symbolic forms. In L.L. Putnam & M.E. Pacanowsky (eds), *Communication and organizations: An interpretive approach* (pp. 173–94). Beverly Hills, CA: Sage.

Conrad, C. & Ryan, M. (1985) Power, praxis, and self in organizational communication theory. In R.D. McPhee & P.K. Tompkins (eds), *Organizational communication: Traditional themes and new directions* (pp. 235–57). Beverly Hills, CA: Sage.

Cooper, R. (1989) Modernism, postmodernism and organizational analysis 3: The contribution of Jacques Derrida. *Organization Studies*, 10: 479–502.

Cooper, R. & Burrell, G. (1988) Modernism, postmodernism and organizational analysis: An introduction. *Organization Studies*, 9: 91–112.

Cooren, F. (2000) *The organizing property of communication*. Amsterdam: John Benjamins.

Czarniawska, B. (1998) *A narrative approach to organization studies*. Thousand Oaks, CA: Sage.

Dahl, R. (1957) The concept of power. *Behavioral Science*, 2: 201–15.

Deetz, S.A. (1982) Critical interpretive research in organizational communication. *The Western Journal of Speech Communication*, 46: 131–49.

Deetz, S.A. (1985) Critical-cultural research: New sensibilities and old realities. *Journal of Management*, 11 (2): 121–36.

Deetz, S.A. (1992) *Democracy in an age of corporate colonization: Developments in communication and the politics of everyday life*. Albany, NY: State University of New York Press.

Deetz, S.A. (1996) Describing differences in approaches to organization science: Rethinking Burrell and Morgan and their legacy. *Organization Science*, 7: 191–207.

Deetz, S. & Kersten, A. (1983) Critical models of interpretive research. In L.L. Putnam & M. Pacanowsky (eds), *Communication and organizations: An interpretive approach* (pp. 147–71). Beverly Hills, CA: Sage.

Deetz, S. & Mumby, D.K. (1985) Metaphors, information, and power. In B. Ruben (ed.), *Information and behavior* (Vol. 1, pp. 369–86). New Brunswick, NJ: Transaction.

Dunford, R. & Palmer, I. (1998) Discourse, organizations and paradox. In D. Grant, T. Keenoy & C. Oswick (eds), *Discourse and organization* (pp. 214–21). London: Sage.

Ehrenhaus, P. (1993) Cultural narratives and the therapeutic motif: The political containment of Vietnam veterans. In D.K. Mumby (ed.), *Narrative and social control* (pp. 77–96). Newbury Park, CA: Sage.

Eisenberg, E. & Goodall, H.L. (2001) *Organizational communication: Balancing creativity and constraint* (3rd edition). New York: Bedford/St Martin's Press.

Ewick, P. & Silbey, S.S. (1995) Subversive stories and hegemonic tales: Toward a sociology of narrative. *Law & Society Review*, 29: 197–226.

Ezzamel, M. & Willmott, H. (1998) Accounting for teamwork: A critical study of group-based systems of organizational control. *Administrative Science Quarterly*, 43: 358–96.

Fairclough, N. (1993) Critical discourse analysis and the marketization of public discourse: The universities. *Discourse and Society*, 4: 133–68.

Fairclough, N. & Wodak, R. (1997) Critical discourse analysis. In T.A. Van Dijk (ed.), *Discourse as social interaction* (pp. 258–84). London: Sage.

Fisher, W.R. (1984) Narration as a human communication paradigm: The case of public moral argument. *Communication Monographs*, 51: 1–22.

Fisher, W.R. (1985) The narrative paradigm: An elaboration. *Communication Monographs*, 52: 347–67.

Forester, J. (1989) *Planning in the face of power*. Berkeley, CA: University of California Press.

Forester, J. (1992) Fieldwork in a Habermasian way. In M. Alvesson & H. Willmott (eds), *Critical management studies* (pp. 46–65). Newbury Park, CA: Sage.

Forester, J. (1993) *Critical theory, public policy and planning practice*. Albany, NY: State University of New York Press.

Frost, P. (1980) Toward a radical framework for practicing organization science. *Academy of Management Review*, 5: 501–8.

Frost, P. (1987) Power, politics, and influence. In F. Jablin, L.L. Putnam, K. Roberts & L. Porter (eds), *Handbook of organizational communication* (pp. 503–47). Newbury Park, CA: Sage.

Frost, P.J., Moore, L.F., Louis, M.R., Lundberg, C.C. & Martin, J. (eds) (1985) *Organizational culture*. Beverly Hills, CA: Sage.

Gabriel, Y. (2000) *Storytelling in organizations: Facts, fictions, and fantasies*. Oxford: Oxford University Press.

Gadamer, H.-G. (1989) *Truth and method* (2nd edition). Trans. J.W.D.G. Marshall. New York: Continuum.

Geuss, R. (1981) *The idea of a critical theory: Habermas and the Frankfurt School*. Cambridge: Cambridge University Press.

Giddens, A. (1979) *Central problems in social theory: Action, structure and contradiction in social analysis*. Berkeley, CA: University of California Press.

Graham, L. (1993) Inside a Japanese transplant: A critical perspective. *Work and Occupations*, 20: 147–73.

Gramsci, A. (1971) *Selections from the prison notebooks*. Trans. Q. Hoare & G.N. Smith. New York: International Publishers.

Grant, D., Keenoy, T. & Oswick, C. (eds) (1998) *Discourse and organization*. London: Sage.

Grossberg, L. (1986) On postmodernism and articulation: An interview with Stuart Hall. *Journal of Communication Inquiry*, 10 (2): 45–60.

Habermas, J. (1979) *Communication and the evolution of society*. Trans. T. McCarthy. Boston, MA: Beacon Press.

Habermas, J. (1984) *The theory of communicative action: Reason and the rationalization of society* (Vol. 1). Trans. T. McCarthy. Boston, MA: Beacon Press.

Habermas, J. (1987) *The theory of communicative action: Lifeworld and system* (Vol. 2). Trans. T. McCarthy. Boston, MA: Beacon Press.

Hall, S. (1983) The problem of ideology: Marxism without guarantees. In B. Matthews (ed.), *Marx: 100 years on* (pp. 57–84). London: Lawrence & Wishart.

Hall, S. (1985) Signification, representation, ideology: Althusser and the poststructuralist debates. *Critical Studies in Mass Communication*, 2: 91–114.

Hardy, C., Palmer, I. & Phillips, N. (2000) Discourse as a strategic resource. *Human Relations*, 53: 1227–48.

Hardy, C. & Phillips, N. (1999) No joking matter: Discursive struggle in the Canadian refugee system. *Organization Studies*, 20: 1–24.

Heidegger, M. (1977) *Basic writings*. New York: Harper & Row.

Hekman, S. (1990) *Gender and knowledge: Elements of a postmodern feminism*. Boston, MA: Northeastern University Press.

Helmer, J. (1993) Storytelling in the creation and maintenance of organizational tension and stratification. *The Southern Communication Journal*, 59: 34–44.

Horkheimer, M. (1986) *Critical theory*. Trans. M. O'Connell et al., New York: Continuum.

Horkheimer, M. & Adorno, T. (1988) *Dialectic of enlightenment*. Trans. J. Cumming. New York: Continuum.

Huspek, M. & Kendall, K. (1991) On withholding political voice: An analysis of the political vocabulary of a 'nonpolitical' speech community. *The Quarterly Journal of Speech*, 77: 1–19.

Jablin, F.M., Putnam, L.L., Roberts, K.H. & Porter, L.W. (eds) (1987) *Handbook of organizational communication: An interdisciplinary perspective*. Newbury Park, CA: Sage.

Jermier, J.M. (1998) Introduction: Critical perspectives on organizational control. *Administrative Science Quarterly*, 43: 235–56.

Keenoy, T., Marchak, R.J., Oswick, C. & Grant, D. (2000) The discourses of organizing. *The Journal of Applied Behavioral Science*, 36: 133–5.

Keenoy, T., Oswick, C. & Grant, D. (1997) Organizational discourses: Text and context. *Organization*, 4: 147–59.

Knights, D. & Morgan, G. (1991) Strategic discourse and subjectivity: Towards a critical analysis of corporate strategy in organizations. *Organization Studies*, 12: 251–74.

Knights, D. & Vurdubakis, T. (1994) Foucault, power, resistance and all that. In J.M. Jermier, D. Knights & W.R. Nord (eds), *Resistance and power in organizations* (pp. 167–98). London: Routledge.

Kondo, D.K. (1990) *Crafting selves: Power, gender, and discourses of identity in a Japanese workplace*. Chicago: University of Chicago Press.

Korsch, K. (1971) *Marxism and philosophy*. New York: Monthly Review Press.

Kunda, G. (1992) *Engineering culture: Control and commitment in a high-tech corporation*. Philadelphia, PA: Temple University Press.

Langellier, K.M. (1989) Personal narratives: Perspectives on theory and research. *Text and Performance Quarterly*, 9: 243–76.

Larrain, J. (1979) *The concept of ideology*. London: Hutchinson.

Linstead, S. & Grafton-Small, R. (1992) On reading organizational culture. *Organization Studies*, 13: 311–55.

Lukács, G. (1971) *History and class consciousness: Studies in Marxist dialectics*. Trans. R. Livingstone. Boston, MA: MIT Press.

Lukes, S. (1974) *Power: A radical view*. London: Macmillan.

Marshak, R.J. (1998) A discourse on discourse: Redeeming the meaning of talk. In D. Grant, T. Keenoy & C. Oswick (eds), *Discourse and organization* (pp. 15–30). London: Sage.

Marx, K. (1967) *Capital*. Trans. S. Moore & E. Aveling. New York: International Publishers.

Merleau-Ponty, M. (1960) *Phenomenology of perception*. Trans. C. Smith. London: Routledge & Kegan Paul.

Mumby, D.K. (1987) The political function of narrative in organizations. *Communication Monographs*, 54: 113–27.

Mumby, D.K. (1988) *Communication and power in organizations: Discourse, ideology, and domination*. Norwood, NJ: Ablex.

Mumby, D.K. (1997a) Modernism, postmodernism, and communication studies: A rereading of an ongoing debate. *Communication Theory*, 7: 1–28.

Mumby, D.K. (1997b) The problem of hegemony: Rereading Gramsci for organizational communication studies. *Western Journal of Communication*, 61: 343–75.

Mumby, D.K. & Clair, R.P. (1997) Organizational discourse. In T.A. van Dijk (ed.), *Discourse as structure and process*, (Vol. 2, pp. 181–205). London: Sage.

Mumby, D.K. & Stohl, C. (1992) Power and discourse in organization studies: Absence and the dialectic of control. *Discourse & Society*, 2: 313–32.

Mumby, D.K. & Stohl, C. (1996) Disciplining organizational communication studies. *Management Communication Quarterly*, 10: 50–72.

Murphy, A.G. (1998) Hidden transcripts of flight attendant resistance. *Management Communication Quarterly*, 11: 499–535.

Newton, T. (1998) Theorizing subjectivity in organizations: The failure of Foucauldian studies? *Organization Studies*, 19: 415–47.

O'Connor, E. (2000) Plotting the organization: The embedded narrative as a construct for studying change. *The Journal of Applied Behavioral Science*, 36: 174–92.

Oswick, C., Keenoy, T. & Grant, D. (2000) Discourse, organizations and organizing: Concepts, objects and subjects. *Human Relations*, 53 (9): 1115–23.

Pacanowsky, M. & O'Donnell-Trujillo, N. (1982) Communication and organizational cultures. *The Western Journal of Speech Communication*, 46: 115–30.

Palmer, R. (1969) *Hermeneutics*. Evanston, IL: Northwestern University Press.

Papa, M.J., Auwal, M.A. & Singhal, A. (1995) Dialectic of control and emancipation in organizing for social change: A multitheoretic study of the Grameen Bank in Bangladesh. *Communication Theory*, 5: 189–223.

Parker, M. (1995) Critique in the name of what? Postmodernism and critical approaches to organization. *Organization Studies*, 16: 553–64.

Pfeffer, J. (1981) *Power in organizations*. Cambridge, MA: Ballinger Publishing.

Putnam, L.L. (1983) The interpretive perspective: An alternative to functionalism. In L.L. Putnam & M. Pacanowsky (eds), *Communication and organizations: An interpretive approach* (pp. 31–54). Beverly Hills, CA: Sage.

Putnam, L.L. & Fairhurst, G. (2001) Discourse analysis in organizations: Issues and concerns. In F.M. Jablin & L.L. Putnam (eds), *The new handbook of organizational communication: Advances in theory, research, and methods* (pp. 78–136). Thousand Oaks, CA: Sage.

Putnam, L.L. & Pacanowsky, M. (eds) (1983) *Communication and organizations: An interpretive approach*. Beverly Hills, CA: Sage.

Ricœur, P. (1970) *Freud and philosophy: An essay on interpretation*. Trans. D. Savage. New Haven, CT: Yale University Press.

Riley, P. (1983) A structurationist account of political culture. *Administrative Science Quarterly*, 28: 414–37.

Rosen, M. (1985) 'Breakfast at Spiro's': Dramaturgy and dominance. *Journal of Management*, 11 (2): 31–48.

Rosen, M. (1988) You asked for it: Christmas at the bosses' expense. *Journal of Management Studies*, 25: 463–80.

Scheibel, D. (1996) Appropriating bodies: Organ(izing) ideology and cultural practice in medical school. *Journal of Applied Communication Research*, 24: 310–31.

Scheibel, D. (1999) 'If your roommate dies, you get a 4.0': Reclaiming rumor with Burke and organizational culture. *Western Journal of Communication*, 63: 168–92.

Schrag, C.O. (1986) *Communicative praxis and the space of subjectivity*. Bloomington, IN: Indiana University Press.

Smircich, L. (1983) Concepts of culture and organizational analysis. *Administrative Science Quarterly*, 28: 339–58.

Smith, F.L. & Keyton, J. (2001) Organizational storytelling: Metaphors for relational power and identity struggles. *Management Communication Quarterly*, 15: 149–82.

Stewart, J. (1991) A postmodern look at traditional communication postulates. *Western Journal of Speech Communication*, 55: 354–79.

Taylor, J.R., Cooren, F., Giroux, N. & Robichaud, D. (1996) The communicational basis of organization: Between the conversation and the text. *Communication Theory*, 6: 1–39.

Therborn, G. (1980) *The ideology of power and the power of ideology*. London: Verso.

Thompson, J.B. (1984) *Studies in the theory of ideology*. Berkeley, CA: University of California Press.

Tompkins, P.K. & Cheney, G. (1985) Communication and unobtrusive control in contemporary organizations. In R. McPhee & P.K. Tompkins (eds), *Organizational communication: Traditional themes and new directions* (pp. 179–210). Beverly Hills, CA: Sage.

Trujillo, N. (1992) Interpreting (the work and talk of) baseball: Perspectives on ballpark culture. *Western Journal of Communication*, 56: 350–71.

Trujillo, N. & Dionisopoulos, G. (1987) Cop talk, police stories, and the social construction of organizational drama. *Central States Speech Journal*, 38: 196–209.

West, C. & Fenstermaker, S. (1995) Doing difference. *Gender & Society*, 9: 8–37.

West, C. & Zimmerman, D. (1987) Doing gender. *Gender & Society*, 1: 125–51.

Willis, P. (1977) *Learning to labor: How working-class kids get working-class jobs*. New York: Columbia University Press.

Witten, M. (1993) Narrative and the culture of obedience at the workplace. In D.K. Mumby (ed.), *Narrative and social control: Critical perspectives* (pp. 97–118). Newbury Park, CA: Sage.

Young, E. (1989) On the naming of the rose: Interests and multiple meanings as elements of organizational culture. *Organization Studies*, 10: 187–206.

Deconstructing Discourse

Martin Kilduff and Mihaela Kelemen

The world into which we are born is structured by the discourse of organizations, a discourse that reaches us through advertising, the speeches of executives, and the repetitions of family and friends who return from places of employment to our homes with tales to tell. How are we to make sense of this discourse, these tales? The organizations themselves seem so varied, ranging from the religious and political to the profit-seeking and the trivial. The struggle to grasp principles behind apparent diversity is one that occupies organizational researchers. In this chapter we revisit one of the pioneering efforts to analyse the universal elements of formal organizations, Chester Barnard's *The Functions of the Executive*, first published in 1938.

Why should we spend time on this book? Let us summarize three answers why attention to the discourses initiated by the classics of social science may be vital for scholarship and for comprehending the contemporary world (see Kilduff & Dougherty, 2000). First, we need to understand the classics of social and organizational science because these works have helped create the world in which we live. The classics, defined as 'earlier works of human exploration which are given a privileged status *vis-à-vis* contemporary explorations' (Alexander, 1989, p. 9), are active tools in the hands of those shaping our societies. Just as Taylorism's effects can be traced in contexts as unexpected as European modern art (Guillen, 1997), so Barnard's effects on contemporary social engineering are wide-ranging and profound (Scott, 1992). Second, an acquaintance with the classics allows us to escape the embarrassment of proclaiming as the 'next advance' truths that were adumbrated 'years, decades, even centuries before' (Sica, 1997, p. 284). The investigation of classics allows us to enlarge our set of concepts and ideas to include those that have fallen out of our collective memory. Third, to the extent that classics such as Barnard's book continue to shape our world, we need to re-evaluate these texts critically in order to prevent taken-for-granted meanings foreclosing alternative discourses. If memory is a moral decision (as argued by Feldman, 2002), then we, as organizational researchers, are morally obliged to maintain a critical awareness of the historical embeddedness of our ideas. In short, the critical examination of classic texts may help us recover, understand and challenge the discourses of theory and practice within which social scientists work.

The discursive turn in organization studies signals the centrality of language in understanding and constructing theories about the social world. But the meaning of the term 'discourse' is often unclear. At least two conventional meanings have been identified (see Alvesson & Kärreman, 2000): (1) discourse as written and spoken text (e.g., speeches by executives of corporations), and (2) discourse as the medium by which social reality is constructed (e.g., technical jargon used by professional engineers). There are also a host of competing versions of discourse analysis derived from such diverse sources as sociolinguistics (e.g., Stubbs, 1983) and critical theory (e.g., Fairclough, 1993). Often overlooked in discussions of discourse and its analysis is deconstruction, a style of thinking and writing that is neither an approach to discourse nor a set of discourse methods, but something altogether more radical. Deconstruction identifies transforming forces within the canonical texts that constitute the discourses of science. The implications of deconstruction move beyond canonical texts into discourses of theory and practice that constitute and shape the lives we lead within and without organizations.

WHAT IS DECONSTRUCTION?

> Deconstruction, a demonstration of the incompleteness or incoherence of a philosophical position using concepts and principles of argument whose meaning and use is legitimated only by the philosophical position. (Wheeler, 1999, p. 209)

Textual deconstruction is often reified, misunderstood and vilified. A fairly typical newspaper reference identifies it as a 'French disease' that has spread 'as French diseases will' (from the *Chicago Tribune*, 29 October 1991, quoted in Naas, 1992, p. ix). Even supposedly reflective academic scholars are apt to blunder when discussing deconstruction. Consider these words from the chair of the department of Culture and Communication at New York University: 'There is, of course, a connection between alien- and devil-believers and a certain variety of deconstructionists' (Postman, 1999, p. 8). In the light of such risible misunderstanding, it is hardly surprising that Derrida wrote to a friend that, 'All sentences of the type "deconstruction is X" or "deconstruction is not X" miss the point, which is to say that they are at the least false' (quoted by Richmond, 1995, p. 180). In this chapter we attempt to avoid such falsehood by offering not merely an inevitably limited introduction to deconstruction and its relation to discourse, but also a brief example of how to deconstruct a classic text.

To dispel one myth immediately, deconstruction is not a set of codified beliefs and practices that can be identified with people called 'deconstructionists'. There is no code, and there are no deconstructionists. As Derrida (1988, p. 141) has cautioned: 'Deconstruction does not exist somewhere, pure, proper, self-identical, outside of its inscriptions in conflictual and differentiated contexts; it "is" only what it does and what is done with it, there where it takes place.' The deconstructive process is adaptable to the exigencies of the text in question and deconstruction, therefore, cannot be boiled down to a formula or a method. In contrast to structuralism, Freudianism or other systematized approaches to texts, the practice of deconstruction remains open and undecided concerning what the text has to offer. A deconstructive reading always emerges from the 'specific complexities of the text itself' (Currie, 1998, p. 11). Rather than seeking to stabilize, reduce or close down discourses, a deconstructive reading opens up complexity and uses it to problematize previous attempts at over-simplification (Currie, 1998, p. 45).

Because a successful deconstruction can open up a text's complexity using only the text's own resources, it sometimes appears to critics of deconstruction that, after all, there is nothing at work but straightforward critical acumen. Deconstruction, at its best, is scaffolding that enables the critic to reach the point at which the text is transformed for the reader allowing the critical apparatus to be dismantled. The traces of deconstruction in the text are ones that were always there. The reader is apt to ask: Where is the deconstruction? All I can see is the text itself commenting on itself.

The gestures of deconstruction are several and varied. Only an outline of these gestures can be offered here, but the reader is referred to the works of Derrida (1976, 1978, 1988) for examples of how logic, close reading in original languages and historical scholarship can illuminate texts. Derrida's 'extravagantly convoluted' writing (Agger, 1991, p. 106) endeavours to both represent the text and expose it. Avoiding oversimplification and reliance on undeclared metaphysical assumptions, Derrida implicates all writing as inherently literary, thereby moving scientific and philosophical texts into the ambit of rhetorical productions.

According to Derrida's (1976) analyses, in producing speech, whether spontaneously or not, people have no direct connection to an interior discourse that is more universal or basic or primary than any other discourse. Speech cannot be privileged as offering more direct access to consciousness than writing. Words build on and refer to other words. Deconstruction tends to be ironic in its use of language to undermine the categories and distinctions that discourse, including social scientific discourse, imposes on shifting and fluid meanings.

In the social sciences, we find deconstruction of classic texts (e.g., Kilduff, 1993), legal doctrines (e.g., Frug, 1984) and psychological theory (e.g., Sampson, 1983). Moving beyond the limits practised by Derrida, but compatible with his idea of an inclusive 'archewriting' that encompasses the textuality not just of written documents but also of speech and action, deconstruction in social science has traced hidden assumptions, metaphysical dependencies, and suppressed voices in a range of contexts that include canonical texts, but also apparently spontaneous discourse (e.g., Martin, 1990).

The practice of deconstruction begins with the premise that all scientific writing is inherently literary. There is no such thing as an unmediated approach to the truth, a neutral style, a mere putting into words the facts of the case. Deconstruction involves 'the epistemological gesture of falsifying the pretensions to truth and completeness of all totalizing principles' (Gasche, 1981, p. 45). Discourse, whether written or spoken, is not, therefore, merely representational and distinct from the objects, thoughts and people referred to. To distinguish categorically between what is inside and outside language becomes an immense and perhaps impossible task, as suggested by Derrida's famous quip, 'Il n'y a pas de-hors texte' (Derrida, 1976, p. 158), interpreted, in one insightful analysis, as: 'There is no outside text' (Currie, 1998, p. 45).

In refusing to grant any discourse immunity from a reliance on rhetoric, Derrida's deconstructions problematize the boundaries between discourses such as the philosophical, the techonological and the literary. In suggesting the embeddedness of human activity in an archewriting that includes speech and writing, Derrida draws our attention to the textuality of everyday life and technology.

In deconstructing a text, the analyst pays special attention to all claims to scientific truth, to obvious principles, to matters too evident to be debated, to arguments so patently clear to everyone that they are relegated to mere footnotes, to gaps in logic, to missing assumptions, and to avoided conclusions. In short, the analyst is interested in what is absent from the text as much as what is present in the text. Derrida, in one of his most original inquiries, asks of texts: Why is this left out? The absence or slighting of inconvenient or apparently negligible issues offers the analyst an opportunity to uncover all that the text has carefully hidden from our view. A characteristic deconstructive gesture is to reintroduce into the discourse the absent other, the missing reference, the excluded category or the avoided conclusion, and thereby expose the apparently seamless prose as steeped in rhetorical moves. One of the standard opening rhetorical flourishes in the social sciences, for example, is the claim, nearly always present in the first few paragraphs, that there is an absence in the previous literature that is waiting to be filled by the providentially provided text in question. Without such an absence, the implication is that the text in question could not be written, would not be accepted, would not be scientific. To pose as science, the text must insist that its presence fills an absence.

Another of the hidden aspects of texts that Derrida has alerted us to is the dependence of the text on sets of hierarchically ordered binary oppositions. Typically, one of the categories is privileged, whereas the other is marginalized or suppressed. Thus, in an example familiar to all of us, a text may persist in calling all the participants by the male gender, excluding all women from consideration. Or the text may implicitly or explicitly privilege the mind over the body, the organic over the mechanistic, those who write programmes over those whose working lives are programmed (see Kilduff, 1993, for an example of such a deconstruction).

A standard deconstructive procedure is to examine carefully the examples used to illustrate the major concepts or processes present in the text. For example, if the text concerns the ways in which speech preceded and gave birth to writing, it is of importance to notice that the examples given to illustrate the characteristics of speech are in fact all examples taken from written rather than spoken statements

(Derrida, 1978). It may become apparent that the text habitually illustrates the privileged member of a hierarchically ordered pair by falling back on the disparaged member of the pair, indicating, at the very least, a discrepancy in the analytical scheme being presented.

Perhaps the most powerful deconstructive gesture is to reveal to the startled reader a hidden text, glossed over countless times by inattentive eyes, but suddenly present for all to see only too clearly once its boundaries, its syntax, its phrasings, and its hiding places are abstracted from the protective embeddedness of the surrounding rhetoric. The hidden text so mysteriously absent and yet so powerfully present may contradict the explicit text, may even undermine the message that the authors have been at such pains to articulate. By bringing the different parts of the hidden text together, the critic is like an archaeologist who reconstructs the skeletons of vanished creatures and brings them to life, creatures that the authors had assured us were banished forever, but who now claim attention from the very pages that the authors have laboured to write. In this sense, deconstruction can be a profoundly creative process that enriches our understanding of texts rather than impoverishing them.

We end this section by repeating a caveat that is often ignored: Deconstruction must follow the contours of the text itself. It cannot impose the critic's political beliefs or prejudices, it cannot follow a rigid code of rules, it cannot be the same from one text to another, it cannot depend on a set of preformed clichés borrowed from other critics, other sources. The deconstructive process is as much a textual appreciation as it is a riveting set of analytical procedures. We are talking about the high art of deconstruction in the hands of Derrida. We do not claim to equal his achievements, but we do claim to take these achievements as our exemplars.

WHO WAS BARNARD AND WHY SHOULD WE CARE?

Deconstruction is sometimes misunderstood to imply that we can analyse texts without knowing anything about the author, the social context or other relevant historical details. The so-called 'death of the author' is taken by some to imply a free-for-all in which any interpretation is as good as any other interpretation. This misunderstanding may have arisen because Derrida's approach to language assumes that what is written has significance beyond what the writer might have intended, and that the writer's intentions (in contrast to the written words) have no privileged status. Words refer to other words and other texts in a network of verbal associations that is beyond the abilities of anyone to control. As Derrida (1981, pp. 129–30) has written concerning the work of Plato: 'Like any text [it] … couldn't not be involved, at least in a virtual, dynamic, lateral manner, with all the words that composed the system of the Greek language.' The resonance of texts within other texts and contexts imposes on the critic an obligation to consider all relevant clues to understanding. Thus, far from freeing the critic to ignore the author's history, deconstruction requires exemplary scholarship.

Derrida makes this quite clear in his statement that anyone wishing to critique the works of the eighteenth-century French philosopher Jean-Jacques Rousseau

> must understand and write, even translate French as well as possible, know the corpus of Rousseau as well as possible, including all the contexts that determine it (the literary, philosophical, rhetorical traditions, the history of the French language, society, history, which is to say, so many other things as well). Otherwise, one could indeed say just about anything at all . ... (Derrida, 1988, p. 144)

Deconstruction, then, operates within strict scholarly limits. An awareness of the context from which a text arises is a necessary aspect of deconstruction.

In the case of *The Functions of the Executive*, knowledge about the author is relevant because the text is based, in large part, on Barnard's own experience as an executive (Wolf, 1994, p. 1042). Beginning his business career in 1910, Barnard became president in 1927 of New Jersey Bell, a position he held until 1948. Barnard's executive experience was paralleled and followed by a career in public service. During the Second World War, he was president of a service organization (the USO) whose purpose was to support the morale of American troops. He held numerous other positions, including Chairman of the National Science Foundation and President of the Rockefeller Foundation.

What sets Barnard apart from other organizational theorists is his executive experience combined with an absence of advanced academic training. Although he attended Harvard, Barnard left after three years without a degree. His intellectual debts to Harvard were many, however. Barnard, in the 1920s and 1930s, was close to many intellectuals at the Harvard Business School, including Elton Mayo, Alfred North Whitehead, Talcott Parsons, Robert Merton, Lloyd Warner, George Homans, William F. Whyte, B.F. Skinner and Fritz Roethlisberger. Interaction with these social scientists formed the intellectual background from which *The Functions* emerged. Like many others at Harvard, Barnard was influenced by the doctrines of Vilfredo Pareto concerning the social engineering of sentiments by elites (Parker, 2000). Consistent with this intellectual legacy, Barnard, in the *The Functions*, describes how the moral and rational superiority of executives justifies their creative control over the changeable parameters that govern the ethical judgements of individuals within organizations (see Feldman, 2002, pp. 37–55, for a commentary).

Barnard is, therefore, an example of that rarity in our field: a relatively self-educated practitioner-theorist, who derived from business experience a systematic approach to organizations that was encouraged and validated by the leading intellectuals of the day. What kinds of experience formed the basis for Barnard's theorizing? As president of New Jersey Bell during the 1930s, Barnard confronted a series of economic and technological changes. During the Depression years, with return on investment declining, Barnard announced a planned reduction in working hours for employees, a plan that avoided lay-offs at the cost of reduced worker income. Barnard oversaw the expansion of the company, and the development of numerous technical innovations in the postwar years. But his go-slow approach to such new developments as the rotary dial phone may have contributed to a large drop in net income in 1947. Overall, Barnard's corporate career has been judged as neither a disaster nor a brilliant success (Scott, 1992, p. 74).

Barnard's public service work during the Depression was characterized by a disapproval of the New Deal policies of Roosevelt and a preference for 'voluntary national coordination and industrial cooperation inspired by the moral authority of leaders in private enterprise' (Scott, 1992, p. 75). He impressed people with his wide knowledge and humane policies, but he has also been described as 'aloof and daunting' (Scott, 1992, p. 84), someone whose 'intolerant, often vague, genius was unappealing to his peers' (Scott, 1992, p. 87).

Barnard's book stands by itself as a foundational document in organizational theory, a monograph commonly credited with initiating the formal analysis of organizations. The relative obscurity of its writing has ensured that 'multiple interpretations are possible' (Feldman, 2002, p. 38) and, indeed, the number of insights discovered by commentators in Barnard's book includes some of the greatest hits of the last half-century's social science: bounded rationality, cognitive dissonance theory, self-perception theory, balance theory, goal-setting, equity theory, and a host of other innovative approaches to informal organization, communication and motivation (see Scott, 1992, for a summary). The book that initiated the floodtide of work on formal organization and management studies is, however, itself curiously preoccupied neither with formal organization nor managerial action but with relatively solitary and pre-industrial activities. This aspect of the book, this discourse of solitude, is highlighted in a critique that serves as a brief illustration of how deconstruction might operate in this particular text.

DECONSTRUCTING THE FUNCTIONS OF THE EXECUTIVE

The absence of organization, the presence of pre-industrial other

'The number of formal organizations in the United States is many millions, and it is possible that the number is greater than that of the total population' (Barnard, 1938, p. 4). Barnard's concept of a formal organization was eclectic enough to include 'families and businesses of more than one person' (p. 4). Because Barnard believed that 'fundamentally the same principles that govern simple organizations may be conceived as governing the structure of complex organizations' (p. 95), much of his book is premised on the analysis of not just any simple organization but of apparently pre-industrial organizations, some of which appear to consist of just one solitary individual (such as a man adrift in a boat – see Barnard, p. 14). The irony of Barnard's book, therefore, is that conclusions about industrial corporations are derived from the analysis of simple pre-industrial activities. When reaching for examples, Barnard falls back on illustrations that are simple in their narrative structure and almost child-like in their appeals to our credulity. To demonstrate his axioms concerning the management of large bureaucracies, Barnard reaches for illustrations from a world untouched by bureaucracy of any kind.

We are told about the boy 'who wants an apple' from the 'farmer's tree – not one at home or in the store' (p. 18). A page later we are introduced to an evidently prehistoric hunter with no shoes who 'running to catch an animal for food gives off heat energy to the atmosphere, pulverizes a small amount of gravel, tears off a bit of skin, and somewhat increases his need for food while attempting to secure it' (p. 19). This man's sad fate pales in comparison to his companion of the same paragraph who, we are informed, 'starts an avalanche which destroys his family, or his dwelling, or his stock of stored food'. What, we may ask, do any of these examples have to tell us about administration, executives or, indeed, the conditions of work in the industrialized West?

Barnard persists throughout the book with his lonely figures engaged in sometimes futile and sometimes comical tasks. In the dry and abstract prose that characterizes his delivery of weighty conclusions, the lonely figures that illustrate his points take on a remarkable life of their own. One of his obsessive themes, for example, is the man who again and again faces the task of moving a stone. Let us dignify this man with an invented name – Sisyphus – even if he remains the *Unnamable* in Barnard's Beckettian morality tale. We are introduced to Sisyphus on page 23, shortly after we are informed that, for the purposes of simplicity, human beings are to be treated 'somewhat as automatons which we manipulate' (p. 23).

The first use of the discourse of Sisyphus and his stone is presented to us in two equivalent versions. The first is, 'Stone too large for man', and the second is 'Man too small for stone' (pp. 23–4). The deliberately simplified English of these equivalent discourses presages the impoverished narratives themselves. In each discourse the man is frustrated and seeks out a companion to help him move the stone. Hence the birth of cooperation, according to Barnard. The possibility that cooperation naturally preceded the effort to move the stone, that cooperation might be an end in itself is specifically ruled out together with all other purposes that are 'social in character' (p. 25). Barnard wants to focus attention only on the biological Sisyphus alone on the stage pushing in vain either because he is too small or the stone is too large.

The possibility that Sisyphus might use technology of some kind to get the stone moving is not, at this stage in the man's developing narrative, allowed by Barnard. We are introduced to a universe where the gods ordain trials of strength that must be undertaken with no outside help. This pitiless universe created and controlled by Barnard allows him to examine systematically the limitations of humans, who are considered as mere biological animals. These proto-humans survive in a world with only the rudiments of comfort. When houses or food or family are referred to they are likely to be used as stage props to increase the grief and loneliness of the individual who, as we have seen, succeeds in moving his stone only to have it precipitate an avalanche that destroys the house, the food or the family. But the lonely man may be a mere anthropomorphic projection from our universe on to the oddly functioning world of Barnard's, where, apparently, companionship may be but an 'unsought-for consequence' of the objective 'such as moving a stone' (p. 45). Sisyphus is condemned not merely to labour, but to a singularity of focus that deprives him of any interest in solidarity with fellow humans, even as this very deprivation is used as a ruse to introduce the necessity of cooperation.

The abnormal condition

In Barnard's universe of isolated automatons, successful organizational cooperation is *abnormal*: 'successful cooperation in or by formal organizations is the abnormal, not the normal, condition' (p. 5). Bearing in mind that formal organizations consist, according to Barnard, not only of families but also of 'associations, clubs, societies, fraternities' and 'many millions of formal organizations of short duration, a few hours at most' (p. 4), his vision of cooperation in organizations as an abnormal condition seems difficult to defend. How can it be that people consistently and continually cooperate in family groups, in clubs, in pick-up basketball games and in work organizations, if the prevalence of cooperation is an 'illusion' (p. 5)?

In order to problematize cooperation, to demonstrate that executives are necessary for the motivation and control of purposive organization, Barnard reduces human beings to bundles of biological and physical characteristics, to 'automatons which we manipulate' (p. 23). Under these conditions of 'artificial simplicity' (p. 36), humans engage in cooperation only in order to overcome physical limitations, to move stones too large for one person, for example. Humans considered as biological caricatures untroubled by any need for association are dominated by the need to consume: 'Everything that an individual does is for consumption' (p. 33). These proto-humans come together to move stones, to plant seeds, to store food and to make weapons such as clubs (p. 32). As each limitation of the environment is overcome and the automatons, having moved the stones, look at each other wondering what to do next, 'special organs known as executives' emerge to provide new purposes, to prevent the disintegration of cooperation (p. 37). Thus, the proto-humans invent formal organizations, complete with cooperative and executive systems, purely from egotistical motives of personal consumption.

This intellectual horror tale allows Barnard to derive the necessity of executive action from the most primitive behaviour. The implication seems to be that purposive formal organizations run by executives are impersonal solutions to consumption problems faced by machine-like drones.

The excluded are always present

Only at this point does Barnard acknowledge what is surely obvious to all: cooperation among humans is the *normal* not the abnormal state of affairs. Barnard begins his fourth chapter by acknowledging the omnipresence of the social factors he repeatedly excluded in the first three chapters: 'In all actual cooperative systems, however, factors thus excluded are always present' (p. 38). He ends the fourth chapter with almost the same words: 'social factors are always present in cooperation' and he goes on to an apparent contradiction of his earlier insistence that cooperation was the essential work of executives. Cooperation, he tells us, is, for individuals, a personal desire and for 'systems of cooperation … a social fact' (p. 45). Even more astounding, in the last few words of the crucial fourth chapter, he recognizes that the social factors so rigorously excluded from his depiction of the proto-humans 'determine cooperation itself' (p. 45). Cooperation is no longer driven by consumption needs and organized by executives.

It is now a self-perpetuating system that rewards its members with personal and sociological 'satisfactions'.

The exclusion and inclusion of 'social factors' from the concept of cooperation, the argument that cooperation was both an abnormal condition and yet an ever-present motivation that perpetuated itself in cooperative systems – these apparent contradictions indicate the difficulties Barnard ran into as he attempted to build a theory of organization that justified executive control.

Perhaps the most famous contribution of Barnard's was his definition of organization. However, we should recognize that, mirroring the conflicted nature of his arguments, he gave us three alternative versions of his definition. First, he argued that 'persons' be excluded from his definition because 'the personal point of view has no pertinence here' (p. 43) given that organizations consist of human activities and forces, not individual humans: 'An organization is defined as *a system of consciously coordinated personal activities or forces*' (p. 72, emphasis in the original). But he no sooner banished persons from organizations than he reintroduced them in a slightly different definition on the next page, which he calls the 'central hypothesis of this book … embodied in the definition of a formal organization as a *system of consciously coordinated activities or forces of two or more persons*' (p. 73, original italics). So the persons are both absent (in the first definition) except as shadows encapsulated in the adjective 'personal', and present (in the second definition) that restores the persons, albeit only to the extent that these persons exhibit themselves as 'activities or forces'. Later we have another definition that removes both the 'personal' and the 'persons' to emphasize that, after all, 'organization, simple or complex, is always *an impersonal system of coordinated human efforts*' (p. 94, original italics).

Note that this definition applies to all organizations, including families: 'Fundamentally the same principles that govern simple organizations may be conceived as governing the structure of complex organizations' (p. 95). The iron hand of bureaucracy reaches deep into the simple family structure and governs it as an 'impersonal system'. Cooperation itself becomes reified. Once it comes into existence, like Frankenstein's monster, 'cooperation requires something to do' (p. 52). Cooperation takes centre stage as a devilish agent in its own right. It 'organizes' (p. 58) and its efficiency 'depends upon what it secures and produces … and how it distributes its resources and how it changes motives' (p. 59). It applies forces to factors in order to be able to furnish 'inducements or satisfactions' (p. 59). Cooperation itself, it seems, is the invisible executive to which the persons must submit, either as '*objects* to be *manipulated* … or as *subjects* to be *satisfied*' (p. 40, emphasis in the original).

Executing the culprit

The reification of cooperation as the self-perpetuating system to which persons as either objects or subjects must submit puts Barnard in the difficult position of both removing persons from his conception of organization and yet promoting certain persons – executives – as the practitioners of the arts and sciences of administration. Barnard starts his book with a quotation that exalts the importance of the leader who brings order where otherwise there is chaos: 'For the efficiency of an army consists partly in the order and partly in the general: but chiefly in the latter, because he does not depend upon the order but the order depends on him' (Aristotle, *Metaphysics*). For Barnard, order is synonymous with formal organization. Order is privileged, disorder is denigrated; order is what counts, disorder is the unimportant other, an other that needs to be appropriated, managed, organized and transformed into order.

The privileging of order, and the nervous remarks throughout the text concerning the 'unrest of the present day' (p. 3), the instability of human desire and human environments (p. 149), and the totalitarian solutions (such as fascism) to such instabilities (p. 9) help explain, perhaps, Barnard's insistence that, after all, it is to the art and craft of specific human actors that cooperative systems owe their survival. Whereas the mass of humanity are helpless victims of random forces, dependent on chance outcomes that they can neither foresee nor control, the executive, like Plato's philosopher kings or Nietzsche's superman, achieves a mastery of affairs that, even at the end of the book, remains mysterious. Consider this concluding quotation: '... in human affairs, chance is everything ... [but] art should be there also: for I should say that in a storm there must be surely a great advantage in having the aid of the pilot's art. You would agree?' (Plato, *Laws*).

Thus the book begins and ends with a recognition of the disorder that characterizes ordinary 'human affairs' and praise for the exemplary figures who find order even in chaos. The romanticism of Barnard's exaltation of the executive is at odds with the persistent depersonalization of his portrayal of organizations. Whereas the executive is the pilot in the storm, the organization is an impersonal electromagnetic field of forces (p. 75). Executive 'organization personality' is quite distinct from 'individual personality' (p. 174), enabling executives to overcome in heroic fashion the 'opposed facts ... opposed thought and emotions of human beings' (p. 21). Rather than being tossed around on the storm of emotions and contradictory forces, the executive, like the switchboard operator who showed 'great moral courage' in continuing to provide uninterrupted service, while watching from her office window her mother's house burn down with the mother inside (p. 269), rises godlike above the emotions of pity and fear. The executive is in thrall to cooperation to such an extent that coercion, including homicide, may be regarded as justifiable to persuade others to submit to authority (p. 151).

As the embodiment of the organization's personality, as the human agent through which impersonal cooperation takes action, the executive represents 'the good of the organization' (p. 171) and must therefore take extreme action when evil threatens. Barnard recognizes that his romantic portrayal of the executive as the embodiment of superior authority is a 'fiction' (p. 170), albeit one that is necessary to protect the illusion that cooperation is natural and inevitable. What is this evil that threatens the acceptance of cooperative authority? It is the situation when 'objective authority is flouted for arbitrary or merely temperamental reasons' (p. 171). Human temperaments have no place in the cooperative system, they threaten the survival of impersonal functions, they represent hostile elements that must be destroyed.

In one of the most remarkable passages in the book, Barnard suggests what should be done to people who bring their individual fallibilities into organizational settings, who threaten the fiction of superior authority, whose behaviour falls outside that coldly impersonal zone of indifference to which employees have surrendered their moral rights of rebellion: 'To fail in an obligation intentionally is an act of hostility. This no organization can permit; and it must respond with punitive action if it can, even to the point of incarcerating or *executing the culprit*' (p. 171, italics added). Barnard adds, so that we are in no doubt what he is referring to: 'Leaving an organization in the lurch is not often tolerable' (p. 171). Better let the mother burn than leave the organization's telephone system (so necessary for cooperation) unattended, even for a moment.

DISCUSSION

Barnard sounds the first notes of a theme later developed by the Carnegie school of theorists (Simon, March and Cyert), a siren-like discourse that has seduced the ears of many managerialists. For Barnard, employees are objects to be manipulated or subjects to be satisfied (p. 40), theory is a powerful tool in the service of the executive, and authority must be insinuated through systems of cooperation. The modern corporation functions much like an army in which the personality of the individual is subjugated to the rationalized systems of offices and objectives. In the army, the troops march at the command of the officers, and in the corporation workers obey within wide latitudes the commands of the executive, irrespective of whether they understand the specific objectives of their orders, their actions, their routines (p. 137). The organization strives above all to survive, and to do this it must overcome the natural inclination of the solitary individual to pursue selfish and unstable desires. The executive must inculcate belief in the real existence of common goals (p. 87) in the service of organizational personality. Through the inculcation of motives, employees become capable of ignoring their own interests in order to enact the routines of the organization, exhibiting at times 'extraordinary moral courage' (p. 269).

In organizations, according to Barnard, the average human being is able to overcome an inherent avoidance of decision-making (p. 189) through training in the routine delivery of 'technologically correct conduct' (p. 192). Thus, the average human is privileged to be part of a formal organization's 'superlative degree' of logical processing (p. 186), planned and executed by top executives, a processing that contrasts favourably with the illogicality of the informal activities in which average humans, left to themselves, engage.

This vision of superlative organization run by Guardian-like executives who inculcate motives through benign propaganda aimed at the narrow-minded employees (see p. 190) has powerful echoes throughout organization theory. In our radical re-reading of Barnard's text, we focused not on these more familiar themes, but on the privileging of organizational behaviour itself in contrast with private individual behaviour. Whether floating in boats, moving stones, pursuing apples, or precipitating catastrophes, the lonely mythical figures that flit through Barnard's book illustrate the absence of formal organization even as they ostensibly serve as paradigmatic examples of cooperation. Can it be that Barnard's discourse, his celebration of organizational rationality and cooperation, rests not on the mysterious systemic power of formal systems but on the inherent cooperative camaraderie of individual persons?

CONCLUSION

Our analysis has had a double aim – to critique a foundational text and to demonstrate how deconstruction can alter established discourse. But the question arises as to whether Derrida's analyses affect the wider discourse of science. Has deconstruction changed the way social science is conducted? The influence of Derrida's analyses is pervasive and subtle. For example, in an examination of Aramis – a proposed new transportation system for Paris – one writer draws our attention to the typical ways in which engineers project text into objects.

> They [engineers] invent a means of transportation that does not exist, paper passengers, opportunities that have to be created, places to be designed (often from scratch), component industries, technological revolutions. They're novelists. With just one difference: their project – which is at first indistinguishable from a novel – will gradually veer in one direction or another. Either it will remain a project in the file drawers (and its text is often less amusing to read than that of a novel) or else it will be transformed into an object … Aramis was a text; it came close to becoming, it nearly became, it might have become, an object, an institution, a means of transportation in Paris. In the archives, it turns back into a text, a technological fiction. (Latour, 1996, p. 24)

Note that if the Aramis project is built, it becomes a taken-for-granted aspect of the urban environment, its textuality hidden from view. In Bruno Latour's analysis of the failure of the Aramis project he invents an approach to technology as text that he calls 'scientifiction' and that involves tracing the proliferation of texts concerning Aramis and their analysis. Latour brings processes and objects created by humans but regarded as inhuman within the realm of sociological textual analysis.

The Derridean emphasis on the pervasiveness of text, and the necessity of understanding this text on its own terms, within its own definitions and contradictions, can therefore engender exciting social science. As the Latour example illustrates, for the researcher to inhabit the world of the text and yet to facilitate the critical analysis of the text requires skill, daring and a comprehensive knowledge of the relevant material. Social science is not trapped within its own text. Rather, social science as text relates to all the other discourse within which we live and move and deliberate and write.

NOTE

The authors thank Gavin Jack, Valerie Fournier, David Boje and an anonymous reviewer for their insightful comments on earlier drafts.

REFERENCES

Agger, B. (1991) Critical theory, poststructuralism, postmodernism: Their sociological relevance. *Annual Review of Sociology*, 17: 105–31.

Alexander, J.C. (1989) *Structure and meaning: Rethinking classical sociology*. New York: Columbia University Press.

Alvesson, M. & Kärreman, D. (2000) Varieties of discourse: On the study of organizations through discourse analysis. *Human Relations*, 53: 1125–50.

Barnard, C. (1938) *The functions of the executive*. Cambridge, MA: Harvard University Press.

Currie, M. (1998) *Postmodern narrative theory*. New York: St Martin's Press.

Derrida, J. (1976) *Of Grammatology*. Baltimore, MD: Johns Hopkins University Press.

Derrida, J. (1978) *Writing and difference*. Chicago: University of Chicago Press.

Derrida, J. (1981) *Positions*. London: Athlone Press.

Derrida, J. (1988) *Limited Inc*. Evanston, IL: Northwestern University Press.

Fairclough, N. (1993) Critical discourse analysis and the marketization of public discourse. *Discourse and Society*, 4: 133–59.

Feldman, S.P. (2002) *Memory as a moral decision: The role of ethics in organizational culture*. New Brunswick, NJ: Transaction.

Frug, G.E. (1984) The ideology of bureaucracy in American law. *Harvard Law Review*, 97: 1277–388.

Gasche, R. (1981) '*Setzung*' and '*Ubersetzung*': Notes on Paul de Man. *Diacritics*, 11: 36–57.

Guillen, M.F. (1997) Scientific management's lost aesthetic: Architecture, organization and the Taylorized beauty of the mechanical. *Administrative Science Quarterly*, 42: 682–715.

Kilduff, M. (1993) Deconstructing *Organizations*. *Academy of Management Review*, 18: 13–31.

Kilduff, M. & Dougherty, D. (2000) Change and development in a pluralistic world: The view from the classics. *Academy of Management Review*, 25: 777–82.

Latour, B. (1996) *Aramis or the love of technology*. Cambridge, MA: Harvard University Press.

Martin, J. (1990) Deconstructing organizational taboos: The suppression of gender conflict in organizations. *Organization Science*, 1: 339–59.

Naas, M.B. (1992) Introduction: For example. In J. Derrida, *The other heading: Reflections on today's Europe* (pp. vii–lix). Bloomington, IN: Indiana University Press.

Parker, M. (2000) *Organizational culture and identity*. London: Sage.

Postman, N. (2000) *Building a bridge to the eighteenth century: How the past can improve our future*. New York: Knopf.

Richmond, S. (1995) Deconstruction. In T. Honderich (ed.), *The Oxford companion to philosophy* (pp. 180–1). New York: Oxford University Press.

Sampson, E.E. (1983) Deconstructing psychology's subject. *The Journal of Mind and Behavior*, 4: 135–64.

Scott, W.G. (1992) *Chester I. Barnard and the guardians of the managerial state*. Lawrence, KS: University of Kansas Press.

Sica, A. (1997) Acclaiming the reclaimers: The trials of writing sociology's history. In C. Camic (ed.), *Reclaiming the sociological classics: The state of scholarship* (pp. 282–98). Malden, MA: Blackwell.

Stubbs, M. (1983) *Discourse analysis: The sociolinguistic analysis of natural language*. Oxford: Blackwell.

Wheeler, S.C. III. (1999) Deconstruction. In R. Audi (ed.), *The Cambridge dictionary of philosophy* (2nd edition) (pp. 209–10). Cambridge: Cambridge University Press.

Wolf, W.B. (1994) Understanding Chester Barnard. *International Journal of Public Administration*, 17: 1035–69.

Part III

DISCOURSES AND ORGANIZING

12

Gender, Discourse and Organization: Framing a Shifting Relationship

Karen Lee Ashcraft

Over the past thirty years, scholars have developed complex accounts of the connections among gender, discourse and organization. Increasingly, discourse is thought to constitute – not simply to reflect – gender, organization, and their seemingly inevitable intersection. Speaking generally, the cumulative impact of this shift in view is that it destabilizes enduring notions of organization and gender as fixed entities and identities that meet in measurable ways. It highlights how discursive activity continuously creates, solidifies, disrupts and alters gendered selves and organizational forms. As such, the discursive turn in this line of inquiry points to possibilities for revising relations of power.

Although many scholars have come to embrace the gender–discourse–organization link, they often diverge, at least implicitly, in how they cast the trifold relationship. Discourse, organization and gender alternately appear as figure and ground, producer and product, subject and context, leading and supporting character, and so forth. This chapter rests on the premise that while diverse views of discourse can enrich inquiry, a guide that characterizes common ways of seeing can enhance dialogue, clarifying points of agreement and tension among perspectives. Although several authors have reviewed literature on gender and organization (Calás & Smircich, 1996; Hearn & Parkin, 1983; Meyerson & Kolb, 2000; Mumby, 1996), few have directly considered varied conceptions of discourse across this work. This chapter is thus distinct in its focus on the relation between gender scholarship and the discursive turn in organization studies.

The chapter combs relevant literature with an eye for tacit depictions of the relationship among discourse, gender and organization. Specifically, I identify four prevailing ways of 'framing', or seeing, the nature and function of discourse; Table 12.1 condenses the key assumptions of each lens. With the term 'fram*ing*', I mean to avoid the image of durable mental maps and, instead, to evoke implicit viewpoints, shared by certain approaches to research, which illuminate particular features yet remain provisional, able to engage the alternate perspectives they obscure. As with any effort to categorize, my model assumes probable risks – for example, reducing complexity and diminishing some commonalties in favour of others. Certainly, I acknowledge the viability of other schemas, as well as the presence of overlap across my own categories. As elaborated in the chapter's conclusion, the four perspectives can be said to circulate in productive tension; they converge *and* conflict, calling attention to different facets of discourse and associated implications. Ultimately, my hope is that this effort to organize and simplify scholarship can stimulate new ways of seeing.

For each of the four modes of framing, I describe basic assumptions, illustrative literature, key contributions and troublesome matters. I order my discussion of perspectives in terms of their relative emphasis on 'micro' to 'macro' dimensions of discourse. A first perspective sees discourse as effect or outcome, stressing how gender shapes such organizational communication habits as linguistic choices and leadership tactics. The remaining three perspectives view discourse as constitutive, though in different ways. A second view underscores how everyday talk manufactures gender subjectivities, and so treats discourse as an ongoing, generative, interactive identity performance. Shifting to an institutional level, a third perspective views discourse as a narrative of gender and power relations that gels into organizational design and thereby fosters gendered interaction among members. Increasingly, this lens promotes a two-dimensional view of discourse – an ongoing dialectic between the abstract 'text' latent in organizational form and the concrete 'conversations' that enact the text (e.g., Taylor, 1993). A fourth way of framing looks beyond organizations *per se* to inspect cultural discourses that arrange gender and labour. Through this lens, discourse is social text – large-scale formations or scripts that engender possible selves and social relations. Across gender and organization research, then, discourse carries at least four meanings: (a) engrained personal communication style; (b) the process of mundane interaction; (c) organizational form; and (d) societal narrative. The last three meanings are most germane to the discursive turn in gender and organization studies, for they inform the constitutive power of micro- (i.e., interactional), meso- (i.e., institutional), and macro- (i.e., societal) levels of discourse.

DISCOURSE AS OUTCOME: GENDER IDENTITY ORGANIZES DISCOURSE

A first way of framing defines discourse as communication style – predispositions towards ways of talking, using language and orienting to human relationships. As it treats discourse primarily as an outcome or reflection of one's gender identity, this perspective downplays the constitutive force of discourse. In this sense, it leans towards a representational view, wherein discourse becomes a vehicle for self-expression. Typically, gender refers to a socialized but relatively fixed identity or cultural membership, which is organized around biological sex and which fosters fairly predictable communication habits. Organization carries a dual meaning here. First, it captures the guiding assumption that discourse is gendered in relatively ordered and consistent ways. In its more overt use, organization is a key context in which gender patterns play out.

The vast literature on gender communication differences best illustrates the outcome lens. Much of the early research in this area took sex/gender as a fixed variable associated with variation.[1] The picture changed as scholars distinguished between biological sex categories and gender identity, developing psychodynamic, social psychological and cultural theories of gender-role socialization that portrayed behavioural differences as learned outcomes or social products, rather than intrinsic traits (Bate, 1988; Ivy & Backlund, 2000; Pearson et al., 1991; Wood, 1997). Of particular prominence in this literature is the focus on 'women's ways' or 'feminine styles' of communicating. Many scholars depict men and women as inhabiting distinct communication cultures (e.g., Bate & Taylor, 1988; Johnson, 1989; Kramarae, 1981; Maltz & Borker, 1982; Tannen, 1990, 1994), painting a binary picture of discursive proclivities. Namely, women tend to approach communication as a process of building and maintaining relationships, prioritizing reciprocal personal disclosure, emotional support and provisional speech. Conversely, men typically view interaction as an instrumental activity and, therefore, stress outcomes like persuasion and adopt more analytical, assertive language. By and large, this dualistic view of gender supports popular images of men and women communicating.

Organization appears as a key site where differences become manifest and consequential. Preoccupation with a particular kind of worker and workplace – female professionals in white-collar settings – is evident in the most prolific literature on gender and organization to date: studies of women in management.[2] A substantial share of this work examines how women's language use, perceptions thereof, and resulting interaction patterns like networking erect barriers (e.g., the 'glass ceiling') to women's professional advancement (e.g., Fitzpatrick, 1983; Horgan, 1990; Reardon, 1997; Staley, 1988; Stewart & Clarke-Kudless, 1993; Wilkins & Andersen, 1991).[3] In her popular account of workplace communication, for example, Tannen (1994) explained that many women avoid self-promotion and use hesitant, self-deprecating language – discursive habits that appear weak, ill-suited to upper management.

Given the overwhelming focus on managerial women, it is no surprise that leadership has engrossed more gender and organization scholars than any other discursive activity. This work has gradually shifted attention from women's dubious capacity to lead to 'women's ways' or 'feminine styles' of leading, claiming that women exhibit distinctive, effective and – in some cases – superior leadership (e.g., Bass & Avolio, 1994; Helgesen, 1990; Loden, 1985; Lynch, 1973; Nelson, 1988; Rosener, 1990). And yet, thirty years of empirical study have yielded inconclusive evidence of difference (Butterfield & Grinnell, 1999; Walker et al., 1996; Wilkins & Andersen, 1991). In a leadership study rare for its explicit attention to discourse, Fairhurst (1993) examined the routine talk of women managers to understand the interactive accomplishment of leader–member relationships.

Her detailed analysis revealed commonality (e.g., the primacy of relational concerns) and variation (e.g., ways of engaging in power games) among study participants, indicating how close readings of discourse in practice can usefully nuance the tidy, dualistic depictions often rendered by studies of communication differences.

The discourse-as-outcome perspective demonstrates how even *perceptions* of gender variance in organizational communication translate into tangible political consequences. Several scholars argue that dominant norms of professional communication privilege men's culture; hence, many women will experience 'double binds' or clashing expectations for femininity and professionalism (e.g., Jamieson, 1995; Marshall, 1993; Murphy & Zorn, 1996; Wiley & Eskilson, 1985). Wood and Conrad (1983), for instance, identified key paradoxes, such as professional women's struggles for coherent definitions of self and suitable mentor relationships; they also considered specific communicative responses that perpetuate, redefine and transcend such paradoxes. In addition to exposing discursive dilemmas that daunt women at work, gender difference scholars have sought to raise esteem for ostensibly feminine modes of leadership communication (e.g., Fine & Buzzanell, 2000; Fletcher, 1994).

The outcome lens, however, rests on a tired and problematic rendition of the relation between discourse and difference. Considering shaky empirical foundations, many authors acknowledge that masculine and feminine speech habits do not fit all males and females. Yet they continue to mark those styles by gender, minimizing within-group variations and reifying a binary logic. Additionally, the outcome view takes gender as an isolated feature of identity, ignoring intersections with race, class, sexuality and age. Coupled with the conventional focus on white women professionals, attention to gender alone has fed a tacit assumption that white, middle-class trends represent universal norms (Calás & Smircich, 1996). Overall, then, the outcome perspective suffers from a general lack of context, placing communication in a cultural, political, institutional, historical and structural vacuum. It neglects the power of discourse to produce difference, as well as how that process implicates power. For instance, if masculine expression has come to involve 'doing dominance' and feminine expression, 'doing deference' (West & Zimmerman, 1987), then valuing difference also entails celebrating asymmetrical power relations (Ashcraft & Pacanowsky, 1996) and a gender-based division of labour (Buzzanell, 1995; Calás & Smircich, 1993).

In sum, the outcome perspective holds that gender identity, while initially learned in interaction, becomes a primary source of communication differences. Organizations appear as impartial housing in which variations assume significance, or in which masculine culture denigrates feminine speech. As this view obscures more complex ways in which institutional discourse organizes gender, it carries several risks. Namely, it divides and essentializes women and men, favouring individual over systemic tendencies; it normalizes the language practices of dominant groups; and it supplies difference as a rationale for organizational control and exclusion. In contrast, a second lens draws attention to how difference gets evoked and towards what ends.

DISCOURSE AS PERFORMANCE: DISCOURSE (DIS)ORGANIZES GENDER IDENTITIES

Like the outcome view, a second way of framing highlights the organization of gender identities around difference. But while the outcome lens sees discursive differences as product and evidence of orderly gender identity, the second view examines how discourse produces and undermines this apparent order. Now a phenomenon with constitutive power, discourse refers to the elastic process of mundane interaction, *not* to entrenched dispositions people bring to that process. On a larger scale, 'a discourse' also suggests a temporarily fixed, relatively coherent, context-specific script that guides situated performances. The performance perspective posits a dialectical relation between these levels of discourse but privileges mundane interaction. On the stage of daily life, actors' talk positions self and other in terms of available gender narratives, which facilitate and delimit possibilities for action (Goffman, 1976, 1977; Weedon, 1987). Thus, identity is a partial, unstable discursive effect. Discourse becomes the process of production and gender, a product always in progress. In this sense, the performance view interrogates the link between symbolic and empirical realms, whereas the outcome view presumed its relative stability. Organization carries a dual meaning here as well, as the ongoing social activity of (dis)ordering gender and as a significant social context for identity formation.

The influential work of West and colleagues (West & Fenstermaker, 1995; West & Zimmerman, 1987) illustrates the major conceptual shift at stake in the move from an outcome to a performance perspective. These authors treat gender as a situated and provisional accomplishment – the continuous activity of managing conduct in light of dominant expectations for behaviour that affirms gender difference. However, particular contexts afford a range of acceptable behaviours, and so, at least some room to manoeuvre. Applying this approach directly to organizational life, Gherardi (1994, 1995) argues that we do gender through 'ceremonial work', which marks men and women as members of separate symbolic orders. This work is largely conversational, performed 'through the verbal appreciation of the "gifts" of the other gender' (1995, p. 132). Because most forms of labour beget ambiguities that breach symbolic divisions, we also perform 'remedial work' to repair such violations (Gherardi, 1994). It is worth noting the radical shift from the outcome view: no longer an expression of a stable identity, 'doing difference' – for example, women's tentative speech – becomes part of an ongoing effort to fix gender identities through interaction. And the apparent veracity of communication difference attests to the tenacity of social scripts, *not* to the presence of some steady internal core. Invoking other theoretical traditions, several scholars have advanced similar accounts of the pivotal role of discourse in producing gender identity (Alvesson & Billing, 1992; Bordo, 1990, 1992; Butler, 1990; Fraser, 1989; Kondo, 1990; Weedon, 1987).

This perspective has stimulated research that explores how women and men construct gender through everyday talk in various organizational settings, 'crafting selves' (Kondo, 1990) in ways that summon, (re)produce and/or resist larger discourses of gender relations (e.g., Alvesson, 1998; Ashcraft & Pacanowsky, 1996; Bell & Forbes, 1994; Edley, 2000; Hossfeld, 1993; Pierce, 1995). A common theme in this literature is the link between discourse and the body and, specifically, the ways in which performing professional identity entails the discursive management of sexed bodies. Scholars have considered a range of discourse practices – such as formal and informal storytelling about maternity leave (Ashcraft, 1999; J. Martin, 1990), or conversational tactics facilitating effective 'passing' (Spradlin, 1998) – that discipline working women with respect to age, attractiveness, emotionality, desire, reproductive capacity and sexuality (e.g., Brewis et al., 1997; Dellinger & Williams, 1997; Hochschild, 1993; Pringle, 1989; Trethewey, 1999, 2000, 2001; Wendt, 1995). Likewise, scholars have usefully re-framed sexual harassment as a discursive activity. Even when it involves physical contact, the reality of harassment – its subjects, meaning, experience, consequences, and responses – gets negotiated among members within the context of specific interactions, organizational cultures and larger social narratives of gender, sex, and power (Bingham, 1994; Clair, 1993; Kramarae, 1992; Strine, 1992; Taylor & Conrad, 1992). More recently, authors have considered organizational sexuality as a unique form, fundamentally discursive in nature (Brewis & Grey, 1994; Brewis et al., 1997; Burrell, 1992; Gherardi, 1995; Pringle, 1989). Notably, much of the 'doing gender at work' literature redresses a common criticism of scholarship on organizational discourse: that it downplays things material (Cloud, 2001). Quite the reverse, these works demonstrate how discursive struggles translate into corporeal practices and effects, as well as how the body becomes a potent symbolic resource for identity formation.

Not surprisingly, most studies of this sort spotlight women. But a growing body of research probes the construction of men's bodies and sexualities in organizational talk (e.g., Alvesson, 1998; Cheng, 1996; Collinson & Collinson, 1989; Collinson & Hearn, 1994, 1996a, 1996b; Gherardi, 1995; Roper, 1996). Scholars have discussed distinctions between technical, managerial and working-class speech communities (Collinson, 1988, 1992; Fine et al., 1997; Gherardi, 1995; Gibson & Papa, 2000; Huspek & Kendall, 1991; Mumby, 1998; Willis, 1977), and several authors have undermined any straightforward conception of men's leadership by explicating particular discourses of masculinity embedded in the norms and symbols of managerial communication (Aaltio-Marjosola & Lehtinen, 1998; Hamada, 1996; Hearn, 1994; Kerfoot & Knights, 1993; Linstead, 1997; Martin, 2001).

In sum, the discourse-as-performance perspective illuminates how discourse constitutes gender. Rejecting essentialist accounts of identity, this view re-frames gender difference as situated social scripts. At the level of institutional context, discourse refers to the scripts themselves; at a micro-level, it is the infinite process of negotiating our accountability to them, often adhering but occasionally improvising and re-writing. Unlike the outcome lens, the performance view encourages analyses that couch gender identities in a political context. Emphasis on the multiplicity of masculinities and femininities also reflects attention to another sort of context: the interplay of gender with race, class, sexuality and age. In these ways, the performance perspective offers a richer account of relations between interactional and institutional facets of discourse. Although the performance lens tends to neglect historical context, recent masculinity scholarship (e.g., Rotundo, 1993) suggests the importance of historical consciousness to studies of gender performance.

A tacit assumption of the performance view is that (re)producing difference inevitably amounts to (re)producing inequality. Some critics contend that, by interrogating difference itself and stressing local performances of it, 'doing gender' studies obscures how dominant groups deploy difference as a hegemonic tool (Collins et al., 1995). Put differently, the performance lens may grant too much constitutive power to discourse, especially its micro dimension, thereby diminishing the role of strategic, institutional, structural and material factors. What's more, this conceptual move may be more easily made from (and comforting to?) white, middle-class standpoints (Collins et al., 1995). Additionally, even as the literature emanating from the performance view insists upon a constitutive view of discourse, it often fails to advance precise claims about discourse *per se* – for example, to make clear methodological distinctions among forms of discourse and discourse analytic approaches, or to elaborate specific mechanisms that link mundane talk to larger social constructions and institutions. Generally, organization emerges as a fairly firm stage – or sometimes, as a changing, unfinished set – that establishes preferences and boundaries for gender identity performance. Rarely does organization appear as an actor in its own right.

DISCOURSE AS TEXT-CONVERSATION DIALECTIC: ORGANIZING (EN)GENDERS DISCOURSE

A third perspective pulls organization out of the shadows, exposing a major figure minimized by the focus on individual identity. Building on insights from the performance view, organization is understood as a precarious social construction. Not inert, organization – like gender identity – is constantly in process, brought to life, sustained and transformed by interaction among members (Weick, 1979). Simultaneously, organization guides interaction, predisposing and rewarding members to practise in particular ways (Barley & Tolbert, 1997). Scholars of the communicative constitution of organization refer to this recursive process as an unfolding dialectic between 'conversation' (i.e., organiz*ing*) and 'text' (i.e., organiza*tion*) (e.g., Taylor, 1993; Taylor & Van Every, 2000). On the one hand, organization emerges as members invoke it in discursive activity; from this angle, organizing is conversation. Concurrently, organization is a prerequisite for communication and collective action in modern society, and, in this sense, it supplies a text that guides discursive activity. Created by the constant interplay of conversation and text, organization becomes a macro agent, which serves to represent, and so to discipline, those who speak it into being (Cooren & Taylor, 1997).

Although the third way of framing increasingly taps the discourse-centred, text-conversation model of organization, until recently it has accentuated the text component of the dialectic. Authors writing in this vein have shown particular concern with theorizing organization not merely as a backdrop but as a kind of actor. Organization-as-text actively (en)genders members whose everyday talk both reflects and reifies it. Organization produces gendered discourse, even as it is also a product of such discourse; put succinctly, organizations are gendered discourse communities (Mumby, 1996). As in the performance view, discourse has two faces, but focus shifts towards discourse as a collective narrative of gender and power relations that crystallizes into organizational form or design. Accordingly, authors in this perspective stress the discursive construction of gender at the 'meso' (i.e., intermediate, institutional) level, where it carries abstract, symbolic, structural and normative force.

The radical idea that institutions, not simply individuals, may be gendered stems from early feminist critiques of organization structure. In a classic review of the renowned Hawthorne studies, Acker and Van Houten (1974) were among the first to consider the 'sex structuring' of organization. They argued that organizations employ gender as a central control mechanism, generating apparent variance in organizational behaviour. Likewise, Kanter (1975, 1977) redefined gender difference as a product of structural relations that concentrate women in the invisible and devalued infrastructure or sprinkle them as tokens near the top. Gender serves as a maintenance tool for this system, supplying potent images of how roles should be enacted and by whom. Ferguson (1984) significantly extended this work, depicting bureaucracy as a form of male domination that feminizes managers, workers and clients by binding them in relations of subordination and dependence. Merging these insights, Acker (1990, 1992) argued that gender symbolism does not simply assist or metaphorically represent organization structure. Rather, organizational designs are fundamentally gendered, and gender is a constitutive principle of organization.

Structural critiques laid a foundation for the discourse-friendly claim that organizational forms offer 'maps' (i.e., text) of ideal relations among gender, power and work, which guide the actual process of organizing (i.e., conversation) (Mills & Chiaramonte, 1991). More specifically, scholars examine how bureaucratic forms control and exclude femininities by privileging hierarchical authority, impersonal relations and biased notions of objectivity and rationality (Britton, 1997; Grant & Tancred, 1992; Ianello, 1992; Morgan, 1996; Pierce, 1995; Pringle, 1989). Some authors extend these critiques to discourses embedded in newer organizational forms, like technocracy (e.g., Burris, 1996). Taken together, feminist critiques of organization-as-text reveal, first, how masculinities are subtly inscribed on specific organizational forms (Maier, 1999) and, second, how those forms tacitly direct member interaction and thus institutionalize gender inequality with tangible consequences (Acker, 1990).

Accompanying much of this scholarship is a call for alternative organizational forms, or new meta-communicative 'maps' that revise oppressive configurations of gendered labour. Abundant research on feminist organizations addresses this call (e.g., Ferree & Martin, 1995). Despite the debate over what distinguishes a 'feminist' form (P.Y. Martin, 1990; Mayer, 1995; Riger, 1994), the literature highlights the structure of feminist communities and, specifically, their preference for collectivist, democratic and other anti- bureaucratic, participatory designs (e.g., Ahrens, 1980; Baker, 1982; Rodriguez, 1988). One major conclusion of this research is the difficulty, if not impossibility, of sustaining such structures in practice (e.g., Mansbridge, 1973; Newman, 1980; Sealander & Smith, 1986). Countless studies concur that a fundamental contradiction between feminist ideology and the demands of organizing amid patriarchal capitalism erodes the best of egalitarian designs (e.g., Kleinman, 1996; Morgen, 1988, 1990; Murray, 1988; Pahl, 1985; Ristock, 1990; Seccombe-Eastland, 1988).

By elucidating the role of discourse in organizational form – and, specifically, by developing the text-conversation dialectic – scholars have begun to re-frame such pessimistic conclusions. This work treats feminist organizing as the constant negotiation of 'alternative discourse communities' that seek emancipatory discourses of gender, power and work amid cultural and material constraints (Fraser, 1989; Mumby, 1996). Mumby and Putnam (1992), for example, theorize a counter-discourse of 'bounded emotionality' – a feminist organizing pattern that reclaims marginalized elements of work experience, including 'nurturance, caring, community, supportiveness, and interrelatedness' (p. 474). Crucially, a discourse-based model investigates how conversation grapples with text – how participants struggle to balance 'the paradoxes and tensions that arise from enacting oppositional forms' (Poole et al., 1997, p. 131) and to 'maintain a complex set of ideals, obligations, regulations, and desires all within a social world that continuously makes demands upon them' (Maguire & Mohtar, 1994, p. 239).

From this vantage point, the contradiction between ideology and practice becomes a situated web of dilemmas. A few scholars have begun to investigate the discursive strategies through which members manage such tensions (Buzzanell et al., 1997; Gottfried & Weiss, 1994; Loseke, 1992; Maguire & Mohtar, 1994; Morgen, 1994; Sotirin & Gottfried, 1999). For example, my own work (Ashcraft, 1998, 2000, 2001) examines how the conflicted 'text' of one feminist community posed acute tensions related to personalizing professional relationships, leading and following, practising diversity and formalizing rules. I contend that several ironic communication practices – such as the articulation of provisional policies in formal documents, or the use of parody to exercise *and* deny decisive influence – enabled members to navigate these tensions, ultimately generating a novel hybrid form. This project demonstrates how, by examining the dynamic interaction of conversation and text, a discursive approach can reveal productive moments in the midst of ostensibly debilitating contradiction.

In sum, the discourse-as-dialectic perspective captures the gendered texture of organizational forms. Although early feminist critiques of organization structure stressed the text side of the dialectic, recent scholarship takes the dialectic more seriously by treating organizational forms as discourse communities, directed by loosely shared narratives that members enact and rewrite in mundane interaction. This discursive model articulates a recursive relation between micro and meso layers of discourse. Through this lens, structure is steady and shaky; practice is inventive and derivative; and organizational form is the productive, promiscuous and fleeting site where structure and practice meet. In short, organization is both the subject and object of gendered discourse. As in the performance view, discourse serves a constitutive function, but the focus of that claim shifts from the productive capacity of mundane interaction to that of institutionalized narratives about how people and labour should be configured. Therein lies a crucial difference; that is, the dialectic lens accentuates what the performance view is said to minimize – the *re*productive function of discourse. As 'maps' become entrenched in organizational forms, mundane interaction moves towards sedimentation and discursive alternatives get obscured as a matter of course. Hence, whereas the performance perspective usefully denies structural determinism, the dialectic view counters the reverse temptation to overestimate the muscle of micro-level discourse, reminding us that daily interaction is never free play.

Perhaps the most jarring implication of the dialectic view is a practical one: it negates the popular image of sexist individuals discriminating in gender-neutral settings. Accordingly, it dispels the notion that sensitivity training is sufficient to induce social change; rather it mandates a system overhaul, a radical revision of the organization-as-text. Additionally, the dialectic lens identifies institutional forces at work in the production of gender difference and identity. Unlike authors in the performance perspective, however, scholars donning the dialectic lens have scarcely considered the ways in which gendered organizational forms are also raced and classed (Ashcraft & Allen, 2003; Cheney, 2000; Nkomo, 1992).[4] The dialectic view also clings to the work*place* by underscoring physical sites where labour is performed and obscuring parallel discursive formations that organize gender and work.

DISCOURSE AS SOCIAL TEXT: SOCIETAL DISCOURSES (EN)GENDER ORGANIZATION

A fourth way of framing looks beyond discrete organization*s* – or actual locations of work and related agencies (e.g., labour unions and professional associations) – to other arenas that interlace gender and labour. The macro face of discourse takes precedence in this view, which shifts to a higher level of abstraction than organizational form. Here, 'a discourse' refers to a broader societal narrative embedded in systems of representation, which offer predictable, yet elastic and lucid, yet contradictory tales of possible subjectivities (Bederman, 1995; Connell, 1995; Mouffe, 1995). Gender and organization are mutually constituted in societal discourse. Manifold discourses (of gendered workers, for example) circulate and entwine at once, and those with greater institutional support 'look' and 'feel' more persuasive than others (Hall, 1997; Laclau & Mouffe, 1985).

From the fourth perspective, the notion of text becomes central to discourse in at least two ways. First, just as the dialectic perspective treats organization as a generative text, so the fourth view sees larger societal narrative as a text that directs the formation of identities (e.g., occupational choice) and organizational forms (e.g., proclivity for bureaucracy). Second, this perspective addresses how broad discursive formations and narrative threads find life in particular texts, such as those drawn from film, literature, museum or scholarship (McGee, 1990). People engage these representations in everyday life and, to some extent, the social text approach depends on such micro practices for its legitimacy. Even so, the micro level of discourse remains mostly implicit in this perspective.

The fourth view shifts attention from communication *in* or *of* organization to communication *about* organization, or how society portrays and debates its institutions and the very notion of work. As such, the social text perspective takes 'organization' less as a particular place and more as the production of apparent order amid chaos; simply put, it investigates the (dis)organization of gender and work. Rather than stress how organization occurs at the site of labour, proponents of the social text view accentuate the organizing properties of public discourse, as it shapes available institutions and our participation in them.

The application of the social text perspective to the study of gender and organization is relatively recent, and scholars have emphasized two representational arenas to date: organization theory and popular culture. Feminist authors often observe that organization scholarship rests on gendered premises, as the 'concepts, explanations, modes of thought, and relevant questions used by organizational researchers are congruent with the everyday ways of thinking of managers' (Acker, 1992, p. 249). Certainly, scholars who embrace other ways of framing challenge these conceptual conditions as well. For example, guided by a logic of difference similar to the outcome view, Marshall (1989) indicts the male-bias of traditional career theory, which silences many women's work experiences and 'female values' by normalizing upward, linear movement through an uninterrupted professional career. Similarly, Ashcraft (1999) contests the gendered basis of executive succession theory, which overlooks maternity leave altogether. And Buzzanell (1994) proposes a turn towards 'feminine/feminist values' – such as community, connectedness and integrative thinking – to confront dominant themes in organizational scholarship.

Seen through the social text lens, scholarly discourse becomes more culpable a willing partner that actively promotes and conceals gendered organization with both the form and content of its representational discourse. As Calás and Smicich ask, ' "Who is watching the watchers?" … Shouldn't we also focus our attention on the social consequences of our own practices – organizational research and theorizing?' (1992a, pp. 222–3). In a series of strategically unsettling essays, one or both of these authors have taken classic organization texts to task (e.g., Calás & Smircich, 1988, 1992b; Calás, 1993), surfaced latent seduction therein (Calás & Smircich, 1991), and upended rhetorical devices of time, race and voice that silence marginalized women in management research (e.g., Calás, 1992). Typically, they follow textual deconstruction with radical alternatives for reconstructive writing. In particular, several critics have converged on the recent discourse of feminine leadership (e.g., Fletcher, 1994; Smith & Smits, 1994). For example, Calás and Smircich (1993) juxtapose contemporary fervour for 'feminine styles' against popular discourses of globalization to reveal a familiar cycle in which women's opportunity depends on their utility to patriarchal aims. Like Rosie-the-Riveter, the feminized manager tends the home fires, while 'real' men fight the international battle of consequence. In contrast, Fondas (1997) contends that popular management texts on re-engineering and team-based organization embrace feminized management but deny its gendered origins, thus maintaining the guise of gender-neutral scholarship. Jointly, such criticism demonstrates how scholarly and popular management discourses intertwine to affirm dominant narratives yet spawn loopholes from which to challenge them.

A second line of study highlights representations of gender and work in popular culture (in the vein of Carlone & Taylor, 1998). For instance, Shuler (2000) explores media portrayals of executive women, Ashcraft and Flores (2003) trace representations of a white-collar masculinity crisis across contemporary films, and Triece (1999) offers a historical analysis of working women as constructed in mail-order magazines. Common across these studies is an attempt to reconstruct larger societal discourses from the analysis of specific texts or discourse fragments. In an innovative project, Holmer-Nadesan and Trethewey (2000) combine analysis of the self-help literature on women's workplace success with in-depth interviews, exploring how women internalize and resist popular discourses as they craft their own professional identities. This study is exceptional in its reach across dimensions and domains of discourse – macro and micro, popular literature and mundane performance. In another promising development, some authors have begun to track historical transformations in discourses of manliness amid shifting political economies and labour arrangements (e.g., Bederman, 1995; Kimmel, 1996).

Although in its infancy, the social text perspective challenges the bounds of conventional organization scholarship. By calling attention to the relevance of 'extra-organizational' texts, it looks beyond 'internal' organizational communication and 'external' public relations messages to the organizing function of texts designed for popular consumption, such as news coverage, film, literature and museums. In this sense, it examines intertextuality across institutional messages, exposing discursive affiliations and tensions ordinarily outside the scope of most organization analyses. Particularly noteworthy is the development of a more holistic and, especially, historical perspective on gender discourse. The social text view also reminds us that 'researchers and theorists are part of the relations of ruling' (Acker, 1992, p. 249). Put differently, it holds scholars accountable for their participation in (en)gendering organization and thus shatters the comfortable vision of scholarship as a mirror of organizational life (Calás & Smircich, 1992a).

This perspective tends to prioritize the textual over the material, macro over micro dimensions of discourse, and deconstruction over reconstruction. As such, it minimizes connections to people and the actual political, economic and bodied conditions they inhabit; it evades tangible possibilities for resistance and social change (Cloud, 2001). Recent projects (e.g., Ashcraft & Mumby, 2004; Holmer-Nadesan & Trethewey, 2000), however, suggest the potential of this perspective to sharpen our understanding of the linkages among discourse, history and material conditions.

RE-FRAMING PERSPECTIVES TOWARDS NEW WAYS OF SEEING

Principally, this chapter aims to clarify the varied meanings of, and assumptions about, discourse in gender and organization studies. I contend that most scholars perceive the gender–discourse–organization relationship through four perspectives that construct a complex of agents, processes, and products, as summarized in Table 12.1. I conclude by considering key tensions and potential alliances that define this complex.

The first two ways of framing share a guiding interest in gender identity and difference, yet they offer opposing accounts of the nature and role of discourse. The outcome perspective views gender as a fairly stable, internalized identity that predictably yields distinct communication habits; here, discourse plays a passive role, reflecting some inner core. The performance lens reverses the relationship, casting identity as a fragile product of situated discourse; here, discourse becomes active, manufacturing the appearance of a steady inner core. Both ways of framing treat organizations as a vital setting for the display of difference, but the outcome view accentuates the *manifestation* of difference and the performance view its discursive *production*. In other words, the former presumes that gender spills into organizational talk, while the latter takes organizational talk as a crucial site in which gendered selves are assembled. It is here that the influence of institutional discourse on identity gains visibility.

The dialectic view treats the organization as a collective actor that produces member discourse rather than a passive or neutral context. Organizations are discourse communities in that their very design yields subtly gendered scripts for routine interaction and identity formation; that is, organizational form-as-text calls difference into being and generates possibilities for responding to it. In the dialectic view, organization directs, but by no means determines, member talk. Consequently, attention to text-in-conversation, or the tension between meso and micro discourses, becomes vital. Generally, the second and third ways of framing seek to balance interactional and institutional aspects of discourse, although they reverse the relative emphasis.

Discourse also serves constitutive functions in the social text lens, which looks beyond particular organizations to related arenas, such as organization theory and popular culture. This approach broadens the scope of analysis, enhancing awareness of societal discourses that (en)gender organization. In particular, the social text view positions gendered selves and organizational forms as part of a larger, historically contingent and ever-unfolding discursive field. Generally speaking, the social text perspective leads to analyses that are abstracted from actual bodies and organizations.

Across gender and organization studies, then, discourse carries at least four meanings that vary in their attention to micro and macro dimensions: (a) engrained personal communication habits; (b) mundane interaction process; (c) organizational form; and (d) societal narrative. The final three meanings stem from the discursive turn in gender and organization scholarship and address the constitutive

Table 12.1 *Four ways of framing the discourse–gender–organization relationship*

Frame	View of discourse	View of gender	View of organization	Discourse level/foci	Illustrative literature
Outcome: *Gender Organizes discourse*	Communication style; an effect of gender	Individual identity and cultural membership, socialized and stable	Physical site of work, where predictable gender discourse patterns become manifest	Micro/systematic variations in personal communication habits, taken to reflect gender identity	Gender differences in organizational communication style; some 'women-in-management' and 'glass ceiling' studies
Performance: *Discourse organizes gender*	Mundane interaction (and context-specific narratives that guide it); constitutive	Individual identity, constantly negotiated; an effect of discourse	Physical site of work, where gender is continually (de)stabilized	Micro/ongoing maintenance of identity through interactive (re)production of gender difference	'Doing gender' at work; routine performance of masculinities and femininities in organizational life
Text-conversation dialectic: *Organizing (en)genders discourse*	Narratives embedded in organizational form and enacted in mundane interaction; constitutive	Relations of control; means and effect of organizing	Subject and object of gendered discourse; physical site of work	Meso/institutional construction of gender relations	Organization as gendered; alternative (especially feminist) forms of organizing
Social text: *Discourse (en)genders organization*	Narratives embedded in societal representations of organization; constitutive	Possible subjectivities, relations and practices; effects of discourse	Subject and object of gendered discourse	Macro/construction of gendered labour relations in 'extra-organizational' sites of practice (especially in scholarship and popular culture)	Organization theory as gendered; cultural studies of gendered organization

power of micro (i.e., interactional), meso (i.e., institutional) and macro (i.e. societal) levels of discourse analysis. The insights and vulnerabilities of each perspective are implied by the definition(s) of discourse to which it adheres. For example, the outcome lens is limited by its rigid and de-contextualized accounts of individual identity, whereas the performance view becomes suspect for excessive faith in interactional flexibility. The dialectic perspective remains susceptible to charges of overstressing organization-as-text, while the social text view risks detachment from organizations and the people who bring them to life.

Distinctions and tensions notwithstanding, much can be gained from exploring how these ways of seeing overlap. Several authors blend perspectives, blurring the needless boundaries between them. For instance, the performance and social text perspectives intermingle when scholars examine how concrete identity performances invoke popular discourses of gender and work (e.g., Holmer-Nadesan & Trethewey, 2000). The outcome, dialectic and social text approaches merge when gender difference theorists advocate organizational forms or theory founded upon 'female values' (e.g., Marshall, 1989, 1993). And studies of doing gender amid specific organizational forms integrate the performance and dialectic views (e.g., Alvesson, 1998; Britton, 1997; Sotirin & Gottfried, 1999). Importantly, such projects indicate the promise of fluid borders among perspectives.

The four perspectives can work together in productive tension, albeit within limits. They illuminate multiple layers, players, processes, functions and products of discourse; they assist one another with respective vulnerabilities. In short, each way of framing generates moments of 'truth' about gendered organization, which also obscure alternating and simultaneous truths. The challenge, then, becomes avoiding the temptation to champion a single understanding. Together, the perspectives elucidate multiple ways in which discourse evokes and follows material conditions, such as environmental factors that shape socialization, economic and institutional changes, and practices of bodily discipline. Another example of useful tension surfaces in discord among the perspectives about the source, function and political nature of difference. Specifically, despite the harsh criticisms levied against it, the outcome lens flags entrenched faith in gender dualisms and its effect on the arrangement, practice and interpretation of work. In this way, it counters the optimism of the performance view, which redresses the deterministic and apolitical tendencies of the outcome frame. In sum, interaction among ways of framing reveals the conflicted realities of gendered organizing. Hence, one promising future direction entails developing projects that traverse perspectives, as modelled by the studies cited above.

Certainly, no way of framing is beyond reproach. Several suggestions gleaned from this analysis can guide scholars to extend existing perspectives in new directions. For instance, studies that focus on difference can devote systematic attention to intersecting forms of identity, disrupting the tendency to naturalize white, middle-class, heterosexual communication. Authors should especially avoid depicting difference as a timeless, universal and politically neutral artifact. Close attention to both discourse in practice (e.g., Fairhurst, 1993) and discourse in socio-political, historical context (e.g., Rotundo, 1993) will focus this effort.

Those who concentrate on organizational form can expand their usual focus on professional subjects and contexts by devoting increased attention to institutional discourses that push the conventional boundaries of work and organization (e.g., volunteerism, domestic labour or gangs). Simultaneously, they can investigate how meta-communicative 'maps' are raced and classed, as well as gendered. Finally, scholars who stress societal discourses of gender and organization can whet the cultural, historical and material consciousness of the literature, bridging macro and micro discursive activities.

This chapter is premised on a particular reading of gender and organization scholarship. On the one hand, discourse analysis has become increasingly pivotal in the wake of the discursive turn, which furnishes a friendly intellectual context for the study of organizing gender and gendering organization. Simultaneously, the literature is often vague on the precise meaning and role of discourse, as well as on particular forms of discourse to examine and ways to study them. For the most part, 'discourse' invokes social constructionist assumptions and marks the constitutive force of such phenomena as language, symbolism, interaction, narrative and text. Assuming that such ambiguity is useful *and* encumbering, I encourage both enhanced precision about discourse *and* resistance to closure. This chapter articulates common ways of framing – dynamic lenses that can transform through interplay. It is not an elusive quest for some optimal perspective, since shifting frames evokes new ways of seeing. With this in mind, I seek to clarify how we already see – to bring the tangled ties among gender, organization and discourse into sharper focus.

NOTES

1 For an appraisal of the literature on sex differences in communication, see Canary and Hause (1993).
2 For extensive reviews of this literature, see Billing and Alvesson (1998) and Calás and Smircich (1996).
3 For a fuller review and critique, see Buzzanell (1995), Powell (1999), and Reuther and Fairhurst (2000).
4 Such neglect is especially evident in feminist critiques of traditional organizational forms, whereas research on feminist organizing offers notable exceptions (e.g., Morgen, 1988; Scott, 1998; West, 1990).

REFERENCES

Aaltio-Marjosola, I. & Lehtinen, J. (1998) Male managers as fathers? Contrasting management, fatherhood, and masculinity. *Human Relations*, 51: 121–36.

Acker, J. (1990) Hierarchies, jobs, bodies: A theory of gendered organizations. *Gender & Society*, 4: 139–58.

Acker, J. (1992) Gendering organizational theory. In A.J. Mills & P. Tancred (eds), *Gendering organizational analysis* (pp. 248–60). Thousand Oaks, CA: Sage.

Acker, J. & Van Houten, D.R. (1974) Differential recruitment and control: The sex structuring of organizations. *Administrative Science Quarterly*, 19: 152–63.

Ahrens, L. (1980) Battered women's refuges: Feminist cooperatives *vs.* social service institutions. *Radical America*, 14: 41–7.

Alvesson, M. (1998) Gender relations and identity at work: A case study of masculinities and femininities in an advertising agency. *Human Relations*, 51: 969–1005.

Alvesson, M. & Billing, Y.D. (1992) Gender and organization: Towards a differentiated understanding. *Organization Studies*, 13: 73–103.

Ashcraft, K.L. (1998) Assessing alternative(s): Contradiction and invention in a feminist organization. Unpublished doctoral dissertation, University of Colorado, Boulder.

Ashcraft, K.L. (1999) Managing maternity leave: A qualitative analysis of temporary executive succession. *Administrative Science Quarterly*, 44: 40–80.

Ashcraft, K.L. (2000) Empowering 'professional' relationships: Organizational communication meets feminist practice. *Management Communication Quarterly*, 13: 347–92.

Ashcraft, K.L. (2001) Organized dissonance: Feminist bureaucracy as hybrid organizational form. *Academy of Management Journal*, 44: 1301–22.

Ashcraft, K.L. & Allen, B.J. (2003) The racial foundations of organizational communication. *Communication Theory*, 13: 5–38.

Ashcraft, K.L. & Flores, L.A. (2003) 'Slaves with white collars': Persistent performances of masculinity in crisis. *Text and Performance Quarterly*, 23: 1–29.

Ashcraft, K.L. & Mumby, D.K. (2004) *Reworking gender: A feminist communicology of organization*. Thousand Oaks, CA: Sage.

Ashcraft, K.L. & Pacanowsky, M.E. (1996) 'A woman's worst enemy': Reflections on a narrative of organizational life and female identity. *Journal of Applied Communication*, 24: 217–39.

Baker, A.J. (1982) The problem of authority in radical movement groups: A case study of a lesbian-feminist organization. *Journal of Applied Behavior Science*, 18: 323–41.

Barley, S.R. & Tolbert, P.S. (1997) Institutionalization and structuration: Studying the links between action and institution. *Organization Studies*, 18: 93–117.

Bass, B. & Avolio, B. (1994) Shatter the glass ceiling: Women may make better managers. *Human Resource Management*, 33: 549–60.

Bate, B. (1988) *Communication and the sexes*. New York: Harper & Row.

Bate, B. & Taylor, A. (eds) (1988) *Women communicating: Studies of women's talk*. Norwood, NJ: Ablex.

Bederman, G. (1995) *Manliness & civilization: A cultural history of gender and race in the United States, 1880–1917*. Chicago: University of Chicago Press.

Bell, E. & Forbes, L.C. (1994) Office folklore in the academic paperwork empire: The interstitial space of gendered (con)texts. *Text and Performance Quarterly*, 14: 181–96.

Billing, Y.D. & Alvesson, M. (1998) *Gender, managers, and organizations*. New York: Walter de Gruyter.

Bingham, S.G. (ed.) (1994) *Conceptualizing sexual harassment as discursive practice*. Westport, CT: Praeger.

Bordo, S. (1990) Feminism, postmodernism and gender-scepticism. In L.J. Nicholson (ed.), *Feminism/postmodernism* (pp. 133–56). New York: Routledge.

Bordo, S. (1992) Postmodern subjects, postmodern bodies. *Feminist Studies*, 18: 159–75.

Brewis, J. & Grey, C. (1994) Re-eroticizing the organization: An exegesis and critique. *Gender, Work and Organization*, 1: 67–82.

Brewis, J., Hampton, M.P. & Linstead, S. (1997) Unpacking Priscilla: Subjectivity and identity in the organization of gendered appearance. *Human Relations*, 50: 1275–304.

Britton, D.M. (1997) Gendered organizational logic: Policy and practice in men's and women's prisons. *Gender & Society*, 11: 796–818.

Butler, J. (1990) *Gender trouble: Feminism and the subversion of identity*. New York: Routledge.

Burrell, G. (1992) The organization of pleasure. In M. Alvesson & H. Willmott (eds), *Critical management studies* (pp. 67–88). London: Sage.

Burris, B.H. (1996) Technocracy, patriarchy, and management. In D.L. Collinson & J. Hearn (eds), *Men as managers, managers as men* (pp. 61–77). Thousand Oaks, CA: Sage.

Butterfield, D.A. & Grinnell, J.P. (1999) 'Re-viewing' gender, leadership, and managerial behavior: Do three decades of research tell us anything? In G.N. Powell (ed.), *Handbook of gender and work* (pp. 223–38). Thousand Oaks, CA: Sage.

Buzzanell, P.M. (1994) Gaining a voice: Feminist organizational communication theorizing. *Management Communication Quarterly*, 7: 339–83.

Buzzanell, P.M. (1995) Reframing the glass ceiling as a socially constructed process: Implications for understanding and change. *Communication Monographs*, 62: 327–54.

Buzzanell, P., Ellingson, L., Silvio, C., Pasch, V., Dale, B., Mauro, G., Smith, E., Weir, N. & Martin, C. (1997) Leadership processes in alternative organizations: Invitational and dramaturgical leadership. *Communication Studies*, 48: 285–310.

Calás, M. (1992) An/other silent voice? Representing 'Hispanic woman' in organizational texts. In A.J. Mills & P. Tancred (eds), *Gendering organizational analysis* (pp. 201–21). Newbury Park, CA: Sage.

Calás, M.B. (1993) Deconstructing charismatic leadership: Re-reading Weber from the darker side. *Leadership Quarterly*, 4: 305–28.

Calás, M.B. & Smircich, L. (1988) Reading leadership as a form of cultural analysis. In J.G. Hunt, R.D. Baliga, H.P. Dachler & C.A. Schriesheim (eds), *Emerging leadership vistas* (pp. 201–26). Lexington, MA: Lexington Press.

Calás, M.B. & Smircich, L. (1991) Voicing seduction to silence leadership. *Organization Studies*, 12: 567–602.

Calás, M.B. & Smircich, L. (1992a) Using the 'F' word: Feminist theories and the social consequences of organizational research. In A.J. Mills & P.Tancred (eds), *Gendering organizational analysis* (pp. 222–34). Thousand Oaks, CA: Sage.

Calás, M. & Smircich, L. (1992b) Rewriting gender into organizational theorizing: Directions from feminist perspectives. In M. Reed & M. Hughes (eds), *Re-thinking organization: New directions in organizational research and analysis* (pp. 227–53). London: Sage.

Calás, M. & Smircich, L. (1993) Dangerous liaisons: The 'feminine-in-management' meets 'globalization'. *Business Horizons*, 36: 71–81.

Calás, M. & Smircich, L. (1996) From 'the woman's' point of view: Feminist approaches to organization studies. In S.R. Clegg, C. Hardy & W.R. Nord (eds), *Handbook of Organization Studies* (pp. 218–57). Thousand Oaks, CA: Sage.

Canary, D.K. & Hause, K.S. (1993) Is there any reason to research sex differences in communication? *Communication Quarterly*, 41: 129–44.

Carlone, D. & Taylor, B. (1998) Organizational communication and cultural studies: A review essay. *Communication Theory*, 8: 337–67.

Cheney, G. (2000) Thinking 'differently' about organizational communication: Why, how, and where? *Management Communication Quarterly*, 14: 132–41.

Cheng, C. (ed.) (1996) *Masculinities in organizations*. Thousand Oaks, CA: Sage.

Clair, R.P. (1993) The use of framing devices to sequester organizational narratives: Hegemony and harassment. *Communication Monographs*, 60: 113–36.

Cloud, D. (2001) Laboring under the sign of the new: Cultural studies, organizational communication, and the fallacy of the new economy. *Management Communication Quarterly*, 15: 268–78.

Collins, P.H., Maldonado, L.A., Takagi, D.Y., Thorne, B., Weber, L. & Winant, H. (1995) Symposium: On West & Fenstermaker's 'Doing Difference'. *Gender & Society*, 9: 491–513.

Collinson, D.L. (1988) 'Engineering humour': Masculinity, joking, and conflict in shop-floor relations. *Organization Studies*, 9: 181–99.

Collinson, D. (1992) *Managing the shop floor: Subjectivity, masculinity, and workplace culture*. New York: De Gruyter.

Collinson, D.L. & Collinson, M. (1989) Sexuality in the workplace: The domination of men's sexuality. In J. Hearn, D. Sheppard, P. Tancred-Sheriff & G. Burell (eds), *The sexuality of organization* (pp. 91–109). Newbury Park, CA: Sage.

Collinson, D.L. & Hearn, J. (1994) Naming men as men: Implications for work, organization and management. *Gender, Work, and Organization*, 1: 2–22.

Collinson, D.L. & Hearn, J. (eds) (1996a) *Men as managers, managers as men*. Thousand Oaks, CA: Sage.

Collinson, D.L. & Hearn, J. (1996b) 'Men' at 'work': Multiple masculinities/multiple workplaces. In M. Mac an Ghail (ed.), *Understanding masculinities: Social relations and cultural arenas* (pp. 61–76). Buckingham: Open University Press.

Connell, R.W. (1995) *Masculinities*. Berkeley, CA: University of California Press.

Cooren, F. & Taylor, J.R. (1997) Organization as an effect of mediation: Redefining the link between organization and communication. *Communication Theory*, 7: 219–60.

Dellinger, K. & Williams, C.L. (1997) Makeup at work: Negotiating appearance rules in the workplace. *Gender & Society*, 11: 151–77.

Edley, P.P. (2000) Discursive essentializing in a woman-owned business: Gendered stereotypes and strategic subordination. *Management Communication Quarterly*, 14: 271–306.

Fairhurst, G.T. (1993) The leader–member exchange patterns of women leaders in industry: A discourse analysis. *Communication Monographs*, 60: 321–51.

Ferguson, K. (1984) *The feminist case against bureaucracy*. Philadelphia, PA: Temple University Press.

Ferree, M.M. & Martin, P.Y. (eds) (1995) *Feminist organizations: Harvest of the new women's movement*. Philadelphia, PA: Temple University Press.

Fine, M.G. & Buzzanell, P.M. (2000) Walking the high wire: Leadership theorizing, daily acts, and tensions. In P.M. Buzzanell (ed.), *Rethinking organizational and managerial communication from feminist perspectives* (pp. 128–56). Thousand Oaks, CA: Sage.

Fine, M., Weis, L., Addelston, J. & Marusza, J. (1997) (In)secure times: Constructing white working-class masculinities in the late 20th century. *Gender & Society*, 11: 568.

Fitzpatrick, M.A. (1983) Effective interpersonal communication for women of the corporation: Think like a man, talk like a lady. In J. Pilotta (ed.), *Women in organizations: Barriers and breakthroughs* (pp. 73–84). Prospect Heights, IL: Waveland Press.

Fletcher, J.K. (1994) Castrating the female advantage: Feminist standpoint research and management science. *Journal of Management Inquiry*, 3: 74–82.

Fondas, N. (1997) Feminization unveiled: Management qualities in contemporary writings. *Academy of Management Review*, 22: 257–82.

Fraser, N. (1989) *Unruly practices: Power, discourse and gender in contemporary social theory*. Minneapolis, MN: University of Minnesota Press.

Gherardi, S. (1994) The gender we think, the gender we do in our everyday organizational lives. *Human Relations*, 47: 591–610.

Gherardi, S. (1995) *Gender, symbolism, and organizational cultures*. Newbury Park, CA: Sage.

Gibson, M.K. & Papa, M.J. (2000) The mud, the blood, and the beer guys: Organizational osmosis in blue-collar work groups. *Journal of Applied Communication Research*, 28: 66–86.

Goffman, E. (1976) Gender display. *Studies in the Anthropology of Visual Communication*, 3: 69–77.

Goffman, E. (1977) The arrangement between the sexes. *Theory & Society*, 4: 301–31.

Gottfried, H. & Weiss, P. (1994) A compound feminist organization: Purdue University's Council on the Status of Women. *Women & Politics*, 14: 23–44.

Grant, J. & Tancred, P. (1992) A feminist perspective on state bureaucracy. In A.J. Mills & P. Tancred-Sheriff (eds), *Gendering organizational analysis* (pp. 112–28). Newbury Park, CA: Sage.

Hall, S. (1997) The work of representation. In S. Hall (ed.), *Representation: Cultural representations and signifying practices* (pp. 13–64). London: Sage/Open University Press.

Hamada, T. (1996) Unwrapping Euro-American masculinity in a Japanese multinational corporation. In C. Cheng (ed.), *Masculinities in organizations* (pp. 160–76). Thousand Oaks, CA: Sage.

Hearn, J. (1994) The organization of violence: Men, gender relations, organizations, and violences. *Human Relations*, 47: 731–54.

Hearn, J. & Parkin, W. (1983) Gender and organizations: A selective review and critique of a neglected area. *Organization Studies*, 4: 219–42.

Helgesen, S. (1990) *The female advantage: Women's ways of leadership.* New York: Doubleday.

Hochschild, A.R. (1993) The managed heart. In A.M. Jaggar & P.S. Rothenberg (eds), *Feminist frameworks: Alternative theoretical accounts of the relations between women and men* (pp. 328–34). New York: McGraw-Hill.

Holmer-Nadesan, M. & Trethewey, A. (2000) Performing the enterprising subject: Gendered strategies for success (?). *Text and Peformance Quarterly*, 20: 223–50.

Horgan, D. (1990) Why women sometimes talk themselves out of success and how managers can help. *Performance & Instruction*, November–December: 20–2.

Hossfeld, K.J. (1993) 'Their logic against them': Contradictions in sex, race, and class in Silicon Valley. In A.M. Jaggar & P.S. Rothenberg (eds), *Feminist frameworks: Alternative theoretical accounts of the relations between women and men* (pp. 346–8). New York: McGraw-Hill.

Huspek, M. & Kendall, K.E. (1991) On withholding political voice: An analysis of the political vocabulary of a 'nonpolitical' speech community. *Quarterly Journal of Speech*, 77: 1–19.

Ianello, K.P. (1992) *Decisions without hierarchy: Feminist interventions in organization theory and practice.* New York: Routledge.

Ivy, D.K. & Backlund, P. (2000) *Exploring genderspeak: Personal effectiveness in gender communication* (2nd edition). Boston, MA: McGraw-Hill.

Jamieson, K.H. (1995) *Beyond the double bind: Women and leadership.* New York: Oxford University Press.

Johnson, F.L. (1989) Women's culture and communication: An analytic perspective. In C.M. Lont & S.A. Friedley (eds), *Beyond boundaries: Sex and gender diversity in communication* (pp. 301–16). Fairfax, VA: George Mason University Press.

Kanter, R.M. (1975) Women and the structure of organizations: Explorations in theory and behavior. In M. Millman & R.M. Kanter (eds), *Another voice: Feminist perspectives on social life and social science* (pp. 34–74). Garden City, NY: Anchor Books.

Kanter, R.M. (1977) *Men and women of the corporation.* New York: Basic Books.

Kerfoot, D. & Knights, D. (1993) Management, masculinity and manipulation: From paternalism to corporate strategy in financial services in Britain. *Journal of Management Studies*, 30: 659–77.

Kimmel, M. (1996) *Manhood in America: A cultural history.* New York: Free Press.

Kleinman, S. (1996) *Opposing ambitions: Gender identity in an alternative organization.* Chicago: University of Chicago Press.

Kondo, D.K. (1990) *Crafting selves: Power, gender, and discourses of identity in a Japanese workplace.* Chicago: University of Chicago Press.

Kramarae, C. (1981) *Women and men speaking: Frameworks for analysis.* Rowley, MA: Newbury House.

Kramarae, C. (1992) Harassment and everyday life. In L.F. Rakow (ed.), *Women making meaning: New feminist directions in communication* (pp. 100–20). New York: Routledge, Chapman and Hall.

Laclau, E. & Mouffe, C. (1985) *Hegemony and socialist strategy: Towards a radical democratic politics.* London: Verso.

Linstead, S. (1997) Abjection and organization: Men, violence, and management. *Human Relations*, 50: 1115–45.

Loden, M. (1985) *Feminine leadership, or how to succeed in business without being one of the boys*. New York: Times Books.

Loseke, D. (1992) *The battered woman and shelters: The social construction of wife abuse*. Albany, NY: SUNY Press.

Lynch, E.M. (1973) *The executive suite – feminine style*. New York: AMACOM.

Maguire, M. & Mohtar, L.F. (1994) Performance and the celebration of a subaltern counterpublic. *Text and Performance Quarterly*, 14: 238–52.

Maier, M. (1999) On the gendered substructure of organization: Dimensions and dilemmas of corporate masculinity. In G.N. Powell (ed.), *Handbook of gender and work* (pp. 69–94). Thousand Oaks, CA: Sage.

Maltz, D. & Borker, R. (1982) A cultural approach to male–female miscommunication. In J.J. Gumpertz (ed.), *Language and social identity* (pp. 196–216). Cambridge: Cambridge University Press.

Mansbridge, J.J. (1973) Time, emotion, and inequality: Three problems of participatory groups. *Journal of Applied Behavioral Science*, 9: 351–67.

Marshall, J. (1989) Re-visioning career concepts: A feminist invitation. In M.B. Arthur, D.T. Hall & B.S. Lawrence (eds), *Handbook of career theory* (pp. 275–91). Cambridge: Cambridge University Press.

Marshall, J. (1993) Viewing organizational communication from a feminist perspective: A critique and some offerings. In S.A. Deetz (ed.), *Communication Yearbook* 16 (pp. 122–43). Newbury Park, CA: Sage.

Martin, J. (1990) Deconstructing organizational taboos: The suppression of gender conflict in organizations. *Organization Science*, 1: 339–59.

Martin, P.Y. (1990) Rethinking feminist organizations. *Gender & Society*, 4: 182–206.

Martin, P.Y. (2001) 'Mobilizing masculinities': Women's experiences of men at work. *Organization*, 8: 587–618.

Mayer, A.M. (1995) Feminism-in-practice: Implications for feminist theory. Paper presented at the annual meeting of the International Communication Association, Albuquerque, NM, May.

McGee, M.C. (1990) Text, context, and the fragmentation of contemporary culture. *Western Journal of Communication*, 54: 274–89.

Meyerson, D.E. & Kolb, D.M. (2000) Moving out of the 'armchair': Developing a framework to bridge the gap between feminist theory and practice. *Organization*, 7: 553–71.

Mills, A. & Chiaramonte, P. (1991) Organization as gendered communication act. *Canadian Journal of Communication*, 16: 381–98.

Morgan, D. (1996) The gender of bureaucracy. In D.L. Collinson & J. Hearn (eds), *Men as managers, managers as men* (pp. 61–77). Thousand Oaks, CA: Sage.

Morgen, S. (1988) The dream of diversity, the dilemma of difference: Race and class contradictions in a feminist health clinic. In J. Sole (ed.), *Anthropology for the nineties* (pp. 370–80). New York: Free Press.

Morgen, S. (1990) Contradictions in feminist practice: Individualism and collectivism in a feminist health center. In C. Calhoun (ed.), *Comparative social research supplement 1* (pp. 9–59). Greenwich, CT: JAI Press.

Morgen, S. (1994) Personalizing personnel decisions in feminist organizational theory and practice. *Human Relations*, 47: 665–84.

Mouffe, C. (1995) Feminism, citizenship, and radical democratic politics. In L. Nicholson & S. Seidman (eds), *Social postmodernism* (pp. 315–31). Cambridge: Cambridge University Press.

Mumby, D.K. (1996) Feminism, postmodernism, and organizational communication studies: A critical reading. *Management Communication Quarterly*, 9: 259–95.

Mumby, D.K. (1998) Organizing men: Power, discourse, and the social construction of masculinity(s) in the workplace. *Communication Theory*, 8: 164–83.

Mumby, D.K. & Putnam, L.L. (1992) The politics of emotion: A feminist reading of bounded rationality. *Academy of Management Review*, 17: 465–86.

Murphy, B.O. & Zorn, T. (1996) Gendered interaction in professional relationships. In J.T. Wood (ed.), *Gendered relationships* (pp. 213–32). Mountain View, CA: Mayfield.

Murray, S.B. (1988) The unhappy marriage of theory and practice: An analysis of a battered women's shelter. *NWSA Journal*, 1: 75–92.

Nelson, M.W. (1988) Women's ways: Interactive patterns in predominantly female research teams. In B. Bate & A. Taylor (eds), *Women communicating: Studies of women's talk* (pp. 199–232). Norwood, NJ: Ablex.

Newman, K. (1980) Incipient bureaucracy: The development of hierarchies in egalitarian organizations. In G.M. Britan & R. Cohen (eds), *Hierarchy & society* (pp. 143–63). Philadelphia, PA: Institute for the Study of Human Issues, Inc.

Nkomo, S.M. (1992) The emperor has no clothes: Rewriting 'race in organizations'. *Academy of Management Review*, 17: 487–513.

Pahl, J. (1985) Refuges for battered women: Ideology and action. *Feminist Review*, 19: 25–43.

Pearson, J.C., Turner, L.H. & Todd-Mancillas, W. (1991) *Gender and communication* (2nd edition). Dubuque, IA: Wm.C. Brown.

Pierce, J.L. (1995) *Gender trials: Emotional lives in contemporary law firms*. Berkeley, CA: University of California Press.

Poole, M.S., Putnam, L.L. & Seibold, D.R. (1997) Organizational communication in the 21st century. *Management Communication Quarterly*, 11: 127–38.

Powell, G.M. (1999) Reflections on the glass ceiling: Recent trends and future prospects. In G.N. Powell (ed.), *Handbook of gender and work* (pp. 325–46). Thousand Oaks, CA: Sage.

Pringle, R. (1989) Bureaucracy, rationality, and sexuality: The case of secretaries. In J. Hearn, D. Sheppard, P. Tancred-Sheriff & G. Burell (eds), *The sexuality of organization* (pp. 158–77). Newbury Park, CA: Sage.

Reardon, K.K. (1997) Dysfunctional communication patterns in the workplace: Closing the gap between men and women. In D. Dunn (ed.), *Workplace/women's place: An anthology* (pp. 165–80). Los Angeles, CA: Roxbury.

Reuther, C. & Fairhurst, G.T. (2000) Chaos theory and the glass ceiling. In P.M. Buzzanell (ed.), *Rethinking organizational and managerial communication from feminist perspectives* (pp. 236–53). Thousand Oaks, CA: Sage.

Riger, S. (1994) Challenges of success: Stages of growth in feminist organizations. *Feminist Studies*, 20: 275–300.

Ristock, J.L. (1990) Canadian feminist social service collectives: Caring and contradictions. In L. Albrecht & R. M. Brewer (eds), *Bridges of power: Women's multicultural alliances* (pp. 172–81). Philadelphia, PA: New Society Publishers.

Rodriguez, N.M. (1988) Transcending bureaucracy: Feminist politics at a shelter for battered women. *Gender & Society*, 2: 214–27.

Roper, M. (1996) 'Seduction and succession': Circuits of homosocial desire in management. In D.L. Collinson & J. Hearn (eds), *Men as managers, managers as men* (pp. 210–26). Thousand Oaks, CA: Sage.

Rosener, J.B. (1990) Ways women lead. *Harvard Business Review*, 68: 119–25.

Rotundo, E.A. (1993) *American manhood: Transformations in masculinity from the revolution to the modern era*. New York: Basic Books.

Scott, E.K. (1998) Creating partnerships for change: Alliances and betrayals in the racial politics of two feminist organizations. *Gender & Society*, 12: 400–23.

Sealander, J. & Smith, D. (1986) The rise and fall of feminist organizations in the 1970s: Dayton as a case study. *Feminist Studies*, 12: 321–41.

Seccombe-Eastland, L. (1988) Ideology, contradiction, and change in a feminist book store. In B. Bate & A. Taylor (eds), *Women communicating: Studies of women's talk* (pp. 251–76). Norwood, NJ: Ablex.

Shuler, S. (2000) Breaking through the glass ceiling without breaking a nail: Portrayal of women executives in the popular business press. Paper presented at the annual meeting of the National Communication Association, Seattle, WA, November.

Smith, P.L. & Smits, S.J. (1994) The feminization of leadership? *Training & Development*, 48: 43–6.

Sotirin, P. & Gottfried, H. (1999) The ambivalent dynamics of secretarial 'bitching': Control, resistance, and the construction of identity. *Organization*, 6: 57–80.

Spradlin, A.L. (1998) The price of 'passing': A lesbian perspective on authenticity in organizations. *Management Communication Quarterly*, 11: 598–605.

Staley, C.C. (1988) The communicative power of women managers: Doubts, dilemmas, and management development programs. In C.A. Valentine & N. Hoar (eds), *Women and communicative power: Theory, research, and practice* (pp. 36–48). Annandale, VA: Speech Communication Association.

Stewart, L.P. & Clarke-Kudless, D. (1993) Communication in corporate settings. In L.P. Arless & D.J. Borisoff (eds), *Women and men communicating*. Fort Worth, TX: Harcourt Brace Jovanovich.

Strine, M.S. (1992) Understanding 'how things work': Sexual harassment and academic culture. *Journal of Applied Communication Research*, 20: 391–400.

Tannen, D. (1990) *You just don't understand: Women and men in conversation*. New York: William Morrow.

Tannen, D. (1994) *Talking from 9 to 5: How women's and men's conversational styles affect who gets heard, who gets credit, and what gets done at work*. New York: William Morrow.

Taylor, B. & Conrad, C. (1992) Narratives of sexual harassment: Organizational dimensions. *Journal of Applied Communication Research*, 20: 401–18.

Taylor, J.R. (1993) *Rethinking the theory of organizational communication: How to read an organization*. Norwood, NJ: Ablex.

Taylor, J.R. & Van Every, E.J. (2000) *The emergent organization: Communication as its site and surface*. Mahwah, NJ: LEA.

Trethewey, A. (1999) Disciplined bodies: Women's embodied identities at work. *Organization Studies*, 20: 423–50.

Trethewey, A. (2000) Revisioning control: A feminist critique of discipline bodies. In P.M. Buzzanell (ed.), *Rethinking organizational and managerial communication from feminist perspectives* (pp. 107–27). Thousand Oaks, CA: Sage.

Trethewey, A. (2001) Reproducing and resisting the master narrative of decline: Midlife professional women's experiences of aging. *Management Communication Quarterly*, 15: 183–226.

Triece, M.E. (1999) The practical true woman: Reconciling women and work in popular mail-order magazines, 1900–1920. *Critical Studies in Mass Communication*, 16: 42–62.

Walker, H.A., Ilardi, B.C., McMahon, A.M. & Fennell, M.L. (1996) Gender, interaction, and leadership. *Social Psychology Quarterly*, 59: 255–72.

Weedon, C. (1987) *Feminist practice and poststructuralist theory*. Oxford: Basil Blackwell.

Weick, K.E. (1979) *The social psychology of organizing* (2nd edition). New York: Random House.

Wendt, R.F. (1995) Women in positions of service: The politicized body. *Communication Studies*, 46: 276–96.

West, C. & Fenstermaker, S. (1995) Doing difference. *Gender & Society*, 9: 8–37.

West, C. & Zimmerman, D.H. (1987) Doing gender. *Gender & Society*, 1: 125–51.

West, G. (1990) Cooperation and conflict among women in the welfare rights movement. In L. Albrecht & R.M. Brewer (eds), *Bridges of power: Women's multicultural alliances* (pp. 149–71). Philadelphia, PA: New Society Publishers.

Wiley, M.G. & Eskilson, A. (1985) Speech style, gender stereotypes, and corporate success: What if women talk more like men? *Sex Roles*, 12: 993–1007.

Wilkins, B.M. & Andersen, P.A. (1991) Gender differences and similarities in management communication. *Management Communication Quarterly*, 5: 6–35.

Willis, P. (1977) *Learning to labor: How working-class kids get working-class jobs*. New York: Columbia University Press.

Wood, J.T. (1997) *Gendered lives: Communication, gender, and culture*. Belmont, CA: Wadsworth.

Wood, J.T. & Conrad, C.R. (1983) Paradox in the experience of professional women. *Western Journal of Speech Communication*, 47: 305–22.

13

Discourse and Power

Cynthia Hardy and Nelson Phillips

In this chapter, we examine the link between power and discourse and propose a framework for understanding the complex relationship between them. Our framework grows out of the observation that power and discourse are mutually constitutive: at any particular moment in time, discourses – structured collections of texts and associated practices of textual production, transmission and consumption – shape the system of power that exists in a particular context by holding in place the categories and identities upon which it rests. In other words, the distribution of power among actors, the forms of power on which actors can draw, and the types of actor that may exercise power in a given situation are constituted by discourse and are, at a particular moment, fixed. Over time, however, discourses evolve as this system of power privileges certain actors, enabling them to construct and disseminate texts. Depending on the dynamics of transmission and consumption, these texts may influence the broader discourse and shape the discursive context. Thus, the power dynamics that characterize a particular context determine, at least partially, how and why certain actors are able to influence the processes of textual production and consumption that result in new texts that transform, modify or reinforce discourses. In other words, discourse shapes relations of power while relations of power shape who influences discourse over time and in what way.

In order to understand the relationship between power and discourse, we need to unpack this complex, mutually constitutive relationship. The discourse literature has been largely preoccupied with one aspect of this relationship: how particular discourses produce systems of power. The work of Foucault has been particularly influential in this regard, focusing attention on the role of discourse in determining the relations of power that characterize a particular social context. However, the way in which the dynamics of power influence discourse has received less attention. Yet, it is clear that some actors will be better able to produce texts that affect discourse because of their access to various kinds of power. Accordingly, we re-examine the power literature from a discursive perspective to draw out the power dynamics that lead actors to produce texts that influence discourse and to understand why some actors are more successful in modifying discourse in ways that are useful to them.

In the remainder of this chapter, we first consider how discourse shapes power, with particular reference to Foucault's work and critical discourse analysis. We then examine how power can shape discourse, integrating both power and discourse literatures to explore the ability of actors to produce texts that influence discourses over time. In exploring these relationships, we develop a model that embodies both in a mutually constitutive relationship and then draw implications for future research.

THE REALM OF DISCOURSE

In this section, we explore the realm of discourse – how discourse produces power relationships and, in so doing, constitutes the social context for action. We define discourses as structured collections of texts, and associated practices of textual production, transmission and consumption, located in a historical and social context (Fairclough, 1992, 1995; Parker, 1992). By text, we refer not only to verbal and written transcriptions but also to 'any kind of symbolic expression requiring a physical medium and permitting of permanent storage' (Taylor & Van Every, 1993, p. 109; also see Fairclough, 1992; Van Dijk, 1997), including cultural artefacts, visual representations buildings, clothes, etc. (e.g., Grant et al., 1998; Wood & Kroger, 2000).

Figure 13.1 depicts how discourse produces a system of power relationships that structures the context in which action takes place. Discourse comprises three sets of practices – the production, transmission, and consumption of texts – that together result in bodies of related texts that invoke, refer to and challenge each other. Discourse also constitutes power relations by holding in place meanings associated with concepts, objects and subject positions, which distribute power and privileges among

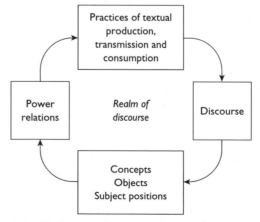

Figure 13.1 *The relationship between discourse and power*

actors. Although discourses change over time, at any single moment the relationship between discourse and power is effectively fixed. Actors may act more or less purposefully to produce texts, but to do so, they can only draw on existing discourses. Therefore the texts they can construct and how they can construct (and interpret) them are limited and shaped by the nature of prevailing discourses. In this way, discourse structures the social space for action. We discuss this model in more detail below.

Discourse

Our view of discourse is heavily influenced by the work of Foucault (1976, 1979, 1982, 1998, 2002). He defines discourses, or discursive formations, as bodies of knowledge that 'systematically form the object of which they speak' (Foucault, 1979, p. 49). They retain a wide range of 'socio-historically contingent linguistic, cultural, technical and organizational resources which actively constitute fields of knowledge and the practices they instantiate' (Reed, 1998, p. 195). In other words, discourses do not simply describe the social world; they constitute it by bringing certain phenomena into being through the way in which they categorize and make sense of an otherwise meaningless reality (Parker, 1992).

Each discourse is defined by a set of rules or principles – the rules of formation – that lead to the appearance of particular objects through the categories and identities that make up recognizable social worlds. Discourse lays down the 'conditions of possibility' that determine what can be said, by whom, and when.

> [Discourse] governs the way that a topic can be meaningfully talked about and reasoned about. It also influences how ideas are put into practice and used to regulate the conduct of others. Just as a discourse 'rules in' certain ways of talking about a topic, defining an acceptable and intelligible way to talk, write or conduct oneself, so also, by definition, it 'rules out', limits and restricts other ways of talking, of conducting ourselves in relation to the topic or constructing knowledge about it. (Hall, 2001, p. 72)

In this way, discourse 'disciplines' subjects in that actors are known – and know themselves – only within the confines of a particular discursive context (Mumby, 2001). Discourse thus influences individuals' experiences or subjectivity, and their ability to think, speak and act, resulting in material effects in the form of practices and interactions.

Writers building on Foucault's work argue that discourses constitute particular types of social category, which we refer to as concepts, objects and subject positions (Fairclough, 1992; Hardy & Phillips, 1999). Concepts are the 'ideas, categories, relationships, and theories through which we understand the world and relate to one another' (Hardy & Phillips, 1999, p. 3). They refer to what Fairclough and Wodak (1997, p. 258) term 'objects of knowledge' and what Taylor (1985, p. 36) calls 'intersubjective meanings'. They are more or less contested social constructions that form culturally and historically situated frames for understanding social reality (Harré, 1979). Concepts reside only in the realm of the ideal but have effects in the material world through the way in which they provide the meanings that underlie social action and influence practices.

Objects are part of the practical realm: they are partially ideal but have a material aspect. When a concept is used to make some aspect of material reality meaningful, an object is constituted. This is not to say that in constituting objects discourse 'reveals' a pre-existing reality, but rather that concepts are discursively attached to particular parts of an ambiguous material world, which has physical existence independent from our experience of it but which can only be understood with reference to prevailing discourses (e.g., Laclau & Mouffe, 1987). For example, in their study of refugee determination, Hardy and Phillips (1999) contrasted the concept of a refugee that existed only in the ideal with the individuals who were constituted as refugees through the discursive practices associated with the refugee determination process. These individuals were not refugees in some essential sense whose refugee status was 'revealed'. Rather, the discourse of refugee determination and the concept of a refugee provided a set of discursive practices that allowed individuals to be constituted as particular objects with the label of 'refugee'.

Subject positions are locations in social space from which certain delimited agents can act. Subjects are socially produced as individuals take up positions within the discourse (Knights & Willmott, 1989; Townley, 1993) and different subjects have different rights:

> These different subject positions have different rights to speak. In other words, some individuals, by virtue of their position in the discourse, will warrant a louder voice than others, while others may warrant no voice at all. (Hardy & Phillips, 1999, p. 4)

For example, the discourse of psychiatry includes the subject position of psychiatrist who has the right to produce texts that determine the sanity of individuals.

In summary, discourse actively constructs a social context through the way in which it constitutes objects of knowledge, categories of social subjects, forms of 'self', social relationships and conceptual frameworks (Deetz, 1992; Fairclough, 1992, 1995; Fairclough & Wodak, 1997). Our framework shows how this process occurs through the construction of concepts, objects and subject positions. We argue that by creating the meanings associated with these basic categories we make sense of and act upon the world. Thus discourse is imprinted on the world through a myriad of social practices that flow from the meaning it creates.

From discourse to power

The social reality constituted by discourse is imbued with power. For Foucault, discourse – or at least the knowledge that it instantiates – is inseparable from power. Power is embedded in knowledge and any knowledge system constitutes a system of power, as succinctly summarized in Foucault's conception of 'power/knowledge'. Knowledge, in the form of broad discourses, constitutes the building blocks of social systems in a profound and inescapable way. In constructing the available identities, ideas and social objects, the context of power is formed: 'it is in discourse that power and knowledge are joined together' (Foucault, 1998, p. 100).

This conception of power 'is not something that is acquired, seized, or shared, something that one holds on to or allows to slip away; power is exercised from innumerable points, in the interplay of nonegalitarian relations' (Foucault, 1998, p. 94). In other words, power is not something connected to agents but represents a complex web of relations determined by systems of knowledge constituted in discourse.

> Power is everywhere; not because it embraces everything, but because it comes from everywhere ... power is not an institution, and not a structure; neither is it a certain strength we are endowed with; it is the name that one attributes to a complex strategical situation in a particular society. (Foucault, 1998, p. 93)

According to this view, power is embedded in discourse in a way that captures advantaged and disadvantaged alike in its web (Deetz, 1992). Each situation has its own politics of truth as the mechanisms that distinguish truth and falsehood and define knowledge vary according to the prevailing discourses (Foucault, 1980). Power relations are therefore constituted in discourse, as is resistance. In fact, power and resistance are inextricably intertwined: 'resistance is never in a position of exteriority in relation to power' (Foucault, 1998, p. 95). Where there is power there is also resistance and, just as power is a broad, agentless web, resistance forms through a myriad of points distributed across the web of power in an irregular, localized fashion; not at a central focal point.

This view emphasizes that an actor is powerful only within a particular discursive context since discourses create the categories of power within which actors operate.

> To the extent that meanings become fixed or reified in certain forms, which then articulate particular practices, agents and relations, this fixity is power. Power is the apparent order of taken-for-granted categories of existence, as they are fixed and represented in a myriad of discursive forms and practices. (Clegg, 1989, p. 183)

It is thus the discursive context, rather than the subjectivity of any individual actor, that influences the nature of political strategy. In fact, for Foucault, the notion of agents acting purposefully in some way not determined by the discourse is antithetical. No statement occurs accidentally (i.e., unconnected to discourse) and the task for the discourse analyst is to ask: 'how is it that one particular statement appeared rather than another?' (Foucault, 2002, p. 30). Discourse forms a cage within which only certain actions are possible. Thus the nature of the discursive formation in place at any point in time is the source of power (and resistance), and the possibilities for speaking and acting that exist at any point in time.

Foucault's work involves a relatively fatalistic view of power (Burman & Parker, 1993), which has been criticized for its failure to recognize that power/knowledge discourses are an expression of strategies of control by identifiable actors within a wider historical and institutional context (Fairclough, 1992; Reed, 1998). Critical discourse analysts, in particular, while sharing Foucault's unique theoretical perspective, argue that it makes it difficult to investigate the role of dominant groups in producing systems of advantage and disadvantage in society, let alone to introduce emancipatory interests (Fairclough, 1992; Fairclough & Wodak, 1997).

Accordingly, critical discourse analysis tempers Foucault's deterministic view of discourse in two ways. First, it argues that discourses are never completely cohesive and devoid of internal tensions, and are therefore never able totally to determine social reality. They are always partial, often cross-cut by inconsistencies and contradiction, and almost always contested to some degree. Second, it argues that actors are commonly embedded in multiple discourses. The tensions between these discourses produces a discursive space in which the agent can play one discourse off against another, draw on multiple discourses to create new forms of interdiscursivity, and otherwise move between and across multiple discourses.

These limits of discourse provide a substantial space within which agents can act self-interestedly and work towards discursive change that privileges their interests and goals. Of interest are the 'dialogical struggle (or struggles) as reflected in the privileging of a particular discourse and the marginalization of others' (Keenoy et al., 1997, p. 150; Mumby & Stohl, 1991), which occur as the meanings of concepts, objects and subject positions are contested and challenged (Phillips & Hardy, 1997).

> Discourse as a political practice establishes, sustains and changes power relations, and the collective entities (classes, blocs, communities, groups) between which power relations obtain. Discourse as an ideological practice constitutes, naturalizes, sustains and changes significations of the world from diverse positions in power relations. (Fairclough, 1992, p. 67)

In other words, critical discourse analysis explores how discursive activity structures the social space within which actors act, how it privileges some actors at the expense of others, as well as the way in which changes in the discourse result in different constellations of advantage and disadvantage.

From this perspective, the study of power 'requires research and theory that examine how communication practices construct identities, experiences and ways of knowing that serve some interests over others' (Mumby, 2001, p. 614). Much of the mainstream work on power has paid little attention to the communicative aspects of power, however, and has instead focused on how the possession of resources allows actors to change the behaviour of others (see, for example, Hardy & Clegg, 1996). However, this behavioural focus obscures how the social categories and meanings around which political struggles take place are constructed.

> The most effective use of power occurs when those with power are able to get those without power to interpret the world from the former's point of view. Power is exercised through a set of interpretive frames that each worker incorporates as part of his or her organizational identity. (Mumby & Clair, 1997, p. 184)

Actors exercise power by 'fixing' the inter-subjective meanings that create a particular reality (Mumby, 2001) and articulating meaning in ways that legitimate their particular views as 'natural' and 'inevitable', link the actions and preferences of other actors to the achievement of their interests, and make particular socially constructed structures take on a neutral and objective appearance (e.g., Hardy, 1985; Deetz & Mumby, 1990).

To conclude, in holding the particular meanings associated with sets of concepts, objects and subject positions in place, discourse shapes the power relations that characterize any setting at a particular moment in time and, in turn, influences what can be said and who can say it. This aspect of discourse is shown in Figure 13.1. While a Foucauldian view largely dismisses agency by self-interested actors, critical discourse analysis suggests there is space for the use of power, albeit within a particular discursive context. This space and the exercise of the power associated with positions within a discourse provide the potential for possible change in discourses over time.

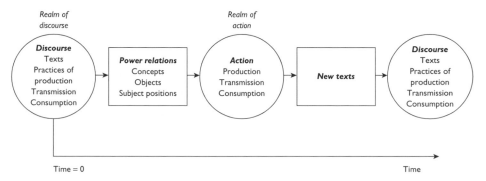

Figure 13.2 *The relationship between power and discourse*

THE REALM OF ACTION

In the realm of action, we examine how action affects discourse through time. We will explore how the practices of textual production, transmission and consumption that provide shared templates for interaction and interpretation are enacted over time, leading to the addition of new texts that reinforce or change discourses and the objects, concepts and subject positions that characterize a social context.

The realm of action is depicted in the right-hand portion of Figure 13.2 where actors engage in the production, transmission and consumption of texts over time. As new texts are added to the discourse, the discourse evolves, leading to changes in the concepts, objects and subject positions – and the power relations – that characterize the social context of action. The left side of Figure 13.2 depicts the relation between discourse and power at a moment in time that provides the context in which practices are enacted as certain actors are able to produce texts that influence discourses (which, in turn, would result in new power relations through changes in concepts, objects and subject positions). In other words, relations of power affect the production of texts and shape discourse through time. Thus discourse and power are in a mutually constitutive relationship where one direction of influence – discourse to power – is revealed when examined at a moment in time, while the other – power to discourse – is revealed over time.

In order to understand how discourses develop over time and the role of action by interested actors in this process, we examine how the production, distribution and consumption of texts contribute 'in varying degrees to the reproduction or transformation ... of the existing order of discourse' (Fairclough, 1992, p. 93). This raises three questions. The first concerns the subject positions that are able to produce and transmit such texts. If power is exercised only as a result of 'the position the agent occupies in the field and by the regularities of the field of discursive production' (Chalaby, 1996, p. 695), what forms of power are relevant to the production of texts. The second question concerns the nature of the texts – many texts are read only by a handful of people in the immediate locality. They may reflect existing discourses, but they certainly do not change them and only reproduce them in a trivial way. What are, then, the characteristics that enable some texts to 'stick', or in Ricœur's (1981, 1986) terms become sufficiently 'fixated', and to displace, transform, modify or reinforce existing discourses? The third question relates to the consumption of texts. More specifically, how do practices of consumption affect the interpretation of texts? Or, to put it another way, what role do consumers of texts play in the determination of their meaning?

Production and transmission

The discussion above suggests that actors can influence discourse by using texts as 'weapons' (Chalaby, 1996, p. 694) to create meanings compatible with their interests (Deetz & Mumby, 1990). Being able to produce and transmit a text, however, requires the exercise of various forms of power. As Taylor and Van Every point out: a text is a technology that requires the mastery of skills and acquisition of tools for its production. It is also 'susceptible to the elaboration of methods in a search for perfectibility, and it lends itself to specialization, and the acquiring of expertise by an elite trained in the procedures of its production' (Taylor & Van Every, 1993, p. 108). As a result, textual production does not only revolve around the use of power in struggles over meaning, but also in the exercise of what Clegg (1989) calls episodic power – the use of the formal power and authority, the manipulation of scarce resources, coalition, co-optation, and even physical coercion that are part and parcel of everyday life (Lawrence et al., 2001). This is not to deny that the constitution of these power sources emanates from the prevailing discourses or that power is associated with the position in a particular discursive context rather than the individual *per se*.

> [A]gents are not sovereign in their texts and their discursive production is not their production. The point is not to suppress the agent, but to understand that his or her discursive production is ultimately determined by the internal rules of the field that he or she belongs to. (Chalaby, 1996, p. 695)

It does, however, suggest that actors who inhabit subject positions associated with (a) formal power; (b) critical resources; (c) network links; and (d) discursive legitimacy are more likely to be able to produce texts that are intended to convey particular meanings and to produce particular effects (even though the actual effects may differ from those intended). We discuss each of these forms of power below.

First, a position may be constructed as possessing *formal power*, by which we refer to authority and decision-making power (French & Raven, 1968; Astley & Sachdeva, 1984) – the recognized right to make a decision as well as access to decision-making processes (Hardy & Leiba-O'Sullivan, 1998). Actors constructed as having formal power within a particular discursive field, that is, those that occupy subject positions that 'warrant voice' (Potter & Wetherell, 1987; Hardy et al., 2000), are more likely to be able to produce texts that stick.

Second, some positions are associated with access to *critical resources*, which may include money, rewards, sanctions, information, credibility, expertise, contacts with members of higher echelons and the control of money (e.g., French & Raven, 1968; Pettigrew, 1973; Pfeffer, 1981), depending on the discursive field. The generation of texts requires some form of physical support system that allows it to be inscribed, whether it is as simple as the human body or pen and paper, or as complex as video conferencing or global publishing networks (Taylor et al., 1996). Accordingly, particular resources will be needed to generate texts, which may range from oratorical expertise to the ownership of telecommunication and media companies.

Third, an actor may be powerful through *network links* and social relationships among actors (Bourdieu, 1993). Such linkages allow actors 'to exercise power through constituting alliances, integrating rather than merely dominating subordinate groups, winning their consent, achieving a precarious equilibrium' (Fairclough, 1992, p. 94).

> [I]t is a question of enlisting enough allies on one's side to become recognized as a legitimate author or spokesperson for the text … A text that passes the networking test is gradually transformed from an artefact of the network into a fact – just part of reality in that organizational world. (Taylor et al., 1996, 26–7)

Finally, a position may be associated with *discursive legitimacy* (Mumby & Stohl, 1991; Fairclough, 1992; Parker, 1992; Phillips & Hardy, 1997).

> To be recognized as the voice of an organization, and its legitimate agent, the aspirant must produce a text and have it authenticated by a sufficient number of people (or at least the right people) to have one's own right to speak become consensually validated. (Taylor et al., 1996, pp. 26–7)

Actors in these positions are understood to be speaking legitimately for issues and organizations affected by the domain (Phillips & Brown, 1993).

These forms of power are distributed among many subject positions; consequently, no single actor is able to determine completely a dominant set of meanings. Instead, multiple actors in a variety of positions are implicated in holding dominant meanings in place (sometimes with considerable struggle among them). As a result, discursive closure is never complete (Clegg, 1989), leaving space for resistance through the production of 'counter'-texts. One such example is whistleblowing: 'the disclosure of illegal, unethical, or harmful practices in the workplace to parties who might take action' (Rothschild & Miethe, 1994, p. 254). In these cases, an actor produces a text contrary to the dominant discourses (often related to organizational compliance and ethicality). Because the actor producing and transmitting this counter-text has discursive legitimacy – as a witness – his or her texts can have a significant and negative effect on the dominant discourse promoted by the organization.

Similarly, Murphy (1998) discusses an example of resistance where a group of flight attendants filed charges of discrimination against their employer for what they saw as the discriminatory application of weight limits on female employees. The company, also worried about negative press reports, reversed its policy. The flight attendants were thus able to formally give voice in the form of texts submitted to the Equal Opportunity Commission, which, in turn, risked sparking the production of other texts in the media. These texts – both actual and threatened – enabled them to resist the dominant discourse in the organization.

Texts

Here we examine some characteristics of texts and the relations among them that make them more likely to influence discourse. What is it about a text that allows it to construct meaning, not just locally, but in a way that embeds it in discourse, producing a broader discursive effect? How do texts become sufficiently categorized, generalized and anonymous (Taylor et al., 1996) to act as trans-situational organizing mechanisms (Cooren & Taylor, 1997) by linking the local circumstances of their production to larger networks? We suggest that the influence of texts on discourse depends on: (a) their connection to other texts and discourses; (b) the genre of the text; (c) the linguistic devices they employ; and (d) the degree to which they become distanced from the circumstances of their original production.

First, one important component of any text concerns the way it connects to other texts and discourses. *Intertextuality* is important because it 'is not just "the text" that shapes interpretation', but also 'those other texts which interpreters variably bring to the interpretation process' (Fairclough, 1992, p. 85). We argue that a text is more likely to influence discourse if it evokes other texts, either explicitly or implicitly, because it will draw on understandings and meanings that are more broadly grounded. Accordingly, Ott and Walter (2000) have shown how intertextuality in film is an identifiable stylistic device consciously employed by the producer to evoke a particular response from the audience. *Interdiscursivity* – drawing on other discourses – also constitutes a conscious strategy in textual production. For example, Fairclough (1992) explores how British Prime Minister Margaret Thatcher's discourse juxtaposed authoritarian, democratic and egalitarian elements, as well as patriarchy and feminism, helping to create a new discourse of political power for a woman leader within a wider context of changed economic and political conditions. Similarly, Livesey (2002) found ExxonMobil's articulation of hybrid discourses, such as eco-efficiency, helped to legitimate 'the market' and de-legitimate radical environmentalism, governmental action and climate science.

Second, the form or *genre* of the text is also important. Genres are recognized types of communication characterized by particular conventions, which are invoked in response to a recurrent set of circumstances, for example, letters, memos, meetings, training seminars, résumés and announcements (Yates & Orlikowski, 1992, 2002), as well as new forms of communication technology, such as electronic mail, online databases, voice mail cellular phones (Rice & Gattiker, 2001). A genre shares similar substance (topics discussed) and form (observable physical and linguistic features) (Kuhn, 1997). While constrained by broader discourse, genres are also 'instruments and outcomes of organizational power' which are 'exercised through the manipulation or selective application of existing genre rules' (Yates & Orlikowski, 1992, p. 321). Accordingly, we suggest that texts are more likely to influence discourse when they conform to particular genres associated with the particular context.

Third, texts enact a variety of *textual devices* that help to shape meaning. A considerable amount of research has, in different ways, explored the performative effects of talk and text by, for example, examining the use of narrative and storytelling (e.g., Boje, 1991, 1995; O'Connor, 1995, 2002), rhetoric (Watson, 1995), and tropes (Oswick et al., 2002), particularly metaphor (Grant & Oswick, 1996; Oswick et al., 2002) and irony (Hatch, 1997). Humour (e.g., Collinson, 1988) and cynicism (Fleming & Spicer, 2003) have been explored, as have such rites and rituals as business planning (Oakes et al., 1998), accounting practices (Hoskins & Maeve, 1987) and Christmas party speeches (Rosen, 1988). Despite the many different approaches, this work converges in its assumptions concerning the organizing properties of language through the ways in which such devices help to shape meaning (Barry & Elmes, 1997), persuade others (Witten, 1993), legitimate interests (Mumby, 1993), and reproduce social structure (Langellier & Peterson, 1993).

Finally, the degree to which the text is *distanced* from the locally situated conversation and 'escapes the finite horizon lived by its author' (Ricœur, 1971, p. 543) objectifies the text, producing a reified representation of 'what is no longer a situated set of conversations but what has instead become an organizational template so abstract that it can be taken to represent not just some but *all* of the conversations it refers to' (Taylor et al., 1996, p. 26). This process occurs in a number of ways: as spoken text is translated into conversational action; as conversation is turned into a narrative representation so the exchange can be understood; and as texts are transcribed in the form of more permanent media to permit storage and relocation. More important for embedding texts in discourse are the creation of media-specific or professional language; materialized physical frame of conversation, for example, office, manuals, software; and formal transmission practices, such as publication, diffusion and broadcasting (see Taylor et al., 1996).

These different features of the text can be employed in ways that make them particularly appealing to potential consumers. Sufficiently seductive texts may actually lead to the transmission and reproduction of texts by consumers rather than the producer. For example, Wittgenstein's early thoughts were originally distributed as mimeographs by his students. These writings, which eventually became known as the Blue and Brown Books, were highly influential despite an almost complete lack of interest in their dissemination on the part of the author and were widely read before they were ever formally published.

Instances of resistance are also linked to seductive texts. Even actors who inhabit low power subject positions can resist dominant meanings through the production of seductive texts For example, Mumby (1997, p. 361) discusses examples of resistance through 'organization graffiti' texts. Two of their examples were 'I have PMS today and a handgun. Any questions?' and 'Mary called in dead today. She used up all her sick days.' In these two cases, seductive texts – that were clever plays on the dominant discourse – represented a 'deconstructive move' that challenged authority and rule-making. Humour often plays an important role in the seductive texts of low power actors (e.g., Collinson, 1988; Hatch, 1997), as does aesthetics, for example, by the way in which independent and underground music texts pass through informal networks.

Consumption

Texts have to be consumed in order for their meaning to be interpreted and established; even dominant discourses involve a struggle in which producers and consumers alike are implicated in the co-construction of their meaning and its reproduction. Consumption is, as a result, unpredictable since there are a number of contradictory ways in which knowledge can be consumed, some of which may be quite different from the intentions of the original producers (Hassard & Keleman, 2002). De Certeau (1984) has shown how the 'tactics of consumption' can subvert and resist the intentions of dominant groups. For example, he points out how the individuals on whom Spanish laws and practices were imposed during the colonization of Latin America neither accepted or rejected them, but transformed them. 'They metaphorized the dominant order: they made it function in another register … The imposed knowledge and symbolisms become objects manipulated by practitioners who have not produced them' (De Certeau, 1984, p. 32). In other words, the meaning of a text is not pre-given, regardless of how powerful the producer of the text may seem or how seductive the text appears – 'disjunctures always exist between dominant readings and individual interpretations' (Mumby, 1997, p. 359). The interpretation of a text is thus a negotiated process of social construction within which there is always scope for resistance to dominant readings through discursive acts that provide alternative meanings (Murphy, 1998).

Sometimes, alternative meanings are constructed in private, in 'hidden transcripts' that power holders do not see directly (Murphy, 1998), but which nevertheless enact localized forms of resistance that can 'lead to the systematic undermining of the dominant hegemony' (Mumby, 1997, p. 17). For example, in her study of flight attendants, Murphy (1998, p. 512) notes that an official regulation was written into the on-board manual, which includes all safety-related procedures, stating that 'the lead flight attendant must assure that all pilots have sufficient beverages before taxi and during cruise to avoid dehydration'. Flight attendants resisted this reinforcement of the subservient female role, as well as the trivialization of their safety role, by mocking the regulation:

> When I ask the pilots if I can get them a drink, I always ask them, 'So, do you need to be hydrated? I don't want you all to die of dehydration in the next hour and a half.' And then I throw in that my father is a urologist, and perhaps they might want me to remind them to go to the bathroom so that they don't get a kidney infection too! Usually, I only have to go in there once. They get their own drinks after that. (Flight attendant quoted in Murphy, 1998; p. 513)

As Murphy points out, while the public discourse reinforced that pilots are in command and the flight attendants are subordinate to them, the cumulative effects of this backstage resistance shifted the power to the extent that many pilots would fetch their own drinks.

In other situations alternative meanings are more widely shared, as in the case study of a *Kaizen* initiative in an automotive plant studied by Ezzamel, Willmott and Worthington (2001, p. 1069). Following disappointing results, the consultants responsible for its introduction organized a feedback presentation during which a drop in production figures was attributed to a 'disciplinary problem' that the plant would 'need to deal with'.

> One of the workers attending this session then invited the consultant to recall how, in his initial presentation … he had emphasized that the success of the initiative would be contingent upon the development of a 'blame-free culture' of mutual management–labour support and responsibility … that he had described *Kaizen* as a 'concept that was very much like a flower, that needed to be *watered* and *nurtured* and that *patience* was needed if it was to grow' … The consultant was then asked: 'well if that's the case, if my flowers in the garden at home don't grow straight away when I water them, should I carry on the watering and wait for them to grow, or do you suggest that I should hit them with the watering can?' (Ezzamel et al., 2001, p. 1069)

In this case, consumers turn the text back on itself – and its producers – by comparing it with an earlier text and drawing attention to inconsistencies between the two.

In both these examples, the original text is not consumed in accordance with the dominant meaning or in the way that the original producers intended. Nor is it rejected or denied in the form of an alternative text. Rather, the original text is subverted as it is consumed. Consumers appropriate parts of the text and use them to reveal 'the partiality of … universal claims and the inadequacies of institutional practices' (Ferguson, 1984, p. 156), leading to changes in the meaning of the original text. In this regard, consumption involves following the ways in which 'meanings are reappropriated and launched again in continuous struggles over meaning' Kondo (1990, p. 225). While many texts may be consumed 'unproblematically' in the sense that the dominant meaning is reinforced and reproduced, in other cases, the role of consumption in constructing the meaning of the text is both visible and subversive, as actors are able to articulate meanings that are taken up by other groups, providing opportunities to shape discourse and altering, if not transforming, power relations (Mumby, 2001).

CONCLUSIONS

In this chapter, we have explored the complex relationship between power and discourse by differentiating two sets of influences: the way in which discourse produces the objects, concepts and subject positions that shape the power relations that characterize a particular social space, and the way that the nature of the power relations in a particular social space affects the production of texts that, over time, influence the discourse. Our model shows both the interconnections and the differences between the discursive context of social reality – the discursive realm – and the material world of social action – the realm of action. These two realms are mutually constitutive but, at the same time, they are characterized by very different dynamics. In providing the context for action, discourse both enables and constrains it through the way in which concepts, objects and subject positions are constituted. However, discourses rely on the exercise of power by actors to support practices of textual production. Discourse and action are distinct but without discourse there can be no action and, without action, there can be no discourse.

What are the implications of this model for future research? A number of areas warrant greater empirical study if we are to develop a better understanding of how discourses develop. As Cooren and Taylor (1997) point out, while there is a considerable amount of well-documented research on the immediate circumstances of textual production and its local effects, we lack a well-developed theory of texts as trans-situational organizing mechanisms. Their concern is with the role of texts in producing organizational reality; our concern is broader, that is, how do texts support and change the broader discourses within which individual organizations exist? While there is agreement in the literature that texts and discourse are related, there is very little discussion of how and why particular texts produce particular discursive effects. For example, we know something about how different genres facilitate the way in which information is conveyed and processed, but very little on exactly how genres impact on discourse. Does the use of an 'appropriate' genre enable it to connect to discourse? If so, how do newly emerging genres, such as those associated with information technology, become meaningful and, over time, influential? Similarly, research suggests that narratives and metaphors are more successful when they possess some form of physicality or materiality (Barry & Elmes, 1997), complement verbal with visual discourse (Jameson, 2000), or when narrators are able to draw on a wide range of narrative competences (O'Connor, 2002), or use particular structures and sub-genres (Jameson, 2000), or have first-mover advantage (Cobb, 1993). But this research tends to focus on the impact of the text on the immediate, local meaning rather than tracking how individual texts embed in discourse.

Another important area for future research concerns the role of consumption in discursive production. Work so far has not explored to any great extent how texts are read or how the social circumstances that surround the act of consumption affect the meanings that result. Blommaert and Bulcaen (2000) argue that readers do not consume a text as a unified whole but instead piece together particular fragments of it. But what does this actually mean in terms of practices of consumption? How do audiences interpret texts and how do the practices of consumption affect the object, concepts and subject positions that are produced? In other words, discourses change as a result of a dynamic process whereby the practices and interests of both the producer and the consumer of the text are played out.

Finally, the role of power in the production of texts leads us to a central question concerning the relation between power and resistance. Mumby (1997) identifies two schools of thought in the literature. The dominance model defines resistance as 'productive acts that reconfigure the terrain of struggle' (Mumby, 1997, p. 362). In these instances, marginalized organizational members attempt to appropriate some of the resources of the organization for their own use in order to create 'spaces of resistance that subvert the dominant social order'. The key here is a dominant organizational discourse that disadvantages some members of the organization, who work to subvert these discourses in their local context. A second view argues that resistance is implicated in dominance in mutually defining ways. The dominant discourse is not simply held in place by power, but by webs of power *and* resistance: '[w]hile meanings may be temporarily fixed and certain interpretations hold sway, there is constant slippage between discourses and meanings, such that alternative and competing definitions of the world arise' (Mumby, 1997, p. 364). This view is much closer to the position of Foucault where resistance is seen as not being separable from power but as an integral part of it. Whether these two views are in opposition or whether they describe alternative types of resistance remains unclear and further research is needed to tease out these dynamics.

In conclusion, the interrelationship between discourse and power is a complex and relatively under-theorized area of research, but one that holds a great deal of potential for extending our understanding of discourse dynamics. In the context of organization studies, this relationship is of particular interest. The study of power has been an integral part of the study of organizations from its inception and a discursive perspective provides a very useful alternative to more mainstream work on power and politics in organizations. It not only provides a framework for understanding how power relations of a particular kind come about, but also how they affect the discourses that constitute organizational reality over time.

REFERENCES

Astley, W.G. & Sachdeva, P.S. (1984) Structural sources of intraorganizational power: A theoretical synthesis. *Academy of Management Review*, 9 (1): 104–13.

Barry, D. & Elmes, M. (1997) Strategy retold: Toward a narrative view of strategic discourse. *Academy of Management Review*, 22 (2): 429–52.

Blommaert, J. & Bulcaen, C. (2000) Critical discourse analysis. *Annual Review of Anthropology*, 29: 447–66.

Boje, D.M. (1991) The storytelling organization: A study of story performance in an office-supply firm. *Administrative Science Quarterly*, 36 (1): 106–26.

Boje, D.M. (1995) Stories of the storytelling organization: A postmodern analysis of Disney as Tamara-land. *Academy of Management Journal*, 38 (4): 997–1035.

Bourdieu, P. (1993) *Sociology in Question*. London: Sage.

Burman, E. & Parker, I. (1993) Against discursive imperialism, empiricism and constructionism: Thirty-two problems with discourse analysis. In E. Burman & I. Parker (eds),

Discourse analytic research: Repertoires and readings of texts in action (pp. 155–72). London: Routledge.

Chalaby, J.K. (1996) Beyond the prison-house of language: Discourse as a sociological concept. *British Journal of Sociology*, 47 (4): 684–98.

Clegg, S.R. (1989) *Frameworks of power*. London: Sage.

Cobb, S. (1993) Empowerment and mediation: A narrative perspective. *Negotiation Journal*, 9: 245–61.

Collinson, D. (1988) Engineering humor: Masculinity, joking and conflict in shop-floor relations. *Organization Studies*, 9: 181–99.

Cooren, F. & Taylor, J.R. (1997) 'Organization as an effect of mediation: Redefining the link between organization and communication. *Communication Theory*, 7 (3): 219–59.

de Certeau, M. (1984) *The practice of everyday life*. Berkeley, CA: University of California Press.

Deetz, S. (1992) *Democracy in an age of corporate colonization: Developments in communication and the politics of everyday life*. Albany, NY: State University of New York.

Deetz, S. & Mumby, D.K. (1990) Power, discourse and the workplace: Reclaiming the critical tradition. *Communication yearbook 13* (pp. 18–47). Thousand Oaks, CA: Sage.

Ezzamel, M., Willmott, H. & Worthington, F. (2001) Power, control and resistance in the factory that time forgot. *Journal of Management Studies*, 38 (8): 1053–79.

Fairclough, N. (1992) *Discourse and social change*. Cambridge: Polity Press.

Fairclough, N. (1995) *Critical discourse analysis: The critical study of language*. London: Longman.

Fairclough, N. & Wodak, R. (1997) Critical discourse analysis. In T.A. van Dijk (ed.), *Discourse as social interaction* (pp. 258–84). London: Sage.

Ferguson, K. (1984) *The feminist case against bureaucracy*. Philadelphia, PA: Temple University Press.

Fleming, P. & Spicer, A. (2003) Working at a cynical distance: Implications for subjectivity, power and resistance. *Organization*, 10 (1): 157–70.

Foucault, M. (1976) *The birth of the clinic*. London: Tavistock.

Foucault, M. (1979) *Discipline and punish: The birth of the prison*. London: Penguin.

Foucault, M. (1980) *Power/knowledge: Selected interviews and other writings 1972–1977*. Brighton: Harvester Press.

Foucault, M. (1982) The subject and power. In R.P. Dreyfus & H.L. Brighton (eds), *Michel Foucault: Beyond structuralism and hermeneutics* (pp. 208–26). Brighton: Harvester Press.

Foucault, M. (1998) *The will to knowledge: The history of sexuality,* volume 1. London: Penguin.

Foucault, M. (2002) *Archeology of knowledge*. London: Routledge.

French, J.R.P. & Raven, B. (1968) The bases of social power. In D. Cartwright & A. Zander (eds), *Group dynamics* (pp. 259–69). New York: Harper & Row.

Grant, D. & Oswick, C. (eds) (1996) *Metaphor and organizations*. London: Sage.

Grant, D., Keenoy, T. & Oswick, C. (1998) Introduction: Organizational discourse: Of diversity, dichotomy and multi-disciplinarity. In D. Grant, T. Keenoy & C. Oswick (eds), *Discourse and organization* (pp. 1–13). London: Sage.

Hall, S. (2001) Foucault: Power, knowledge and discourse. In M. Wetherell, S. Taylor & S.J. Yates (eds), *Discourse theory and practice: A reader* (pp. 72–81). London: Sage.

Hardy, C. (1985) The nature of unobtrusive power. *Journal Management Studies*, 22 (4): 384–99.

Hardy, C. & Clegg, S. (1996) Some dare call it power. In S. Clegg, C. Hardy & W. Nord (eds), *Handbook of organization studies* (pp. 622–41). London: Sage.

Hardy, C. & Leiba-O'Sullivan, S. (1998) The power behind empowerment: Implications for research and practice. *Human Relations*, 51 (4): 451–83.

Hardy, C. & Phillips, N. (1999) No joking matter: Discursive struggle in the Canadian refugee system. *Organization Studies*, 20 (1): 1–24.

Hardy, C., Palmer, I. & Phillips, N. (2000) Discourse as a strategic resource. *Human Relations*, 53 (9): 1227–47.

Harré, R. (1979) *Social being: A theory for social psychology*. Oxford: Basil Blackwell.

Hassard, J. & Kelemen, M. (2002) Production and consumption in organizational knowledge: the case of the 'paradigms debate'. *Organization*, 9 (2): 331–55.

Hatch, M.J. (1997) Irony and the social construction of contradiction in the humor of a management team. *Organization Studies*, 8 (3): 275–88.

Hoskins, K. & Maeve, R. (1987) The genesis of accountability: The West Point connections. *Accounting, Organizations and Society*, 12: 37–73.

Jameson, D.A. (2000) Telling the investment story: A narrative analysis of shareholder reports. *Journal of Business Communication*, 37 (1): 7–38.

Keenoy, T., Oswick, C. & Grant, D. (1997) Organizational discourses: Text and context. *Organization*, 4 (2): 147–57.

Knights, D. & Willmott, H. (1989) Power and subjectivity at work: From degradation to subjugation in social relations. *Sociology*, 23 (4): 535–58.

Kondo, D. (1990) *Crafting selves: Power, gender and discourse of identity in a Japanese workplace*. Chicago: University of Chicago Press.

Kuhn, T. (1997) The discourse of issues management: A genre of organizational communication. *Communication Quarterly*, 45 (3): 188–210.

Laclau, E. & Mouffe, C. (1987) *Hegemony and socialist strategy: Towards a radical democratic politics*. London: Verso.

Langellier, K.M. & Peterson, E.E. (1993) Family storytelling as a strategy of social control. In D. Mumby (ed.), *Narrative and social control: Critical perspectives* (pp. 49–76). Newbury Park, CA: Sage.

Lawrence, T.B., Winn, M. & Jennings, P.D. (2001) The temporal dynamics of institutionalization. *Academy of Management Review*, 26 (4): 626–44.

Livesey, S.M. (2002) Global warming wars: Rhetorical and discourse analytic approaches to ExxonMobil's corporate public discourse. *Journal of Business Communication*, 39 (1): 117–48.

Mumby, D. (1993) *Narrative and social control: Critical perspectives*. Newbury Park, CA: Sage.

Mumby, D. (1997) The problem of hegemony: Rereading Gramsci for organizational communication studies. *Western Journal of Communication*, 61 (4): 343–75.

Mumby, D. (2001) Power and politics. In F. Jablin & L.L. Putnam (eds), *The new handbook of organizational communication* (pp. 585–623). Thousand Oaks, CA: Sage.

Mumby, D. & Clair, R.P. (1997) Organizational discourse. In T.A. van Dijk (ed.), *Discourse as structure and process* (pp. 181–205). London: Sage.

Mumby, D. & Stohl, C. (1991) Power and discourse in organization studies: Absence and the dialectic of control. *Discourse and Society*, 2 (3): 312–22.

Murphy, A.G. (1998) Hidden transcripts of flight attendant resistance. *Management Communication Quarterly*, 11: 499–535.

O'Connor, E.S. (1995) Paradoxes of participation: Textual analysis and organizational change. *Organization Studies*, 16 (5): 769–803.

O'Connor, E.S. (2002) Storied business: Typology, intertextuality, and traffic in entrepreneurial narrative. *Journal of Business Communication*, 39 (1): 36–54.

Oakes, L.S., Townley, B. & Cooper, D.J. (1998) Business planning as pedagogy: Language and control in a changing institutional field. *Administrative Science Quarterly*, 43 (2): 257–92.

Oswick, C., Keenoy, T. & Grant, D. (2002) Metaphor and analogical reasoning in organization theory: Beyond orthodoxy. *Academy of Management Review*, 27 (2): 294–303.

Ott, B. & Walter, C. (2000) Intertexuality: Interpretive practice and textual strategy. *Critical Studies in Media Communication*, 17 (4): 429–43.

Parker, I. (1992) *Discourse dynamics*. London: Routledge.

Pettigrew, A.M. (1973) *The politics of organizational decision making*. London: Tavistock.

Pfeffer, J. (1981) *Power in organizations*. Marshfield, MA: Pitman.

Phillips, N. & Brown, J. (1993) Analyzing communication in and around organizations: A critical hermeneutic approach. *The Academy of Management Journal*, 36 (6): 1547–76.

Phillips, N. & Hardy, C. (1997) Managing multiple identities: Discourse, legitimacy and resources in the UK refugee system. *Organization*, 4 (2): 159–86.

Potter, J. & Wetherell, M. (1987) *Discourse and social psychology: Beyond attitudes and behaviour*. London: Sage.

Reed, M. (1998) Organizational analysis as discourse analysis: A critique. In T.K.D. Grant & C. Oswick (eds), *Discourse and organization* (pp. 193–213). London: Sage.

Rice, R.E. & Gattiker, U.E. (2001) New media and organizational structuring. In F. Jablin & L. Putnam (eds), *The new handbook of organizational communication* (pp. 544–81). Thousand Oaks, CA: Sage.

Ricœur, P. (1971) The model of the text: Meaningful action considered as text. *Social Research*, 38: 529–62.

Ricœur, P. (1981) *Hermeneutics and the human sciences: Essays on language, action and interpretation*. New York: Cambridge University Press.

Ricœur, P. (1986) *From text to action: Essays in hermeneuticss II*. Evanston, IL: Northwestern University Press.

Rosen, M. (1988) You asked for it: Christmas at the boss's expense. *Journal of Management Studies*, 25: 463–80.

Rothschild, J. & Miethe, T.D. (1994) Whistleblowing as resistance in modern work organizations: The politics of revealing organizational deception and abuse. In J.M. Jermier, D. Knights & W.R. Nord (eds), *Resistance and power in organizations* (pp. 252–74). London: Routledge.

Taylor, Charles (1985) *Philosophy and the human sciences*. Cambridge: Cambridge University Press.

Taylor, J.R. & Van Every, E.J. (1993) *The vulnerable fortress: Bureaucratic organization in the information age*. Toronto, Canada: University of Toronto.

Taylor, J.R., Cooren, F., Giroux, N. & Robichaud, D. (1996) The communicational basis of organization: Between the conversation and the text. *Communication Theory*, 6 (1): 1–39.

Townley, B. (1993) Foucault, power/knowledge and its relevance for human resource management. *Academy Management Review*, 18 (3): 518–45.

Van Dijk, T.A. (1997) Discourse as interaction in society. In T.A. van Dijk (ed.), *Discourse as structure and process* (pp. 1–37). London: Sage.

Watson, T.J. (1995) Rhetoric, discourse and argument in organizational sense making: A reflexive tale. *Organizational Studies*, 16 (5): 805–21.

Witten, M. (1993) Narrative and the culture of obedience at the workplace. In D. Mumby (ed.), *Narrative and social control: Critical perspectives* (pp. 97–118). Newbury Park, CA: Sage.

Wood, L.A. & Kroger, R.O. (2000) *Doing discourse analysis: Methods for studying action in talk and text*. Thousand Oaks, CA: Sage.

Yates, J. & Orlikowski, W.J. (1992) Genres of organizational communication: A structurational approach to studying communication and media. *Academy of Management Review*, 17 (2): 299–326.

Yates, J. & Orlikowski, W. (2002) Genre systems: Structuring interaction through communication norms. *Journal of Business Communication*, 39 (1): 13–35.

14

Organizational Culture and Discourse

Mats Alvesson

Organizational culture may, as organizational discourse analysis, mean many things and is very hard to delimit and specify. A lot of writings labelled 'organizational culture' share with discourse analysis a strong interest in language use in organizational settings, but many texts sidestep any theme related to language and focus on something else: behaviour, minds, emotions, values, cognitions. Again, other authors are more vague on how they conceive language: more general notions of meanings, expressions or communications are used. As I see it, a cultural approach to organizations would be language-sensitive, but not necessarily language-focused.

This chapter contains a comparison between a cultural and a discursive approach. Very briefly, my point is that a cultural approach focuses more broadly on shared, moderately stable forms of meaning that are only partially verbalized. Culture concerns systems of meanings and symbolism involving taken-for-granted elements in need of deciphering. Myths, basic assumptions about human nature, the environment, etc. are seldom directly espoused. They are partly non-conscious and occasionally 'language-distant', that is, not necessarily directly espoused, but call for reading between and behind the lines. A discursive understanding looks more specifically on language in use and views meaning as discursively constituted and typically as unstable. This understanding would call not so much for 'deeper' analysis, but for the identification and tracing of discourses and their effects.

In this chapter I argue that understandings of culture often call for a careful interpretation of language use in social contexts, while any view on discourse benefits from taking the historical cultural context into account. The two perspectives nevertheless invite different research agendas and organizational theorizing. A discourse approach would, at least in its stronger versions, assume that meaning just does not exist, but is constituted by and within discourse, which tends to be seen as a meaning-creating force. From a cultural perspective, meaning is seen as partly a product of tradition and partly the synthesis of people's symbolizing powers. Cultural meaning goes beyond a one-to-one relationship between language use and cognitive or affective meaning. Still, it makes sense to preserve the integrity of a cultural discourse approach and avoid mixing language use and cultural meaning.

The chapter is divided into four sections. The first section includes an overview of the organizational culture field. The second section identifies and reviews four key themes of relevance for most theoretical approaches to, and empirical studies on, organizational culture. The third section provides a brief overview and discussion of organizational discourse. The fourth section relates organizational culture to organizational discourse. Here I take the position that (many versions of what are labelled/framed as) culture and discourse are similar and overlapping, but that it may be productive to identify and focus on differences and alternative interpretive options of a cultural and discursive approach in organization studies.

THE MEANING(S) OF CULTURE

A glance at just a few works that use the term 'organizational culture' will reveal enormous variation in the definitions of this term and even more in the use of the term 'culture'. 'Culture' has no fixed or broadly agreed meaning even in anthropology (Borowsky, 1994; Ortner, 1984), but variation in its use is especially noticeable in the literature on organizational culture (Alvesson & Berg, 1992).

I use the term 'organizational culture' as an umbrella concept for a way of thinking which takes a serious interest in cultural and symbolic phenomena. This term directs the spotlight in a particular direction rather than mirroring a concrete reality for possible study. Culture refers to a socially shared orientation to social reality created through the negotiation of meaning and the use of symbolism in social interactions. This position is in line with the view broadly shared by many modern anthropologists (especially Geertz, 1973). Culture is then understood to be a system of common symbols and meanings, not the totality of a group's way of life. It provides 'the shared rules governing cognitive and affective aspects of membership in an organization, and the means whereby they are shaped and expressed' (Kunda, 1992, p. 8). Culture is not, according to this view, primarily 'inside' people's heads, but somewhere 'between' the heads of a group of people where symbols and meanings are publicly expressed, for example, in work group interactions and in board meetings, but also in material objects. Culture is thus closely related to communication and language use, even though it means more than 'discourse' – a point I will come back to.

The key term *meaning* refers to how an object or an utterance is interpreted. Meaning has a subjective referent in the sense that it appeals to an expectation, a way of relating to things. Meaning makes an object relevant and meaningful. Yanow defines meaning as 'what values, beliefs, and/or feelings an artifact represents beyond any "literal", non-symbolic referent' (2000, p. 252).

The second important term '*symbol*' intensifies the idea of meaning. A symbol can be defined as an object – a word or statement, a kind of action or a material phenomenon – that stands ambiguously for something else and/or something more than the object itself (Cohen, 1974). A symbol is rich in meaning – it condenses a more complex set of meanings in a particular object and thus communicates meaning in an economic way. A symbol can be linguistic, behavioural or material.

Despite the emphasis on culture set forth by Geertz and others as an ideational phenomenon, cultural analysis is, of course, not limited to studying the shared meanings and ideas of people or forms of communication with a strong symbolic element, such as 'exotic' rituals or metaphors, stories and slogans functioning as key symbols for a particular group (Ortner, 1973). As Eisenberg and Riley (2001) and others emphasize, a cultural approach does not 'limit its interest to overt constructions with "extra meaning" such as central metaphors or key stories' (2001, p. 295). Cultural analysis may be applied to all kinds of organizational phenomena, for example, the meanings and understandings of bureaucratic rules, information technology, products, gender, objectives, performance measures, etc. (Alvesson, 2002; Gregory, 1983).

Viewing culture broadly as a shared and learned world of experiences, meanings, values and understandings which inform people and which are expressed, reproduced and communicated partly in symbolic form is consistent with a variety of approaches to the conduct of concrete studies. (It does, of course, also leave out many versions of culture.) More precise ways of viewing culture and what it can reveal will be reviewed and discussed.

SOME KEY THEMES IN ORGANIZATIONAL CULTURE

The research field of organizational culture is complex, hard to delimit and there are no self-evident ways to divide the field into various theoretical perspectives or schools. Overviews range from focusing on different perspectives (Alvesson & Berg, 1992; Smircich, 1983; Smircich & Calás, 1987) to proceeding from Habermas's model of cognitive interests (Knights & Willmott, 1987; Stablein & Nord, 1985). Ouchi and Wilkins (1985) emphasized levels of analysis – from micro to macro approaches. An influential distinction between three paradigms or perspectives was put forward by Martin and co-authors (e.g., Martin, 1992, 2002; Martin & Frost, 1996; Martin & Meyerson, 1988) that divided cultural studies of organizations into integrative differentiation and fragmentation camps. Still another, more recent, review of the field, emphasizing a communicative perspective, proceeds from six versions of culture: culture as symbolism and performance, culture as text, culture as critique, culture as identity, culture as cognition, and culture as climate and effectiveness (Eisenberg & Riley, 2001). In this section, I chose to review a few themes of profound significance for culture research, at least as the field is delimited here, that is with an interpretive and language-sensitive orientation.

Organizational culture and language

Within the organizational culture literature it is common to identify cultural forms. Trice and Beyer (1993) use the categories of language, symbols, narratives and practices. Symbols refer to objects, natural and manufactured settings, performers and functionaries. Language refers to jargon, slang, gestures, signals, signs, songs, humour, gossip, rumours, metaphors, proverbs and slogans. Narratives are exemplified by stories, legends, sagas and myths. Practices include rituals, taboos, rites and ceremonies. Martin (2002) refers to four cultural forms: rituals, stories and scripts, jargon and humour. Language is viewed as a major set of cultural forms or manifestations and there are a wealth of studies under the label of organizational culture that at least partly treat what organizational discourse proponents refer to as discursive phenomena or aspects. I will address the relationship later.

Many organizational culture studies – at least studies incorporated in books framed as being about organizational culture or organizational symbolism – treat language use as an important element of culture. In speeches and other forms of communication cultural meanings are expressed and (re-)created. Van Maanen (1991), for example, also takes into account the role of organizational language in a study of Disneyland:

> Customers at Disneyland are for example never referred to as such, they are 'guests'. There are no rides at Disneyland, only 'attractions'. Disneyland itself is a 'park', not an amusement center, and it is divided into 'back-stage', 'on-stage' and 'staging' regions. (Van Maanen, 1991, pp. 65–6)

Language is here typically seen as a part of organizational culture – on equal footing with other cultural expressions such as actions, settings and material objects. This larger cultural 'whole' is privileged and is involved in order to adequately interpret the meaning of language. There is seldom a strict focus on language, as the interpretation of meaning is very much a matter of making skilful guesses and assessments of broad, implicit meanings, only partially mirrored or espoused in the form of explicit language use. Frequently, the ambition is to address a wider cultural terrain than 'only' language use.

Metaphors

In a classic overview of concepts of culture in organizational analysis, Smircich (1983) has distinguished between culture as a variable and culture as a root metaphor. Researchers who see culture as a variable draw upon a more traditional objectivist and functionalist view of social reality and try to improve models of organization by taking socio-cultural sub-systems, in addition to traditionally recognized variables, into account. In contrast, researchers who see culture as a root metaphor approach organizations as if they were cultures and draw upon anthropology in developing radically new theories or paradigms.

Instead of considering culture as something that an organization *has*, researchers proceeding from the root metaphor idea stress that the organization *is* a culture or, rather, can be seen as if it is a culture: 'Culture as a root metaphor promotes a view of organizations as expressive forms, manifestations of human consciousness. Organizations are understood and analyzed not mainly in economic or material terms, but in terms of their expressive, ideational, and symbolic aspects' (Smirchich, 1983, p. 348). According to this perspective, 'organizational culture is not just another piece of the puzzle, it is the puzzle' (Pacanowsky & O'Donnell-Trujillo, 1983, p. 146). Therefore, the research agenda is to explore organization as socially shared – intersubjective – experience.

One way of increasing or improving the metaphorical qualities of culture is to consider how the broad and fluffy concept of culture is further structured through an additional metaphorical layer, what may be referred to as a second-level metaphor. I have argued for the need for, and helpfulness of, looking at the image or gestalt behind the idea of organizational culture, that is the metaphor of the metaphor (Alvesson, 2002). The point is that a (culture) metaphor also comes from somewhere and the metaphorical nature of the thinking and framework behind any definition and surface-level use of the culture concept in organization studies can be made more explicit. Being conscious about a second-order metaphor behind the gestalt informing one's thinking, together with the definitions applied, is one way of sharpening culture as an interpretive framework. Examples of second-level metaphors include compass, sacred cow, social glue and world closure. There are other ways of considering metaphors in cultural (and discourse) studies. Metaphors explicitly used in organizations – metaphors of the field – are seen as crucial, either as indicators of cultural meanings or as powerful vehicles for sense-making and/or control (Manning, 1979). There is also research using metaphors for conceptualizing empirical phenomena based less on a theoretical, a priori idea of culture – as in the second-level metaphors – and more on the empirical observations. Trujillo (1992), for example, using multiple perspectives, studied a baseball park as a site of capitalist labour, communitas at home and as theatre.

Organizational culture and level of analysis

It is important to think through themes of organizational culture in relationship to social groups/communities on various levels and culture-producing forces acting on various kinds of scale: from watercooler everyday talk to new messages expressed by powerful media on a global range. Some authors see organizations as micro-entities embedded in a larger societal culture; others regard the work group as an entire culture with certain idiosyncrasies and strong boundary lines between itself and other groups. Most authors fall between these two extremes. Wilkins and Ouchi (1983) speak of 'local cultures', and Martin, Sitkin and Boehm (1985, p. 101) of 'umbrellas for (or even arbitrary boundary lines around) collections of subcultures'.

The expressions used for culture frame our understanding of phenomena. Cultural studies are very much a matter of discovering subtle patterns, and our conceptualizations must encourage sensitivity for these. Van Maanen and Barley

(1985), for example, explicitly reject the label 'organizational culture' because it suggests that organizations bear unity and unique cultures, something which they find difficult to justify empirically. Parker (2000) is uncomfortable with the term 'organizational sub-cultures', as it assumes that organizational culture is the 'natural' starting point for culture talk, which may be quite misleading, as there typically is much cultural variation within most organizations (Young, 1989). Many studies do give priority to a particular level of analysis. It would seem beneficial to take into account the combination of a variety of 'macro-elements', such as professions, mass media, social movements and gender ideologies, that put their imprints on organizational life, and at the same time pay close attention to the local production of culture, which is constrained or informed by these broader forces and affiliations (Alvesson, 2002).

Culture, power and domination

As argued, the basic idea of a cultural understanding of organizations gives considerable weight to more or less integrated patterns of ideas and meanings that provide some stability and a point of departure for coordination. These ideas and meanings tend to be taken for granted and the social world will be regarded as natural, neutral and legitimate (Alvesson & Deetz, 2000; Deetz, 1992; Frost, 1987).

Several authors have argued that the creation and utilization of existing as well as novel ideologies and symbolic means of control are crucial features of management and leadership (e.g., Kunda, 1992; Rosen, 1985; Willmott, 1993). In some modern organizations symbolic power is particularly salient, compared to technical and bureaucratic means of control, although all kinds of control typically co-exist. The use of modes of control not primarily targeted at consciousness and meaning but on output, rules and other constraining measures also involve cultural control. The interface between cultural and technostructural control needs to be emphasized (Alvesson & Kärreman, 2004).

Corporate culture as an expression of power may be seen as taking the form of systematic efforts to establish a certain world view, a particular set of values and/or emotions among corporate employees. Ray (1986) refers to corporate culture as 'the last frontier of control'. Critics have called this management strategy 'cultural engineering' (Alvesson & Berg, 1992; Kunda, 1992). Quite a lot of critical research focuses on the use of language by managers and other dominant actors in establishing a particular version of social reality (e.g., Alvesson, 1996; Knights & Willmott, 1987; Rosen, 1985), sometimes focusing on intentions and actions rather than outcomes and receptions.

There are, however, good reasons to point at the limitations of managers in their ability to control culture. As stated by Batteau (2001, p. 726): 'Being evocative and dynamically related, the cultures of an organization can be navigated and negotiated but not controlled'.

Ambiguity and fragmentation

There is an increasing awareness about the multiplicity of cultural orientations in organizations. Not only the idea that a single, overall organizational culture creates unity among people in organizations, but also the counter-idea that organizations are typically characterized by stable and well-demarcated sub-cultures is increasingly being disputed.

Emphasis on ambiguity and the instability of meaning and values is a response to the dominance of the idea that a culture (or a sub-culture) is a clear and known entity that creates unity and harmony within an organization (or a group within it) and solves problems. In several writings, Martin and co-authors (1992, 2002; Martin & Meyerson, 1988) have emphasized an ambiguity perspective on culture. (In later writings they talk about fragmentation instead.) They point to the 'black hole' in our definitions of culture produced by the exclusion of ambiguity – uncertainty, contradiction and confusion. Instead of culture creating order, rather it is seen as disorder. Culture is not a matter of consensus, or of group conflicts based on clearly differentiated groups (sub-cultures), but is characterized by shifting positions and incoherence. Still, it could be argued that some modest degree of shared meanings is a precondition for it being meaningful to use the term 'culture' as well as for organizations to exist and produce something (Trice & Beyer, 1993, p. 14).

The diversity of groups and the multitude of group identifications means that there is considerable variation and fluidity in what sets of meanings and values become salient in people's organizational life in different situations. As Anthony (1994, p. 31) comments, 'in the course of work, people walk out of one cultural enclosure and into another at different times of the day and periods of their lives'. This is partly related to the multiplicity of group distinctions and partly to identifications with associated ideas and values: '...the "culture" of an organization is displayed through a huge variety of contested "us" and "them" claims. In some cases the organization will be "us", but ideas about similarity and difference can call upon other sources as well' (Parker, 2000, p. 227). Ybema (1996) points out the joint occurences of unity and division in work relations and Batteau (2001) emphasizes the synthesis and capacities to attain understanding to what on one level may be seen as manifestations of ambiguity and fragmentation. Alvesson (2002) suggests bounded ambiguity as a concept to capture this aspect.

The four themes addressed highlight key issues in organizational culture studies, but are useful for illuminating certain aspects of discourse. I will to some extent connect these themes when thus moving on to the organizational discourse literature.

ORGANIZATIONAL DISCOURSE

Even though 'culture' – like many other popular terms – is happily used to cover wide and diverse grounds, the label 'discourse' probably outperforms it in terms of the almost endless number of ways in which it is used. As many people have pointed out (e.g., Potter & Wetherell, 1987), texts on what is labelled 'discourse' may have nothing whatsoever in common, apart from perhaps taking some interest in language and language use in one sense or another. See, for example, the broad range of studies in the review of Putnam and Fairhurst (2001). It is clearly not the primary purpose of this chapter to explore the various meanings of discourse, but in order to relate organizational culture to organizational discourse, some dominant – or at least commonly used – views of discourse must be identified and specified.

Grant, Keenoy and Oswick define organizational discourse as 'the languages and symbolic media we employ to describe, represent, interpret and theorize what we take to be the facticity of organizational life' (1998, p. 1). Oswick, Keenoy and Grant talk about a discursive epistemology 'that illuminate[s] the fragility, rather than the solidity, of organizations or organizing processes' (2000, p. 1115). They also, however, refer to Mumby and Clair, who view organizational discourse as 'the principal means by which organization members create a coherent social reality that frames their sense of who they are...' and 'is both an expression and a creation of organizational structure' (1997, p. 181). This last citation indicates a view of discourse as very powerful, creating a coherent social reality. If we follow Mumby and Clair and reserve the term 'discourse' for something that creates and reflects organizational structures, discourse indeed becomes a rare, though powerful, phenomenon. It has very little in common with a definition such as that of Potter and Wetherell: 'all forms of spoken interaction, formal and informal, and written texts of all kinds' (1987, p. 7).

I think it is productive to consider two significant dimensions or areas of variation within the literature on discourse: (1) the power and coherence versus fragility and processuality dimension, and (2) the focus on broader structural (poststructurally framed) concerns associated with an interest in the details of discourse in local contexts versus an interest in a certain version of macro and structure (see Alvesson & Kärreman, 2000).

Notions of discourse I: muscular versus fragile

Starting with the first dimension, we see here considerable variation within organizational discourse studies. Oswick, Keenoy and Grant's (2000) claim about the fragility of organizations is very far from the view of Mumby and Clair (1997), which indicates almost the opposite, 'a coherent social reality' created by discourse. The centrality of discourse may mean a fragile reality *or* a strong grip of social reality produced by and held in place by muscular discourse. The organizational discourse literature moves between these views. A key dimension in making sense of the variety of discourse talk is thus *the degree of muscularity of discourse* – is it, by definition, high-powered or is discourse viewed as loosely connected to structures and not necessarily the decisive element in reality-creation? In metaphorical terms, we can refer to this dimension of discourse as muscular versus fragile (Alvesson & Kärreman, 2000). This could perhaps to some extent be seen as an empirical question (and not about assumptions/theoretical focus), but it is clearly not just a matter of going out there to find out, as it is related to the theoretical positioning on discourse guiding empirical inquiry.

We see here a loose parallel to the interest in power in parts of organizational culture studies. Two connections can be made. The first is that cultural meaning as well as discourse may be seen as the key element in how domination is exercised. Critical culture and critical discourse researchers, sharing this focus on domination, typically have more in common than they have with 'neutral', 'descriptive' or 'managerial' students of culture and discourse, respectively (Alvesson & Deetz, 2000).

The second connection relates to the theme of a stable and integrated organizational reality – whether through domination or 'organic consensus' – in relation to a view that stresses instability and disorganization. We can see a parallel to the debate in organizational culture studies between positions assuming the 'unitary and unique' versus the 'ambiguous and fragmented' nature of values, beliefs and meanings in organizations. The assumption of discourse as related to (as an expression and creation of) a coherent social reality has considerable similarities with the former cultural position, and the fragility and fluidity exhibit commonalities with the ambiguous/ fragmented position. This is not to say that there are not substantive differences between culture and discourse people – we need to consider both shared and dissimilar concerns.

Notions of discourse II: local versus wide-ranging

The second key dimension in various positions on discourse concerns what can be labelled *the formative range of discourse*. One option is to take an interest in discourse at close range, considering and emphasizing the local, situational context. Language use, then, is understood in relationship to the specific process and social context in which discourse is produced. This means that the nuances of language use are focused (Potter & Wetherell, 1987). At the other extreme we see discourse as a rather universal, if historically situated, language constituting a particular phenomenon. We may talk about long-range, macro-systemic discourse. We may, for example, talk about a discourse on 'the New Economy'. In order to clarify the difference between discourse in these two senses, I refer to long-range discourse as Discourse (with a capital D). A Discourse, or rather indications of it, shows up at a large number of sites in more or less different ways, and is, methodologically, treated as being of a more or less standardized nature. The idea is that it is possible to cut through the variation at the local levels through summaries and synthetizations pointing at overall themes turning up at the specific situations. Language use becomes less strongly focused. Overall categories and standards then tend to be privileged in the treatment of empirical material. As Miller (1997, p. 34) describes Foucault-inspired work: 'Whatever the form of the data, Foucauldian discourse studies involve treating the data as expressions of culturally standardized discourses that are associated with particular social settings'. This is, of course, accomplished at the expense of paying attention to variations at the local and meso levels. The organizational level in itself is not of primary interest. Close-range studies focus on these. They emphasize the need to take social context and interactions seriously. The rich, detailed picture aimed for, sensitive to the local nature of the discourse, makes viewing it as culturally standardized difficult. For those interested in close-range studies, discourse is local business, not expressions of imperialism. Boje (1991), for example, advocates the study of stories documenting the way in which storytelling is performed, which calls for paying attention to detail and to local context. The richness of the material and considerations of uniqueness seriously make the quest for standards in the particular not an easy one. In a similar manner, long-range conceptions of Discourse do not deny local variation. The point is, however, that it is seen as of limited interest compared to the need to address Big issues. As the extremely detailed study on social text of type conversation analysis means a too narrow focus for organization studies, as conventionally understood, it is arguably the somewhat more generalizable patterns and contradictions of language use in action in specific social contexts that are of interest. How people tend to use and respond to language is thus of greater interest than the exact wordings and breaks in specific utterances.

Sometimes researchers want to address both micro and macro levels. Fairclough (1993) is interested in discourse, in the sense of spoken or written language use at the level of discursive practice, as well as what he refers to as 'the order of discourse', 'the totality of discursive practice of an institution, and relationships between them' (1993, p. 138). There is a tension between these two levels and it is not easy to take both equally seriously in the same study, unless one assumes that the social world hangs intimately and orderly together.

This theme is to some extent similar to the issue of levels in organizational cultural analysis. Many influential organizational culture studies do, however, take the meso level seriously (e.g., Kunda, 1992; Martin, 1992; Watson, 1994). Within discourse work, there are tendencies either to go strongly in a micro orientation or to treat micro events as indications of a more standardized form of discourse (Discourse) and thus neglect local variation or even meso-level analysis to look at more general phenomena, for example, Discourses on strategy and HRM (Knights & Morgan, 1991; Townley, 1994). Fairclough in a sense goes in both directions, and some discursivists emphasize a meso, organizational level (e.g., Hardy et al., 2000), but discourse analysts tend to spread quite widely over the local–universal spectrum. This dimension is frequently not explicitly addressed in the discourse literature.

Organizational discourse as a catch-all

That discourse studies are widely dispersed along the key dimensions described is not a problem in itself, although it may lead to some confusion. It may be partly responsible for a tendency for discourse students to use rather broad-ranging and indistinct concepts of discourse, incorporating a somewhat wide set of aspects and themes, including non-linguistic dimensions. Fairclough (1993), for example, suggests that any discursive event is analysed on the basis of its being 'simultaneously a piece of text, an instance of discursive practice, and an instance of social practice' (quoted in Grant et al., 2001, p. 7). Van Dijk (1993) remarks that discourse can be seen as a way of thinking. Clegg goes further and includes '"discursive practices": practices of talk, text, writing, cognition, argumentation, and representation generally' (Clegg, 1989, p. 151).

There is a risk that the term 'discourse' becomes a 'catch-all', similar to old-fashioned uses of culture (forms of life, including behaviours), accused of covering too much and revealing too little (Geertz, 1973). One may be sympathetic to the ambition to relate discourse analysis to broader concerns, such as ideologies, ways of thinking and social practices, but still reserve the term 'discourse' for a more specific meaning around the analysis of language use in social settings. Discourse can then be related to something that is not included in a 'discourse-package' that stipulates a close connection between language use and social practice, where discourse is viewed as forming social reality. Perhaps it is to be preferred, as for example Watson (1994) does, to define discourse as 'a connected set of statements, concepts, terms and expressions which constitutes a way of talking and writing about a particular issue, thus framing the way people understand and act with respect to that issue' (1994, p. 113). In what follows, I mainly use discourse in the ways suggested here – fairly close to language use (in opposition to a way of thinking about the world) and as somewhat open in terms of constitutive effects. This view then differs from both a 'weak' view, marginalizing it as 'mere talk', as well as from more high-powered ideas about the strong world-creating effects of discourse. The focus here is on language and language use and with a modest interest in the effects. I avoid strong assumptions about discourse including or directly producing cognitions, practices, etc.

ORGANIZATIONAL CULTURE AND DISCOURSE

It is now time to connect organizational culture and discourse. I'll start with briefly discussing an unfortunate tendency to overlap and conflate, and then go on to identify/suggest some ideas for distinctive, alternative positions.

Organizational discourse as the re-labelling of organizational culture?

Within the organizational discourse literature Oswick, Keenoy and Grant (2000) mention a set of approaches analysing, among other themes, metaphor, stories, novels and sagas, narratives, rituals and myths, rhetoric, texts, drama and sense-making. Apart from these authors having more examples of language themes, their list is very similar to lists of cultural manifestations and forms (e.g., Martin, 2002; Trice & Beyer, 1993, briefly summarized above). These similarities are seldom pointed out and organizational discourse is often portrayed as a new field in organization studies: we may see signs of social amnesia here – not uncommon in social science.

Sometimes one may get the impression that what may appear to be theoretical themes or developments may just be a matter of shifting labels. The terms 'organizational culture' and 'organizational discourse' are sometimes used at random, implying that titles and key vocabulary reflect fashion and the supply of conference and publication possibilities, as much as the specific intellectual interests of the authors. This may not be seen as a problem. It can be argued that we cannot fix meaning or police how we use words. But if we conflate different interpretive possibilities, it may undermine the use of discourse analysis as something new, offering an alternative to, for example, the more language- and communication-sensitive parts of organizational culture research. The following section tries to position the two approaches.

A case for distinctive organizational culture and discourse approaches

Moving within the overlapping zones between culture and discourse calls for a nuanced unpacking of the differences in focus between a cultural and a discursive approach. In order to avoid too much complexity, I will concentrate on typical versions of organizational culture and discourse thinking and will disregard most of the considerable variation in the use of cultural and discursive approaches. (A more thorough treatment would have worked with a *set* of distinctive cultural and discursive approaches.)

MEANING IN CULTURE AND DISCOURSE   One way of highlightening similar concerns, but also the different foci between organizational culture and discourse, is to say that cultural analysis concentrates on meaning while discourse addresses language and language use. Obviously there is overlap as it is difficult to imagine meaning altogether outside language and all language and language use are about meaning – its transmission or construction. But an interest in cultural meaning goes beyond manifest language use. From a cultural point of view meaning is not only based in language, but also in actions and artifacts, in taken-for-granted assumptions and ideas that people may have a problem in verbalizing. Moreover, much of the learning and transmission of cultural meaning is tacit. A cultural framework assumes the existence of ideas and meanings that construct a version of the object without a specific, explicit and present 'text' producing it. Although it is not assumed that meanings construct or reproduce themselves, culturalists argue that there is a tendency for meaning systems to be expressed through a variety of subtle means, of which some are 'non-discursive', and also to show considerable atemporality.

A discourse approach 'examines how language constructs phenomena, not how it reflects and reveals it' (Phillips & Hardy, 2002, p. 6). It does not assume the existence of meanings just 'being there', outside language. Meaning becomes constituted in discursive acts. Meaning connected to discourse is created through language use, it is explicit and tends to closely follow discourse in operation. Discourse emphasizes the 'process of differentiating, fixing, labelling, classifying and relating – all intrinsic processes of discursive organization – that social reality is systematically constructed' (Chia, 2000, p. 513). Without a discourse in operation, meaning would not appear. It would disappear as a consequence of the discontinuation of the use of a specific vocabulary, according to a discourse perspective. If certain words are dropped, certain meanings would, in principle, vanish. Meaning becomes intimately tied to, indeed driven by, language use and is local in nature. Specific meanings are not, as assumed by culturalists, established and existing prior to specific uses of language, nor are they grounded in a broader meaning system.

LANGUAGE AS REFLECTION VERSUS EFFECT-PRODUCING While language use from a cultural perspective *reveals* (or expresses) underlying meanings, a discursive perspective emphasizes how language use *creates* temporal meanings. A culture position would give more space for internalizations and inertia, including the influence of taken-for-granted assumptions, although it is important not to overstress the stability of cultural meanings, as culturalists emphasizing ambiguity, fragmentation and the processuality of meaning suggest (Alvesson, 2002; Martin, 2002). This means that culture is viewed as 'being' there and is manifested in, for example, language use, even though ambiguity-focused culture theorists say that this 'being' takes the form of a reservoir of unstable, sometimes contradictory meanings. Language use can then be seen as clues or indications of an underlying cultural meaning system. This is, of course, not static but is changeable and changes over time. Changes in language use thus also drive change, but slowly and indirectly. New uses of language tend slowly to change established cultural meanings, the latter being a source of inertia and resistance.

A discourse position would say that language and other symbolic media must consistently fuel people and social institutions with meanings – through constant acts of labelling, classifying, differentiating, etc. – in order to exercise power. Language is thus not so much a manifestation of something established 'being there', but rather is an active producer of temporary order. To the extent one finds a stable social system or structure, it would be an effect of one dominant discourse being constantly in operation and thus holding a steady grip over social reality (meaning patterns).

A FRAGMENTED *VS* A PATTERNED ORGANIZATIONAL REALITY Compared to work on discourse, cultural studies would be more oriented towards broader, more holistic concerns. Even though many cultural theorists nowadays emphasize the negotiated and shifting nature of meaning systems, there is, in general, a greater interest in connectedness and synthesis among those favouring culture vocabularies. The fragmentation view differs from the 'average' view on culture, but when culture students take ambiguities and fragmentations seriously, these are seen as variations of 'patterns' rather than directly contingent upon the flows of language use.

Discourse analysis, emphasizing the local, more specific impact of discourse, would limit the range of analytical interest, providing space for a multitude of discourses in operation in organizations. As language use, presumably, is frequently much varied and locally situated, discourse analysis that is sensitive to this level of analysis would probably in many cases indicate local variation and a multitude of socially-constructed realities, producing a rather fragmented and fragile organization – pushing this point even further than fragmentation-oriented culture people.

As indicated above, there are discourse advocates that aim for wide-ranging Discourses, but these are not the major focus in this chapter. Although one should not over-stress this point, discourse often signals an interest in variation and fragmentation, while the use of the term 'culture' often points towards a search for less fluid, more integrated patterns of meaning.

HUMAN BEINGS AND LANGUAGE   Many culture researchers emphasize the subjectivity of organizational life and place human subjects who collectively develop and reproduce shared meanings at the centre of their study. This approach tends to be humanistic and emphasizes how people interpret their social world based on tradition. As Geertz (1973), in one of the most frequently cited passages in the literature of social science, has put it, culture means that human beings are caught in the web of significance that they themselves have spun. Within the organizational culture literature, few authors assume full-scale sovereignty of people in culture creation and interpretation. People are 'doing culture' within the constraints of historically-dominated meanings and taken-for-granted ideas, and the more critically-minded culture researchers emphasize how dominant social interests, powerful groups and ideologies put their imprints on meaning creation.

Some discourse researchers and especially Foucauldians (e.g., Knights & Morgan, 1991), on the other hand, are inclined to reject humanism and see subjects as not the creator-interpreter of their reality and the bearers of meaning, but reserve this role for discourse. Human beings are driven/constituted by discourses that somehow have appeared. However, the picture is not consistent, and authors relate to 'discourse' in all sorts of ways. Hardy, Palmer and Phillips, for example, assume that 'individuals do engage in discursive activity in ways that produce outcomes that are beneficial to them' (2000, p. 1232) and also that 'the activities of actors shape discourses, while those discourses also shape the actions of those actors' (p. 1228). As regarding the other themes discussed here, there are a variety of positions taken by people framing their work in culture discourse terms, and there is no easy way to separate the 'groups'. Still, there is a tendency for culture researchers to associate themselves with interpretivist humanism and discourse researchers to see subjects as (temporary) effects of discourse. While the former assume that people are caught in the webs of meaning they themselves have spun, discursivists, at the moment where discourse is invoked, say that subjects are caught in the net of distinctions and categories that language – more than human beings – bring about.

Summing up

Let me summarize my efforts, partly to make sense of, and partly to suggest a view of, the differences between an interest in organizational culture and organizational discourse:

- *Culture.* Broadly shared meanings and symbolism, often partly or fully taken-for-granted. Language is central in producing culture, but discourse can often be seen as expressing/revealing 'deeper' meanings that have been developed over time and have 'been there' prior to a particular linguistic act. But there are also other elements than language – material practices and conditions, non-verbal aspects of social interaction, etc. – active in culture production and repro-duction. Culture provides a subtext to language use – a prestructured under-standing and an inclination to read discourse in a particular way.
- *Discourse.* Specific use of language structuring a chunk of the world in a particular way. Discourse frames and constitutes identity and elements in sub-jectivity through specific communicative acts and thus expresses micro power. Language to a lesser extent refers to or expresses already existing cultures as creating meaning. The discourse-driven nature of meaning implies its temporal character.

Having emphasized some analytical differences, some common grounds and interactive effects can be identified. Culture is put into action, carried and changed partly or perhaps mainly through discourses. Cultural meanings frame, restrict and give meta-meaning to discourses. The same discourse (language use) in different cultures (meaning contexts) may lead to different receptions and thus meanings. A cultural view would not assume any distinct effects of Discourse, but would take seriously that a variety of receptions and meanings are possible. Discourses – both with a capital and lower-cased – are ordered and integrated by cultures, but also represent a (perhaps even *the* most important) medium in which cultures are constructed, reproduced, contested and changed. In discourse, ideo-logies and other cultural elements are developed, modified and expressed. It is at this level that the subject is 'hit' by linguistic acts carrying and applying cultural themes and more or less elaborated or fragmented ideologies.

CONCLUSION

'Culture' is often seen as a broad and vague term and it is important, of course, to think through how one uses a cultural framework in order to attain interpretive distinctiveness and depth. Elements in a thoughtful cultural approach to organi-zations may include the following points:

- To be careful of cultural levels and 'entities', and avoid emphasizing a single 'unit' such as society, industry, company, social group or a symbol, and to take seriously the relevance of considering a multitude of levels or contexts.

- To consider the images or metaphors behind culture (second-level metaphors), giving the concept a more distinct meaning.
- To (sometimes) view cultural meanings in the context of power and politics, and to see ideas and meanings as outcomes of power relations and a key element in social domination.
- To struggle with language and the problems of representation, acknowledging that meanings are diffuse and hard to articulate for interviewees and also for researchers to describe.
- To focus on meanings and symbolism and relate these to everyday life and social practices, and to dig behind public statements and social scripts being available and in circulation for culture talk.
- To take issues of ambiguity, fragmentation and discontinuities around culture seriously, and to be careful about prematurely ascribing unity, stability and coherence to meaning systems.

The discourse literature even outperforms organizational culture studies in the varied and frequently broad-brushed way the term is used. A list of recommendations that may increase the analytical distinctiveness and novelty of a discourse approach – going beyond discourse as a sexy re-labelling of earlier approaches – could include the following points:

- To think through the level of discourse. Is discourse close to the specific language in use or is it a broader line of reasoning/summary (a narrative or a 'paradigm') abstracted from specific texts and talks?
- To try to sharpen the idea of (or behind) discourse through considering and/or developing alternative labels or metaphors for discourse. In the above I have proposed 'language use' and 'muscularity' as examples, illuminating some discourse thinking.
- To be clear about how language is studied – what language use to follow and, when relevant, the analytical steps in moving from specific language use to talking about Discourse.
- To address the connectedness or various loose couplings between language uses and 'non-discursive' phenomena. Does discourse mirror/create organizational structures or may discourses circulate in organizations without any necessary connections to other phenomena?
- To consider the tension between discourse creating/reflecting an ordered, regulated and fixed world accomplished through the powers of discourse, and discourse as a way of getting an understanding of a fragile, discontinuous and fluid social world.

It is important to see similarities as well as differences in cultural and discursive understandings. Let me end this chapter by illustrating this using Chia's point of view on the operations of discourse:

> Discourse works to create some sense of stability, order and predictability and to thereby produce a sustainable, functioning and liveable world from what would otherwise be an amorphous, fluxing and undifferentiated reality indifferent to our causes. (Chia, 2000, p. 514)

Discourse accomplishes this 'through the material inscriptions and utterances that form the basis of language and exchanges' (2000, p. 514). Culture performs almost the same fantastic trick, but through shared meanings produced and communicated partly through language, and also through more tacit means and non-discursive forms of symbolism. While discourse people think that constant re-fuelling of inscriptions and utterances is necessary, culture people have more faith in history, tradition and the interpretive capacity of people to do some of the work. At an overall level, discourse and culture are intellectual tools for addressing similar concerns about the magic of social life, but with different emphasis. I think we have richer analytical opportunities at our disposal if we maintain a distinction between a cultural and discursive approach. We must at the same time realize that further distinctions need to be made and that these are never unproblematic, as they slice the world in a particular way, creating a kind of order which discourse studies, in particular, problematizes.

REFERENCES

Alvesson, M. (1996) *Communication, power and organization*. Berlin/New York: De Gruyter.

Alvesson, M. (2002) *Understanding organizational culture*. London: Sage.

Alvesson, M. & Berg, P.O. (1992) *Corporate culture and organizational symbolism*. Berlin/New York: De Gruyter.

Alvesson, M. & Deetz, S. (2000) *Doing critical management research*. London: Sage.

Alvesson M. & Kärreman, D. (2000) Varieties of discourse: On the study of organizations through discourse analysis. *Human Relations*, 53 (9): 1125–49.

Alvesson, M. & Kärreman, D. (2004) Interfaces of control: Technocratic and socio-ideological control in a global management consultancy firm. *Accounting, Organization and Society*, 29: 423–44.

Anthony, P. (1994) *Managing organizational culture*. Buckingham: Open University Press.

Batteau, A. (2001) Negations and ambiguities in the cultures of organizations. *American Anthropologist*, 102 (4): 726–40.

Boje, D. (1991) The story-telling organization: A study performance in an office-supply firm. *Administrative Science Quarterly*, 36. 106–26.

Borowsky, R. (ed.) (1994) *Assessing cultural anthropology*. New York: McGraw-Hill.

Chia, R. (2000) Discourse analysis as organizational analysis. *Organization*, 7 (3): 513–18.

Clegg, S. (1989) *Frameworks of power*. London: Sage.

Cohen, A. (1974) *Two-dimensional man: An essay on the anthropology of power and symbolism in complex society*. London: Routledge & Kegan Paul.

Deetz, S. (1992) *Democracy in an age of corporate colonization*. Albany, NY: State University of New York Press.

Eisenberg, E. & Riley, P. (2001) Organizational culture. In F. Jablin & L. Putnam (eds), *The new handbook of organizational communication* (pp. 291–322). Thousand Oaks, CA: Sage.

Fairclough, N. (1993) Critical discourse analysis and the marketization of public discourse. *Discourse and Society*, 4: 133–59.

Frost, P.J. (1987) Power, politics, and influence. In F. Jablin, L.L. Putnam, K. Roberts & L. Porter (eds), *Handbook of organizational communication* (pp. 503–47). Newbury Park, CA: Sage.

Geertz, C. (1973) *The interpretation of culture*. New York: Basic Books.

Grant, D., Keenoy, T. & Oswick, C. (1998) Defining organizational discourse: Of diversity, dichotomy and multi-disciplinarity. In D. Grant, T. Keenoy & C. Oswick (eds), *Discourse and organization* (pp. 1–13). London: Sage.

Grant, D., Keenoy, T. & Oswick, C. (2001) Organizational discourse: Key contributions and challenges. *International Studies of Management and Organization*, 31 (3): 6–24.

Gregory, K.L. (1983) Native-view paradigms: Multiple cultures and culture conflicts in organizations. *Administrative Science Quarterly*, 28: 359–76.

Hardy, C., Palmer, I. & Phillips, N. (2000) Discourse as a strategic resource. *Human Relations*, 53 (9): 1227–48.

Knights, D. & Morgan, G. (1991) Corporate strategy, organizations and subjectivity: A critique. *Organization Studies*, 12: 251–73.

Knights, D. & Willmott, H.C. (1987) Organizational culture as management strategy: A critique and illustration from the financial service industries. *International Studies of Management and Organization*, 17 (3): 40–63.

Kunda, G. (1992) *Engineering culture: Control and commitment in a high-tech corporation*. Philadelphia, PA: Temple University Press.

Manning, P. (1979) Metaphors of the field: Varieties of organizational discourse. *Administrative Science Quarterly*, 24: 660–71.

Martin, J. (1992) *The culture of organizations: Three perspectives*. New York: Oxford University Press.

Martin, J. (2002) *Organizational culture*. Thousand Oaks, CA: Sage.

Martin, J. & Frost, P. (1996) The organizational culture wars: A struggle for intellectual dominance. In S. Clegg, C. Hardy & W. Nord (eds), *Handbook of organization studies* (pp. 599–621). London: Sage.

Martin, J. & Meyerson, D. (1988) Organizational cultures and the denial, channelling and acknowledgement of ambiguity. In L.R. Pondy, R.J. Boland & H. Thomas (eds), *Managing ambiguity and change* (pp. 93–125). New York: Wiley.

Martin, J., Sitkin, S. & Boehm, M. (1985) Founders and the elusiveness of a cultural legacy. In P.J. Frost, L. Moore, M. Louis, C. Lundberg & J. Martin (eds), *Organizational culture* (pp. 99–124). Beverly Hills, CA: Sage.

Miller, G. (1997) Building bridges: The possibility of analytic dialogue between ethnography, conversation analysis and Foucault. In D. Silverman (ed.), *Qualitative research* (pp. 24–44). London: Sage.

Mumby, D. & Clair, R. (1997) Organization and discourse. In T.A. van Dijk (ed.), *Discourse as structure and process* (Vol. 2, pp. 181–205). London: Sage.

Ortner, S. (1973) On key symbols. *American Anthropologist*, 75: 1338–46.

Ortner, S. (1984) Theory in anthropology since the sixties. *Comparative Studies in Society and History*, 26: 126–66.

Oswick, C., Keenoy, T. & Grant, D. (2000) Discourse, organizations and organizing: Concepts, objects and subjects. *Human Relations*, 53 (9): 1115–23.

Ouchi, W. & Wilkins, A. (1985) Organizational culture. *Annual Review of Sociology*, 11: 457–83.

Pacanowsky, M. & O'Donnel-Trujillo, N. (1983) Organizational communication as cultural performance. *Communication Monographs*, 50: 126–47.

Parker, M. (2000) *Organizational culture and identity*. London: Sage.

Phillips, N. & Hardy, C. (2002) *Discourse analysis*. Thousand Oaks, CA: Sage.

Potter, J. & Wetherell, M. (1987) *Discourse and social psychology*. London: Sage.

Putnam, L. & Fairhurst, G. (2001) Discourse analysis in organizations: Issues and concerns. In F. Jablin & L. Putnam (eds), *The new handbook of organizational communication* (pp. 78–136). Thousand Oaks, CA: Sage.

Ray, C.A. (1986) Corporate culture: The last frontier of control. *Journal of Management Studies*, 23 (3): 287–96.

Rosen, M. (1985) Breakfirst at Spiro's: Dramaturgy and dominance. *Journal of Management*, 11 (2): 31–48.

Smircich, L. (1983) Concepts of culture and organizational analysis. *Administrative Science Quarterly*, 28: 339–58.

Smirchich, L. & Calás, M. (1987) Organizational culture: A critical assessment. In F. Jablin, L. Putnam, K. Roberts & L. Porter (eds), *The handbook of organizational communication* (pp. 228–63). Beverly Hills, CA: Sage.

Stablein, R. & Nord, W. (1985) Practical and emancipatory interests in organizational symbolism. *Journal of Management*, 11 (2): 13–28.

Townley, B. (1994) *Reframing human resource management*. London: Sage.

Trice, H.M. & Beyer, J.M. (1993) *The culture of work organizations*. Englewood Cliffs, NJ: Prentice-Hall.

Trujillo, N. (1992) Interpreting the work and talk of baseball: Perspectives on baseball park culture. *Western Journal of Communication*, 56: 350–71.

Van Dijk, T. (1993) Principles of critical discourse analysis. *Discourse and Society*, 4: 249–83.

Van Maanen, J. (1991) The smile factory. In P.J. Frost, L. Moore, M. Louis, C. Lundberg & J. Martin (eds), *Reframing organizational culture* (pp. 58–76). Thousand Oaks, CA: Sage.

Van Maanen, J. & Barley, S.R. (1985) Cultural organization: Fragments of a theory. In P.J. Frost, L. Moore, M. Louis, C. Lundberg & J. Martin (eds), *Organizational culture* (pp. 31–54). Beverly Hills, CA: Sage.

Watson, T. (1994) *In search of management*. London: Routledge.

Wilkins, A.L. & Ouchi, W.G. (1983) Efficient cultures: Exploring the relationship between culture and organizational performance. *Administrative Science Quarterly*, 28: 468–81.

Willmott, H. (1993) Strength is ignorance; slavery is freedom: Managing culture in modern organizations. *Journal of Management Studies*, 30 (4): 515–52.

Yanow, D. (2000) Seeing organizational learning: A 'cultural' view. *Organization*, 7: 247–68.

Ybema, S. (1996) A duck-billed platypus in the theory and analysis of organizations: Combinations of consensus and dissensus. In W. Koot, I. Sabelis & S. Ybema (eds), *Contradictions in context: Puzzling over paradoxes in contemporary organizations* (pp. 39–61). Amsterdam: VU University Press.

Young, E. (1989) On the naming of the rose: Interests and multiple meanings as elements of organizational culture. *Organization Studies*, 10: 187–206.

15

Tools, Technologies and Organizational Interaction: The Emergence of 'Workplace Studies'

Christian Heath, Paul Luff and Hubert Knoblauch

In this chapter, we will discuss a growing corpus of research concerned with the ways in which tools and technologies, ranging from paper documents through to complex multimedia systems, feature in day-to-day work and interaction. This body of research has come to be known as 'workplace studies'. They are relatively unknown in organizational analysis and yet include detailed empirical studies of action and interaction in such diverse settings as air traffic control, emergency dispatch centres, control rooms on rapid urban transport networks, international telecommunication centres, financial institutions, newsrooms, construction sites, law firms and hospitals. They explore the ways in which artefacts are 'made at home' in the workplace, and demonstrate how the use of even the most seemingly 'personal computer' rests upon a complex social organization, an indigenous and tacit body of practice and procedures through which tools and technologies gain their occasioned sense and relevance within workplace activities. These studies, with their interest in the detailed social and interactional character of organizational activities, embody a distinctive shift in empirical studies of work and discourse, placing the object and the material environment at the heart of the analysis of discourse, talk and bodily conduct.

While drawing upon methodological developments within the social sciences, in particular ethnomethodology and conversation analysis, workplace studies have a curious provenance, a provenance that accounts, in part, for their underlying analytic concerns as well as the relative lack of awareness of them within organizational analysis and, more generally, management. We begin by providing some background to these studies and then in the second part of the chapter we discuss their analytic and substantive contribution with regard to one or two examples. We are particularly concerned with giving a sense of the range of empirical workplace studies and the ways in which they provide a distinctive and detailed analytic approach to taking the artefact at work seriously; that is in examining the ways in which they feature in the practical and contingent accomplishment of workplace activity and interaction.

BACKGROUND: TECHNOLOGY AND SITUATED ACTION

Technology has been a central concern for the social sciences since their inception and with the emergence of the computer and digital systems we have seen a wide-ranging commitment to (re)developing theories, models and concepts to encompass the impact of technology on work, organization and society. In sociology, for example, there is an impressive and substantial body of research concerned with the impact of computing and telecommunication systems on contemporary society and organizational life. These 'macro theories' reflect approaches and debates which have arisen more specifically within organizational analysis and the ways in which we conceptualize the post-bureaucratic organization. As Barley and Kunda (2001, p. 78) suggest, there has been a tendency 'to account for new organizational forms and practices solely as responses to changing environments', including the emergence of new technologies. So, for example, a range of significant developments – changes in the division of labour, job specification, skilling, automation and the like – is attributed to the widespread deployment of digital technologies. Unfortunately, however, as Barley and Kunda go on to suggest, these manifestations of contemporary organization theory distract attention from a 'detailed understanding of work and the ways in which technology is used and interpreted in specific organizational contexts' (2001, p. 79).

There is a small but important body of research within organizational studies concerned with the ways in which tools and technologies feature and fail to feature in everyday activity within the workplace. For example, Orlikowski (1992) examines the ways in which a groupware system, Lotus Notes, is exploited by members of a major consulting organization, and in particular addresses how certain features of the system fail to resonate with working practice and conventions within the firm. In a series of papers, Barley and colleagues (e.g., Barley 1990, 1996; Barley & Bechky, 1994) have examined the ways in which technologies feature in work and technical work, and have powerfully explored how conventional ideas and concepts of work, technology and organization have to be reconfigured with regard to detailed studies of practice. These and related initiatives are by and large relatively unusual within organizational analysis and to a large extent are, understandably, primarily concerned with the structures of work and the impact, or potential impact, of technologies on occupations and professional practice. They are also concerned with delineating how particular technologies achieve sense and significance, a sort of interpretive framework that arises through practice and achieves a certain resilience. The ways in which tools and technologies are used within particular actions and activities, their occasioned intelligibility, and in particular the ways in which they feature in interaction and collaboration within the workplace, remain relatively unexplored. There is, however, a discipline, and a substantial corpus of research, that does indeed address technology and interaction, and in part it is debate emerging within this research that led to the emergence of workplace studies.

To a large extent our understanding of the use of computers and, more generally, new technologies is largely dominated by cognitive science and in particular HCI (human–computer interaction). HCI has had pervasive academic and practical influence and its models and theories underlie, implicitly and explicitly, much of the research and development of technologies developed for the workplace. In HCI, studies of the use of computers are largely experimental and driven by a concern with developing cognitive models of the users' activities. Underlying the analysis is the idea that human action is governed by rules, scripts and plans, and that through manipulation of symbols and the development of representations, individuals are able to execute intelligent action and interaction. The operation of the computer serves therefore both as a metaphor to characterize human reasoning and conduct, as well as a substantive domain in which to discover cognitive processes. The approach is perhaps best exemplified in the influential study of human–computer interaction by Card, Moran and Newell (1980, 1983) where they develop 'GOMS': a model which differentiated system use with regard to the 'goals' of the individual user, the basic 'operators' through which the user attempts to accomplish his or her goals, the 'methods' by which the operators are combined to achieve the goals, and the cognitive processes of their 'selection'. Underlying these analyses is the assumption that by looking at how individuals use or 'interact' with technology, one might be able to discover the 'grammar of the head' (Payne & Green, 1986) or the 'structure and process of a person's mind' (Carroll 1990). It is also suggested that by studying the use of technology in terms of the mental models of the user, it could be possible to design a system which 'mirrors' the cognitive processes of its user (Norman, 1988).

This general approach has been subject to sustained criticism over some years, and these debates have increasingly led to the emergence of a variety of methodological developments. For example, Dreyfus (1972), Coulter (1979), Winograd and Flores (1986), Searle (1985) and the contributors to Still and Costall (1991) in very different ways build a wide-ranging critique of the pretensions of cognitive science and the idea that computers provide a suitable model of, or can even reflect, intelligence and practical reasoning. However, it is perhaps Suchman, in her monograph *Plans and Situated Action* (1987), who has had the most profound impact on the prevailing approach to human–computer interaction and in facilitating the emergence of a distinctive body of naturalistic studies of technology and social action, namely workplace studies. Drawing on ethnomethodology and conversation analysis, in particular the writings of Garfinkel (1967), Suchman suggests that the goal-oriented, plans-based models of human conduct which form the basis of HCI and cognitive science have a number of shortcomings. In the first place, they diminish the importance of the immediate context, or 'situation', of conduct and, in particular, the ways in which plans and schemas have to be applied with regard to the contingencies which emerge during the execution of practical action. Second, she shows how the meaning of plans, scripts, rules and the like are dependent upon the circumstances in which they are invoked; they do not determine conduct, but rather provide a resource through which individuals organize their own actions and interpret the conduct of others. Third, she argues, that by ignoring how individuals use and reason with plans and scripts in actual circumstances, human agency and the array of common-sense competencies on which it relies are cast from the analytic agenda. She demonstrates that formalisms, however detailed, are subject to the contingencies which arise in actual 'practical situations of choice', and that rules, plans, scripts etc. depend upon the ordinary common-sense abilities and reasoning of individuals for their deployment and intelligibility. The implication of Suchman's argument is that we can only understand technologies, and the various formalisms which may be involved, by considering how they feature within practical action and with regard to circumstances in which mundane activities are produced. The methodological consequences of Suchman's thesis are clear; it is necessary to turn from the experimental, the cognitive and the deterministic to the naturalistic, the social and the contingent.

The experimental thrust of HCI, Suchman's (1987) thesis, and a concern in computer science and engineering that technologies often fail to support the activities for which they are designed, has led to a growing recognition in the social sciences that we know relatively little about how people use tools and technologies in mundane circumstances. Even sociology, for example, with its burgeoning interest in the object over the past couple of decades, has not generated a substantial body of research concerned with the ways in which objects and artefacts are used in practice in everyday settings such as the workplace. Button (1993) speaks, for example, of the 'disappearing technology', where the social sciences posit tools, artefacts, objects etc. as the topic of interest, but analytically disregard how technologies are embedded in the practical accomplishment of social action and interaction. Consider the document. As Weber and others demonstrate, the document is central to the emergence of the modern organization from the mid-nineteenth century onwards, and is the artefact, *par excellence*, which has been transformed by digital technology. Curiously, however, we have relatively little understanding of the ways in which documents are assembled, read and exchanged within the developing course of practical activities, still less of the ways in which documents feature in interactional and collaborational organizational environments. For those with an academic or practical interest in documents, there is little research within the social sciences to which they can turn to discover how documents are embedded within organizational activities or how the technical transformation of such seemingly mundane artefacts resonates with indigenous work practices and procedures.

The growing recognition that we need to take technology in action seriously and consider the social and interactional organizations through which tools, systems and the like are used within the workplace has informed the emergence of a new field, namely CSCW (computer supported cooperative work). CSCW had become a forum for some of the more innovative developments in computing, ranging from early attempts to develop systems for group decision-making, through to the implementation of media spaces which provide a vehicle for real-time collaborative work among distributed personnel. It has also provided a field in which more conventional models of organizational conduct have been subject to some debate, both with regard to their inability to successfully inform the development of systems to support such activities as decision-making, but more importantly perhaps, their disregard for the fine details of workplace activities and the ways in which tools and technologies underpin their practical accomplishment. Since these early beginnings, CSCW has provided an opportunity for close collaboration between the social and computer sciences and, through this collaboration and the requirements of developing complex systems, has underscored the necessity to understand, in detail, the practical and socially organized accomplishment of workplace activities. Indeed, it is increasingly recognized that the successful, that is usable, design and development of advanced technologies to support communication and collaboration needs to be based upon an empirically founded body of knowledge and findings concerning the practices through which everyday activities are produced and coordinated. In consequence, CSCW, more than any other field of inquiry has provided a vehicle for the development of workplace studies and a re-flowering of the sociology of work, unparalleled perhaps save for the initiatives of E.C. Hughes in Chicago following the Second World War.

EXAMINING TECHNOLOGY AND SOCIAL INTERACTION

The general disregard in the social sciences for how technologies are used in practice, the growing debate within HCI and the development of CSCW have had an important influence on the emergence of workplace studies. A burgeoning body of empirical studies has arisen which is concerned with the analysis of how tools and technologies feature in social action and interaction in organizational settings. In large part these studies are ethnographies, involving extensive field studies of work settings, in some cases augmented by detailed video-based analyses of particular activities. The studies serve as a foundation with which to consider how artefacts, ranging from seemingly mundane tools such as pen and paper, through to highly complex systems, feature in the production and coordination of social actions and activities. In some cases they are also used to inform the design and development of new technologies and to consider how innovative systems might be exploited and deployed. In general, however, the substantive and, in some cases, applied concerns of these workplace studies, their interest in technologies in action and their commitment to the naturalistic analysis of human conduct serve to mask the diversity of these ethnographies, ethnographies that have drawn from such diverse traditions as symbolic interactionism, activity theory and distributed cognition.

However, it is ethnomethodology and conversation analysis, more than other analytic orientations, which have had the most prevailing influence on workplace studies and, more generally, social science research in CSCW. This is hardly surprising. Suchman's (1987) original critique of cognitive science and HCI drew on ethnomethodology and conversation analysis, and these analytic commitments have informed the development of a number of workplace studies facilitated by Suchman at Xerox and Rank Xerox research laboratories in the USA and Britain. Like other workplace studies, this body of research is naturalistic, concerned with building, as Geertz (1973) suggests, 'thick descriptions' of human activities, based an extensive field studies, and in general addresses the ways in which tools and technologies feature in social action and interaction. The analytic focus, however, shifts from the interest in meaning, representation and the social construction of tools and artefacts to a concern with the practical accomplishment of workplace activities and the ways in which participants themselves constitute the sense or intelligibility of tools and technologies in and through their conduct and interaction. It reflects a more radical conception of 'situated action', which places the emergent and reflexive character of practical action at the forefront of the analytic agenda. The concern therefore is to examine the practices and procedures, the socially organized competencies, in and through which participants themselves use tools and technologies in the emergent production and coordination of social action and activities, practices and procedures which give objects and artefacts their occasioned and determinate sense. This central concern, with the occasioned and accomplished sense of technology in action, has led to a particular interest in social interaction, talk, visual and material conduct, and the ways in which tools and artefacts feature, moment by moment, in the developing and collaborative production of workplace activities.

Despite the variety of approaches found within workplace studies, they all reflect a prevailing commitment to the analysis of technology in action, and in particular to the investigation of the ways in which tools and artefacts feature in the accomplishment of practical organizational conduct. They also reflect a concern with the practicalities of technology, and in particular with the design and deployment of advanced systems. These more applied commitments may primarily consist of re-specifying our understanding of system use and, through this re-specification, inform how designers and software engineers configure innovative tools and technologies. They may involve a more substantive practical commitment, contributing to the design and assessment of prototype systems (see, for example, Button & Dourish, 1996; Hughes et al., 1992; Jirotka & Wallen, 2000). In many cases, these naturalistic studies of work and technology necessarily involve close collaboration between social and computer scientists, where, alongside detailed empirical research, there is an underlying concern with the design of complex systems and how those systems feature, or may turn out to feature, in organizational activities and interaction.

USERS AND TASKS: SYSTEMS IN ACTION

To give a sense of these workplace studies, we will briefly consider two areas in which they have made an important contribution to our understanding of tools and technologies in action. The first arises in light of the ways in which documents feature in organizational conduct, the second with the real-time coordination of complex co-located and distributed activities. In passing, we will suggest ways in which these empirical studies bear upon a number of key concepts and ideas in organizational theory.

Perhaps the most wide-ranging impact of digital technologies in organizational environments is in recording, storing and retrieving textual information. The document, in both its paper and digital forms, has formed a central concern of workplace studies, and there is a growing body of research which examines how documents are assembled and used and how they provide a critical resource in the coordination of inter- and intra-organizational activities. For example, Harper's (1998) study of the International Monetary Fund powerfully examines how data collected about indigenous economies are transformed into extensive reports, the conventions of which point to standard policy recommendations and form a vehicle through which a disparate collection of organizational actions are coordinated. Button and Sharrock (1994) have examined how both paper and electronic documents feature in the coordination of large-scale software projects, and, more recently have considered how various 'formalizations' are embedded in artefacts and used to produce a range of complex activities on the shopfloor in the printing industry (Button & Sharrock, 1997). Other workplace studies concerned with the ways in which documents feature and are constituted through organizational activities include analyses of the introduction of information systems into customer service departments of high street banks (Randall & Hughes, 1995), the use of official, computer-based reports in handling calls to emergency dispatch centres (Whalen, 1995a, 1995b; Zimmerman, 1992), and the use of paper tickets for capturing the trading details in financial institutions (Jirotka et al., 1993). More generally, Sellen and Harper (2002) have undertaken a range of studies as part of a programme of research with Xerox Research Laboratories that is concerned with the affordances of paper and the ways in which paper facilitates practical action and interaction in organizations.

Consider, for example, the introduction of information systems into primary healthcare in the UK. Over the past decade almost all practices have introduced a computer-based system, which was designed largely to replace the conventional paper medical record card. Like the paper record, the computer-based system is designed to enable doctors to document aspects of the patient's illness and its management, and also access more general information concerning treatment programmes and the like. The computer-based system, like its precursor, the paper record, is not simply a report that documents the details of a patient's illness, but is a critical resource in the accomplishment of the consultation. For example, before a patient enters the consulting room a practitioner will glance at the last entries on the record to determine whether the patient is returning for a particular reason; the very design of the beginning of the consultation is sensitive to the information the doctor retrieves. Or, for example, during the consultation, the doctor will glance at the record to check the patient's treatment or even look for a hint as to the nature of a current complaint. Moreover, practitioners enter information into the system during the consultation, including the patient's symptoms, the diagnosis or assessment and details concerning the management of the complaint, including the necessary information to issue the prescription before the patient leaves (Heath & Luff, 1996). The computer-based record, like the paper document, therefore not only depends upon

Fragment 1

Dr: That's great
    (2.0)   *(Dr turns to keyboard)*
→ P: The only thing other problem I <u>do</u> have u::hm I
    sleep quite fitfully.
    (0.2)

Dr: uh huh
    (0.6)

P: Aa;nd (0.2) with my previous doctor I did
   occasionally go to him:: (.) for: (0.2) sleeping
   tablets::
Dr: Ye rs:
P: (hh)but <u>not</u> often.
Dr: Ri:ght
   (0.6)

P: And *er. (0.3) then again it was only prescription
   for: (0.2) maybe a weeks::: (0.6) supply just to
   get me back into (0.2) so:…
Dr: O.kay:…

the doctor's specialized skills and practices in detailing information, but also on his
or her abilities to use and coordinate the technology in his interaction with the
patient, interaction that is inevitably highly contingent and emergent.

Both patient and doctor are not only sensitive to the use of the system, but sensitive
to how the other orients to its use. Consider the following fragment drawn from an
ordinary general practice consultation. We join the action following the diagnosis and
discussion of treatment. The doctor inquires whether there is anything else the patient
might need (the patient has recently registered with the practice). The patient initially
shakes his head and says 'no', the doctor says 'That's great' and turns to the keyboard
and begins to type the prescription for the patient. As the doctor begins to type, the
patient raises a new problem for which he might occasionally need treatment.

The patient begins the utterance 'The only thing …' just as the doctor completes
a series of key strokes and lifts his right hand momentarily from the keyboard. The
doctor then continues to type until the patient utters 'occasionally'. He then lifts
his left hand from the keyboard. At this moment, the patient turns to the doctor. The
doctor strikes two keys and the patient hesitates 'him:: (.) for: (0.2)'. As if sensitive to patient hesitation, the doctor appears to delay further key strokes until the
patient continues. Then just as the word 'sleeping' is uttered, the doctor once again
begins to type. The fragment suggests therefore that the use of the system is
closely coordinated with the talk and interaction of the participants.

It is worthwhile considering the subsequent interaction in a little more detail.
The Xs indicate key strokes.

Fragment 1. Transcript 2

Dr	Dr begins to		Dr	Dr
Types	reposition fingers		nods head	turns to P.
↓	↓		↓	↓

XX   X X   X X X

P: --------- And er --- then again it was only prescription for -- maybe a weeks:::---------supply:

                        ↑...........↑
                      P. turns to Dr

On the word 'right' the doctor produces a sequence of four key strokes. The key strokes have a rhythm – two quick, two slow. The first two appear to project the second two, and the fourth, a final stroke. On the fourth stroke, the doctor begins to reposition his fingers. Just as the sequence is audibly complete and the doctor begins to lift his fingers, the patient produces 'And', projecting continuation. The doctor continues to type with the word 'prescription'. On the word 'maybe' the patient turns towards the doctor and the doctor stops typing. He retains his orientation towards the screen, but nods in response to the patient. Despite the typing being arrested and the head nod, the patient withholds further talk. The patient's pause would appear to elicit the orientation of the doctor; he turns from the screen to the patient and at that moment the patient continues with the word 'supply'.

The patient therefore is highly sensitive to the use of the system by the doctor. He articulates his talk with regard to the moment by-moment use of the system by the doctor and attempts (and is able) to anticipate potential boundaries within the activity, boundaries that project a shift in the activity that might enable the patient to secure a more involved and attentive recipient. For his own part, the doctor, in using the system, orients to the actions and activities of the patient. He delays, for example, beginning the activity until the patient has declined the opportunity to raise further issues or problems. When the patient does begin to speak and then stalls, the doctor temporarily delays typing. And, when the patient continues a little later and then withholds further talk, the doctor shifts his visual alignment from the screen to the patient. The use of the system, the technology, by the doctor arises within and through his interaction with the patient; the ways in which the details of the prescription are entered into the system are embedded within this emergent and contingent interaction. The brief and seemingly trivial moment of interaction points to some interesting issues with regard to conventional ideas concerning systems use and workplace activity.

In the first place, 'human–computer interaction', in this setting as in many others – for example call centres, reception areas, travel agencies and the like – does not simply consist of 'interaction' between the user and the system. The 'interaction' between the system and the user is accomplished with regard to the action of the co-participant(s). The use of the system is subject to the contributions of the co-participant, just as the co-participant – the patient, caller, client or whoever – produces his or her actions with regard to the use of system. For example, it is widely recognized that callers to call centres orient to the sounds of tapping on the keyboard when disclosing their reason for the call and associated information, just as call takers will delay keystrokes or even attempt to modulate their sound to encourage the caller to continue. The use of the system is embedded within the (social) interaction between doctor and patient and, fundamentally, the contingent and situated aspects of system use, discussed by Suchman (1987) and others, arise, in part, by virtue of that interaction. To ignore how the system is used with regard to, and becomes intelligible by virtue of, that interaction would seem to disregard the very ways in which the technology comes to feature in action and organizational conduct.

In the second place, the fragment raises some interesting issues concerning the organizational tasks and activities. In cognitive science and certain strands of organizational theory, tasks are primarily conceptualized as individual activities that follow a series of pre-specified procedures, rules or scripts. They also necessitate specific (and specialized) bodies of skill and knowledge. If, for example, 'writing a prescription' is a specialized activity undertaken by medical practitioners that follows a set of conventions and rules, it would seem reasonable to characterize the activity as a task. We can begin to see, however, that the actual accomplishment of this task, its *in situ* occasioned production, involves a complex and highly contingent interaction between doctor and patient. It is not simply that the prescription relies upon information provided by the patient, but rather its articulation is dependent on the emerging contributions of the co-participant. The task is a collaborative accomplishment and the system is a critical resource in its production and is used with regard to the ongoing participation of the patient. The task is accomplished in and through this interaction.

Finally, and perhaps most critically, the fragment raises issues with regard to the concept of the 'user' and the skills that 'users' rely upon in using the technology. The doctor is the principal user of the system and yet his use of the system is inextricably bound to the actions and contributions of the patient. The patient himself orients to the system and its use; he glances at the keyboard and screen, monitors the sounds emanating from the system, and is highly sensitive to the actions performed by the doctor when entering or retrieving information. In a sense, therefore, the patient is also a user of the system, and certainly the doctor's use of the system emerges in and through the patient's participation (for a related discussion, see Woolgar, 1991). Moreover, the skills or better competencies, which the doctor deploys to use the system, are not simply bound to the technology, but are interwoven with the interaction with the patient. They rely upon the patient's ability to act in particular ways and to make sense of the doctor's actions with the system. These skills and competencies are relied upon by the doctor and are not individual or idiosyncratic. Rather they are socially organized, interactionally embedded resources that enable doctor and patient contingently to coordinate the system's use in and through their (social) interaction. The individualistic and cognitive conception of the user found within certain forms of HCI and organizational analysis that pervades our current understanding of system use, provides a curiously impoverished image of the ways in which tools and technologies are used, removing the practical intelligence critical to the competent deployment of artefacts in practical circumstances. The seemingly simple use of an information system as an integral feature of professional conduct therefore provides a vehicle with which to reconsider the idea of a 'user' and the skills on which he or she relies, and begins to reveal the complex array of social, technical and interactional resources which inform the mundane and accountable use of the technology.

TEAMWORK AND COLLABORATION

The concern with both paper and electronic documents in workplace studies has also informed a substantial corpus of research concerned with what Suchman (1993) has characterized as 'centres of coordination'. These include studies of air traffic and ground control, in the UK, North America, Scandinavia and France, financial trading centres, network control centres, call centres, the control rooms of London Underground and RER in Paris, 911 centres in California, NASA control centres, and surveillance centres (see, for example, Fillippi & Theureau, 1993; Heath et al., 1993; Hughes et al., 1988, Suchman, 1993; Watts et al., 1996; Zimmerman, 1992; and contributions found in Engeström & Middleton, 1996; Luff et al., 2000). Personnel in domains such as these are responsible for coordinating a complex array of co-located and distributed activities. They have certain common characteristics, a strict division of labour coupled with the necessity to coordinate a complex array of simultaneous and sequential tasks and activities, both within the centre and between the centre and other domains, a wide range of technological resources, including paper documents (such as flight strips and timetables), information systems (diagrams, schedules, maps, etc.), CCTV (of docking bays, platforms, public entrances and walkways), large-scale digital or mechanical displays (which display rail traffic, telecommunication lines, etc.), and various communication devices (such as touch-screen telephones, radios and alarms). They are 'multimedia' environments *par excellence*, and provide an opportunity to examine how co-located and distributed personnel are able to draw on such resources to oversee or survey distributed events and activities and develop a coordinated response to problems and emergencies.

Examples drawn from command and control are widely discussed in the literature so it might be worthwhile discussing an example from a related but very different setting which raises parallel issues. The case in question is the editorial office of a major, international news agency in London, namely Reuters (see, for example, Heath & Luff, 2000). The editorial section consists of a number of 'desks', each desk specializing in particular types of financial news. Desks receive certain stories from bureaux throughout the world, and journalists edit the material using a basic information system. They then transmit those stories to particular customers who are primarily based in financial institutions in London and elsewhere in Europe. Journalists edit the material alone, although it is critical that they remain aware of stories being handled by other journalists and on other desks in the newsroom, and where necessary, they inform colleagues of potentially relevant items they may have received. Journalists handle a substantial number of news stories during the day and, given the speed with which some of these have to be 'turned round' and transmitted to customers (two or three minutes in some cases), they may have little time to explicitly inform colleagues of stories which may be of some relevance. Moreover, if they did, they run the danger of bombarding colleagues with unnecessary, even obtrusive, information. In consequence, they have developed a range of practices through which they delicately render stories visible to others within the newsroom.

Consider the following example. Things are relatively quiet in the newsroom and as he works on a story about a fall in Israeli interest rates, Peter begins to make a joke of the text he is editing on-screen. Peter's remarks, which are produced in a mock Jewish accent, are not explicitly addressed to colleagues on his own desk (Money and Capital), nor to those on the adjoining desk, Equities. While talking aloud, he continues to looks at his monitor and edit the story.

Fragment 2. Transcript 1

Peter: *Bank* of (.) *Israel* interest ra(i)te drops.
        (0.3)
Peter: Down, down, down.
        (0.4)
Peter: Didn't it do this last week.
        (13.0)

In talking aloud, Peter gives voice to the story on which he is working. Peter's remarks are loud enough to be audible to colleagues sitting at adjoining and surrounding desks. By talking aloud, he renders aspects of the text that is documented on his screen 'publicly' accessible, or at least audible to others within the immediate location. In so doing, he does not simply talk through the text, but provides a selective rendition which animates aspects of the story, giving it the character of a joke. Interestingly, the way in which the story is voiced and animated, its lighthearted rendition coupled with Peter's continuing orientation to and work on the text, does not demand that his colleagues respond, or even acknowledge, what has been said. It places no one under an obligation to respond or, more technically, to produce a sequentially appropriate response. It neither identifies a particular recipient nor an appropriate next action or activity. The question, 'Didn't it do this last week' is rhetorical. It elaborates the joke and perhaps provides a framework for Peter's remarks, but does not demand or encourage a response. In some sense Peter's remarks render the materials on which he is working selectively 'visible' to his colleagues within the local milieu, but through the ways in which it is accomplished, it places no one under any particular obligation to respond.

Peter continues to work on the story. Roughly twelve seconds later, Alex, who is sitting some six feet away at the Equities desk, momentarily changes his orientation. He glances towards Peter and then turns back to his own monitor. Peter appears to treat the action as relevant to the story that he voiced some moments ago. He utters 'er:::' and after pausing for one second, perhaps to relocate the potentially relevant part of the text, tells part of the story on which he is working. In the illustrations, Peter is on the right, and Alex second from the right.

Fragment 2. Transcript 2

(13.0)

Peter:
er

(1.0)

Bank of Israel er.
(3.2)
cut its er daily (0.4) the rate on its daily
money tender, (0.2) to commercial banks.

(0.6)

Alex: Yeah. Got that now. Thanks Peter
(0.6)
Peter: O.kay?

Peter's talk is now addressed specifically to Alex. He no longer makes a joke of the story, nor characterizes the text on which he is working, but rather delivers a quote from the material itself. The quote provides a more precise and potentially factual report of the events. Peter's delivery sharply contrasts with the earlier version. It is not rendered as a joke or as a précis, but rather as part of the original, authentic story. The ways in which the talk is produced, coupled with the accompanying visual conduct, provides colleagues with the resources to differentiate the status of the two renditions and in particular their 'relationship' to the textual version of the story.

The exposition of the story is occasioned by Alex's momentary orientation to Peter. Peter treats Alex's action as requesting further information concerning the story and in particular its relevance and potential newsworthiness. Although the original joke is not specifically addressed, the informing is designed to enable Alex to receive accurate and authentic information concerning the recent change in Israeli interest rates.

It looks as if the telling is over following Alex's acknowledgement of the story with 'Yeah. Got that now. Thanks Peter'. However, some seconds later, Peter reads aloud the sentence that describes the actual fall in interest rates. By pausing in the delivery of the sentence, Peter momentarily renders the description problematic and, on completing the sentence, he goes on to correct the story. The correction involves the speaker realigning his position to the text, from narrator to commentator. Peter differentiates his version from the original text and publicizes, at least across the two desks, the editorial correction.

Fragment 2   **Transcript 3**
    Peter: Half a percent, (1.2) to eleven percent.
                (0.2)
    Peter: I think they mean a half a percentage Point
                (15:04)
    Peter: Ser<u>v</u>ice Jerusalem (0.5) with a <u>drop</u> copy to Nicosia, right?
                (0.7)
    Alex: Yes

Finally, Peter marks the completion of the handling of the Israeli interest rate story by checking with Alex as to which Reuters' bureau should receive copies of the corrected version.

What begins as a joke therefore turns out to have some serious import for news production. The Israeli interest rate story gets publicly corrected, distributed to more than one desk and subsequently to the customers of both Money and Capital and Equities. It also features, and is referred to, in other stories that are handled by the two desks on that day. The story achieves its wider circulation by virtue of Peter's joke. The joke is delicately designed to establish these possibilities. It does not demand that others abandon the activities in which they are engaged or even take up the story. Rather, Peter's joke renders visible the gist of the story which he is currently editing. It momentarily displays the activity in which he is engaged. It provides colleagues with news concerning the Israeli interest rates but does not project a response. The talk is produced by Peter (and treated by his colleagues) as if devoid of sequential relevance and yet invites others to consider the import of the story with respect to their own activities and responsibilities.

In gaining some indication that a colleague is interested in hearing more of the story, Peter transforms the way in which he presents the text to the others. Instead of continuing the joke, he provides an authentic rendition of the text, (re)presenting the change in interest rates. The speaker therefore differentiates the informing by virtue of the ways in which he presents the text, although in both cases it is as if he is simply reading aloud the story on the screen. In the final part of the informing, the speaker once again alters his standpoint *vis-à-vis* the text, visibly locating and correcting an error in the original copy. In rendering his activity visible, the speaker exploits, through the ways in which he talks through the story, different standpoints with respect to the text itself. In this way he ongoingly tailors the sequential significance and sense of the story for those within the local milieu. In this way a textual story, located temporarily on the screen, is transformed into talk and rendered visible to others within the local domain. It informs the activities in which the journalists engage both individually and collaboratively.

Once again, we can see the ways in which competent use of the system relies upon the ability of the journalist to coordinate its use with the presence and (potential) contribution of others. The use of the system is interactionally and communicatively oriented; it is accomplished with regard to the practical interests and activities of others. Simply being able to edit text, that is having the requisite skills to use a basic information system, is a small part of being able to use competently the technology within the practical constraints and circumstances of the editorial office. The task of receiving, selecting and editing stories using the technology relies upon a complex social and interactional organization that allows journalists to coordinate their contributions, in real time, with the interests, responsibilities and conduct of others. It should be added that in editing and writing stories the journalists are simultaneously oriented to the interests and concerns of the recipients, that is the 'readers' of the stories and the practical constraints under which such people work. In orienting, for example, to the interests of colleagues on separate desks, the journalists consider and anticipate what may be of interest to the 'readers' who will use the materials issued by commodities, minerals, equities, etc.

We can begin to see how the (conventional) use of the system is bound into and addresses teamwork and collaboration. Conventional computing technology, in this case a simple information system, is designed to provide individual users with particular forms of information and editorial capabilities and to restrict the access that others have to that information through screen size and the like. Moreover, in the case at hand, to avoid overloading and bombarding journalists with irrelevant stories (at least for their particular customers), stories are coded and directed towards certain desks. Journalists have redeveloped a body of practice that addresses the design and configuration of the system and provides the possibility of the unobtrusive (or better, undemanding) distribution of potentially relevant stories. Through their conduct, they selectively render information on, and editorial activity with, the system, providing colleagues not only with a sense of the activity in which others are involved, but also with news stories that may in turn have some relevance for their customers. Trivial as it may seem, making jokes, talking out loud, producing occasional exclamations and such like, turn out to have important organizational consequences; they provide the resources through which coordination and collaboration are accomplished within the editorial office. They provide resources that enable journalists to use the system in concert with the activities of colleagues and thereby to provide a coherent, timely and relevant news service for the trading rooms in London and elsewhere.

As Anderson, Hughes and Sharrock (1989) point out, these issues also bear upon our understanding of the division of labour. Despite growing debates concerning new forms of the division of labour emerging within contemporary developments in organizational arrangements, it remains an important heuristic in the analysis of work and organizations. Workplace studies have begun to explore the ways in which participants themselves orient to, use and rely upon the division of labour within the practical accomplishment of their daily activities. So, for example, in their ongoing project concerned with air traffic control, Hughes and others (Hughes et al., 1988; Harper et al., 1991) show how the division of labour is not encountered as a coherent and integrated totality, but rather as a stream of differentiated and discrete tasks. The differentiation of work activities, as a hierarchy of responsibility, is an ongoing and contingent allocation of responsibility, of both self and others. Seen from within, the division of labour is a fluid gestalt and is evidenced in innumerable locally produced ways, known in common and seen at a glance (Anderson et al., 1989). In the editorial office, we can see ways in which the formal division of responsibility and labour is ongoingly accomplished in and through the interaction of the participants. Journalists are highly sensitive to the responsibilities of colleagues; they scrutinize and selectively render visible stories that may be of relevance to the activities, the labour, of others, and provide co-participants with the resources to discriminate what is indeed relevant and appropriate. Interestingly, the practical accomplishment of the division of labour by the journalists themselves within the course of their work is itself sensitive to the divisions of responsibility and labour found within financial institutions in London and elsewhere. The delicate forms of collaboration and co-participation that arise within the editorial office contribute to and preserve conventional divisions of labour and activity within the trading rooms.

Teamwork has been a critical theme of organizational studies since their inception and its analysis reflects many of the traditional theories of structure, interdependence and integration, coordination and action (see, for example, Boden 1994). Surprisingly, perhaps, the ways in which teamwork is accomplished, by the participants themselves in the course of their everyday work, remain relatively neglected, despite a long-standing recognition that social interaction was critical to its organization. Indeed, even the highly insightful and more general ethnographic studies of work that emerged in the light of the initiatives of E.C. Hughes and others in Chicago following the Second World War, a tradition that continues in organizational analysis, tend to gloss over the practicalities and, in particular, the interactional accomplishment of teamwork (Hughes, 1958). Workplace studies, including studies of control centres, operating theatres, trading rooms, etc., have begun to reveal and explicate the highly contingent character of teamwork and the ways it emerges, and is sustained, in and through the talk and interaction. They point to the complex forms of participation and co-participation entailed in teamwork and the ways in which these are ongoingly accomplished with regard to the emerging practicalities at hand. Perhaps most critically, they demonstrate how the formal, the informal and the tacit are embedded in and inseparable from the ongoing interaction of the participants themselves; to disregard this interaction is to ignore the practices and reasoning through which work and teamwork are accomplished.

DISCOURSE, ORGANIZATION AND COMMUNICATION WORK

As the chapters in this volume suggest, over the past decade or so there has been a burgeoning interest within various disciplines concerned with language, discourse and communication in organizations (Keenoy et al., 1997). A diverse range of interests and approaches have informed this 'linguistic' turn, and have served to generate a rich and varied re-specification of a number of the key concepts which traditionally have informed organizational analysis. A significant strand of this work has focused on the interaction and, in particular, the ways in which 'organization' is accomplished in and through the talk of the participants. Conversation analysis has been particularly important in this regard. We have witnessed the emergence of a wide range of empirical studies of talk at work, studies which addressed such diverse organizational environments as news interviews, medical consultations and business meetings (e.g., Boden, 1994; Boden & Zimmerman, 1991; Drew & Heritage, 1992; Heritage & Maynard, in press). The studies have powerfully explicated the sequential organization of talk in interaction, through which participants' accomplish a range of workplace activities. Like other approaches to talk and discourse at work (e.g., Edwards & Potter, 1992) the visual and material aspects of action in organizations have received less attention. Workplace studies complement these developments. They preserve and enhance the commitment to unpacking the interactional accomplishment of workplace activities and reshape our understanding of organizational conduct while avoiding the relativism that Silverman (1997) and Reed (1992), among others, suggest increasingly pervades studies of institutional activities.

In the first place, workplace studies build on earlier research (e.g., Goodwin, 1982; Heath, 1986) to reveal the ways in which bodily conduct – glances, gestures, etc. – is an integral feature in the practical accomplishment of workplace activities; the articulation and intelligibility of talk produced in and through the visual as well as vocal. Second, workplace studies direct analytic attention towards the ways in which objects and artefacts, tools and technologies, are not simply constituted through talk, but rather inform the very ways in which participants produce and recognize social action and activities – the collaborative accomplishment of workplace activities emerging in and though the material environment. In this regard, it is worth mentioning that the ecological foundations of action and interactional and organizational settings still remain a curiously neglected concern for studies of work, language and discourse, achieving an analytic primacy which remains empirically untenable. In particular, workplace studies have begun to reveal how tools and technologies, and other features of the local environment, are brought to bear and are reflexively constituted in action and interaction within the workplace. Perhaps, most importantly, they have also begun to address rather different forms of interaction and communication in organizations. In control rooms, for example, communicational activities do not necessarily involve 'focused interaction', but rather highly variable forms of emerging and contingent participation in which individuals, who may be co-located or dispersed, more or less participate in the production of a number of concurrent, interdependent activities. In various ways workplace studies powerfully demonstrate how the fine details of interaction lie at the heart of a broad range of organizational activities, and that discourse, talk and interaction are embedded in the material environment. These analytic and substantive developments demand methodological innovations which still leave a number of key questions unanswered.

The concern with the contingent and interactional character of organizational conduct contributes to related developments in organizational theory (Knoblauch, 1997; Reed, 1992). There is a growing recognition that globalization, changes in the nature of the market and the emergence of new communication technologies are generating new forms of organizational arrangement and conduct, which require flexible and temporary forms of cooperation within and between firms and the components of desegregated corporations. As yet, however, there is little research concerned with the ways in which different forms of collaboration emerge, coalesce, evolve and fragment, and how individuals in concert with each other use various tools and technologies to assemble temporary forms of cooperation in order to, for example, develop a particular product for a niche in the market. Workplace studies may provide a conceptual and empirical vehicle for addressing these new forms of organization and cooperation, allowing us to reconsider institutional forms and their associated baggage of roles, rules and goals. Such concerns have strong parallels with 'new institutionalism' (DiMaggio & Powell, 1991), but as Silverman (1997) suggests, workplace studies provide an opportunity to build fine-grained, empirically-grounded studies of institutional conduct alongside the more programmatic and theoretical work found increasingly within some areas of contemporary organizational analyses.

In a recent and important collection of workplace studies, Engeström and Middleton suggest that these new forms of organizational analyses provide a vehicle for interweaving 'microsociological analysis of locally constructed and negotiated work activities' with 'macro-level discussions of the impact of technological development on the skills and the organization of work' (Engeström & Middleton, 1996, p. 1). While we have reservations concerning the so-called 'micro–macro' distinction, we can begin to see how the analysis of technologically-oriented work may provide a vehicle for reconsidering some of the key ideas in our understanding of such concepts as information, information work and the information society. At their most basic, we can see how workplace studies provide the possibility of recovering 'information' from its reified status as a theoretical construct, by considering how participants themselves, in the course of the organizational actions and activities, orient to, use and disseminate information. So, for example, a range of studies have begun to examine how individuals collect and constitute particular types of information, how they configure facts and findings, reports and descriptions, how such information is managed and on what occasions and for what purposes it is retrieved, and how information is deployed within practical action and interaction. In this regard, information as a blanket term – to encapsulate a disparate and unbounded array of materials, matters, and the like – becomes untenable, as we turn analytic attention to the ways in which particular organizationally-relevant information gains its significance and determinate character in actual courses of action and interaction. Information is inextricably embedded in practice and practical action.

Alongside their empirical and conceptual contributions, workplace studies are having an increasing influence on the design and development of advanced technologies, in particular perhaps, systems to support cooperative work. While it is probably undesirable that we will witness the emergence of a practical ethnography for technology akin to the methods and guidelines we find in HCI and cognate disciplines, it is perhaps heartening to note that naturalistic studies of work and interaction, sometimes derided for being insignificant, if not trivial, are found to have important implications for such seemingly practical matters as the design and deployment of advanced technology. By turning attention to the details of work, and in particular the tacit, 'seen but unnoticed' social and interactional resources on which participants rely in the practical accomplishment of organizational activities, we can begin to (re)consider how particular tools and technologies might support, enhance, even transform what people do and the ways in which they do it. Moreover, shifting attention from the cognitive to the social, from the individual to the collaborative, provides a vehicle for exploring more innovative ways of supporting action and interaction in the workplace and, in particular, the new forms of synchronous and asynchronous cooperation increasingly demanded by fragmented, disaggregated organizations. More importantly perhaps, these newly emerging workplace studies provide a distinctive body of sociological research which directs analytic attention towards the ways in which tools and technologies feature in practical action and interaction and help expose an important, yet largely unexplored, realm of social organization.

NOTE

We would like to thank Jon Hindmarsh, Dirk vom Lehn and David Greatbatch for their wide-ranging contributions to the discussion of many of the issues and materials addressed here.

REFERENCES

Anderson, R., Hughes, J. & Sharrock, W. (1989) *Working for profit.* Farnborough: Avebury.

Barley, S.R. (1990) The alignment of technology and structure through roles and networks. *Administrative Science Quarterly*, 35: 65–103.

Barley, S.R. (1996) Technicians in the workplace: ethnographic evidence for bringing work into organization studies. *Administrative Science Quarterly*, 41: 404–41.

Barley S.R. & Bechky, B.A. (1994) In the backrooms of science: The work of technicians in science labs. *Work and Occupations*, 21: 85–126.

Barley, S.R. & Kunda, G. (2001) Bringing work back in. *Organization Science*, 12 (1): 76–95.

Boden, D. (1994) *The business of talk: Organizations in action.* Oxford and Cambridge, MA: Polity Press.

Boden, D. & Zimmerman, D.H. (eds) (1991) *Talk and social structure: Studies in ethnomethodology and conversation analysis.* Cambridge: Polity Press.

Button, G. (1993) The curious case of the disappearing technology. In G. Button (ed.), *Technology in the working order* (pp. 10–28). London: Routledge.

Button, G. & Dourish, P. (1996) Technomethodology: Paradoxes and possibilities. *Proceedings of CHI 1996* (pp. 19–26). Vancouver, Canada. New York: ACM Press.

Button G. & Sharrock, W. (1994) Occasioned practices in the work of software engineers. In M. Jirotka & J. Goguen (eds), *Requirements engineering: Social and technical issues* (pp. 217–40). London: Academic Press.

Button, G. & Sharrock, W. (1997) The production of order and the order of production. *Proceedings of the European Conference in Computer Supported Cooperative Work 1997* (pp. 1–16). Lancaster. New York: Kluwer.

Card, S.K., Moran, T.P. & Newell, A. (1980) Computer text-editing: An information processing analysis of a routine cognitive skill. *Cognitive Psychology*, 12: 32–74.

Card, S.K., Moran, T. & Newell, A. (1983) *The psychology of human–computer interaction.* Hillsdale, NJ: Lawrence Erlbaum Associates.

Carroll, J.M. (1990) Infinite detail and emulation in an ontologically minimized HCI. *Proceedings of CHI 1990* (pp. 321–7). Seattle. Cambridge, MA: ACM Press.

Coulter, J. (1979) *The social construction of mind: Studies in ethnomethodology and linguistic philosophy.* London: Macmillan.

DiMaggio, P.J. & Powell, W.W. (1991) Introduction. In W.W. Powell & P.J. DiMaggio, (eds), *The new institutional in organizational analysis* (pp. 1–38). Chicago and London: University of Chicago Press.

Drew, P. & Heritage, J.C. (eds) (1992) *Talk at work: Interaction in institutional settings.* Cambridge: Cambridge University Press.

Dreyfus, H.L. (1972) *What computers still can't do: A critique of artificial reason* (2nd edition). Cambridge, MA: MIT Press.

Edwards, D. & Potter, J. (1992) *Discursive psychology.* London: Sage.

Engeström, Y. & Escalante, V. (1996) Mundane tool or object of affection? The rise and fall of the postal buddy. In B.A. Nardi, (ed.), *Context and consciousness: Activity and human–computer interaction* (pp. 325–73). Cambridge, MA: MIT Press.

Engeström, Y. & Middleton, D. (eds) (1996) *Cognition and communication at work.* Cambridge: Cambridge University Press.

Filippi, G. & Theureau, J. (1993) Analysing cooperative work in an urban traffic control room for the design of a coordination support system. *Proceedings of the European conference on computer supported cooperative work 1993* (pp. 171–86). Milan, Italy, 13–17 September.

Garfinkel, H. (1967) *Studies in ethnomethodology.* Englewood Cliffs, NJ: Prentice-Hall.

Geertz, C. (1973) *The interpretation of cultures.* New York: Basic Books.

Goodwin, C. (1982) *Conversational interaction: The interactions between speakers and hearers.* New York: Academic Press.

Goodwin, C. & Goodwin, M.H. (1996) Seeing as a situated activity: Formulating planes. In Y. Engeström & D. Middleton (eds), *Cognition and communication at work* (pp. 61–95). Cambridge: Cambridge University Press.

Harper, R.H.R. (1998) *Inside the IMF: An ethnography of documents, technology and organizational action.* London: Academic Press.

Harper, R., Hughes, J. & Shapiro, D. (1991) Working in harmony: An examination of computer technology and air traffic control. In J. Bowers & S.D. Benford (eds), *Studies in computer supported cooperative work. Theory practice and design* (pp. 225–34). Amsterdam: North Holland.

Health, C.C. (1986) *Body movement and speech in medical interactions*. Cambridge: Cambridge University Press.

Heath, C.C. & Luff, P. (1996) Documents and professional practice: 'bad' organizational reasons for 'good' clinical records. *Proceedings of the conference on computer supported cooperative work 1996* (pp. 354–63). Boston, MA, 16–20 November. New York: ACM Press.

Heath, C.C. & Luff, P.K. (2000) *Technology in action*. Cambridge: Cambridge University Press.

Heath, C.C., Jirotka, M., Luff, P. & Hindmarsh, J. (1993) Unpacking collaboration: the interactional organization of trading in a city dealing room. *Proceedings of the European conference on computer supported cooperative work 1993* (pp. 155–70). Milan, Italy, 13–17 September. New York: Kluwer.

Heritage, J.C. & Maynard, D. (in press) *Practising medicine: Talk and action in primary care encounters*. Cambridge: Cambridge University Press.

Hughes, E.C. (1958) *Men and their work*. Glencoe, IL: Free Press.

Hughes, J.A., Randall, D.R. & Shapiro, D. (1992) Faltering from ethnography to design. *Proceedings of the conference on computer supported cooperative work 1992* (pp. 115–22). Toronto, Canada, 31 October – 4 November. New York: ACM Press.

Hughes, J.A., Shapiro, D.Z., Sharrock, W.W., Anderson, R.A., Harper, R.R. & Gibbons, S.C. (1988) *The automation of air traffic control*. Final Report, Department of Sociology, Lancaster University.

Jirotka, M., Luff, P. & Heath, C. (1993) Requirements for technology in complex environments: Tasks and interaction in a city dealing room. *SIGOIS Bulletin* (Special Issue: *Do users get what they want? (DUG 1993)*), 14 (2): 17–23.

Jirotka, M. & Wallen, L. (2000) Analysing the workplace and user requirements: Challenges for the development of methods for requirements engineering. In P. Luff, J. Hindmarsh & C. Heath (eds), *Workplace studies: Recovering work practice and informing system design* (pp. 242–62). Cambridge: Cambridge University Press.

Keenoy, T., Oswick, C. & Grant, D. (1997) Organizational discourse: Text and context. *Organization*, 4: 147–57.

Knoblauch, H. (1997) Die kommunikative Konstruktion postmoderner Organizationen. Institutionen, Aktivitätssysteme und kontextuelles Handeln. *Österreichische Zeitschrift für Soziologie*, 22 (2): 6–23.

Luff, P., Hindmarsh, J. & Heath, C. (eds) (2000) *Workplace studies: Recovering work practice and informing system design*. Cambridge: Cambridge University Press.

Norman, D.A. (1988) *The psychology of everyday things*. New York: Basic Books.

Norman, D.A. (1998) *The invisible computer*. Cambridge, MA: MIT Press.

Orlikowski, W.J. (1992) Learning from notes: Organizational issues in groupware implementation. *Proceedings of the conference on computer supported cooperative work 1992* (pp. 362–9). Toronto, Canada, 31 October – 4 November. New York: ACM Press.

Payne, S.J. & Green, T.R.G. (1986) Task-action grammars: A model of the mental representation of task languages. *Human–Computer Interaction*, 2 (2): 93–133.

Randall, D. & Hughes, J.A. (1995) Sociology, CSCW and working with customers. In P. Thomas (ed.), *The social and interaction dimensions of human–computer interfaces* (pp. 142–60). Cambridge: Cambridge University Press.

Reed, M.I. (1992) *The sociology of organizations: Themes, perspectives and prospects*. London: Harvester Wheatsheaf.

Searle, J.R. (1985) *Minds, brains and science*. Cambridge, MA: Harvard University Press.

Sellen, A. & Harper, R.H.R. (2002) *The myth of the paperless office*. Cambridge, MA: MIT Press.

Silverman, D. (1997) Studying organizational interaction: Ethnomethodology's contribution to the 'new institutionalism'. *Administrative Theory and Praxis*, 19 (2): 178–95.

Still, A. & Costall, A. (eds) (1991) *Against cognitivism: Alternative foundations for cognitive psychology*. London: Harvester Wheatsheaf.

Suchman, L. (1987) *Plans and situated actions: The problem of human–machine communication.* Cambridge: Cambridge University Press.

Suchman, L. (1993) Technologies of accountability: On lizards and aeroplanes. In G. Button (ed.), *Technology in working order* (pp. 113–26). London: Routledge.

Watts, J.C., Woods, D.D., Corban, J.M., Patterson, E.S., Kerr, R.L. & Hicks, L.C. (1996) Voice loops as cooperative aids in space shuttle mission control. *Proceedings of the conference on computer supported cooperative work 1996* (pp. 48–56). Cambridge, MA. New York: ACM Press.

Whalen, J. (1995a) Expert systems *vs* systems for experts: Computer-aided dispatch as a support system in real-world environments. In P. Thomas (ed.), *The social and interactional dimensions of human–computer interfaces* (pp. 161–83). Cambridge: Cambridge University Press.

Whalen, J. (1995b) A technology of order production: Computer-aided dispatch in public safety communications. In P. ten Have & G. Psathas (eds), *Situated order: Studies in the social organization of talk and embodied activities* (pp. 187–230). Washington, DC: University Press of America.

Winograd, T. & Flores, F. (1986) *Understanding computers and cognition: A new foundation for design.* Reading, MA: Addison-Wesley.

Woolgar, S. (1991) Configuring the user: The case of usability trials. In J. Law (ed.), *A sociology of monsters: Essays on power, technology and domination* (pp. 58–97). London: Routledge.

Zimmerman, D.H. (1992) The interactional organization of calls for emergency assistance. In P. Drew & J. Heritage (eds), *Talk at work: Interaction in institutional settings* (pp. 418–69). Cambridge: Cambridge University Press.

16

Organizational Discourse and New Media: A Practice Perspective

Pablo J. Boczkowski and Wanda J. Orlikowski

We open this chapter with what we believe is a telling observation from the field. In a study of the communicative practices of a large, geographically-distributed, high-tech company, Woerner (2002) reports that her participants routinely refer to their use of instant messaging, phone conferences and in-person meetings as 'face-to-face communication'. What are we to make of this apparent mis-labelling? Is this simply a categorical error on the part of the participants, or an expression of the transformative efforts undertaken by these workers to deal with new media in their everyday organizational lives? We believe the latter: that the participants, far from being 'in error', are engaged in a practical recategorization of media use to reflect their current and emerging communicative practices.

Stories like Woerner's underscore not only the central role of new media innovations in organizational practices, but also the parallel innovations in sense-making enacted by the actors to deal with their changing workplace. Woerner's findings suggest that for her participants the most salient aspect of communicating is not whether it is face-to-face or not, but whether it is synchronous or not. Synchronicity affords, among other things, immediacy of interaction, direct connection to others, and relative control over the pace, timing and content of the conversation. As these are elements that have become more pressing in contemporary organizational work, participants' interest in synchronicity is not surprising. What is surprising, however, is the extent to which academic scholarship has not kept pace with actors' innovative efforts, by insisting, for instance, on privileging 'face-to-face' communication and preserving a central distinction between 'face-to-face' and 'mediated' communication.

Even though research in the last twenty years has yielded important contributions to understanding new media and organizational discourse, we believe its current innovative capacity lags behind that of both technology production and use. Put differently, the current state of the art in this domain of inquiry presents some under-explored areas which recent developments like those portrayed in this chapter's opening story make more visible. We address these through a literature review and a programmatic essay. Our review of the literature highlights under-explored areas in existing scholarship, areas that become particularly acute in light of organizational innovations and media developments. Our programmatic statement suggests the value of developing a more practice-oriented understanding of the recursive interaction between people, new media and organizational discourse. By focusing on the everyday activities of situated actors, a practice orientation can provide insights into the dynamic, emergent and enacted nature of organizational discourse as it unfolds through a complex array of new and evolving media.

The study of discourse has been variously conceived. Following Putnam and Fairhurst (2001), in this chapter we will broadly understand discourse analysis as 'the study of words and signifiers, including the form or structure of these words, the use of language in context, and the meanings or interpretation of discursive practices' (2001, p. 79). The creation, circulation and appropriation of these words and signifiers within organizational contexts takes place in both unmediated and mediated fashion. In this chapter, we focus on one variant of mediated discourse, that which employs relatively new media – instead of media that have been around for a long time, such as print. We conceive new media broadly as the convergence and hybridization of information and telecommunication technologies that result in technologies such as electronic mail, videoconferencing, instant messaging and voice mail (Lievrouw et al., 2001).

Since research on new media and organizational discourse is reviewed extensively elsewhere, we focus on specific areas in the current state of the literature that seem particularly under-explored and which a practice perspective may develop further. Following a review of these areas, we introduce the fundamentals of a practice perspective and illustrate it with examples from research on the use of new media in the workplace. Then, we draw from relatively recent empirical research to reflect on how a practice perspective may contribute to understanding discourse and new media as well as to advancing new scholarly avenues. In the concluding section of this chapter we offer some closing remarks on the future of this domain of inquiry.

CONTEXT, TECHNOLOGY AND COMMUNICATION

Research on new media and organizational discourse has been reviewed extensively, especially in the last few years (see, for instance, Fulk & Collins-Jarvis, 2001; O'Mahony & Barley, 1999; Rice & Gattiker, 2001; Roberts & Grabowski, 1996; Wellman et al., 1996). These reviews assess many strengths and weaknesses of work in this area. Hence, in this section we focus on three issues which (a) seem relatively under-developed in the current state of the literature, (b) have become particularly salient in the light of contemporary organizational and technological innovations, and (c) may benefit from a practice perspective. These issues stem from a relatively narrow characterization of context, a somewhat atomized view of the communication process, and a tendency to compartmentalize technology's discursive potentials.

Context

The vast majority of the existing literature constructs the context of organizational discourse and new media in either one of two ways. First, experimental studies tend to construct an 'artificial' context that facilitates the occurrence of specific discursive patterns. This work has made important contributions by bringing these patterns to the foreground, and making more visible their key elements and dynamics. For example, in a series of laboratory experiments, Sproull and Kiesler (1991) demonstrate that the reduction of non-verbal information in computer-mediated communication could lead, under certain circumstances, to an intensification of flaming behaviour. Furthermore, although we normally associate experimental designs with laboratory settings, experimental studies in non-laboratory settings also generate important insights on specific patterns. For example, in a study of team projects by MBA students located in different universities, Cramton (2001) observes the processes and mechanisms through which unrecognized social differences can lead to negative outcomes in situations of dispersed work arrangements.

Second, work done through field studies has mostly analysed processes and outcomes located within the 'natural' context, as bounded by the focal organization in which research was conducted. For example, in a study of the structural configuration of virtual organizations, Ahuja and Carley (1999) examine the discursive patterns evident in the electronic mail of the Soar group, a research and development enterprise composed of scholars located in an array of educational and corporate settings. Through a network analysis of communication among group members, they show that contrary to much speculation about the demise of hierarchy in virtual teams, the informal structure becomes hierarchically stratified with regard to role distribution and task knowledge. In an example from a qualitative, interpretive tradition of inquiry, Orlikowski, Yates, Okamura and Fujimoto (1995) focus on the relations among users of a new computer conferencing system in the R&D laboratory of a Japanese corporation. By analysing electronic messages, they identified the role played by a self-organizing group of technical support experts who structured the discursive practices enacted with the new communication medium by other members of the R&D laboratory.

Despite their valuable contributions to understanding differences among media and dynamics of organizational discourse, these approaches focus on intra-organizational practices and pay comparatively little attention to extra-organizational factors that are not fully captured in either experimental settings or field studies focused on intra-organizational processes. Hence, we know more about the inter-personal dynamics of flaming behaviour than about variations in the discourse across ethnic or organizational groups. Similarly, there has been more research about group processes that lead to negative outcomes in geographically displaced teams than about the potential of different occupational and industrial characteristics to affect these processes and outcomes. Along these lines, more research exists on the communication structures of a single virtual organization or the discursive patterns of helping behaviour among employees of a focal organization than about the possible influence of broader cultural formations in accounting for these kinds of phenomenon.

Communication

The second issue centres on the way existing research often embraces a relatively atomistic view of organizational discourse and new – or old – media. This view emerges in two intertwined scholarly preferences. First, researchers tend to study one medium in isolation from the others normally co-present in organizational life. For instance, analysts compare the use of electronic mail with that of meetings, letters, telephone calls, facsimile, and so on. This approach has made an important contribution by isolating the potential effects that the different media have in organizational discourse. For instance, Treviño, Webster and Stein (2000) examine communication in four 'media': electronic mail, facsimile, letters and face-to-face meetings.[1] To this end, they conducted surveys on media choice, attitude and use in a wide range of organizational settings. Although the authors recognized that actors communicate using all four media in their work routines, the respondents answered questions about only one medium, and on just one message in the assigned medium. That is, 'respondents were then asked to think about the last message they had sent via the particular medium. They answered a series of questions regarding their choice of that medium in that situation. This provided a realistic context and point of reference for the survey questions and allowed us to investigate the variables that differentiate among choices of multiple media' (Treviño et al., 2000, p. 169). Through this approach, the authors are able to tease out some of the differential effects of diverse combinations of technological, personal and contextual factors.

Second, researchers frequently treat face-to-face communication as the benchmark against which mediated communication should be assessed. This assumption is particularly prevalent in the two most prolific research programmes in this area: media richness theory (Daft & Lengel, 1986) and the reduced-cues approach (Sproull & Kiesler, 1991). By using discursive practices enacted in face-to-face situations as a baseline, this scholarly preference yields valuable insights about what might be novel and unique about new media such as electronic mail, videoconferencing and voice mail, and their links to pre-existing media and discursive structures.

Despite their significant contributions to understanding new media, this focus on isolated media leaves some dimensions of mediated discourse relatively unexamined. First, it segments what is a more complex ensemble of media, practices, artifacts and experiences, where organizational discourse emerges as situated human actors use intersecting, overlapping and dynamic arrays of multiple media. Studies of actors' discrete engagements with separate media are then less equipped to account for the dynamics of such a complex ensemble.

Furthermore, positing face-to-face interaction as the standard against which all other interactions are to be compared limits attention to communication features that are salient in face-to-face encounters, thus overlooking new discursive capabilities of electronic media (Reder & Schwab, 1988; Walther, 1996) and disregarding any novel interaction patterns that may emerge from using new media (Orlikowski & Yates, 1994). As Culnan and Markus (1987) argued more than fifteen years ago, features of electronic media – such as large-scale synchronous conferencing and the storage, manipulation and retrieval of interaction traces – have virtually no analogue in traditional communication modes. And this concern is likely to be even more prevalent in the current age of networked computing, instant messaging and the World Wide Web.

Finally, this segmentation of media along with the use of a face-to-face benchmark also triggers an apparent dualism between off- and on-line communications. As Haythornthwaite put it, the concentration of most existing research 'on CMC versus face-to-face, online versus offline, and virtual versus real has perpetuated a dichotomized view of human behavior' (2001, p. 363). For instance, much recent work focuses on the supposed distinctiveness of 'virtual' teams and organizations that results from the use of new media (DeSanctis & Monge, 1999), as if non-electronic work practices do not rely on communication artifacts. This work overlooks seminal studies like Yates's (1989) on the constitutive role of media in the non-virtual modern corporation, or more recent studies on the use of media in the virtual pre-modern corporation (O'Leary et al., 2002).

Technology

The third issue relates to the atomized view of communication, that is, researchers tend to compartmentalize technology's expressive potentials by looking at the textual, audio or visual capabilities of new media in isolation from each other. In other words, analysts focus on technologies like electronic mail, voice mail and video-conferencing, but do not look as closely at the integration of text, audio, visual and other capabilities of new media. In addition, most scholarship concentrates on text-based new media. This research expands our knowledge of the specific discursive consequences associated with the affordances of different technical capabilities. For example, Flanagin, Tiyaamornwong, O'Connor and Seibold (2002) examine the interaction between gender and anonymity in computer-mediated group work. The study aims to adjudicate between the competing claims of the reduced-cues (Sproull & Kiesler, 1991) and the social identity and deindividuation models (Spears & Lea, 1994) on the issue of status equalization. To this end, the authors examine variation among groups of female and male college students using text-based new media to collaborate in course-related activities. Computer-mediation communication (CMC) 'is taken here to mean largely text-based electronic interaction conducted across space and time' (Flanagin et al., 2002, p. 88). Partly as a result of concentrating on text-based new media, the authors reveal that 'men and women differ in their perceptions and experiences of CMC and act strategically with regard to a key feature of the technology – anonymity' (2002, p. 82).

Even though valuable contributions have emerged from compartmentalizing technical capabilities, this approach under-emphasizes two significant dimensions of organizational discourse with new media. First, the emphasis on text, or audio, or video is somewhat at odds with the increasing use of multimedia tools that typifies the recent evolution of organizational settings. Second, this compartmentalization could generate an image of mediated organizational discourse that fragments the complex interrelationships among technology's material and symbolic capabilities. Although the new media of the not-so-distant past were characterized by a correspondence between technology type and expressive potentials (e.g., electronic mail was textual and the telephone was aural), today's new media challenge this neat correspondence: electronic mail increasingly includes visual elements and cellular telephony encompasses a complex intermingling of audio, text and video messaging. Therefore, to continue advancing our understanding of new media in organizational discourse, it is important to build on the insights generated by compartmentalizing technology to examine these current trends in technological and workplace innovations.

A PRACTICE VIEW OF DISCOURSE AND MEDIA

In the previous section we highlighted three relatively under-explored areas of new media and organizational discourse. We believe that alternative approaches can shed light on these issues in new ways that may be particularly useful in revealing the changing patterns that link organizations, discourse and new media in the contemporary workplace. In particular, as the pace of change in organizational forms continues (DiMaggio, 2001), we are confronted not with traditional hierarchies and entrenched divisions of authority but with dynamic relations of interdependence (Stark, 2001), a turn to projects and networks (Powell, 2001), and regimes of distributed construction (Boczkowski, 2004). As the nature, location and processes of work change (Barley & Kunda, 2001), knowledge and skills become embedded in a variety of collaborative endeavours that transcend organizational, temporal and geographic boundaries. Finally, as innovations in electronic media accelerate and expand, evolving configurations of technological artifacts become – at the same time – increasingly interconnected, heterogeneous, embedded and fixed, as well as increasingly fragmented, invisible, provisional and fluid (Bowker & Star, 1999; Levy, 1994).

Such a changing organizational and technological landscape calls for investigations that: (a) problematize the multiple, dynamic contexts of interaction within and across organizational as well as occupational, regional and national boundaries; (b) investigate the emerging features of new electronic technologies within their complex interconnections and criteria of effectiveness; and (c) take seriously the multimedia nature of new media which embody multiple expressive modes in the form of text, still and moving images, animation, audio, tactile sensations and bodily experiences.

Scholarship in such fields as anthropology, classics, cognitive science, communication, philosophy and science and technology studies contends that transformations in media artifacts are inextricably tied to alterations in cognition, communication, and culture (Clark, 1997; Engeström & Middleton, 1996; Goody, 1977; Hutchins, 1995; Latour, 1994; Ong, 1982; Suchman, 1996). One corollary of this research is that action results from the relationships among ensembles of material and social elements, rather than from the effect of one element's agency upon the others. Put differently, action has a distributed and emergent character. Applied to this chapter, it shifts the locus of discourse from people or media to their relationships, and the nature of discourse from possessed to performed. A practice perspective, because it assumes a recursive interaction between people, activities, artifacts and contexts, is particularly well positioned to address social phenomena that are relational, emergent and enacted.

In essence, a practice approach examines the enactment of discursive structures with and about new media through patterns of localized actions. Drawing on such social theorists as Giddens (1976, 1984) and Bourdieu (1977, 1990), a practice approach privileges the situated and recurrent activities through which people constitute their everyday lives. When applied to the study of technologies in organizations, a practice approach builds on existing technology scholarship that has looked at the everyday activities associated with using new artifacts. While not explicitly adhering to a practice orientation, research conducted from structurational and ethnomethodological perspectives has examined the situated interactions that characterize people's use of new technology. For example, Barley's now classic (1986) study of the implementation of CT scanning technology into two hospital radiology departments showed how the use of the same technology within organizational settings that shared certain basic features could lead to dramatically different structural outcomes. Informed by a structurational perspective, Barley defined his unit of analysis as the everyday interactions (which he labelled 'scripts') of radiologists and technicians as they used the new scanning technology. By focusing on actors' recurrent discursive practices, Barley was able to articulate the distinct interpretive and institutional processes that differentially shaped the use of new technology in the two organizational settings.

Also drawing on a structurational perspective is Poole and DeSanctis's (1990, 1992; DeSanctis & Poole, 1994) Adaptive Structuration Theory (AST). Developed to study information technology in organizations, AST assumes that technologies are best understood in terms of how the social structures embedded in their design are, or are not, reproduced in specific social contexts. This theory focuses on the micro-level appropriations that users make in their ongoing use of technology; that is, on appropriations of the structures incorporated into the design of the technology and ones embedded within social institutions. The theory is labelled 'adaptive' to acknowledge the ongoing and often intended modifications that users engage in as they interact with their technologies over time. This recognition of users' artful adaptations echoes Rice and Rogers' (1980) observation that people often 're-invent' the artifacts they use in their everyday activities.

The work of Taylor and his colleagues (Taylor & Van Emery, 1993, 2000; Taylor et al., 2001) has blended structurational approaches with actor–network and distributed cognition theories to offer a novel lens on organizational life that foregrounds the everyday communication practices of its members. In this lens, the organization emerges as the site and surface of these practices: site because it is constituted in the discursive engagements of its members and surface because it is available to them in multiple discursive embodiments, such as memos, databases and conversations. In addition, Taylor and his colleagues have suggested that the structuring of organizational life in communication practices is an inherently contradictory process in which individual, group and organizational dimensions are frequently in tension. In their application of this lens to examine the effects of workplace computerization, Taylor and his colleagues have found that these contradictions and tensions are central to understanding how new technologies adopted to alter elements in one dimension (e.g., at the level of the entire organization) end up having unanticipated consequences in other dimensions (individual and group, in this hypothetical case).

Numerous studies conducted from within an ethnomethodological orientation have also examined the everyday activities of actors engaging with various artifacts. Many of these studies, performed under the rubric of 'Computer Supported Cooperative Work' (CSCW), focus on the ways that actors use technological artifacts to structure complex work systems (Suchman et al., 1999), for example, air traffic control (Harper & Hughes, 1993), airport ground operations (Goodwin & Goodwin, 1996; Suchman, 1993), subway management (Heath & Luff, 1992), and naval navigation (Hutchins, 1990, 1995). These studies typically focus on the situated and moment-by-moment coordination of workers as they orient to each other and their tasks using the technologies at hand. What emerges from such grounded observations is a way of understanding how concrete activities simultaneously shape, and are shaped by, the properties of the technologies that people use and how these situated interactions tend to (re)produce particular social orders.

These prior studies that examine everyday interactions with technologies represent important antecedents to the practice approach. Following what is called 'the practice turn' in contemporary social theory (Schatzki et al., 2001), practices are defined as 'embodied, materially mediated arrays of human activity centrally organized around shared practical understandings' (Schatzki, 2001, p. 2). Practices are situated within institutional contexts and enact a multiplicity of social structures. Actors generate them as part of the ongoing structuring processes through which groups, organizations and communities are (re)produced and transformed. Practices are constitutive of the micro-level interactions of human agents, but they reflect and reconstruct macro-level influences. In this sense, structures are both the medium and outcome of the everyday practices that constitute social life (Giddens, 1984).

In contrast to existing approaches to new media and organizational discourse, a practice lens invites us to focus on different dimensions of discursive activity: its ongoing character; its embodiment within human bodies; its embeddedness in social-political contexts; its relation to the material and symbolic capabilities of artifacts; its dependence on shared practical understandings; its capacity for improvised responses to emergent situations; and its enactment – generation, reinforcement, renewal and transformation – of social structures through everyday action.

A practice view of new media and organizational discourse might focus on two distinct aspects of discourse: *discourse with new media*, or how everyday communication practices are enacted with new media, and *discourse about new media*, or the rhetorical construction of new media in recurrent discourse. We articulate each below, drawing on examples to provide detail on what such studies might look like.

A focus on *discursive practices* would examine the recurrent practices of organizational actors as they engage with various media to accomplish their everyday work. To illustrate, we draw on a recent article by Orlikowski (2000) in which she sets forth a view of technology structures as enacted by the ongoing practices of a community of users rather than as embedded in technological artifacts (DeSanctis & Poole, 1994; Orlikowski, 1992). In this view, the use of artifacts is constituted by recurrent organizational practices, focusing attention on what people do with the artifacts in their everyday work activities. This approach departs from prior studies that examine why and how a given artifact is more or less likely to be adopted or appropriated in various circumstances and with what consequences. In contrast, Orlikowski's practice lens focuses on the knowledgeable action of organizational members embedded within particular institutional contexts, and how their recurrent engagement with new media artifacts – such as electronic mail, conferencing systems and Lotus Notes – (re)constitutes particular emergent structures of technology use, which Orlikowski referred to as *technologies-in-practice*. As Orlikowski (2000, p. 421) noted, 'thus, the research orientation is inverted – from a focus on given technologies, embodied structures, and their influence on use – to a focus on human agency and the enactment of emergent structures in the use of technologies'.

In her study, Orlikowski (2000) centres on the ways that four groups of organizational actors within three different organizations use the Lotus Notes groupware to get their work done. She reports that the groups (developers, technical support staff, management consultants and software specialists) enacted six different technologies-in-practice with Notes over time: limited-use, productivity aid, collective problem-solving tool, collaboration, process support and improvisation. The practice lens Orlikowski develops allows her to ask when, where, how and why these different structures of technology use are constituted through the users' interaction with particular material properties of the new medium, specific institutional contexts, and various understandings of the artifact and their organizations. In addition, the practice lens affords the examination of the institutional, interpretive and technological conditions that shape users' enactment, and how such enactment, in turn, reinforces or modifies the institutional, interpretive and technological conditions.

A focus on *discourse about new media* examines the production and consumption of new media through everyday discourse. This work builds on the research associated with introducing or using new computer technology (Hayes & Walsham, 2000; Kling, 1994, 2002; Prasad, 1993, 1995; Turkle, 1984). Research conducted by Boczkowski (2003) serves as an example of a study that focuses specifically on the discourse associated with new media. He examines how personnel of three online newspapers attribute meaning to the notion of interactivity, and the effects that different meaning attributions have on actors' use of technological capabilities and the subsequent construction of various media artifacts for the newspaper's audience.

The analysis reveals the existence of three ideal typical interpretations of interactivity in these settings. First, actors conceive interactivity as a technical attribute of the online news site that, in contrast with a traditional newspaper, enables audience members to select the kinds and amount of content on a given topic or service. Personalization and search features are examples of such technical attributes. Second, actors interpret interactivity as a communication alternative in the exchanges between journalists and audience members, as well as among the audience members themselves, that expands the kinds and amounts of information flows from the usual unidirectional mode of traditional newspapers. Exchanges by electronic mail and in forums and chatrooms illustrate such communication alternatives. Third, actors see interactivity as combining the first and second ideal types, that is, as both technical feature and communication alternative. The study shows that the prevalence of these ideal types is influenced by factors such as gender and workers' occupational background, with varying consequences for work and technology.

IMPLICATIONS OF A PRACTICE VIEW OF ORGANIZATIONAL DISCOURSE AND NEW MEDIA

The uses of new electronic media already facilitate the interaction and blurring of traditional categories such as face-to-face and mediated communication, authors and readers, synchronicity and asynchronicity, time and space, resulting in various hybrid forms of discourse that incorporate novel and multiple aspects of media, genres, roles and times/locales. As noted earlier, we believe that discourse and media studies should be expanded to account for the range of organizational, technical and categorical innovations evident in use. We suggest that a practice perspective on organizational discourse and media may offer one way to do this. In what follows, we draw from prior empirical work to illustrate the potential of a practice perspective to push forward new scholarly avenues in the study of organizational discourse and new media.

Context: a practice view

Examining human practices involves attending to the flow of activities engaged in by organizational actors, and the range of social, material and power relations that shape such activities. This approach requires paying attention to more than just the proximal context of the local situation (e.g., group interaction or team dynamics) but also to the broader contexts in which discursive activities are embedded, most notably the extra-organizational, occupational and national contexts, as reflected, for example, in political interests, patterns of stratification, network ties, professionalized standards and vocabularies, ethnic and gender orientations, and macro-institutional norms. A practice approach does not presume to know a priori which contexts matter; this determination is an empirical issue. However, a practice approach predisposes researchers to be attentive to the range of influences on discursive work, whether acknowledged or not, whether anticipated or not.

For example, Boczkowski's (1999) study focuses on the interplay between the larger context of national identity and the discursive dynamics of a virtual community. Boczkowski conducted a 14-month ethnographic study of the Argentine Mailing List – a text-based virtual community of Argentine people living abroad – and examined the multiple ways in which the interplay between context and community appears in the content, form and material infrastructure of actors' discursive practices. At the beginning of the study, several technical problems arose in relation to an increasing number of messages in the mailing list. This increase in volume stemmed in part from the growth of soccer-related communication: 'given the function that soccer has in the socialization of many Argentine people, accessing the transmission of a game while living abroad plays a significant role in the reconstruction' of members' nationhood (1999, p. 97). A group of community volunteers emerged to examine the problems, and they proposed that the community adopt a new administrative structure and buy its own network server (until then the mailing list had been hosted on a machine at one member's workplace). A worldwide fundraising campaign resulted in donations by more than 400 members. After an intense discussion on topics ranging from the desired specifications of the new server to how the new technical and organizational capabilities related to what it meant to being an Argentine, the new server was put in place and named after one of Argentina's most popular cartoon characters. According to Boczkowski, this name 'embodied yet one more attribute of nationality in a crucial piece of the infrastructure through which they interacted … [which in turn] reinforced their sense of national belonging' (1999, p. 99).

The development of a CD-ROM to serve as a 'multimedia album' of the community was another event that Boczkowski analysed. Many exchanges about this matter started as technical discussions and then rapidly morphed into exercises of 'collectively remembering' (Middleton & Edwards, 1990) a wide array of elements of Argentine culture. One key element was attending to words and phrases that were typical of Spanish in Argentina. Boczkowski noted that members of the community repeatedly 'discussed the importance that being in touch with "their language" had for their psychological well-being' (1999, p. 102), and thus argued that the reconstruction of national identity in cyberspace partly happens by 'heightening the use of those discursive markers that distinguish one national group from others and through making their use a matter of public discussion … [as if members] compensate for their semiotic deprivations in everyday life by increasing their attention on Argentine discursive resources' (1999, p. 102).

These brief vignettes show that the content, form and material infrastructure of discursive practices in this virtual community could be made intelligible only by focusing on the way actors dealt with their larger context. Nationhood was neither automatically reproduced nor constructed *de novo*, but was enacted through the reconstructive practices that locally appropriated key elements of national culture.

Communication: a practice view

A practice view examines the set of activities engaged in by organizational members, without singling out specific, discrete interactions. As noted earlier, discursive practices constitute a complex ecology of media activities, artifacts and experiences. Understanding this ecology requires making sense of the complex interdependence of ongoing human activities as they engage with multiple media across multiple contexts to get particular communicative work done. Focusing on discursive practices precludes singling out a particular medium and examining its use in isolated contexts, or in comparison to face-to-face interaction. Following Dobres (2000, p. 1), there is a profound difference between saying that new media shape organizational discourse and saying that people shape their discourse through the production and use of new media. A practice view focuses on the latter and is interested in the variety of ways in which people accomplish skilled performances in their ongoing activities. As the production of such skilled performances unavoidably requires actors' engagement with a range of media – including face-to-face interaction – such engagement and their complex interplay in practice becomes the focus of analysis.

To illustrate, Heath and Luff (2000) examine the interaction of workers in the control room of the London Underground. Even though these actors were co-located, their work was thoroughly mediated by an array of multimedia technologies, including digital displays of train locations and service operation, closed-circuit television of stations and routes, radios, touch-screen telephones and public address systems. Informed by ethnomethodology and conversational analysis, the research examines the practices and reasoning drawn on by the actors to accomplish their ongoing collaborative work.

Heath and Luff show how, despite the formal tasks and prescribed division of labour in the control room, the everyday practices of the participants are both flexible and emergent as they make sense of and respond to each other and the emergent local contingencies. This detailed ethnographic examination of *in situ* control room work practices yields important insights into the way participants simultaneously produce their own activities as well as participate in the activities of their colleagues. This participation affords an engagement, both explicit and implicit, in the collective accomplishment of each other's tasks and thus helps the group as a whole cope with unexpected difficulties and emergencies. Through monitoring their own and others' practices, as well as monitoring the status of multiple tools, participants 'produce and preserve the mutual intelligibility of emergent events and activities' (Heath & Luff, 2000, p. 105). Heath and Luff's examination also includes a careful consideration of how these activities are embedded within the multimedia material environment of their workplace, allowing them to consider the ways in which participants, through their actions, make particular features of the local environment relevant at specific times (2000, p. 90).

This brief description indicates that understanding the communication of any group, organization or community cannot be accomplished by looking at the use of a single medium, or by looking at the activities of a single actor. The focus on discourse and new media directs attention to the interaction of situated practices, the collective character of contemporary work and the norms associated with using multiple, different media. It offers insights into how, when and why actors structure – implicitly and explicitly – their discourse by attending to the conduct and interests of their co-participants and how this structuring shapes their uses of various media over time.

Technology: a practice view

To the extent that more and more organizational communication is achieved through multimedia technologies, an examination of actors' skilled accomplishments of discursive practices with whatever media is at hand will require attending to the way in which actors work with and integrate the variety of textual, audio and visual elements available to them. Current literature in this area has bounded the term 'discourse' fairly narrowly as textual discourse, a boundary that is now at odds with the increasing importance of multimedia design in all forms of organizational discourse, but particularly in discourse mediated by networked technologies. Because a practice perspective focuses attention on what people do to communicate, discourse is enacted through the ongoing activities of humans, using multiple, dynamic and emergent media.

Nardi and Whittaker illustrate this approach (2002; Nardi et al., 2000, 2002) through a number of studies that use various methods – interviews, observations and electronic logs. These researchers examine everyday communication activities of distributed organizational participants using a wide range of communication media: fax, express mail, pagers, telephones, cell phones, voice mail, teleconferencing, videoconferencing, email, instant messaging, the Internet, FTP, the Web, chat, intranets, extranets, and face-to-face contact. As an analytic lens, Nardi and Whittaker develop the concept of a 'communication zone' which they define as 'a virtual "space" in which a series of conversations can take place' (2002, p. 86), and in which attention, availability and commitment among the interacting partners are negotiated. Communication zones are mutually constituted by the participants to communicate and shape the history, context, work processes, temporal conditions and media use. The research examines, for example, how participants change their use of media when conversational conditions change, shifting from instant messaging to telephone when a longer discussion is called for, or from email to face-to-face communication when participants want to signal high-level commitment through physical engagement and eye contact. Examining participants' use of various media in different contexts, Nardi and Whittaker's work builds an understanding of how communication zones are enacted, sustained and reduced over time. They show that communication zones are constituted by participants through interaction, are dynamic and fragile, and can decay over time (2002, p. 94). Communication zones thus require ongoing attention and adaptive use of media to continue to be effectively constituted over time.

In addition to offering rich empirical material and conceptual insights, Nardi and Whittaker's programme of research also offers interesting implications for organization practice. In particular, they propose that participants think about the design of 'media ecologies' 'where a particular mix of media is specified depending on the nature of the work and contextual aspects of the workplace situation' (2002, p. 102). They argue that no single medium or single media ecology can adequately serve the dynamic complexity of organizational communication, and recommend that participants take into account three key aspects of organizing – work practices, relationships among participants and temporal flow of work – when designing what they term as, following Illich, ' "convivial" media ecologies' (2002, p. 107).

CONCLUSION

This chapter examines the scholarship on new media and organizational discourse. More specifically, it focuses on three under-explored areas – the treatment of context, communication processes and discursive potentials of technology – which have become increasingly salient in making sense of actors' innovative, dynamic and mediated discursive practices.

With respect to context, we contend that the current, relatively narrow characterization of context precludes consideration of elements that critically influence how people shape their discourse through the use of new media, for example, national identities, regional variations, ethnic boundaries, occupational distinctions, professional vocabularies, network linkages, power relations and institutional norms. Inattention to such contextual elements runs the risk of inappropriately attributing observed discursive outcomes to internal processes or to particular media. Attending to a broader view of context does not presume that the salient elements are pre-given or known a priori. Rather, identifying the range of contextual influences on actors' discursive work becomes an important part of any empirical investigation.

With respect to communication processes, we argue that the existing literature often treats communication through an atomized and under-socialized lens. This practice leads to studying the use or effects of one medium in isolation, and thus to segmenting discursive practices into independent and discrete encounters with separate new media artifacts. Such segmentation 'isolates' the effects and experiences of distinct media, with the potential danger of ignoring the more complex ecology at work, one in which discursive practices emerge from actors' dynamic and situated engagements with multiple, intersecting and overlapping new media artifacts.

Finally, with respect to the discursive potentials of new media, we emphasize the limitations of the current tendency to compartmentalize them. In particular, we highlight how an almost exclusive focus on text-based electronic media inhibits an understanding of uses and consequences of multimedia tools that have become increasingly prevalent in the workplace. Furthermore, this singular view of technology's discursive potentials prevents us from conceptualizing the multiple and variable interactions among the multimedia capabilities of tools, interactions that have critical implications for how actors shape their discourse through the production and use of new media.

In response to these concerns, we offer a practice perspective that addresses these limitations. This perspective is not a cure-all, but by emphasizing the embedded, embodied, emergent and enacted aspects of organizational life, it affords a different orientation to, and even reconceptualization of, the study of organizational discourse and new media. Such an orientation comes from focusing on the situated, distributed and emergent character of organizational discourse and its constitutive relationship with media artifacts. It requires looking at the broader context of discursive activity, the interpenetration of communication processes by an array of multiple media, and the potentials of recent technical developments for multi-mediated discourse.

This chapter's opening story highlights the ways in which new media afford innovations in both understandings and practices of contemporary organizational actors. Taking advantage of these transformations to innovate our own scholarly understandings and practices is an opportunity we cannot afford to miss.

NOTES

We appreciate the helpful comments of Linda Putnam, Scott Poole and Robert Kraut on earlier drafts of this chapter, which was presented at the 2003 annual meeting of the International Communication Association, where it received a Top Three Paper Award from the Organizational Communication Division.

1 We have put 'media' in quotes here because, as Yates and Orlikowski (1992) have argued, these four are not all media. While electronic mail and facsimile may be seen to be media, letters and meetings are not media but genres of communication.

REFERENCES

Ahuja, M. & Carley, K. (1999) Network structure in virtual organizations. *Organization Science*, 10: 741–57.

Barley, S.R. (1986) Technology as an occasion for structuring: Evidence from observation of CT scanners and the social order of radiology departments. *Administrative Science Quarterly*, 31: 78–108.

Barley, S.R. & Kunda, G. (2001) Bringing work back in. *Organization Science*, 12 (1): 76–95.

Boczkowski, P. (1999) Mutual shaping of users and technologies in a national virtual community. *Journal of Communication*, 49: 86–108.

Boczkowski, P. (2003) Technical attribute, communication alternative, or both? The discourse and practice of interactivity in three online newspapers. Paper presented at the annual meeting of the Academy of Management, Seattle, WA.

Boczkowski, P. (2004) *Digitizing the news: Innovation in online newspapers*. Cambridge, MA: MIT Press.

Bourdieu, P. (1977) *Outline of a theory of practice.* New York: Cambridge University Press.

Bourdieu, P. (1990) *The logic of practice.* Stanford, CA: Stanford University Press.

Bowker, G.C. & Star, S.L. (1999) *Sorting things out: Classification and its consequences.* Cambridge, MA: MIT Press.

Clark, A. (1997) *Being there: Putting brain, body, and world together again.* Cambridge, MA: MIT Press.

Cramton, C. (2001) The mutual knowledge problem and its consequences for dispersed collaboration. *Organization Science,* 12: 346–71.

Culnan, M.J. & Markus, M.L. (1987) Information Technologies. In F.M. Jablin, L.L. Putnam, K.H. Roberts & L.W. Porter (eds), *Handbook of organizational communication: An interdisciplinary perspective* (pp. 420–43). Newbury Park, CA: Sage.

Daft, R.L. & Lengel, R.H. (1986) Organizational information requirements, media richness and structural design. *Management Science,* 32 (5): 554–71.

DeSanctis, G. & Monge, P. (1999) Introduction to the special issue: Communication processes for virtual organizations. *Organization Science,* 10: 693–703.

DeSanctis, G. & Poole, M.S. (1994) Capturing the complexity in advanced technology use: Adaptive structuration theory. *Organization Science,* 5 (2): 121–47.

DiMaggio, P. (2001) Conclusion: The futures of business organization and the paradoxes of change. In P. DiMaggio (ed.), *The twenty-first century firm: changing economic organization in international perspective* (pp. 210–43). Princeton, NJ: Princeton University Press.

Dobres, M.A. (2000) *Technology and social agency: Outlining a practice framework for archeology.* Oxford: Blackwell Publishers.

Engeström, Y. & Middleton, D. (eds) (1996) *Cognition and communication at work.* New York: Cambridge University Press.

Flanagin, A., Tiyaamornwong, V., O'Connor, J. & Seibold, D. (2002) Computer-mediated group work: The interaction of member sex and anonymity. *Communication Research,* 29: 66–93.

Fulk, J. & Collins-Jarvis, L. (2001) Wired meetings: Technological mediation in organizational gatherings. In F. Jablin & L. Putnam (eds), *The new handbook of organizational communication: Advances in theory, research, and methods* (pp. 624–63). Thousand Oaks, CA: Sage.

Giddens, A. (1976) *New rules of sociological method.* London: Hutchinson (2nd edition, 1993, Cambridge: Polity Press).

Giddens, A. (1984) *The constitution of society: Outline of the theory of structure.* Berkeley CA: University of California Press.

Goodwin, C. & Goodwin, M.H. (1996) Seeing as situated activity: Formulating planes. In Y. Engeström & D. Middleton (eds), *Cognition and communication at work* (pp. 61–95). New York: Cambridge University Press.

Goody, J. (1977) *The domestication of the savage mind.* Cambridge: Cambridge University Press.

Harper, Richard H.R. & Hughes, John A. (1993) What a f-ing system! Send 'em all to the same place and then expect us to stop 'em hitting. In G. Button (ed.), *Technology in working order: Studies of work, interaction and technology* (pp. 127–43). London: Routledge.

Hayes, N. & Walsham, G. (2000) Competing interpretations of computer-supported cooperative work in organizational contexts. *Organization,* 7 (1): 49–67.

Haythornthwaite, C. (2001) Introduction: The Internet in everyday life. *American Behavioral Scientist,* 45: 363–82.

Heath, C. & Luff, P. (1992) Collaboration and control: Crisis management and multimedia technology in London Underground line control rooms. *Computer Supported Cooperative Work Journal,* 1 (1–2): 69–94.

Heath, C. & Luff, P. (2000) *Technology in action*. Cambridge: Cambridge University Press.

Hutchins, E. (1990) The technology of team navigation. In J. Galegher, R.E. Kraut & C. Egido (eds), *Intellectual teamwork: Foundations of cooperative work* (pp. 191–220). Hillsdale, NJ: Lawrence Erlbaum Associates.

Hutchins, E. (1995) *Cognition in the wild*. Cambridge, MA: MIT Press.

Kling, R. (1994) Reading 'all about' computerization: How genre conventions shape social analyses. *The Information Society*, 10 (3): 147–72.

Kling, R. (2002) Critical professional discourses about information and communications technologies and social life in the US. In K. Brunnstein & J. Berleur (eds), *Human choice and computers: Issues of choice and quality of life in the information society* (pp. 1–20). Amsterdam: Kluwer Academic Publishers.

Latour, B. (1994) On technical mediation: Philosophy, sociology, genealogy. *Common Knowledge*, 3: 29–64.

Levy, D.M. (1994) Fixed or fluid? Document stability and new media. *Proceedings of the European Conference on Hypermedia Technology*, Edinburgh, Scotland, 18–23 September.

Lievrouw, L., Bucy, E., Finn, T.A., Frindte, W., Gershon, R., Haythornthwaite, C., Köhler, T., Metz, J.M. & Sundar, S.S. (2001) Bridging the subdisciplines: An overview of communication and technology research. In W. Gudykunst (ed.), *Communication yearbook 24*, (pp. 272–96). Thousand Oaks, CA: Sage.

Middleton, D. & Edwards, D. (1990) Conversational remembering: A social psychological approach. In D. Middleton & D. Edwards (eds), *Collective remembering* (pp. 23–45). London: Sage.

Nardi, B.A. & Whittaker, S. (2002) The place of face-to-face communication in distributed work. In S. Kiesler & P. Hinds (eds), *Distributed work* (pp. 83–111). Cambridge, MA: MIT Press.

Nardi, B.A., Whittaker, S. & Bradner, E. (2000) Interaction and outeraction: Instant messaging in action. *Proceedings of the Conference on Computer Supported Cooperative Work* (pp. 79–88). New York: ACM Press.

Nardi, B.A., Whittaker, S. & Schwarz, H. (2002) NetWORKers and their activity in intensional networks. *Journal of Computer Supported Cooperative Work*, 11: 205–42.

O'Leary, M.B., Orlikowski, W.J. & Yates, J. (2002) Distributed work over the centuries: Trust and control in the Hudson's Bay Company, 1670–1826. In S. Kiesler & P. Hinds (eds), *Distributed work* (pp. 27–54). Cambridge, MA: MIT Press.

O'Mahony, S. & Barley, S. (1999). Do digital telecommunications affect work and organization? The state of our knowledge. *Research in Organizational Behavior*, 21: 125–61.

Ong, W. (1982) *Orality and literacy: The technologizing of the word*. New York and London: Routledge.

Orlikowski, W. (1992) The duality of technology: Rethinking the concept of technology in organizations. *Organization Science*, 3: 397–427.

Orlikowski, W.J. (2000) Using technology and constituting structures: A practice lens for studying technology in organizations. *Organization Science*, 11 (4): 404–28.

Orlikowski, W.J. & Yates, J. (1994) Genre repertoire: Examining the structuring of communicative practices in organizations. *Administrative Science Quarterly*, 39: 541–74.

Orlikowski, W., Yates, J., Okamura, K. & Fujimoto, M. (1995) Shaping electronic communication: The metastructuring of technology in the context of use. *Organization Science*, 6: 423–44.

Poole, M.S. & DeSanctis, G. (1990) Understanding the use of Group Decision Support Systems: The theory of adaptive structuration. In J. Fulk & C. Steinfeld (eds), *Organizations and communication technology* (pp. 173–93). Beverly Hills, CA: Sage.

Poole, M.S. & DeSanctis, G. (1992) Microlevel structuration in computer-supported group decision-making. *Human Communication Research*, 19: 5–49.

Powell, W. (2001) The capitalist firm in the 21st century: Emerging patterns. In P. DiMaggio (ed.), *The twenty-first century firm: Changing economic organization in international perspective* (pp. 33–68). Princeton, NJ: Princeton University Press.

Prasad, P. (1993) Symbolic processes in the implementation of technological change: A symbolic interactionist study of work computerization. *Academy of Management Journal*, 36: 1400–29.

Prasad, P. (1995) Working with the 'smart' machine: computerization and the discourse of anthropormorphism in organizations. *Studies in Cultures, Organizations, and Societies*, 1: 253–65.

Putnam, L.L. & Fairhurst, G.T. (2001) Discourse analysis in organizations: Issues and concerns. In F.M. Jablin & L. Putnam (eds), *The new handbook of organizational communication: Advances in theory, research and methodology* (pp. 78–136). Thousand Oaks, CA: Sage.

Reder, S. & Schwab, R.G. (1988) The communicative economy of the workgroup: Multichannel genres of communication. *Proceedings of the Conference on Computer Supported Cooperative Work* (pp. 354–68). Portland, OR.

Rice, R. & Gattiker, U. (2001) New media and organizational structuring. In F. Jablin & L. Putnam (eds), *The new handbook of organizational communication: Advances in theory, research, and methods* (pp. 544–81). Thousand Oaks, CA: Sage.

Rice, R.E. & Rogers, E.M. (1980) Reinvention in the innovation process. *Knowledge*, 1 (4): 499–514.

Roberts, K. & Grabowski, M. (1996) Organizations, technology and structuring. In S. Clegg, C. Hardy & W. Nord (eds), *Handbook of organization studies* (pp. 409–23). London: Sage.

Schatzki, T.R. (2001) Practice theory. In T.R. Schatzki, K. Knorr Cetina & E. von Savigny (eds), *The practice turn in contemporary theory* (pp. 1–14). London: Routledge.

Schatzki, T.R., Knorr Cetina, K. & von Savigny, E. (eds) (2001) *The practice turn in contemporary theory*. London: Routledge.

Spears, R. & Lea, M. (1994) Panacea or panopticon? The hidden power in computer-mediated communication. *Communication Research*, 21: 427–59.

Sproull, L. & Kiesler, S. (1991) *Connections: New ways of working in the networked organization*. Cambridge, MA: The MIT Press.

Stark, D. (2001) Ambiguous assets for uncertain environments: Heterarchy in postsocialist firms. In P. DiMaggio (ed.), *The twenty-first century firm: Changing economic organization in international perspective* (pp. 69–104). Princeton, NJ: Princeton University Press.

Suchman, L.A. (1993) Technologies of accountability: Of lizards and airplanes. In G. Button (ed.), *Technology in working order: Studies of work, interaction and technology* (pp. 113–43). London: Routledge.

Suchman, L.A. (1996) Constituting shared workspaces. In Y. Engeström and D. Middleton (eds), *Cognition and communication at work* (pp. 35–59). New York: Cambridge University Press.

Suchman, L., Blomberg, J., Orr, J.E. & Trigg, R. (1999) Reconstructing technologies as social practice. *American Behavioral Scientist*, 43 (3): 392–408.

Taylor, J. & Van Every, E. (1993) *The vulnerable fortress: Bureaucratic organization and management in the information age*. Toronto: University of Toronto Press.

Taylor, J. & Van Every, E. (2000) *The emergent organization: Communication as its site and surface*. Mahwah, NJ: Lawrence Erlbaum Associates.

Taylor, J., Groleau, C., Heaton, L. & Van Every, E. (2001) *The computerization of work: A communication perspective*. Thousand Oaks, CA: Sage.

Treviño, L., Webster, J. & Stein, E. (2000) Making connections: Complementary influences on communication media choices, attitudes, and use. *Organization Science*, 11: 163–82.

Turkle, S. (1984) *The second self: Computers and the human spirit.* New York: Simon & Schuster.

Walther, J.B. (1996) Computer-mediated communication: Impersonal, interpersonal, and hyperpersonal interaction. *Communication Research*, 23: 3–43.

Wellman, B., Salaff, J., Dimitrova, D., Garton, L., Gulia, M. & Haythornthwaite, C. (1996) Computer networks as social networks: Collaborative work, telework, and virtual work. *Annual Review of Sociology*, 22: 213–38.

Woerner, S.L. (2002) Private communication.

Yates, J. (1989) *Control through communication: The rise of system in American firms.* Baltimore, MD: Johns Hopkins University Press.

Yates, J. & Orlikowski, W.J. (1992) Genres of organizational communication: A structurational approach to studying communication and media. *The Academy of Management Review*, 17 (2): 299–326.

17

The Discourse of Globalization and the Globalization of Discourse

Norman Fairclough and Pete Thomas

Globalization has been described as an idea whose time has come (Held et al., 1999). It has been pored over by economists, social scientists, geographers and business analysts, and many, often imprecise, definitions of the phenomenon have been offered. It has generated fierce debate between adherents to at least three standpoints, and the meaning to be derived from empirical data has been argued over to such a degree that what the term 'globalization' actually describes of the world around us is far from clear and very much further from consensus. The term has been used somewhat glibly at times, but also has been wielded as a heavyweight rhetorical resource, both in the context of scholarly work and in the wider practices and events of day-to-day life.

In this chapter we examine globalization from the perspective of discourse, with particular reference to the process of organizing, looking in turn at what we shall call the 'discourse of globalization' and the 'globalization of discourse'. Held, McGrew, Goldblatt and Perraton (1999) usefully outline the main standpoints in the debate about what globalization is, identifying three broad schools of thought: hyperglobalists, sceptics and transformationists. The hyperglobalist thesis sees globalization as a new epoch of human history characterized by significant changes in trade, finance and governance (Ohmae, 1990, 1995; Greider, 1997). Economic factors linked to global competition in a single global marketplace are seen as driving changes in social and political organization. The school sub-divides into a discourse that celebrates these developments as a neo-liberal utopia of autonomy and free market principles, and a neo-Marxist discourse of opposition that highlights issues of oppression. It might be argued that hyperglobalist discourse, both pro and anti, is the loudest discourse as it is that which tends to reach the widest number of people via the media. This in itself is an important point and will be returned to later.

The sceptical thesis rests on an interpretation of evidence that suggests current developments are by no means new (Hirst & Thompson, 1996). Again, taking a largely economistic view, sceptics argue that globalization is exaggerated and is a contemporary myth. From a discourse point of view, what seems of interest here is why there is a need for such a myth at this point in time and, more specifically, what is it that the myth-makers hope to achieve? The transformationalist thesis sees globalization as the transformative force that is behind social, economic, political and cultural changes (Giddens, 1990). This force is a long-term historical process born out of the coming together of many different phenomena. The grand view of the hyperglobalists is tempered, but the sceptical standpoint is seen as understating the transformations involved; changes of great magnitude are evident but the trajectories of those changes are uncertain.

Both the hyperglobalist and sceptic arguments tend to be unacceptably teleological and empiricist (Held et al., 1999). They suggest conceptualizations of globalization that present current events as part of a linear progression towards a given end-state, and see statistical evidence of global trends as unproblematically confirming or disproving the globalization thesis. The transformationist approach acknowledges the contingency and open-endedness of the process or flow of events that we have come to call globalization, and in this respect comes closer to a dialectical understanding of the phenomenon that we believe is a more fruitful way of thinking about it. However, even authors within this school of thought find it tempting or necessary to propose definitions and outline typologies of 'possible' globalizations. For example, Held et al., construct their own definition of globalization as:

> A process (or set of processes) which embodies a transformation in the spatial organization of social relations and transactions – assessed in terms of their extensity, intensity, velocity and impact – generating transcontinental or interregional flows and networks of activity, interaction, and the exercise of power. (Held et al., 1999, p. 16)

The transformations that make up globalization are many and varied, and are gauged against the extent to which networks spread, the intensity of interconnectedness between activities within networks, the speed of change and the impact changes have on communities. Different types of globalization can emerge from these transformations (Held et al., 1999 dub these types as thick, diffused, expansive and thin), and can exist concurrently as different levels of transformation take place in different contexts. Held et al.'s (1999) main point is that globalization is not a singular condition, but is multifaceted and highly diverse. This conceptualization is sophisticated and allows us to explore the many different experiences of globalization that we may have.

In view of this we should not be asking what globalization is, but why certain versions of it seem to dominate our thinking in relation to the issue of organization. At the same time we need to be sensitive to the changeability of discourse and to the diverse ways in which the discourse develops. In short, we should consider the potential diversity of the discourse, but also seek to explain why this potential is not necessarily realized. To explore the phenomenon we propose a dialectical view of the processes of organizing, globalization and discourse, and the interrelationships between these issues. In the first section we describe Harvey's (1996) account of dialectics, which we draw upon to explore the relation between discoursal and non-discoursal moments of globalization. In the next section we employ this approach to consider the 'discourse of globalization', that is, to examine and theorize the role of discourse in relation to globalization, illustrating our approach with certain globalization texts that are specifically related to organization. We argue that such representations tend to crystallize 'globalization' as a reified object from an ongoing process or flow, that is, as a temporary permanence that itself becomes part of the process of globalization. We suggest that discursive representations of globalization are resources that are developed by social agents in order to accomplish social objectives, and that they contribute to the process of globalizing itself, though sometimes in ways that agents did not intend or anticipate. In the third section we employ the dialectical approach once again to analyse the possible emergence of organizational discourses as global in reach and penetration. From these analyses we argue that the relations between discoursal and non-discoursal moments of globalization are problematic, as the discourses are not translatable into other moments in any simple, predictable and uniform way. This translation gap opens up space for counter-discourses, and for the hybridization of discourses and social practices. We conclude by reiterating the importance of this approach to analysis for understanding contemporary globalization processes.

DIALECTICS OF DISCOURSE

In the management and organizational literature, and particularly in the discourse of consultants and gurus, it is often claimed that the degree and extent of contemporary change is unprecedented, though rarely does anyone provide compelling empirical evidence to support this assertion. It might be argued that change has always taken place, change and flow and movement are constants, and therefore contemporary events are no different from those observable throughout history. From a dialectical point of view, what needs to be explained is not the extent of change, but what forces impede change or give it a certain direction when it could have gone in another (Harvey, 1996). According to Harvey (1996), dialectical thinking gives flows and processes precedence over things or elements, and in particular it seeks to explain how things and elements come to be constituted out of those flows and processes. Starting with a view of the world as an ongoing flux leads us to question how things (such as organizations and globalization) come to be constituted as things at all, that is, how and why they become 'permanences', even if only temporarily. Identifying the generative principles that produce order (things and systems) from flow and flux is the focus of dialectical thinking, and in part this involves discourse. This process of *crystallization* forms one of the foci for this chapter, particularly in terms of the role discourse plays in it. For example, the crystallization of a set of multiple processes we might call 'organizing' into an entity we call an organization is a complex matter, but it certainly involves discursive practice, and we can usefully explore what the role of discourse is in the process (Chia, 1996, 2000).

In paying special attention to discourse, we are not claiming that globalization or organization, or anything else for that matter, is reducible to discourse. Discourse is one 'moment' among several that comprise social processes, events and practices, the others being power, beliefs/ values/desires, institutions/rituals, material practices and social relations (Harvey, 1996). All human activity is made up of these moments, involving representation through discourse, the playing out of power relations, the possession or giving up of beliefs or values, the building of institutions, the transformation and movement of materials and the engagement in social relations with others. Dialectically, each moment internalizes the others in the flow of human activity – they are different but not discrete. For example, beliefs have a partially discursive character without being reducible to discourse; beliefs can be expressed discursively and the holding of beliefs within our minds has a discursive aspect to it as our thoughts are internal but contextually influenced expressions of discourse (Potter & Wetherall, 1987).

The relationships between moments involve what Harvey (1996) calls *translation*. As translations take place between moments, we may experience slippage; the translation of effects is never an exact mimesis, but is a metamorphosis according to certain correspondence rules. In the case of globalisation, for example, we might translate material relations into a discourse of globalization, perhaps via the discourse of statistical method, but the resulting discourse never exactly replicates or captures the material conditions. Indeed, with different rules of correspondence the same material practices can be translated into different discourses, in other words different crystallizations can be formed from the same flow of social processes. Thus, it becomes a key aim of dialectical investigation to ask how translations take place and why certain crystallizations occur and gain currency while others do not.

All discursive work involves some degree of crystallization, as texts represent a very explicit crystallization of a phenomenon, but again this should not be taken as a privileging of the discursive moment over others. Other moments are not reducible to discourse, nor is discourse reducible to other moments. However, the articulated ensemble of moments of the social is crystallized and given meaning in discourse, which means discourse has special significance, but this is not to argue that discourse *determines* other moments. Language and other semiotic modes (see Iedema, 2001, 2003 for more on the broader semiotic processes at work in social practices) give meaning to the world, and also mediate and mobilize action upon it. If we find it necessary to focus on discourse in exploring how the world is given meaning and is understood, we must nevertheless also interpret discourse, and concrete texts, against the background of the other moments of the social, that is, we must put them in context. Fairclough (2001) uses the example of the knowledge economy to illustrate this. Knowledge has been a long-standing part of economic production, but a discourse has emerged in recent years that suggests that it has become more significant. For this to happen the discourse must translate from other moments of social practice in a way that seems meaningful, reasonable and convincing to those interpreting the discourse. Put simply, the discourse of the knowledge economy must have some consistency with people's experiences of other moments of social practice.

It should be stressed, however, that discourse does not simply represent aspects of other moments; it also contributes to their constitution. The emergence of a knowledge society gains impetus from discursive representations of that society, and discursive resources are produced which may have constitutive, 'performative', effects on other moments; they may change them. The perspectives of '*verstehen*' and '*erklären*' are both relevant for discourse and texts – the latter both figure in processes of meaning-making, and thereby have causal effects on the world (in a non-Humean sense of causality, see Sayer, 2000; Fairclough et al., forthcoming). Discourse internalizes beliefs and desires, and discourses constitute not only representations of existing realities but also imaginaries, projections of possible alternative realities, visions of possible futures (for instance, in policy texts), as well as misrepresentations (deliberate or not, and potentially ideological) of existing realities. Discourses are positioned, interested, and imaginaries are tied to particular projects and purposes, though a stake in hegemonic struggles is to universalize the particular, to claim a universal status for particulars (Butler et al., 2000; Fairclough, 2003). Imaginaries may be enacted, inculcated and materialized through networks of social practices (Fairclough, 2001) so as to change ways of acting and interacting, social relations, social and personal identities, and the material world. In this way, discourses may come to be internalized in other moments. For example, discursive imaginaries of the 'knowledge economy' may be enacted in new ways of managing, inculcated in new managers and materialized in physical transformations of working environments. But there is nothing inevitable about this dialectical process of internalization: thus, although organizations are of course socially constructed, once they are constructed they become 'intransitive' realities which may be more or less open to, or resistant to, discourse-led transformations. We would advocate a 'moderate' version of social constructivism that recognizes both the performative power of discourse, and the intransitivity of the socially constructed world (Sayer, 2000; Fairclough et al., forthcoming).

A dialectical view of discourse and globalization, then, involves developing an understanding of how and why the discourse of globalization has crystallized from the flows of social activity at this point in time, and how this crystallization may affect those flows. However, in so far as we can talk of a 'discourse of globalization', we must acknowledge that it is not unitary and homogeneous – there are many different discourses, and counter-discourses, produced from various positions within various social practices and in various locations, and associated with a variety of projects, motives and interests (Hay & Rosamond, 2002). There are problems of sheer scale and complexity facing an analysis of this sort –globalizing processes as well as discursive representations and imaginaries of these process are myriad and cannot be mapped or tracked in any comprehensive way. What we can do is examine specific texts in order to explore how those texts come to be produced, and what cumulative influence those texts may or may not have. There are two interrelated and inseparable aspects to this analysis then: on the one hand, an analysis of crystallization, particularly the crystallization of social processes into texts, and on the other, an analysis of how discourse translates from and into other moments of social practice. We now move on to consider both aspects in relation to the discourse of globalization and the globalization of discourse.

THE DISCOURSE OF GLOBALIZATION

As we have indicated, globalization is a heavily contested phenomenon and has provoked much debate and argument. There is relatively little analysis of the phenomenon from a discourse perspective, and even less that connects globalization discourse to organization, yet language is an important facet of the phenomenon. Bourdieu and Wacquant (2001) describe globalization discourse as a 'planetary vulgate'. They suggest that the original conditions of production have become obscured as the discourse circulates around government, multinationals, non-governmental agencies, universities and think-tanks. They argue that an American imperialism is obscured by: '... the trappings of cultural oecumenicism [sic] or economic fatalism ... [making] ... a transnational relation of economic power appear like a natural necessity' (2001, p. 4). The suggestion is that the discourse of globalization is founded on belief and social fantasy (in a dialectical sense it internalizes these moments), yet by invoking economic and political reasoning it seems to have far more basis in material reality than it actually does. Then, as the discourse gains ground, it takes on the performative power to make these fantasies real. Bourdieu and Wacquant (2001) are pointing to the internalization of desire and imagination in discourse, and the subsequent internalization of discourse into social relations, material conditions, institutions and power (and, again, in desires and beliefs).

From the imagined to the crystallized

Let us look at a particular example, Kenichi Ohmae's book *The Borderless World* (1994), which was an early contribution to the now expansive literature on globalization and organization. In his text Ohmae, then managing director of McKinsey in Japan and a regular contributor to the *Harvard Business Review*, 'begins to describe the economic world toward which we are moving' (1994, p. ix). At the end of the book Ohmae presents a 'Declaration of Interdependence Toward the World 2005' (pp. 21–217) in which he claims that increasing free trade across economies and an erosion of national sovereignty 'enhances the well-being of individuals and institutions ... stands open to all who wish to participate ... [and] ... creates no absolute winners or losers as market mechanisms adjust participating nation's competitiveness' (1994, p. 216). He argues that consumers are becoming more powerful, technology more dispersed, companies more cost-sensitive and countries less important. Suggesting that a few elite companies are global in the way in which they operate, Ohmae argues that to be successful other companies should follow their example. Those that continue to use words such as 'overseas', 'subsidiaries' and 'affiliates' exhibit symptoms that truly global firms do not; all but the global are 'sick' in some way.

Clearly hyperglobalist and teleological, Ohmae's vision is a hymn to free market economics. Customers are lionized, and regulators and bureaucracy are criticized for placing ideology in the way of invention, in a way that is consistent with a much wider consultancy discourse that rubbishes bureaucracy so as to create space for the consultants' alternative mode of organizing. Ohmae is employing the 'golden opportunity' metaphor (Oswick, 2001): globalization represents a chance to restructure the world to make it more amenable to business imperatives, and also a chance for managers of corporations to embrace changes that will deliver business success. However, as in other examples (Ghoshal & Bartlett, 1998), the metaphor is neatly coupled with an implied threat, namely, that managers have no choice but to embrace these changes if they and their companies are to survive. Thus, a positive utopian message marginalizes alternative critical readings of globalization (Oswick, 2001), while a form of coercive persuasion (Pardo, 2001) heightens anxiety among managers and reinforces adherence to the positive view. Within an organizational context managers are placed in a position of weakness and power simultaneously. On the one hand, they are too fearful to resist changes that may or may not happen and cannot take the chance that events may overtake them if they do not respond. Of course, few will appreciate the irony that rather than responding to changes they are actually constituting those changes, enacting Ohmae's vision, as they alter the way in which they manage. On the other hand, however, the managers also become powerful locally as they are invested with a potent discursive resource (Hardy et al., 2000). The threat of globalization can be used as leverage over employees so as to gain commitment and, because of their privileged access to the discursive resources, reinforce managerial prerogative (Oswick, 2001). In this sense the discourse is recontextualized within the conjuncture of managerial practices as an ideological resource (Astley, 1984; Thomas, 2003a). In this recontextualized form the discourse can become a means of overcoming resistance, which can be marginalized as out of step with a changing world and perverse in the face of the 'golden opportunity' that waits to be taken or the threat that cannot be ignored. Recontextualization may include the translation of the discourse into non-discursive moments of managerial and work practice, but also an 'internal' dialectic operates within the discoursal moment (Fairclough, 2001): discourses can be enacted as genres (ways of *(inter)acting* in their discoursal aspect, for example, ways of conducting meetings) and inculcated as styles (ways of *being* in their discoursal aspect, for example, the communicative styles of managers).

Ohmae claims to be 'describing' the new world to which we are moving, when it might be more accurate to say he is 'imagining' a possible version of that world. The slippage between description and imagination, between 'realis' statements about what is the case and 'irrealis' predictions or imaginings of what might or will be the case (Graham, 2001), endows Ohmae's vision with the persuasive credibility of fact. Extrapolating from relatively little, largely personal and anecdotal evidence drawn from his experience as a consultant in the distinctly atypical environment of the corporate boardroom, he gives his version of globalization the appearance of inevitability. In this respect Ohmae's work is typical of a consultancy-led discourse that is popular with a managerial elite and, perhaps, with a growing number of politicians.

This is a significant element in talking globalization into being (Bauman, 1998) and it is also part of the discourse generated by what Bourdieu and Wacquant (2001) describe as the 'communication consultants to the prince', often defectors from academia who give an academic veneer to the political projects of governments and a business elite. It also raises the question of authorial motive. The decision to write a book is not taken lightly, and presumably the desire to crystallize a certain version of globalization has something to do with Ohmae's own needs and wants. We can only speculate about his motives, and we do not doubt the good faith in which he puts his case, but we should at least be cognizant of his need to maintain a high profile as a business thinker and of the need of consultancy businesses to create the right context for the delivery of their services. Similarly, we need to be mindful of how discourses such as Ohmae's might be contextualized at an institutional level. The links between the consultancy industry and non-governmental organizations are exemplified by Malloch-Brown, former Vice-President of the World Bank and head of the UN Development Programme, who argued that the UNDP must become '... a kind of McKinsey for the developing world' (cited in Cooke, 2003). Further, the links with government are exemplified by the fact that McKinsey itself played a central role in the decentralization of local government in Tanzania (Max, 1990), highlighting the fact that texts such as Ohmae's need to be contextualized into the structures of power and influence that they help create and sustain. For many, Ohmae's text (and others like it) is very persuasive. Few managers are likely to want to take a chance on Ohmae being wrong; that way there is everything to lose, and the power of the discursive resource that he offers, its pervasive promotion by those with social power, makes it most seductive. Better to contribute to the enactment of his vision by internalizing the discourse into organizational life than to risk missing out.

We should not, however, imagine that the hegemonic imposition and internalization (enactment, inculcation) of the globalization discourse of such texts goes without challenge. For example, Hirst and Thompson (1996) critique Ohmae's version of globalization as a myth, and Tomlinson (1999) criticizes Ohmae's impoverished and instrumental view of the world as a business opportunity. Also globalization has generated a counter-discourse of opposition and resistance. Popular books like *One World Ready or Not* (Greider, 1997) or *No Logo* (Klein, 2000) provide a discursive backdrop to the direct action of anti-globalization protesters and provide a foil to the utopian visions of neo-liberals like Ohmae. Bourdieu and Wacquant (2001) are dismissive of the anti-globalization movement because it relies on reproducing the globalization myth rather than seeking to expose the mechanisms and power groups that produce and reproduce the rhetoric.

Harvey (1996) also expresses concern that the movement is too fragmented, being made up of all sorts of 'militant particularisms', and runs the risk of failing to engage with the forces of globalization in an effective manner. Despite these concerns, there is at least a counter-discourse that can reach a fairly broad audience. As Harvey (1996) argues, discourse is the realm in which we become conscious of political issues and, primarily, that in which they are fought out, so these counter-discourses cannot be discounted. However, it has to be admitted that these counter-discourses seem to carry far less weight than the hyperbolic output of Ohmae and writers like him, at least within the context of business, governmental and non-governmental organizations. All too often such discourse is dismissed as unrealistic, idealistic or seditious.

There is another obstacle to the hegemony of hyperglobalization discourse: the process of translating the discourse into other moments, into institutional forms and material practices, is not in any way a simple or mechanical matter. Ohmae's book has been influential in terms of being cited in many academic analyses of globalization as well as more popular writings, but its effects on other moments of organization are not easy to discern. Ohmae himself anticipates this in relation to the moment of belief, noting that old beliefs are difficult to let go of. Translation from discourse to belief is rendered problematic if the discourse fails to connect with other moments of social practice. Despite the rhetorical and persuasive power of the discourse, it does meet with resistance, and efforts to homogenize organizations globally seem fraught with difficulty, as we will describe later. Beyond the corporate environment its enactment seems negligible. Although governments seem unwilling to stand in the way of a globalization imperative or to regulate it in anyway, the 'borderless world' has not transpired in the way in which Ohmae (1994) suggested or recommended. National particularity is as evident as ever, and most corporations seem to continue to preserve some form of national identity despite operating across the globe. Further, despite acknowledgement of the globalization imperative, the discourse cannot easily translate into the belief system of government, because it is at odds with the power that governors have, are keen to preserve, and which benefits them in material and social ways; turkeys don't vote for Christmas! Also, the discourse has to compete against other discourses such as those of nationalism and trade protectionism. Popular nationalistic movements and those who seek to preserve economic well-being within national borders continue to propagate alternative discourses that may be favoured and internalized by politicians.

Ohmae's text represents a crystallization of a version of globalization that stems partly from his experience and observation of social practices and partly from his imagination. Ohmae extrapolates from his experience through a process of imagining, the result being a text that presents a particular vision of globalization. This vision and others like it correspond to the hyperglobalist position described by Held et al. (1999). As such they are strident and persuasive, not necessarily because they are true, but because of their rhetorical strength, say compared to the sceptical thesis, the appeal of which is undermined by the very scepticism, doubt and measured analysis that characterizes it. The hyperglobalist view is also persuasive because of the manner in which it is perceived and the beliefs that it fosters among those to whom it is addressed. It is less risky to believe in the hyperglobalist vision and to prepare for it, and thereby bring it into being. However, as we have also shown, the translation from discourse to other moments of social practice is uncertain and difficult. The discourse may fail to find purchase in a wider range of moments of social action, it may not chime with contemporary power and social relations, or it may not be internalized into institutions because it questions and undermines those very institutions. The translation failure creates the space for alternative discourses, such as the sceptical criticism of Hirst and Thompson (1996) to exist, but it also creates an opportunity for others to develop new discursive resources that can aid the enactment of the discourse.

From the crystallized to social practice

Ohmae's (1994) discourse of an imagined globalization is not the only form of globalization discourse that exists or is of particular relevance to organization. In response to texts like Ohmae's, many authors have come to see globalization as a significant issue for management and organization. For some this involves using the rhetoric of the discourse to repackage existing knowledge, using the 'global' prefix to differentiate material (e.g., Stonehouse et al., 2000). For others it means taking a prescriptive approach, offering advice on how to cope with the changes that are said to be taking place. A typical example of this prescriptive approach is a twin volume set, *Globalization*, produced by the Ashridge Business School (Kirkbride, 2001; Kirkbride & Ward, 2001). Such texts recontextualize the globalization discourse to produce a discourse that can be translated into social action by managers in order to secure business success. Assuming that globalization is happening and that it carries significant managerial consequences, the texts produce prescriptions for a wide range of managerial tasks. Covering issues such as labour management, marketing, e-business, forming alliances and 'parenting' new ventures, the tone of the Ashridge text is highly normative, presenting what, from the experience of the authors, is thought to be 'best practice'.

Such texts might be seen as handbooks for managerial practice, and in this sense there should be a relatively easy translation from the moment of discourse into material practice and social action. In the marketing chapter (Hennessey, 2001), for example, straightforward advice is provided on: screening for global opportunities using a range of data sources; approaches to strategy; and marketing mix management. These are key issues that could form the basis of managerial action, perhaps the definition of an agenda, or even more direct action such as the acquisition of market data. This text, with its emphasis on the action that a manager might take, is very different from Ohmae's. What is crucial here is that the text is perceived to be credible and its lessons are easily internalized into management practice. Various aspects of the text support the establishment of credibility. First, the Ashridge 'brand', which is deliberately highlighted in the preface – 'one of the world's leading business schools … leading-edge thinking … practical focus … expertise in globalization … developed from research, observation, hands-on experience and passion' (Kirkbride, 2001, p. xi) – is likely to be perceived as an indicator of quality by readers. Second, the consultancy-oriented background of the contributors, which is elaborated upon at some length in 'notes on contributors', seems designed to appeal to those managerial readers who seek authoritative but practical information. Third, the clear and 'unacademic' mode of writing seems oriented to making the translation process from discourse to action easier.

In many ways Ohmae's text opens up the conditions that make a text such as this possible. Ohmae's imaginary opens up a space that such prescriptive texts fill, and those prescriptions are framed within a reproduction of Ohmae's thesis. Intertextually, Ohmae opens the space and also reinforces the need for the prescriptive text. There is far less of the imaginary internalized in such texts, instead the material practices and institutions of successful enterprises are internalized into the discourse in order to stand as 'best practice' and thus be re-internalized into the material practices, social relations and institutional setting of a new set of managers. The appeal of such 'recycled' practice may seem counter-intuitive: one might expect management practitioners to be reluctant to reproduce the practices of others as this provides little in the way of competitive advantage. However, if those managers are experiencing high anxiety, they might prefer the safe discourse of best practice and tried-and-tested ideas (Abrahamson, 1996), and also this sort of prescriptive 'best practice' discourse appears, at least, to be far more translatable into the moments of social activity that make up managerial action in organizations (Thomas, 2003b). However, as with the translation of Ohmae's discourse into other moments of social activity, the evidence suggests that translation problems still and will always remain. The globality of prescriptions seems problematic: ideal types of management and organization often fail to make the transition from discourse to action as prescribed, a phenomenon to which we now turn.

THE GLOBALIZATION OF DISCOURSE?

The globalization discourse is often thought of as a global discourse. However, it is doubtful whether any discourse is really global, in the sense of it being dispersed to every corner of the world. Evidence also suggests that the discourse is not always translated into other moments of social action in quite the way envisaged by the producers of the discourse, particularly in the organizational context.

In his 1995 book on globalization, Malcolm Waters wrote of a single idealized form of organizational behaviour that would tend to transcend cultural and economic differences. We might label this idealization 'managerialism', though this is a somewhat simplistic term that encompasses a range of sub-discourses. Waters regarded the idealization as being centred on what we think of as 'flexible specialization' (Piore & Sabel, 1984), coupling strategic management practices with Japanese organizational approaches (teamworking, just-in-time, quality circles) and workforce flexibility (functional and numerical) in order to enhance responsiveness to global consumers. Alternatively, we might see the knowledge economy and the knowledge/learning organization as an aspect of this managerialism (Jessop, 2003). In the public sector this managerialism is found in the discourse of New Public Management (NPM) (Ferlie et al., 1996; Salskov-Iversen et al., 2000), focusing on responsiveness and efficiency. These sub-discourses are changeable and can be somewhat transient, and they each reflect only part of the managerialist meta-discourse. However, they do tend to be perceived as globalizing discourses, with lasting universal appeal and application. Indeed, these First World discourses are increasingly seen as the solutions to Third World problems and as models for organization and governance at various levels (Cooke, 2003). However, the emergence of the idealized organization associated with managerialism seems problematic. In this section we examine two examples of this meta-discourse: the discourse of flexible specialization, which has not translated into material practice and institution building quite as envisaged; and NPM, which has developed unevenly (Salskov-Iversen et al., 2000), suggesting that Waters' (1995) view of an idealized form subsuming all others was mistaken.

With respect to flexible specialization, some analysts have questioned the conceptual polarity between this model and the more traditional Fordist form of organization (Williams et al., 1987), but even if we accept the polarity, the emergence of flexible specialization as a global discourse and practice is not in evidence in quite the totalizing way we might imagine. First, many different modes of organizing continue to exist despite the dissemination of some global 'ideal type'. Clegg (1990) describes very different forms of enterprise to be found in the cultural contexts of France, Italy and South-East Asia. Such forms may be under threat perhaps, but Clegg (1990) is at pains to highlight the embeddedness of organization in cultural conditions that are not easily swept aside. Similarly in the public sector, there is continuing adherence to a discourse of welfare or public service.

This leads to a second point: the flexible specialization model is largely a Japanized version of organizing, itself embedded culturally and therefore not easily transferable to different cultures. As with any discourse, it emerges first within some local setting and then becomes more widely disseminated, but because of this it is never a global discourse as such, but a local one that becomes dispersed, and as ever, dispersal or translation into new contexts are always problematic. Even Japanese 'transplants' to other countries have been unable to import a model Japanese mode of organization without encountering resistance and being forced to modify practices (Stephenson, 1996), so to expect non-Japanese organizations to unproblematically translate the discourse into practice seems naive. In a recent case study of Matsushita, a major Japanese corporation, the tension between global discourse and local practice is made very evident (Holden, 2001). Within a single organization we can find contradictory forces and discourses in tension with each other; in the case of Matsushita a desire to adapt to local needs and the inculcation of a global organizational philosophy seems at odds. The need to adapt to local conditions and to be responsive is evident in company initiatives, but is undermined by a strong conservative discourse of global standardization and conformity, stemming from a Head Office belief that Japanese ways are best and that local managers are untrustworthy.

Such tensions give rise to what is sometimes referred to as a rhetoric–reality gap (Watson, 1994), and the tensions are dealt with and played out in many ways. For example, in his ethnography of ZTC, Watson (1994) found that a new discourse or rhetoric did not displace that which already existed, but became fused with it in complex and confusing ways. The discourses co-existed and were translated into social action in endlessly inventive ways that attempted to dissipate the tension that lay between them. Similarly, De Cock's (1998) analysis of the implementation of the Total Quality Management (TQM) and Business Process Re-engineering (BPR) discourses in two large British manufacturing organizations also illustrates the ways in which so-called hegemonic discourses fail to be totalizing, and how space for creativity remains. In De Cock's (1998) case we see explicitly the problems which might surround the translation of discourse into the moment of beliefs and values. On the basis of the discourses of TQM and BPR stakeholders in the organizations came to have expectations about them being implemented so as to enhance ways of managing. In simple terms, the discourses became internalized into the belief structures of certain stakeholders in positive ways, offering a means of improving performance. However, De Cock (1998) suggests that senior managers had not internalized the discourse uniformly; some were sceptical of the discourses and as such there was in some cases a failure to translate the discourse into the intended belief structures. In addition, and of great significance here, the generic discourses of TQM and BPR were rearticulated to fit into local conditions, there being an '...asymmetry between the rules-as-represented ... and the rules-as-guide-in-practice ...' (De Cock, 1998, p. 18). From Watson's (1994) and De Cock's (1998) analyses it becomes clear that even though a discourse might be hegemonic in intent, it may not be in practice, as it competes against alternative discourses and is modified to comply with 'local' discourses and practices. These cases also demonstrate that what we sometimes tend to regard as homogeneous locales are often no such thing, but are made up of various and sometimes conflicting or contradictory social processes and actors.

In the case of NPM there are also doubts about the hegemonic nature of the discourse, as the transferability of the 'private sector as role model' discourse into the different cultural milieu of the public sector is questionable (Pollitt, 1993; Clarke & Newman, 1997), as is the translation of First World managerialist prescriptions for Third World development (Cooke, 2003). In their analysis of NPM, Salskov-Iversen, Hansen and Bislev (2000) examine the role of transnational discourse communities (TDCs), such as the OECD, the World Bank and the UN Public Administration Division, as disseminating vehicles. Coupled with globalization, it might be expected that the discourse of NPM would involve a 'cascade of change' (Clarke & Newman, 1997) from the global through national and sub-national, and through layers of government. As with TQM and BPR in De Cock's (1998) example, the discourse creates an expectation, with globalization becoming a meta-narrative that frames all other orders of discourse (Clarke & Newman, 1997), that some version of managerialism will solve many different problems in different contexts. The shift to NPM is naturalized by the globalization imperative, but as with TQM and BPR, the assimilation of NPM and its internalization into social practices responds to local phenomena as well as the 'universal' logic of globalization. Salskov-Iverson, Hansen and Bislev (2000) show that in municipal organizations in Mexico and the UK, the NPM discourse is rearticulated according to local conditions, with the local 'generating sites' translating the global discourse into a local discourse that is internalized into social processes.

The globality of any discourse, therefore, seems to be limited in any totalizing sense. The hegemony of various types of global managerialist discourse is not solid or stable but involves a process of re-negotiation within local contexts (Chouliaraki & Fairclough, 1999; Salskov-Iversen et al., 2000). This involves a global/local dialectic that acknowledges the contested nature of discourse and its ambiguity. Global discourses such as flexible specialization and NPM might be conceptualized as colonizing discourses that move into local areas and occupy the space within which discourse operates. However, we should acknowledge that discourse is appropriated and drawn into local spaces by actors who may treat the discourse as a resource. We should also acknowledge that discourse unfolds in complex ways and for it to become a resource it must find common ground within the local context (Hardy et al., 2000). Appropriation and colonization are not different phenomena, for as Chouliaraki and Fairclough (1999) argue, all forms of colonization are simultaneously forms of appropriation. This means that conceptualizing any 'global' discourse involves attending to local as well as global phenomena. However, as well as acknowledging a possible gap between the global and the local we should also be mindful of the conflicts and contradictions that might exist within the local context. What might be a positive and helpful resource to one social agent in a locale may not be to another in that same locale. Within a local context we are likely to encounter heterogeneous interests and perspectives.

Robertson (1995) argues that our tendency to conceptualize globalization as a large-scale phenomenon is misplaced, as globalization does not override locality. According to Robertson (1995), the process of homogenization does not displace the process of heterogenization, as both tendencies take place at the same time and, further, are mutually implicative. Employing the notion of 'glocalization', he explores the tensions evident between the 'global' and the 'local' but avoids the view that there is a polarity between the two. For example, the glocalization of marketing, that is, the customizing of marketing efforts to meet the needs of differentiated customers, does not simply reflect local differences but constructs them. Consumers can internalize invented consumer traditions to their advantage or they can reject them, causing us to recognize that not all marketing initiatives are successful. Again, the capacity of some local agents to appropriate discourse rather than be colonized by it, and to regard it as a resource rather than a threat, ought to be considered.

In this complex situation of the global/local dialectic, and the interrelationship between colonization and appropriation, it would seem that discourses that we might regard as hegemonic, totalizing and standardized rarely are. Following Nederveen Pieterse (1995), globalization of discourse involves a process of hybridization rather than standardization. Hybridization involves certain forms becoming separated from existing practices and then being combined with new forms into new practices (Nederveen Pieterse, 1995). The resulting practices are a hybrid form of human activity, sometimes emerging unintentionally perhaps, but at other times being designed as a hybrid by social agents. Hybridization of discourse involves a process were discourses are combined to produce new discourses. For example, we might regard the New Public Management discourse as combining managerialist and public service discourses. Hybridization also involves the combining of different genres and styles, the creation of new texts that do the social tasks that people want them to do. The key point to consider here is that a hegemonic discourse is not reproduced as dominant and does not overlay or push aside existing discourses in any general sense. As Chouliaraki and Fairclough argue, this means that we must 'be as fully open as possible to the specificity of events, at the same time as reiterating how they are constrained by and reproductive as well as productive of structures' (1999, p. 144).

CONCLUSION

In this chapter we have tried to analyse globalization using a dialectical approach. In doing so we have placed special emphasis on two phenomena: crystallization and translation. Both phenomena stem from our desire to conceptualize globalization as a process rather than an entity. We have tried to present globalization as a process that involves several moments of social action, including a discursive moment, which has been our primary focus here. We have explored how discourse crystallizes versions of globalization from other moments of social practice, and why certain crystallizations appear to be more important or influential than others.

The production of texts involves translating other moments of social practice into discourse and we have briefly explored the crystallization of Ohmac's imagined form of globalization and the inscription of managerial practice in the form of the Ashridge texts. A key point to be made here is that we should attend very carefully to what moments of social practice are translated into discourse and crystallized into texts. It is insufficient to consider only discourse as the focus of analysis as the form of the discourse is shaped by the social practices within which it is dialectically imbricated. Thus, Ohmae's 'imagined' discourse and the Ashridge crystallization of a practical discourse are very different, because they are fashioned in different contexts and for different reasons. Analysis of discourse generally, and the globalization discourse specifically, should focus on the translation process involved in making discourse, attending to the social reasons that make such translations necessary or desirable, and the motivations that drive agents to carry out the process.

As well analysing how the discourse of globalization is formed, we have also considered the extent to which it can be said that discourse can become globalized. In this case we find that so-called global discourses of managerialism tend to be translated, first, by recontextualization into new forms of discourse that take account of pre-existing local discourses, and which may also mix styles and genres in a creative process of language use. Second, discourse may be translated into different moments of social action, changing belief systems or social structures, for example. But once again this is not a predictable process; agents selectively enact discourse and modify it to local conditions. The motives and desires of social agents are also a factor.

The translation processes we have outlined seem to be crucial to understanding globalization, and probably any other social phenomenon. But these processes are not simply of conceptual importance, within the context of critical discourse analysis they are also politically important. First, the inherent unpredictability and uncertainty of the translation process is a reason for optimism, for it suggests that discourses that appear to be dominant and hegemonic may not be so. They exhibit frailties and weaknesses that can be exploited and which give scope for resistance and the development of new counter-discourses. Hegemony is, in any case, always a precarious and contingent accomplishment that is never total. This is not to say we should be complacent; discourses have to be actively resisted and countered, actively spoken against in the variety of ways we have described above. Second, translation is important because it is through translation that social agents appropriate discourse. Discourse is not simply dropped blanket-like on to a situation, nor is it necessarily imposed by colonizing forces. It can be actively acquired by agents and used by them in ways that are unpredictable and that can be emancipatory. However, once again caution is required because we remain alive to the possibility that appropriation may involve cooption by powerful agents. While we acknowledge the power of institutions, we reject deterministic conceptions of discourse analysis that underplay the potential of active agents, and while we see scope for local resistance, we do not underestimate institutionalized power (Reed, 2000).

REFERENCES

Abrahamson, E. (1996) Management fashion. *Academy of Management Review*, 21 (1): 254–85.

Astley, G. (1984) Subjectivity, sophistry and symbolism in management science. *Journal of Management Studies*, 21 (3): 259–72.

Bauman, Z. (1998) *Globalization: The human consequences*. Cambridge: Polity Press.

Bourdieu, P. & Wacquant, L. (2001) NewLiberalSpeak: Notes on the new planetary vulgate. *Radical Philosophy*, 105 (January/February): 2–5.

Butler, J., Laclau, E. & Zizek, D. (2000) *Contingency, hegemony, universality*. London: Verso.

Chia, R. (1996) *Organizational analysis as deconstructive practice*. Berlin: Walter de Gruyter.

Chia, R. (2000) Discourse analysis as organizational analysis. *Organization*, 7 (3): 513–18.

Chouliaraki, L. & Fairclough, N. (1999) *Discourse in late modernity*. Edinburgh: Edinburgh University Press.

Clarke, J. & Newman, J. (1997) *The managerial state*. London: Sage.

Clegg, S.R. (1990) *Modern organizations*. London: Sage.

Cooke, B. (2002) *Managing the neo-liberalism of the third world.* Working Paper No. 3. University of Manchester: Institute for Development Policy and Management.

De Cock, C. (1998) Organizational change and discourse: Hegemony, resistance and reconstitution. *M@n@gement*, 1 (1): 1–22.

Fairclough, N. (2001) The dialectics of discourse. *Textus*, XIV: 231–42.

Fairclough, N. (2003) *Analyzing discourse: Textual analysis for social research.* London: Routledge.

Fairclough, N., Jessop, R. & Sayer, A. (forthcoming) Semiosis and critical realism. In J. Roberts (ed.), *discourse, deconstruction and realism.* London: Routledge.

Ferlie, E., Pettigrew, A., Ashburner, L. & Fitzgerald, L. (1996) *The new public management in action.* Oxford: Oxford University Press.

Ghoshal, S. & Bartlett, C.A. (1998) *Managing across borders: The transnational solution.* London: Random House.

Giddens, A. (1990) *The consequences of modernity.* Cambridge: Polity Press.

Graham, P. (2001) Space: Irrealis objects in technology policy and their role in new political economy. *Discourse and Society*, 12 (6): 761–88.

Greider, W. (1997) *One world ready or not: The manic logic of global capitalism.* London: Penguin.

Hardy, C., Palmer, I. & Phillips N. (2000) Discourse as a strategic resource. *Human Relations*, 53 (9): 1227–48.

Harvey, D. (1996) *Justice, nature and the geography of difference.* Oxford: Blackwell.

Hat, C. & Rosamond, B. (2002) Globalization, European integration and the discursive construction of economic imperatives. *Journal of European Public Policy*, 9 (9): 147–67.

Held, D., McGrew, A., Goldblatt, D. & Perraton, J. (1999) *Global transformations.* Cambridge: Polity Press.

Hennessey, H.D. (2001) Global marketing. In P. Kirkbride (ed.), *Globalization: The external pressures.* (pp. 197–222). Chichester: John Wiley.

Hirst, P. & Thompson, G. (1996) *Globalization in question.* Cambridge: Polity Press.

Holden, N. (2001) Why globalizing with a conservative corporate culture inhibits localization of management: The telling case of Matsushita Electric. *International Journal of Cross Cultural Management*, 1 (1): 53–72.

Iedema, R. (2001) Resemiotization. *Semiotica*, 137 (1–4): 23–39.

Iedema, R. (2003) Multimodality, resemiotization: Extending the analysis of discourse as multi-semiotic practice. *Visual Communication*, 2 (1): 29–57.

Jessop, B. (2003) Post-Fordismus und wissensbasierte Ökonomie: eine Reinterpretation des Regulationsansatzes. In U. Brand & W. Raza (eds), *Fit für den Post-Fordismus? Theoretisch-politische Perspektiven des Regulationsansatzes.* Münster: Westfälisches Dampfboot.

Kirkbride, P.S. (ed.) (2001) *Globalization: The external pressures.* Chichester: John Wiley.

Kirkbride, P.S. & Ward, K. (eds) (2001) *Globalization: The internal dynamic.* Chichester: John Wiley.

Klein, N. (2000) *No logo.* London: Flamingo.

Nederveen Pieterse, J. (1995) Globalization as hybridization. In M. Featherstone, S. Lash & R. Robertson (eds), *Global modernities* (pp. 45–68). London: Sage.

Ohmae, K. (1994) *The borderless world: Power and strategy in the global marketplace.* London: Harper Collins.

Oswick, C. (2001) The globalization of globalization: An analysis of a managerialist trope in action. In J. Biberman & A. Alkhafaji (eds), *The business research yearbook.* IABD Press.

Pardo, M.L. (2001) Linguistic persuasion as an essential political factor in democracies: Critical analysis of the globalization discourse in Argentina at the turn and at the end of the century. *Discourse and Society*, 12 (1): 91–118.

Piore, M.J. & Sabel, C.F. (1984) *The second industrial divide: Possibilities for prosperity.* New York: Basic Books.

Pollitt, C. (1993) *Managerialism and the public services.* (2nd edition). Oxford: Blackwell.

Potter, J. & Wetherall, M. (1987) *Discourse and social psychology: Beyond attitudes and behaviour*. London: Sage.

Robertson, R. (1995) Glocalization: Time–space and homogeneity–heterogeneity. In M. Featherstone, S. Lash & R. Robertson (eds), *Global modernities*. London: Sage.

Salskov-Iversen, D., Hansen, H.K. & Bislev, S. (2000) Governmentality, globalization and local practice: Transformations of a hegemonic discourse. *Alternatives*, 25: 183–222.

Sayer, A. (2000) *Realism and social theory*. London: Sage.

Stephenson, C. (1996) The different experience of trade unionism in two Japanese transplants. In P. Ackers, C. Smith & P. Smith (eds), *The new workplace and trade unionism*. London: Routledge.

Stonehouse, G., Hamill, J., Campbell, D. & Purdie, T. (2000) *Global and transnational business*. Chichester: John Wiley.

Thomas, P.S. (2003a) The recontextualization of management: A discourse-based approach analysing the development of management thinking. *Journal of Management Studies*,

Thomas P.S. (2003b) Organizational learning and knowledge as a social practice: A dialectical discourse-based framework. Paper presented to the Organizational Learning and Knowledge Fifth International Conference, Lancaster University, Lancaster.

Tomlinson, J. (1999) *Globalization and culture*. Oxford: Polity Press.

Waters, M. (1995) *Globalization*. London: Routledge.

Watson, T. (1994) *In search of management*. London: Routledge.

Williams, K., Cutler, T., Williams, J. & Haslam, C. (1987) The end of mass production? *Economy and Society*, 16 (3): 405–39.

Part IV

REFLECTIONS

Turning to Discourse

Barbara Czarniawska

Dis-cursus – originally the action of running here and there, comings and goings, measures taken, 'plots and plans'... (Barthes, 1978, p. 3)

Barthes finds this description of *discursus* to be perfectly fitting the actions of a lover. But isn't it a fair description of the actions of an organizer as well? Running here and there, coming and going, taking measures, plotting and planning ... True, organizers do more than that – they become involved with things and bodies, not merely plots and plans – but it is nevertheless a good beginning.

The 'discursive turn' brought many good things into organization and management studies. Let me enumerate a few.

The interest in discourse turned the attention of communication studies away from the mechanical model of information transfer, with its three heroes – 'the sender', 'the addressee' and 'the message' – and its villain, 'the noise'. The perfect communication was assumed to occur when the message sent by the sender arrived at the receiver in its identical shape. As pointed out by Umberto Eco (1979), such a theory assumes that the information carried by a message is the negative of entropy and is equivalent to meaning. Accordingly, language is an order (a code) imposed upon the disorder of noise. Consequently, reiteration (redundancy) increases the possibility of the message being received and understood. Herein lies the hitch: 'the very order which allows a message to be understood is also what makes it absolutely predictable – that is, extremely banal. The more ordered and comprehensive a message, the more predictable it is' (Eco, 1979, p. 5). In a real interaction situation (as opposed to a machine simulation), information is *additive*: its value depends on its novelty to the receiver. The new text cannot be interpreted according to previously accepted rules; it is open to new interpretations, and new interpretations tend to be called *misunderstandings*. In time, some of these interpretations may win over others and acquire legitimacy; a new order is established and the information becomes predictable. Temporarily, however, meaning and information are opposed to each other. It is ambiguity that makes the world go on; perfect information is redundant. George Steiner takes this reasoning to the extreme, claiming that mistranslation is a source of human creativity. The Tower of Babel is a frustrating situation but, he says, perhaps the right way of managing such a situation is pidgin rather than Pentecost (Steiner, 1975/1992, p. 495). Running here and there, translating and misunderstanding, sowing order together with chaos: all of this becomes visible once discourse is in focus.

Steiner's reasoning is in tune with Latour's (1986) suggestion that each translation is a transformation, and as such injects energy into the translator and that which is translated. The picture of the organizer as someone who runs in between also helps to corroborate the point that Latour (2004) is making so forcefully: they are mediators, not intermediaries. An intermediary, in his vocabulary, is what transports meaning or force without transformation (an 'ideal' messenger); mediators transform, translate, distort and modify the meaning – or whatever they are supposed to carry. In the 1971 Joseph Losey movie, *The Go-Between*, the young messenger transports letters – but also bridges worlds and changes destinies, including his own. Class discourses clash with love discourses and with generation discourses, but it is Leo Colston's organizing that activates them and transforms them simultaneously.

Another gain concerns those of us who were interested in powerful insights reached by ethnomethodology, but were alarmed by its formalistic approach or discouraged by its apparent incapacity to recognize connections between conversations. Conversation analysis captures and analyses a concrete speech situation located in a point in time and space. Discourse analysis addresses many conversations that take place over time in different locations and yet seem to be connected. Conversation analysis uses transcripts or videotapes of a concrete interaction, whereas discourse analysis collects various types of inscription of 'conversations' that may never have been enacted in the ordinary meaning of the word. In ethnomethodology, actors (interlocutors) are visible and central. In discourse analysis, discourse is impersonal: no actors (interlocutors) need be visible. But ethnomethodology and discourse analysis can support one another. The institutionalized discourse serves as a repertoire for actual conversations; these in turn reproduce and change the discourse. A research report is a conversation within the social science discourse: a written exchange of sentiments, observations, opinions and ideas. The exchange is a forced one because it has been arranged by the writer of the report: texts authored by people who never speak to one another and are forced to converse in yet another text.

Last but not least, the focus on discourse has helped those of us who are interested in narratives to envision a useful difference between spoken and written discourse. I am following here the thought of Paul Ricœur (1981), who emphasized that each text is primarily a work of *discourse*, which means that it is a structured entity that cannot be reduced to a sum of the sentences that created it. This entity is structured according to rules that permit its recognition of belonging to some kind of a literary *genre*: a novel, a dissertation, a play. Even if each text can be classified as belonging to or transgressing some genre, it has its unique *composition*, and when such a composition is repeated in the work of the same author, one can speak of a *style*. Composition, genre and style reveal the work that was entailed in the creation of a given specimen of discourse.

It is important to notice, however, that the text is a *written* work of discourse, which means that it is more than the inscription of an earlier speech (this is why such inscriptions cannot be read and analysed in the same way that proper texts are). Speaking and writing are two separate modes of discourse. Ricœur introduced the concept of *distanciation* to highlight the difference between the two. Text has acquired a distance from speech, even if it might have originated in a speech.

The first form of distanciation depends on that meaning acquiring through a text a longer life than just the event of the speech. The institution of minutes is a good example of this distanciation. *The second form of distanciation* concerns the intentions of the speaker and the inscribed speech. In the case of speech it makes sense to check if one understood the author's intentions because the speaker can always deny having said a concrete thing. When it comes to interpreting the text, however, the author and the reader assume more or less equal status. (This is, by the way, why sending the transcripts of the interview to the interviewees is a risky procedure: the interviewee considers the transcript of the interview to be a written text, and corrects it accordingly.) The corrected text has little to do with the original speech, not because the interviewer heard wrongly, but because the two are different forms of discourse.

The third form of distanciation concerns the distance between the two audiences: a speech is addressed to a concrete audience, whereas a written text is potentially addressed to anybody who can read. A (common) conviction that texts can be written for a concrete audience is based either on a belief in repetition of the past (past readers of John Grisham's novels will most likely be the readers of John Grisham's future novels) or on a belief in the possibility of creating the text's own audience, of shaping the reader, as Flaubert said of Balzac. In authors who are neither Grishams nor Balzacs, such a conviction is an expression of either naïveté or hubris.

The fourth form of distanciation concerns the separation of the text from the frame of reference that the speaker and the audience may have shared or may have created together. During a talk, it is enough to ask the audience if they are familiar with a certain segment of reality, and adapt the speech accordingly. The frame of reference of future readers remains unknown to the writer. Texts intended for a certain audience can be unexpectedly adopted by quite another type of audience.

This way of defining the text – and distinguishing it from spoken discourse – has consequences for interpretation of the text. The two first forms of distanciation mean that 'the problem of the right understanding can no longer be solved by a simple return to the alleged intentions of the author' (Ricœur, 1981, p. 211). The other two forms of distanciation, the unknown audience and its unknown frame of reference, can be dealt with in two different ways. One is the way of the structuralists and the poststructuralists: concentrate on the text alone, leaving aside the question of its possible referents. The second is the one proffered by Ricœur himself: 'to situate explanation and interpretation along a unique *hermeneutical arc* and to integrate the opposed attitudes of explanation and understanding within an overall conception of reading as the recovery of meaning' (Ricœur, 1981, p. 161). Here, Ricœur introduces an analogy that is crucial for organization theorists: the text as action, the action as text.

Meaningful action shares the constitutive features of the text: it becomes objectified by inscription, which liberates it from its agent; it has relevance beyond its immediate context and it can be read like an open work. Similarly, a text can be attributed to an agent (the author) it is possible to ascribe rather than establish intentions to its author and it has consequences – often unexpected consequences. In such a conceptualization, a text does not 'stand for' an action; the relationship between them is that of an analogy, not a reference. A text inscribes the trajectories of the organizers, their plans and plots, their comings and goings. Doing organization studies, we can follow not only the work of distanciation, but also its opposite: texts that are the starting point for new conversations, new speeches, new spoken discourse. From action to text, from text to action.

Is a focus on discourse bringing only gifts? As usual, with each new fashion, some unintended consequences are bound to follow. One is the mystification of the term 'discourse', following its transfer from Romance to Anglo-Saxon languages. Desperate for a 'definition' of discourse, young scholars peruse Foucault, seeking the final word, and often mistake various pragmatic descriptions of its functioning ('discourse creates its own object') for the definition. Far be it from me to try to guess the intentions of the great scholar, it seems obvious that he had no need to define the term, which is used in everyday parlance in the Romance languages The point was to show how it works, rather than to provide an ostensive definition. This transfer between different languages, however, might become a source of some new creative mis-translations. This is not just a pious hope. The mis-translation has already paid off. Whereas the Romance languages understand discourse, in its vernacular sense, as a one-way communication (basically, a speech, a talk), the Anglo-Saxon usage recovered the etymology of the concept, focusing on its function of binding, of connecting – even if such connection might take the form of oppressing or constraining.

More problematic, from my point of view, is a possibility that the attention turned towards discourse might further the idealization of organization theory. Things and bodies might once more avoid inspection, covered by a veil of words. This development, however, is neither unavoidable nor necessary, as shown in at least two chapters in this volume. The present volume can be seen as an excellent example of variety and richness of approaches born out of the interest for discourse.

REFERENCES

Barthes, Roland (1978) *A lover's discourse. Fragments.* New York: Hill and Wang.
Eco, Umberto (1979) *The role of the reader. Explorations in the semiotics of texts.* London: Hutchinson.
Latour, Bruno (1986) The powers of association. In John Law (ed.), *Power, action and belief* (pp. 264–80). London: Routledge and Kegan Paul.

Latour, Bruno (2004) *How to trace social connections by using Actor-Network-Theory.* Oxford: Oxford University Press.

Ricœur, Paul (1981) The model of the text: Meaningful action considered as text. In John B. Thompson (ed.), *Hermeneutics and the human sciences* (pp. 197–221). Cambridge: Cambridge University Press.

Steiner, George (1975/1992) *After Babel. Aspects of language and translation.* Oxford: Oxford University Press.

A Bias for Conversation: Acting Discursively in Organizations

Karl E. Weick

Peters and Waterman (1982), in their best-selling book *In Search of Excellence*, spent much of their time talking about a 'bias for action' and almost none of it talking about 'a bias for talk'. That imbalance reflects a reality in organizational life. In most organizations practitioners act as if talk is cheap, things are easier said than done, you can't start acting until you stop talking, action is preferable to talk, discourse is passive while 'doing' is active, and talking and doing are consecutive rather than concurrent. A bias towards action is visible in the language of 'actionable issues' and 'action lists'. Robert Marschak (1998, p. 19) has summarized the folk model that lies behind these outcroppings: 'The folk model implicitly structures talk and action as: (i) separate states, disjoint in time and space, (ii) where talk is an initial or earlier location(s) on a path or journey (iii) to the goal or destination of action, and (iv) where talk must be gone through, gotten over or finished before one is able to move on to the goal of action.' People assume that, at best, talk may lead to action and at worse can block or prevent getting to action. If organizational life follows a sequence wherein discussion → deciding → doing → deed accomplished, then the final stage is the most worthy and most valued and the first stage is least valued and least worthy since it is the farthest removed from the good outcome.

Given the context created by these assumptions, advocates of discourse analysis face an uphill battle for legitimacy. But they have the means to change this. What they need to do is make explicit several assumptions that they take for granted which would help a wider audience appreciate that conversation *is* the action in organizing. People who maintain a bias for action are astonished that anyone would assert that something as trivial as talk could ever do something as important as constitute organizations or be equivalent to organization or be the medium through which organizing and activity are talked into existence. They would be less astonished if they knew more about the orienting assumptions that make such assertions plausible.

This brief commentary reviews a sample of orienting assumptions that students of discourse routinely make, assumptions that are typically invisible to those who equate organizing with action rather than conversation. My contention is that if assumptions such as these were more visible, the central role of talk in action would be more apparent and practitioners would be less casual about their talk when they strive to organize more effectively. My hunch is that a deeper appreciation of the infrastructure of discourse analysis would lead to less talk about a 'bias for action', and more talk about a 'bias for acting discursively'. Key assumptions to be discussed include limiting conditions between which organizing unfolds, the nature of raw materials that are organized, how organizing gives shape to these raw materials, the unity of acts of organizing, enactment as a central form of action in organizing, and conceptual imagery that preserves organizational becoming.

One way to specify the limiting conditions of organizing is to adopt the poetic imagery that Taylor and Van Every found so useful in depicting the emergent organization, the contrast between crystal and smoke (2000, pp. 31, 324–6). They introduce this distinction, borrowed from Atlan (1979) in the context of self-organizing systems where life occupies the space created by the boundary conditions of crystal and smoke.

> *Crystal* is a perfectly structured material, in its repeated symmetry of pattern, but because its structure is perfect, it never evolves: It is fixed for eternity. It is not life. But it is order. *Smoke* is just randomness, a chaos of interacting molecules that dissolves as fast as it is produced. It is not life either. But it is dynamic. Life appears when some order emerges in the dynamic of chaos and finds a way to perpetuate itself, so that the orderliness begins to grow, although never to the point of fixity (because that would mean the loss of the essential elasticity that is the ultimate characteristic of life. (Taylor & Van Every, 2000, p. 31)

Applied to issues of organization, the boundaries formed by smoke and crystal become the limiting conditions between which organizing unfolds. Taylor and Van Every equate *crystal* with repetition, regularity, redundancy and the materialization of many distributed conversations in the form of texts that stabilize and reproduce states of the world. They equate *smoke* with variety, unpredictability, complexity and a conversation whose outcomes are not predictable and can only be saved in texts. Organization resides between smoke and crystal just as it resides between conversation and text in discourse analysis and just as it resides between redundancy and complexity in everyday life. Organization is talked into existence when portions of smoke-like conversation are preserved in crystal-like texts that are then articulated by agents speaking on behalf of an emerging collectivity. Repetitive cycles of texts, conversations and agents define and modify one another and jointly organize everyday life.

If we translate this picture into the sense-making recipe (Weick, 1995), 'how can I know what I think until I see what I say', we find that organizing assumes an odd character. In the sense-making recipe, the smoke of saying is converted into the crystal of thinking by means of the intermediate activity of seeing, which by Taylor and Van Every's logic becomes a surrogate for organizing. Organizing as seeing? Well, yes, sort of. One of Putnam, Phillips and Chapman's (1996, pp. 380–2) seven metaphors for communication and organizing is the lens metaphor. People who use this metaphor focus on perceptual filtering that protects, shields, guides, screens, scans, sifts and relays information.

A basic assumption of the lens metaphor is that information is incomplete. In transmitting a message different backgrounds and goals of senders and receivers increase the likelihood that information will be converted, simplified, reduced or summarized ... The inevitability of misperception challenges traditional notions of accuracy, clarity, and communication effectiveness by introducing meaning and interpretation into message transmission. (Putnam et al., 1996, p. 381).

The authors go on to note that

'the image of organizations for the lens metaphor is the *eye* or the visual organ of sight. The eye represents perception, point of view, the center of visual processing. Even though it is part of the brain's information processing system ... the eye is the center or the core in which activities function, like 'the eye of the storm', or 'the eye of the flower'. Information processing in organizations, although linked to cognition, is a visual process in that the eye performs the critical perceptual functions. The lens metaphor, however, highlights the boundaries and structural properties of organizations: scanning and screening occur across static borders. Perception, the locus of organizing, alters the way that information is conceived. (1996, p. 382)

It is not until the final sentence that Putnam et al., start to inch away from a wholly conduit view of organization towards 'organizing' as a plausible setting for a lens. What is crucial about a lens metaphor is that it moves away from the prevailing view of organization as computational and thought-driven, towards an image of organizations as ocular and perception-driven. Discourse is not just pure saying, it is also seeing what one says. If discourse is treated as an act of seeing, then the importance of text-like structures that embody organization become more apparent. And with text in the foreground, it is easier to imagine that the content of organizing consists of activities such as editing, reading, writing and talking, in which roles of editors, readers, writers and speakers are enacted with differential power to speak on behalf of texts. My point is that a lens is a conduit of sorts, but it is not a static container. Filtering is emergent just as ordering is emergent. Discourse analysts take this for granted, practitioners easily miss it.

Just what is the raw material that gets filtered in the interest of order? Robert Chia (2000, p. 517) argues that phenomena 'have to be forcibly carved out of the undifferentiated flux of raw experience and conceptually fixed and labeled so that they can become the common currency for communicational exchanges'. This means that when we talk about a social world, we are referring to an abstraction that has already been carved out and named. Viewed this way, discourse is a hybrid of smoke and crystal. Since it starts with undifferentiated flux, we can differentiate that flux into many different concepts. Yet, we seldom encounter flux as smoke, and more often encounter the crystallized concepts of predecessors. (For an exception see Weschsler's (1982) study of the artist Robert Irwin entitled *Seeing is forgetting the name of the thing seen*.) Nevertheless, much of the original vagueness and undifferentiatedness remains. That remainder provides the continuing grist for art, intuition and aesthetics; it provides the basis on which confusion and ambiguity rather than ignorance and uncertainty are the primary issues in organizations, and it provides the warrant for defining wisdom as the realization that an increase in knowledge produces an increase in ignorance (Meacham, 1990).

Given the existence of flux and undifferentiated vagueness, how does organizing produce order and make human behaviour more predictable? 'Organization is an attempt to order the intrinsic flux of human action, to channel it towards certain ends, to give it a particular shape, through generalizing and institutionalizing particular meanings and rules. At the same time organization is a pattern that is constituted, shaped, emerging from change' (Tsoukas & Chia, 2002, p. 570). Viewed in this way, organization does not precede communication nor is communication produced by organization. Instead, organization emerges through communication. There is a conversation world (the site of an organization) that consists of 'a lived world of practically focused collective attention to a universe of objects, presenting problems and necessitating responses to them'. And there is a text-world (the surface of an organization), that consists of 'an interpreted world of collectively held and negotiated understandings that link the community to its past and future and to other conversational universes of action by its shared inheritance of a common language' (Taylor & Van Every, 2000, p. 34).

Said differently, order emerges when collectively negotiated interpretations of flux turn circumstances into a situation that is comprehensible and that serves as a springboard for action. What is important is that texts produced in interaction effectively represent both the world around the conversation and the conversation itself and provide a surface that affords narrative reasoning (Taylor & Van Every, 2000, pp. 40–5).

Narrative reasoning is not just about stories. Instead, it is about reducing differences among actors by means of institutionalized cognitive representations. 'For an activity to be said to be organized, it implies that types of behavior in types of situation are systematically connected to types of actors ... An organized activity provides actors with a given set of cognitive categories and a typology of actions' (Tsoukas & Chia, 2002, p. 573). Narrative reasoning comes into play because categories and types have considerable latitude for interpretation. Categories are malleable because they are socially defined, because they are adapted to local circumstances, and because they have a radial structure with a few prototypical examples that contain all of the features of the category and many peripheral examples that contain fewer defining features. It is these peripheral members of any category that exert continuing pressure for narrative elaboration. If people act on the basis of central prototypic cases, then action is stable. If, however, they act on the basis of peripheral cases, then their action is more variable, more indeterminate, more likely to alter organizing (Tsoukas & Chia, 2002, p. 574). It is this sense in which organizing implies generalizing, and this sense in which discourse enacts transient ordering (Lanzara, 1999).

Thus, organizing viewed as acting discursively transforms a difficult and infrangible reality into a resource that people can use. 'Through its strategy of differentiation and simple-location, identification and classification, regularizing and routinization, discursive action works to translate the difficult and intransigent, the remote or resistant, the intractable or obdurate into a form that is more amenable to functional deployment. This is the fundamental role of discourse *as* organization' (Chia 2000, p. 517, original italics).

To treat discourse *as* organization does not mean that discourse *is* organization. When we combine discourse and organizing we must be careful not to commit the same mistake that psychologists did when they talked about acts akin to organizing, and actions akin to discourse. John Dewey (1896/1998) argued persuasively that psychologists made a big mistake when they posited that the foundation of all action was the reflex arc, a sequence that had three parts: (1) sensation or stimulus, (2) idea or central activity, (3) reaction or response. Dewey argued that researchers who assumed a reflex arc were misguided because they had the sequence backwards; they mistook shifting functions for discrete, sequential parts, and they ignored unified acts that were cycles rather than arcs. The sequence was backwards because the so-called originating 'sensations' did not become clear until the outcome was known, which meant that they could hardly have controlled the unfolding act. In Dewey's words:

> the reflex arc idea, as commonly employed, is defective in that it assumes sensory stimulus and motor response as distinct psychical existences, while in reality they are always inside a co-ordination and have their significance purely from the part played in maintaining or reconstituting the co-ordination ... This circuit is more truly organic than reflex, because response determines the stimulus, just as truly as sensory stimulus determines movement. Indeed, the movement is only for the sake of determining the stimulus, of fixing what kind of a stimulus it is, of interpreting it. (Dewey, 1896/1998, pp. 5, 6)

I mention Dewey's analysis because I think there is a danger that discourse theorists could fall into the same trap. Discourse, like sensation, is neither self-contained nor de-contextualized nor originative. Instead, it is a becoming, its functioning is known only late, and that functioning is affected by what was already underway and disrupted. Just as the eventual physiological response belatedly defines the 'earlier' stimulus, the organizing of flux belatedly defines the 'earlier' discourse that mattered. The discourse that counts in acts of organizing is known more in the aftermath than in the moment. And it is known through its embedding in and articulating of organizing activities. While there is a strong temptation to treat discourse as a master trigger in organizational analysis, Dewey's analysis conveys an important caution. If organizing is a unified act that blends repetition and variety, and if discourse – much like sensation – is a part of organizing that gets singled out, defined, and labelled *post hoc*, then discourse still remains crucial but what is crucial about it depends on its embedding (Pye, 1993). Thus, when an investigator extracts significant conversational exchanges as data for further study, there is the danger that the very context which made the conversation organizational will get elided. We could, therefore, commit the opposite error to that of Peters and Waterman. Namely, we could mistakenly conclude that the selected fragment of conversation occurred earlier and more distinctly and was more determinative in the process of organizing than in fact was the case. Equivalent attention to organizing and discourse is crucial to maintain relevance and validity.

Organizing does involve more than discourse and we need to remain mindful that organizational action is an ontological activity. The apparent solidity of an organization stems from the stabilizing effects of discursive acting (see Putnam et al., 1996, pp. 384–6 on 'the metaphor of performance'). To act discursively is to engage in what has been called, elsewhere, enactment. Enactment has been described (Nicholson, 1995, p. 155) as a concept developed 'to connote an organism's adjustment to its environment by directly acting upon the environment to change it. Enactment thus has the capacity to create ecological change to which the organism may have subsequently to adjust ... Enactment is thus often a species of self-fulfilling prophecy (and it involves) the reification of experience and environment through action'. Enactment is about both direct and indirect organizing. Direct organizing through enactment occurs through direct changes of flux and indirect organizing occurs through changing oneself. Enactment is about direct action in the service of differentiating flux into an environment and an organization. Enactment is also about indirect action in the sense that it resembles closely the mechanism associated with *self*-fulfilling prophecies. It is the resemblance to self-fulfilling prophecies that explains why enactment, which may begin as an expectation embedded in a reification, often has material, textual consequences. To focus on enactment and acting discursively is to better position oneself to pick up emergence, change, agency and open-ended interactions as lived in everyday organizational life.

In concluding, I want to call attention to a recurring form of language that may help bridge the disconnect between talk and action. That form is the adverb. Action is ongoing, which means renderings of action have to capture this flavour. John Dewey was aware of this when he said:

> Intelligence is incarnate in overt action, using things as means to affect other things. 'Thought', reason, intelligence, whatever word we choose to use, is existentially an adjective (or better an adverb,) not a noun. It is a disposition of activity, a quality of that conduct which foresees consequences of existing events and which uses what is foreseen as a plan and method of administering affairs. (Dewey, 1925/1958, pp. 158–9).

Dewey made the same point even more compactly when he said, 'the infinitive and the imperative develop from the participle, present tense. Perfection means perfecting, fulfillment, fulfilling, and the good is now or never' (Dewey, 1922/2002, p. 290). We see similar sensitivity to motion, unfolding, and the quality of the act when Grant, Keenoy and Oswick argue that:

> [Discourse is significant in] constructing, situating, facilitating and communicating the diverse cultural, institutional, political, and socio-economic parameters of 'organizational being'. Thus, discourse not only shapes and directs organizational behaviours, but also *constitutes* actors' contested and contestable meanings. With such a reading 'organization' can be seen as a continuous process of social accomplishment which, in both senses of the term, is 'articulated' by and through the deployment of discursive resources. (Grant et al., 1998, p. 12)

Robert Chia is sensitive to movement when he says, 'It is through this process of differentiating, fixing, naming, labeling, classifying, and relating – all intrinsic processes of discursive organization – that social reality is systematically constructed' (Chia, 2000, p. 513). Goffman describes conversation as 'a strip or tract of referencings, each referencing tending to bear, but often deviously, some retrospectively perceivable connection to the immediately preceding one' (cited in Taylor & Van Every, 2000, p. 36). Weick and Roberts (1993) describe collective mind as embodied in heedful interrelating. Considered together, these depictions suggest that the phrase 'discourse analysis' may convey a more static picture of discourse than is intended. It may be harder to see the dynamics of smoke when conversation rather than conversing is the object. We may be in a stronger position to bridge talk and action if we describe organizational conversation as 'the total universe of shared interaction-through-languaging of the people who together identify with a given organization' (Taylor & Van Every, 2000, p. 35).

Everyday life, whether it consists of conceptualizing or organizing, means dealing with disorder, equivocality and ambiguity through selective attention in the interest of pattern-making. Selective attention often takes the form of seeing what we believe which means that beliefs crystallized in earlier texts tend to edit what is 'seen' in current conversations. Each of us edit in order to get some sense of order, which removes some of the confusion we confront when we try to figure out what we are dealing with and who we are. Both researchers and practitioners talk environments and organizations into existence as presumptive entities by means of conversations edited by older texts.

Whether researchers claim that their object of study is acting thinkingly (Weick, 1983) or acting discursively, those claims will have more resonance with the human condition to the extent that they grasp more fully the dynamic, transient smoke-like character of unfolding contextualized conversation. Researchers already have reasonable control of conceptual images that depict more stable, crystal-like texts (for example, the technology of content analysis). The problem is that we have less control over images that capture dynamics and flux (complexity theory represents an attempt to remedy this, for example, McDaniel, 1997). That's why adverbs and participles are important. Failure to represent conversing within flux and conversing about flux makes our textual analyses less complete than they could be. If we remind ourselves of the stubbornly changing character of organizational life, we will be in a better position to talk about discoursing as well as discourse, and to demonstrate that talking is organizing.

REFERENCES

Atlan, H. (1979) *Entre le cristal et la fumée* (*Between crystal and smoke*). Paris: Editions de Seuil.

Chia, R. (2000) Discourse analysis as organizational analysis. *Organization*, 7 (3): 513–18.

Dewey, J. (1896/1998) The reflex arc concept in psychology. In L.A. Hickman & T.M. Alexander (eds), *The essential Dewey: Ethics, logic, psychology* (Vol. 2, pp. 3–10). Bloomington, IN: Indiana University Press.

Dewey, J. (1922/2002) *Human nature and conduct*. Mineola, NY: Dover.

Dewey, J. (1925/1958) *Experience and nature*. Mineola, NY: Dover.

Grant, D., Keenoy, T. & Oswick, C. (eds) (1998) *Discourse and organization*. London: Sage.

Lanzara, G.F. (1999) Between transient constructs and persistent structures: Designing systems in action. *Journal of Strategic Information Systems*, 8: 331–49.

Marschak, R.J. (1998) A discourse on discourse: Redeeming the meaning of talk. In D. Grant, T. Keenoy & C. Oswick (eds), *Discourse and Organization* (pp. 15–30). London: Sage.

McDaniel, R.R. Jr. (1997) Strategic leadership: A view from quantum and chaos theories. *Health Care Management Review*, 22 (1): 21–37.

Meacham, J.A. (1990) The loss of wisdom. In R.J. Sternberg (ed.), *Wisdom* (pp. 181–211). New York: Cambridge University Press.

Nicholson, N. (1995) Enactment. In N. Nicholson (ed.), *Blackwell Encyclopedic Dictionary of Organizational Behavior* (pp. 155–6). Cambridge, MA: Blackwell.

Peters, T.J. & Waterman, R.H. Jr. (1982) *In Search of Excellence*. New York: Harper and Row.

Putnam, L.L., Phillips, N. & Chapman, P. (1996) Metaphors of communication and organization. In S.R. Clegg, C. Hardy & W.R. Nord (eds), *Handbook of Organization Studies* (pp. 375–408). London: Sage.

Pye, A.J. (1993) 'Organizing as explaining' and the doing of managing: An integrative appreciation of processes of organizing. *Journal of Management Inquiry*, 2 (2): 157–68.

Taylor, J.R. & Van Every, E.J. (2000) *The emergent organization: Communication as its site and surface*. Mahwah, NJ: Lawrence Erlbaum Associates.

Tsoukas, H. & Chia, R. (2002) Organizational becoming: Rethinking organizational change. *Organization Science*, 13 (5): 567–82.

Weick, K.E. (1983) Managerial thought in the context of action. In S. Srivastava (ed.), *The executive mind* (pp. 221–42). San Francisco: Jossey-Bass.

Weick, K.E. (1995) *Sensemaking in organizations*. Thousand Oaks, CA: Sage.

Weick, K.E. & Roberts, K.H. (1993) Collective mind in organizations: Heedful interrelating on flight decks. *Administrative Science Quarterly*, 38: 357–81.

Weschler, L. (1982) *Seeing is forgetting the name of the thing one sees: A life of contemporary artist Robert Irwin*. Berkeley, CA: University of California Press.

Getting Real about Organizational Discourse

Mike Reed

Much of the intellectual inspiration and drive for the development of discursive forms of analysis in social science and organization studies has come from an avowedly anti-realist ontology and epistemology (Potter, 1997; Westwood & Linstead, 2001). Considered in relation to its social ontology, epistemological priorities and explanatory rationale, discourse analysis has drawn on a social constructionist paradigm that is, in its essentials, anti-realist, subjectivist, relativist and ideationalist. What matters, from the point of view of the social constructionist paradigm on which discourse analysis draws so extensively, is to define and explore social reality as an effect of language. Crucially, this necessarily entails walking a very fine line between 'discourse reductionism/determinism' and 'discursive constructionism'. While the former is more than happy to assert, indeed insist, that social reality – and, perhaps, even material reality? – is *constituted* through language (as expressed through talk or text), the latter recoils from the 'solipsistic vortex' that seductively beckons those who enthusiastically embrace such a radical ontological relativism. Instead, supporters of 'discursive constructionism' carefully avoid this radical ontological relativism by constantly reminding us that language does not exhaust our interest in social reality. It merely provides the primary communicative mechanism and medium through which social reality can be accessed and described. As the editors of this *Handbook* are scrupulously careful to remind us in their introductory chapter:

> Studies of organizational discourse are interested in the social constructionist (Berger and Luckmann, 1967; Searle, 1995) effects of language in organizational settings. As Mumby and Clair point out:

> Organizations exist only in so far as their members create them through discourse. This is not to claim that organizations are 'nothing but' discourse, but rather that discourse is the principle means by which organization members create a coherent social reality that frames their sense of who they are. (Mumby & Clair, 1997, p. 181)

There are several interesting elisions in this use of Mumby and Clair's syllogism to deny the accusation of 'discourse reductionism or determinism'. First, it conflates an ontological axiom – 'organizations only exist in so far as their members create them through discourse' – with an epistemological assertion – 'discourse is the principle means by which organization members create a coherent social reality that frames their sense of who they are'. Secondly, it interpolates an ontological disclaimer – 'this is not to claim that organizations are nothing but discourse' – as a pre-emptive response to the possible charge of discourse reductionism/determinism. Thirdly, it concludes with an inference from the previous two statements – axiomatic assertion and inserted qualifying disclaimer – which implies that *'social reality' per se is synonymous with a socially constructed sense of shared meaning and identity* – 'a coherent sense of social reality that frames their sense of who they are'. Ontology is collapsed into epistemology, which, in turn, is equated with the discursive means, mechanisms and forms through which members – of a society or an organization – fabricate and sustain a collectively meaningful social and institutional identity. The circle is complete; 'it' – that is, social reality – all comes back to discourse, or language, in its manifold forms and practices. Nothing remains, except what Westwood and Linstead (2001, pp. 4–5) call the 'ontological interrogation of organization' through which 'the turn to language' is at its most radical and complete:

> Organization has no autonomous, stable or structural status outside of the text that constitutes it. The text of organization itself consists of a shifting network of signifiers in dynamic relations of difference. Text does not have an entitive status either; it is a process, a process in which meanings are emergent, deferred and dispersed ... The notion of structure is illusionary, representing only an ideological practice that pretends to stand in the place of the flux of shifting and seamless textual relationships ... Organization is structure, but only when structure is recognized to be an effect of language, a tropological achievement. (Westwood & Linstead, 2001, pp. 4–5)

The fine line between 'discourse reductionism/ determinism' and 'discursive construtionism' has become so gossamer thin that its meaning and significance has been virtually obliterated. All we are left with is a strident anti-realism/materialism and a sub-Foucauldian discourse analysis that typically advances 'from the assumption that discourses, or sets of statements, *constitute* objects and subjects ... Language, put together as discourses, arranges and naturalizes the social world in a specific way and informs social practices. These practices *constitute* particular forms of subjectivity in which human subjects are managed and given a certain form, as self-evident and natural' (Alvesson & Kärreman, 2000, p. 1128, emphasis added). Such an approach fundamentally undermines the proposition that societies and organizations consist of social structures that position social actors within 'authoritative and allocative orders' constraining their ability to act in pursuit of collectively shared values and interests. Indeed, if we remain within the philosophical confines of the anti-realist/materialist paradigm, then it is difficult to see how the central explanatory aspiration of 'critical discourse analysis' can possibly be realized. How are we to make 'explicit the connections among everyday discourse, sense-making practices, larger social structures and the enactment of power relations' (Mumby & Clair, 1997, p. 202) if social structure is collapsed into discursive agency?

It is in response to concerns such as these that a 'critical realist' approach to discourse analysis has emerged and been developed over the last decade or so (Fairclough, 1995; Fairclough & Wodak, 1997; Chouliarki & Fairclough, 1999;

Fairclough et al., 2002; Reed, 1998). While possessing distinct affinities to the forms of 'critical discourse analysis' outlined by Mumby in this volume, the critical realist perspective on discourse analysis in institutions and organizations has several defining features that distinguish it from the former.

First, the realist-based approach to discourse analysis starts from the argument that the philosophical idealism that underpins the constructionist-based paradigm consistently blurs, if not obliterates, the crucial distinction between 'reality' and 'knowledge'. Realists insist that the material and social worlds of which we are a constituent, but only one, part cannot be treated as if they are ultimately dependent on, and indeed constituted through, consciousness or language. As Trigg puts it.

> No realist, in any sphere, will countenance the running together of the reality that can be known with our knowledge of it. Otherwise, 'our world', limited as it is, will become synonymous with 'the world'. No distinction can be then made between reality and our conceptions of it (whoever 'we' may be). We suddenly, by definition, become omniscient, without the ability to distinguish between what there is and what we know. (Trigg, 2001, p. 238)

Thus, the realist-based view of organizational discourse analysis is based on the pivotal argument that 'the social world comes *previously structured*' (Trigg, 2001, p. 235, emphasis added). This pre-structuring process, and the material conditions and social structures that it reproduces, cannot be collapsed into language or discourse. If they are so collapsed or conflated, then the 'generative power' inherent in social structures cannot be accessed or explained because it remains imprisoned within its 'discursive moment' – within the linguistic and textual forms through which it is communicated and represented. Discourse cannot be assigned ontological primacy and explanatory sovereignty over socio-material reality and the structures or mechanisms through which it is generated, elaborated and transformed. Once this happens, then any form of discourse analysis beginning from such a position will inevitably degenerate into an 'idealist regress'. As a result, the independent ontological status and strategic explanatory role of generative structures or mechanisms – such as bureaucratic hierarchies, modes of capital accumulation and social stratification systems – will be lost from analytical view.

The second major defining characteristic of a realist-based approach to organizational discourse analysis, that sets it firmly apart from a constructionist-based approach, is its underlying conception of what discourse 'is' and the explanatory task that 'it' is required to perform. As Fairclough (1992, p. 60) argued more than a decade ago, discursive practices are necessarily 'constrained by the fact that they inevitably take place within a constituted material reality, with pre-constituted objects and pre-constituted social subjects'. Considered in this light, discourse is necessarily dependent on a pre-constituted set of separable, yet interdependent, material conditions and social structures. This suggests that the interplay between social structure and discursive innovation must be analysed dialectically. That is, as a complex and dynamic relationship of antagonistic tension and opposition which is grounded in very real material and social constraints that confront actors as obdurate and recalcitrant obstacles in their everyday organizational lives.

At any particular point in historical time and in any social and spatial location, actors will be faced with a set of *institutionalized* economic, political and cultural constraints that will limit the range of strategic and tactical discursive options available to them. This becomes even more evident as they struggle to 'move things on' in the light of their perceived material interests and normative values and the structural obstacles that stand in the way of their progression. Actors will have to mobilize creative discursive resources and forms as they attempt to intervene in pre-structured social situations to their relative advantage. This will, necessarily, create tension and opposition between the pre-existing authoritative and allocative orders generated by earlier phases of 'institution building' and the power structures through which they were previously established and legitimated. Innovative discursive practices and forms are necessarily embedded in and emerge from pre-existing material conditions and social structures. New discursive genres and symbolic orders cannot avoid 'inheriting' what cultural and political capital has been deposited by older and long-established discursive regimes. But, again of necessity, they will also, in the fullness of time, come to undermine and challenge that very inheritance in their quest to change the institutional status quo in some shape or form. Thus, institutional fields and organizational forms will be shaped and reshaped as a result of the complex dialectical interplay between pre-existing structural constraints and the combined collective efforts of corporate agents to engage in new modes of discursive practice that will inevitably change them, to some degree or another. As Fairclough, Jessop and Sayer argue:

> …it does not follow that language and ways of thinking are unconstrained by the world. Not just anything can be constructed … A critical realist account of social structuration must be sensitive to the complex dialectic that is entailed in the emergence, reproduction and transformation of social structures from social actions and the reciprocal influence of these emergent structures on ongoing social action … Discourses are positioned ways of representing – representing other social practices as well as the material world, and reflexively representing this social practice, from particular positions in social practices … What enters a practice as a new discourse, such as the discourse of 'new public management', may become enacted as new ways of interacting, which will in part be new genres (new ways of interacting discursively) … both the production and consumption of symbolic systems (orders of discourse etc.) are over-determined by a range of factors that are more or less extra-semiotic. (2002, pp. 5–9)

Within this realist-based approach to the analysis of organizational discourse, discourses are now regarded as real, objective entities with 'fateful' socio-material consequences for social action, depending on their inherent capacities and powers to shape and reshape the social relations and practices in which corporate agents are collectively engaged. As Scott (2000, p. 32) suggests, 'discourses or traditions of thought, therefore, are manifested in real human behaviour, are subject to change and decay, and may be hierarchically organized and, more importantly, are nested within supra-discourses'.

This brings us to the third defining characteristic of a realist-based approach to organizational discourse – that is, the underlying conception of 'social structuration' that it works with and the implications of this for its commitment to the historical explanation of discursive innovation and change. Approaches to organizational discourse analysis that have been developed within the social constructionist paradigm rely heavily on a conception of 'social structuration', in which the production and reproduction of social structures are determined by the social practices through which this 'making and re-making process' occurs. 'Structure' is collapsed into 'practice' and the latter, in turn, is conflated with the linguistic means and discursive forms through which it is enacted. 'Organization' is fused with language in a way that denies its status as a distinctive institutional form, with necessary causal properties and powers of its own. As a distinctive social structure generating innate capacities and powers, 'organization' emerges out of the complex interplay between enduring structural conditioning, creative collective agency and the contingencies of socio-historical context (Reed, 1997, 1998, 2002b and 2002c). For the realist, the social structuration of 'organization' has to be understood as the outcome of a historical process in which:

> [r]eality is attributed to whatever exerts a causal force, enabling what is relational, detectable only through its effects, to be recognized as real ... Social ontology must regulate explanatory methodology. Language is *a* but not *the* condition of knowledge, since it must be used to refer to something other than itself ... Structures are real constraining conditions of action, which cannot be grasped adequately by regarding them simply as effects of systems of representation or 'discourse' ... Institutional and distributional positioning conditions agency by defining interests and access to resources. This means that the stringency of constraint and the powers of agency vary from case to case ... Explaining structuration in these terms demands facing the complexities of each historical case. There is a 'necessary historicity' in social explanation. There are no 'lazy' alternatives to the painstaking investigation of the interaction between the relevant agents, structural conditions and contingencies. Every case is unique, requiring its own narrative of the temporal process of its formation. (Parker, 2000, pp. 117–19)

Parker's specification of realist social ontology and explanation demands that the analysis of discursive innovation and change be focused on particular historical cases, in all their uniqueness and contingencies. But these 'analytical histories of emergence, of why it is so and not otherwise' (Parker, 2000, p. 119), must be conducted within a general social theory. The latter analytically guides and disciplines the meticulous construction and evaluation of particular historical narratives, identifying the 'kinds of constraints and agents in play during the emergence of what is being investigated' (Parker, 2000, p. 119). Within this explanatory methodology, the major focus will be on the irreducible and autonomous 'intermediate terrain' of middle-range institutional structures and positions that cannot be conflated into the social practices, including discursive practices, through which collective agency is expressed. Realist social and organizational theory can only deliver on its explanatory promise by providing a detailed understanding and account of the strategic role that intermediate relations and forms (such as 'organization') play in the making and remaking of social structures. At the core of this analysis must lie an in-depth appreciation of power struggles over the institutional status quo engaged in by corporate agents and their longer-term impact on the trajectories of structural change and innovation emerging in specific socio-historical contexts. Relocated within this realist-based ontological, analytical and methodological context, organizational discourse analysis now becomes an exercise in historical reconstruction. It's overriding explanatory aim is to reconstruct and evaluate the discursive genres and mechanisms through which collective agents have struggled to restructure established power relations and the distributional outcomes that they produce and legitimate.

One prime illustration of realist-based organizational discourse analysis can be discovered in the ongoing interpretation and explanation of 'new public management' over the last decade or so. The latter can be seen as a powerful discursive regime and genre engaged in the 'technologization' of political debate and policy development in Anglo-American welfare states during the 1980s and 1990s (Clarke & Newman, 1997; McLaughlin et al., 2002; Reed, 2002a). Fairclough (1995) argues the technologization of discourse has five interrelated features. First, it is 'expert-based and driven'. Secondly, it entails a discernible shift towards more detailed, intrusive and intensive forms of 'discourse regulation or policing'. Thirdly, it pushes towards the design and projection of 'context-free' discourse techniques that are potentially universalistic in their application. Fourthly, it furthers experimentation in strategically motivated 'discourse simulation and hybridization'. Finally, it generates an underlying dynamic and trajectory of discursive rationalization and standardization.

Recent sociological and historical research on new public management, as an innovative discursive genre and policy paradigm, in Anglo-American welfare states has revealed all of these five interconnected characteristics in operation. But the specific developmental trajectories followed by 'discursive technologization' through the articulation and interpolation of 'new public management' into policy debate and decision-making over the last two decades is highly variable between national-level welfare states/ systems and within different sectors within the same state/system (McLaughlin et al., 2002). The localized impact of these system/sector-specific discursive trajectories on policy formulation and implementation – even more their innate capacity and power to change the organization, management and delivery of service practice – is as, if not more, subject to historical variability and situational contingency. Nevertheless, any realist-based explanation of the organizational impact of 'discursive technologization' through 'new public management', whether at the macro, meso or micro levels of analysis, will share a common rationale and logic. That is, to generate analytically structured historical narratives focusing on the complex interplay between relatively enduring structural conditioning, creative collective agency and the contingencies of context within and between different levels of social organization. By following this explanatory rationale and logic, realist-based organizational discourse analysts attempt to access and evaluate the 'generative properties and capacities' of new discursive mechanisms and practices, such as 'new public management'. In particular, they aspire to provide insightful historical accounts of the ways in which discursive change and innovation enter into and reshape ongoing power struggles to make and remake the institutional status quo and the configuration of power relations that it reproduces.

In this respect, organizational discourse analysis conducted within a realist paradigm can be seen to share a number of intellectual and ideological affinities with the 'critical discourse perspective' outlined by Mumby in this volume. This is clearly the case in relation to the common explanatory focus on the 'underlying structures of domination, resistance and interest-driven discursive strategies that lurk beneath ostensibly consensual meaning systems' (Mumby, this volume). But realists would wish to develop *a much stronger structural and historical account* of the pre-existing institutional forms and material conditions that inevitably constrain the discursive options available to corporate agents as they struggle to maintain and challenge the institutional status quo. These power structures and their material foundations are not 'all encompassing and determining' (Mumby, this volume) in relation to the creative potential inherent in collective agency. But they do need to be given a much stronger ontological status and explanatory role than seems to be envisaged in Mumby's characterization of the 'critical discourse tradition'. We should not allow an understandable fear of structural determinism and reification to prevent us from fulfilling the explanatory promise of organizational discourse analysis conducted within the broad philosophical and methodological terms of reference provided by critical social realism. To fulfil that explanatory promise, we require a social ontology, research methodology and explanatory theory that are based upon, and advance a much more robust conception of social structuration as the outcome of a dynamic interaction between 'structure' and 'agency' over historical time (Reed, 2003). We need 'to get real about organizational discourse'.

REFERENCES

Alvesson, M. & Kärreman, D. (2000) Varieties of discourse: On the study of organizations through discourse. *Human Relations*, 53 (9): 1125–49.

Berger, P. & Luckmann, T. (1967) *The social construction of reality*. London: Penguin.

Chouliarki, L. & Fairclough, N. (1999) *Discourse in late modernity: Rethinking critical discourse analysis*. Edinburgh: Edinburgh University Press.

Clarke, J. & Newman, J. (1997) *The managerial state*. London: Sage.

Fairclough, N. (1992) *Discourse and social change*. Cambridge: Polity Press.

Fairclough, N. (1995) *Language and power*. London: Longman.

Fairclough, N. & Wodak, R. (1997) Critical discourse analysis. In T. Van Dijk (ed.), *Discourse as social interaction* (pp. 258–84). London: Sage.

Fairclough, N., Jessop, B. & Sayer, A. (2002) Critical realism and semiosis. *Journal of Critical Realism*, 5 (1): 2–10.

McLauhglin, K., Osborne, S. & Ferlie, E. (eds) (2002) *New public management: Current trends and future prospects*. London: Routledge.

Mumby, D. (2004, this volume) Discourse, power and ideology: Unpacking the critical approach. In D. Grant, C. Hardy, C. Oswick & L. Putnam (eds), *The Sage handbook of organizational discourse* (pp. 237–58). London: Sage.

Mumby, D. & Clair, R. (1997) Organizational discourse. In T. Van Dijk (ed.), *Discourse as structure and process* (pp. 181–205). London: Sage.

Parker, J. (2000) *Structuration*. Buckingham: Open University Press.

Potter, J. (1997) Discourse analysis as a way of analysing naturally occurring talk. In D. Sliverman (ed.), *Qualitative research: Theory, method and practice* (pp. 144–60). London: Sage.

Reed, M. (1997) In praise of duality and dualism: Rethinking agency and structure in organizational analysis. *Organization Studies*, 18 (1): 21–42.

Reed, M. (1998) Organizational analysis as discourse analysis. In D. Grant, T. Keenoy & C. Oswick (eds), *Discourse and Organization* (pp. 193–213). London: Sage.

Reed, M. (2002a) New managerialism and the management of UK universities. In M. Dewatripont, F. Thys-Clement & L. Wilkin (eds), *European universities: Change and convergence?* (pp. 69–83). Bruxelles: Éditions De L'Université De Bruxelles.

Reed, M. (2002b) New managerialism, professional power and organizational governance in UK universities. In A. Amaral, G. Jones & B. Karsath (eds), *Governing Higher Education: National perspectives on institutional governance* (pp. 181–203). Netherlands: Kluwer.

Reed, M. (2002c) New managerialism and technologies of management in universities: Looking forward to virtuality? In K. Robins & F. Webster (eds), *The virtual university: Information, markets and management* (pp. 126–47). Oxford: Oxford University Press.

Reed, M. (2003) The agency/structure dilemma in organization theory: Open doors and brick walls. In H. Tsoukas & C. Knudsen (eds), *The Oxford handbook of organization theory: Meta-theoretical perspectives* (pp. 289–309). Oxford: Oxford University Press.

Scott, D. (2000) *Realism and educational research*. London: Sage.

Searle, J.R. (1995) *The Construction of Social Reality*. London: Allen Lane.

Trigg, R. (2001) *Understanding social science* (2nd edition). Oxford: Blackwell.

Westwood, R. & Linstead, S. (eds) (2001) *The language of organization*. London: Sage.

Index

Indexed by Caroline Eley